WREN & MARTIN

LARGE FORMAT

High School

English Grammar & Composition

Wren & Martin

by

P.C. WREN, M.A. (OXON)

and

H. MARTIN, M.A. (OXON), O.B.E.

Revised by

N.D.V. PRASADA RAO, M.A., D.T.E., Ph.D.

BLACKIE®
ELT BOOKS
(An imprint of S Chand Publishing)

BLACKIE ELT BOOKS
(An imprint of S Chand Publishing)
A Division of S Chand And Company Limited
(An ISO 9001 Certified Company)
Head Office : D-92, Sector 2, Noida, Uttar Pradesh-201 301
Phone : 0120-468 2700, **e-mail :** info@schandpublishing.com
Registered Office : A-27, 2nd Floor, Mohan Co-operative Industrial Estate, New Delhi–110 044
www.schandpublishing.com; **e-mail :** helpdesk@schandpublishing.com

Marketing Offices :

Chennai	:	Ph: 044-2363 2120, chennai@schandpublishing.com
Guwahati	:	Ph: 0361-406 6369, guwahati@schandpublishing.com
Hyderabad	:	Ph: 040-4018 6018, hyderabad@schandpublishing.com
Jalandhar	:	Ph: 0181-464 5630, jalandhar@schandpublishing.com
Kolkata	:	Ph: 033-2335 7458, kolkata@schandpublishing.com
Lucknow	:	Ph: 0522-400 3633, lucknow@schandpublishing.com
Mumbai	:	Ph: 022-2500 0297, mumbai@schandpublishing.com
Patna	:	Ph: 0612-226 0011, patna@schandpublishing.com

First Published 1936
Revised Edition 1973, 1982, 1990, 1998
This New Edition 2024
First Impression 2025

ISBN : 978-93-58701-55-5 **Product Code :** SCS3WMP090ENGAR24CBN

PRINTED IN INDIA
By Vikas Publishing House Private Limited, Plot 20/4, Site-IV, Industrial Area Sahibabad, Ghaziabad–201 010
and Published by S Chand And Company Limited, A-27, 2nd Floor, Mohan Co-operative Industrial Estate, New Delhi–110 044.

PREFACE

Wren and Martin's monumental work **High School English Grammar and Composition** is available in two editions. One is a multicolour illustrated edition, and the other is a regular edition without illustrations.

The material in the book has been further updated wherever it has been felt necessary, particularly in the chapters dealing with adjectives, active and passive voice, articles and prepositions.

It was in the year 1972 that the revision of this book was contemplated and the publishers commissioned me to revise it thoroughly. The revised edition came out in 1973 and was very well received. One of the main features of the revised edition was the addition of a great deal of new material (such as the three chapters on structures) based on the new developments in the study of English structure and usage. Subsequently the book was revised several times and most extensively for this edition.

Unlike many traditional grammar books, this book in the present form helps the student to use the language as well as giving detailed information about the language. It provides ample guidance and practice in sentence building, correct usage, comprehension, written composition and other allied areas so as to equip the student with the ability to communicate effectively in English.

It is gratifying to learn that this classic work, though primarily intended for use in the Indian subcontinent, is also used in Sri Lanka, Maldives, Nepal, Bhutan, Indonesia, the Philippines, Myanmar, Malaysia, Singapore, Mauritius, the Middle East, African countries, etc. It is hoped that the book will be found useful in many more countries where English is used as a second or foreign language.

Dr N.D.V. Prasada Rao

Contents

Book I. Grammar

	CHAPTERS		PAGES
1.	THE SENTENCE	...	10
2.	SUBJECT AND PREDICATE	...	10
3.	THE PHRASE AND THE CLAUSE	...	11
4.	PARTS OF SPEECH	...	12
5.	THE NOUN: KINDS OF NOUNS	...	13
6.	THE NOUN: GENDER	...	16
7.	THE NOUN: NUMBER	...	18
8.	THE NOUN: CASE	...	22
9.	THE ADJECTIVE	...	26
10.	COMPARISON OF ADJECTIVES	...	30
11.	ADJECTIVES USED AS NOUNS	...	38
12.	POSITION OF ADJECTIVES	...	39
13.	THE CORRECT USE OF SOME ADJECTIVES	...	39
14.	ARTICLES	...	42
15.	PERSONAL PRONOUNS	...	48
16.	REFLEXIVE AND EMPHATIC PRONOUNS	...	53
17.	DEMONSTRATIVE, INDEFINITE AND DISTRIBUTIVE PRONOUNS	...	54
18.	RELATIVE PRONOUNS	...	56
19.	INTERROGATIVE PRONOUNS	...	64
20.	THE VERB: TRANSITIVE AND INTRANSITIVE VERBS	...	66
21.	VERBS OF INCOMPLETE PREDICATION	...	70
22.	ACTIVE AND PASSIVE VOICE	...	71
23.	MOOD	...	75
24.	TENSES: INTRODUCTION	...	77
25.	THE USES OF THE PRESENT AND PAST TENSES	...	80
26.	THE FUTURE	...	84
27.	THE VERB: PERSON AND NUMBER	...	86
28.	THE INFINITIVE	...	87
29.	THE PARTICIPLE	...	90
30.	THE GERUND	...	95
31.	IRREGULAR VERBS	...	97
32.	AUXILIARIES AND MODALS	...	103
33.	CONJUGATION OF THE VERB LOVE	...	108
34.	THE ADVERB	...	110
35.	COMPARISON OF ADVERBS	...	115
36.	FORMATION OF ADVERBS	...	116
37.	POSITION OF ADVERBS	...	117
38.	THE PREPOSITION	...	119
39.	WORDS FOLLOWED BY PREPOSITIONS	...	126
40.	THE CONJUNCTION	...	137
41.	SOME CONJUNCTIONS AND THEIR USES	...	145
42.	THE INTERJECTION	...	149
43.	THE SAME WORD USED AS DIFFERENT PARTS OF SPEECH	...	150

Book II. Composition

PART I: ANALYSIS, TRANSFORMATION AND SYNTHESIS

1. ANALYSIS OF SIMPLE SENTENCES ... 157-165
    Exercises 1-7 ... 157
2. PHRASES ... 165-170
    Adjective Phrases ... 165
        Exercises 8-12 ... 166
    Adverb Phrases ... 167
        Exercises 13-19 ... 167
    Noun Phrases ... 169
        Exercises 20-22 ... 169
3. CLAUSES ... 170-177
    Adverb Clauses ... 170
        Exercises 23-26 ... 171
    Adjective Clauses ... 172
        Exercises 27-30 ... 173
    Noun Clauses ... 174
        Exercises 31-36 ... 174
4. SENTENCES: SIMPLE, COMPOUND AND COMPLEX ... 177-179
    Exercise 37 ... 178
5. MORE ABOUT NOUN CLAUSES ... 179-181
    Exercises 38-39 ... 180
6. MORE ABOUT ADJECTIVE CLAUSES ... 181-183
    Exercises 40-42 ... 182
7. MORE ABOUT ADVERB CLAUSES ... 183-190
    Adverb Clauses of Time ... 183
        Exercise 43 ... 183
    Adverb Clauses of Place ... 184
        Exercise 44 ... 184
    Adverb Clauses of Purpose ... 184
        Exercise 45 ... 184
    Adverb Clauses of Cause or Reason ... 184
        Exercise 46 ... 184
    Adverb Clauses of Condition ... 184
        Exercise 47 ... 184
    Adverb Clauses of Result and Consequence ... 185
        Exercise 48 ... 185
    Adverb Clauses of Comparison ... 185
        Exercises 49-50 ... 186
    Adverb Clauses of Supposition or Concession ... 186
        Exercises 51-55 ... 186
8. ANALYSIS OF COMPLEX SENTENCES (Clause Analysis) ... 190-193
    Exercise 56 ... 192
9. ANALYSIS OF COMPOUND SENTENCES (Clause Analysis) ... 193-196
    Exercise 57 ... 195
    Exercise 58 (Miscellaneous) ... 195
10. TRANSFORMATION OF SENTENCES ... 196-203
    Sentences Containing the Adverb 'too' ... 196
        Exercise 59 ... 196
    Interchange of the Degrees of Comparison ... 197

	Exercise 60	...	197
	Interchange of Active and Passive Voice	...	198
	Exercises 61-63	...	199
	Interchange of Affirmative and Negative Sentences	...	200
	Exercises 64-65	...	200
	Interchange of Interrogative and Assertive Sentences	...	200
	Exercises 66-67	...	201
	Interchange of Exclamatory and Assertive Sentences	...	201
	Exercises 68-69	...	201
	Interchange of One Part of Speech for Another	...	202
	Exercise 70	...	202
11.	TRANSFORMATION OF SENTENCES (CONTD.)	...	203-216
	Conversion of Simple Sentences to Compound (Double) Sentences	...	203
	Exercises 71-72	...	203
	Conversion of Compound (Double) Sentences to Simple Sentences	...	204
	Exercises 73-74	...	204
	Conversion of Simple Sentences to Complex	...	206
	Exercises 75-78	...	206
	Conversion of Complex Sentences to Simple Sentences	...	208
	Exercises 79-82	...	209
	Conversion of Compound Sentences to Complex	...	212
	Exercises 83-84	...	212
	Conversion of Complex Sentences to Compound	...	214
	Exercises 85-86	...	214
	Exercise 87 (Miscellaneous)	...	215
12.	SYNTHESIS OF SENTENCES	...	216-222
	Combination of Two or More Simple Sentences into a Single Simple Sentence	...	216
	Exercises 88-93	...	217
	Exercise 94 (Miscellaneous)	...	220
13.	SYNTHESIS OF SENTENCES (CONTD.)	...	222-224
	Combination of Two or More Simple Sentences into a Single Compound Sentence	...	222
	Exercise 95	...	223
14.	SYNTHESIS OF SENTENCES (CONTD.)	...	224-230
	Combination of Two or More Simple Sentences into a Single Complex Sentence	...	224
	Exercises 96-100	...	225
15.	THE SEQUENCE OF TENSES	...	230-232
	Exercises 101-103	...	231
16.	DIRECT AND INDIRECT SPEECH	...	232-239
	Exercises 104-109	...	235

PART II: CORRECT USAGE

17.	AGREEMENT OF THE VERB WITH THE SUBJECT	...	241-243
	Exercise 110	...	243
18.	NOUNS AND PRONOUNS	...	243-247
	Exercises 111-114	...	246
19.	ADJECTIVES	...	247-249
20.	VERBS	...	249-252
	Exercise 115	...	252
21.	ADVERBS	...	252-254
	Exercise 116	...	253
22.	CONJUNCTIONS	...	254-255
23.	ORDER OF WORDS	...	255-257

Exercises 117-118 ... 256
24. IDIOMS ... 257-263
25. IDIOMS (CONTD.) ... 263-276
26. PUNCTUATION ... 277-282
Exercises 119-122 ... 280
27. SPELLING RULES ... 283-284
28. THE FORMATION OF WORDS ... 284-296
Exercises 123-124 ... 285
29. FIGURES OF SPEECH ... 296-301
Exercise 125 ... 301

PART III: STRUCTURES

30. VERB PATTERNS ... 303-309
Exercise 126 ... 309
31. QUESTION TAGS, SHORT ANSWERS, ETC. ... 309-311
Exercises 127-130 ... 310
32. MORE STRUCTURES ... 312-315
Exercise 131 ... 315

PART IV: WRITTEN COMPOSITION

33. PARAGRAPH-WRITING ... 317-320
Principles of Paragraph Structure ... 317
Examples ... 318
The Writing of Single Paragraphs ... 319
Exercise 132 ... 320
34. STORY-WRITING ... 320-323
Hints ... 320
Specimen Outline ... 320
Exercise 133 ... 321
35. REPRODUCTION OF A STORY-POEM ... 323-327
Hints ... 323
Specimens ... 324
Exercise 134 ... 326
36. LETTER-WRITING ... 327-349
The Form of Letters ... 327
Classification of Letters ... 330
Social Letters ... 330
Exercise 135 ... 332
Exercise 136 ... 334
Exercises 137-139 ... 336
Exercises 140-141 ... 339
Notes of Invitations ... 340
Business Letters ... 341
Exercise 142 ... 344
Letters of Application ... 345
Exercise 143 ... 345
Further Official Letters ... 346
Exercise 144 ... 346
Letters to Newspapers ... 346
Exercise 145 ... 347
More Letters ... 347
Exercise 146 ... 348
37. COMPREHENSION ... 349-362
Specimen ... 349
Exercise 147 ... 350
38. PRECIS-WRITING ... 362-376

	Uses of Precis-Writing	...	363
	Method of Procedure	...	363
	To Sum Up	...	365
	Specimens	...	366
	Exercise 148	...	367
39.	EXPANSION OF PASSAGES	...	376-378
	Method of Procedure	...	376
	Specimens	...	377
	Exercise 149	...	378
40.	ESSAY-WRITING	...	379-389
	Characteristics of a Good School Essay	...	379
	Classification of Essays	...	380
	Example	...	382
	The Elephant	...	382
	Bare Outline	...	383
	Full Outline	...	383
	Writing the Essay	...	384
	Summary of Method of Procedure	...	385
	Holidays	...	385
	Books and Reading	...	385
	A Visit to a Book Fair	...	386
	A House on Fire	...	386
	The Elephant	...	387
	Population Growth	...	387
	"Spreading Greenery for a Healthy Living"	...	388
	Exercises 150-151	...	388
41.	AUTOBIOGRAPHIES	...	389-391
	Specimens	...	389
	Exercises 152-154	...	390
42.	DIALOGUE-WRITING	...	391-399
	Method of Procedure	...	391
	Special Hints	...	391
	Specimens	...	392
	Exercises 155-162	...	396
43.	THE APPRECIATION OF POETRY	...	399-409
	Appreciation of the Poem	...	404
	Specimens	...	404
	Exercise 163	...	406
44.	PARAPHRASING	...	409-429
	Uses of Paraphrasing	...	409
	Characteristics of a Good Paraphrase	...	410
	The Paraphrase of Poetry	...	411
	Special Hints	...	412
	Method of Procedure	...	413
	Specimens	...	414
	Exercise 164	...	415
45.	COMMON ABBREVIATIONS	...	419-420

English Grammar

This section presents the various grammatical forms and relates them to meanings and uses. The clear explanations and examples, followed by a lot of practice material, will help you to understand the grammatical system and make correct sentences.

Can we say 'two dozens bananas'? We can't. We should say 'two dozen bananas'. **Dozen score, hundred, thousand** and **million** don't take **-s** when a number comes before them. You will find this point in chapter 7.

We normally use **any** (not **some**) in questions, e.g.

Have you bought **any** biscuits ?

But we can't say to our guests :

Would you like **any** biscuits ?

We should say :

Would you like **some** biscuits ?

We should use **some** in questions when we expect people to say 'yes', for example, in offers and requests. (Chapter 13)

Can you correct this sentence ?

Gopal usually goes to the college by bus.

We should omit **the** before **college**. We can't use **the** or **a/an** before **school, college, university, church, hospital** and **prison** when we think about the normal purpose of these places. (Chapter 14)

Read the following conversation :

'Have you decided what to do ?' - 'Yes. I will resign the job.'

The second speaker has made a mistake. The sentence should be : 'I **am going to** resign the job'. We should use **will** when we decide to do something at the time of speaking. When we have decided to do something before talking about it, we should use the **going to** form, not **will**. (Chapter 26)

The following sentence is incorrect :

It has been raining since two hours.

We should use **for**, not **since**. **Since** is used with a point of time and **for** with a period of time (Chapter 38).

And there are a lot of points like these to learn. You will find the usage points woven into the description of the grammatical system. Note that you can't master grammar by merely reading the rules and examples. You should PRACTISE. Don't neglect to do the exercises.

Book 1

Grammar

Chapter 1 THE SENTENCE

1. When we speak or write we use words. We generally use these words in groups; as,

Little Jack Horner sat in a corner.

A group of words like this, which makes *complete sense*, is called a **sentence**.

Kinds of Sentences

2. Sentences are of four kinds:

(a) Those which make *statements* or *assertions;* as,

Humpty Dumpty sat on a wall.

(b) Those which ask *questions;* as

Where do you live?

(c) Those which express *commands, requests,* or *entreaties;* as,

Be quiet.

Have mercy upon us.

(d) Those which express *strong feelings; as,*

How cold the night is!

What a shame!

A sentence that makes a *statement* or *assertion* is called a **declarative** or **assertive** sentence.

A sentence that asks a *question* is called an **interrogative** sentence.

A sentence that expresses a *command* or an *entreaty* is called an **imperative** sentence.

A sentence that expresses *strong* feeling is called an **exclamatory** sentence.

Chapter 2 SUBJECT AND PREDICATE

3. When we make a sentence:

(a) We name some *person* or *thing;* and

(b) *Say* something about that person or thing.

In other words, we must have a *subject* to speak about and we must *say* or *predicate* something about that subject.

Hence every sentence has *two* parts:

(a) The part which names the person or thing we are speaking about. This is called the **subject** of the sentence.

(b) The part which tells something about the subject. This is called the **predicate** of the sentence.

4. The subject of a sentence usually comes first, but occasionally it is put after the predicate; as,

Here comes the bus.

Sweet are the uses of adversity.

5. In imperative sentences the subject is left out; as,

Sit down. [Here the subject You *is understood.]*

Thank him. [Here too the subject You *is understood.]*

Here comes the bus.
Sit down.
Thank him

EXERCISE IN GRAMMAR 1

In the following sentences separate the subject and the predicate.

1. The cackling of geese saved Rome.
2. The boy stood on the burning deck.
3. Tubal Cain was a man of might.
4. Stone walls do not make a prison.
5. The singing of the birds delights us.
6. Miss Kitty was rude at the table one day.
7. He has a good memory.
8. Bad habits grow unconsciously.
9. The earth revolves round the sun.
10. Nature is the best physician.
11. Edison invented the phonograph.
12. The sea hath many thousand sands.
13. We cannot pump the ocean dry.
14. Borrowed garments never fit well.
15. The early bird catches the worm.
16. All matter is indestructible.
17. Islamabad is the capital of Pakistan.
18. We should profit by experience.
19. All roads lead to Rome.
20. A guilty conscience needs no excuse.
21. The beautiful rainbow soon faded away.
22. No man can serve two masters.
23. A sick room should be well aired.
24. The dewdrops glitter in the sunshine.
25. I shot an arrow into the air.
26. A barking sound the shepherd hears.
27. On the top of the hill lives a hermit.

Chapter 3 THE PHRASE AND THE CLAUSE

6. Examine the group of words "in a corner". It makes sense, but not complete sense. Such a group of words, which makes sense, but not complete sense, is called a **phrase**.

In the following sentences, the groups of words in **bold** are phrases:

The sun rises ***in the east.***

Humpty Dumpty sat ***on a wall.***

There came a giant ***to my door.***

It was a sunset ***of great beauty.***

The tops ***of the mountains*** *were covered with snow.*

Show me ***how to do it.***

It was a sunset of great beauty.

7. Examine the groups of words in bold in the following sentences:

He has a chain ***of gold.***

He has a chain ***which is made of gold.***

We recognize the first group of words as a phrase.

The second group of words, unlike the phrase *of gold*, contains a subject (*which)* and a predicate (*is made of gold*).

He has a chain which is made of gold.

Such a group of words which forms part of a sentence, and contains a subject and a predicate, is called a **clause**.

In the following sentences, the group of words in bold are clauses:

*People **who pay their debts** are trusted.*

*We cannot start **while it is raining**.*

*I think that you **have made a mistake**.*

Chapter 4 PARTS OF SPEECH

8. Words are divided into different kinds or classes, called **parts of speech**, *according to their use*; that is, *according to the work they do in a sentence.* The parts of speech are eight in number.

1. noun	3. pronoun	5. adverb	7. conjunction
2. adjective	4. verb	6. preposition	8. interjection

9. A **noun** is a word used as the *name* of a person, place, or thing; as,

***Akbar** was a great **king**.*

***Kolkata** is on the banks of the river **Hooghly**.*

*The **rose** smells sweet.*

*The **sun** shines brightly.*

*His **courage** won him **honour**.*

> **Note**— The word *thing* includes (i) all objects that we can see, hear, taste, touch, or smell; and (ii) something that we can th*ink* of, but cannot perceive by the senses.

10. An **adjective** is a word used to *add something* to the meaning of a noun; as,

*He is a **brave** boy.* *There are **twenty** boys in **this** class.*

11. A **pronoun** is a word used *instead of a noun*; as,

*John is absent, because **he** is ill.* *The books are where you left **them**.*

12. A **verb** is a word used to express an action, event or state; as,

*The girl **wrote** a letter to her cousin.*

*Kolkata **is** a big city.*

*Iron and copper **are** useful metals.*

13. An **adverb** is a word used to *add something* to the meaning of a verb, an adjective, or another adverb; as,

*He worked the sum **quickly**.*

*This flower is **very** beautiful.*

*She pronounced the word **quite** correctly.*

14. A **preposition** is a word used with a noun or a pronoun to show how the person or thing denoted by the noun or pronoun stands in relation to something else; as,

*There is a cow **in** the garden.*

*The girl is fond **of** music.*

*A fair little girl sat **under** a tree.*

15. A **conjunction** is a word used to *join* words or sentences; as,

*Rama **and** Hari are cousins.*

*Two **and** two make four.*

*I ran fast, **but** missed the train.*

16. An **interjection** is a word which expresses some sudden feeling; as,

***Hurrah**! We have won the game.*

***Alas** ! She is dead.*

17. Some modern grammars include **determiners** among the parts of speech. Determiners are words like *a, an, the, this, that, these, those, every, each, some, any, my, his, one, two,* etc., which determine or limit the meaning of the nouns that follow. In this book, as in many traditional grammars, all determiners except *a, an* and *the* are classed among adjectives.

18. As words are divided into different classes according to the work they do in sentences, it is clear that we cannot say to which part of speech a word belongs unless we see it used in a sentence.

*They arrived soon **after**. (Adverb)*

*They arrived **after** us. (Preposition)*

*They arrived **after** we had left. (Conjunction)*

From the above examples we see that *the same word can be used as different parts of speech.*

EXERCISE IN GRAMMAR 2

Name the part of speech of each italicized word in the following sentences, giving in each case your reason for the classification.

1. *Still* waters run deep.
2. He *still* lives in that house.
3. *After* the storm comes the calm.
4. The *after* effects of the drug are bad.
5. The *up* train is late.
6. It weighs *about* a pound.
7. He told us all *about* the battle.
8. He was only a yard *off* me.
9. Suddenly one of the wheels came *off.*
10. Muslims *fast* in the month of Ramzan.
11. He kept the *fast* for a week.
12. He is *on* the committee.
13. Let us move *on.*
14. Sit down and rest a *while.*
15. I will watch *while* you sleep.
16. They *while* away their evenings with books and games.

Chapter 5 THE NOUN: KINDS OF NOUNS

19. A noun is a word used as the *name* of a person, place, or thing.

Note—The word *thing* is used to mean anything that we can think of.

20. Look at the following sentence.

***Asoka** was a wise **king**.*

The noun *Asoka* refers to a *particular* king, but the noun *king* might be applied to any other king as well as to Asoka. We call *Asoka* a **Proper Noun**, and *king* a **Common Noun.**

Similarly,

***Sita** is a Proper Noun, while **girl** is a Common Noun.*

***Hari** is a Proper Noun, while **boy** is a Common Noun.*

***Kolkata** is a Proper Noun, while **city** is a Common Noun.*

***India** is a Proper Noun, while **country** is a Common Noun.*

The word *girl* is a Common Noun, because it is a name *common* to all girls, while *Sita* is a Proper Noun because it is the name of a *particular* girl.

Def.—A **Common Noun** is a name *given in common* to every person or thing *of the same class* or *kind.*

[Common here means shared by all.]

Def.—A **Proper Noun** is the name of some *particular* person or place.

[*Proper* means *one's own.* Hence a Proper Name is a person's *own* name.]

Note 1—Proper nouns are always written with a capital letter at the beginning.

Note 2—Proper nouns are sometimes used as common nouns; as,

1. He was the *Lukman* (= the wisest man) of his age.
2. Kalidas is often called the *Shakespeare* (= the greatest dramatist) of India.

Common Nouns include what are called Collective Nouns and Abstract Nouns.

21. A **collective noun** is the name of a number (or *collection)* of persons or things taken together and spoken of as *one whole;* as,

crowd, mob, team, flock, herd, army, fleet, jury, family, nation, parliament, committee.

a fleet = a collection of ships or vessels.

an army = a collection of soldiers.

a crowd = a collection of people.

The police dispersed the ***crowd****.*

The French ***army*** *was defeated at Waterloo.*

The ***jury*** *found the prisoner guilty.*

A ***herd*** *of cattle is passing.*

22. An **Abstract Noun** is usually the name of a *quality, action, or state* considered apart from the object to which it belongs; as,

quality *— goodness, kindness, whiteness, darkness, hardness, brightness, honesty, wisdom, bravery.*

action *— laughter, theft, movement, judgement, hatred.*

state *— childhood, boyhood, youth, slavery, sleep, sickness, death, poverty.*

The names of the Arts and Sciences (*e.g.*, grammar, music, chemistry, etc.) are also Abstract Nouns.

[We can speak of a *brave* soldier, a *strong* man, a *beautiful* flower. But we can also think of these *qualities* apart from any particular person or thing, and speak of *bravery, strength, beauty* by themselves. So also we can speak of what persons do or feel apart from the persons themselves, and give it a name. The word *abstract* means *drawn off.*]

23. Abstract Nouns are formed—

(1) from Adjectives; as,

kindness from kind; honesty from honest.

[Most abstract nouns are formed thus.]

(2) from Verbs; as,

obedience from obey; growth from grow.

(3) from Common Nouns; as,

childhood from child; slavery from slave.

24. Another classification of nouns is whether they are "countable" or "uncountable".

Countable nouns (or **countables**) are the names of objects, people, etc. that we can count, *e.g.*, book, pen, apple, boy, sister, doctor, horse.

Uncountable nouns (or **uncountables**) are the names of things that we cannot count, *e.g.*, milk, oil, sugar, gold, honesty. They mainly denote substances and abstract things.

Countable nouns have plural forms while uncountable nouns do not. For example, we say "books" but we cannot say "milks".

EXERCISE IN GRAMMAR 3

Point out the Nouns in the following sentences, and say whether they are common, proper, collective or abstract.

1. The crowd was very big.
2. Always speak the truth.
3. We all love honesty.
4. Our class consists of twenty pupils.
5. The elephant has great strength.
6. Solomon was famous for his wisdom.
7. Cleanliness is next to godliness.
8. We saw a fleet of ships in the harbour.
9. The class is studying grammar.
10. The Godavari overflows its banks every year.
11. A committee of five was appointed.
12. Jawaharlal Nehru was the first Prime Minister of India.
13. The soldiers were rewarded for their bravery.
14. Without health there is no happiness.
15. He gave me a bunch of grapes.
16. I recognized your voice at once.
17. Our team is better than theirs.
18. Never tell a lie.
19. Wisdom is better than strength.
20. He sets a high value on his time.
21. I believe in his innocence.
22. This room is thirty feet in length.
23. I often think of the happy days of childhood.
24. The streets of some of our cities are noted for their crookedness.
25. What is your verdict, gentlemen of the jury ?

EXERCISE IN COMPOSITION 4

Write the collective nouns used to describe a number of

(1) cattle; (2) soldiers; (3) sailors.

Write the qualities that belong to boys who are

(1) lazy; (2) cruel; (3) brave; (4) foolish.

EXERCISE IN COMPOSITION 5

Form Abstract Nouns from the following Adjectives.

long	strong	wide	broad	high	young
true	wise	free	poor	humble	short
good	proud	just	decent	prudent	vacant
brave	vain	cruel	dark	sweet	novel
sane	bitter	deep	human	quick	ignorant

Form Abstract Nouns from the following Verbs.

laugh	believe	choose	defend	free	obey
serve	move	think	see	live	hate
conceal	protect	judge	expect	please	seize
advise	pursue	excel	act	flatter	punish
relieve	now	starve	depart	die	converse
steal	occupy	persevere	succeed	discover	

Form Abstract Nouns from the following Common Nouns.

king	infant	mother	priest	friend	man
owner	agent	boy	captain	thief	rogue
hero	bond	rascal	woman	regent	beggar
pirate	patriot	bankrupt	author	coward	pilgrim
glutton					

Chapter 6 THE NOUN: GENDER

25. You know that living beings are of either the *male* or the *female* sex. Now compare the words in the following pairs.

boy	*lion*	*hero*	*cock-sparrow*
girl	*lioness*	*heroine*	*hen-sparrow*

lion

What do you notice ?

The first word of each pair is the name of a *male* animal.

The second word of each pair is the name of a *female* animal.

A noun that denotes a *male* animal is said to be of the **Masculine Gender.** [*Gender* comes from Latin *genus*, kind or sort.]

A noun that denotes a *female* animal is said to be of the **Feminine Gender.**

male female

26. A noun that denotes *either a male or a female* is said to be of the **Common Gender**; as
parent, child, friend, pupil, servant, thief, relation, enemy, cousin, person, orphan, student, baby, monarch, neighbour, infant.

27. A noun that denotes a thing that is *neither male nor female (i.e.,* ***thing without life****)* is said to be of the **Neuter Gender**; as,
book, pen, room, tree.
*[****Neuter*** *means* ***neither****, that is, neither male nor female.]*

It will be thus seen that in modern English the gender of a noun is entirely a matter of sex or the absence of sex. It has nothing to do with the *form* of a noun, which determines its gender in many other languages, *e.g.*, in Urdu where *bagiche* is masculine and *lakri* is feminine.

28. Objects without life are often **personified**, that is, spoken of as if they were living beings. We then regard them as males or females.

The Masculine Gender is often applied to objects remarkable for strength and violence ; as,
The Sun, Summer, Winter, Time, Death,
The ***sun*** *sheds* ***his*** *beams on rich and poor alike.*

The Feminine Gender is sometimes applied to objects remarkable for beauty, gentleness, and gracefulness ; as,
The Moon, the Earth, Spring, Autumn, Nature, Liberty, Justice, Mercy, Peace, Hope, Charity.
The ***moon*** *has hidden* ***her*** *face behind a cloud.*
Spring *has spread* ***her*** *mantle of green over the earth.*
Peace *hath* ***her*** *victories no less renowned than war.*

This use is most common in poetry but certain nouns are personified in prose too. A ship is often spoken of as *she* ; as,
The ship lost all ***her*** *boats in the storm.*

Ways of Forming the Feminine of Nouns

29. There are three ways of forming the Feminine of Nouns:-
(1) *By using an entirely different word* ; as

Masculine	Feminine
Bachelor	maid (old use)
	spinster
Boy	girl
Brother	sister
Buck	doe
Bull (or ox)	cow
Bullock	heifer
Cock	hen
Colt	filly
Dog	bitch
Drake	duck
Drone	bee
Earl	countess
Father	mother
Gander	goose
Gentleman	lady

Masculine	Feminine
Hart	roe
Horse	mare
Husband	wife
King	queen
Lord	lady
Man	woman
Monk (or friar)	nun
Nephew	niece
Papa	mamma
Ram	ewe
Sir	madam
Son	daughter
Stag	hind
Uncle	aunt
Wizard	witch

(2) By adding a syllable (-ess, -ine, -trix, -a, etc.) as,

Masculine	Feminine
Author	authoress
Baron	baroness
Count	countess
Giant	giantess
Heir	heiress
Host	hostess
Jew	Jewess
Lion	lioness
Manager	manageress

Masculine	Feminine
Mayor	mayoress
Patron	patroness
Peer	peeress
Poet	poetess
Priest	priestess
Prophet	prophetess
Shepherd	shepherdess
Steward	stewardess
Viscount	viscountess

Note— In the following *-ess* is added after *dropping* the vowel of the masculine ending.

Masculine	Feminine
Actor	actress
Benefactor	benefactress
Conductor	conductress
Enchanter	enchantress
Founder	foundress
Hunter	huntress
Instructor	instructress
Negro	negress
Abbot	abbess
Duke	duchess
Emperor	empress

Masculine	Feminine
Preceptor	preceptress
Prince	princess
Songster	songstress
Tempter	temptress
Seamster	seamstress
Tiger	tigress
Traitor	traitress
Waiter	waitress
Master	mistress
Murderer	murderess
Sorcerer	sorceress

Note — The suffix *-ess* is the commonest suffix used to form feminine nouns, from the masculine, and is the only one which we now use in forming a new feminine noun.

Masculine	Feminine
Hero	heroine
Testator	testatrix
Czar	czarina

Masculine	Feminine
Sultan	sultana
Signor	signora
Fox	vixen

(3) By placing a word before or after; as,

Masculine	*Feminine*
Grandfather	grandmother
Greatuncle	greataunt
Manservant	maidservant
Landlord	landlady

Masculine	*Feminine*
Milkman	milkwoman
Peacock	peahen
Salesman	saleswoman
Washerman	washerwoman

Chapter 7 THE NOUN: NUMBER

30. Notice the change of form in the second word of each pair.

tree	box	ox	man
trees	boxes	oxen	men

The first word of each pair denotes *one* thing, the second word of each pair denotes *more than one.*

A Noun that denotes *one* person or thing, is said to be in the **Singular Number**; as,
boy, girl, cow, bird, tree, book, pen.

A Noun that denotes *more than one person* or thing, is said to be in the Plural Number ; as,
boys, girls, cows, birds, trees, books, pens.

Thus there are *two* numbers in English—the Singular and the Plural.

How Plurals are Formed

31. *(i)* The Plural of nouns is generally formed *by adding -s to the singular* ; as,

boy, boys ; girl, girls ; book, books ;
pen, pens ; desk, desks ; cow, cows.

(ii) But Nouns ending in *-s, -sh, -ch* (soft), or -x form the plural by adding *-es* to the singular ; as,

class, classes; kiss, kisses; dish, dishes;
brush, brushes; match, matches; watch, watches;
branch, branches; tax, taxes; box, boxes.

(iii) Most Nouns ending in *-o* also form the plural *by adding -es to the singular* ; as,

buffalo, buffaloes; mango, mangoes; hero, heroes;
potato, potatoes; cargo, cargoes, echo, echoes;
negro, negroes; volcano, volcanoes.

(iv) A few nouns ending in *-o* merely add *-s*, ; as,

dynamo, dynamos ; solo, solos ; ratio, ratios ;
canto, cantos ; memento, mementos ; quarto, quartos ;
piano, pianos ; photo, photos ; stereo, stereos.
kilo, kilos ; logo, logos ; commando, commandos

ladies

(v) Nouns ending in *-y*, preceded by a *consonant*, form their plural *by changing -y into -i and adding -es* ; as,

baby, babies ; lady, ladies ; city, cities ;
army, armies ; story, stories ; pony, ponies.

(*vi*) The following nouns ending in *-f* or *-fe* form their plural *by changing -f or -fe into v and adding -es* ; as,

thief, thieves ; wife, wives ; wolf, wolves ;
life, lives ; calf, calves ; leaf, leaves ;
loaf, loaves ; knife, knives ; shelf, shelves.
half, halves ; elf, elves ; self, selves
sheaf, sheaves

The nouns *dwarf, hoof, scarf* and *wharf* take either *-s* or *-ves* in the plural.

dwarfs or dwarves ; hoofs or hooves ; scarfs or scarves ;
wharfs or wharves

handkerchief

Other words ending in *-f* or *-fe* add *-s*; as,

chief, chiefs ; safe, safes ; proof, proofs
gulf, gulfs ; cliff, cliffs ; handkerchief, handkerchiefs

32. A few nouns form their plural *by changing the inside vowel of the singular* ; as,

man, men ; woman, women; foot, feet ; tooth, teeth ;
goose, geese ; mouse, mice ; louse, lice.

33. There are a few nouns that form their plural *by adding -en* to the singular ; as,

ox, oxen; child, children.

The plural of *fish* is *fish* or *fishes.* In currrent English fish is the usual plural. *Fishes* can be used to refer to different kinds of fish.

34. Some nouns have the singular and the plural *alike* ; as,

swine, sheep, deer ; cod, trout, salmon; aircraft, spacecraft, series, species.
pair, dozen, score, gross, hundred, thousand (when used after numerals).
I bought three dozen oranges.
Some people reach the age of three score and ten.
The sari cost me five thousand rupees.
stone, hundredweight.
He weighs above nine stone.
Twenty hundredweight make one ton.

fish

35. Some nouns are used only in the plural.

(1) Names of instruments which have two parts forming a kind of pair; as,
bellows, scissors, tongs, pincers, spectacles.

(2) Names of certain articles of dress ; as,
trousers, drawers, breeches, jeans, tights, shorts, pyjamas.

trouser

(3) Certain other nouns ; as,
Annals, thanks, proceeds (of a sale), tidings, environs, nuptials, obsequies, assets, chattels.

36. Some nouns originally singular are now generally used in the plural ; as,

Alms, riches, eaves.
***Riches** do many things.*

37. The following nouns look plural but are in fact singular:

(1) Names of subjects
mathematics, physics, electronics, etc.

(2) The word *news*

(3) Names of some common diseases
measles, mumps, rickets

(4) Names of some games
billiards, draughts

spectacles

Mathematics **is** *his favourite study.*
No news **is** *good news.*
India won by **an** *innings and three runs.*
Measles **is** *infectious.*
Billiards **is** *my favourite game.*

'Means' is used either as singular or plural. But when it has the meaning of 'wealth' it is always plural ; as,

He succeeded by **this** *means (or, by* **these** *means) in passing the examination.*
His means **are** *small, but he has incurred no debt.*

38. Certain Collective Nouns, though singular in form, are always used as plurals ; as,

poultry, cattle, vermin, people, gentry.
These **poultry are** *mine.*
Whose **are** *these* **cattle** *?*
Vermin *destroy our property and carry disease.*
Who **are** *those* **people** *(= persons) ?*
There **are** *few* **gentry** *in this town.*

Note—As a Common Noun 'people' means a 'nation' and is used in both singular and plural ; as,

1. The Japanese are a hard-working *people.*
2. *There are many different peoples in Europe.*

39. A Compound Noun generally forms its plural *by adding -s to the principal word* ; as,

Singular	*Plural*
Commander-in-chief	commanders-in-chief
Coat-of-mail	coats-of-mail
Son-in-law	sons-in-law
Daughter-in-law	daughters-in-law
Step son	step sons
Step daughter	step daughters
Maid servant	maid servants (but man servant, plural men servants)
Passer-by	passers-by
Looker-on	lookers-on
Man-of-war	men-of-war

We say *spoonfuls* and *handfuls,* because *spoonful* and *handful* are regarded as one word.

Note that the Proper Nouns *Brahman* and *Mussulman* are not compounds of *man*; therefore their plurals are *Brahmans* and *Mussulmans.*

40. Many nouns taken from foreign languages keep their original plural form ; as,

From Latin—

erratum, errata ; *formula, formulae (or formulas) :*
index, indices ; *memorandum, memoranda ;*
radius, radii ; *terminus, termini (or terminuses)*

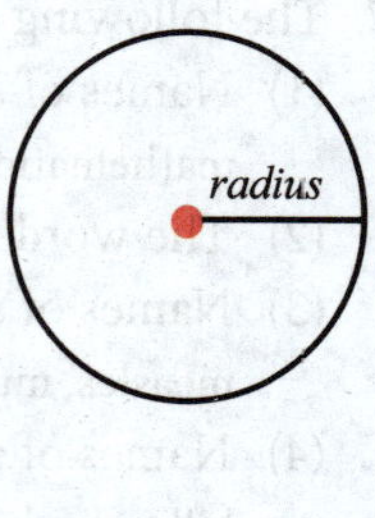

From Greek—

axis, axes ; *parenthesis, parentheses ;*
crisis, crises ; *hypothesis, hypotheses ;*
basis, bases ; *phenomenon, phenomena ;*

analysis, analyses; *criterion, criteria*

From Italian—

Bandit, banditti, (or bandits)

From French—

Madame (madam), mesdames; monsieur, messieurs

From Hebrew—

Cherub, cherubim (or cherubs); seraph, seraphim (or seraphs).

41. Some nouns have two forms for the plural, each with a somewhat different meaning.

Singular	***Plural***
Brother	brothers, sons of the same parent. brethren, members of a society or a community.
Cloth	cloths, kinds or pieces of cloth. clothes, garments.
Die	dies, stamps for coining. dice, small cubes used in games.
Index	indexes, tables of contents to books indices, signs used in algebra.
Penny	pennies, number of coins. pence, amount in value.

brothers

42. Some nouns have two meanings in the singular but only one in the plural.

	Singular	***Plural***	
Light :	(1) *radiance* ; (2) *a lamp.*	Lights :	*lamps.*
People :	(1) *nation* ; (2) *men and women.*	Peoples :	*nations.*
Powder :	(1) *dust* ; (2) *a dose of medicine in fine grains like dust.*	Powders :	*doses of medicine.*
Practice :	(1) *habit* ; (2) *exercise of a profession.*	Practices :	*habits.*

brethren

43. Some nouns have one meaning in the singular, two in the plural.

	Singular		***Plural***
Colour :	*hue.*	Colours :	(1) *hues* ; (2) *the flag of a regiment.*
Custom :	*habit.*	Customs :	(1) *habits* ; (2) *duties levied on imports.*
Effect :	*result.*	Effects :	(1) *results* ; (2) *property.*
Manner :	*method.*	Manners:	(1) *methods* ; (2) *correct behaviour.*
Moral :	*a moral lesson.*	Morals :	(1) *moral lessons* ; (2) *conduct*
Number :	*a quantity.*	Numbers :	(1) *quantities* ; (2) *verses.*
Pain :	*suffering.*	Pains :	(1) *sufferings.*

eye glasses

			(2)	*care, exertion.*
Premise :	*proposition*	Premises :	(1)	*propositions ;*
			(2)	*buildings.*
Quarter :	*fourth part.*	Quarters :	(1)	*fourth parts ;*
			(2)	*lodgings.*
Spectacle :	*a sight.*	Spectacles :	(1)	*sights ;*
			(2)	*eye-glasses.*
Letter :	(1) *letter of the alphabet ;*	Letters :	(1)	*letters of the alphabet ;*
	(2) *epistle.*		(2)	*epistles ;*
			(3)	*literature.*
Ground :	(1) *earth ;*	Grounds :	(1)	*enclosed land attached to house.*
	(2) *reason.*		(2)	*reasons ;*
			(3)	*dregs.*

44. Some nouns have different meanings in the singular and the plural.

Singular	***Plural***
Air : atmosphere.	Airs : affected manners.
Good : benefit, well-being.	Goods : merchandise.
Compass : extent, range.	Compasses : an instrument for drawing circles.
Respect : regard.	Respects : compliments.
Physic : medicine.	Physics : natural science.
Iron : a kind of metal.	Irons : fetters.
Force : strength.	Forces : troops.

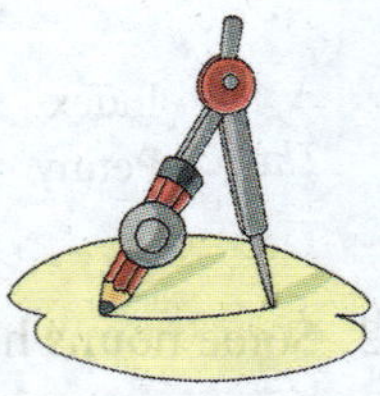
compass

45. Letters, figures and other symbols are made plural by adding an apostrophe and *s*; as,
There are more e's than a's in this page.
Dot your i's and cross your t's.
Add two 5's and four 2's.

tin

46. It is usual to say —
The Miss Smiths. (Singular, Miss Smith.)

47. Abstract Nouns have no plural. They are uncountables.
hope, charity, love, kindness.
When such words do appear in the plural, they are used as countables; as
Provocations = instances or cases of provocation.
Kindnesses = acts of kindness.
Names of substances are also uncountables and are not therefore used in the plural.
Copper, iron, tin, wood.
When such words are used in the plural, they become countables with changed meanings ; as,
Coppers = copper coins ; irons = fetters ;
tins = cans made of tin ; woods = forests.

Chapter 8 THE NOUN: CASE

48. Examine these sentences:
1. John threw a stone.
2. The horse kicked the boy.
In sentence 1, the noun *John* is the Subject. It is the answer

to the question, "Who threw a stone ?"

The group of words *threw a stone* is the Predicate.

The Predicate contains the verb *threw.*

What did John *throw?—A stone. Stone* is the object which John threw. The noun *stone* is therefore called the **Object**.

In sentence 2, the noun *horse* is the Subject. It is the answer to the question, "Who kicked the boy ?"

The noun *boy* is the Object. It is the answer to the question, "Whom did the horse kick ?"

49. When a noun (or pronoun) is used as the Subject of a verb, it is said to be in the **Nominative Case.**

When a noun (or pronoun) is used as the Object of a verb, it is said to be in the **Objective** (or **Accusative) Case.**

Note—To find the Nominative, put Who ? or What ? before the verb.

To find the Accusative, put *Whom* ? or *What* ? before the verb and its subject.

50. A noun which comes after a preposition is also said to be in the Accusative Case ; as,

The book is on the desk.

The noun *desk* is in the Accusative Case, governed by the preposition *on.*

The book is on the desk.

51. Read the following sentences :

Hari broke the window. (Object)

The window was broken. (Subject)

It will be seen that Nouns in English have the *same form* for the Nominative and the Accusative.

The Nominative generally comes *before* the verb, and the Accusative *after* the verb. Hence they are distinguished by the *order* of words, or by the sense.

52. Compare—

1. Rama gave a ball.

2. Rama gave Hari a ball.

In each of these sentences the noun *ball* is the Object of *gave.*

In the second sentence we are told that *Hari* was the person *to whom* Rama gave a ball.

The noun *Hari* is called the **Indirect Object** of the verb *gave.*

The noun *ball,* the ordinary Object, is called the **Direct Object.**

It will be noticed that the position of the Indirect Object is immediately after the verb and before the Direct Object.

Note—

Rama gave Hari a ball. = Rama gave a ball to Hari.

Will you do me a favour ? = Will you do a favour to me ?

I bought Rama a ball. = I bought a ball for Rama.

Fetch the boy a book. = Fetch a book for the boy.

She made Ruth a new dress. = She made a new dress for Ruth.

Get me a taxi. = Get a taxi for me.

We see that the Indirect Object of a verb denotes the person *to whom* something is given, or *for whom* something is done.

53. Examine the sentence :

This is Rama's umbrella.

Ram's umbrella

Rama's umbrella = the umbrella *belonging to* Rama.

The *form* of the noun *Rama* is changed to *Rama's* to show ownership or *possession.* The Noun *Rama's* is therefore said to be in the **Possessive** (or **Genitive**) **Case**.

The Possessive answers the question, 'Whose ?'

Whose umbrella ? — Rama's.

54. The Possessive Case does not always denote possession. It is used to denote authorship, origin, kind, etc. as,

Shakespeare's plays	=	*the plays written by Shakespeare*
A mother's love	=	*the love felt by a mother*
The President's speech	=	*the speech delivered by the President*
Mr Aggarwal's house	=	*the house where Mr. Aggarwal lives*
Ashok's school	=	*the school where Ashok goes*
A children's playground	=	*a playground for children*
A week's holiday	=	*a holiday which lasts a week*

Formation of the Possessive Case

55. (1) When the noun is Singular, the Possessive Case is formed by adding *'s* to the noun ; as,

The *boy's* book ; the *king's* crown.

Note—The letter s is omitted in a few words where too many hissing sounds would come together ; as,

For conscience' sake ; for goodness' sake ;
For justice' sake ; for Jesus' sake ; Moses' laws.

(2) When the noun is Plural, and ends in *s*, the Possessive Case is formed by adding only an apostrophe ; as,

Boys' school ; girls' school ; horses' tails.

(3) When the noun is Plural but does not end in *s*, the Possessive sign is formed by adding *'s;* as,

Men's club ; children's books.

56. When a noun or a title consists of several words, the Possessive sign is attached only to the last word; as,

The King of Bhutan's visit.

The Prime Minister of Mauritius' speech.

57. When two nouns are in apposition, the possessive sign is put to the latter only ; as,

That is Tagore the poet's house.

58. Also when two nouns are closely connected, the possessive is put to the latter ; as,

Karim and Salim's bakery.

William and Mary's reign.

59. Each of two or more connected nouns implying *separate* possession must take the possessive sign ; as,

Raja Rao's and R.K. Narayan's novels.

Goldsmith's and Cowper's poems.

Narayan's and Rao's novels

Use of the Possessive Case

60. The Possessive Case is now used chiefly with the names of *living things ;* as,

The Governor's bodyguard ; the lion's mane.

So we must say :

The leg of the table [not, the table's leg].

The cover of the book [not, the book's cover].

house's roof

The roof of the house [not, the house's roof].

61. But the Possessive is used with the names of *personified** *objects;* as,

India's heroes ; Nature's laws ; Fortune's favourite ; at duty's call ; at death's door.

62. The Possessive is also used with nouns denoting time, space, or weight ; as,

A day's march ; a week's holiday ; in a year's time ; a stone's throw ; a foot's length ; a pound's weight.

63. The following phrases are also in common use :

At his fingers' ends ; for mercy's sake ; to his heart's content ; at his wit's end ; a boat's crew.

64. The possessive of a proper name or of a noun denoting a trade, profession, or relationship may be used to denote a building or place of business (church, house, school, college, shop, hospital, theatre, etc.); as,

She has gone to the baker's (= baker's shop).

Tonight I am dining at my uncle's (= uncle's house).

Can you tell me the way to St .Paul's (= St. Paul's church)?

I attend the Town High School but my cousin attends St. Xavier's.

He was educated at St. Joseph's.

65. When you are in doubt whether to use a noun in the possessive case or with the preposition *of,* remember that, as a general rule, the possessive case is used to denote possession or ownership. Thus it is better to say 'the defeat of the enemy' than 'the enemy's defeat', even though no doubt as to the meaning would arise.

Sometimes, however, a noun in the possessive case has a different meaning from a noun used with the preposition *of;* as,

'The Prime Minister's reception in Delhi' means a reception held by the Prime Minister in Delhi.

'The reception of the Prime Minister in Delhi' means the manner in which the people welcomed him when he entered Delhi.

The phrase 'the love of a father' may mean either 'a father's love of his child' or 'a child's love of his father'.

a child's love of his father

Nouns in Apposition

66. Read the following sentence.

Rama, our captain, made fifty runs.

We see that *Rama* and our *captain* are one and the same person. The noun *captain* follows the noun *Rama* simply to explain which *Rama* is referred to.

When one noun follows another to describe it, the noun which follows is said to be **in apposition** to the noun which comes before it.

[*Apposition* means *placing near.*]

A noun in apposition is in the *same* case as the noun which it explains.

In the above sentence the noun *captain* is in apposition to the noun *Rama,* and is in the Nominative Case (because *Rama* is in the Nominative Case).

Further examples:

1. *Kabir, the great reformer, was a weaver.*
2. *Yesterday I met your uncle, the doctor.*
3. *Have you seen Ganguli, the artist's drawings ?*

In sentence 1, the noun in apposition is in the Nominative Case.

In sentence 2, the noun in apposition is in the Accusative Case. [Why?]

In sentence 3, the noun in apposition is in the Genitive Case. [Why?]

* When an inanimate thing has ascribed to it the attributes of a person, it is said to be personified. (See § 28).

Chapter 9 THE ADJECTIVE

67. Read the following sentences :

1. Sita is a *clever* girl. (Girl of *what kind* ?)
2. I don't like *that* boy. (*Which* boy ?)
3. He gave me *five* mangoes. (*How many* mangoes ?)
4. There is *little* time for preparation. (*How much* time ?)

In sentence 1, 'clever' shows *what kind* of girl Sita is ; or, in other words, 'clever' *describes* the girl Sita.

In sentence 2, 'that' *points out* which boy is meant.

In sentence 3, 'five' shows *how many* mangoes he gave me.

In sentence 4, 'little' shows *how much* time there is for preparation.

A word used with a noun to *describe* or *point out*, the person, animal, place or thing which the noun names, or to tell the *number* or *quantity*, is called an **Adjective**.

So we may define an Adjective as a word used with a noun to *add something for its meaning*.

[*Adjective* means *added to*.]

68. Look at the following sentences:

1. The *lazy* boy was punished.
2. The boy is *lazy*.

In sentence 1, the Adjective *lazy* is used along with the noun *boy* as an *epithet* or *attribute*. It is, therefore, said to be used **Attributively.**

In sentence 2, the Adjective *lazy* is used along with the verb *is*, and forms part of the Predicate. It is, therefore, said to be used **Predicatively.**

Some Adjectives can be used only Predicatively ; as,

She is *afraid* of ghosts.

I am quite *well*.

Kinds of Adjectives

Adjectives may be divided into the following classes :

69. **Adjectives of Quality** (or **Descriptive Adjective**) show the *kind* or *quality* of a person or thing ; as,

Kolkata is a *large* city.

He is an *honest* man.

The *foolish old* crow tried to sing.

This is a Grammar of the *English** language.

[*Adjectives formed from Proper Nouns (*e.g., French* wines, *Turkish* tobacco, *Indian* tea, etc.) are sometimes called **Proper Adjectives.** They are generally classed with Adjectives of Quality.]

Adjectives of Quality answer the question : *Of what kind ?*

70. **Adjectives of Quantity** show *how much* of a thing is meant; as,

I ate *some* rice.

He showed *much* patience.

He has *little* intelligence.

We have had *enough* exercise.

He has lost *all* his wealth.

You have *no* sense.

He did not eat *any* rice.

Take *great* care of your health.

He claimed his *half* share of the booty.

There has not been *sufficient* rain this year.

The *whole* sum was expended.

Adjectives of Quantity answer the question : *How much* ?

71. **Adjectives of Number** (or **Numeral Adjectives**) show *how many* persons or things are meant, or *in what order* a person or thing stands ; as,

The hand has *five* fingers.

Few cats like cold water.

There are *no* pictures in this book.

I have taught you *many* things.

All men must die.

Here are *some* ripe mangoes.

Most boys like cricket.

There are *several* mistakes in your exercise.

Sunday is the *first* day of the week.

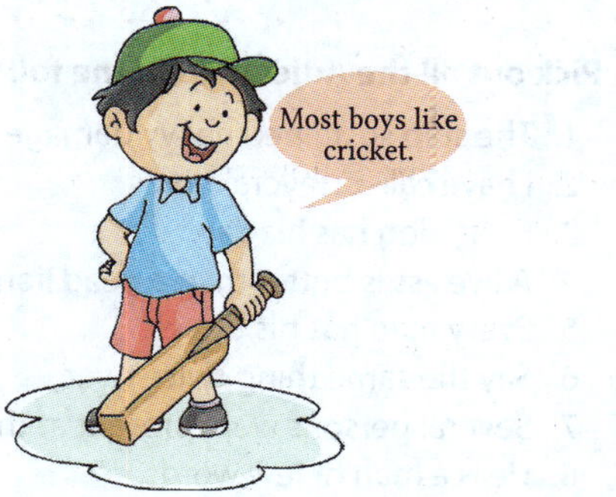

Adjectives of Number answer the question : *How many* ?

72. Adjectives of Number (or Numeral Adjectives) are of three kinds.

(i) **Definite Numeral Adjectives,** which denote an *exact* number ; as,

One, two, three, etc. These are called **Cardinals.**

First, second, third, etc. These are called **Ordinals.**

[A Cardinal denotes *how many,* and an Ordinal the *order* of things in a series. It will be seen that Ordinals really do the work of Demonstrative Adjectives. See 74]

(ii) **Indefinite Numeral Adjectives,** which do *not* denote an exact number ; as,

All, no; many, few; some, any; certain, several, sundry.

(iii) **Distributive Numeral Adjectives,** which refer to each one of a number; as.,

Each boy must take his turn.

India expects *every* man to do his duty.

Every word of it is false.

Either pen will do.

On *either* side is a narrow lane.

Neither accusation is true.

73. The same Adjective may be classed as of Quantity or Number, according to its use.

Adjectives of Quantity	*Adjectives of Number*
I ate *some* rice.	*Some* boys are clever.
He has lost *all* his wealth.	All men must die.
You have *no* sense.	There are *no* pictures in this book.
He did not eat *any* rice.	Are there *any* mango-trees in this garden ?
I have *enough* sugar.	There are not *enough* spoons.

74. **Demonstrative Adjectives** *point out* which person or thing is meant ; as,

This boy is stronger than Hari.

That boy is industrious.
These mangoes are sour.
Those rascals must be punished.
Yonder fort once belonged to Shivaji.
Don't be in *such* a hurry.
I hate *such* things.

industrious

Demonstrative Adjectives answer the question : *Which* ?

[It will be noticed that *this* and *that* are used with Singular nouns and *these* and *those* with Plural nouns.]

75. *What, which* and *whose*, when they are used with nouns to ask questions, are called **Interrogative Adjectives**; as,

Whose book is this?

What manner of man is he ?
Which way shall we go ?
Whose book is this ?

[It will be seen that *what* is used in a general sense, and *which* in a selective sense.]

EXERCISE IN GRAMMAR 6

Pick out all the Adjectives in the following sentences, and say to which class each of them belongs.

1. The ship sustained heavy damage.
2. I have called several times.
3. Every dog has his day.
4. A live ass is better than a dead lion.
5. Every man has his duties.
6. Say the same thing twice over.
7. Several persons were present at the time.
8. He is a man of few words.
9. Neither party is quite in the right.
10. What time is it ?
11. Which pen do you prefer ?
12. The way was long, the wind was cold, the minstrel was infirm and old.
13. He comes here every day.
14. I have not seen him for several days.
15. There should not be much talk and little work.
16. Abdul won the second prize.
17. The child fell down from the great height.
18. He was absent last week.
19. He died a glorious death.
20. A small leak may sink a great ship.
21. Good wine needs no bush.
22. I like the little pedlar who has a crooked nose.
23. King Francis was a hearty King, and loved a royal sport.
24. In the furrowed land the toilsome and patient oxen stand.
25. My uncle lives in the next house.
26. Some dreams are like reality.
27. A cross child is not liked.
28. It is an ill wind that blows nobody any good.

76. In the following sentences, the words *own* and *very* are used as **Emphasizing Adjectives.**

I saw it with my *own* eyes.
He was beaten at his *own* game.
Mind your *own* business.
He is his *own* master.
That is the *very* thing we want.
"When all else left my cause,
My *very* adversary took my part''.

I saw it with my own eyes.

77. The word *what* is sometimes used as an **Exclamatory Adjective;** as,

What genius !
What folly !
What an idea !
What a blessing !
What a piece of work is man !

What genius!

78. As already pointed out (§ 74), *this* and *that* are the only Adjectives which are inflected or changed in form to show number.

This girl sings. *These* girls sing.

That boy plays. *Those* boys play.

This, these indicate something near to the speaker.

That, those indicate more distant objects.

Formation of Adjectives

79. *(i)* Many Adjectives are formed from Nouns.

Noun	*Adjective*
Boy	boyish
Fool	foolish
Care	careful
Play	playful
Hope	hopeful
Venture	venturesome
Trouble	troublesome
Shame	shameless
Sense	senseless
Silk	silken
Gold	golden

Noun	*Adjective*
Dirt	dirty
Storm	stormy
Pardon	pardonable
Laugh	laughable
Outrage	outrageous
Courage	courageous
Glory	glorious
Envy	envious
Man	manly
King	kingly
Gift	gifted

(ii) Some Adjectives are formed from Verbs.

Verb	*Adjective*
Tire	tireless
Talk	talkative

Verb	*Adjective*
Cease	ceaseless
Move	moveable

(iii) Some Adjectives are formed from other Adjectives.

Adjective	*Adjective*
Tragic	tragical
Whole	wholesome
Three	threefold

Adjective	*Adjective*
Black	blackish
White	whitish
Sick	sickly

EXERCISE IN COMPOSITION 7

Supply suitable Adjectives.

1. The town stood a____siege.
2. The____prize was won by a Hindu.
3. The____woman lives in a wretched hut.
4. This is a very____matter.
5. The battle of Waterloo ended in a____victory.
6. Suddenly there arose a____storm.
7. It is a____lie.
8. The____tidings were a heavy blow to the old man.
9. Here is Rs. 50 : pay the fare and keep the____money.
10. His reading is of a very____range.
11. The injured man wants____advice.
12. You cannot have it____ways.
13. India expects____man to do his duty.
14. The____bird catches the worm.
15. Have you any____reason to give ?
16. ____anxiety has undermined his health.
17. There were riots in____places.
18. An____man will not reason calmly.
19. He stands____feet in his stockings.
20. Nelson won for himself____fame.
21. I have no____cash.
22. He always walks with a____step.
23. ____errors are not easily corrected.
24. Every cloud has a____lining.
25. He was a man of____ambition.
26. He was listened to in____silence.

EXERCISE IN COMPOSITION 8

Form Adjectives from the following Nouns.

[Attach each Adjective to a suitable noun.]

ease, pity, time, heaven, health, wealth, love, hill, need, green, room, cost, pain, doubt, wonder, peace, child, prince, mountain, ridicule, picture, labour, wood, pomp, artist, progress, slave, contempt, tempest, sense, quarrel, thought, hope, friend

EXERCISE IN COMPOSITION 9

Use each of the following Adjectives in a sentence.

[Models — A *soft* answer turneth away wrath.

His *polite* manners have endeared him to all.

Swimming is a *healthy* exercise.

A *certain* man fell among thieves.]

happy, sad, industrious, lazy, big, small, soft, harsh, hard, polite, rude, wise, foolish, rich, poor, young, new, old, long, short, quick, slow, strong, weak, handsome, ugly, clever, dull, kind, cruel, healthy, dutiful, distant, certain.

EXERCISE IN COMPOSITION 10

Use a suitable Adjective with each of the following Nouns.

[Models — A violent storm.

A long siege.

A decisive victory.

A populous city.

A devoted husband.]

storm, siege, sleep, victory, advice, blow, silence, hands, water, servant, flower, city, artist, dealer, voice, husband, subject, child, king, dog

EXERCISE IN COMPOSITION 11

Use as many suitable Adjectives as you can with each of the following Nouns.

[Models — A narrow street, a wide street, a crooked street, a dirty street.

A clean street.

A deliberate lie, a black lie, a white lie.]

fortune, man, news, storm, health, novel, progress, room, incident

EXERCISE IN COMPOSITION 12

Write down the Adjectives opposite in meaning to the following.

courageous, many, wild, hot, lean, heavy, costly, barren, beautiful, patient, honest, civilized, careful, strong, experienced, slow, friendly, cruel, soft

Chapter 10 COMPARISON OF ADJECTIVES

80. Read these sentences :

1. Rama's mango is *sweet.*
2. Hari's mango is *sweeter* than Rama's.

Hari's mango is sweeter than Rama's.

3. Govind's mango is the *sweetest* of all.

In sentence 1, the adjective *sweet* merely tells us that Rama's mango has the quality of sweetness, without saying how much of this quality it has.

In sentence 2, the adjective *sweeter* tells us that Hari's mango, compared with Rama's, has more of the quality of sweetness.

In sentence 3, the adjective *sweetest* tells us that of *all* these mangoes Govind's mango has the greatest amount or highest degree of the quality of sweetness.

We thus see that Adjectives change in form (*sweet, sweeter, sweetest*) to show *comparison.* They are called the three **Degrees of Comparison.**

The Adjective *sweet* is said to be in the **Positive Degree.**

The Adjective *sweeter* is said to be in the **Comparative Degree.**

The Adjective *sweetest* is said to be in the **Superlative Degree.**

The Positive Degree of an Adjective is the Adjective in its simple form. It is used to denote the mere existence of some quality of what we speak about. It is used when no comparison is made.

The Comparative Degree of an Adjective denotes a *higher* degree of the quality than the Positive, and is used when *two* things (or sets of things) are compared ; as,

This boy is *stronger* than that.

Which of these two pens is the *better* ?

Apples are *dearer* than oranges.

The Superlative Degree of an Adjective denotes the highest degree of the quality, and is used when *more than two* things (or sets of things) are compared ; as,

This boy is the *strongest* in the class.

Note 1—There is another way in which we can compare things. Instead of saying 'Rama is stronger than Balu', we can say 'Balu is less strong than Rama'. Instead of saying 'Hari is the laziest boy in the class', we can say 'Hari is the least industrious boy in the class'.

Note 2—The Superlative with most is sometimes used where there is no idea of comparison, but merely a desire to indicate the possession of a quality in a very high degree; as,

This is *most* unfortunate.

It was a *most* eloquent speech.

Truly, a *most* ingenious device !

This usage has been called the *Superlative of Eminence*, or the *Absolute Superlative.*

Formation of Comparative and Superlative

81. Most Adjectives of *one* syllable, and some of more than one, form the Comparative by adding *er* and the Superlative by adding *est* to the Positive.

Positive	*Comparative*	*Superlative*
Sweet	sweeter	sweetest
Small	smaller	smallest
Tall	taller	tallest
Bold	bolder	boldest
Clever	cleverer	cleverest
Kind	kinder	kindest
Young	younger	youngest
Great	greater	greatest

When the Positive ends in *e,* only *r* and *st* are added.

Brave	braver	bravest
Fine	finer	finest
White	whiter	whitest
Large	larger	largest
Able	abler	ablest
Noble	nobler	noblest
Wise	wiser	wisest

When the Positive ends in *y*, preceded by a consonant, the *y* is changed into *i* before adding *er* and *est*.

Happy	happier	happiest
Easy	easier	easiest
Heavy	heavier	heaviest
Merry	merrier	merriest
Wealthy	wealthier	wealthiest

heavy heavier heaviest

When the Positive is a word of one syllable and ends in a *single* consonant, preceded by a *short vowel*, this consonant is doubled before adding *er* and *est*.

Red	redder	reddest
Big	bigger	biggest
Hot	hotter	hottest
Thin	thinner	thinnest
Sad	sadder	saddest
Fat	fatter	fattest

Sad Sadder Saddest

82. Adjectives of more than *two* syllables form the Comparative and Superlative by putting *more* and *most* before the Positive.

Positive	*Comparative*	*Superlative*
Beautiful	more beautiful	most beautiful
Difficult	more difficult	most difficult
Industrious	more industrious	most industrious
Courageous	more courageous	most courageous

Two-syllable adjectives ending in *ful* (e.g. useful), *less* (e.g. hopeless), *ing* (e.g. boring) and *ed* (e.g. surprised) and many others (e.g. modern, recent, foolish, famous, certain) take *more* and *most*.

The following take either *er* and *est* or *more* and *most*.

polite	simple	feeble	gentle	narrow
cruel	common	handsome	pleasant	stupid

She is *politer/more polite* than her sister.

He is the *politest/most polite* of them.

83. The Comparative in *er* is not used when we compare two qualities in the same person or thing. If we wish to say that the courage of Rama is greater than the courage of Balu, we say,

Rama is *braver* than Balu.

But if we wish to say that the courage of Rama is greater than his prudence, we must say,

Rama is *more brave* than prudent.

84. When two objects are compared with each other, the latter term of comparison must exclude the former; as,

Iron is more useful than any *other* metal.

If we say,

Iron is more useful than any metal,

Iron is more useful than any metal,

that is the same thing as saying 'Iron is more useful than iron' since iron is itself a metal.

Irregular Comparison

85. The following Adjectives are compared *irregularly*, that is, their Comparative and Superlative are not formed from the Positive.

Positive	*Comparative*	*Superlative*
Good, well	better	best
Bad, evil, ill	worse	worst
Little	less,lesser	least
Much	more	most (quantity)
Many	more	most (number)
Late	later, latter	latest, last
Old	older, elder	oldest, eldest
Far	farther	farthest
(Nigh)	(nigher)	nighest, next
(Fore)	(former)	foremost, first
(Fore)	further	furthest
(In)	inner	inmost, innermost
(Up)	upper	upmost, uppermost
(Out)	outer, (utter)	utmost, uttermost

Note—The forms nigh, nigher, nighest, fore and utter are outdated.

EXERCISE IN GRAMMAR 13

Compare the following Adjectives.

black, excellent, ill, gloomy, mad, safe, bad, unjust, gay, able, dry, timid, ugly, true, severe, exact, agreeable, difficult, little, few, numerous, merry

86. The double forms of the Comparative and Superlative of the Adjectives given in § 85 are used in different ways.

Later, latter; latest, last — *Later* and *latest* refer to time; *latter* and *last* refer to position.

He is *later* than I expected.

I have not heard the *latest* news.

The *latter* chapters are lacking in interest.

The *last* chapter is carelessly written.

Ours is the *last* house in the street.

Elder, older ; eldest, oldest — *Elder* and *eldest* are used only of persons, not of animals or things; and are now confined to members of the same family. *Elder* is not used with *than*. *Older* and *oldest* are used of both persons and things.

John is my *elder* brother.

Tom is my *eldest* son.

He is *older* than his sister.

Rama is the *oldest* boy in the eleven.

This is the *oldest* temple in Kolkata.

Farther, further — Both *farther* and *further* are used to express distance. *Further*, not *farther*, is used to mean "additional".

Kolkata is *farther/further* from the equator than Colombo.

After this he made no *further* remarks.

I must have a reply without *further* delay.

Nearest, next —*Nearest* means the shortest distance away. *Next* refers to one of a sequence of things coming one after the other.

Mumbai is the seaport *nearest* to Europe.

Where is the *nearest* phone box?

Karim's shop is *next* to the post office.

My uncle lives in the *next* house.

EXERCISE IN COMPOSITION 14

(a) Fill the blank spaces with 'later' or 'latter'.

1. The majority accepted the____proposal.
2. The_____part of the book shows signs of hurry.
3. At a_____date, he was placed in charge of the whole *taluka.*
4. I prefer the______proposition to the former.
5. Is there no_____news than last week's ?

(b) Fill the blank spaces with 'older' or 'elder'.

1. I have an_____sister.
2. Rama is_____than Hari by two years.
3. His_____brother is in the Indian Civil Service.
4. She is the_____of the two sisters.
5. The nephew is______than his uncle.

(c) Fill the blank spaces with 'oldest' and 'eldest'.

1. Rustam is the_____of my uncle's five sons.
2. He is the_____member of the School Committee.
3. That is Antonio, the duke's______son.
4. The_____mosque in the town is near the railway station.
5. Mr. Smith is the______ teacher in the school.

(d) Fill the blank spaces with 'farther' or 'further'.

1. I can't walk any _____.
2. No_____reasons were given.
3. He walked off without_______ceremony.
4. Until______orders Mr K S Dave will act as Headmaster of Nira High School.
5. To let, a bungalow at Ridge Road. For____particulars apply to Box No. 65.

(e) Fill the blank spaces with 'latest' or 'last'.

1. The_____news from China is very disquieting.
2. The_____time I saw him, he was in high spirits.
3. Today is the_____day for receiving tenders.
4. We expect to get the______news in a few hours.
5. The______Moghul Emperor came to an ignominious end.

(f) Fill the blank spaces with 'nearest' or 'next'.

1. This is the_____post office to my house.
2. The pillar-box is_____to my house.
3. The burglar was taken to the____police station.
4. His house is_____to mine.
5. The_____railway station is two miles from here.

87. Certain English Comparatives have lost their comparative meaning and are used as Positive. They cannot be followed by *than*. These are:

former, latter, elder, hinder, upper, inner, outer, utter.

Both the tiger and the leopard are cats; the *former* animal is much larger than the *latter.*

The *inner* meaning of this letter is not clear.

The soldiers ran to defend the *outer* wall.

My *elder* brother is an engineer.

This man is an *utter* fool.

88. Certain Comparatives borrowed from Latin have no Positive or Superlative degree. They all end in *or*, not *er*. They are twelve in all. Five of them have lost their Comparative meaning, and are used as Positive Adjectives. These are:

interior, exterior, ulterior, major, minor.

The *exterior* wall of the house is made of stone; the *interior* walls are of wood.

His age is a matter of *minor* importance.

I have no *ulterior* motive in offering you help.

The other seven are used as Comparative Adjectives but are followed by *to* instead of *than* (See § 89).

89. The comparative degree is generally followed by *than;* but Comparative Adjectives ending in *-or* are followed by the preposition *to;* as,

inferior, superior, prior, anterior, posterior, senior, junior.

Hari is *inferior* to Ram in intelligence.

Rama's intelligence is *superior* to Hari's.

His marriage was *prior* to his father's death.

He is *junior* to all his colleagues.

All his colleagues are *senior* to him.

All his colleagues are senior to him.

90. Adjectives expressing qualities that do not admit of different degrees cannot, strictly speaking, be compared; as,

square, round, perfect, eternal, universal, unique.

strictly speaking, a thing cannot be more *square*, more *round*, more *perfect*. But we say, for instance,

This is the *most perfect* specimen I have seen.

EXERCISE IN GRAMMAR 15

Point out the Adjectives and name the Degree of Comparison of each.

1. The poor woman had seen happier days.
2. Do not talk such nonsense.
3. Make less noise.
4. That child has a slight cold.
5. A live ass is stronger than a dead lion.
6. Say the same thing twice over.
7. Solomon was one of the wisest men.
8. Hunger is the best sauce.
9. His simple word is as good as an oath.
10. There was not the slightest excuse for it.
11. My knife is sharper than yours.
12. Small people love to talk of great men.
13. Of two evils choose the less.
14. I hope the matter will be cleared up some day.
15. Your son makes no progress in his studies.
16. Open rebuke is better than secret love.
17. We never had such sport.
18. I have other things to attend to.
19. Hari is the idlest boy in the class.
20. I promise you a fair hearing.
21. There is much to be said on both sides.
22. He gave the boys much wholesome advice.
23. He thinks he is wiser than his father.
24. No news is good news.
25. Bangladesh has the largest tea garden in the world.
26. Lead is heavier than any other metal.
27. I congratulated him on his good fortune.
28. He has many powerful friends.
29. The longest lane has a turning.

EXERCISE IN GRAMMAR 16

Make three columns, and write the following Adjectives in the Positive, Comparative and Superlative Degrees.

[Be careful to use the form of comparison that is pleasing to the ear.]

shameful, clever, pretty, interesting, hopeful, honest, important, patient, rude, delightful, stupid, attractive, heavy, beautiful, fortunate, pleasant.

EXERCISE IN COMPOSITION 17

Supply the proper form (Comparative or Superlative) of the Adjective.

[Note:—The Comparative and not the Superlative should be used to compare two things.]

1. *Good* — How is your brother today ? Is he____?
2. *Hot* — May is____here than any other month.
3. *Pretty* — Her doll is____than yours.
4. *Idle* — Hari is the____boy in the class.
5. *Sharp* — Your knife is sharp, but mine is____.
6. *Dear* — Honour is____to him than life.
7. *Rich* — He is the_____man in our town.
8. *Old* — Mani is two years_____than Rati.
9. *Large* — Name the____city in the world.
10. *Good* — He is the_____friend I have.
11. *Bad* — He is the______boy of the two.
12. *Bad* — Raman's work is bad, Hari's is_____, but Govind's is the _____.
13. *Ferocious* — There is no animal_____than the tiger.
14. *Bad* — The trade is in a_____condition today than it was a year ago.
15. *Tall* — He is the______of the two.
16. *Dry* — Sind is the_____part of Pakistan.
17. *Useful* — Iron is_____than any other metal.
18. *Useful* — Iron is the_____of all metals.
19. *Great* — Who is the_____living poet ?
20. *Nutritious* — I think he requires a_____diet.
21. *Proud* — It was the_____moment of his life.
22. *Good* — The public is the_____judge.
23. *Little* — That is the_____price I can take.
24. *Light* — Silver is______than gold.

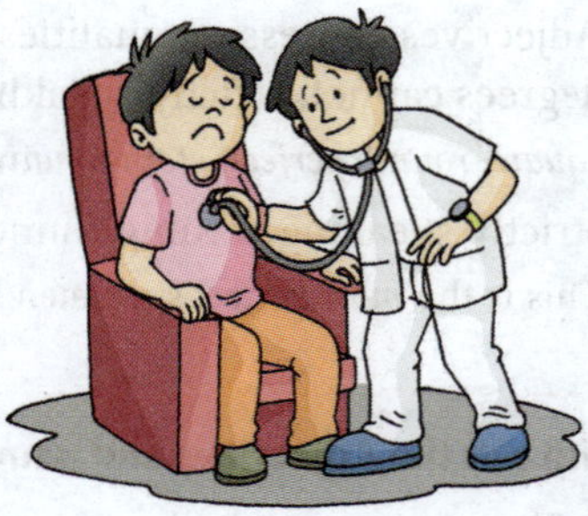

EXERCISE IN COMPOSITION 18

Supply appropriate Comparatives or Superlatives to each of the following.

1. Prevention is_____than cure.
2. Akbar had a_____reign than Babar.
3. Sachin Tendulkar is the ______ batsman in the world.
4. The pen is______than the sword.
5. The______buildings are found in America.
6. The Pacific is_____than any other ocean.
7. Which of the two girls has the______dress ?
8. Honour is_____to him than life.
9. This pen is_____than the other.
10. Who is the_____boy in the class ?

EXERCISE IN COMPOSITION 18

11. The Eiffel Tower is______than Qutab Minar.
12. My uncle is______than my father.
13. The multi-millionaire Mr. Sen is the______in this town.
14. Wordsworth is a______poet than Cowper.
15. Balu is the______bowler in the eleven.
16. The streets of Mumbai are______than those of Ahmedabad.
17. Ooty is ______ than Chennai.
18. The piano was knocked down to the______bidder.
19. Mount Everest is the______peak of the Himalayas.
20. He writes a______hand than his brother.
21. He writes the______hand in his class.
22. He is one of the_______speakers in Punjab.
23. Who was the______general, Alexander or Caesar?
24. The_______fables are those attributed to Aesop.
25. *The Arabian Nights* is perhaps the______story-book.
26. Shakespeare is______than any other English poet.
27. Of all countries, China has the______population in the world.
28. Clouds float in the sky because they are______than the air.
29. There are two ways of doing the sum, but this one is the______.
30. It is good to be clever, but it is______to be industrious.
31. This is the______of my two sons.
32. This is the_____that I can do.

EXERCISE IN COMPOSITION 19

Change the following sentences by using 'less' or 'least' without changing the meaning.

1. The mango is sweeter than the pineapple.
2. Silver is more plentiful than gold.
3. This is the most useless of all my books.
4. Wolfram is one of the rarest minerals.
5. The wild-apple is the sourest of all fruits.
6. Iron is more useful than copper.

Interchange of the Degrees of Comparison

91. As the following examples show, it is possible to change the Degree of Comparison of an Adjective in a sentence, without changing the meaning of the sentence.

Superlative — Lead is the heaviest of all metals.
Comparative — Lead is heavier than all other metals.
Comparative — Mahabaleshwar is cooler than Panchgani.
Positive — Panchgani is not so cool as Mahabaleshwar.
Positive — He is as wise as Solomon.
Comparative — Solomon was not wiser than he is.
Superlative — *Shakuntalam* is the best drama in Sanskrit.
Comparative — *Shakuntalam* is better than any other drama in Sanskrit.
Positive — No other drama in Sanskrit is as good as *Shakuntalm.*
Superlative — Chennai is one of the biggest of Indian cities.
Comparative — Chennai is bigger than most other Indian cities.
Positive — Very few Indian cities are as big as Chennai.

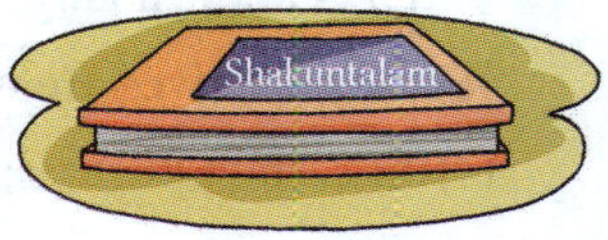

Positive — Some poets are at least as great as Tennyson.
Comparative — Tennyson is not greater than some other poets.
— Some poets are not less great than Tennyson.
Superlative — Tennyson is not the greatest of all poets.

EXERCISE IN COMPOSITION 20

Change the Degree of Comparison, without changing the meaning.

1. Malacca is the oldest town in Malaysia.
2. Soya beans are at least as nutritious as meat.
3. No other planet is as big as Jupiter.
4. Very few boys are as industrious as Latif.
5. He would sooner die than tell a lie.
6. India is the largest democracy in the world.
7. Shakespeare is greater than any other English poet.
8. Samudra Gupta was one of the greatest of Indian kings.
9. The tiger is the most ferocious of all animals.
10. Australia is the largest island in the world.
11. Lead is heavier than any other metal.
12. Some people have more money than brains.
13. A wise enemy is better than a foolish friend.
14. The Marwaries are not less enterprising than any other community in India.
15. I know him quite as well as you do.
16. You do not know him better than I do.
17. No other man was as strong as Bhim.
18. Some boys are at least as industrious as Suresh.
19. Mount Everest is the highest peak of the Himalayas.
20. Very few animals are as useful as the cow.
21. America is the richest country in the world.
22. It is easier to preach than to practise.
23. Iron is more useful than all the other metals.
24. Open rebuke is better than secret love.
25. This is the tallest building in the city.
26. Sir Surendranath was at least as great an orator as any other Indian.
27. Ooty is as healthy as any resort in India.
28. The pen is mightier than the sword.

Chapter 11 ADJECTIVES USED AS NOUNS

Blessed are the meek.

92. Adjectives are often used as Nouns.

(1) As Plural Nouns denoting a class of persons; as,

The *cautious* (= cautious persons) are not always cowards.

The rich (= rich people) know not how *the poor* (= poor people) live.

The wicked (= wicked people) flee when no man pursueth, but *the righteous* (= righteous people) are bold as a lion.

Blessed are the *meek*.

(2) As Singular Nouns denoting some abstract quality; as,

The future (= futurity) is unknown to us.

He is a lover of the *beautiful* (= beauty in general).

(3) Some Adjectives actually become Nouns, and are hence used in both numbers.

(a) Those derived from Proper Nouns; as, *Australians, Canadians, Italians.*

(b) Some denoting persons; as, *juniors, seniors, mortals, inferiors, superiors, nobles, criminals, savages, elders, minors.*

(c) A few denoting things generally; as, *secrets, totals, liquids, solids, valuables.*

[Some adjectives are used as Nouns only in the plural; as, *sweets, bitters, valuables, eatables.*]

(4) In certain phrases; as,

in *general;* in *future;* in *short;* in *secret;* before *long;* at *present;* for *good* ; at *best;*
through *thick and thin;* for *better* or for *worse;*
in *black* and *white; right* or *wrong;* from *bad* to *worse;* the *long* and *short.*

Next time I will charge you.

In future I shall charge you for medical advice.

In short, we know nothing.

The negotiations were carried on *in secret.*

I shall see you *before* long.

Before long, he will be appointed to a higher post.

At present, he is in pecuniary difficulties.

I do not want any more at *present.*

He has left India *for good.*

We can't arrive before Saturday *at best.*

It must be said to his credit that he stood by his friend *through thick and thin.*

I must have your terms down in *black and white.*

Right or wrong, my country.

I am afraid the young man is going from *bad to worse.*

The long and short of it is that I distrust you.

Nouns used as Adjectives

93. The use of Nouns as Adjectives is very common in English; as,

I met a little *cottage* girl.

He is always playing *computer* games.

Chapter 12 POSITION OF ADJECTIVES

94. A single Adjective used attributively is generally placed immediately *before* the noun; as,

King Francis was a *hearty* king, and loved a royal sport.

Where are you going, my *pretty* maid, with your *rosy* cheeks and *golden* hair ?

O Captain ! my Captain ! our *fearful* trip is done.

Observe the difference in meaning between:

(i) a great nobleman's son, and

(ii) a nobleman's great son.

95. In poetry, however, the Adjective is frequently placed after the noun; as,

Children *dear,* was it yesterday?

We heard the sweet bells over the bay.

O man with sisters *dear* !

96. When several Adjectives are attached to one noun they are generally placed after it for emphasis; as,

There dwelt a miller *hale* and *bold.*

The King, *fearless* and *resolute,* at once advanced.

Franklin had a great *genius, original, sagacious,* and *inventive.*

97. When some word or phrase is joined to the Adjective to explain its meaning, the Adjective is placed after its noun; as,

He was a man *fertile* in resource.

A Sikh, *taller* than any of his comrades, rushed forward.

98. In certain phrases the Adjective always comes after the noun; as,

heir apparent, time immemorial, lord paramount, viceroy elect, letters patent, knights temporal, notary public, body politic, God Almighty.

Chapter 13 THE CORRECT USE OF SOME ADJECTIVES

99. **Some, any**—To express quantity or degree *some* is used normally in *affirmative* sentences, *any* in *negative* or *interrogative* sentences.

I will buy some mangoes.

I will buy *some* mangoes.

I will not buy *any* mangoes.

Have you bought *any* mangoes ?

But *any* can be used after *if* in affirmative sentences.

If you need *any* money I will help you.

Some is used in questions which are really offers/requests or which expect the answer "yes".

Will you have some ice-cream?

Will you have *some* ice-cream? (Offer)

Could you lend me *some* money? (Request)

Did you buy *some* clothes? (= I expect you did.)

100. **Each, every.**— *Each* and *every* are similar in meaning, but *every* is a stronger word than *each;* it means, 'each without exception'. *Each* is used in speaking of two or more things; *every* is used only in speaking of *more than two. Each* directs attention to the individuals forming any group, *every* to the total group. Each is used only when the number in the group is limited and definite ; *every* when the number is indefinite.

It rained every day during my holidays.

Every seat was taken.

Five boys were seated on *each* bench.

Each one of these chairs is broken.

Leap year falls in *every* fourth year.

He came to see us *every* three days [*i.e.,* once in every *period* of three days].

It rained *every* day during my holidays.

I was away ten days and it rained *each* day.

101. **Little, a little, the little** — Note carefully the use of—

(1) little, (2) a little, (3) the little.

Little = *not* much (*i.e.,* hardly any). Thus, the adjective *little* has a negative meaning.

HOSPITAL

There is little hope of his recovery, *i.e.,* he is not likely to recover.

He showed *little* concern for his nephew.

He has *little* influence with his old followers.

He showed *little* mercy to the vanquished.

He has *little* appreciation of good poetry.

A little = some though not much. 'A little' has a positive meaning.

There is *a little* hope of his recovery, *i.e.*, he may possibly recover.

A little tact would have saved the situation.

A little knowledge is a dangerous thing.

The little = not much, but all there is.

The little information he had was not quite reliable.

The little knowledge of carpentry that he possessed stood him in good stead.

[The sentence means—The knowledge of carpentry he possessed was not much; but all that knowledge stood him in good stead.]

EXERCISE IN COMPOSITION 21

Insert 'a little', or 'the little' whichever is suitable.

1. ______grain they had was damaged by sea water.
2. ______precaution is necessary in handling that machine.
3. ______care could have prevented the catastrophe.
4. ______influence that he has, he uses to the best advantage.
5. ______knowledge of French that he has is likely to be very useful to him on the continent.

102. **Few, a few, the few** —Note carefully the use of —

(1) few, (2) a few, (3) the few.

Few men are free from faults

Few = not many, hardly any, 'Few' has a negative meaning.

Few persons can keep a secret.

Few people are so hopeless as drunkards.

Few towns in India have public libraries.

Few works of reference are so valuable as the *Encyclopaedia Britannica.*

Few men are free from faults.

Few men reach the age of one hundred years.

Few Parsees write Gujarati correctly.

A few = some. 'A few' has a positive meaning, and is opposed to 'none'.

A few words spoken in earnest will convince him.

A few Parsees write Gujarati correctly.

The few = not many, but all there are.

The few remarks that he made were very suggestive.

[The sentence means—The remarks that he made were not many; but all those remarks were very suggestive.]

The few friends he has are all very poor.

The few clothes they had were all tattered and torn.

EXERCISE IN COMPOSITION 22

Insert 'a few' or 'the few' whichever is suitable.

1. _____ public libraries that we have are not well equipped.
2. _____days that are left to him he spends in solitude and meditation.
3. Many Hindus study Sanskrit, but only_____Parsees study Avesta.
4. _____days' rest is all that is needed.
5. Have you got _____ potatoes left ?
6. It is a question of spending _____rupees.
7. _____hints on essay-writing are quite to the point.
8. _____months that he spent in Ooty did him a lot of good.
9. When I met him _____years after, he looked old and haggard.
10. _____short poems in the volume show signs of genius.
11. In _____words he expressed his gratitude to his friends.
12. _____Americans have their offices in Kolkata.
13. _____trinkets she has are not worth much.
14. _____ poems he has written are all of great excellence.

Chapter 14 ARTICLES

103. The Adjectives *a* or *an* and *the* are usually called **Articles.** They are really Demonstrative Adjectives.

104. There are two Articles—*a* (or *an*) and *the.*

105. *A* or *an* is called the **Indefinite Article,** because it usually leaves *indefinite* the person or thing spoken of; as, *a* doctor; that is, *any* doctor.

106. *The* is called the **Definite Article,** because it normally points out some *particular* person or thing; as,

He saw *the* doctor; meaning some *particular* doctor.

The indefinite article is used before singular countable nouns, *e.g.,*
a book, *an* orange, *a* girl

The definite article is used before singular countable nouns, plural countable nouns and uncountable nouns, *e.g.,*

the book, *the* books, *the* milk

A or An

107. The choice between *a* and *an* is determined by *sound.* Before a word beginning with a vowel sound *an* is used; as,

an ass, *an* enemy, *an* inkstpad, *an* orange, *an* umbrella, *an* hour, *an* honest man, *an* heir.

It will be noticed that the words *hour, honest, heir* begin with a vowel sound, as the initial consonant *h* is not pronounced.

108. Before a word beginning with a consonant sound *a* is used; as,

a boy, *a* reindeer, *a* woman, *a* yard, *a* horse, *a* hole,

also *a* university, *a* union, *a* European, *a* ewe, *a* unicorn, *a* useful article;

because these words (*university, union,* etc.) begin with a consonant sound, that of *yu.* Similarly we say,

a one-rupee note, such *a* one, *a* one-eyed man.

because *one* begins with the consonant sound of *w.*

109. Some native speakers use *an* before words beginning with *h* if the first syllable is not stressed.

An hotel (More common : *a* hotel)

an historical novel (More common : *a* historical novel)

Use of the Definite Article

110. The Definite Article *the* is used—

(1) When we talk about a particular person or thing, or one already referred to (that is, when it is clear from the context which one we mean); as,

The book you want is out of print. (Which book ? The one you want.)

Let's go to *the* park. (= the park in this town)

The girl cried. (*the* girl = the girl already talked about)

(2) When a *singular* noun is meant to represent a whole class; as,

The cow is a useful animal.

[Or we may say, "Cows are useful animals."]

The horse is a noble animal.

The cat loves comfort.

The rose is the sweetest of all flowers.

The banyan is a kind of fig tree.

[Do not say, "a kind of a fig tree". This is a common error.]

The two nouns *man* and *woman* can be used in a general sense without either article.

Man is the only animal that uses fire.

Woman is man's mate.

But in present-day English *a man* and *a woman* (or *men* and *women*) are more usual.

A woman is more sensitive than *a* man.

(3) Before some proper names, viz., these kinds of place-names :

(a) oceans and seas, e.g. *the* Pacific, *the* Black Sea
(b) rivers, e.g. *the* Ganga, *the* Nile
(c) canals, e.g. *the* Suez Canal
(d) deserts, e.g. the Sahara
(e) groups of islands, e.g. *the* West Indies
(f) mountain ranges, e.g. *the* Himalayas, *the* Alps
(g) a very few names of countries, which include words like *republic* and *kingdom* (e.g. *the* Irish Republic, *the* United Kingdom) also: *the* Ukraine, *the* Netherlands (and its seat of government *the* Hague)

(4) Before the names of certain books; as,

the Vedas, *the* Puranas, *the* Iliad, *the* Ramayana.

But we say—

Homer's Iliad, Valmiki's Ramayana.

(5) Before names of things unique of their kind; as,

The sun, *the* sky, *the* ocean, *the* sea, *the* earth.

Note—Sometimes *the* is placed before a Common noun to give it the meaning of an Abstract noun; as,

At last *the warrior* (the warlike or martial spirit) in him was thoroughly aroused.]

(6) Before a Proper Noun when it is qualified by an adjective or a defining adjectival clause; as,

The great Caesar : *the* immortal Shakespeare.

The Mr. Roy *whom* you met last night is my uncle.

(7) With Superlatives ; as,

The darkest cloud has a silver lining.

This is *the* best book of elementary chemistry.

(8) With ordinals; as,

He was *the* first man to arrive.

The ninth chapter of the book is very interesting.

(9) Before musical instruments; as,

He can play *the* flute.

He can play the flute.

(10) Before an adjective when the noun is understood; as,

The poor are always with us.

(11) Before a noun (with emphasis) to give the force of a Superlative; as,

The Verb *is the* word (= the chief word) in a sentence.

(12) As an Adverb with Comparatives; as,

The more the merrier.

(= *by how much* more, *by so much* the merrier)

The more they get, *the* more they want.

Use of the Indefinite Article

111. The Indefinite Article is used—

(1) In its original numerical sense of *one;* as,

Twelve inches make *a* foot.

Not *a* word was said.

A word to the wise is sufficient.

A bird in the hand is worth two in the bush.

(2) In the vague sense of *a certain;* as,

A Kishore Kumar (= a certain person named Kishore Kumar) is suspected by the police.

One evening *a* beggar came to my door.

(3) In the sense of *any,* to single out an individual as the representative of a class; as,

A pupil should obey his teacher.

A cow is a useful animal.

(4) To make a common noun of a proper noun; as,

A Daniel come to judgement ! (A Daniel = a very wise man)

Omission of the Article

112. The Article is omitted—

(1) Before names of substances and abstract nouns (*i.e.* uncountable nouns) used in a general sense; as,

Sugar is bad for your teeth.

Gold is a precious metal.

Wisdom is the gift of heaven.

Honesty is the best policy.

Virtue is its own reward.

Note 1—Uncountable nouns take *the* when used in a particular sense (especially when qualified by an adjective or adjectival phrase or clause); as,

Would you pass me *the* sugar? (= the sugar on the table)

The wisdom of Solomon is great.

I can't forget *the* kindness with which he treated me.

(2) Before plural countable nouns used in a general sense; as,

Children like chocolates.

Computers are used in many offices.

Note—Note that such nouns take the when used with a particular meaning; as,

Where are *the* children? (= our children)

(3) Before most proper nouns (except those referred to earlier), namely, names of people (e.g. Gopal, Rahim), names of continents, countries, cities, etc. (e.g. Europe, Pakistan, Nagpur), names of individual mountains (e.g. Mount Everest), individual islands, lakes, hills, etc.

(4) Before names of meals (used in a general sense); as,

What time do you have lunch ?

Dinner is ready.

Note—We use *a* when there is an adjective before breakfast, lunch, dinner, etc. We use *the* when we specify

I had *a late lunch* today.

The dinner we had at the Tourist Hotel was very nice.

(5) Before languages; as,

We are studying *English.*

They speak *Punjabi* at home.

(6) Before *school, college, church, bed, table, hospital, market, prison,* when these places are visited or used for their primary purpose; as,

I learnt French at *school.*

We go to *church* on Sundays.

He stays in *bed* till nine every morning.

My uncle is still in *hospital.*

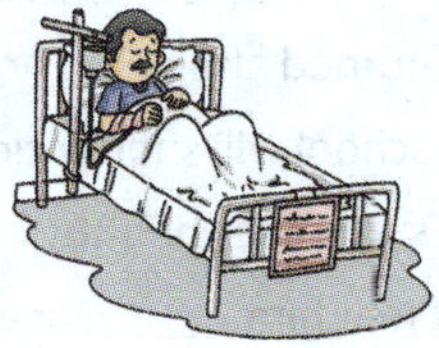

Note— *The* is used with these words when we refer to them as a definite place, building or object rather than to the normal activity that goes on there; as,

The school is very near my home.

I met him at *the* church.

The bed is broken.

I went to *the* hospital to see my uncle.

(7) Before names of relations, like *father, mother, aunt, uncle,* and also *cook* and *nurse,* meaning 'our cook', 'our nurse'; as,

Father has returned.

Aunt wants you to see her.

Cook has given notice.

Cook has given notice.
SALARY

(8) Before predicative nouns denoting a unique position, *i.e.*, a position that is normally held at one time by one person only; as,

He was elected *chairman* of the Board.

Mr Banerji became *Principal* of the college in 1995.

(9) In certain phrases consisting of a transitive verb followed by its object; as,

to catch fire, to take breath, to give battle, to cast anchor, to send word, to bring word, to give ear, to lay siege, to set sail, to lose heart, to set foot, to leave home, to strike root, to take offence.

(10) In certain phrases consisting of a preposition followed by its object; as,

at home, in hand, in debt, by day, by night, at daybreak, at sunrise, at noon, at sunset, at night, at anchor, at sight, on demand, at interest, on earth, by land, by water, by river, by train, by steamer, by name, on horseback, on foot, on deck, in jest, at dinner, at ease, under ground, above ground.

EXERCISE IN COMPOSITION 23

Complete the following sentences by filling in *a, an* or *the* as may be suitable.

1. Copper is___useful metal.
2. He is not____honourable man.
3. ____able man has not always a distinguished look.
4. ____reindeer is a native of Norway.
5. Honest men speak_____truth.
6. Rustum is_____young Parsee.
7. Do you see_____blue sky ?
8. Varanasi is_____holy city.
9. Aladdin had____wonderful lamp.
10. The world is____happy place.
11. He returned after_____hour.
12. ____school will shortly close for the Puja holidays.
13. ____sun shines brightly.
14. I first met him_____year ago.
15. Yesterday _____ European called at my office.
16. Sanskrit is_____difficult language.
17. ____Ganga is____sacred river.
18. ____lion is____king of beasts.
19. You are_____fool to say that.
20. French is_____easy language.
21. Who is ____ girl sitting there?
22. Which is___longest river in India ?
23. Rama has come without ____ umbrella.
24. Mumbai is_____very costly place to live in.
25. She is_____untidy girl.
26. The children found____egg in the nest.
27. I bought ____ horse, ____ox, and____buffalo.
28. If you see him, give him____ message.
29. English is___language of__ people of England.
30. The guide knows _____ way.
31. Sri Lanka is _____ island.
32. Let us discuss _____ matter seriously.
33. John got ____ best present.
34. Man, thou art ____ wonderful animal.
35. India is one of ____ most industrial countries in Asia.
36. He looks as stupid as ____ owl.
37. He is _____ honour to this profession.

EXERCISE IN COMPOSITION 24

Insert Articles where necessary.

1. While there is life there is hope.
2. Her knowledge of medicine had been acquired under aged Jewess.
3. Sun rises in east.
4. The brave soldier lost arm in battle.
5. The doctor says it is hopeless case.
6. I like to live in open air.
7. Get pound of sugar from nearest grocer.
8. Set back clock; it is hour too fast.
9. The poor woman has not rupee.
10. You must take care.
11. Eskimos make houses of snow and ice.
12. Where did you buy umbrella?
13. Have you never seen elephant?
14. Draw map of India.
15. Do not look gift horse in mouth.
16. Have you told him about accident?
17. Tagore was great poet.
18. How blue sky looks!
19. Who wishes to take walk with me?
20. What beautiful scene this is!
21. The musician was old Mussalman.
22. The river was spanned by iron bridge.
23. Moon did not rise till after ten.
24. Like true sportsmen they would give enemy fair play.
25. They never fail who die in great cause.
26. There is nothing like staying at home for comfort.
27. He likes to picture himself as original thinker.
28. It is never thankful office to offer advice.
29. Umbrella is of no avail against thunderstorm.
30. I have not seen him since he was child.
31. For Brutus is honourable man.
32. Neil Armstrong was first man to walk on moon.
33. Man has no more right to say uncivil thing than to act one.
34. We started late in afternoon.
35. It is a strange thing how little, in general, people know about sky.
36. Scheme failed for want of support.
37. Tiger, animal equal to lion in size, is native of Asia.
38. Time makes worst enemies friends.
39. My favourite flower is rose.
40. Time we live ought not to be computed by number of years, but by use that has been made of them.
41. Mumbai is largest cotton textile centre in country.
42. Men are too often led astray by prejudice.
43. Only best quality is sold by us.
44. What kind of bird is that ?
45. Wild animals suffer when kept in captivity.
46. May we have pleasure of your company?
47. It was proudest moment of my life.
48. Andamans are group of islands in Bay of Bengal.
49. He started school when he was six years old.
50. He neglects attending church, though church is only few yards from his house.
51. March is third month of year.
52. Dr Arnold was headmaster of rugby.
53. Man cannot live by bread alone.
54. When will father be back?
55. Appenines are in Italy.

Repetition of the Article

113. If I say—

I have *a* black and white dog.

I mean a dog that is partly black and partly white.

But if I say—

I have *a* black and *a* white dog,

I mean *two* dogs, one black and the other white.

Hence when two or more adjectives qualify the *same* noun, the Article is used before the *first adjective only*; but when they qualify *different* nouns, expressed or understood, the Article is normally used before *each adjective.*

114. Compare:

1. *The* Secretary and Treasurer is absent.
2. *The* Secretary and *the* Treasurer are absent.

The first sentence clearly indicates that the posts of Secretary and Treasurer are held by *one* person. The repetition of the article in the second sentence indicates that the two posts are held by *two* different persons.

Hence we see that when two or more connected nouns refer to the *same* person or thing, the Article is ordinarily used before *the first only* ; but when two or more connected nouns refer to *different* persons or things, the Article is used before *each.*

Also examine the following sentences.

Sir Surendranath was *a* great orator and statesman.

There are on the committee among others *a* great economist and *a* great lawyer.

115. We may either say—

The third and *the* fourth *chapter.*

[Or] *The* third and fourth *chapters.*

116. In expressing a comparison, if two nouns refer to the same person or thing, the Article is used before *the first noun only;* as,

He is a better mechanic than clerk.

He is a better poet than novelist.

He is a better thinker than debater.

He would make a better engineer than lawyer.

But if they refer to *different* persons or things, the Article must be used with *each noun;* as,

He is a better mechanic than a clerk (would make).

He would make a better statesman than a philosopher (would make).

Chapter 15 PERSONAL PRONOUNS

117. We may say —

Hari is absent, because Hari is ill.

But it is better to avoid the repetition of the Noun *Hari*, and say—

Hari is absent, because *he* is ill.

Hari is ill.

A word that is thus used *instead of a noun* is called a **Pronoun.** [*Pronoun* means *for-a-noun.*]

Def.—A **Pronoun** is a word used instead of a Noun.

118. Read the following sentences.

I am young. *We* are young.

You are young. *They* are young.

He (she, it) is young.

We are young.

I, we, you, he, (*she, it*), *they* are called **Personal Pronouns** because they stand for the three *persons,*

(*i*) the person speaking,

(*ii*) the person spoken to, and

(*iii*) the person spoken of.

The Pronouns *I* and *we,* which denote the person or persons *speaking,* are said to be Personal Pronouns of the First Person.

The Pronoun *you,* which denotes the person or persons spoken to, is said to be a Personal Pronoun of the Second Person.

You is used both in the singular and plural.

The pronouns *he (she)* and *they,* which denote the person or persons *spoken of,* are said to be Personal Pronouns of the **Third Person.** *It,* although it denotes the thing spoken of, is also called a *Personal* Pronoun of the Third Person. [The Personal Pronouns of the Third Person are, strictly speaking, Demonstrative Pronouns.]

Forms of the Personal Pronouns

119. The following are the different forms of the Personal Pronouns.

FIRST PERSON *(Masculine or Feminine)*

	Singular	Plural
Nominative	I	we
Possessive	my, mine	our, ours
Accusative	me	us

SECOND PERSON (Masculine or Feminine)

SINGULAR/PLURAL

Nominative	you
Possessive	your, yours
Accusative	you

THIRD PERSON

	Singular			Plural
	Masculine	*Feminine*	*Neuter*	*All Genders*
Nominative	he	she	it	they
Possessive	his	her, hers	its	their, theirs
Accusative	him	her	it	them

Note 1—It will be seen that the Possessive Cases of most of the Personal Pronouns have two forms. Of these the forms *my, our, your, her, their* are called Possessive Adjectives because they are used with nouns and do the work of Adjectives; as,

This is *my* book.
Those are *your* books.
That is *her* book.

Possessive Adjectives are sometimes called **Pronominal Adjectives,** as they are formed from Pronouns.

Note 2—The word *his* is used both as an Adjective and as a Pronoun; as

This is *his* book. (Possessive Adjective)
This book is *his.* (Possessive Pronoun)

In the following sentences the words in italics are Possessive Pronouns,

This book is *mine.*
Those books are *yours.*
That book is *hers.*
That idea of *yours* is excellent.

120. The Pronoun of the Third Person has three *Genders* :

Masculine : *he*
Feminine : *she*
Neuter : *it*

121. **It** —The Pronoun *it* is used:

(1) For things without life; as,

Here is your book; take *it* away.

(2) For animals, unless we clearly wish to speak of them as male and female; as,

He loves his dog and cannot do without *it.*

The horse fell and broke *its* leg.

The horse fell and broke its leg.

(3) For a young child, unless we clearly wish to refer to the sex; as,

When I saw the child *it* was crying.

That baby has torn *its* clothes.

(4) To refer to some statement going before; as,

He is telling what is not true; and he knows *it.*

He deserved his punishment; and he knew *it.*

(5) As a provisional and temporary subject before the verb *to be* when the real subject follows; as,

It is easy to find fault. [To find fault is easy.]

It is doubtful whether he will come.

It is certain that you are wrong.

(6) To give emphasis to the noun or pronoun following ; as,

It was you who began the quarrel.

It was I who first protested.

It was at Versailles that the treaty was made.

It is a silly fish that is caught twice with the same bait.

It is an ill wind that blows nobody good.

(7) As an indefinite nominative of an impersonal verb; as,

It rains. *It* snows. *It* thunders.

The Pronoun *it* here seems to stand for no noun whatever, though this can be readily supplied from the verb. Thus, 'It rains' means 'The rain rains.'

It so used is called an **Impersonal Pronoun**. So also the verb *rains* is here called an **Impersonal Verb.**

(8) In speaking of the weather or the time; as,

It is fine.

It is winter.

It is ten o'clock.

122. Since a Personal Pronoun is used instead of a Noun, it must be of the same *number, gender* and *person* as the Noun for which it stands; as,

Rama is a kind boy. *He* has lent his bicycle to Govind.

Sita helps her mother in household work. *She* also does her lesson.

Those beggars are idle. *They* refuse to work for their living.

123. When a Pronoun* stands for a Collective Noun, it must be in the Singular Number (and Neuter Gender) if the Collective Noun is viewed as a *whole;* as,

The army had to suffer terrible privations in *its* march.

The fleet will reach *its* destination in a week.

The crew mutinied and murdered *its* officers.

After a few minutes the jury gave *its* verdict.

jury

* It will be noted that we use the word 'Pronoun' in § 123-128 without observing the distinction pointed out in § 119 between the forms, *my, her, our, your, their* (which are called Possessive Adjectives) and the forms *mine, hers, ours, yours, theirs* (which are called Possessive Pronouns).

If the Collective Noun conveys the idea of *separate individuals* comprising the whole, the Pronoun standing for it must be of the Plural Number ; as,

The jury were divided in *their* opinions.

The committee decided the matter without leaving *their* seats.

124. When two or more Singular Nouns are joined by *and*, the Pronoun used for them must be Plural; as,

Rama and Hari work hard. *They* are praised by their teacher.

Both Sita and Savitri are tired; *they* have gone home.

But when two Singular Nouns joined by *and* refer to the same person or thing, the Pronoun used must of course be Singular; as,

The Secretary and Treasurer is negligent of *his* duty.

125. When two Singular Nouns joined by *and* are preceded by *each* or *every*, the Pronoun must be Singular; as,

Every soldier and *every* sailor was in *his* place.

126. When two or more Singular Nouns are joined by *or* or *either...or, neither... nor*, the Pronoun is generally Singular; as,

Rama or Hari must lend *his* hand.

Either Sita or Amina forgot to take *her* parasol.

Neither Abdul nor Karim has done *his* lesson.

127. When a Plural Noun and a Singular Noun are joined by *or* or *nor*, the Pronoun must be in the Plural; as,

Either the manager or his assistants failed in *their* duty.

128. When a pronoun refers to more than one noun or pronoun of different persons, it must be of the first person plural in preference to the second, and of the second person plural in preference to the third; as,

You and *I* have done our duty.

You and *Hari* have idled away your time.

129. Good manners require that we should say—

'You and I' *not* 'I and you'.

'You and he' *not* 'he and you'.

'Hari and I' *not* 'I and Hari'.

'He and I' *not* 'I and he'.

You and *I* must work together.

You and *he* must mend your ways.

Hari and *I* are old school friends.

He and *I* can never pull on together.

130. Each of the personal pronouns, *I, he, she, we, they* has a different form for the accusative case, namely, *me, him, her, us, them*. It is a common mistake to use *I* for *me*, when the pronoun is connected by a conjunction (*and, or*) with some other word in the accusative case.

Study the following correct sentences.

The presents are for you and *me* (not, I).

My uncle asked my brother and *me* to dinner.

131. Note that *but* is a preposition in the following sentence:

Nobody will help you but *me*. (not : *I*)

Take care to use the accusative form after *but* in such cases.

EXERCISE IN GRAMMAR 25

In the following sentences, point out the Pronouns and say for what each stands.

1. Alice was not a bit hurt, and she jumped up on to her feet in a moment.
2. There were doors all round the hall, but they were all locked.
3. Alice opened the door and found that it led into a small passage.
4. "I wish I hadn't cried so much," said Alice.
5. "You are not attending", said the Mouse to Alice severely. "What are you thinking of ?"
6. "Come back!" the Caterpillar called after her. Alice turned and came back again.
7. Hari brought his book and laid it on the table.
8. Karim has lost his dog and cannot find it.
9. Suresh is at the head of his class, for he studies hard.
10. Rama, you are a lazy boy.
11. The camel is a beast of burden. It is used to carry goods across the desert.
12. The female lion is called a lioness. She has no mane.
13. The horse fell down and broke its leg.
14. Birds build their nests in trees.
15. If the thief is caught, he will be punished.
16. Train up a child in the way he should go.
17. And Nathan said to David, Thou art the man.

EXERCISE IN COMPOSITION 26

In the following sentences, use Pronouns in place of nouns wherever you can.

1. Rama had taken his watch out of his pocket, and was looking at the watch uneasily, shaking the watch every now and then, and holding the watch to his ear.
2. The boys went into the garden, where the boys saw a snake.
3. Very soon the Rabbit noticed Alice as Alice went hunting about, and called out to Alice in an angry tone.

EXERCISE IN COMPOSITION 27

Write the correct form of Pronoun in the following.

1. We scored as many goals as_____. (they, them)
2. Rama and_____ were present. (I, me)
3. Can you sing as well as_____ ? (they, them)
4. Let you and_____ try what we can do. (I, me)
5. Wait for Hari and_____. (I, me)
6. You know that as well as_____. (I, me)
7. It was_____ that gave you the alarm. (I, me)
8. Between you and_____, I do not believe him. (I, me)
9. We are not as poor as_____. (they, them)
10. Rama is as old as_____. (I, me)
11. He is known to my brother and_____. (I, me)
12. He is as good as_____. (I, me)
13. Nobody but_____ was present. (he, him)
14. He and_____ were great friends. (I, me)
15. Whom can I trust, if not_____? (he, him)
16. Let_____ answer this question. (he, him)
17. There isn't much difference between you and_____. (He, him)
18. None so blind as_____ that will not see. (they, them)
19. It isn't for such as_____ to dictate to us. (they, them)

Chapter 16 REFLEXIVE AND EMPHATIC PRONOUNS

132. When *-self* is added to *my, your, him, her, it,* and *-selves* to *our, your, them,* we get what are called Compound Personal Pronouns.

They are called **Reflexive Pronouns** when the action done by the subject turns back (*reflects*) upon the subject; as,

I hurt *myself.*	We hurt *ourselves.*
You will hurt *yourself.*	You will hurt *yourselves.*
He hurt *himself.*	
She hurt *herself.*	They hurt *themselves.*
The horse hurt *itself.*	

It will be noticed that each of these Reflexive Pronouns is used as the *Object* of a verb, and refers to the same person or thing as that denoted by the Subject of the verb.

133. Sometimes, in older English, especially in poetry, a simple pronoun was used reflexively; as;

Now I lay *me* down to sleep.

134. The word *self* is sometimes used as a Noun; as,

To thine own *self* be true.
He cares for nothing but *self.*
He thinks much of *self.*

Emphatic Pronouns

135. Now look at the following sentences.

I will do it *myself.*
I *myself* saw him do it.
We will see to it *ourselves.*
You *yourself* can best explain.
He *himself* said so.
She *herself* says so.
It was told so by the teacher *himself.*
We saw the Prime Minister *himself.*
The town *itself* is not very large.
They *themselves* admitted their guilt.

It will be seen that here Compound Personal Pronouns are used for the sake of *emphasis,* and are therefore called **Emphatic Pronouns.**

EXERCISE IN GRAMMAR 28

Tell which Pronouns in the following sentences are Reflexive and which Emphatic.

[Emphatic Pronouns are also called Emphasizing Pronouns.]

1. I will go myself.
2. Rama has hurt himself.
3. We often deceive ourselves.
4. I myself heard the remark.
5. You express yourself very imperfectly.
6. I wash myself when I get up.
7. The boys hid themselves.
8. They have got themselves into a mess.
9. Boadicea poisoned herself.
10. They loved themselves so much that they thought of no one else.
11. The prisoner hanged himself.
12. The poor widow poisoned herself.
13. They enjoyed themselves.
14. Don't you deceive yourself ?
15. I myself heard the remark.
16. He set himself a hard task.
17. We exerted ourselves.
18. The dog choked itself.
19. They gave themselves a lot of trouble.
20. We seldom see ourselves as others see us.

21. A house divided against itself cannot stand.
22. He that wrongs his friend wrongs himself more.
23. Some people are always talking about themselves.
24. Xerxes himself was the last to cross the Hellespont.
25. He has landed himself in difficulties.
26. Thou shalt love thy neighbour as thyself.
27. Acquit yourselves like men.

Chapter 17 DEMONSTRATIVE, INDEFINITE AND DISTRIBUTIVE PRONOUNS

136. Consider the following sentences.

This is a present from my uncle.

These are merely excuses.

Both cars are good; but *this* is better than *that.*

Mumbai mangoes are better than *those* of Bengaluru.

Make haste, *that's* a good boy.

[Here *that* = one who makes haste.]

There is no period in ancient Indian history so glorious as *that* of the Guptas. [Do not write,"as the Guptas"]

My views are quite in accordance with *those* of the University Commission.

I may have offended, but *such* was not my intention.

He was the representative of the King, and as *such* (= the representative of the King) they honoured him.

The stranger is welcomed as *such.*

That is the Red Fort.

It will be noticed that the Pronouns in italics are used to *point out* the objects to which they refer, and are, therefore, called **Demonstrative Pronouns.** (Latin *demonstrare*, to show clearly)

137. *This, that,* etc. are (Demonstrative) *Adjectives* when they are used with nouns; as,

This book is mine.

That pen is yours.

These books are mine.

Those pens are yours.

What was *that* noise ?

This horse is better *than* that horse.

All *such* people ought to be avoided.

138. *This* refers to what is close at hand, and nearest to the thought or person of the speaker; *that* refers to what is 'over there', farther away, and more remote.

This is better *than* that.

139. *That,* with its plural *those,* is used to avoid the repetition of a preceding Noun; as,

The climate of Belgaum is like *that* of Pune.

The streets of this city are worse than *those* of Ahmedabad.

Our soldiers were better drilled than *those* of enemies.

The rivers of America are larger than *those* of Europe.

140. When two things which have been already mentioned are referred to, *this* refers to the thing last mentioned, *that* to the thing first mentioned; as,

Virtue and vice offer themselves for your choice ; *this* (*i.e.,* vice) leads to misery, *that* (*i.e.,* virtue) to happiness.

Alcohol and tobacco are both injurious; *this* perhaps, less than *that.*

Indefinite Pronouns

141. Consider the following sentences:

One hardly knows what to do.
One does not like to say so, but it is only too true.
One cannot be too careful of *one's* (not, his) good name.
One must not boast of *one's* own success.
One must use *one's* best efforts if one wishes to succeed.
One must not praise *one's self.*
None of his poems are well known.
None but fools have ever believed it.
[*None* is a shortened form of *not one;* yet it is commonly used with plural verbs.]
They (= people in general) say he has lost heavily.
They say that one of the local banks has stopped payment. [They say = it is said by some persons.]
All were drowned.
Some are born great.
Some say he is a sharper.

Somebody has stolen my watch.
Nobody was there to rescue the child.
Few escaped unhurt.
Many of them were Gurkhas.
We did not see *any* of them again.
One or *other* of us will be there.
Do good to *others.*
Did you ask *anybody* to come ?
What is *everybody's* business is *nobody's* business.
His words are in *everyone's* mouth.

All these Pronouns in italics refer to persons or things in a *general* way, but do not refer to any person or thing in particular. They are, therefore, called **Indefinite Pronouns.**

142. Most of these words may also be used as Adjectives.

I will take you there *one* day.
Any fool can do that.
He is a man of *few* words.
Some milk was spilt.

143. In referring to *anybody, everybody, everyone, anyone, each* etc., the pronoun *he* or *she* is used according to the context; as,

I shall be glad to help *everyone* of my boys in *his* studies.

Note that today it is more usual to use a plural pronoun (*they/them/their*) except in very formal English.

Anybody can do it if *they* try.
Each of them had *their* share.

Distributive Pronouns

144. Consider the following sentences:

Each of the boys gets a prize.
Each took it in turn.
Either of these roads leads to the railway station.
Either of you can go.
Neither of the accusations is true.

Each, either, neither are called **Distributive Pronouns** because they refer to persons or things *one at a time.* For this reason they are always *singular* and as such followed by the verb in the *singular.*

Note—*Each* is used to denote every one of a number of persons or things taken singly.

Either means the one or the other of two.

Neither means not the one nor the other of two. It is the negative of *either*.

Hence *either* and *neither* should be used only in speaking of *two* persons or things. When *more than two* are spoken of, *any, no one, none* should be used.

145. The position of the pronoun *each* should be noticed. It may have three positions.

1. *Each* of the men received a reward.
   Each of these horses cost five thousand rupees.
   I bought *each* of these mangoes for three rupees.
2. These men received *each* a reward.
   These horses cost *each* five thousand rupees.
3. These horses cost five thousand rupees *each*.
   I bought these mangoes for three rupees *each*.

The third order is usual after a numeral. We do not say, 'The men received a reward each'; but we say, 'The men received five hundred rupees each'.

146. In the following sentences, *each, either* and *neither* are used as Adjectives; they are followed by nouns of the *singular* number.

Each boy took his turn. *Neither* accusation is true.

At *either* end was a marble statue. (Here *either* = *each* or *both*.)

147. Study the following sentences.

1. The two men hate *each other*.
2. They cheated one another.

If we analyse them, they mean—

1. The two men hate, *each* hates the *other*.
2. They cheated, *one* cheated *another*.

Each and *one* really belong to the subject, *other* and *another* are objects. But *each other* and *one another* have become in practice compound pronouns (called **Reciprocal Pronouns)** and are rarely separated even by a preposition. Thus we say :

The brothers quarrelled *with each other*.

They all gave evidence *against one another*.

Note – The one-time rule that *each other* should be used in speaking of two persons or things, *one another* in speaking of more than two is no longer strictly observed. 'The three brothers quarrelled with *each other*' is now accepted as idiomatic.

Chapter 18 RELATIVE PRONOUNS

148. Read the following pairs of sentences.

1. I met Hari. Hari had just returned.
2. I have found the pen. I had lost the pen.
3. Here is the book. You lent me the book.

I have found the pen. I lost the pen.

Let us now combine each of the above pairs into one sentence. Thus:

1. I met Hari *who* had just returned.
2. I have found the pen *which* I had lost.
3. Here is the book *that* you lent me.

Now let us examine the work done by each of the words, *who, which* and *that*.

The word *who* is used instead of the noun *Hari*. It, therefore, does the work of a Pronoun.

The word *who* joins or connects two statements. It, therefore, does the work of a Conjunction.

The word *who*, therefore, does double work—the work of a Pronoun and also the work of a Conjunction.

We might, therefore, call it a Conjunctive Pronoun.

It is, however, called a **Relative Pronoun** because it *refers* or *relates* (*i.e.*, carries us back) to some noun going before (here, the noun *Hari*), which is called its **Antecedent.**

Let the pupil show why *which* and *that* are also Relative Pronouns in the second and third sentences.

What is the Antecedent of *which* in the second sentence ?

What is the Antecedent of *that* in the third sentence ?

Forms of the Relative Pronouns

149. The Relative Pronoun *who* has different forms for Accusative and Genitive.

		Singular and Plural
Nominative	:	who
Genitive	:	whose
Accusative	:	whom/who*

This is the boy whom all praise.

This is the boy (or girl) *who* works hard.

This is the boy (or girl) *whose* exercise is done well.

This is the boy (or girl) *whom / who* all praise.

These are the boys (or girls) *who* work hard.

These are the boys (or girls) *whose* exercises are done well.

These are the boys (or girls) *whom / who* all praise.

It will be noticed that the forms are the same for singular and plural, masculine and feminine.

150. The Relative Pronoun *which* has the same form for the Nominative and Accusative cases.

This is the house *which* belongs to my uncle.

The house *which* my uncle built cost him Rs. 3,50,000.

The Relative Pronoun *which* has no Genitive Case, but *whose* is used as a substitute for 'of which' ; as,

A triangle *whose* three sides are equal is called an equilateral triangle.

151. The Relative Pronoun *that* has the same form in the Singular and Plural, and in the Nominative and Accusative. It has no Genitive case.

He *that* is content is rich.

They *that* touch pitch will be defiled.

Take anything *that* you like.

I don't know what happened.

152. The Relative Pronoun *what* is used only in the Singular, and has the same form in the Nominative and Accusative.

What has happened is not clear.

I say *what* I mean.

He failed in *what* he attempted.

Use of the Relative Pronouns

153. As a general rule, *who* is used for *persons* only. It may refer to a Singular or a Plural Noun.

The man *who* is honest is trusted.

Blessed is he *who* has found his work.

He prayeth best *who* loveth best.

He *who* hesitates is lost.

They never fail *who* die in a great cause.

The man who is honest is trusted.

---

* *Who* replaces *whom* in informal English.

They are slaves *who* dare not be
In the right with two or three.

Who is sometimes used in referring to animals.

Whose (the Possessive form of *who*) is used in speaking of persons, animals and also things without life (see § 150); as,

The sun, *whose* rays give life to the earth, is regarded by some people as a god.

This is the question *whose* solution has baffled philosophers of all ages.

[More properly, 'This is the question the solution *of which* has baffled philosophers of all ages'.]

154. *Which* is used for *things without life* and for *animals.* It may refer to a Singular or Plural Noun.

The moment *which* is lost is lost for ever.

The books *which* help you most are those which make you think most.

The horse *which* I recently bought is an Arab.

The moment which is lost is lost for ever.

Which was sometimes formerly used to refer to persons ; as,

Our Father, *which* art in heaven.

Which may also refer to a sentence ; as,

The man was said to be drunk, *which* was not the case.

He said he saw me there, *which* was a lie.

He is here, *which* is fortunate.

Note—The Relative Pronouns *who* and *which* can be used—

(i) To restrict, limit, or define more clearly the antecedent ; that is, where the clause introduced by a relative pronoun is **restrictive** or **defining** ; as,

The man *who* had cheated me was yesterday arrested by the police.

The book *which* you see on the table cost me ninety rupees.

(ii) To give some additional information about the antecedent ; that is, where the clause introduced by a relative pronoun is **continuative** or **non-defining** ; as,

The teacher sent for the boy, *who* (= and he) came at once.

I gave him a rupee, *which* (= and it) was all I had with me.

Note—That non-defining clauses are separated from the main clause by commas.

Compare:

My brother who is a doctor has gone to America.

My brother, who is a doctor, has gone to America.

The first sentence implies that the speaker has several brothers, and the clause *who is a doctor* distinguishes a particular one of them. In the second, the clause does not define and the implication is that the speaker has only one brother.

155. *That* is used for *persons* and *things.* It may refer to a Singular or a Plural Noun. (See § 151)

That has no genitive case and it is never used with a preposition preceding.

This is the boy *that* I told you of.
I know the house *that* he lives *in.*
Uneasy lies the head *that* wears a crown.
I have lost the watch *that* you gave me.
Thrice is he armed *that* hath his quarrel just.
A city *that* is set on a hill cannot be hid.
He *that* is not with me is against me.
Happy is the man *that* findeth wisdom.
He *that* is slow to anger is better than the mighty.
The crowd *that* gathered cheered him to the echo.

Who *that* has met him can escape his influence ?
All *that* I said had no effect on him.
He was the most eloquent speaker *that* I ever heard.

It will be noticed that the relative pronoun *that* is used only in defining clauses, *i.e.*, clauses that restrict, limit, or define the antecedent.

156. *That* may be used as an adverbial accusative = *on which, in which, at which ;* as,
I remember the day *that* he came.
On the day *that* thou eatest thereof thou shalt surely die.

157. As the Relative Pronoun *that* has a restrictive force it sometimes becomes unsuitable as the substitute for *who* or *which.* Thus I cannot say—
My father *that* is a schoolmaster is fifty years old.

I must say—
My father, *who* is a schoolmaster, is fifty years old.

But if I happen to have more than one sister, I can say—
My sister *that* has been adopted by my uncle is ill.

158. The Relative Pronoun *that* is used in preference to *who* or *which*—

(1) After Adjectives in the Superlative Degree ; as,
He was the most eloquent speaker *that* I ever heard.
The wisest man *that* ever lived made mistakes.
This is the best *that* we can do.

(2) After the words *all, same, any, none, nothing, (the) only ;* as,
All is not gold *that* glitters.
He is the same man *that* he has been.
It is only donkeys *that* bray.
It was not for nothing *that* he studied philosophy.
Man is the only animal *that* can talk.

(3) After the Interrogative Pronouns *who, what* ; as,
Who *that* saw her did not pity her ?
Who am I *that* I should object ?
What is it *that* troubles you so much ?
What is there *that* I do not know ?

(4) After two antecedents, one denoting a *person* and the other denoting an *animal* or a *thing ;* as,
The boy and his dog *that* had trespassed on the club premises were turned out.

159. *What* refers to *things* only. It is used without an antecedent expressed, and is equivalent to *that which* (or the *thing which*).
What (= that which) cannot be cured must be endured.
I say *what* (= that which) I mean.
I mean *what* I say.
What is done cannot be undone.
What man has done man can do.
What is one man's meat is another man's poison.

Give careful heed to *what* I say.
What I have written, I have written.
He found *what* he was looking for.

It will be noticed that *what* is used in the Nominative and Accusative singular only.

160. In older English, the word *as* was used as a relative pronoun after *such*; as,
Tears *such as* angels weep burst forth.
These mangoes are not *such as* I bought yesterday.
He is *such* a man *as* I honour.
We have never had *such* a time *as* the present.

His answer was *such as* I expected him to give.

These mangoes are not such as I bought yesterday.

The word *as* can be used as a Relative Pronoun after *same*; as,

My trouble is *the same as* yours [is].
This is not *the same as* that [is].
[But] I played with *the same* bat *that* you did.

'The same as' usually means 'of the same kind'.
'The same...that' means 'one and the same'.

The word *as* is also used as a Relative Pronoun after *as* followed by an adjective ; as,

I collected *as* many specimens *as* I could find.

Note—The first *as* here is an Adverb.

161. In older English, the word *but* was used as a relative pronoun after a negative; it often had the force of a relative pronoun.

There is none *but* will agree with me. (*but* will agree = *who* will *not* agree)
There is no Hindu *but* knows the story of the Ramayana. (That is, there is no Hindu who does not know, etc.)
There is no man *but* wishes to live.
There is no rose *but* has some thorn. (*but* = which...no)
There is scarcely a child *but* likes candy.
There is no man *but* knows these things. (*but* = who does not)

It will be seen that the pronoun *but* is here equivalent to *who...not, which...not*.

Omission of the Relative Pronoun

contented mind

162. The Relative Pronoun is generally omitted when it would be in the accusative case ; as,

Few and short were the prayers ^ we said.
A contented mind is the greatest blessing ^ a man can enjoy in the world.
I am monarch of all ^ I survey.
Men must reap the things ^ they sow.

"*That* is used preferably with reference to persons. Thus, we tend to say 'the meeting *which* I attended yesterday,' rather than 'the meeting *that* I attended yesterday.' But more frequently still do we say 'the meeting I attended yesterday,' the Accusative Relative being as a rule omitted altogether."—*Onions.*

This tendency to omit the Accussative Relative is more marked in the spoken language. In the written language its omission is often felt to be undignified.

163. In the following examples from poetry a Relative Pronoun in the nominative case is omitted.

"Tis distance ^ lends enchantment to the view."
"I have a brother ^ is condemned to die."

Note— The omission of a Relative Pronoun in the nominative case is now quite exceptional except in colloquial speech.

There's somebody at the door ^ wants to see you.

Omission of the Antecedent

164. In older English, the Antecedent of a Relative Pronoun was sometimes left out ; as,

Who works not shall not eat.
= (He) who works not shall not eat.
Whom the gods love, die young.
= (Those) whom the gods love die young.
Who steals my purse, steals trash.
Who laughs last, laughs best.
Who has lost all hope has also lost all fear.
Be good, sweet maid, and let who will be clever.

Who laughs last, laugh best.

Agreement of the Relative Pronoun and its Antecedent

165. As the Relative Pronoun refers to a Noun or Pronoun (called its Antecedent) it must be of the same *number* and *person* as its Antecedent. [Remember that the verb shows the number and person of the Relative Pronoun.]

The *boy who was* lazy was punished.
The *boys who were* lazy were punished.
I, who am your king, will lead you.
I am the *person that is* to blame.
We who seek your protection, are strangers here.
O thou that leadest Israel !
You who are mighty, should be merciful.
You who seek wisdom, should be humble.
He that is not with me is against me.
He that is down, needs fear no fall.
He that eats till he is sick must fast till he is well.
They who live in glass houses should not throw stones.
They who seek only for faults see nothing else.
The *flowers which grow* in our gardens are not for sale.
This is the only *one* of his poems *that* is worth reading.
[= Of his poems this is the only one that is worth reading.]

But the *case* of the Relative Pronoun depends upon its relation to the verb in the clause in which it occurs.

Rama is the boy *who* did it.
Rama is the boy *whom* I want.
Rama is the boy *whose* pencil I have.
Rama is the boy to *whom* I spoke.
He *whom* we worship, by *whose* gift we live, is the Lord.

Position of the Relative Pronoun

166. To prevent ambiguity, the Relative Pronoun should be placed as near as possible to its Antecedent ; as,

The *boy who won* the first prize in English is the son of my friend, Mr Joshi.

It would mean something quite different if we separate the Relative Pronoun from its Antecedent and say:

The boy is the son of my friend Mr Joshi who won the first prize.

Again such a sentence as "I have read Gokhale's speeches, who was a disciple of Ranade" would be improved if changed to "I have read the speeches of Gokhale, who was a disciple of Ranade".
So also the following sentence requires to be rearranged.

I with my family reside in a village near Pune which consists of my wife and three children.

Compound Relative Pronouns

167. Pronouns formed by adding *ever, so,* or *soever* to *who, which* and *what* are called **Compound Relative Pronouns.** They are:

whoever, whoso, whosoever; whichever ; whatever, whatsoever.

These Relatives have no antecedent expressed.

Whosoever (= any and every person who) exalteth himself shall by abased.
Whoso diggeth a pit shall fall therein.
Whatsoever thy hand findeth to do, do it with thy might.

168. The forms *whoever, whichever,* and *whatever* are now ordinarily used ; as,

Whoever (*i.e.,* any person who) comes is welcome.
Take *whichever* (*i.e.,* any which) you like.
I will take with me *whomsoever* you choose.
Whatever (*i.e,* anything which) he does, he does well.

EXERCISE IN GRAMMAR 29

Name the Relative Pronouns in the following sentences, tell the case of each, and mention its antecedent.

1. The pen that you gave me is a very good one.
2. The answer which you gave is not right.
3. I know the woman whose child was hurt.
4. Bring me the letters which the postman left.
5. This is the house that Jack built.
6. Hari saw the man who had been hurt.
7. We met the sailors whose ship was wrecked.
8. Here are the books which I found.
9. The cat killed the rat that ate the corn.
10. Bring me the books which lie on the table.
11. Here is the book that you lent me.
12. I hate children who are cruel.
13. Show me the knife that you have bought.
14. He has not brought the knife that I asked for.
15. Dogs soon know the persons by whom they are kindly treated.
16. This is the juggler whom we saw yesterday.
17. They that seek wisdom will be wise.

EXERCISE IN COMPOSITION 30

Fill the blanks with suitable Relative Pronouns.

1. We always like boys ____ speak the truth.
2. We saw the dog ____ worried the cat.
3. He ____ does his best shall be praised.
4. I know ____ you mean.
5. She has gone to Chennai, ____ is her birthplace.
6. I have seen the bird ____ you describe.
7. I do not know the man ____ hit the boy.
8. He gave away ____ he did not need.
9. There is no one ____ has not lost a friend.
10. Here is the pen ____ you lost.
11. Most people get ____ they deserve.
12. Time ____ is lost is never found again.
13. I did not know the person ____ called.
14. He is a man ____ you can trust.
15. Where is the book ____ I gave you ?
16. Is this the street ____ leads to the station ?
17. The letter ____ you wrote never arrived.
18. Listen to ____ I say.
19. He ____ is merciful shall meet mercy.
20. Did you receive the letter ____ I sent yesterday ?
21. ____ I have said, I have said.
22. ____ he was I could never find out.
23. ____ do you believe him to be ?
24. Do you know ____ has happened ?
25. ____ is done cannot be undone.
26. Do the same ____ I do.
27. For my purpose I need such a man ____ he is.
28. God helps those ____ help themselves.
29. No man can lose ____ he never had.
30. You should not imitate such a boy ____ he.

EXERCISE IN COMPOSITION 31

Fill the blanks with suitable Relative Pronouns.

1. That man ____ will not work must starve.
2. Such a man ____ he should be honoured.
3. These mangoes are not such ____ I bought yesterday.
4. It is not such a pretty place ____ I had expected.
5. We have need of more such men ____ he.
6. He plays the game ____ he likes best.
7. I do not believe ____ you say.
8. My uncle, ____ I loved, is dead.
9. The farmer is cutting the corn ____ has ripened.
10. ____ you say is not true.
11. A lady ____ I know nursed the child.
12. He says ____ he means, and means ____ he says.
13. ____ pleases you will please me.
14. I gave it to the man ____ I saw there.

15. I know _____ you are seeking.
16. They _____ touch pitch will be defiled.
17. You have not brought the book _____ I asked for.
18. Only he _____ bears the burden knows its weight.
19. Such books _____ you read are not worth reading.
20. When you speak to him remember to _____ you are speaking.
21. I regard that man as lost _____ has lost his sense of shame.
22. Wealth is not his _____ has it, but his _____ enjoys it.
23. People _____ are too sharp cut their own fingers.
24. Truth provokes those _____ it does not convert.
25. We do not know _____ he intends to do.
26. It is an ill wind _____ blows nobody good.
27. Is this a dagger _____ I see before me ?
28. I know to _____ you are alluding.
29. _____ the gods would destroy they first make mad.
30. He is the very man _____ we want.
31. Please recite _____ you have learned.
32. They always talk _____ never think.
33. Such _____ have pure hearts shall inherit the kingdom of heaven.

EXERCISE IN COMPOSITION 32

Join together each of the following pairs of sentences by means of a Connective.

1. I know a man. The man has been to Iceland.
2. The thief stole the watch. The thief was punished.
3. Show the road. The road leads to Delhi.
4. Here is the doctor. The doctor cured me of malaria.
5. I met a boy. He was very cruel.
6. He does his best. He should be praised.
7. The man is honest. The man is trusted.
8. My father is dead. I loved my father.
9. The teacher sent for the boy. The boy came at once.
10. Wellington was a great general. He defeated Napoleon at the Battle of Waterloo.
11. The dog bit the burglar. The burglar had broken into the house.
12. Once upon a time there lived a giant. The giant was very powerful and cruel.
13. We met a girl. The girl had lost her way.
14. Kalidas is famous. He wrote some fine dramas.
15. He is a rogue. No one trusts him.
16. The child is dead. The child came here yesterday.
17. The child is dead. I saw the child yesterday.
18. I know the man. He stole the bicycle.
19. The man stole the bicycle. He has been arrested.
20. I have found the umbrella. I lost it.
21. I saw a soldier. He had lost an arm.
22. This is the path. He came by this path.
23. The horse was lame. We saw the horse.
24. Those boys were kept in. They had been very lazy.
25. I saw a girl. She was singing.
26. That boy bowls very well. You see him there.
27. Here is the book. You were asking for the book.
28. Here is the pencil. You lost it yesterday.
29. The man is deaf. You spoke to the man.
30. Coal is found in West Bengal. It is a very useful mineral.

EXERCISE IN COMPOSITION 33

Join together each of the following pairs of sentences by means of a Connective.

1. This is the building. It was built in a single month.
2. The letter reached me this morning. You sent the letter.
3. Karim is always idle. He was punished.
4. I met my uncle. He had just arrived.
5. This is the house. Jack built it.
6. The boy is my cousin. You see him there.
7. The ladies have arrived. I was speaking of them.
8. The boys clapped heartily. They were watching the match.
9. The boy tells lies. He deserves to be punished.
10. I heard a song. The song pleased me.
11. I heard some news. The news astonished me.
12. I know a man. The man has a wooden leg.
13. Here is a book. The book contains pictures.
14. Give me the ruler. The ruler is on the desk.
15. The bicycle is a new one. Hari rode it.
16. We got into a bus. It was full of people.
17. He has a friend. He is a clever artist.

18. He is a well-known man. His generosity is the talk of the town.
19. The cat caught the mouse. The cat was pursuing the mouse.
20. Can I borrow the book ? You are reading it.
21. The boy was very proud. He had won the first prize.
22. Little Red Riding Hood went to visit her grandmother. Her grandmother was ill in bed.
23. This is my cousin. I was speaking of him.
24. We all despise a cowardly boy. He is one.
25. This is the cat. It killed the rat.

26. Those grapes were very sweet. You brought them.
27. Hari spoke to the soldier. The soldier's arm was in a sling.
28. The captain praised Balu. Balu's bowling was very good.
29. A man came running up. He heard me calling.

EXERCISE IN COMPOSITION 34

Split each of the following sentences into two.

1. The boys gave a loud shout, which was heard across the river.
2. Bring me the book that is on the table.
3. It was a wretched hut in which she lived.
4. The boy who fell off his bicycle has hurt his leg.
5. The elephant that was sick died.
6. The farmer is cutting the corn which has ripened.
7. Napoleon, whom the French honour, died at St. Helena.
8. The crow dropped the cheese, which the fox immediately snapped up.
9. John, who is my cousin, is a diligent boy.
10. Where is the parcel that I left here yesterday ?
11. I have found the book which I lost.
12. We visited Cox's Bazar, which is the most attractive spot in Bangladesh.
13. The boy whom you see there made the top score in the last match.

14. Dadabhai Naoroji, who was the first Indian to enter the British Parliament, was a Parsee.
15. He is a poet whose works are widely known.
16. The Taj Mahal, which was built by Shah Jahan, is the finest mausoleum in the world.
17. Last year we visited the Moti Masjid, which is a mosque of great architectural beauty.
18. The meeting, which was held in the Town Hall, was a great success.
19. The rope, which was old, snapped.

20. The task which you have to do is easy.
21. People who live in glass houses must not throw stones.

Chapter 19 INTERROGATIVE PRONOUNS

169. Consider the following sentences.

Who is there ? *Who* are you ?
About *whom* are you talking?/ *Who* are you talking about?
Whom do you want ?/ *Who* do you want?
Whose is this book ?
Which is the house ?

Which do you prefer, tea or coffee ?
What is the matter ?
What do you want ?
What will all the neighbours say ?

It will be noticed that the Pronouns in italics are similar in form to Relative Pronouns. But the work which they do is different. They are here used for *asking questions,* and are, therefore, called **Interrogative Pronouns.**

170. In the following sentences the Interrogative Pronouns are used in asking *indirect* questions.

I asked *who* was speaking.
I do not know *who* is there.
Tell me *what* you have done.
Ask *what* he wants.
Say *which* you would like best.

Who is speaking?

171. Again consider the following sentences.

Who gave you that knife ?	(Nominative)
Whose is this book ?	(Possessive)
Whom did you see?/ *Who* did you see?	}
To *whom* were you speaking?/ *Who* were you speaking to?	(Accusative)
What is that ?	(Nominative)
What do you want ?	(Accusative)
Which is he ?	(Nominative)
Which do you prefer ?	(Accusative)

Nominative :	who	Masc. and Fem.
Possessive :	whose	Singular and Plural.
Accusative :	whom/who	

Today the accusative *who* is more usual than *whom,* especially in spoken English.

What and *which* do not have different forms for different cases.

172. *Who* is used of *persons* only.

Who spoke ? (We expect the answer to be the name of a person.)
Who goes there ? *Who* made the top score ?
Who is knocking at the door ? *Who* says so ?
Whose is this umbrella ? *Whom* did you see ?

173. *Which* is used of both *persons* and *things.* It implies selection, that is, it implies a question concerning a limited number.

Which is your friend ? *Which* are your books ?
Which of the boys saw him ?
Which of you has done this ?
Which of these books is yours ?
Which of the pictures do you like best ?
Which of you by taking thought can add one cubit unto his stature ?
Which will you take ?

Who is knocking at the door?

174. *What* is used of *things* only.

What have you found ? (We expect the answer to be the name of a thing.)
What do you want ? *What* did you say ?
What was it all about ?
What is sweeter than honey ?
What are those marks on your coat ?

175. In such expressions as, 'What are you ?', 'What is he ?', 'What is this man ?' the word *what* does not refer to the person but to his *profession* or *employment**.

What are you ? ____I am a doctor.
What is he ? ____He is an engineer.

An engineer

* Today it is more usual to say 'What do you do?', 'What does he do?' etc.

But–

Who is he ? (= What is his name and family ?) –He is Mr K P Roy.

176. In the following sentences *which* and *what* are used as Interrogative Adjectives.

Which book are your reading ?

Which way shall we go ?

What books have you read ?

What pranks are you playing ?

What manner of man is this, that even the wind and the sea obey him ?

What pranks are you playing?

177. In the following sentences the words in italics are used as **Compound Interrogative Pronouns.**

Whoever told you so ?

Whatever are you doing ?

Note–The forms *whoever, whichever, whatever* are intensive.

EXERCISE IN COMPOSITION 35

Use the correct form of the Interrogative Pronoun in the following.

1. ____wishes to see you ?
2. ____do you wish to see ?
3. ____did she say was the winner ?
4. ____did he invite ?
5. ____shall I give this to ?
6. ____do men say that I am ?
7. ____do you believe did this ?
8. About ____are you speaking ?
9. ____did you see ?
10. ____do you mean ?
11. To ____did you give the key ?
12. ____of the girls can sew the best ?
13. By ____was the book written ?
14. ____are you seeking ?
15. ____of you has done this ?
16. ____have you seen ?
17. ____of our dogs is ill ?
18. ____do you think they are ?
19. ____do you think I am ?
20. ____did you find there ?
21. ____was that speaking to you ?
22. ____came here yesterday ?
23. ____do you consider in the right ?
24. ____, do you consider, is right ?
25. ____did you speak to ?
26. ____is life worth ?
27. ____of these bats will you take ?
28. ____ did he say ?
29 ____is that for ?
30. ____have you decided to do ?
31. ____stole the bird's nest ?
32. ____do you prefer ?
33. ____are you doing ?
34. ____has my book ?
35. ____ is an Island ?
36. ____is your book ?
37. ____do you want ?
38. With ____were you talking ?
39. ____did they fight each other for ?
40. ____is better, honour or riches ?
41. ____am I speaking to, please ?

178. A Pronoun used as an *exclamation* is called an **Exclamatory Pronoun** ; as,

What ! Still here ! I thought you had gone home long ago.

What ! You don't know Rama ?

Chapter 20 THE VERB: TRANSITIVE AND INTRANSITIVE VERBS

179. A **Verb** is a word that *tells* or *asserts* something about a person or thing. *Verb* comes from the Latin *verbum*, a *word.* It is so called because it is the most important word in a sentence.

A Verb may tell us–

(1) What a person or thing *does ;* as,

Hari *laughs.* The clock *strikes.*

(2) What *is done* to a person or thing ; as,

Hari is *scolded.* The window *is broken.*

Hari laughs

(3) What a person or thing *is ;* as,

The cat *is dead.* Glass *is* brittle. I *feel* sorry.

Def —A Verb is a word used to tell or assert something about some person or thing.

180. A Verb often consists of more than one word; as,

The girls were *singing.*

I *have learnt* my lesson.

The watch *has been found.*

181. Read these sentences.

1. The boy *kicks* the football.
2. The boy *laughs* loudly.

In sentence 1, the action denoted by the verb *kicks passes over* from the doer or subject *boy* to some Object *football.* The verb *kicks* is, therefore, called a **Transitive Verb.** *(Transitive* means *passing over.)*

In sentence 2, the action denoted by the verb *laughs* stops with the doer or Subject *boy* and *does not pass over* to an Object. The verb *laughs* is, therefore, called an **Intransitive Verb**. *(Intransitive* means *not passing over.)*

Def —A Transitive Verb is a Verb that denotes an action which *passes over* from the doer or Subject to an Object.

Def —An Intransitive Verb is a Verb that denotes an action which does not pass over to an object, or which expresses a *state* or *being ;* as,

He *ran* a long distance.	*(Action)*
The baby *sleeps.*	*(State)*
There *is* a flaw in this diamond.	*(Being)*

Note—Intransitive Verbs expressing being take the same cases after them as before them.

182. Most Transitive Verbs take a single object. But such Transitive Verbs as *give, ask, offer, promise, tell*, etc., take *two* objects after them—an Indirect Object which denotes the *person to whom* something is given or *for whom* something is done, and a Direct Object which is usually the name of some *thing;* as,

His father gave *him* (Indirect) a *watch* (Direct).

He told *me* (Indirect) a *secret* (Direct).

183. Most verbs can be used both as Transitive and as Intransitive verbs. It is, therefore, better to say that a verb is *used* Transitively or Intransitively rather than that it *is* Transitive or Intransitive.

Used Intransitively Feminine	*Used Transitively Feminine*
1. Some ants fight very fiercely.	1. The ants fought the wasps.
2. The ship sank rapidly.	2. The shot sank the ship.
3. The bell rang loudly.	3. Ring the bell, Rama.
4. The train stopped suddenly.	4. The driver stopped the train.
5. He spoke haughtily.	5. He spoke the truth.
6. This horse never kicks.	6. The horse kicked the man.
7. How do you feel ?	7. I feel a severe pain in my head.

Note— Some Verbs, e.g., *come, go, fall, die, sleep, lie*, denote actions which cannot be done to anything ; they can, therefore, never be used Transitively.

184. In such a sentence as 'The man killed himself' where the Subject and the Object both refer to the same person, the verb is said to be used *reflexively.*

Sometimes, though the verb is used reflexively, the Object is not expressed. In the following examples the reflexive pronoun understood is put in brackets:

The bubble burst [itself].

The guests made [themselves] merry.

Please keep [yourselves] quiet.

With these words he turned [himself] to the door.

The Japanese feed [themselves] chiefly on rice.

These verbs may, however, be regarded as pure Intransitives without any reflexive force whatever.

185. Certain verbs can be used reflexively and also as ordinary transitive verbs ; as,

Do not *forget* his name.

I *forget* his name.

Acquit yourself as man.

The magistrate *acquitted* him of the charge against him.

I *enjoy myself* sitting alone.

He *enjoys* good health.

He *interested himself* in his friend's welfare.

His talk does not *interest* me.

EXERCISE IN GRAMMAR 36

Name the Verbs in the following sentences, and tell in each case whether the Verb is Transitive or Intransitive. Where the Verb is Transitive name the Object.

1. The sun shines brightly.
2. The boy cut his hand with a knife.
3. The clock stopped this morning.
4. The policeman blew his whistle.
5. The sun rises in the east.
6. An old beggar stood by the gate.
7. The clock ticks all day long.
8. I looked down from my window.
9. Put away your books.
10. The moon rose early.
11. The cat sleeps on the rug.
12. Cocks crow in the morning.
13. Your book lies on the table.
14. The fire burns dimly.
15. Time changes all things.
16. We eat three times a day.
17. Tell the truth.
18. The birds sing in the green trees.
19. The little bird hopped about and sang.
20. My new watch does not keep good time.
21. The beggar sat down by the side of the road.
22. I could not spare the time.
23. He took shelter under a tree.
24. The boy easily lifted the heavy weight.
25. Balu wrote a letter to his uncle.
26. A tiny bird lived under the caves.
27. I know a funny little man.
28. Birds fly in the air.
29. A light rain fell last night.
30. I shall bring my camera with me.
31. You speak too loudly.
32. The dog ran after me.

EXERCISE IN COMPOSITION 37

Write five sentences containing Transitive Verbs, and five containing Intransitive Verbs.

Intransitive Verbs Used as Transitives

186. When an Intransitive Verb is used in a *causative* sense it becomes Transitive.

1. The horse *walks*.	1. He *walks* the horse.
2. The girl *ran* down the street.	2. The girl *ran* a needle into her finger (*ran* a needle = *caused* a needle to run).
3. Birds fly.	3. The boys *fly* their kites (*i.e., cause* their kites to fly).

187. A few verbs in common use are distinguished as Transitive or Intransitive by their spelling, the Transitive being causative *forms* of the corresponding Intransitive verbs.

Intransitive	*Transitive*
1. Many trees *fall* in the monsoon.	1. Woodmen *fell* trees. (Fell = cause to fall)
2. *Lie* still.	2. *Lay* the basket there. (Lay = cause to lie)
3. *Rise* early with the lark.	3. *Raise* your hands. (Raise = cause to rise)
4. *Sit* there.	4 *Set* the lamp on the table. (Set = cause to sit)

188. Some Intransitive Verbs may become Transitive by having a Preposition added to them ; as,

All his friends *laughed at* (= derided) him.
He will soon *run through* (= consume) his forture.
Please *look into* (= investigate) the matter carefully.
We *talked about* (= discussed) the affair several times.
I *wish for* (= desire) nothing more.
The Police Inspector *asked for* (= demandded) his name.

Sometimes the Preposition is *prefixed* to the Verb ; as,

Shivaji *over*came the enemy.
He bravely *with*stood *the attack.*
The river *over*flows its banks.

189. Intransitive Verbs sometimes take after them an Object *akin* or *similar in meaning* to the Verb. Such an Object is called the **Cognate Object** or **Cognate Accusative.** (Latin *Cognatus,* akin)

I have *fought* a good *fight.*
He *laughed* a hearty *laugh.*
I *dreamt* a strange *dream.*
He *sleeps* the *sleep* of the just.
Let me *die* the *death* of the righteous.
She *sighed* a deep *sigh.*
She *sang* a sweet *song.* He *ran* a *race.*
Aurangzeb *lived* the *life* of an ascetic.

The noun used as a Cognate Object is in the Accusative Case.

The following are examples of partially Cognate Objects:

He *ran* a great *risk* (= he ran a *course* of great risk).
The children *shouted applause* (= the children shouted a *shout* of applause).

190. A noun used adverbially to modify a verb, an adjective, or an adverb denoting *time, place, distance, weight, value* etc., is called an **Adverbial Object** or **Adverbial Accusative,** and is said to be in the Accusative Case adverbially ; as,

He held the post ten *years.*
I can't wait a *moment* longer.
He went *home.*
He swam a *mile.*
He weighs seven *stone.*
The watch cost nine hundred *rupees.*

191. There are a few Transitive Verbs which are sometimes used as Intransitive Verbs.

Transitive	*Intransitive*
1. He *broke* the glass.	1. The glass *broke.*

2. He *burnt* his fingers.
3. *Stop* him from going.
4. *Open* all the windows.

2. He *burnt* with shame.
3. We shall *stop* here a few days.
4. The show *opens* at six o'clock.

Chapter 21 VERBS OF INCOMPLETE PREDICATION

192. Read the following sentences.

1. The baby *sleeps.*
2. The baby *seems* happy.

The verbs in both these sentences are Intransitive.

But when I say 'The baby sleeps' I do make complete sense.

On the other hand if I say 'The baby seems' I do not make complete sense.

The Intransitive Verb *seems* requires a word (*e.g., happy*) to make the sense complete. Such a verb is called a **Verb of Incomplete Predication.**

The word *happy,* which is required to make the sense complete, is called the **Complement of the Verb** or the **Completion of the Predicate.**

193. Verbs of Incomplete Predication usually express the idea of *being, becoming, seeming, appearing.* The Complement usually consists of a Noun (called a **Predicative Noun**) or an Adjective (called a **Predicative Adjective**). When the Complement describes the Subject, as in the following sentences, it is called a **Subjective Complement.**

1. Tabby is a *cat.*
2. The earth is *round.*
3. John became a *soldier.*
4. Mr. Mehta became mayor.
5. The man seems *tired.*
6. You look *happy.*
7. The sky grew *dark.*
8. Roses smell *sweet.*
9. Sugar tastes *sweet.*
10. She appears *pleased.*
11. This house is to *let.*

Note— When the Subjective Complement is a Noun (as in 1, 3, 4) it is in the same case as the Subject, i.e., in the Nominative Case.

194. Certain Transitive Verbs require, besides an Object, a Complement to complete their predication ; as,

1. The boys made Rama *captain.*
2. His parents named him *Hari.*
3. This made him *vain.*
4. The jury found him *guilty.*
5. Rama called his cousin a *liar.*
6. Exercise has made his muscles *strong.*
7. I consider the man *trustworthy.*
8. God called the light *day.*
9. We thought him a *rascal.*
10. They chose him their *leader.*

Here, in each case, the Complement describes the *Object,* and is, therefore, called an **Objective Complement.**

Note— When the Objective Complement is a noun (as in 1, 2, 5, 8, 9, 10) it is in the Objective (or Accusative) Case in agreement with the object.

EXERCISE IN GRAMMAR 38

Say whether the Verbs in the following sentences are Transitive or Intransitive, name the Object of each Transitive Verb, and the Complement of each Verb of Incomplete Predication.

1. The hungry lion roars.
2. The report proved false.
3. The boy stood on the burning deck.
4. The child had fallen sick.
5. The ass continued braying.
6. The wind is cold.
7. The results are out.
8. He tried again and again.
9. We see with our eyes.
10. The child fell asleep

11. The weather is hot.
12. They are Europeans.
13. The rumour seems true.
14. Owls hide in the daytime.
15. Bad boys hide their faults.
16. The poor woman went mad.
17. We waited patiently at the station.
18. He told a lie.
19. They elected him president.
20. I found her weeping.
21. He struck the man dead.
22. The crow flew down and stole the cheese.
23. The sky looks threatening.
24. They made him general.
25. He waited an hour.
26. New brooms sweep clean.

waited patiently at the station

Chapter 22 ACTIVE AND PASSIVE VOICE

195. Compare:

1. Rama *helps* Hari.
2. Hari is *helped* by Rama.

It will be seen that these two sentences express the same meaning.

But in sentence 1, the form of the Verb shows that the person denoted by the subject **does** *something*.

Rama (the person denoted by the subject) does *something*.

The Verb *helps* is said to be in the Active Voice.

In sentence 2, the form of the Verb shows that something **is done to** the person denoted by the Subject.

Something is *done* to Hari (the person denoted by the Subject.)

The Verb *helped* is said to be in the **Passive Voice.**

Def—A verb is in the Active Voice when its form shows (as in sentence 1) that the person or thing denoted by the Subject *does something*; or, in other words, is the *doer* of the action.

The Active Voice is so called because the person denoted by the Subject *acts*.

Def— A Verb is in the Passive Voice when its form shows (as in sentence 2) that *something is done to* the person or thing denoted by the Subject.

The Passive Voice is so called because the person or thing denoted by the Subject is not active but *passive,* that is, suffers or receives some action.

Def—Voice is that form of a Verb which shows whether what is denoted by the Subject *does something* or *has something done to it.*

Note the change from the Active Voice to the Passive Voice in the following sentences.

Active Voice	*Passive Voice*
1. Sita *loves* Savitri.	1. Savitri *is loved* by Sita.
2. The mason *is building* the wall.	2. The wall *is being built* by the mason.
3. The peon *opened* the gate.	3. The gate *was opened* by the peon.
4. Some boys *were helping* the wounded man.	4. The wounded man was being helped by some boys.
5. He *will finish* the work in a fortnight	5. The work *will be finished* by him in a fortnight.
6. Who *did* this ?	6. By whom *was* this *done?*
7. Why *did* your brother *write* such a letter ?	7. Why *was* such a letter written by your brother ?

It will be noticed that when the Verb is changed from the Active Voice to the Passive Voice, the *Object* of the Transitive Verb in the *Active* Voice becomes the *Subject* of the Verb in the *Passive* Voice.

[Thus in sentence 1, *Savitri,* which is the object of *loves* in the Active Voice, becomes the Subject of *is loved in the Passive Voice.]*

Since the Object of a verb in the active voice becomes the Subject of the passive form, it follows that *only Transitive Verbs can be used in the Passive Voice,* because an Intransitive Verb has no Object.

196. The passive voice is formed with the suitable tense of the verb *be* followed by the past participle. Study this table.

Tense (or Modal + base)	*Active Voice*	*Passive Voice*
	take	am taken
Simple present	takes	is taken
	are taken	
	am taking	am being taken
Present continuous	is taking	is being taken
	are taking	are being taken
Present perfect	has taken	has been taken
	have taken	have been taken
Simple past	took	was taken
	were taken	
Past continuous	was taking	was being taken
	were taking	were being taken
Past perfect	had taken	had been taken
Simple future	will take	will be taken
	shall take	shall be taken
can/may/	can take	can be taken
must, etc. + base	must take	must be taken

197. Students must know when to use the Active Voice and when to use the Passive: the ability to change the Active Voice into the Passive and *vice versa* is not sufficient.

The Active Voice is used when the agent (*i.e.,* doer of the action) is to be made prominent ; the Passive, when the person or thing acted upon is to be made prominent. The Passive is, therefore, generally preferred when the active form would involve the use of an indefinite or vague pronoun or noun (*somebody, they, people, we,* etc.) as subject ; that is, when we do not know the agent or when it is clear enough who the agent is.

My pen has been stolen. (Somebody has stolen my pen.)
I was asked my name. (They asked me my name.)
English is spoken all over the world. (People speak English all over the world.)
I have been invited to the party. (Someone has invited me to the party.)
All orders will be executed promptly. (We will execute all orders promptly.)

In such cases the agent with *by* is usually avoided.

Note, however, that, as in the examples given earlier, the *by*-phrase cannot be avoided where the agent has some importance and is necessary to complete the sense.

EXERCISE IN GRAMMAR 39

Name the Verbs in the following sentences, and tell whether they are in the Active or in the Passive Voice.

1. The cat killed the mouse.
2. We compelled the enemy to surrender.
3. The boy was bitten by a dog.
4. The thief was caught.
5. The boy made a kite.
6. The ship was burned.
7. The young man made a disturbance at the meeting.
8. The captive was bound to a tree.
9. The bird was killed by a cruel boy.
10. The sudden noise frightened the horse.
11. He is loved by all.
12. The exhibition was opened by the Governor.
13. I see a dark cloud.
14. His command was promptly obeyed.

15. Some of the cargo had been damaged by the sea water.
16. Nothing will be gained by hurry.
17. The dog chased the sheep.
18. This letter was posted last night.
19. The field is ploughed.
20. The dog was teased by the boy.
21. The cat drank all the milk.
22. A stone struck me on the head.
23. The old gentleman takes snuff.
24. The money was lost.
25. The letter has just been posted.

EXERCISE IN GRAMMAR 40

Turn the following sentences from the Active Voice to the Passive Voice.

(Note—The agent with by should be omitted in Nos. 7, 12, 25, 29, 30, 31, 32, 33, 34 and 35.)

1. The cat killed the mouse.
2. The man cut down the tree.
3. Columbus discovered America.
4. His teacher praised him.
5. The boy teased the dog.
6. The syce feeds the horse every day.
7. The police arrested him.
8. Rama was making a kite.
9. The boy caught the ball.
10. My father will write a letter.
11. I will conquer him.
12. He kept me waiting.
13. The hunter shot the lion.
14. Hari opened the door.
15. A policeman caught the thief.
16. Sohrab threw the ball.
17. He scored twenty runs.
18. Your behaviour vexes me.

19. Manners reveal character.
20. He made a very remarkable discovery.
21. Little strokes fell great oaks.
22. Dhondu will bring the pony.
23. Everyone loves him.
24. My cousin has drawn this picture.
25. We expect good news.
26. The farmer gathers the harvest.
27. His own brother swindled him.
28. The recitation pleased the inspector.
29. Somebody has put out the light.
30. The enemy have defeated our army.
31. They sell TVs here.
32. I have sold my bicycle.
33. People will soon forget it.
34. They opened the theatre only last month.
35. We prohibit smoking.

198. When verbs that take both a direct and an indirect object in the Active Voice are changed to the Passive, either object may become the subject of the Passive verb, while the other is *retained.*

Active	*Passive*
The guard refused him admittance.	Admittance was refused to him by the guard. He was refused admittance by the guard.
Mr. Krishnaji teaches us grammar.	Grammar is taught to us by Mr Krishnaji. We are taught grammar by Mr Krishnaji.
The manager will give you a ticket.	A ticket will be given to you by the manager. You will be given a ticket by the manager.
Who taught you French ?	By whom was French taught to you ? / Who were you taught French by? By whom were you taught French ?
He handed her a cheque.	A cheque was handed to her. She was handed a cheque.

An indirect object denotes the person to whom or for whom something is given or done, while a direct object usually denotes a thing. In cases like the above, it is probably more usual for passive constructions to begin with the person.

199. Note that we use *with* (not *by*) to talk about an instrument used by the agent. Compare :

The dog was hit *with* a stick. (Active Voice : Somebody hit the dog with a stick.)

The dog was hit *by* a boy. (Active Voice : A boy hit the dog.)

200. There are a few Transitive verbs which, even in an Active form, are sometimes used in a Passive sense ; as,

These mangoes *taste* sour (*i.e.*, are sour when they are tasted).

The rose *smells* sweet (*i.e.*, is sweet when it is smelt).

The cakes *eat* short and crisp (*i.e.*, are short and crisp when they are eaten).

At least the play *reads* well (*i.e.*, affects the reader well when it is read).

EXERCISE IN COMPOSITION 41

Change the following sentences so that the Verbs will be in the Passive Voice.

1. We saw you and him.
2. They asked me my name.
3. We refused them admission.
4. I bought the baby a doll.
5. They found him guilty of murder.
6. A thunderstorm often turns milk sour.
7. You cannot pump the ocean dry.
8. They saw the storm approaching.
9. He keeps me waiting.
10. They painted the house red.
11. He told me to leave the room.
12. He promised me a present.
13. I shall order the carriage.
14. The boy is climbing the cliff.
15. One may accomplish many things by a little effort.
16. I am watching you very carefully.

EXERCISE IN COMPOSITION 42

Rewrite the following sentences so that the Verbs will be in the Active Voice.

1. He was praised by his father.
2. The first railway was built by George Stephenson.
3. The horse was frightened by the noise.
4. Not a word was spoken by Latif.
5. The teacher was pleased with the boy's work.
6. He was taken to the hospital by his friends.
7. The town was destroyed by an earthquake.
8. The road was lined with people.
9. The President was welcomed by the people.
10. *Shakuntalam* was written by Kalidas.
11. The building was damaged by the fire.
12. I was struck by his singular appearance.
13. Those cars were built by robots.
14. The streets were thronged with spectators.
15. The trees were blown down by the wind.
16. We shall be blamed by everyone.
17. The child was knocked down by a car.
18. Alice was not much surprised at this.
19. He will be greatly surprised if he is chosen.

EXERCISE IN COMPOSITION 43

Write three sentences with the Verbs in the Active Voice, and rewrite them with the Verbs in the Passive Voice.

201. We give below further examples of the interchange of Active and Passive Voice.

Active — All his friends laughed at him.
Passive — He was laughed at by all his friends.
Active — They made him king.
Passive — He was made king.
Active — They use video for teaching the students.
Passive — Video is used for teaching the students.
Active — One should keep one's promises.
Passive — Promises should be kept.
Active — When will you return the book?
Passive — When will the book be returned?
Active — Someone has picked my pocket.
Passive — My pocket has been picked.
Active — Circumstances will oblige me to go.
Passive — I shall be obliged to go.

EXERCISE IN COMPOSITION 44

In the following sentences change the Voice.

1. We elected Balu captain.
2. I saw him opening the box.
3. We must listen to his words.
4. Shall I ever forget those happy days ?
5. By whom was this jug broken ?
6. His subordinates accused him of various offences.
7. One cannot gather grapes from thistles.
8. The telegraph wires have been cut.
9. Alas ! We shall hear his voice no more.
10. The 1998 Asian Games were held in Bangkok, Thailand.
11. Without effort nothing can be gained.
12. Do not insult the weak.
13. All desire wealth and some acquire it.
14. Why should I be suspected by you ?
15. The information is kept on our computer.
16. The legend tells us how the castle received its name.
17. My watch was lost.
18. Why did he defraud you of your earnings ?
19. The public will learn with astonishment that war is imminent.
20. He made his wife do the work.
21. The teacher appointed him monitor.
22. The doctor despaired of his recovery.
23. He was refused admittance.
24. They laughed at his warnings and objected to all his proposals.
25. The people regarded him as an impostor and called him a villain.

Chapter 23 MOOD

202. The simplest use of a Verb is to make a *statement of fact* or ask a *question* ; as,

I *write* to my brother every week.

Who *wrote* that letter ?

But a Verb may also be used to express a *command* ; as,

Write neatly.

Or a Verb may be used to express a *mere supposition* ; as,

If I *were* you, I would not do it.

These different *modes* or *manners* in which a Verb may be used to express an action are called **Moods.** (Lat. *modus,* manner.)

Def.—Mood is the *mode* or *manner* in which the action denoted by the Verb is represented.

203. There are three Moods in English:

Indicative, Imperative, Subjunctive.

Indicative Mood

204. The Indicative Mood is used :

(1) To make a statement of *fact* ; as,

Rama *goes* to school daily.

We *are taught* Arithmetic.

Rama goes to school daily.

He *writes* legibly.
Napoleon *died* at St. Helena.
The child *is* alive.

(2) To ask a question ; as,
Have you *found* your book ?
Are you well ?

Have you found your book?

In each of these sentences the Verb in italics is said to be in the **Indicative Mood.**

205. The Indicative Mood is also used in expressing a supposition which is *assumed as a fact* ; as,
If [= assuming as a fact that] I *am* to be a beggar, it shall never make me a rascal.
If it *rains,* I shall stay at home. [Assuming as a fact that it will rain, etc.]
If my friend *wants* it, I shall give it to him. [Assuming as a fact that my friend wants it, etc.]
If he *is* the ring-leader, he deserves to be punished. [Assuming as a fact that he is the ring-leader, etc.]

A Verb which makes a *statement of fact* or asks a *question,* or expresses a *supposition which is assumed as a fact,* is in the Indicative Mood.

Imperative Mood

206. The Imperative Mood is used to express—

(1) A Command ; as,
Wait there.
Come here.
Open your book at page 7.

Try to do better.

(2) An exhortation ; as,
Be steady.
Take care of your health.
Try to do better.

Take care of your health.

(3) An entreaty or prayer ; as,
Have mercy upon us.
Give us this day our daily bread.

In each of these sentences the Verb in italics is said to be in the **Imperative Mood.**

A Verb which expresses a *command,* an *exhortation,* an *entreaty* or *prayer,* is in the Imperative Mood.

Note 1—The Imperative mood can strictly be used only in the Second Person, since the person commanded must be the person spoken to. But in the First and Third Persons a like sense is expressed by the use of the Auxiliary Verb let ; as,

Let me go. Let us go. Let him go. Let them go.

Note 2—The Subject of a Verb in the Imperative Mood (you) is usually omitted.

Subjunctive Mood

207. The following are the forms of the Subjunctive.

Present Subjunctive		*Past Subjunctive*	
the verb 'be'	*other verbs*	*the verb 'be'*	*other verbs*
I be	I speak	I were	I spoke
We be	We speak	We were	We spoke
You be	You speak	You were	You spoke
He be	He speak	He were	He spoke
They be	They speak	They were	They spoke

The Subjunctive Mood scarcely exists in present-day English.

208. The Present Subjunctive occurs

(1) In certain traditional phrases, where it expresses a wish or hope ; as,

God bless you !
God save the King !
Heaven help us !

(2) In formal English, in a noun clause dependent on a verb expressing desire, intention, resolution, etc. ; as,

I move that Mr Gupta be appointed Chairman.
It is suggested that a ring road be built to relieve the congestion.
We recommended that the subscription be increased to ten rupees.

209. The Past Subjunctive is used

(1) After the verb *wish*, to indicate a situation which is unreal or contrary to fact ; as,

I wish I knew his name. (= I'm sorry I don't know his name.)
I wish I were a millionaire.
She wishes the car belonged to you.

(2) After *if*, to express improbability or unreality in the present ; as,

If I were you I should not do that (but I am not you, and never can be).
If we started now we would be in time (but we cannot start now).

(3) After *as if/as though*, to indicate unreality or improbability ; as,

He orders me about as if I were his wife (but I am not).
He walks as though he were drunk (but he is not).

(4) After *it is time* + subject, to imply that it is late ; as,

It is time we started.

(5) After *would rather* + subject, to indicate preference ; as,

I would rather you went by air (= I should prefer you to go by air).
They would rather you paid them by cheque.

Chapter 24 TENSES : INTRODUCTION

210. Read the following sentences.

1. I *write* this letter to please you.
2. I *wrote* the letter in his very presence.
3. I *shall write* another letter tomorrow.

In sentence 1, the Verb *write* refers to **present** time.
In sentence 2, the Verb *wrote* refers to **past** time.
In sentence 3, the Verb *shall write* refers to **future** time.

Thus a Verb may refer

(1) to **present** time, (2) to **past** time, or (3) to **future** time.

211. A Verb that refers to *present* time is said to be in the **Present Tense;** as,

I *write*. I *love*.

[The word *tense* comes from the Latin *tempus*, time.]

A Verb that refers to *past* time is said to be in the **Past Tense;** as,

I *wrote*. I *loved*.

A Verb that refers to *future* time is said to be in the **Future Tense;** as,

I *shall write*. I *shall love*.

212. Thus there are three main Tenses:

The **Present,** the **Past,** the **Future.**

The Tense of a Verb shows the *time* of an action or event.

Note—Sometimes a past tense may refer to present time, and a present tense may express future time, as:

I wish I *knew* the answer. (=I'm sorry I don't know the answer. Past tense – Present time)
Let's wait till he *comes*. (Present tense – future tense)

213. Below we give the chief Tenses (Active Voice, Indicative Mood) of the verb *to love*.

PRESENT TENSE

	Singular Number	*Plural Number*
1st Person	I love	We love
2nd person	You love	You love
3rd Person	He loves	They love

PAST TENSE

	Singular Number	*Plural Number*
1st Person	I loved	We loved
2nd Person	You loved	You loved
3rd Person	He loved	They loved

FUTURE TENSE

	Singular Number	*Plural Number*
1st Person	I shall/will love	We shall/will love
2nd Person	You will love	You will love
3rd Person	He will love	They will love

214. Read these sentences :

1. I love. **(Simple Present)**
2. I am loving. **(Present Continuous)**
3. I have loved. **(Present Perfect)**
4. I have been loving. **(Present Perfect Continuous)**

The Verbs in all of these sentences refer to the *present* time, and are therefore said to be in the *present tense.*

In sentence 1, however, the Verb shows that the action is mentioned simply, without anything being said about the completeness or incompleteness of the action.

In sentence 2, the Verb shows that the action is mentioned as *incomplete or continuous,* that is, as still *going on.*

In sentence 3, the Verb shows that the action is mentioned as *finished, complete,* or *perfect,* at the time of speaking.

The tense of the Verb in sentence 4 is said to be *Present Perfect Continuous,* because the verb shows that the action is going on continuously, and not completed at this present moment.

Thus we see that the Tense of a verb shows not only the *time* of an action or event, but also the *state* of an action referred to.

215. Just as the Present Tense has four forms, the Past Tense also has the following four forms :

1. I loved. **(Simple Past)**
2. I was loving. **(Past Continuous)**
3. I had loved. **(Past Perfect)**
4. I had been loving. **(Past Perfect Continuous)**

Similarly, the Future Tense has the following four forms :

1. I shall/will love. **(Simple Future)**
2. I shall/will be loving. **(Future Continuous)**
3. I shall/will have loved. **(Future Perfect)**
4. I shall have been loving. **(Future Perfect Continuous)**

We may now define Tense as that form of a Verb which shows the *time* and the *state* of an action or event.

216. A verb agrees with its subject in number and person. Study the verb forms of various tenses:

Simple Present Tense	*Present Continuous Tense*
I speak	I am speaking

You speak
He speaks
We speak
They speak

Present Perfect Tense

I have spoken
You have spoken
He has spoken
We have spoken
They have spoken

Simple Past Tense

I spoke
You spoke
He spoke
We spoke
They spoke

Past Perfect Tense

I had spoken
You had spoken
He had spoken
We had spoken
They had spoken

Simple Future Tense

I shall/will speak
You will speak
He will speak
We shall/will speak
They will speak

Future Perfect Tense

I shall/will have spoken
You will have spoken
He will have spoken
We shall/will have spoken
They will have spoken

You are speaking
He is speaking
We are speaking
They are speaking

Present Perfect Continuous Tense

I have been speaking
You have been speaking
He has been speaking
We have been speaking
They have been speaking

Past Continuous Tense

I was speaking
You were speaking
He was speaking
We were speaking
They were speaking

Past Perfect Continuous Tense

I had been speaking
You had been speaking
He had been speaking
We had been speaking
They had been speaking

Future Continuous Tense

I shall/will be speaking
You will be speaking
He will be speaking
We shall/will be speaking
They will be speaking

Future Perfect Continuous Tense

I shall/will have been speaking
You will have been speaking
He will have been speaking
We shall/will have been speaking
They will have been speaking

EXERCISE IN GRAMMAR 45

Point out the Verbs in the following sentences and name their Moods and Tenses.

1. The river flows under the bridge.
2. I shall answer the letter to night.
3. I knew he was there, for I had seen him come.
4. It has been raining all night.
5. I hear he has passed all right.
6. I had finished when he came.
7. He takes but little pride in his work.
8. I have been living here for months.
9. Be good, sweet maid.
10. By this time to morrow I shall have reached my home.
11. It is time we left.
12. He told me that he had finished the work.
13. God forgive you !
14. He is waiting for you in the compound.
15. Piper, pipe that song again.

16. I am hoping to get a holiday soon.
17. Perhaps it were better to obey him.
18. Do noble deeds, not dream them all the day.
19. I shall have plenty of time tomorrow.
20. Though this be madness, yet there is method in it.
21. The king had never before led his troops in battle.
22. If he was guilty, his punishment was too light.
23. We have heard a strange story.
24. The travellers, all of whom had seen the chameleon, could not agree about its colour.
25. Beware lest something worse should happen to you.
26. The farmer is cutting the corn which has ripened.
27. I wish my brother were here.
28. She would rather we stayed till tomorrow.

Chapter 25 THE USES OF THE PRESENT AND PAST TENSES

PRESENT TENSES

Simple Present Tense

217. The Simple Present is used:

(1) To express a habitual action ; as,

He *drinks* tea every morning.
I *get up* everyday at five o'clock.
My watch *keeps* good time.

He drinks tea.

(2) To express general truths ; as,

The sun rises in the east.
Honey is sweet.
Fortune *favours* the brave.

(3) In exclamatory sentences beginning with *here* and *there* to express what is actually taking place in the present ; as,

Here *comes* the bus !
There she *goes* !

flight

(4) In vivid narrative, as substitute for the Simple Past ; as,

Sohrab now *rushes* forward and *deals* a heavy blow to Rustam.
Immediately the Sultan *hurries* to his capital.

(5) To express a future event that is part of a fixed timetable or fixed programme,

The next flight *is* at 7.00 tomorrow morning.
The match *starts* at 9 o'clock.
The train *leaves* at 5.20.
When *does* the coffee house *reopen*?

218. Note also the other uses of the Simple Present Tense.

(1) It is used to introduce quotations ; as,

Keats *says*, 'A thing of beauty is a joy for ever'.

(2) It is used, instead of the Simple Future Tense, in clauses of time and of condition ; as,

I shall wait till you *finish* your lunch.
If it *rains* we shall get wet.

(3) As in broadcast commentaries on sporting events, the Simple Present is used, instead of the Present Continuous, to describe activities in progress where there is stress on the succession of happenings rather than on the duration.

(4) The Simple Present is used, instead of the Present Continuous, with the type of verbs referred to in (§ 221) below.

Present Continuous Tense

219. The Present Continuous is used:

(1) For an action going on at the time of speaking ; as,

She *is singing* (now).
The boys *are playing* hockey.

(2) For a temporary action which may not be actually happening at the time of speaking; as,

I *am reading* 'David Copperfield' (but I am not reading at this moment).

(3) For an action that has already been arranged to take place in the near future ; as,

I *am going* to the cinema tonight.
My uncle *is arriving* tomorrow.

220. It has been pointed out before that the Simple Present is used for a habitual action. However, when the reference is to a particularly obstinate habit—something which persists, for example, in spite of advice or warning—we use the Present Continuous with an adverb like *always, continually, constantly.*

My dog is very silly ; he *is* always *running* out into the road.

221. The following verbs, on account of their meaning, are not normally used in the continuous form:

(1) Verbs of perception, *e.g., see, hear, smell, notice, recognize.*

(2) Verbs of appearing , *e.g., appear, look, seem.*

(3) Verbs of emotion, *e.g., want, wish, desire, feel, like, love, hate, hope, refuse, prefer.*

(4) Verbs of thinking, *e.g., think, suppose, believe, agree, consider, trust, remember, forget, know, understand, imagine, mean, mind.*

(5) *have* (= possess), *own, possess, belong to, contain, consist of, be* (except when used in the passive).

e.g.

Wrong	*Right*
These grapes *are tasting* sour.	These grapes *taste* sour.
I *am thinking* you are wrong.	I *think* you are wrong.
She *is seeming* sad.	She *seems* sad.
He *is having* a cellphone.	He *has* a cellphone.

However, the verbs listed above can be used in the continuous tenses with a change of meaning:

She *is tasting* the soup to see if it needs more salt.

(taste = test the flavour of)

I *am thinking* of going to Malaysia.

(think of = consider the idea of)

They *are having* lunch. (*have* = eat)

Present Perfect Tense

222. The Present Perfect is used:

(1) To indicate completed activities in the immediate past (with *just*); as,

He *has* just *gone* out.

It *has* just *struck* ten.

(2) To express past actions whose time is not given and not definite; as,

Have you *read* 'Gulliver's Travels'?

I *have* never *known* him to be angry.

Mr. Hari *has been* to Japan.

(3) To describe past events when we think more of their effect in the present than of the action itself ; as,

Gopi *has eaten* all the biscuits (*i.e.,* there aren't any left for you).

I *have cut* my finger (and it is bleeding now).

I *have finished* my work (= now I am free).

(4) To denote an action beginning at some time in the past and continuing up to the present moment (often with *since*- and *for*-phrases); as,

I *have known* him for a long time.

He *has been* ill since last week.

We *have lived* here for ten years.

We *haven't seen* Padma for several months.

223. The following adverbs or adverb phrases can also be used with the Present Perfect (apart from those mentioned above): *never, ever* (in questions only), *so far, till now, yet* (in negatives and questions), *already, today, this week, this month,* etc.

Note—The Present Perfect is never used with adverbs of past time. We should not say, for example, 'He has gone to Kolkata yesterday'. In such cases the Simple Past should be used ('He went to Kolkata yesterday').

Present Perfect Continuous Tense

224. The Present Perfect Continuous is used for an action which began at some time in the past and is still continuing ; as,

He *has been sleeping* for five hours (and is still sleeping).

They *have been building* the bridge for several months.

They *have been playing* since four o'clock.

He has been sleeping for five hours (and is still sleeping).

225. This tense is also sometimes used for an action already finished. In such cases the continuity of the activity is emphasized as an explanation of something.

'Why are your clothes so wet ?'– 'I *have been watering* the garden'.

PAST TENSES

Simple Past Tense

226. The Simple Past is used to indicate an action completed in the past. It often occurs with adverbs or adverb phrases of past time.

The steamer *sailed* yesterday.

I *received* his letter a week ago.

She *left* school last year.

227. Sometimes this tense is used without an adverb of time. In such cases the time may be either implied or indicated by the context.

I *learnt* Hindi in Nagpur.

I *didn't* sleep well (*i.e.*, last night).

Babar *defeated* Rana Sanga at Kanwaha.

228. The Simple Past is also used for past habits ; as,

He *studied* many hours everyday.

She always *carried* an umbrella.

He always carried an umbrella.

Past Continuous Tense

229. The Past Continuous is used to denote an action going on at some time in the past. The time of the action may or may not be indicated.

We were *listening* to the radio all evening.

It *was getting* darker.

The light went out while I *was reading*.

When I saw him, he *was playing* chess.

As in the last two examples above, the Past Continuous and Simple Past are used together when a new action happened in the middle of a longer action. The Simple Past is used for the new action.

230. This tense is also used with *always, continually*, etc. for persistent habits in the past.

He *was* always *grumbling*.

Past Perfect Tense

231. The Past Perfect describes an action completed before a certain moment in the past ; as,

I met him in New Delhi in 1996. I *had seen* him last five years before.

232. If two actions happened in the past, it may be necessary to show which action happened earlier than the other. The Past Perfect is mainly used in such situations. The Simple Past is used in one clause and the Past Perfect in the other ; as,

When I reached the station the train *had started* (so I couldn't get into the train).

I *had done* my exercise when Hari came to see me.

I *had written* the letter before he arrived.

Past Perfect Continuous Tense

233. The Past Perfect Continuous is used for an action that began before a certain point in the past and continued up to that time ; as,

At that time he *had been writing* a novel for two months.

When Mr Mukerji came to the school in 1995, Mr Anand *had* already *been teaching* there for five years.

EXERCISE IN COMPOSITION 46

Choose the correct verb form from those in brackets.

1. The earth ____round the sun. (move, moves, moved)
2. My friends ____the Prime Minister yesterday. (see, have seen, saw)
3. I ____him only one letter up to now. (sent, have sent, send)
4. She ____ worried about something. (looks, looking, is looking)
5. It started to rain while we ____tennis. (are playing, were playing, had played)
6. He ____ fast when the accident happened. (is driving, was driving, drove)
7. He ____asleep while he was driving. (falls, fell, has fallen)
8. I'm sure I ____him at the party last night. (saw, have seen, had seen)
9. He ____a mill in this town. (have, has, is having)
10. He ____here for the last five years. (worked, is working, has been working)
11. He thanked me for what I ____. (have done, had done, have been doing)
12. I ____a strange noise. (hear, am hearing, have been hearing)
13. I ____him for a long time. (know, have known, am knowing)
14. I ____English for five years. (study, am studying, have been studying)
15. Don't disturb me. I ____my homework. (do, did, am doing)
16. Abdul ____to be a doctor. (wants, wanting, is wanting)
17. The soup ____ good. (taste, tastes, is tasting)
18. He ____ TV most evenings. (watches, is watch, is watching)
19. He ____out five minutes ago. (has gone, had gone, went)
20. When he lived in Hyderabad, he ____to the cinema once a week. (goes, went, was going)
21. The baby ____all morning. (cries, has been crying)
22. I ____ Rahim at the zoo. (saw, have seen, had seen)
23. I ____Kumar this week. (haven't seen, did't see, am not seeing)
24. This paper ____twice weekly. (is appearing, appearing, appears)
25. Ashok fell off the ladder when he ____ the roof. (is mending, was mending, mended)

EXERCISE IN COMPOSITION 47

Choose the correct alternative from those given in brackets.

1. The Headmaster ____to speak to you. (wants, is wanting, was wanting)
2. I ____a new bicycle last week. (bought, have bought, had bought)
3. Here are your shoes ; I ____them. (just clean, just cleaned, have just cleaned)
4. It ____ since early morning, (rained, is raining, has been raining)
5. I ____a lot of work today. (did, have done, had done)
6. I ____something burning. (smell, am smelling, have been smelling)
7. Look! The sun ____ over the hills. (rises, is rise, is rising)
8. She ____unconscious since four o'clock. (is, was, has been)
9. He used to visit us every week, but he ____now. (rarely comes, is rarely coming, has rarely come)
10. We ____ for his call since 4.20. (are waiting, have been waiting, were waiting)
11. Everyday last week my aunt ____a plate. (breaks, broke, was breaking)
12. I know all about that film because I ____it twice. (saw, have seen, had seen)
13. Our guests ____; they are sitting in the garden. (arrived, have arrived, had arrived)
14. I ____him since we met a year ago. (didn't see, haven't seen, hadn't seen)
15. We ____our breakfast half an hour ago. (finished, have finished, had finished)

16. She jumped off the bus while it ____. (moved, had moved, was moving)
17. When we went to the cinema, the film ____. (already started, had already started, would already start)
18. I ______ for half an hour when it suddenly started to rain. (have walked, have been walking, had been walking)
19. Did you think you ____me somewhere before ? (have seen, had seen, were seeing)
20. The town ____its appearance completely since 1980. (is changing, changed, has changed)
21. Sheila ______ her case, look. (packed, has packed, had packed)
22. When I was in Sri Lanka, I ______ Negombo, Beruwela and Nilaveli. (visited, was visited, have visited)
23. I meant to repair the radio, but ____time to do it today (am not having, haven't had, hadn't)
24. When I ______ my dinner I went to bed. (had, have had, had had)
25. Men ____to abolish wars up to now, but maybe they will find a way in the future. (never managed, have never managed, will have never managed)

Chapter 26 THE FUTURE

234. There are several ways of talking about the future in English: the Simple Future Tense, the *going to* form, the Simple Present Tense, etc.

Simple Future Tense

235. The Simple Future Tense is used to talk about things which we cannot control. It expresses the future as fact.

I *shall be* twenty next Saturday.
It *will be* Diwali in a week.
We *will know* our exam results in May.

236. We use this tense to talk about what we think or believe will happen in the future.

I think Pakistan *will win* the match.
I'm sure Helen *will get* a first class.

As in the above sentences, we often use this tense with *I think*, and *I'm sure*. We also say *I expect* ______, *I believe* ______, *Probably* ______, etc.

237. We can use this tense when we decide to do something at the time of speaking.

It is raining. I *will take* an umbrella.
"Mr Sinha is very busy at the moment." – "All right. *I'll wait*."

Going to

238. We use the *going to* form (*be going to* + base of the verb) when we have decided to do something before talking about it.

"Have you decided what to do?" – "Yes. *I am going to resign* the job."
"Why do you want to sell your motorbike?" – "*I'm going to buy* a car."

Remember that if the action is already decided upon and preparations have been made, we should use the *going to* form, not the Simple Future Tense. The Simple Future Tense is used for an instant decision.

239. We also use the *going to* form to talk about what seems likely or certain, when there is something in the present which tells us about the future.

It *is going to rain*; look at those clouds.
The boat is full of water. It *is going to sink*.
She *is going to have* a baby.

240. The *going to* form may also express an action which is on the point of happening.

Let's get into the train. It'*s going to leave*.
Look! The cracker *is going to explode*.

The boat is full of water.It is going to sink.

Be about to

241. *Be about to* + base form can also be used for the immediate future.

Let's get into the train. It's *about to leave*.
Don't go out now. We *are about to have lunch*.

Simple Present Tense

242. The Simple Present Tense is used for official programmes and timetables.

The college *opens* on 23rd June.

The film *starts* at 6.30 and *finishes* at 9.00.

When *does* the next train *leave* for Chennai?

243. The Simple Present is often used for future time in clauses with *if, unless, when, while, as* (= *while*), *before, after, until, by the time* and *as soon as*. The Simple Future Tense is not used in such cases.

I won't go out if it *rains*. (not: will *rain*)

Can I have some milk before I *go* to bed?

Let's wait till he *finishes* his work.

Please ring me up as soon as he *comes*.

Present Continuous Tense

244. We use the Present Continuous Tense when we talk about something that we have planned to do in the future.

I *am going* to Shimla tomorrow.

We *are eating* out tonight.

Mr Abdul Rehman *is arriving* this evening.

We are eating out tonight.

You are advised to use the Present Continuous (not the Simple Present) for personal arrangements.

Future Continuous Tense

245. We use the Future Continuous Tense to talk about actions which will be in progress at a time in the future.

I suppose it *will be raining* when we start.

This time tomorrow I *will be sitting* on the beach in Singapore.

"Can I see you at 5 o'clock?" – "Please don't come then. I *will be watching* the tennis match on TV."

246. We also use this tense to talk about actions in the future which are already planned or which are expected to happen in the normal course of things.

I *will be staying* here till Sunday.

He *will be meeting* us next week.

The postman *will be coming* soon.

I will be staying here till Sunday.

Be to

247. We use *be to* + base form to talk about official plans and arrangements.

The Prime Minister *is to visit* America next month.

The conference *is to discuss* "Nuclear Tests."

Be to is used in a formal style, often in news reports. *Be* is usually left out in headlines, e.g. "Prime Minister to visit America".

Future Perfect Tense

248. The Future Perfect Tense is used to talk about actions that will be completed by a certain future time.

I *shall have written* my exercise by then.

He *will have left* before you go to see him.

By the end of this month I *will have worked* here for five years.

Future Perfect Continuous Tense

249. The Future Perfect Continuous tense is used for actions which will be in progress over a period of time that will end in the future.

By next March we *shall have been living* here for four years.

I'*ll have been teaching* for twenty years next July.

This tense is not very common.

EXERCISE IN GRAMMAR 48

Choose the correct or more suitable forms of the verbs to fill in the blanks.

1. The plane ______ at 3.30. (arrives, will arrive)
2. I will phone you when he _____ back. (comes, will come)
3. When I get home, my dog _____ at the gate waiting for me. (sits, will be sitting)
4. I _____ the Joshis this evening. (visit, am visiting)
5. Look at those black clouds. It _____. (will rain, is going to rain)
6. The train _______ before we reach the station. (arrives, will have arrived)
7. Perhaps we ______ Mahabaleshwar next month. (visit, will visit)
8. Unless we _____ now we can't be on time. (start, will start)
9. I _____ into town later on. Do you want a lift? (drive, will be driving)
10. The next term _____ on 16th November. (begins, is beginning)
11. Oh dear! I _____. (will sneeze, am going to sneeze)
12. By 2020, robots _____ many of the jobs that people do today. (will be taking over, will have taken over)
13. I'm sure she ______ the exam. (passes, will pass)
14. I _____ home next Sunday. (go, am going)
15. I _____ you one of these days, I expect. (see, will be seeing)
16. Help! I _____ fall. (will, am going to)
17. She has bought some cloth; she ______ herself a blouse. (will make, is going to make)
18. I _____ your house this afternoon. It is on my way home from work. (will be passing, am passing)
19. Hurry up! The programme _____. (will start, is about to start)
20. This book is not long. I _____ it by lunch time. (will be reading, will have read)

For information about verb forms in conditionals, see Book II, Chapter 32.

Chapter 27 THE VERB : PERSON AND NUMBER

250. The Verb, like the Personal Pronouns, has three Persons —the First, the Second and the Third. Thus, we say

1. I *speak*. 2. You *speak*. (Old English: Thou speakest.) 3. He *speaks*.

This is because of the difference in *Person* of the Subjects, as all the three are subjects of the singular number.

In sentence 1, the Subject is of the First Person, therefore the Verb is also of the First Person.

In sentence 2, the Subject is of the Second Person, therefore the verb is also of the Second Person.

In sentence 3, the Subject is of the Third Person, therefore the Verb is also of the Third Person.

We thus see that the Verb takes the same Person as its Subject; or, that *the Verb agrees with its Subject in Person.*

251. The Verb, like the Noun and the Pronoun, has two Numbers: the Singular and the Plural. Thus we say —

1. He *speaks.* 2. They *speak.*

This is because of the difference in *Number* of the subjects (as both the Subjects are of the third person).

In sentence 1, the Subject is Singular, therefore the Verb is Singular.

In sentence 2, the Subject is Plural, therefore the Verb is Plural.

We thus see that the Verb takes the same Number as its Subject ; or, that *the Verb agrees with its Subject in Number.*

252. But we have already seen that *the Verb also agrees with its Subject in Person* ; hence we have the important rule. **The Verb must agree with its Subject in Number and Person**; that is, the Verb must be of the same Number and Person as its Subject. Thus, if the Subject is of the Singular Number, First Person, the Verb must be of the Singular Number, First Person ; as,

I *am* here. I *was* there. I *have* a bat. I *play* cricket.

If the Subject is of the Singular Number, Third Person, the Verb must be of the Singular Number, Third Person ; as,

He *is* here. He *was* there. He *has* a bat. He *plays* cricket.

If the Subject is of the Plural Number, Third Person, the Verb must be of the Plural Number, Third Person ; as,

They *are* here. They *were* there. They *have* bats. They *play* cricket.

Note— In some languages the form of the Verb changes with the Number and Person of the Subject. In modern English verbs have lost all their inflections for number and person, except in the third person of the singular number. Thus we have—

I speak.	We speak.
You speak.	You speak. (*You* is both singular and plural in current English.)
He speaks.	They speak.

The only exception is the verb *to be*. We say—

I *am*.	We *are*.
You *are*.	You *are*.
He *is*.	They *are*.

For further study of the agreement of the verb with the subject, see Book II, Chapter 17.

Chapter 28 THE INFINITIVE

253. Read these sentences:

I want *to go*.

They tried *to find* fault with us.

The forms *to go* and *to find* are "infinitives."

The **infinitive** is the base of a verb, often preceded by *to*.

254. Read the following sentences:—

1. *To err* is human.
2. Birds love *to sing*.
3. *To respect* our parents is our duty.
4. He refused *to obey* the orders.
5. Many men desire *to make* money quickly.

In sentence 1, the Infinitive, like a noun, is the Subject of the verb *is*.

In sentence 2, the Infinitive, like a noun, is the Object of the verb *love*.

In sentence 3, the Infinitive, like a noun, is the Subject of the verb *is*, but, like a verb, it also takes an object.

In sentence 4, the Infinitive, like a noun, is the Object of the verb *refused*, but, like a verb, it also takes an object.

In sentence 5, the Infinitive, like a noun, is the Object of the verb *desire*, but, like a verb, it also takes an Object and is modified by an Adverb.

It will be seen that the Infinitive is a kind of noun with certain features of the verb, especially that of taking an object (when the verb is Transitive) and adverbial qualifiers. In short, the Infinitive is a Verb-Noun.

255. The word *to* is frequently used with the Infinitive, but is not an essential part or sign of it.

Thus, after certain verbs (*bid, let, make, *need, *dare, see, hear*), we use the Infinitive without *to*; as,

Bid him *go* there.
I *bade* him *go*.
Let him *sit* here.
I will not *let* you *go*.
Make him *stand*.
I *made* him *run*.

* Except when they are conjugated with *do*.

We *need* not *go* today.
You *need* not *do it.*
You *dare* not *do it.*
I *saw* him *do* it.
I *heard* him *cry.*

256. The infinitive without *to* is also used after the verbs *will, would, shall, should, may, might, can, could* and *must.*
I will *pay* the bill.
You *should* work harder.
He *can* speak five languages.
You *must* come to the office at nine tomorrow.

He will pay the bill.

The Infinitive without *to* is also used after *had better, had rather, would rather, sooner than, rather than*; as,
You had better *ask* permission.
I had rather *play* than *work.*
I would rather *die* than *suffer* so.

Use of the Infinitive

257. The Infinitive, with or without adjuncts, may be used, like a Noun –

(1) As the Subject of a Verb; as,
To find fault is easy.
To err is human.
To reign is worth ambition.

(2) As the Object of a transitive Verb; as
I do not mean *to read.*
He likes *to play* cards.

(3) As the Complement of a Verb; as,
Her greatest pleasure is *to sing.*
His custom is *to ride* daily.

Bring me some water.

(4) As the Object of a Preposition; as,
He had no choice but (= except) *to obey.*
The speaker is about *to begin.*

(5) As an Objective Complement; as,
I saw him *go.*

When the infinitive is thus used, like a Noun, it is called the **Simple Infinitive**.

258. The Infinitive is also used–

(1) To qualify a Verb, usually to express *purpose*; as,
He called *to see* my brother (= for the purpose of seeing my brother).
We eat *to live.* (*Purpose*)
I come *to bury* Caesar. (*Purpose*)
He wept *to see* the desolation caused by the flood. (*Cause*)

It is pleasant to take.

(2) To qualify an Adjective; as,
Figs are good *to eat.*
This medicine is pleasant *to take.*
The boys are anxious *to learn.*
He is too ill *to do* any work.

(3) To qualify a Noun; as,
This is not the time *to play.*

You will have cause *to repent.*

He is a man *to be admired.*

Here is a house *to let.*

This house is *to let.*

(4) To qualify a Sentence; as,

To tell the truth, I quite forgot my promise.

He was petrified, *so to speak.*

When the Infinitive is thus used it is called the **Gerundial** or **Qualifying Infinitive**.

It will be seen that in 1 and 2 the Gerundial Infinitive does the work of an Adverb; in 3 it does the work of an Adjective; in 4 it is used absolutely.

259. The Infinitive may be active or passive. When active it may have a present and a perfect form, and may merely name the act, or it may represent progressive or continued action.

Active

Present: to love — ***Perfect:*** to have loved

Present Continuous: to be loving

Perfect Continuous: to have been loving

When passive the Infinitive has a present and a perfect form.

Passive

Present: to be loved

Perfect: to have been loved

EXERCISE IN GRAMMAR 49

State how the Infinitive is used in the following sentences.

1. There was nothing for it to fight.
2. Let us pray.
3. The mango is fit to eat.
4. I heard her sing.
5. I have come to see you.
6. The order to advance was given.
7. Men must work and women must weep.
8. I am sorry to hear this.
9. He is slow to forgive.
10. A man severe he was and stern to view.
11. And fools who came to scoff remained to pray.
12. Thus to relieve the wretched was his pride.
13. Full many a flower is born to blush unseen.
14. Music hath charms to soothe the savage beast.
15. Never seek to tell thy love.
16. To retreat was difficult; to advance was impossible.

17. Everybody wishes to enjoy life.
18. My desire is to see you again.
19. There was not a moment to be lost.
20. The counsel rose to address the court.
21. My right there is none to dispute.
22. The ability to laugh is peculiar to mankind.
23. He has the power to concentrate his thoughts.
24. He was quick to see the point.
25. I am not afraid to speak the truth.
26. Better dwell in the midst of alarms
    Than reign in this horrible place.
27. Can you hope to count the stars?
28. To toil is the lot of mankind.
29. It is delightful to hear the sound of the sea.
30. It is a penal offence to bribe a public servant.

EXERCISE IN COMPOSITION 50

Combine together the following pairs of sentences by using Infinitives.

[*Example* — Napoleon was one of the greatest of generals. He is universally acknowledged so. = Napoleon is universally acknowledged to have been one of the greatest of generals.

Note—It will be noticed that we have turned one of the sentences into a phrase containing an infinitive.]

1. He did not have even a rupee with him. He could not buy a loaf of bread.
2. Every cricket team has a captain. He directs the other players.
3. You must part with your purse. On this condition only you can save your life.
4. He went to Amritsar. He wanted to visit the Golden Temple.
5. The robber took out a knife. He intended to frighten the old man.
6. I speak the truth. I am not afraid of it.
7. The insolvent's property was sold by the official Assignee. The insolvent's creditors had to be paid.
8. He wants to earn his livelihood. He works hard for that reason.
9. The strikers held a meeting. They wished to discuss the terms of the employers.
10. He has five children. He must provide for them.
11. The old man has now little energy left. He cannot take his morning constitutional exercises.
12. The Rajah allowed no cows to be slaughtered in his territory. It was his custom.
13. He formed a resolution. It was to the effect that he would not speculate any more.
14. Everyone should do his duty. India expects this of every man.
15. She visits the poor. She is anxious to relieve them of their sufferings.
16. He collects old stamps even at great expense. This is his hobby.
17. He must apologise for his misconduct. It is the only way to escape punishment.
18. I have no aptitude for business. I must speak it out frankly.
19. He was desirous of impressing his host. So he was on his best behaviour in his presence.
20. That young man has squandered away all his patrimony. He must have been very foolish.
21. He has risen to eminence from poverty and obscurity. It is highly creditable.

Chapter 29 THE PARTICIPLE

260. Read this sentence.

Hearing the noise, the boy woke up.

The word *hearing* qualifies the noun *boy* as an Adjective does.

It is formed from the Verb *hear*, and governs an object.

The word *hearing*, therefore, partakes of the nature of both a Verb and an Adjective, and is called a **Participle**. It may be called a Verbal Adjective.

Def— A participle is that form of the Verb which partakes of the nature both of a Verb and of an Adjective.

[Or] A participle is a word which is partly a Verb and partly an Adjective.

Note— The phrase 'Hearing the noise', which is introduced by a Participle, is called a Participle Phrase. According to its use here, it is an Adjective Phrase.

261. Study the following examples of Participles:

1. We met a girl *carrying* a basket of flowers.
2. Loudly *knocking* at the gate, he demanded admission.
3. The child, *thinking* all was safe, attempted to cross the road.
4. He rushed into the field, and foremost *fighting* fell.

The above are all examples of what is usually called the **Present Participle,** which ends in *-ing* and represents an action as *going on* or *incomplete* or *imperfect.*

If the verb from which it comes is Transitive, it takes an object, as in sentence 1.

Notice also that in sentence 2, the Participle is modified by an adverb.

262. Besides the Present Participle, we can form from each verb another Participle called its **Past Participle**, which represents a completed action or state of the thing spoken of.

The following are examples of Past Participles:

Blinded by a dust storm, they fell into disorder.
Deceived by his friends, he lost all hope.
Time *misspent* is time lost.
Driven by hunger, he stole a piece of bread
We saw a few trees *laden* with fruit.

It will be noticed that the Past Participle usually ends in *-ed, -d, -t, -en,* or *-n.*

Besides these two simple participles, the Present and the Past, we have what is called a Perfect Participle that represents an action as completed at some past time; as,

Having rested, we continued our journey.

263. In the following examples the Participles are used as simple qualifying adjectives in front of a noun; thus used they are called **Participle Adjectives.**

A *rolling* stone gathers no moss.
We had a drink of the *sparkling* water.
His *tattered coat* needs mending.
The *creaking* door awakened the dog.
A *lying* witness ought to be punished.
He played a *losing* game.
A *burnt* child dreads the fire.
His *finished* manners produced a very favourable impression.
He wears a *worried* look.
Education is the most *pressing* need of our country.
He was reputed to be the most *learned* man of his time.

From the last two examples it will be noticed that a Participle admits of degrees of comparison.

264. Used adjectivally the Past Participle is Passive in meaning, while the Present Participle is Active in meaning; as,

a *spent* swimmer = a swimmer who is tired out;
a *burnt* child = a child who is burnt;
a *painted* doll = a doll which is painted;
a *rolling* stone = a stone which rolls.

265. Let us now recapitulate what we have already learnt about the Participle.

(1) A participle is a Verbal Adjective.

(2) Like a Verb it may govern a noun or pronoun; as,
Hearing the *noise*, the boy woke up. [The noun *noise* is governed by the participle *Hearing*].

(3) Like a Verb it may be modified by an adverb; as,
Loudly knocking at the gate, he demanded admission. [Here the participle *knocking* is modified by the adverb *Loudly*.]

(4) Like an adjective it may qualify a noun or pronoun; as,
Having rested, the *men* continued their journey

(5) Like an Adjective it may be compared; as,
Education is the *most pressing* need of our time. [Here the participle *pressing* is compared by prefixing *most*.]

266. Below are shown the forms of the different Participles:

Active	**Passive**
Present: loving	*Present*: being loved
Perfect: having loved	*Perfect*: having been loved
	Past: loved

Use of the Participle

267. It will be noticed that the Continuous Tenses (Active Voice) are formed from the Present Participle with tenses of the verb *be*; as,

I am loving. I was loving. I shall be loving.

The Perfect Tenses (Active Voice) are formed from the Past Participle with tenses of the verb *have*; as,

I have loved. I had loved. I shall have loved.

The Passive Voice is formed from the Past Participle with tenses of the verb *be*; as,

I am loved. I was loved. I shall be loved.

268. We have seen that Participles qualify nouns or pronouns. They may be used—

(1) Attributively; as,

A *rolling* stone gathers no moss.
His *tattered* coat needs mending.
A *lost* opportunity never returns.

(2) Predicatively; as,

The man seems *worried.* (Modifying the Subject)
He kept me *waiting.* (Modifying the Object)

(3) Absolutely with a noun or pronoun going before; as,

The weather *being fine,* I went out.
Many *having arrived,* we were freed from anxiety.
Weather *permitting,* there will be a garden party at Government House tomorrow.
God *willing,* we shall have another good monsoon.
The sea *being smooth,* we went for sail.
The wind *having failed,* the crew set to work with a will.
His master *being absent,* the business was neglected.
The wind *being favourable,* they embarked.

It will be seen that in each of the above sentences the Participle with the noun or pronoun going before it, forms a phrase independent of the rest of the sentence. Such a phrase is called an **Absolute Phrase**; and a noun or pronoun so used with a participle is called a **Nominative Absolute**.

269. An Absolute Phrase can be easily changed into a subordinate clause; as,

Spring advancing, the swallows appear. [When spring advances. – Clause of Time]
The sea being smooth, we went for a sail. [Because the sea was smooth. – Clause of Reason]
God willing, we shall meet again. [If God is willing. – Clause of Condition]

Errors in the Use of Participles

270. Since the participle is a verb-adjective it must be attached to some noun or pronoun; in other words, it must always have a proper 'subject of reference'.

The following sentences are *incorrect* because in each case the Participle is left without proper agreement:

1. Standing at the gate, a scorpion stung him. (As it is, the sentence reads as if the scorpion was standing at the gate.)
2. Going up the hill, an old temple was seen.
3. Entering the room, the light was quite dazzling.

We should, therefore, recast these sentences as shown below:

1. Standing at the gate, he was stung by a scorpion.

Or: While he was standing at the gate, a scorpion stung him.

2. When we went up the hill, we saw an old temple.
3. Entering the room, I found the light quite dazzling.

Or: When I entered the room, the light was quite dazzling.

271. Usage, however, permits in certain cases such constructions as the following where the participle is left without a proper 'subject of reference'. [The Participle in such cases is called an **Impersonal Absolute.**]

Taking everything into consideration, the Magistrate was perfectly justified in issuing those orders.

Considering his abilities, he should have done better.
Roughly *speaking*, the distance from here to the nearest railway station is two miles.

It will be noticed that in the above instances the unexpressed subject is indefinite.

Thus, 'Roughly speaking' = If one speaks roughly.

272. Sometimes, as in the following examples, the Participle is understood:

Sword (being) in hand, he rushed on the jailor.
Breakfast (having been) over, we went out for a walk.

EXERCISE IN GRAMMAR 51

Pick out the Participle in each of the following sentences. Tell whether it is a Present or a Past participle, and also how it is used.

1. Generally speaking, we receive what we deserve.
2. Having gained truth, keep truth.
3. I saw the storm approaching.
4. Hearing a noise, I turned round.
5. Considering the facts, he received scant justice.
6. The enemy, beaten at every point, fled from the field.
7. Being dissatisfied, he resigned his position.
8. The rain came pouring down in torrents.
9. Having elected him President, the people gave him their loyal support.
10. The traveller, being weary, sat by the woodside to rest.

EXERCISE IN GRAMMAR 52

Pick out the Participle in each of the following sentences. Tell whether it is a Present or a Past Participle, and also how it is used.

1. The fat of the body is fuel laid away for use.
2. Being occupied with important matters, he had no leisure to see us.
3. The children coming home from school look in at the open door.
4. Michael, bereft of his son Luke, died of a broken heart.
5. Books read in childhood seem like old friends.
6. Lessons learned easily are soon forgotten.
7. A word fitly spoken is like apples of gold in pictures (baskets) of silver.
8. Seeing the sunshine, I threw open the window.
9. Seizing him by the arm, his friend led him away.
10. Encouraged by his wife, he persevered.
11. Overcome by remorse, he determined to atone for his crime by liberality to the church.

EXERCISE IN COMPOSITION 53

Combine the following pairs of sentences by making use of a Participle.

[*Examples:* The magician took pity on the mouse. He turned it into a cat.
= *Taking* pity on the mouse, the magician turned it into a cat.
The train was ready to leave the station. The people had taken their seats.
= The people *having taken* their seats, the train was ready to leave the station.]

1. The porter opened the gate. We entered.
2. We started early. We arrived at noon.
3. We met a man. He was carrying a log of wood.
4. The stable door was open. The horse was stolen.
5. He seized his stick. He rushed to the door.
6. The hunter took up his gun. He went out to shoot the lion.

7. A crow stole a piece of cheese. She flew to her nest to enjoy the tasty meal.
8. The wolf wished to pick a quarrel with the lamb. He said, "How dare you make the water muddy?"
9. A passenger alighted from the train. He fell over a bag on the platform.
10. Nanak met his brother in the street. He asked him where he was going.
11. My sister was charmed with the silk. She bought ten yards.
12. The steamer was delayed by a storm. She came into port a day late.
13. He had resolved on a certain course. He acted with vigour.
14. He staggered back. He sank to the ground.
15. The letter was badly written. I had great difficulty in making out its contents.
16. They had no fodder. They could give the cow nothing to eat.
17. A hungry fox saw some bunches of grapes. They were hanging from a vine.
18. Cinderella hurried away with much haste. She dropped one of her little glass slippers.

273. Participles sometimes contain an implied meaning, which can be more fully expressed by changing the participle phrase into a clause of: (*a*) time, (*b*) cause, (*c*) concession, or (*d*) condition.[See § 269]

(*a*) Having done his lesson (= *after* he had done his lesson), he went out to play cricket.
Walking along the street one day (= *while* I was walking along the street one day) I saw a dead cobra.

(*b*) Being overpowered (= *because* he was overpowered), he surrendered.
Running at top speed (= *because* he ran at top speed), he got out of breath.

(*c*) Possessing all the advantages of education and wealth (= although he possessed all the advantages of education and wealth), he never made a name.

(*d*) Following my advice (= *if* you follow my advice), you will gain your object.
Seven were killed, including the guard (= *if* the guard is included).

EXERCISE IN COMPOSITION 54

Rewrite each of the following sentences, by changing the Participle into a Finite Verb.

[*Examples*: Quitting the forest, we advanced into the open plain. = We quitted the forest and advanced into the open plain. Driven out of his country, he sought asylum in a foreign land. = As he was driven out of his country, he sought asylum in a foreign land.

1. Going up the stairs, the boy fell down.
2. Having lost my passport, I applied for a new one.
3. I once saw a man walking on a rope.
4. Walking on the roof, he slipped and fell.
5. Having no guide with us, we lost our way.
6. The stable door being open, the horse was stolen.
7. Being paralytic, he could not walk.
8. Hearing the noise, I woke up.
9. Caesar being murdered, the dictatorship came to an end.
10. Working all day, I was fatigued.
11. We met an old *Sadhu* walking to Varanasi.
12. Having come of age, his son entered into partnership with him.
13. Having failed in the first attempt, he made no further attempts.
14. Walking up to the front door, I rang the bell.
15. Winter coming on, the grasshopper had no food.
16. Enchanted with the whole scene, I lingered on my voyage.
17. The enemy disputed their ground inch by inch, fighting with the fury of despair.
18. Mounting his horse, the bandit rode off.
19. The policeman, running with all his speed, was scarcely able to overtake the thief.
20. Not knowing my way, I asked a policeman.

Chapter 30 THE GERUND

274. Read this sentence.

Reading is his favourite pastime.

The word *reading* is formed from the Verb *read*, by adding *ing*.

We also see that it is here used as the Subject of a verb, and hence does the work of a Noun. It is, therefore, a Verb-Noun, and is called a **Gerund**.

Further examples of Gerund:

1. *Playing* cards is not allowed here.
2. I like *reading* poetry.
3. He is fond of *hoarding* money.

In sentence 1, the Gerund, like a noun, is the subject of a verb, but, like a verb, it also takes an object, thus clearly showing that it has also the force of a verb.

In sentence 2, the Gerund, like a noun, is the object of a verb but, like a verb, it also takes an object, thus clearly showing that it has also the force of a verb.

In sentence 3, the Gerund, like a noun, is governed by a preposition, but, like a verb, it also takes an object.

It will be noticed that the Infinitive and the Gerund are alike in being used as Nouns, while still retaining the power that a Verb has of governing another noun or pronoun in the objective case.

Def. — A Gerund is that form of the verb which ends in -ing, and has the force of a Noun and a Verb.

275. As both the Gerund and the Infinitive have the force of a Noun and a Verb, they have the same uses. Thus in many sentences either of them may be used without any special difference in meaning; as,

Teach me *to swim*.
Teach me *swimming*.
To give is better than *to receive*.
Giving is better than *receiving*.

To see is *to believe*.
Seeing is *believing*.

276. The following sentences contain examples of Compound Gerund forms:

I heard of his *having gained* a prize.
We were fatigued on account of *having walked* so far.
They were charged with *having sheltered* anarchists.
He is desirous of *being praised*.

It will be noticed that Compound Gerund forms are formed by placing a Past Participle after the Gerunds of *have* and *be*.

277. The Gerund of a Transitive verb has the following forms:

Active	Passive
Present: loving	*Present:* being loved
Perfect: having loved	*Perfect:* having been loved

278. As both the Gerund and the Present Participle end in -ing, they must be carefully distinguished.

The Gerund has the force of a Noun and a verb; it is a Verbal *Noun*.

The Present Participle has the force of an Adjective and a Verb; it is a Verbal *Adjective*.

Examples of Gerund:

He is fond of *playing* cricket.
The old man was tired of *walking*.
We were prevented from *seeing* the prisoner.
Seeing is believing.

Examples of Participle:

Playing cricket, he gained health.
Walking along the road, he noticed a dead cobra.
Seeing, he believed.

279. Read this sentence.

The indiscriminate *reading of* novels is injurious.

Here *reading* is used like an ordinary Noun.

Notice that *the* is used before and *of* after it.

Further examples of Gerunds used like ordinary Nouns.

The *making* of the plan is in hand.
The time of the *singing* of the birds has come.
Adam consented to the *eating* of the fruit.
The middle station of life seems to be the most advantageously situated for the *gaining* of wisdom.

280. In such Compound nouns as:

walking stick	frying pan	hunting whip
fencing-stick	writing-table	

walking, frying, hunting, fencing, writing are Gerunds.

They mean 'a stick for walking,' 'a pan for frying,' 'a whip for hunting,' 'a stick for fencing,' and 'a table for writing.'

281. Compare the following two sentences:

1. I hope you will excuse *my* leaving early.
2. I hope you will excuse *me* leaving early.

In the first sentence the word preceding the gerund is in the possessive case, while in the second sentence it is in the objective case. Both the sentences are correct. We can use either the possessive case or objective case of nouns and pronouns before gerunds. The possessive is more formal, and it is less usual in everyday speech. Here are further examples:

We rejoiced at *his/him* being promoted.
I insist on *your/you* being present.
Do you mind *my/me* sitting here?
All depends on *Karim's/Karim* passing the exam.
I disliked the *manager's/manager* asking me personal questions.
The accident was due to the *engine-driver's/engine-driver* disregarding the signals.

Use of the Gerund

282. A Gerund being a verb-noun may be used as —

(1) Subject of a verb: as,

Seeing is believing.
Hunting deer is not allowed in this country.

(2) Object of a transitive verb; as,

Stop *playing*.
Children love *making* mud castles.
I like *reading* poetry.
He contemplated *marrying* his cousin.

(3) Object of a preposition ; as,

I am tired of *waiting*.
He is fond of *swimming*.
He was punished for *telling* a lie.
We were prevented from *seeing* the prisoner.
I have an aversion to *fishing*.

(4) Complement of a verb ; as,

Seeing is *believing*.
What I most detest is *smoking*.

(5) Absolutely ; as,

Playing cards being his aversion, we did not play bridge.

EXERCISE IN GRAMMAR 55

Point out the Participles and Gerunds in the following sentences. In the case of the Participle, name the noun or pronoun which it qualifies. In the case of the Gerund, state whether it is subject, object, complement, or used after a preposition.

1. He was found fighting desperately for his life.
2. He has ruined his sight by reading small print.
3. Hearing the noise, he ran to the window.
4. We saw a clown standing on his head.
5. Asking questions is easier than answering them.
6. Waving their hats and handkerchiefs, the people cheered the king.
7. Walking on the grass is forbidden.
8. Jumping over the fence, the thief escaped.
9. The miser spends his time in hoarding money.
10. Much depends on Rama's returning before noon.
11. Amassing wealth often ruins health.
12. I was surprised at Hari's being absent.
13. We spent the afternoon in playing cards.
14. The miser hated spending money.
15. She was angry at Saroja trying to lie to her.
16. Praising all alike is praising none.
17. Are you afraid of his hearing you ?
18. I determined to increase my salary by managing a little farm.
19. Success is not merely winning applause.
20. The year was spent in visiting our rich neighbours.
21. Singing to herself was her chief delight.
22. He preferred playing football to studying his lessons.
23. I thank thee, Jew, for teaching me that word.
24. I cannot go on doing nothing.

Chapter 31 IRREGULAR VERBS

283. Verbs can be regular or irregular.

284. Regular verbs form their past tense and past participle by adding *ed*.

Base Form	*Past Tense*	*Past Participle*
walk	walked	walked
laugh	laughed	laughed
paint	painted	painted

285. Irregular verbs form their past tense and past participle in a different way from adding *ed*.

Base Form	*Past Tense*	*Past Participle*
sit	sat	sat
ring	rang	rung
come	came	come
cut	cut	cut

We distinguish three types of irregular verbs:

(1) Verbs in which all three forms are the same (e.g. cut - cut - cut)

(2) Verbs in which two of the three forms are the same (e.g. sit - sat - sat)

(3) Verbs in which all three forms are different (e.g. ring - rang - rung)

286. Below is a list of irregular verbs divided into the three types mentioned above. Some of them can also be regular. In such cases the regular forms are also given.

Type (1) – All three forms are the same.

Base Form	*Past Tense*	*Past Participle*
bet	bet	bet
burst	burst	burst
cost	cost	cost
cut	cut	cut
hit	hit	hit
hurt	hurt	hurt
let	let	let
put	put	put
read	read	read
set	set	set
shut	shut	shut
split	split	split
spread	spread	spread

Type (2) – Two of the forms are the same.

Base Form	*Past Tense*	*Past Participle*
beat	beat	beaten
become	became	become
bend	bent	bent
bleed	bled	bled
breed	bred	bred
bring	brought	brought
build	built	built
burn	burnt/burned	burnt/burned
buy	bought	bought
catch	caught	caught
come	came	come
creep	crept	crept
deal	dealt	dealt
dig	dug	dug
dream	dreamt/dreamed	dreamt/dreamed
feed	fed	fed
feel	felt	felt
fight	fought	fought
find	found	found
get	got	got
hang	hung	hung
have	had	had
hear	heard	heard
hold	held	held
keep	kept	kept
lay	laid	laid
lead	led	led
lean	lent/leaned	lent/leaned
learn	learnt/learned	learnt/learned
leap	leapt/leaped	leapt/leaped
leave	left	left
lend	lent	lent
light	lit	lit
lose	lost	lost
make	made	made
mean	meant	meant
meet	met	met
pay	paid	paid

run	ran	run
say	said	said
sell	sold	sold
send	sent	sent
shine	shone	shone
shoot	shot	shot
sit	sat	sat
sleep	slept	slept
smell	smelt/smelled	smelt/smelled
spell	spelt	spelt
spend	spent	spent
spill	spilt/spilled	spilt/spilled
speed	sped	sped
spell	spelt/spelled	spelt/spelled
spit	spat	spat
spoil	spoilt/spoiled	spoilt/spoiled
stand	stood	stood
stick	stuck	stuck
sting	stung	stung
strike	struck	struck
sweep	swept	swept
swing	swung	swung
teach	taught	taught
tell	told	told
think	thought	thought
understand	understood	understood
win	won	won
wind	wound	wound

Type (3) – All three forms are different.

Base Form	*Past Tense*	*Past Participle*
be	was/were	been
begin	began	begun
bite	bit	bitten
blow	blew	blown
break	broke	broken
choose	chose	chosen
do	did	done
draw	drew	drawn
drink	drank	drunk
drive	drove	driven
eat	ate	eaten
fall	fell	fallen
fly	flew	flown
forbid	forbade	forbidden
forget	forgot	forgotten
forgive	forgave	forgiven
freeze	froze	frozen
give	gave	given
go	went	gone
grow	grew	grown
hide	hid	hidden
know	knew	known
lie	lay	lain

mistake	mistook	mistaken
ride	rode	ridden
ring	rang	rung
rise	rose	risen
see	saw	seen
sew	sewed	sewn/sewed
shake	shook	shaken
show	showed	shown
shrink	shrank	shrunk
sing	sang	sung
sink	sank	sunk
speak	spoke	spoken
spring	sprang	sprung
steal	stole	stolen
stink	stank	stunk
swear	swore	sworn
swim	swam	swum
take	took	taken
tear	tore	torn
throw	threw	thrown
wake	woke	woken
wear	wore	worn
write	wrote	written

287. The following verbs have an alternative past participle form (ending in *en*), which can only be used adjectivally.

Verb Participle	*Usual Past Past Participle*	*Adjectival*
drink	drunk	drunken
melt	melted	molten
prove	proved	proven
shave	shaved	shaven
shear	sheared	shorn
shrink	shrunk	shrunken
sink	sunk	sunken
strike	struck	stricken

Compare the following:

(a)	(b)
He has *drunk* liquor.	a *drunken* soldier
The iron has *melted.*	*molten* iron
He has *proved* it.	a *proven* fact
He has *shaved* off his beard.	a clean-*shaven* face
They have *sheared* the sheep.	a *shorn* sheep
The cloth has *shrunk.*	a *shrunken* head
The ship has *sunk.*	a *sunken* ship
The clock has *struck* five.	a grief-*stricken* widow

EXERCISE IN COMPOSITION 56

In the following sentences change the verbs to the Past Tense.

1. Rama writes to his mother every week.
2. The wind blows furiously.
3. The boy stands on the burning deck.
4. The door flies open.
5. She sings sweetly.
6. The old woman sits in the sun.
7. Abdul swims very well indeed.
8. His voice shakes with emotion.
9. He drives a roaring trade.

10. He bears a grudge against his old uncle.
11. He spends his time in idleness.
12. He feels sorry for his faults.
13. A portrait of Mahatma Gandhi hangs on the wall.
14. The kite flies gaily into the air.
15. He wears away his youth in trifles.
16. What strikes me is the generosity of the offer.
17. He sows the seeds of dissension.
18. They all tell the same story.
19. He lies in order to escape punishment.
20. He comes of a good line.
21. The boy runs down the road at top speed.
22. I do it of my own free will.
23. His parents withhold their consent to the marriage.
24. I forget his name.
25. He gets along fairly well.
26. They choose Mr. Malik to be their chairman.
27. He throws cold water on my plan.
28. The child clings to her mother.
29. Judas, overwhelmed with remorse, goes and hangs himself.
30. I know him for an American.
31. He swears a solemn oath that he is innocent.
32. In a fit of rage she tears up the letter.
33. Her head sinks on her shoulder.
34. She hides her face for shame.
35. My master bids me work hard.
36. The books lie in a heap on the floor.
37. She lays her working on the table.

EXERCISE IN COMPOSITION 57

Fill in the Past Tense or Past Participle of the verb given.

1. *see* It is years since I _____him. He has _____his best days.
2. *fall* Of late the custom has _____into disuse. The lot _____upon him.
3. *drink* The toast was _____with great enthusiasm.
4. *speak* He _____freely when he had drunk alcohol. Marathi is _____in Maharashtra.
5. *wear* My patience _____out at last. The inscription has _____away in several places.
6. *tear* In a fit of rage she _____up the letter. The country is _____by factions.
7. *sting* He has been _____by a scorpion. The remark _____him.
8. *run* You look as if you had _____all the way home. He _____for his life.
9. *forget* Once Sydney Smith, being asked his name by the servant, found to his dismay that he had _____his own name.
10. *choose* A better day for a drive could not have been _____.
11. *come* Computer technology has ________ a long way since the 1970s.
12. *bite* The old beggar was _____by a mad dog. A mad dog _____him.
13. *swim* The boy has _______ across the Indus.
14. *write* I think he should have _____and told us. Honesty is _____on his face.
15. *lay* He _____the book on the table. He had not _____a finger on him. They _____ their heads together.
16. *lie* We _____beneath a spreading oak. He has long _____under suspicion.
17. *take* A beautiful shot from cover-point _____off the balls.
He has _____a fancy to the boy.
18. *go* Recently the price of sugar has _____up. The argument _____home. The verdict _____against him.
19. *begin* He had _____his speech before we arrived. He _____to talk nonsense.
20. *bid* Do as you are _____. He _____us goodbye.
He _____two thousand rupees for the pony.

21. *ring* Has the warning-bell _____? I _____him up last night.
22. *steal* Someone has _____my purse. She _____his heart.
23. *sow* You must reap what you have _____.
24. *drive* Poor fellow ! he was – very hard. They say he _____a hard bargain.
25. *sing* It seemed to me that she had never _____so well. Our bugles _____truce.
26. *shake* He was much _____by the news. His voice _____as he spoke.
27. *eat* He is _____up with pride. In the end he _____his words.
28. *do* Let us have _____with it. I _____my duty.

29. *spring.* Homer describes a race of men who _____from the gods. The ship _____a leak.
30. *show* Has Rustum _____you his camera ? He _____a clean pair of heels.
31. *freeze* The explorers were _____to death. The blood _____in their veins.
32. *strike* I was _____by a stone. It never _____me before that he was old.
33. *mistake* I found upon inquiry that I had _____the house. He _____me for my brother.
34. *shoe* Go, ask the ferrier whether he has _____the horses yet.
35. *strew* His path was _____with flowers.

36. *sink* His voice gradually ____ to a whisper.
And thousands had ____ to the ground overpower'd.
37. *tread* Walking through the jungle, he ____ on a snake.
38. *rise* He has ____ from the ranks. As his friends expected he ____ to the occasion.
39. *beat* On the arrival of a policeman, he ____ a hasty retreat. He ____ the Afghans in a bloody battle
It was not the only battle in which they were ____.
40. *blow* The tempest ____ the ship ashore.
41. *catch* Walking on the beach, we ____ sight of a strange bird. He has ____ a Tartar.
42. *have* After the storm we ____ a spell of fine weather.
43. *meet* I ____ a little cottage girl. The poor fellow has ____ with many reverses.
44. *sleep* We thought her dying when she ____.
45. *get* He has ____ hold of the wrong end of the stick.
46. *lead* The faithful dog ____ his blind master.
47. *awake* And his disciples came to him, and ____ him. I was soon ____ from this disagreeable reverie.
48. *bear* I was ____ away by an impulse.
49. *stand* It has ____ the test of time.
50. *sit* He has ____ for the examination.
51. *know* He says he has never ____ sickness. I ____ his antecedents.
52. *bind* The prisoner was ____ hand and foot.
53. *break* He has ____ his collar-bone.
54. *breed* What is ____ in the bone will not wear out of the flesh.
55. *strive* I ____ with none, for none was worth my strife.
56. *give* He never ____ me a chance to speak.
He is ____ to opium-smoking.
57. *dream* I ____ I was in love again.
58. *weep* I have ____ a million tears.

EXERCISE IN COMPOSITION 58

Fill in the Past Tense or Past Participle of the verb given.

1. *spin* The story is tediously ____ out.
2. *mean* I ____ it for a joke. He was ____ for a lawyer.
3. *arise* Suddenly the wind ____.
There never has ____ a great man who has not been misunderstood.
4. *draw* Who ____ the first prize ? He has ____ a wrong inference.
The train ____ up to the station.
5. *understand* I certainly ____ you to make that promise. I am afraid I did not make myself ____.
6. *shoot* He was accidentally ____ in the arm.
7. *shrink* He is not known ever to have ____ from an encounter. There was no cruelty from which the robber chief ____.
8. *smell* I noticed that he ____ of brandy.
9. *stick* The cart ____ in the mud.
10. *swear* The soldiers ____ allegiance to the Constitution of India. He was yesterday ____ in as a member of the Legislative Assembly.
11. *sweep* The waves ____ the pier. The pier was ____ away. Plague ____ off millions.
12. *cost* Often a lie has ____ a life. His folly ____ him years of poverty.
13. *buy* A rupee ____ twice as much fifteen years ago.
14. *crow* His enemies ____ over his fall.
15. *deal* He ____ unfairly with his partner.
The robber ____ him a blow on the head.
16. *lose* His rashness ____ him his life. ____ time is never found again. The man who yields to the fascination of the gaming-table is ____.
17. *find* Sir, I have ____ you an argument ; but I am not obliged to find you an understanding.
The picture ____ its way to the auction-room.

18. *forgive* Christ ____ his crucifiers.
19. *sleep* It is said of Akbar that he rarely ____ more than three hours at a time.
20. *seek* His company is greatly ____ after.
    It might be truly said of him that he never ____ honour.
21. *hide* Adam and his wife ____ themselves from the presence of the Lord God.
22. *fall* He ____ never to rise again. A certain man went down from Jerusalem to Jericho, and ____ among thieves. He has ____ asleep.
23. *set* He has ____ his heart on success. The teacher ____ them an example.
24. *die* He ____ at a ripe old age.
25. *see* I ____ her singing at her work. He has ____ the ups and downs of life.
26. *spoil* The news ____ my dinner.
27. *leave* He has ____ a large family. The police ____ no stone unturned to trace the culprits.
28. *grow* Three years she ____ in sun and shower. Some of these wars have ____ out of commercial considerations.
29. *think* I have ____ of a plan.
    I ____ of Chatterton, the marvellous boy.
30. *become* He ____ the slave of low desires.
31. *hear* Not a drum was ____, not a funeral note. He hopes his prayer will be ____.
32. *fight* He ____ for the crown. He has a good fight.
33. *forsake* His courage ____ him. He has ____ his old friends.
34. *teach* The village master ____ his little school.
    They have ____ their tongue to speak lies.
35. *wring* She ____ her hands in agony. Any appeal for help ____ her heart.
36. *wind* He ____ up by appealing to the audience to contribute to the fund.
37. *thrust* He was ____ through with a javelin.
38. *say* He has ____ the last word on the matter.
39. *fly* The bird has ____ away. The bird ____ over the tree.
40. *flee* The murderer has ____ to Australia.
    The terrified people ____ to the mountains.
41. *overflow* During the night the river had ____ its banks.

Chapter 32 AUXILIARIES AND MODALS

288. The verbs *be* (*am, is, was,* etc), *have* and *do*, when used with ordinary verbs to make tenses, passive forms, questions and negatives, are called **auxiliary verbs** or **auxiliaries**. (*Auxiliary* = helping)

289. The verbs *can, could, may, might, will, would, shall, should, must* and *ought* are called **modal verbs** or **modals**. They are used before ordinary verbs and express meanings such as permission, possibility, certainty and necessity. *Need* and *dare* can sometimes be used like modal verbs.

Modals are often included in the group of auxiliaries. In some grammars they are called "modal auxiliaries".

290. The modals *can, could, may, might, shall, should, will, would, must* and *ought* are termed Defective Verbs, because some parts are wanting in them. They have no *-s* in the third person singular; they have no *-ing* and *-ed* forms.

Be

291. The auxiliary *be* is used

(1) In the formation of the continuous tenses ; as,
He *is* working. I *was* writing.

(2) In the formation of the passive ; as,

The gate *was* opened.

Be followed by the infinitive is used

(1) To indicate a plan, arrangement, or agreement ; as,

I *am* to see him tomorrow.

We *are* to be married next month.

(2) To denote command ; as,

You *are* to write your name at the top of each sheet of paper.

Mother says you *are* to go to market at once.

292. Be is used in the past tense with the perfect infinitive to indicate an arrangement that was made but not carried out ; as,

They *were* to have been married last month but had to postpone the marriage until June.

Have

293. The auxiliary *have* is used in the formation of the perfect tenses; as,

He *has* worked. He *has* been working.

294. *Have to* is used with the infinitive to indicate obligation ; as,

I *have* to be there by five o'clock.

He *has* to move the furniture himself.

295. The past form *had to* is used to express obligation in the past.

I had to be there by five o'clock.

He had to move the furniture himself.

296. In negatives and questions, *have to* and *had to* are used with *do, does, did*; as,

They have to go. → They don't have to go. Do they have to go?

He has to go. → He doesn't have to go. Does he have to go?

He had to go. → He didn't have to go. Did he have to go?

Do

297. The auxiliary *do* is used

(1) To form the negative and interrogative of the simple present and simple past tenses of ordinary verbs ; as,

He *doesn't* work.	He *didn't* work.
Does he work ?	*Did* he work ?

(2) To avoid repetition of a previous ordinary verb ; as,

Do you know him ?	Yes, I *do*.
She sings well.	Yes, she *does*.

You met him, *didn't* you ?

He eats fish and so *do* you.

298. Do is also used to emphasize the affirmative nature of a statement ; as,

You *do* look pale.

I told him not to go, but he *did* go.

299. In the imperative, *do* makes a request or invitation more persuasive ; as,

Do be quiet,

Oh, *do* come ! It's going to be such fun.

In such cases *do* is strongly stressed.

Can, Could, May, Might

300. *Can* usually expresses ability or capacity ; as,

I *can* swim across the river.

He *can* work this sum.

Can you lift this box ?

301. *Can* and *may* are used to express permission. *May* is rather formal.
You can/may go now.
Can/May I borrow your umbrella?

302. *May* is used to express possibility in affirmative sentences. *Can* is used in the corresponding interrogative and negative sentences.
It *may* rain tomorrow.
He *may* be at home.
Can this be true ?
It *cannot* be true.

Compare 'It *cannot* be true' with 'It *may not* be true'. *Cannot* denotes impossibility, while *may not* denotes improbability.

303. In very formal English, *may* is used to express a wish; as,
May you live happily and long !
May success attend you !

304. *Could* and *might* are used as the past equivalents of *can* and *may* ; as,
I *could* swim across the river when I was young. (Ability)
He said I *might/could* go. (Permission)
I thought he *might* be at home. (Possibility)
She wondered whether it *could* be true. (Possibility)

305. *Could*, as in the first example above, expresses only ability to do an act, but not the performance of an act. We should use *was/were able to* for ability +action in the past.
When the boat was upset, we *were able to* (or *managed to*) swim to the bank. (not : we *could* swim to the bank)

In negative statements, however, either *could* or *was/were able to* may be used.
I *couldn't* (or: *wasn't able to*) solve the puzzle. It was too difficult.

306. In present time contexts *could* and *might* are used as less positive versions of *can* and *may* ; as,
I *could* attend the party. (Less positive and more hesitant than 'I *can* attend the party'.)
Might/Could I borrow your bicycle ? (A diffident way of saying '*May/Can* I.......')
It *might* rain tomorrow. (Less positive than 'It *may* rain......')
Could you pass me the salt ? (Polite request)

307. *Might* is also used to express a degree of dissatisfaction or reproach ; as,
You *might* pay a little more attention to your appearance.

308. Note the use of *can, could, may* and *might* with the perfect infinitive.
He is not there. Where *can* he *have gone*? (= Where is it possible that he has gone? - *May* expresses annoyance.)
You *could have accepted* the offer. (= Why didn't you accept the offer?)
Fatima *may/might have gone* with Saroja. (= Possibly Fatima has gone/went with Saroja.)
Why did you drive so carelessly? You *might have run* into the lamp post. (= It is fortunate that you didn't run into the lamp post.)

Shall, Should, Will, Would

309. *Shall* is used in the first person and *will* in all persons to express pure future.
Today *I/we shall* is less common than *I/we will*.
I *shall/will* be twenty-five next birthday.
We *will* need the money on 15th.
When *shall* we see you again ?
Tomorrow *will* be Sunday.
You *will* see that I am right.

In present day English, however, there is a growing tendency to use *will* in all persons.

310. *Shall* is sometimes used in the second and third persons to express a command, a promise, or threat ; as,
He *shall* not enter my house again. (Command)
You *shall* have a holiday tomorrow. (Promise)
You *shall* be punished for this. (Threat)

Note—that these uses of shall are old-fashioned and formal and generally avoided in modern English.

311. Questions with *shall I/we* are used to ask the will of the person addressed ; as,

Shall I open the door ? (*i.e.,* Do you want me to open it ?)

Which pen *shall* I buy ? (*i.e.,* What is your advice ?)

Where *shall* we go ? (What is your suggestion ?)

312. *Will* is used to express

(1) Volition ; as,

I *will* (=am willing to) carry your books.
I *will* (=promise to) try to do better next time.
I *will* (=am determined to) succeed or die in the attempt.

In the last example above, *will* is strong-stressed.

(2) Characteristic habit ; as,

He *will* talk about nothing but films.
She *will* sit for hours listening to the wireless.

(3) Assumption or probability ; as,

This *will* be the book you want, I suppose.

That *will* be the postman, I think.

313. *Will you* indicates an invitation or a request ; as,

Will you have tea ?

Will you lend me your scooter ?

314. *Should* and *would* are used as the past equivalents of *shall* and *will* ; as,

I expected that I *should* (more often : *would*) get a first class.
He said he *would* be twenty-five next birthday.
She said she *would* carry my books.
She *would* sit for hours listening to the wireless. (Past habit)

315. *Should* is used in all persons to express duty or obligation ; as,

We *should* obey the laws.
You *should* keep your promise.
Children *should* obey their parents.

316. In clauses of condition, *should* is used to express a supposition that may not be true.

If it *should* rain, they will not come.
If he *should* see me here, he will be annoyed.

317. *Should* and *would* are also used as in the examples below.

(*i*) I *should* (or : *would*) like you to help her. ('*Should/would* like' is a polite form of 'want'.)

(*ii*) *Would* you lend me your scooter, please ? ('Would you ?' is more polite than 'Will you')

(*iii*) You *should* have been more careful. (*Should*+perfect infinitive indicates a past obligation that was not fulfilled.)

(*iv*) He *should* be in the library now. (Expresses probability)

(*v*) I wish you *would* not chatter so much. (*Would* after *wish* expresses a strong desire.)

Must, Ought to

318. *Must* is used to express necessity or obligation.

You *must* improve your spelling.
We *must* get up early.

318A. *Must* refers to the present or the near future. To talk about the past we use *had to* (the past form of *have to*); *must* has no past form.

Yesterday we *had to* get up early.

319. *Must* is often used when the obligation comes from the speaker. When the obligation comes from somewhere else, *have to* is often used. Compare:

I *must* be on a diet. (It is my own idea.)

I *have to* be on a diet. (The doctor has told me to be on a diet.)

319A. *Must* can also express logical certainty.

Living in such crowded conditions *must* be difficult. (=I am sure it is difficult.)

She *must have left* already. (I am sure she *has left* already.)

320. *Ought (to)* expresses moral obligation or desirability ; as,

We ought to love our neighbours.

We ought to help him.

You *ought* to know better.

321. *Ought (to)* can also be used to express probability.

Prices *ought to* come down soon.

This book *ought* to be very useful.

Used (to), Need, Dare

322. The auxiliary *used (to)* expresses a discontinued habit.

There *used* to be a house there.
I *used* to live there when I was a boy.

Used to, as an auxiliary verbs is old-fashioned and very formal. Today we normally used *did* in negatives and question (e.g. *Did* you *used* to swim?)

323. The auxiliary *need*, denoting necessity or obligation, can be conjugated with or without *do*.When conjugated without *do*, it has no *-s* and *-ed* forms and is used with an infinitive without *to* only in negative and interrogative sentences and in sentences that contain semi-negative words like 'scarcely' and 'hardly'.

He *need* not go. (=It is not necessary for him to go.)

Need I write to him ?

I *need* hardly take his help.

324. When conjugated with *do*, *need* has the usual forms *needs, needed* and is used with a to-infinitive. It is commonly used in negatives and questions ; it sometimes occurs in the affirmative also.

Do you *need* to go now ?

I *don't need* to meet him.

One *needs* to be careful.

325. Compare :

(*i*) I didn't need to buy it. (=It was not necessary for me to buy it and I didn't buy it.)

(*ii*) I needn't have bought it. (=It was not necessary for me to buy it, but I bought it.)

326. The auxiliary *dare* (=be brave enough to), as distinct from the ordinary verb *dare* (=challenge), does not take *-s* in the third person singular present tense. It is generally used in negative and interrogative sentences. When conjugated without *do*, it is followed by an infinitive without *to* ; when conjugated with *do*, it takes an infinitive with or without *to* after it.

He *dare* not take such a step.

How *dare* you contradict me ?

He *dared* not do it.

He *doesn't dare* speak to me.

EXERCISE IN COMPOSITION 59

Choose the correct alternative.

1. I don't think I (shall, should, can) be able to go.
2. He (shall, will, dare) not pay unless he is compelled.
3. You (should, would, ought) be punctual.
4. I wish you (should, would, must) tell me earlier.
5. (Shall, Will, Would) I assist you ?
6. (Shall, should, would) you please help me with this ?
7. You (ought, should, must) to pay your debts.
8. He said I (can, might, should) use his telephone at any time.
9. If you (shall, should, would) see him, give him my regards.
10. He (need, dare, would) not ask for a rise, for fear of losing his job.
11. I (needn't to see, needn't have seen, didn't need to see) him, so I sent a letter.
12. (Shall, Might, Could) you show me the way to the station.
13. To save my life, I ran fast, and (would, could, was able to) reach safely.
14. I (would, used, ought) to be an atheist but now I believe in God.
15. You (needn't, mustn't, won't) light a match ; the room is full of gas.
16. The Prime Minister (would, need, is to) make a statement tomorrow.
17. You (couldn't wait, didn't need to wait, need't have waited) for me ; I could have found the way all right.
18. I was afraid that if I asked him again he (can, may, might) refuse.
19. She (shall, will, dare) sit outside her garden gate for hours at a time, looking at the passing traffic.
20. (Should, Would, Shall) you like another cup of coffee ?
21. I wish he (should, will, would) not play his wireles so loudly.
22. I (am to leave, would leave, was to have left) on Thursday. But on Thursday I had a terrible cold, so I decided to wait till Saturday.
23. He (used, is used, was used) to play cricket before his marriage.
24. (Shall, Will, Would) I carry the box into the house for you ?
25. He (will, can, might) come, but I should be surprised.

EXERCISE IN COMPOSITION 59A

Rewrite each of these sentences, using a modal verb. (In 2 and 9, use another modal.)

1. Possibly she isn't Anil's sister.
2. Perhaps we will go to Shimla next month.
3. My sister was able to read the alphabet when she was 18 months old.
4. It is necessary that you do not wash the car. (The paint is still wet.)
5. It is not necessary for you to wash the car. (It is clean.)
6. I am certain that they have left already.
7. Do you allow me to use your phone?
8. I was in the habit of going to the beach every day when I was in Chennai.
9. He will probably pass his driving test easily.
10. Perhaps he forgot about the meeting.
11. I suggest visiting Qutab Minar.
12. Nobody has answered the phone; perhaps they have gone out.
13. I am sure he is over seventy.
14. It was not necessary for me to meet him but I met him.
15. It was not necessary for me to meet him (and I didn't meet him).

Chapter 33 CONJUGATION OF THE VERB LOVE

327. The **conjugation** of a verb shows the various forms it assumes, either by inflection or by combination with parts of other verbs, to mark Voice, Mood, Tense, Number, and Person ; and to those must be added its Infinitives and Participles. Below is given the complete conjugation of the verb *love,* with a view to helping the pupil to systematize the knowledge already acquired by him.

(I) TENSES

Simple Present

Active

I love
You love
He loves
They love

Passive

I am loved
You are loved
He is loved
They are loved

Present Continuous

Active

I am loving
You are loving
He is loving
We are loving
They are loving

Passive

I am being loved
You are being loved
He is being loved
We are being loved
They are being loved

Present Perfect

Active

I have loved
You have loved
He has loved
We have loved
They have loved

Passive

I have been loved
You have been loved
He has been loved
We have been loved
They have been loved

Present Perfect Continuous

Active

I have been loving
You have been loving
We have been loving
They have been loving

Passive

......
......
......
......

Simple Past

Active

I loved
You loved
He loved
We loved
They loved

Passive

I was loved
You were loved
He was loved
We were loved
They were loved

Past Continuous

Active

I was loving
You were loving
He was loving
They were loving

Passive

I was being loved
You were being loved
He was being loved
They were being loved

Past Perfect

Active

I had loved
You had loved
He had loved
We had loved
They had loved

Passive

I had been loved
You had been loved
He had been loved
We had been loved
They had been loved

Past Perfect Continuous

Active	*Passive*
I had been loving	......
You had been loving	......
He had been loving	......
We had been loving	......
They had been loving	......

Simple Future

Active	*Passive*
I shall/will love	I shall/will be loved
You will love	You will be loved
He will love	He will be loved
We shall love	We shall be loved
They will love	They will be loved

Future Continuous

Active	*Passive*
I shall/will be loving	......
You will be loving	......
He will be loving	......
We shall be loving	......
They will be loving	......

Future Perfect

Active	*Passive*
I shall/will have loved	I shall/will have been loved
You will have loved	You will have been loved
He will have loved	He will have been loved
We shall have loved	We shall have been loved
They will have loved	They will have been loved

Future Perfect Continuous

Active	*Passive*
I shall/will have been loving	......
You will have been loving	......
He will have been loving	......
We shall have been loving	......
They will have been loving	......

(II) The Imperative

Love	Be loved

(III) Non-Finites

Present Infinitive	to love	to be loved
Continuous Infinitive	to be loving	......
Perfect Participle	to have loved	to have been loved
Present Participle	loving	being loved
Perfect Participle	having loved	having been loved

Chapter 34 THE ADVERB

328. Read the following sentences.

1. Rama runs *quickly*.
2. This is a *very* sweet mango.
3. Govind reads *quite* clearly.

In sentence 1, *quickly* shows **how** (or **in what manner**) Rama *runs* ; that is, *quickly* modifies the **Verb** *runs.*

In sentence 2, *very* shows **how much** (or **in what degree**) the mango is *sweet* ; that is, *very* modifies the **Adjective** sweet.

In sentence 3, *quite* shows **how far** (or **to what extent**) Govind reads *clearly* ; that is, *quite* modifies the **Adverb** *clearly.*

A word that modifies the meaning of a verb, an adjective, or another Adverb is called an **Adverb.** The words *quickly, very,* and *quite* are, therefore, Adverbs.

Def—An Adverb is a word which modifies the meaning of a Verb, an Adjective or another Adverb.

329. In the following sentences Adverbs modify phrases.

She was sitting *close* beside him.
At what hour is the sun *right* above us ?
Have you read *all* through this book ?
She was dressed *all* in pink.
He paid his debts *down* to the last penny.

330. Adverbs standing at the beginning of sentences sometimes modify *the whole sentence,* rather than any particular word ; as,

Probably he is mistaken. [=It is probable that he is mistaken.]
Possibly it is as you say.
Certainly you are wrong.
Evidently the figures are incorrect.
Unfortunately no one was present there.
Luckily he escaped unhurt.

Kinds of Adverbs

331. Adverbs may be divided into the following classes, according to their *meaning.*

(1) **Adverbs of Time** (which show *when)*

I have heard this *before.*
We shall *now* begin to work.
I had a letter from him *lately.*
He comes here *daily.*
I have spoken to him *already.*
He once met me in Cairo ;
Mr. Gupta *formerly* lived here.
That day he arrrived *late.*
He called here a few minutes *ago.*
The end *soon* came.
I hurt my knee *yesterday.*
Wasted time *never* returns.
I have not seen him *since.*

(2) **Adverbs of Frequency** (which show *how often)*

I have told you *twice.*
He *often* makes mistakes.
The postman called *again.*
He *frequently* comes unprepared.
I have not seen him *once.*
He *seldom* comes here.
He *always* tries to do his best.

(3) **Adverbs of Place** (which show *where*)

Stand *here.*
The little lamb followed Mary *everywhere.*
He looked *up.*
Is Mr. Das *within* ?
The horse galloped *away.*
Go *there.*
My brother is *out.*
Come *in.*
Walk *backward.*

(4) **Adverbs of Manner** (which show *how* or in what *manner)*

Govind reads *clearly.*
This story is *well* written.
The child slept *soundly.*
Slowly and *sadly* we laid him down.
You should not do *so.*
The Sikhs fought *bravely.*
The boy works *hard.*
I was *agreeably* disappointed.
Is that *so* ?
Thus only, will you succeed.

Note—This class includes nearly all those Adverbs which are derived from adjectives and end in *-ly.*

(5) **Adverbs of Degree** or **Quantity** (which show *how much,* or *in what degree* or *to what extent)*

He was *too* careless.
These mangoes are *almost* ripe.
I am *fully* prepared.
The sea is *very* stormy.
He is good *enough* for my pupose.
I am *so* glad.
You are *altogether* mistaken.
Things are *no better* at present.
She sings *pretty* well.

Is that *any* better ?
You are *quite* wrong.
I am *rather* busy.
You are *partly* right.

He is *as* tall as Rama.

(6) **Adverbs of Affirmation and Negation**

Surely you are mistaken.
He *certainly* went.
I do *not* know him.

(7) **Adverbs of Reason**

He is *hence* unable to refute the charge.
He *therefore* left school.

332. Some of the above Adverbs may belong to more than one class.

She sings *delightfully.*	(Adverb of Manner)
The weather is *delightfully* cool.	(Adverb of Degree)
Don't go *far.*	(Adverb of Place)
He is *far* better now.	(Adverb of Degree)

Note—The above are all examples of Simple Adverbs. (See § 336)

333. *Yes* and *no,* when they are used by themselves, are equivalents of sentences.

Have you typed the letter ? *Yes.*
[Here *yes* stands for the sentence 'I have typed the letter'.]
Are you going to Japan ? *No.*
[Here *no* means 'I am not going to Japan'.]

EXERCISE IN GRAMMAR 60

In the following sentences (1) pick out the Adverbs and tell what each modifies ; (2) tell whether the modified word is a Verb, an Adjective, or an Adverb ; (3) classify each Adverb as an Adverb of time, place, manner, degree, etc.

1. He was ill pleased.
2. Try again.
3. He is too shy.
4. We rose very early.
5. I am so glad to hear it.
6. Cut it lengthwise.
7. Too many cooks spoil the broth.
8. Are you quite sure ?
9. That is well said.
10. Once or twice we have met alone.
11. The railway station is far off.
12. I have heard this before.
13. Father is somewhat better.
14. I am much relieved to hear it.
15. The walk was rather long.
16. The patient is much worse today.
17. She arrived a few minutes ago.
18. Ambition urges me forward.
19. She was dressed all in black.
20. We were very kindly received.
21. Her son is out in Iran.
22. I surely expect him tomorrow.
23. He could not speak, he was so angry.
24. You are far too hasty.
25. The secret is out.
26. He is old enough to know better.
27. I would much rather not go.
28. You need not roar.
29. Your watch is five minutes too fast.
30. He went off on Monday.
31. His health is no worse than before.
32. Wisdom is too high for a fool.
33. There is a screw loose somewhere.
34. I see things differently now.
35. Rome was not built in a day.
36. The door burst open and in they came.
37. We have scorched the snake, not killed it.
38. Do not crowd your work so closely together.
39. The patient is no better today.
40. He needs to do it.
41. Do not walk so fast.
42. Put not your trust in princes.
43. Order the carriage round.
44. He has been shamefully treated.
45. I wonder you never told me.

334. When Adverbs are used *in asking questions* they are called **Interrogative Adverbs ; as,**

Where is Abdul ?	[Inter. Adverb of Place]
When did you come ?	[Inter. Adverb of Time]
Why are you late ?	[Inter. Adverb of Reason]
How did you contrive it ?	[Inter. Adverb of Manner]
How many boys are in your class ?	[Inter. Adverb of Number]
How high is Rajabai Tower ?	[Inter. Adverb of Degree]

335. Read the sentences.

Show me the house *where* (=in which) he was assaulted.

Here the Adverb *where* modifies the verb *was assaulted.*

Further the Adverb *where,* like a Relative Pronoun, here relates or refers back to its antecedent *house.* It is, therefore, called a **Relative Adverb.**

Further examples of Relative Adverbs :—

This is the reason *why* I left.

Do you know the time *when* the Punjab Mail arrives ?

336. It will be now seen that according to their *use,* Adverbs are divided into three classes—

(1) Simple Adverbs, used to modify the meaning of a verb, an adjective, or an adverb; as,
I can *hardly* believe it. You are *quite* wrong.
How brightly the moon shines!

(2) Interrogative Adverbs, used to ask questions; as,
Why are you late ?

(3) Relative Adverbs, which refer back to a noun as their antecedent ; as,
I remember the house *where* I was born.

337. It will be noticed that –

(1) A Simple Adverb merely modifies some word.

(2) An Interrogative Adverb not only modifies some word, but also introduces a question.

(3) A Relative Adverb not only modifies some word, but also refers back to some antecedent.

Forms of Adverbs

338. Some Adverbs are the *same in form* as the corresponding Adjectives ; that is, some words are used sometimes as Adjectives, sometimes as Adverbs.

Adjectives	*Adverbs*
He spoke in a *loud* voice.	Don't talk so *loud.*
Rama is our *fast* bowler.	Rama can bowl *fast.*
He lives in the *next* house.	When I *next* see him, I shall speak to him.
He went to the *back* entrance.	Go *back.*
Every *little* difficulty ruffles his temper.	He is *little* known outside India.
This is a *hard* sum.	He works *hard* all day.
It's an *ill* wind that blows nobody good.	I can *ill* afford to lose him.
He is the *best* boy in this class.	He behaves *best.*
He is *quick* to take offence.	Run *quick.*
Are you an *early* riser ?	We started *early.*
The teacher has a *high* opinion of that boy.	Always aim *high.*
He is the *only* child of his parents.	You can *only* guess.
We have food *enough* to last a week.	She sings well *enough.*
He is no *better* than a fool.	He knows me *better* than you.
There is *much* truth in what he says.	The patient is *much* better.

Remember that it is only by noticing *how a word is used* that we can tell what Part of Speech it is.

EXERCISE IN COMPOSITION 61

Form sentences to illustrate the use of the following words (1) as Adjectives, (2) as Adverbs.

very, near, ill, only, clean, long, late, early, fast

339. Some Adverbs have two forms, the form ending in *ly* and the form which is the same as the Adjective ; as,

He sings very *loud.* He sings very *loudly.*

Sometimes, however, the two forms of the Adverb have *different meanings* ; as,

Rama works *hard* (= diligently).
I could *hardly* (= scarcely) recognize him.
Stand *near.* (Opposed to *distant)*
Rama and Hari are *nearly* (= closely) related.
He arrived *late.* (Opposed to *early*).
I have not seen him *lately* (= recently).
I am *pretty* (= tolerably, fairly) sure of the fact.
She is *prettily* (= neatly, elegantly) dressed.

340. Some Adverbs are used as Nouns after prepositions ; as,

He lives far from *here* (= this place).
He comes from *there* (= that place).
I have heard that before *now* (= this time).
By *then* (= that time) the police arrived on the scene.
Since *when* (= what time) have you taken to smoking ?
The rain comes from *above.*

Note– The common use of from with thence and whence is wrong. Thence= from there; whence = from where. Thus the addition of from to either of these words is incorrect.

341. Certain Adverbs sometimes seem to be used as Adjectives, when some participle or adjective is understood.

The *then* king = the king *then reigning.*
A *down* train = a *down-going* train.
An *up* train = an *up-going* train.
The *above* statement = the statement *made above.*

342. In the following sentences *the* is not the definite article, but an old demonstrative pronoun used as an Adverb.

The more *the* merrier [= *by how much* the more *by so much* the merrier; that is, the more numerous a party is, the more enjoyable it is].

The fewer *the* better = [*by how much* the fewer *by so much* the better].
The sooner *the* better = [*by how much* the sooner *by* so much the better].
He has tried it and is [so much] *the* better for it.

It will be noticed that *the* is used as an Adverb only with an adjective or another adverb in the comparative degree.

343. Nouns expressing adverbial relations of *time, place, distance, weight, measurement, value, degree,* or the like, are often used as Adverbs. Thus—

The siege lasted a *week.*
He went *home.*
The load weighs three *tonnes.*
The cloth measures three *metres.*
The wound was *skin* deep.
This will last me a *month.*
We walked five *miles.*
It measures five *feet.*
The watch is only fifty *rupees.*

A noun so used is called an **Adverbial Accusative.**

344. Sometimes Verbs are used as Adverbs ; as,

Smack went the whip.

Chapter 35 COMPARISON OF ADVERBS

345. Some Adverbs, like Adjectives, have three degrees of comparison. Such Adverbs are generally compared like Adjectives.

346. If the Adverb is of one syllable, we form the Comparative by ending *er*, and the Superlative by adding *est*, to the Positive ; as,

Fast	faster	fastest	Hard	harder	hardest
Long	longer	longest	Soon	sooner	soonest

Rama ran *fast*. (Positive)

Arjun ran *faster*. (Comparative)

Hari ran *fastest* of all. (Superlative)

347. Adverbs ending in *ly* form the Comparative by adding *more* and the Superlative by adding *most* ; as,

Swiftly	more swiftly	most swiftly
Skilfully	more skilfully	most skilfully

Abdul played *skilfully*. (Positive)

Karim played *more skilfully* than Abdul. (Comparative)

Of all the eleven Ahmed played *most skilfully*. (Superlative)

But note *early, earlier, earliest.*

I came *early* this morning.
Ram came *earlier*.
Abdul came *earliest* of all.

348. It will be noticed that only Adverbs of *Manner, Degree,* and *Time* admit of comparison.

Many Adverbs, from their nature, cannot be compared ; as,

Now, then, where, there, once.

349. Some of the commonest Adverbs form their Comparative and Superlative Degrees *irregularly*.

Positive	*Comparative*	*Superlative*
Ill, badly	worse	worst
Well	better	best
Much	more	most
Little	less	least
(Nigh), near	nearer	next
Far	{ farther further	{ farthest furthest
Late	later	latest

Rama writes *well*.
Arjun writes *better* than Rama.
Hari writes *best* of all.
Do you work *much* ?
I work *more* than you do.
Hari works *most* of the three of us.

EXERCISE IN GRAMMAR 62

Compare the following Adverbs.

suddenly, often, near, loud, hard, wisely, patiently.

Chapter 36 FORMATION OF ADVERBS

350. Adverbs of Manner are mostly formed from Adjectives by adding *ly* (a corruption of *like*) ; as,
Clever, cleverly; wise, wisely ; kind, kindly ; foolish, foolishly ; quick, quickly; beautiful, beautifully.

Akbar was a *wise* king.
He ruled *wisely* for many years.

When the Adjective ends in *y* preceded by a consonant, change *y* into *i* and add *ly* ; as,
Happy, happily ; ready, readily ; heavy, heavily.

When the Adjective ends in *le,* simply change *e* into *y* ; as,
Single, singly ; double, doubly.

351. Some Adverbs are made up of a Noun and a qualifying Adjective ; as,
Sometimes, meantime, meanwhile, yesterday, midway, otherwise.

352. Some Adverbs are compounds of *on* (weakened to *a*) and a Noun ; as,
Afoot (= on foot), abed, asleep, ahead, aboard, away.

Similarly there are other Adverbs which are also compounds of some a Preposition and a Noun ; as,
betimes, besides, today, tomorrow, overboard.

Note—The word be is an old form of the Preposition *by.*

353. Some Adverbs are compounds of a Preposition and an Adjective ; as,
abroad, along, aloud, anew, behind, below, beyond.

354. Some Adverbs are compounds of a Preposition and an Adverb; as,
within, without, before, beneath.

355. There is a class of Adverbs which are derived from the Pronouns *the* (= that), *he, who.*

PRONOUNS	ADVERBS				
	Place	*Motion*	*Motion*	*Time*	*Manner*
to	*from*				
The	there	thither	thence	then	thus
He	here	hither	hence	......	......
Who	where	whither	whence	when	how

356. Many of the above Adverbs are compounded with Prepositions. Thus we get—
Thereby, therefrom, therein, thereof, thereon, thereto, therewith ; hereafter, hereby, herein, hereupon, herewith ;
wherefore, wherein, whereon, whereof :
hitherto ;
thenceforth, thenceforward ;
henceforth, henceforward.

357. Two Adverbs sometimes go together, joined by the Conjunction *and* ; as,
again and again (= more than once, repeatedly),
by and by (= before long, presently, after a time),
far and near (= in all directions),
far and wide (= comprehensively),
far and away (= by a great deal, decidedly, beyond all comparison),
first and foremost (= first of all),
now and then (= from time to time, occasionally),
now and again (= at intervals, sometimes, occasionally),
off and on (= not regularly, intermittently),

once and again (= on more than one occasion, repeatedly),
out and away (= beyond comparison, by far),
out and out (= decidedly, beyond all comparison),
over and above (= in addition to, besides, as well as),
over and over (= many times, frequently, repeatedly),
through and through (= thoroughly, completely),
thus and thus (= in such and such a way).
to and fro (= backwards and forwards, up and down).

Good books should be read *again and again.*
I warned him *again and again.*
By and by the tumult will subside.
His fame has spread *far and near.*

As a statesman he saw *far and wide.*
This is *far and away* the best course.
He is *far and away* the best bowler in our eleven.
He *now and then* writes on fiscal questions.
I write to him *now and then.*
He worked ten years, *off and on,* on his Pali Dictionary.
I have told you *once and again* that you must not read such trash.
This is *out and away* the best work on Astronomy.
He gained *over and above* this, the goodwill of all people.
Over and above being hard-working he is thoroughly honest.
He reads all the novels of Scott *over and over.*
I believe he is *out and out* the best Indian batsman.
He has read Milton *through and through.*
Thus and thus only we shall succeed.
He walked *to and fro,* meditating.

Chapter 37 POSITION OF ADVERBS

358. Adverbs of manner, which answer the question 'How' (*e.g., well, fast, quickly, carefully, calmly)* are generally placed after the verb or after the object if there is one ; as,

It is raining *heavily.*
The ship is going *slowly.*
She speaks English *well.*
He does his work *carefully.*

359. Adverbs or adverb phrases of place (*e.g., here, there, everywhere, on the wall)* and of time (*e.g., now, then, yet, today, next Sunday)* are also usually placed after the verb or after the object if there is one ; as,

He will come *here.*
I looked *everywhere.*
Hang the picture *there.*
I met him *yesterday.*
They are to be married *next week.*

360. When there are two or more adverbs after a verb (and its object), the normal order is : adverb of manner, adverb of place, adverb of time.

She sang well in the *concert.*
We should go *there tomorrow evening.*
He spoke earnestly at the meeting last night.

361. Adverbs of frequency, which answer the question 'How often?' (*e.g., always, never, often, rarely, usually, generally)* and certain other adverbs like *almost, already, hardly, nearly, just, quite* are normally put between the subject and the verb if the verb consists of only one word; if there is more than one word in the verb, they are put after the first word.

His wife *never* cooks.
He has *never* seen a tiger.

I have *often* told him to write neatly.
We *usually* have breakfast at eight.
My uncle has *just* gone out.
I *quite* agree with you.

362. If the verb is *am/are/is/was,* these adverbs are placed after the verb; as,
I am *never* late for school.
He is *always* at home on Sundays.
We are *just* off.

363. These adverbs are usually put before an auxiliary or the single verb *be,* when it is stressed ; as,
"Abdul has come late again." "Yes, he *always* does come late."
"When will you write the essay ?" "But I *already* have written it."
"Will you be free on Sundays ?" "I *usually* am free on Sundays."
"Do you eat meat ?" "Yes, I *sometimes* do."

When an auxiliary is used alone in short responses, as in the last example above, it is stressed and therefore the adverb comes before it.

364. The auxiliaries *have to* and *used to* prefer the adverb in front of them.
I *often* have to go to college on foot.
He *always* used to agree with me.

365. When an adverb modifies an adjective or another adverb, the adverb usually comes before it ; as
Rama is a rather lazy boy.
The dog was quite dead.
The book is very interesting.
Do not speak *so* fast.

366. But the adverb *enough* is always placed after the word which it modifies ; as,
Is the box big *enough* ?
He was rash *enough* to interrupt.
He spoke loud *enough* to be heard.

367. As a general rule, the word *only* should be placed immediately before the word it modifies ; as,
I worked *only* two sums.
He has slept *only* three hours.

In spoken English, however it is usually put before the verb. The required meaning is obtained by stressing the word which the *only* modifies ; as,
I *only* worked two sums.
He has *only* slept three hours.

EXERCISE IN COMPOSITION 63

Insert the given adverbs (or adverb phrases) in their normal position.

1. He invited me to visit him (often).
2. I am determined to yield this point (never).
3. I know the answer (already).
4. We have seen her (just, in the square).
5. I have to reach the office (by 9.30, usually).
6. Will he be (there, still) ?
7. I shall meet you (this evening, in the park).
8. The train has left (just).
9. "Can you park your car near the shops ?" "Yes, I can (usually)."
10. You have to check your oil before starting (always).
11. He is in time for meals (never).
12. We should come (here, one morning).
13. He has recovered from his illness (quite).

14. She goes to the cinema (seldom).
15. That is not good (enough).
16. You must say such a thing (never, again).
17. Suresh arrives (always, at 9 o'clock, at the office).
18. He played the violin (last night, brilliantly, in the concert).

Chapter 38 THE PREPOSITION

368. Read:

1. There is a cow *in* the field.
2. He is fond *of* tea.
3. The cat jumped *off* the chair.

In sentence 1, the word *in* shows the relation between two things —*cow* and *field.*

In sentence 2, the word *of* shows the relation between the attribute expressed by the adjective *fond* and *tea.*

In sentence 3, the word *off* shows the relation between the action expressed by the verb *jumped* and the *chair.*

The words *in, of, off* are here used as **Prepositions.**

Def— A Preposition is a word *placed before* a noun or a pronoun to show in what *relation* the person or thing denoted by it stands in regard to something else.

[The word Preposition means 'that which is placed before'.]

It will be noticed that—

in sentence 1, the Preposition joins a Noun to another Noun ;
in sentence 2, the Preposition joins a Noun to an Adjective ;
in sentence 3, the Preposition joins a Noun to a Verb.

369. The Noun or Pronoun which is used with a Preposition is called its Object. It is in the Accusative case and is said to be governed by the Preposition.

Thus, in sentence 1, the noun *field* is in the Accusative case, governed by the Preposition *in.*

370. A Preposition may have two or more objects ; as,

The road runs over *hill* and *plain.*

371. A Preposition is usually placed *before* its object, but sometimes it follows it ; as,

1. Here is the watch *that* you asked *for.*
2. That is the boy *(whom)* I was speaking *of.*
3. *What* are you looking *at* ?
4. *What* are you thinking *of* ?
5. *Which* of these chairs did you *sit on* ?

Note 1 — When the object is the Relative Pronoun that, as in sentence 1, the Preposition is always placed at the end.

The Preposition is often placed at the end when the object is an interrogative pronoun (as in sentences 3, 4 and 5) or a Relative Pronoun understood (as in sentence 2).

Note 2 — Sometimes the object is placed first for the sake of emphasis; as,

This I insist *on*. He is known all the *world over.*

372. The Prepositions *for, from, in, on* are often omitted before nouns of place or time; as,

We did it last *week*. I cannot walk a *yard*. Wait a *minute*.

Kinds of Prepositions

373. Prepositions may be arranged in the following classes:

(1) Simple Prepositions

at, by, for, from, in, of, off, on, out, through, till, to, up, with.

(2) Compound Prepositions which are generally formed by prefixing a Preposition (usually *a* = no or *be* = by) to a Noun, an Adjective or an Adverb.

About, above, across, along, amidst, among, amongst, around, before, behind, below, beneath, beside, between, beyond, inside, outside, underneath, within, without.

(3) Phrase Prepositions (Groups of words used with the force of a single preposition.)

according to	in accordance with	in place of
agreeably to	in addition to	in reference to
along with	in (on) behalf of	in regard to
away from	in case of	in spite of
because of	in comparison to	instead of
by dint of	in compliance with	in the event of
by means of	in consequence of	on account of
by reason of	in course of	owing to
by virtue of	in favour of	with a view to
by way of	in front of	with an eye to
conformably to	in lieu of	with reference to
for the sake of	in order to	with regard to

He succeeded *by dint of* perseverance and sheer hard work.
In case of need, phone 32567.
By virtue of the power vested in me, I hereby order, etc.
In consequence of his illness he could not finish the work in time.
Owing to his ill health, he retired from business.
With reference to your letter of date, we regret we cannot allow any further rebate.
In order to avoid litigation, he accepted Rs. 30,000 in full settlement of his claim for Rs. 42,000.
In course of time he saw his mistake.
He died fighting *on behalf of* his country.
On behalf of the staff he read the address.
He persevered *in spite of* difficulties.
In the event of his dying without an issue, his nephew would inherit the whole property.
Instead of talking, prove your worth by doing something.
By reason of his perverse attitude, he estranged his best friends.
He acted *according to* my instructions.
Why don't you *go along with* your brother ?
In accordance with your instructions, we have remitted the amount to your bankers.
There is a big tree *in front of* his house.
Agreeably to the terms of the settlement, we herewith enclose our cheque for Rs. 1000.
By way of introduction, he made some pertinent remarks.
By means of rope ladders they scaled the wall.
For the sake of their beliefs, the Puritans emigrated to America.
In course of his researches he met with many difficulties.
He abdicated the throne *in favour of* his eldest son.
He could not attend school *because of* his father's serious illness.
He accepted the car *in lieu of* his claim for Rs. 3,25,000.
With a view to an amicable settlement, we offer you without prejudice Rs. 7,500 in full settlement of all your claims uptodate.
On account of his negligence the company suffered a heavy loss.
Whatever he does, he does *with an eye to* the main chance.

He died fighting on behalf of his country.

374. *Barring, concerning, considering, during, notwithstanding, pending, regarding, respecting, touching,* and a few similar words which are present participles of verbs, are used absolutely without any noun or pronoun being attached to them. For all practical purposes, they have become Prepositions, and are sometimes distinguished as **Participial Prepositions.**

Barring (= excepting, apart from) accident, the mail will arrive tomorrow.
Concerning (= about) yesterday's fire, there are many rumours in the bazar.
Considering (= taking into account) the quality, the price is not high.
Ulysses is said to have invented the game of chess *during* the siege of Troy.
Notwithstanding (= in spite of) the resistance offered by him, he was arrested by the police.
Pending further orders, Mr. Desai will act as Headmaster.
Regarding your inquiries, we regret to say that at present we are not interested in imitation silk.
Respecting the plan you mention, I shall write to you hereafter.
Touching (= with regard to) this matter, I have not as yet made up my mind.

375. Several words are used sometimes as Adverbs and sometimes as Prepositions. A word is a Preposition when it governs a noun or pronoun ; it is an Adverb when it does not.

Adverb	*Preposition*
Go, and run *about.*	Don't loiter *about* the street.
I could not come *before.*	I came the day *before* yesterday.
Has he come *in* ?	Is he *in* his room ?
The wheel came *off.*	The driver jumped *off* the car.
Let us move *on.*	The book lies *on* the table.
His father arrived soon *after.*	*After* a month he returned.
Take this parcel *over* to the postoffice.	He rules *over* a vast empire.
I have not seen him *since.*	I have not slept *since* yesterday.

EXERCISE IN GRAMMAR 64

Name the Prepositions in the following sentences, and tell the word which each governs.

1. Little Jack Horner sat in a corner.
2. Old Mother Hubbard, she went to the cupboard.
3. The lion and the unicorn fought for the crown.
4. Humpty Dumpty sat on a wall.
5. Wee Willie Winkie runs through the town.
6. She sat by the fire, and told me a tale.
7. Rain, rain, go to Spain, and never come back again.
8. A fair little girl sat under a tree.
9. Such a number of rocks came over her head.
10. John Gilpin was a citizen of credit and renown.
11. "Will you walk into my parlour ?" said the spider to the fly.
12. Into the street the Piper stepped.
13. I can never return with my poor dog Tray.
14. He worked and sang from morn till night.
15. They all ran after the farmer's wife, who cut off their tails with a carving knife.
16. One day the boy his breakfast took, and ate it by a purling brook which through his mother's orchard ran.
17. Old John with white hair, does laugh away care, sitting under the oak, among the old folk.
18. They rise with the morning lark, and labour till almost dark.
19. By the Nine Gods he swore.
20. Under a spreading chestnut-tree the village smithy stands.
21. He goes on Sunday to church, and sits among his boys.
22. I bring fresh showers for the thirsting flowers, from the seas and the streams.
23. Her arms across her breast she laid.
24. Mine be a cot beside the hill.
25. Around my ivied porch shall spring each fragrant flower that drinks the dew.
26. One crowded hour of glorious life is worth an age without a name.
27. I tried to reason him out of his fears.

EXERCISE IN GRAMMAR 65

Distinguish the Prepositions from Adverbs in the following sentences.

1. Come down.
2. We sailed down the river.
3. The man walked round the house.
4. He sat on a stool.
5. The carriage moved on.
6. The soldiers passed by.
7. The man turned round.
8. We all went in.
9. He is in the room.
10. He hid behind the door.
11. I left him behind.
12. She sat by the cottage door.
13. The path leads through the woods.
14. I have read the book through.
15. The storm is raging without.
16. We cannot live without water.

EXERCISE IN COMPOSITION 66

Form sentences to illustrate the use of the following words (1) as Prepositions, and (2) as Adverbs.

Behind, up, by, along, in, about, beyond, under, before, after.

376. We have seen that the object to a Preposition is a Noun or Pronoun. Sometimes, however, the object to a Preposition is an Adverb of Time or Place (See § 340); as,

I will be done by *then* (= that time).
Since *then* (= that time) he has not shown his face.
Come away from *there* (= that place).
He must have reached there by *now* (= this time).
How far is it from *here* (= this place) ?
It cannot last for *ever*.

377. Sometimes the object to a Preposition is an Adverbial Phrase ; as,

Each article was sold at *over a pound*.
The noise comes from *across the river*.
He was not promoted to the rank of a colonel till *within a few months of his resignation*.
I sold my car for *under its half cost*.
He swore from dawn till *far into the night*.
He did not see her till a *few days ago*.
I was thinking about *how to circumvent him*.

378. A clause can also be the object to a Preposition ; as,

Pay careful attention to *what I am going to say*.
There is no meaning in *what you say*.

379. The object to a Preposition, when it is a relative pronoun, is sometimes omitted ; as,

He is the man I was looking for. [Here *whom* is understood.]
These are the good rules to live by. [Here *which* is understood.]

EXERCISE IN COMPOSITION 67

Fill in blanks with suitable Prepositions.

1. The dog ran ____the road.
2. The river flows ____the bridge.
3. The work was done ____haste.

4. He is afraid ____the dog.
5. I am fond ____music.
6. He goes ____Sunday ____ church.
7. He died ____his country.
8. The steam engine was invented ____James Watt.
9. The burglar jumped ____the compound wall.

10. The village was destroyed ____fire.
11. What is that ____me ?
12. It cannot be done ____offence.
13. He spoke ____me ____Urdu.
14. They live ____the same roof.
15. I have not seen him ____Wednesday last.
16. I have known him ____a long time.
17. The moon does not shine ____its own light.

18. This is a matter ____little importance.
19. I am tired ____walking.
20. He has not yet recovered ____his illness.
21. I shall do it ____pleasure.
22. God is good ____me.
23. I will sit ____my desk to do my lesson.
24. I am sorry ____what I have done.
25. O God ! Keep me ____sin.
26. I bought it ____ seventy rupees.
27. He broke the jug ____a hundred pieces.
28. It has been raining ____yesterday.
29. I have been working hard ____arithmetic.
30. We suffered ____your neglect.
31. The exercise was written ____me ____a Camlin pen.
32. "Will you walk ____my parlour ?" said the spider ____the fly.
33. It is ten o'clock ____my watch.
34. There is nothing new ____the sun.
35. Do not cry ____spilt milk.
36. You, boys, must settle it ____yourselves.
37. The public are cautioned ____pickpockets.
38. They drove ____Mumbai ____Pune.

380. Prepositions are very commonly used in composition with verbs, to form new verbs. Sometimes they are prefixed ; as,

outbid, overcome, overflow, overlook, undergo, undertake, uphold, withdraw, withhold, withstand.

More frequently Prepositions follow the verbs and remain separate; as,
boast of, laugh at, look for, send for.

He *boasted of* his accomplishments.
He *looked for* his watch everywhere.
Please *send for* Rama.
Everyone *laughed at* him.

Relations expressed by Prepositions

381. The following are some of the most common relations indicated by Prepositions:

(1) Place ; as,

Went *about* the world ; ran *across* the road ; leaned *against* a wall ; fell *among* thieves ; quarrelled *among* themselves ; *at* death's door ; *sit on* the deck ; stood *before* the door ; stood *behind* the curtain ; lies *below* the surface ; sat *beside* me ; plies *between* Mumbai and Alibag ; stand *by* me; rain comes *from* the clouds ; *in* the sky ; fell *into* a ditch ; lies *near* his heart ; Kolkata is *on* the Hooghly ; the cliff hangs *over* the sea ; tour *round* the world ; marched *through* the town ; came *to* the end of the road ; put pen *to* paper ; travelled *towards* Nasik ; lay *under* the table ; climbed *up* the ladder ; lies *upon* the table ; *within* the house.

(2) Time ; as,

After his death ; *at* an early date ; arrived *before* me ; *behind* time ; *by* three o'clock; *during* the whole day ; *for* many years ; *from* 1st April ; *in* the afternoon ; sat watching far on *into* the night ; lived *under* the Moghuls; *on* Monday ; *pending* his return ; *since* yesterday ; lasted *through* the night ; *throughout* the year ; wait *till* to-morrow ; ten minutes *to* twelve; *towards* evening ; *until* his arrival ; rise *with* the sun ; *within* a month.

(3) Agency, instrumentality ; as,

Sell goods *at* auction ; sent the parcel *by* post ; was stunned *by* a blow ; was destroyed *by* fire ; heard this *through* a friend ; cut it *with* a knife.

(4) Manner ; as,

Dying *by* inches ; fought *with* courage ; worked *with* earnestness, won *with* ease.

(5) Cause, reason, purpose ; as,

Laboured *for* the good of humanity ; died *of* fever ; the very place *for* a picnic; did it *for* our good ; suffers *from* gout ; died *from* fatigue ; does it *from* perversity; retreated *through* fear of an ambush; concealed it *through* shame; lost his purse *through* negligence ; shivers *with* fever ; took medicine *for* cold.

(6) Possession ; as,

There was no money *on* him ; the mosque *of* Omar ; a man *of* means ; the boy *with* red hair.

(7) Measure, standard, rate, value ; as,

He charges interest *at* nine per cent. Stories like these must be taken *at* what they are worth. Cloth is sold *by* the yard. I am taller than you *by* two inches. It was one *by* the tower-clock.

(8) Contrast, concession ; as,

After (in spite of, notwithstanding) every effort, one may fail. *For* one enemy he has a hundred friends. *For* (in spite of) all his wealth he is not content. *With* (in spite of) all his faults I admire him.

(9) Inference, motive, source, or **origin** ; as,

From what I know of him, I hesitate to trust him. The knights were brave *from* gallantry of spirit. He did it *from* gratitude. Light emanates *from* the sun. *From* labour health, from health contentment springs. This is a quotation *from* Milton. His skill comes *from* pracitce.

Note— It will be seen that the same Preposition, according to the way in which it is used, would have its place under several heads.

EXERCISE IN GRAMMAR 68

Explain the force of the Preposition in:

1. I will do it *for* all you may say.
2. This work is *beyond* his capacity.
3. I would do anything *before* that.
4. *After* this I wash my hands *of* you.
5. It is cool *for* May.
6. She made grand preparations *against* his coming.
7. It was all *through* you that we failed.
8. He was left *for* dead on the field.
9. All that they did was piety *to* this.
10. The lifeboat made straight *for* the sinking ship.
11. I shall do my duty *by* him.
12. He married *for* money.
13. A man is a man *for* all that.
14. Nothing will come *of* nothing.
15. *With* all his faults I still like him.

382. The following Prepositions require special notice:

(1) We can use *in* or *at* with the names of cities, towns or villages. In most cases *in* is used. We use *in* when we are talking about a place as an area; we use *at* when we see it as a point.
We stayed *in* Mumbai for five days.
Our plane stopped *at* Mumbai on the way to Iran. (Mumbai = Mumbai airport)
How long have you lived *in* this village?

(2) We use *at* to talk about group activities and shops/workplaces.

Did you see Shobha *at* the party?
There weren't many people *at* the meeting.
I saw him *at* the baker's.

(3) We use *in* with the names of streets and *at* when we give the house-number.

He lives *in* Church Street.
He lives *at* 45 Church Street.

(4) We use *on* when we think of a place as a surface.

The dog is lying *on* the floor.
Put this picture *on* the wall.

(5) *Till* is used of *time* and *to* is used of *place*; as

He slept *till* eight o'clock.
He walked *to* the end of the street.

(6) *With* often denotes the *instrument* and *by* the *agent* ; as,

He killed two birds *with* one shot.
He was stabbed *by* a lunatic *with* a dagger.

(7) *Since* is used before a noun or phrase denoting some *point* of time, and is preceded by a verb in the *perfect* tenses ; as,

I have eaten nothing *since* yesterday.
He has been ill *since* Monday last.
I have not been smoking *since* last week.

(8) *In* before a noun denoting a period of time, means *at the end of* ; *within* means *before the end of* ; as,

I shall return *in* an hour. I shall return *within* an hour.

(9) *Beside* means *at* (or *by*) *the side of*, while *besides* means *in addition to* ; as,

Beside the ungathered rice he lay.
Besides his children, there were present his nephews and nieces.
Besides being fined, he was sentenced to a term of imprisonment.

Note—Be careful not to use beside for besides.

EXERCISE IN GRAMMAR 69

Fill in the blanks with appropriate Prepositions.

1. He lives _____ Hyderabad. He lives _____ 48 Tilak Street.
2. He started _____ six _____ the morning.
3. He hanged himself _____ a piece of cloth.
4. The portrait was painted _____ a famous artist who flourished _____ the sixteenth century.
5. I must start _____ dawn to reach the station in time.
6. I hope to reach the station _____ an hour at the outside.
7. The child has been missing _____ yesterday.
8. The caravan must reach its destination _____ sunset.
9. The mail train is due _____ 3 P.M.
10. He travelled thirty kilometres _____ two hours.
11. He rushed _____ my room, panting for breath.
12. He does not leave his house _____ 9 o'clock.
13. The Express departs _____ 3 P.M. _____ Delhi.
14. Human sacrifices were practised _____ the Nagas.
15. I received his message _____ eight o'clock _____ the morning.
16. _____ last month I have seen him but once.
17. _____ rice they had curry.
18. The fever has taken a turn for the better _____ yesterday.

19. He has spent his life ____Kolkata.
20. I saw him felling a big tree ____a hatchet.
21. Come and sit ____me.
22. Nobody ____you knows the truth.
23. While I was ____Delhi he was ____Mumbai.
24. He was killed ____the robber ____a hatchet.
25. We shall stay three months ____America.
26. ____Rustam and Sohrab, there were three other boys present.
27. ____a Ford he has a Fiat car.

Prepositions with forms of transport

383. We use *by* + noun when we talk about means of transport. We do not use *the* or *a*/ *an* before the noun.

We travelled *by* train. (not : by *the/a* train)
We say *by bicycle, by car/ taxi/bus/train, by boat/ ship/ plane, by air/sea.*

We do not use *by* when the reference is to a specific bicycle, car, train, etc.
Suresh went there *on* my bike. (not : by my bike)
We travelled *in* Mr. Joshi's car. (not : by Mr. Joshi's car)
They came *in* a taxi.
I'll go *on* the 7.30 bus.

We use *on* to mean a specific bicycle, bus, train, ship or plane, and *in to mean* a specific car, taxi, van, lorry or ambulance.

We say *on foot* (not *by foot).*
He goes to the office *on* foot. (= He walks to the office.)

Chapter 39 WORDS FOLLOWED BY PREPOSITIONS

384. Certain Verbs, Nouns, Adjectives, and Participles are always followed by particular Prepositions. Read the following sentences, noting appropriate Prepositions:

Mumbai is famous *for* its textiles.
The goat subsists *on* the coarsest of food.
Jawaharlal Nehru was fond *of* children.
India is a noble, gorgeous land, teeming *with* natural wealth.
Being apprised *of* our approach, the whole neighbourhood came out to meet their minister.
In the classical age the ideal life of the Brahman was divided *into* four stages or *ashrams.*
It is natural in every man to wish *for* distinction.
He was endowed *with* gifts fitted to win eminence in any field of human activity.
The writer is evidently enamoured *of* the subject.
These computers are cheap enough to be accessible *to* most people.
Ambition does not always conduce *to* ultimate happiness.
The true gentleman is courteous and affable *to* his neighbours.
Newly acquired freedom is sometimes liable *to* abuse.
Little Jack proved quite a match *for* the giant.
Camels are peculiarly adapted *to* life in the desert.
He is a man of deep learning, but totally ignorant *of* life and manners.
The income derived *from* the ownership of land is commonly called rent.
The Moors were famous *for* their learning and their skill in all kinds of industries.
Alexander profited *by* the dissensions of the Punjab Rajas.
Few things are impossible *to* diligence and skill.
I am indebted to you *for* your help.
Ashoka, although tolerant *of* competing creeds, was personally an ardent Buddhist.
The celebrated grammarian Patanjali was a contemporary *of* Pushyamitra Sunga.
The African elephant is now confined *to* Central Africa.
Ivory readily adapts itself *to* the carver's art.
Coleridge's poetry is remarkable *for* the perfection of its execution.
The holy tree is associated *with* scenes of goodwill and rejoicing.

The noise from downstairs prevented me *from* sleeping.
I am already acquainted *with* the latest developments of the situation.
His duties were of a kind ill-suited *to* his ardent and daring character.
Man is entirely different *from* other animals in the utter helplessness of his babyhood.
A residence of eight years in Sri Lanka had inured his system *to* the tropical climate.
The ancient Greeks, though born in a warm climate, seem to have been much addicted *to* the bottle.
He (Dr. Johnson) was somewhat susceptible *to* flattery.
A man who always connives *at* the faults of his children is their worst enemy.
Naples was then destitute *of* what are now, perhaps, its chief attractions.
The cat appears to have originated in Egypt or *in* the East.
Judged *by* its results the policy of Hastings was eminently successful.
In his work Charak often hints *at* the value of sweet oil.
There is still no cure *for* the common cold.
It was formerly supposed that malaria was due *to* poisonous exhalations.
People who are averse *to* hard work, generally do not succeed in life.
Buddhism teaches that freedom *from* desires will lead to escape *from* suffering.

EXERCISE IN COMPOSITION 70

Construct sentences containing the following expressions.

afflicted with leprosy ; sanguine of success ; commit to memory ; specific for malaria ; allowance for short weight ; appropriate to the occasion ; abstain from animal food ; antipathy to dogs ; convulsed with laughter ; contrary to expectation ; infested with vermin ; touched with pity ; subversive of discipline ; beneficial to health ; tantamount to a refusal; worthy of praise; beset with difficulties ; accountable to God ; atone for misdeeds ; addicted to opium ; entitled to consideration ; heedless of consequences ; deaf to entreaties ; aptitude for business ; incentive to hard work ; sensitive to criticism ; indifferent to praise or blame

EXERCISE IN COMPOSITION 71

The following nouns take the preposition *for* after them. Use them in sentences.

affection, ambition, anxiety, apology, appetite, aptitude, blame, candidate, capacity, compassion, compensation, contempt, craving, desire, esteem, fitness, fondness, guarantee, leisure, liking, match, motive, need, opportunity, partiality, passion, pity, predilection, pretext, relish, remorse, reputation, surety

EXERCISE IN COMPOSITION 72

The following nouns take the preposition *with* after them. Use them in sentences.

acquaintance, alliance, bargain, comparison, conformity, enmity, intercourse, intimacy, relations

EXERCISE IN COMPOSITION 73

The following nouns take the preposition *of* after them. Use them in sentences.

abhorrence, assurance, charge, distrust, doubt, experience, failure, observance, proof, result, want

EXERCISE IN COMPOSITION 74

The following nouns take the preposition *to* after them. Use them in sentences.

access, accession, allegiance, alternative, antidote, antipathy, approach, assent, attachment, attention, concession, disgrace, dislike, encouragement, enmity, exception, incentive, indifference, invitation, key, leniency, likeness, limit, menace, obedience, objection, obstruction, opposition, postscript, preface, reference, repugnance, resemblance, sequel, submission, succession, supplement, temptation, traitor

EXERCISE IN COMPOSITION 75

The following nouns take the preposition *from* after them. Use them in sentences.

abstinence, cessation, deliverance, descent, digression, escape, exemption, inference, respite

EXERCISE IN COMPOSITION 76

The following adjectives and participles take the preposition *to* after them. Use them in sentences.

(*a*) abhorrent, acceptable, accessible, accustomed, addicted, adequate, adjacent, affectionate, agreeable, akin, alien, alive, amenable, analogous, applicable, appropriate, beneficial, callous, common, comparable, condemned.

(*b*) conducive, conformable, congenial, consecrated, contrary, creditable, deaf, derogatory, detrimental, devoted, disastrous, due, entitled, equal, essential, exposed, faithful, fatal, foreign, hostile, impertinent, incidental, inclined.

(*c*) indebted, indifferent, indispensable, indulgent, inimical, insensible, immune, irrelevant, favourable, hurtful, immaterial, impervious, indigenous, liable, limited, lost, loyal, material, natural, necessary.

(*d*) obedient, obliged, offensive, opposite, painful, partial, peculiar, pertinent, pledged, preferable, prejudicial, prior, profitable, prone, reduced, related, relevant, repugnant, responsible, restricted, sacred, sensitive, serviceable, subject, suitable, suited, supplementary, tantamount, true

EXERCISE IN COMPOSITION 77

The following adjectives and participles take the preposition *in* after them. Use them in sentences.

absorbed, abstemious, accomplished, accurate, assiduous, backward, bigoted, correct, defective, deficient, experienced, diligent, enveloped, fertile, foiled, honest, implicated, interested, involved, lax, proficient, remiss, temperate, versed

EXERCISE IN COMPOSITION 78

The following adjectives and participles take the preposition *with* after them. Use them in sentences.

acquainted, afflicted, beset, busy, compatible, compliant, consistent, contemporary, content, contrasted, conversant, convulsed, delighted, deluged, disgusted, drenched, endowed, fatigued, fired, gifted., infatuated, infected, infested, inspired, intimate, invested, overcome, popular, replete, satiated, satisfied

EXERCISE IN COMPOSITION 79

The following adjectives and participles take the preposition *of* after them. Use them in sentences.

accused, acquitted, afraid, apprehensive, apprised, assured, aware, bereft, cautious, certain, characteristic, composed, confident, conscious, convicted, convinced, covetous, defrauded, deprived, desirous, destitute, devoid, diffident, distrustful, dull, easy, envious, fearful, fond, greedy, guilty, heedless, ignorant, informed, innocent, irrespective, lame, lavish, negligent, productive, proud, regardless, sanguine, sensible, sick, slow, subversive, sure, suspicious, tolerant, vain, void, weary, worthy

EXERCISE IN COMPOSITION 80

The following adjectives and participles take the preposition *for* after them. Use them in sentences.

anxious, celebrated, conspicuous, customary, designed, destined, eager, eligible, eminent, fit, good, grateful, notorious, penitent, prepared, proper, qualified, ready, sorry, sufficient, useful, zealous

EXERCISE IN COMPOSITION 81

The following verbs take the preposition *to* after them. Use them in sentences.

accede, adapt, adhere, allot, allude, apologize, appoint, ascribe, aspire, assent, attain, attend, attribute, belong, conduce, conform, consent, contribute, lead, listen, object, occur, prefer, pretend, refer, revert, stoop, succumb, surrender, testify, yield

EXERCISE IN COMPOSITION 82

The following verbs take the preposition *from* after them. Use them in sentences.

abstain, alight, cease, debar, derive, derogate, desist, detract, deviate, differ, digress, dissent, elicit, emerge, escape, exclude, preserve, prevent, prohibit, protect, recoil, recover, refrain

EXERCISE IN COMPOSITION 83

The following verbs take the preposition *with* after them. Use them in sentences.

associate, bear, clash, coincide, comply, condole, cope, correspond, credit, deluge, disagree, dispense, expostulate, fill, grapple, intrigue, meddle, part, quarrel, remonstrate, side, sympathize, trifle, vie

EXERCISE IN COMPOSITION 84

The following verbs take the preposition *of* after them. Use them in sentences.

acquit, beware, boast, complain, despair, die, disapprove, dispose, divest, dream, heal, judge, repent, taste

EXERCISE IN COMPOSITION 85

The following verbs take the prepositions *for* after them. Use them in sentences.

atone, canvass, care, clamour, feel, hope, mourn, pine. start, stipulate, sue, wish, yearn

EXERCISE IN COMPOSITION 86

The following verbs take the preposition *in* after them. Use them in sentences.

acquiesce, dabble, delight, employ, enlist, excel, fail, glory, increase, indulge, involve, persevere, persist

EXERCISE IN COMPOSITION 87

The following verbs take the preposition *on* after them. Use them in sentences.

comment, decide, deliberate, depend, determine, dwell, embark, encroach, enlarge, impose, insist, intrude, resolve, subsist, trample

EXERCISE IN COMPOSITION 88

Fill in the blanks with appropriate Prepositions.

1. Mr. Ram Lal subscribed a handsome sum ____the Flood Relief Fund.

2. His friends condoled ____him ____his bereavement.
3. He quarrelled ____me ____a trifle.
4. He readily complied ____my request.
5. He dispensed ____the services of his dishonest clerk.
6. He yielded ____superior force.
7. He despaired ____success.
8. He supplies the poor ____clothing.
9. His friends disagreed ____him on that point.
10. He acceded ____my request.
11. He abstains ____liquor.
12. He was found guilty ____manslaughter.
13. He is incapable ____doing good work.
14. He is married ____my cousin.
15. He is sensible ____your kindness.
16. He is true ____his king.
17. He is involved ____difficulties.
18. The auditor is entitled ____his remuneration.
19. I prefer tea ____coffee.

20. I don't concur ____you ____that opinion.
21. There is no exception ____this rule.
22. I am obliged ____you ____your kindness.
23. I am not envious ____his success.
24. I am convinced ____the necessity of prudence.

25. We should rely ____our own efforts.
26. I inquired ____the servant if his master was at home.
27. I purposely refrained ____saying more.
28. I insisted ____going.
29. I exchanged ____him my calculator ____a camera.
30. I assented ____his proposal.
31. I am not satisfied ____your explanation.
32. You must conform ____the regulations.
33. He did not profit ____experience.
34. We should all aim ____excellence.
35. Alcohol is injurious ____health.

36. He is innocent ____the crime.
37. The stories in that book are full ____interest.
38. Don't associate ____disreputable people.
39. Do not indulge ____strong language.
40. He is grateful ____his master ____many favours.
41. He is dependent ____his parents.
42. He is abstemious ____eating and drinking.
43. He is prompt ____carrying out orders.
44. He is vain ____his attainments.
45. He is deficient ____common sense.
46. He is vexed ____me.
47. He is indifferent ____his own intere
48. He is proficient ____mathematics.

49. He is not ashamed ____his neighbours.
50. He is devoid ____sense.
51. He is suspicious ____all his neighbours.
52. He has a passion ____arguing.
53. Recently there has been a reduction ____ the price of milk.

54. He proved false ____his friend.
55. A square may be equivalent ____a triangle.
56. The avaricious man is greedy—gain.
57. He is very different ____his brother.
58. The head-dress of the Cossacks is similar ____that of the ancient Persians.
59. He was born ____humble parents in Nasik.
60. His views do not accord ____mine.

EXERCISE IN COMPOSITION 89

Fill in the blanks with appropriate Prepositions.

1. Temperance and employment are conducive ____health.
2. A policeman rescued the child ____danger.

3. Dogs have antipathy ____cats.
4. He promised not to do anything repugnant ____the wishes of his parents.
5. He is not the man to allow any one to encroach ____ his rights.
6. Some of the members of the Assembly complained ____increased military expenditure.
7. Even the enemies admit that he is endowed ____rare talents.
8. He inspires respect ____his friends.
9. Our path is beset ____difficulties.
10. He was not able to give a satisfactory explanation ____his absence.

11. His illness is a mere pretext ____his absence.
12. He has been very much indulgent ____his children.
13. This discussion is hardly relevant ____the subject
14. Contentment is essential ____happiness.
15. Early rising is beneficial ____health.
16. He is not likely to do anything detrimental ____our interests.
17. His benefactions must redound ____his credit.
18. Only graduates are eligible ____the post.
19. He is capable as a leader, but intolerant ____opposition.

20. Boys over sixteen are debarred ____competing.
21. Father Damien consecrated his life ____ ameliorating the lot of lepers.
22. That rule is not applicable ____your case.
23. A public man should be tolerant ____criticism.
24. He is willing to make a concession ____the demands of his employees.
25. I often find him absorbed ____thought.
26. The accommodation is adequate ____our needs.
27. The hotel is adjacent ____the station.
28. The authorship of the book is wrongly ascribed ____him.
29. Never do anything that is not compatible ______public safety.

30. His father often connives ____ his follies.
31. Some public men are very sensitive ____ criticism.

32. He is addicted ____ gambling.
33. You need not be afraid ____ being late.
34. Death is preferable ____ disgrace.
35. Cats are tenacious ____ life.
36. It is not true that the study of science tends ____ atheism.
37. Some films are an incitement ____ crime.
38. He was angry ____ me, because he thought my remark was aimed ____ him.
39. The climate of Rangoon does not agree ____ him.
40. His plans are adverse ____ my interests.
41. The question of unemployment bristles ____ difficulties.

42. Although he was bred ____ the law, he became a successful journalist.
43. Generally, the rich are more covetous ____ money than the poor.
44. He is still smarting ____ rebuke.
45. He scoffed ____ the idea of revolution.
46. He has reverted ____ his former post.
47. The battle resulted ____ a victory for the Allies.
48. He restored the article ____ its rightful owner.
49. The whole theory rests ____ no firmer foundation than mere conjecture.
50. The ultimate decision rests ____ the board of directors.
51. Only when persuasions failed the police resorted ____ force.
52. Superstitious fears preyed ____ his mind and made him miserable.
53. He piques himself ____ his artistic taste.
54. They now jeered ____ him whom they had once acclaimed as their hero.
55. His followers now began to intrigue ____ his adversary.
56. She interceded ____ her husband on behalf of the people.
57. It is not easy to infer ____ his account the real state of affairs.
58. He died without imparting ____ anyone the secret of his process.

59. His statement was tantamount ____ a confession.
60. The facts point ____ a different explanation.
61. His friends prevailed ____ him to withdraw his resignation.
62. Few boys are not amenable ____ discipline.

EXERCISE IN GRAMMAR 90

Fill in the blanks with appropriate Prepositions.

1. Silkworms feed ____ mulberry trees.
2. Pavlova excels ____ dancing.
3. The wild boar abounds ____ some parts of Europe.
4. He has no special liking ____ mathematics.

5. Ashoka is worthy ____ remembrance.
6. The godown is infested ____ rats.
7. There is no exception ____ this rule.
8. Nothing conduces ____ happiness so much as contentment.
9. Alcohol is injurious ____ health.
10. Oil is good ____ burns.
11. Invalids are not capable ____ continued exertion.
12. The British Parliament is composed ____ two Houses.
13. Do not confide your secrets ____ everyone.
14. He is abstemious ____ his habits.

15. He is ignorant ____ what he pretends to know.
16. My brother is weak ____ mathematics.
17. He has conceived an aversion ____ all kinds of profitable labour.
18. Birbal is celebrated ____ his witty sayings.
19. The avaricious man is greedy ____ gain.
20. The Atlantic separates Europe ____ America.
21. Adam assigned ____ every creature a name peculiar ____ its nature.
22. Temperance and employment are conducive ____ health.
23. A brave boy rescued the child ____ danger.

24. Industry is the key _____ success.

25. The customs were searching _______ drugs at the airport.

26. Elizabeth knew how to inspire her soldiers _____ hope.

27. Long indulgence _____ vice impaired his once robust constitution.

28. Early rising is beneficial _____ health.

29. We should live in a style suited _____ our condition.

30. Examinations act as an incentive _____ diligence.

31. Hard work and perseverance are indispensble _____ success in life.

32. He is too miserly to part _____ his money.

33. He is a clever man, but unfortunately diffident _____ his powers.

34. Suddenly we were enveloped _____ dense fog.

35. Many aspire _____ greatness, but few attained.

36. His income is not adequate _____ his wants.

37. The soil of Pune is favourable _____ roses.

38. I am sick _____ the whole business.

39. A car will be a great convenience _____ a busy man like him.

40. Whoever acts contrary _____ nature does not go unpunished.

41. The accident resulted _______ the death of five people.

42. These derelict houses are reproach _____ the city.

43. The Germans were called baby-killers and their methods of warfare stigmatized as a reproach _____ civilization.

44. The mule was partially relieved _____ the load.

45. America has raised a tariff wall to protect home industries _____ foreign competition.

46. The facts point _____ a different conclusion.

47. Your wish is tantamount _____ a command.

48. This state is committed _______ the policy of total prohibition.

49. One is sure _____ what one sees.

50. He is indifferent alike _____ praise and blame.

EXERCISE IN COMPOSITION 91

Fill in the blanks with appropriate Prepositions.

1. No doubt he has achieved much, but I cannot give him credit _____ all that he boasts _____.
2. The despotism of custom is everywhere the standing hindrance _____ human achievement.
3. He is indebted _____ his friend _____ a large sum.
4. What Dr. Arnold mainly aimed _____, was to promote the self-development of the young minds committed _____ his charge.
5. He was so much enamoured _____ her that he forgot his duties _____ his children.
6. It is difficult to agree _____ those critics who ascribe the work of Shakespeare _____ Bacon.
7. In his autobiography he refers _____ his abhorrence _____ animal diet.

8. He conversed _____ us _____ subjects _____ varied interest.
9. The accident happened _____ him _____ a late hour and _____ an out-of-the-way place.
10. A cashier is liable to render account _____ the money received _____ him.
11. The soldiers _____ the fort were provided _____ provisions to last them a year.
12. We are accountable _____ God _____ our actions.
13. Let us vie _____ one another _____ doing good.
14. His thirst _____ knowledge left him no leisure _____ anything else.
15. The rich and the poor alike nobly responded _____ the call _____ further funds.
16. For those who suffer _____ nerves the remedy lies _____ perfect rest.
17. A slave lies _____ the necessity _____ obeying his master's orders.
18. The heir _____ the throne was free _____ physical or moral taint.

19. He impressed ____them that sorcery was vital ____their success.
20. Methylated spirit is spirit of wine made undrinkable by mixing it ____methyl to exempt it ____duty.
21. To love our country, to be interested ____its concerns, is natural ____all men.
22. He complained ____his weak eyes and lamented the necessity ____spectacles.
23. Samudragupta was known ____his skill ____music and song ; he was equally proficient ____the allied art of poetry.
24. It is the grasping of power combined ____the thirst ____fame which constitutes ambition.
25. It would be well for us to admire what is worthy ____admiration in such a people, rather than to carp ____their errors.
26. The common fallacy is that intimacy dispenses ____the necessity of politeness. The truth is just the opposite ____this.
27. The title Master was originally prefixed ____the name of a person of rank or learning ; it is now restricted ____boys.
28. This ticket will entitle you _____ a free seat at the concert.
29. History, as well as daily experience, furnishes instances of men endowed ____the strongest capacity ____business and affairs, who have all their lives crouched under slavery to the grossest superstition.
30. He has no liking ____cards, and lately he has taken a dislike—outdoor exercise.
31. At first they refused to acquience ______ the terms, but finally yielded ______ the logic of facts.
32. The hippopotamus feeds chiefly____aquatic plants, but also seeks its food on land and is sometimes destructive ____cultivated crops.
33. Learning is knowledge especially as acquired ____study ; it is frequently contrasted ____knowledge or wisdom gained ____experience.
34. At the eleventh hour he retired ____the contest, leaving the field open ____his opponent.
35. Coriolanus, with all his greatness, was entirely devoid ____all sympathy ____the people.
36. From this time he became habitually depressed and moody and addicted ____the frequent use ____ alcohol.
37. The first acts of the new administration were characterized rather ____vigour than ____judgement.
38. They were statesmen accustomed ____the management ____great affairs.
39. Measure yourself ____your equals ; and learn ____frequent competition the place which nature has allotted ____you.
40. Contrary ____my instructions, he went ____his depth and would certainly have met ____a fatal mishap but for the timely help rendered ____him.

385. Sometimes a word takes a certain Preposition after it in one context and a different Preposition in another context.

We should accommodate ourselves *to* circumstances. My friend accommodated me *with* a loan.

I differ *with* you *on* this question. Your car differs *from* mine *in* several respects.

I am anxious *about* the result. Her parents are anxious *for* her safety.

He has retired *from* business. He has retired *into* private life.

He has great influence *over* his disciples. He has hardly any influence *with* the Vizier. The remarks of his critics had considerable influence *on* his writings.

All his life he laboured *for* the good of humanity. He is labouring *under* a misapprehension. He laboured *at* his dictionary for twelve years.

Trespassers are liable *to* a fine of Rs. 500. He is liable *for* his wife's debts.

EXERCISE IN COMPOSITION 92

Fill in the blanks with appropriate Prepositions.

1. A child is not able to distinguish good ____evil. Death does not distinguish ____the rich and the poor. Sir Ronald Ross is distinguished ____his medical researches. Punch is distinguished ____his hunchback. (between, by, for, from)
2. On account of his age he is disqualified ____competing. Ill health disqualified the body ____labour and the mind ____study. (for, from).
3. Innocence is not proof ____scandal. He was discharged as there was no proof ____his guilt. (against, of)

4. He has no good cause ____complaint. Darkness was the cause______his losing his way. (for, of)
5. True charity does not consist_____indiscriminate alms-giving. Brass consists ______copper and zinc. (in, of)
6. I am not concerned ____his affairs. I am not concerned ____him ____that business. He was much concerned ____ hearing the sad news. His parents are naturally concerned ____his safety. (about, at, for, in, with)
7. He parted___his friends in high spirits. He parted___his property and went on pilgrimage to Dwarka. (from, with.)
8. He acted___fear. He acted____my suggestion. He acted____compulsion. (from, under, upon)
9. He succeeded____the throne of his uncle. He succeeded____his object. (in, to)
10. He agreed_____my proposal. He agreed____me on that question. They could not agree____themselves. (among, to, with)
11. The patient is now free___danger. He is free___his money. The goods were passed free___duty (from, of, with)
12. I prevailed___him to join our Union. He prevailed___me in the dispute. The peculiar custom prevails___the Todas. (among, over, upon)
13. I was angry _____ him _____ lying to me. (for, with)
14. The city is well provided___corn. We should provide___risk of fire by insuring our goods. He has provided_____his children. (against, for, with)
15. The police is entrusted___the enforcement of law and order. The children were entrusted___the care of their uncle. (to, with)
16. The edition of *Ivanhoe* is adapted___Indian boys. The form and structure of nests are adapted___the wants and habits of each species. Many Urdu plays are adapted___English. (for, from, to)
17. We are all slaves___convention. No man should be a slave___his passions. (of, to)
18. He is blind___one eye. Are you blind___your own interests ? (of, to)
19. There is no exception___the rule. All the ministers were present at the function with the exception___Mr. Smith. He took exception___the presence of an outsider. (against, of, to)
20. His creditors became impatient___payment. Impatient___delay, he knocked at the door rather loudly. The people became impatient___the burden of heavy taxation. (at, for, under)

EXERCISE IN COMPOSITION 93

Fill in the blanks with appropriate Prepositions.

1. He invested his patrimony____jute shares. The Police Commissioner is invested ____magisterial powers. (in, with)
2. Let us talk____something else. For a while they talked____politics. I will talk ____my son respecting his conduct. (about, of, to)
3. He takes no interest____politics. What you say has no interest____me. I have no interest____the agents of the firm. (for, in, with)
4. He has a reputation____honesty. He has the reputation ____being a good teacher. (for, of)
5. He exercises complete authority____his followers. There is no authority____this use. I say this on the authority____ the Oxford English Dictionary. Dr. Bridge is an authority____English prosody. (for, of, on, over)
6. He fell a victim____his own avarice. The victims ____cholera were mostly poor people. (of, to)
7. I have no use____it. He has lost the use____his right arm. (for, of)
8. There are some diseases that proceed ____dirt. After visiting Agra we proceed ____Delhi. Let us proceed ____the work in hand. (from, to, with)
9. He supplied the poor ____clothing. He supplied clothing ____the poor. (to, with)
10. She was greatly afflicted ____the loss of her only child. The old man is afflicted ____gout. (at, with)
11. The teacher impressed ____us the value of discipline. We were impressed ____what he said. (on, with)
12. The operation was accompanied ____little or on pain. She was accompanied ____her brother. (by, with.)
13. The English allied themselves ____the French. Elementary Algebra is allied ____Arithmetic. (to, with)
14. Napoleon had a genius ____military tactics. Without doubt he is a genius ____mathematics. (for, in)
15. The idea originated ____him while he was travelling in Japan. The fire originated ____a haystack. (in, with)
16. He jumped ____a conclusion not warranted by facts. The child jumped ____joy when I gave him sweets. He jumped ____my offer. (at, for, to)

17. He is negligent ____whatever he does. He is negligent ____his duties. (in, of)
18. Contentment is requisite ____happiness. He is told that prolonged treatment is requisite ____effecting a cure. (for, to)
19. His shattered health is the result ____intemperance. Jealousy results ____unhappiness. No good is likely to result ____this union. (from, in, of)
20. It does not rest ____the Collector to order his release. His whole case rests ____alibi. (on, with)
21. Most of the roads in that district are not suitable ____motor-cars. He lives in a style suitable ____his position. (for, to)
22. He responded ____the ladies in a humorous speech. The boy immediately responded ____a blow. He responded ____his toast in a neat little speech. (for, to, with)

386. Some related words take different Prepositions after them.

I acted *according to* his advice.
In *accordance with* his advice I took quinine.
She has great *affection for* her grandchildren.
The old lady is *affectionate to* all.
The flood and ebb tides *alternate with* each other.
The *alternative to* submission is death.
It is all due to his *ambition for* fame.
He is *ambitious of* fame.
He is *capable* of anything.
He has not the requisite *capacity for* this work.
He has great *confidence in* his assistant.
He is quite *confident of* success.
What a *contrast to* his brother !
What a *contrast between* them !
The present speech is mild *contrasted with* his past utterance on the same subject.
It is not likely to *derogate from* his merit.
He never said or did anything *derogatory to* his high position.
He is *descended from* a noble family.
He is a *descendant of* Mahatma Gandhi.
He has no *desire for* fame.
He is *desirous of* visiting Agra.
He was *equal to* the occasion.
He is to be blamed *equally with* his brother.
The coat fits me well *except for* the collar.
I take *exception to* your remark.
The child is *fond of* sweets.
She has great *fondness* for children.
The drama is *founded on* an episode in the Ramayana.
It has, however, no *foundation in* fact.
He *hindered* me *from* going.
Child marriage is a great *hindrance to* progress.
He is quite *infatuated with* her.
His *infatuation for* that girl led him astray.
He has no *liking for* cards.
His *dislike to* her continued to increase.
He is *neglectful of* his dress.
I have often found him *negligent in* his work.
They say he is *partial to* his friends.
Children show a *partiality for* sweetmeats.
I have no *prejudice against* foreigners.
Such a step will be *prejudicial to* your interests.
He is *prepared for* anything.
Preparatory to taking extreme measures, his father once again warned him.
Pursuant to our conversation, I now send you a cheque for Rs. 500 as my contribution to the fund.
In *pursuance of* your instructions, we are writing to-day to the Collector.
I am of opinion that he is *qualified for* the post.
He is *disqualified from* practising as a pleader.
As a *result of* the injury received by him, he died of tetanus.

It is said that nothing *resulted from* the conference.
I have great *respect for* his learning.
He is *respectful to* his superiors, without being servile.
He *seized upon* the opportunity offered to him.
The *seizure of* his property was carried out under direct orders from the Rajah.
I assure you that I am *sensible of* your kindness.
His paralysed arm is *insensible to* feeling.
Subsequent to the meeting he wrote a letter to *The Hindu.*
Consequent upon this letter, the agents of the company filed a suit against him for defamation.
Trust in God and do what is right.
His *distrust of* his assistants is perhaps unfounded.
The country suffers for *want of* skilled labour.
He is *wanting in* a little common sense.

387. Sometimes a verb is followed by a preposition ; sometimes no preposition follows it. The meaning, however, is not always the same in both cases.

I *call* that mean. I *called on* him at his office.
I don't *catch* your meaning. A drowning man *catches* at a straw.
This *closed* the proceedings. After a little higgling he *closed with* my offer.
He *commenced* life as a shop assistant. The proceedings *commenced with* a song.
Have you *counted* the cost ? I *count upon* your advice and cooperation.
He *deals* fairly *with* his customers. He *deals* in cotton and cloth.
The compounder *dispenses* medicines. His master *dispensed with* his services.
He *gained* his object by persuasion. He *gained upon* his rich uncle by his suave manners.
He *grasped* the meaning of the passage in no time. Like a shrewd man of business he *grasped at* the opportunity.
I *met* him on my way to the station. His appeals for funds *met with* a poor response.
He always prepares his speech. Our soldiers prepared themselves for the offensive.
The police *searched* the house of the suspect. We *searched for* the lost article.

388. Do not use the infinitive with certain words which require a preposition followed by a gerund or by a verbal noun.

He is addicted to gambling. [Not : to gamble.]
I assisted her in climbing the hill.
He is averse to playing cards.
I do not believe in pampering servants.
I am bent on attending the meeting.
He has hardly any chance of succeeding.
He is confident of securing the first prize.
The custom of tipping is prevalent everywhere.
He is desirous of visiting Japan.
He despaired of achieving his object.
There is some difficulty in perceiving his meaning.
Hereafter he is disqualified for holding any government post.
Remember the duty of helping the poor.
Sudha excels in dancing.
You can have no excuse for talking bluntly.
He is expert in inventing stories.
I am fond of reading novels.
The firm was fortunate in securing the government's support.
What hindered you from visiting the Museum ?
He was disappointed in the hope of being rewarded.
He felt the humiliation of withdrawing his words.
We should be indefatigable in doing good.
I insisted on having my say.
He is intent on visiting Norway.
You were not justified in imputing motives to him.
He has a knack of doing it.
He appreciated the necessity of acting promptly.
He persisted in disobeying the orders.
He lacks the power of imparting, although he is a good mathematical scholar.
The practice of cramming is rightly regarded as an evil.
It was only a pretext for delaying the matter.

What is there to prevent him from leaving Chennai ?
I had the privilege of knowing him intimately.
They were prohibited from entering the village.
I refrained from hurting his feelings.
You were right in suspecting him.
There is little satisfaction in sitting idle.
He has no scruple in begging.
He succeeded in convincing his critics.
He thought of eluding his pursuers.
I am tired of writing letters to him.

> **Note**—Sometimes both constructions are allowable ; e.g.
>
> He was afraid of telling the truth.
> He was afraid to tell the truth.
> He at last got the opportunity of meeting him.
> He at last got the opportunity to meet him.

389. On the other hand, certain words always take the infinitive after them; as,

He advised us to desist from that attempt.
I decline to say anything further.
I expect to meet opposition.
It is hard to get access to him.
He hopes to win the first prize.
We are all inclined to judge of others as we find them.
He intends to compile a Marathi dictionary.

390. Prepositions are sometimes inserted where they are not required; as,

Where have you been to ? [Here *to* is not required.]
My eldest son is a boy of about eighteen years old. [Here *of* is not required.]
After having finished my work I went home. [Here *after* is not required.]

391. Note that the verbs *discuss*, *order* and *stress* are transitive and therefore they are not followed by prepositions. We *discuss* a topic (**not** *discuss about* a topic), *order* tea (**not** *order for* tea), *stress* a point (**not** *stress on* a point).

Chapter 40 THE CONJUNCTION

392. Read the following sentences.

1. God made the country *and* man made the town.
2. Our hoard is little, *but* our hearts are great.
3. She must weep, *or* she will die.
4. Two *and* two make four.

In 1, 2 and 3, the Conjunctions join together two sentences.

In 4, the Conjunction joins together two words only. [See § 393]

Def—A Conjunction is a word which merely *joins* together sentences, and sometimes words.

393. Conjunctions join together sentences and often make them more compact ; thus,

'Balu *and* Vithal are good bowlers'

is a short way of saying

'Balu is a good bowler *and* Vithal is a good bowler'.

So,

'The man is poor, *but* honest'

is a contracted way of saying

'The man is poor, *but* he is honest.'

Sometimes, however, the Conjunction *and* joins words only; as,

Two *and* two make four.

Hari *and* Rama are brothers.

Hari *and* Rama came home together.

Such sentences cannot be resolved in two sentences.

394. Conjunctions must be carefully distinguished from Relative Pronouns, Relative Adverbs, and Prepositions, which are also connecting words.

1. This is the house *that* Jack built. (Relative Pronoun)
2. This is the place *where* he was murdered. (Relative Adverb)
3. Take this *and* give *that.* (Conjunction)

In sentence 1, the Relative Pronoun *that* refers to the noun *house,* and also joins the two parts of the sentence.

In sentence 2, the Relative Adverb *where* modifies the verb *was murdered* and also joins the two parts of the sentence.

In sentence 3, the Conjunction *and* simply joins the two parts of the sentence ; *it does no other work.*

It will thus be seen that–

Relative Pronouns and Relative Adverbs also join ; but they do more.

Conjunctions merely join : they do no other work.

Observe that a Preposition also joins two words, but it does more ; it governs a noun or pronoun ; as,

He sat *beside* Rama. He stood *behind* me.

395. Some Conjunctions are used in pairs ; as,

Either —or.	*Either* take it *or* leave it.
Neither —nor.	It is *neither* useful *nor* ornamental.
Both —and	We *both* love *and* honour him.
Though—yet. (rare in current English)	*Though* he is suffering much pain, *yet* he does not complain.
Whether—or.	I do not care *whether* you go *or* stay.
Not only—but also.	*Not only* is he foolish, *but also* obstinate.

Conjunctions which are thus used in pairs are called **Correlative Conjunctions** or merely **Correlatives.**

396. When Conjunctions are used as Correlatives, each of the correlated words should be placed *immediately before* the words to be connected ; as,

He visited *not only* Agra, *but also* Delhi.

(*Not*) He *not only* visited Agra, *but also* Delhi.

397. We use many compound expressions as Conjunctions ; these are called **Compound Conjunctions.**

In order that.	The notice was published *in order that* all might know the facts.
On condition that.	I will forgive you *on condition that* you do not repeat the offence.
Even if.	Such an act would not be kind *even if* it were just.
So that.	He saved some bread *so that* he should not go hungry on the morrow.
Provided that.	You can borrow the book *provided that* you return it soon.
As though.	He walks *as though* he is slightly lame.
Inasmuch as.	I must refuse your request, *inasmuch as* I believe it unreasonable.
As well as.	Rama *as well as* Govind was present there.
As soon as.	He took off his coat *as soon as* he entered the house.
As if.	He looks *as if* he were weary.

Classes of Conjunctions

398. As we shall see Conjunctions are divided into two classes : Co-ordinating and Subordinating.

Read the sentence :

Birds fly *and* fish swim.

The sentence contains two *independent* statements or two statements of *equal rank* or importance. Hence the Conjunction joining together these two statements or clauses of *equal rank* is called a **Co-ordinating Conjunction** ['Co-ordinating' means of *equal rank.*]

Def — A Co-ordinating Conjunction joins together clauses of equal rank.

399. The chief Co-ordinating Conjunctions are:
and, but, for, or, nor, also, either.....or, neither......nor.

400. Co-ordinating Conjunctions are of four kinds :

(1) **Cumulative** or **Copulative** which merely *add* one statement to another ; as,

We carved not a line, *and* we raised not a stone.

(2) **Adversative** which express opposition or *contrast* between two statements ; as,

He is slow, *but* he is sure.
I was annoyed, *still* I kept quiet.
I would come ; *only* that I am engaged.
He was all right ; *only* he was fatigued.

(3) **Disjunctive** or **Alternative** which express a *choice* between two alternatives ; as,

She must weep, *or* she will die.
Either he is mad, *or* he feigns madness.
Neither a borrower, *nor a* lender be.
They toil not, *neither* do they spin.
Walk quickly, *else* you will not overtake him.

(4) **Illative** which express an *inference ;* as,

Something certainly fell in : *for* I heard a splash.
All precautions must have been neglected, *for* the plague spread rapidly.

401. Any of the Co-ordinating Conjunctions, with the exception of *or, nor,* may be omitted and its place taken by a comma, semi-colon, or colon ; as,
Rama went out to play ; Hari stayed in to work.

402. Read the sentence :
I read the paper *because* it interests me.

The sentence contains two statements or clauses one of which, 'because it interests me', is *dependent* on the other. Hence the Conjunction introducing the *dependent* or *subordinate* clause is called a **Subordinating Conjunction.**

Def —A Subordinating Conjunction joins a clause to another on which it depends for its full meaning.

403. The chief Subordinating Conjunctions are:
after, because, if, that, though, although, till, before, unless, as, when, where, while.
After the shower was over the sun shone out again.
A book's a book, *although,* there is nothing in it.
As he was not there, I spoke to his brother.
He ran away *because* he was afraid.
Answer the first question *before* you proceed further.
Take heed *ere* it be too late.
Except ye repent, you shall all likewise perish.
You will pass *if* you work hard.
Sentinels were posted *lest* the camp should be taken by surprise.
Since you say so, I must believe it.
Tell them *that* I will come.
He finished first *though* he began late.
Will you wait *till* I return ?
He will not pay *unless* he is compelled.

Since you say so, I must believe it.

I waited for my friend *until* he came.
When I was younger, I thought so.
I do not know *whence* he comes.
He found his watch *where* he had left it.
I do not understand *how* it all happened.
Make hay *while* the sun shines.
I shall go *whither* fancy leads me.
I know not *why* he left us.

404. The word *than* is also a Subordinating Conjunction.
He is taller *than* I (am tall).
I like you *better than* he (likes you).
I like you better *than* (I like) him.
Hari is more stupid *than* Dhondu (is stupid).
His bark is worse *than* his bite (is bad).

405. Subordinating Conjunctions may be classified according to their meaning, as follows:

(1) Time
I would die *before* I lied.
No nation can be perfectly well governed *till* it is competent to govern itself.
Many things have happened *since* I saw you.
I returned home *after* he had gone.
Ere he blew three notes, there was a rustling.

(2) Cause or Reason
My strength is as the strength of ten, *because* my heart is pure.
Since you wish it, it shall be done.
As he was not there, I spoke to his brother.
He may enter, *as* he is a friend.

Since you wish it, it shall be done.

(3) Purpose
We eat so *that* we may live.
He held my hand *lest* I should fall.

(4) Result or Consequence
He was so tired *that* he could scarcely stand.

(5) Condition
Rama will go *if* Hari goes.
Grievances cannot be redressed *unless* they are known.

(6) Concession
I will not see him, *though* he comes.
Though He slay me, yet will I trust Him.
A book's a book, *although* there's nothing in it.

(7) Comparison
He is stronger *than* Rustum [is].

406. Certain words are used both as Prepositions and Conjunctions. [See § 375]

Preposition	*Conjunction*
Stay *till* Monday.	We shall stay here *till* you return.
I have not met him *since* Monday.	We shall go *since* you desire it.
He died *for* his country.	I must stay here, *for* such is my duty.
The dog ran *after* the cat.	We came *after* they had left.
Everybody *but* Govind was present.	He tried, *but* did not succeed.
He stood *before* the painting.	Look *before* you leap.

EXERCISE IN GRAMMAR 94

Point out the Conjunctions in the following sentences, and state whether they are Co-ordinating or Subordinating.

1. You will not succeed unless you work harder.
2. We arrived after you had gone.
3. I waited till the train arrived.
4. Bread and milk is wholesome food.
5. You will get the prize if you deserve it.
6. When you are called, you must come in at once.
7. Do not go before I come.
8. I cannot give you any money, for I have none.
9. Since you say so, I must believe it.
10. He fled lest he should be killed.
11. I shall be vexed if you do that.
12. We got into the port before the storm came on.
13. He was sorry after he had done it.
14. I did not come because you did not call me.
15. He is richer than I am.
16. My grandfather died before I was born.
17. I will stay until you return.
18. Catch me if you can.
19. Tom runs faster than Harry.
20. Is that story true or false ?
21. You will be late unless you hurry.
22. He asked whether he might have a holiday.
23. Give me to drink, else I shall die of thirst.
24. If I feel any doubt, I ask.
25. He deserved to succeed, for he worked hard.
26. He will be sure to come if you invite him.
27. We can travel by land or water.
28. The earth is larger than the moon.
29. Either you are mistaken, or I am.
30. I shall go, whether you come or not.
31. Unless you tell me the truth, I shall punish you.
32. I hear that your brother is in London.
33. Blessed are the merciful, for they shall obtain mercy.

EXERCISE IN GRAMMAR 95

Use these Conjunctions in complex sentences.

(1) But, either..............or, neither...........nor, whether...........or.
(2) That, before, how, as, unless, until, though, when , while, where, if, than.

EXERCISE IN GRAMMAR 96

Fill the blanks with appropriate Conjunctions.

1. Be just _____fear not.
2. I ran fast, ______I missed the train.
3. He fled, ______he was afraid.
4. Make haste, ______you will be late.

5. ____you try, you will not succeed.
6. I am sure ____he said so.
7. Wait ____I return.
8. Do not go ____I come.
9. He finished first ____he began late.
10. Take care ____you fall.
11. Take a lamp, ____the night is dark.
12. ____he was ambitious I slew him.
13. Open rebuke is better ____secret love.
14. ____you eat too much you will be ill.
15. I shall not go ____I am invited.
16. He has succeeded better ____he hoped.
17. I do it ____I choose to.
18. ____duty calls us we must obey.
19. Live well ____you may die well.
20. Think nought a trifle, ____it small appear.
21. The purse has been lost ____stolen.
22. Rustum is slow ____sure.
23. He remained at home ____he was ill.
24. ____he was industrious, I encouraged him.

EXERCISE IN GRAMMAR 97

Fill each blank in the following sentences with an appropriate Conjunction :—

1. Three ____three make six.
2. Is his name Sen ____Gupta ?
3. He will not come ____it rains.
4. ____you run, you will not overtake him.
5. He is very rich ____he is not happy.
6. ____I return, stay where you are.
7. He was punished, ____he was guilty.
8. He behaved ____a brave man should do.
9. There is no doubt ____the earth is round.
10. I wonder ____he will come.
11. He is witty ____vulgar.
12. Will you kindly wait ____I return?
13. Karim is tall, ____Abdul is taller.
14. He lost his balance ____fell off the bicycle.
15. He tried hard ____did not succeed.
16. Is this my book ____yours ?
17. Water ____oil will not mix.

18. They left ____we returned.
19. The vase will break ____you drop it.
20. I shall not go out now ____it is raining very heavily.
21. Trains run from this station every few minutes ____ we shall not have to wait.
22. Man proposes ____God disposes.
23. Time ____tide do not wait for anybody.
24. Virtue ennobles, ____vice degrades.
25. This ____that must suffice.
26. The train was derailed ____no one was hurt.
27. She writes slowly ____neatly.
28. I believe him ____he is truthful.
29. You will not get the prize ____you deserve it.
30. Send for me ____you want me.
31. Hari will do all right, ____he perseveres.
32. Catch me ____you can.
33. He told me ____you had arrived an hour ago.

34. You will never succeed _____ you try.
35. _____ I were you, I'd keep quiet.
36. Wait _____ I come.
37. Be just _____ fear not.
38. Tell me _____ you understand.
39. We will come, _____ it rains _____ not.
40. Make hay _____ the sun shines.
41. It is a long time _____ we last saw him.
42. Please write _____ I dictate.
43. It is hoped _____ all will go well.
44. Give me _____ poverty _____ riches.
45. He is taller _____ I (am).
46. _____ I cannot get away, I will go next week.
47. _____ you wish it, it shall be done.
48. Why is our food so sweet ? _____ we earn before we eat.
49. Take heed _____ you fall.
50. He gazed so long _____ both his eyes were dazzled.
51. _____ there is life there is hope.
52. Walk on _____ you come to the gate.
53. They say _____ he is better.
54. I have been in such a pickle _____ I saw you last.
55. His plans, _____ vast, were never visionary.
56. Some people live _____ they may eat.
57. He went _____ I came.
58. He will starve _____ he will steal.
59. There were more people _____ we had expected.
60. _____ there is something to be done, the world knows how to get it done.
61. _____ I grant his honesty I suspect his memory.

62. _____ I am poor, I am not dishonest.
63. No one knows _____ he went.
64. Come _____ you please.
65. Do _____ you are bidden.
66. He must have passed this way, _____ there is no other road.
67. _____ respected, he is not liked.
68. We all know _____ sin and sorrow go together.
69. I don't know _____ he will be here.
70. Grievances cannot be redressed _____ they are known.
71. We shall fail _____ we are industrious.
72. _____ it was late we decided to set out.
73. I am well, _____ I do not feel very strong.
74. _____ he is there, I shall see him.
75. How can he buy it _____ he has no money ?
76. _____ you are not ready, we must go on.

77. The building has been razed _____ I visited the city.
78. Love not sleep, _____ thou come to poverty.
79. He bled so profusely _____ he died.
80. I know you better _____ he (does).

EXERCISE IN GRAMMAR 98

Join each pair of the following sentences by means of a suitable Conjunction. Make such changes as are necessary.

1. My brother is well.	My sister is ill.
2. He sells mangoes.	He sells oranges.
3. He did not succeed.	He worked hard.
4. Rama played well.	Hari played well.
5. I honour him.	He is a brave man.
6. You may go.	I will stay.
7. Rama reads for pleasure.	Hari reads for profit.
8. We decided to set out.	It was late.
9. He was poor.	He was honest.

10.	He is not a knave.	He is not a fool.
11.	We love Bahadur.	He is a faithful dog.
12.	Rustum made twelve runs.	He was caught at the wicket.
13.	He is rich.	He is not happy.
14.	The sheep are grazing.	The oxen are grazing.
15.	He is poor.	He is contented.
16.	This mango is large.	This mango is sweet.
17.	My brother was not there.	My sister was not there.
18.	The boy is here.	The girl is here.
19.	The piper played.	The children danced.
20.	You must be quiet.	You must leave the room.
21.	He sat down.	He was tired.
22.	Rama works hard.	Hari is idle.
23.	I lost the prize.	I tried my best.
24.	I like him.	He is dangerous.
25.	I went to the shop.	I bought a slate.
26.	He is slow.	He is sure.
27.	I know.	He does not think so.
28.	You are tall.	My brother is taller.
29.	Hari went to school.	Sita stayed at home.
30.	He must start at once.	He will be late.
31.	I shall sit still.	I shall listen to the music.
32.	Hari did not come.	He did not send a letter.
33.	I ran fast.	I missed the train.
34.	Karim works hard.	Abdul works harder.
35.	He must be tired.	He has walked twelve miles.
36.	It is autumn.	The leaves are falling.
37.	I will come.	I am not ill.
38.	I will bring your umbrella.	You wish it.
39.	He remained cheerful.	He has been wounded.
40.	He went out.	The train stopped.
41.	He ran to the station.	He missed the train.
42.	I came.	I was unwilling.
43.	Men have fought for their country.	Men have died for their country.
44.	He was afraid of being late.	He ran.
45.	Hari does not write fast.	He writes very well.
46.	The boy is dangerously ill.	The boy's head was hurt.
47.	The old man fell down the steps.	He broke his leg.
48.	He tried to get up.	He could not.
49.	Mother is at home.	Father is at home.
50.	I have a cricket bat.	I have a set of stumps.
51.	We went early to the circus.	We could not get a seat.
52.	He must do as he is told.	He will be punished.
53.	The prisoner fell down on his knees.	The prisoner begged for mercy.
54.	Sita goes to school.	Ganga goes to school.
55.	Rama may be in the house.	Rama may be in the garden.

EXERCISE IN GRAMMAR 99

Distinguish as Adverb, Preposition, or Conjunction, each of the italicized words in the following sentences.

1. He came *before* me.
2. He came two hours *before.*
3. He came *before* I left.
4. Have you ever seen him *since* ?
5. I have not seen him *since* Monday.
6. I have not seen him *since* he was a child.
7. Man wants *but* little here below.
8. He yearns for nothing *but* money.
9. We shall go, *but* you will remain.
10. He arrived *after* the meeting was adjourned.
11. He arrived *after* the meeting.
12. He arrived soon *after.*

Chapter 41 SOME CONJUNCTIONS AND THEIR USES

407. **Since,** as a Conjunction, means—

(1) *From and after the time when* ; as

I have been in such a pickle *since* I saw you last.
Many things have happened *since* I left school.
I have never seen him *since* that unfortunate event happened.

Note— *Since*, when used as a Conjunction in this sense, should be preceded by a verb in the present perfect tense, and followed by a verb in the *simple past tense.*

(2) *Seeing that, in as much as* ; as,

Since you wish it, it shall be done.
Since you will not work, you shall not eat.
Since that is the case, I shall excuse you.

408. **Or** is used—

(1) To introduce an alternative, as,

Your purse *or* your life.
You must work *or* starve.
You may take this book *or* that one.

Note— There may be several alternatives each joined to the preceding one by or, presenting a choice between any two in the series ; as,

He may study law *or* medicine *or* engineering *or* he may enter into trade.

(2) To introduce an alternative name or synonym ; as,

The violin *or* fiddle has become the leading instrument of the modern orchestra.

(3) To mean *otherwise* ; as,

We must hasten *or* night will overtake us.

(4) As nearly equivalent to *and* ; as,

The troops were not wanting in strength *or* courage, but they were badly fed.

409. **If** is used to mean—

(1) *On the condition or supposition that* ; as,

If he is there, I shall see him.
If that is so, I am content.

(2) *Admitting that,* as,

If I am blunt, I am at least honest.
If I am poor, yet I am honest.

(3) *Whether* ; as,

I asked him *if* he would help me.
I wonder *if* he will come.

(4) *Whenever* ; as,

If I feel any doubt I inquire.

If is also used to express wish or surprise : as,
If I only knew !

410. **That**, as a Conjunction, retains much of its force as a Demonstrative Pronoun. Thus the sentence 'I am told that you are miserable' may be transposed into 'You are miserable : I am told *that*.'
That is used—

(1) To express a Reason or Cause, and is equivalent to *because, for that, in that* ; as,

Not *that* I loved Caesar less, but *that* I loved Rome more.
He was annoyed *that* he was contradicted.

(2) To express a Purpose, and is equivalent to *in order that* ; as,

We sow *that* we may reap.
He kept quiet *that* the dispute might cease.

Note—Today *that* is rarely used for reason or purpose.

(3) To express a Consequence, Result, or Effect ; as,

I am so tired *that* I cannot go on.
He bled so profusely *that* he died.
He was so tired *that* he could scarcely stand.

411. **Than** as a Conjunction, follows adjectives and adverbs in the comparative degree ; as,
Wisdom is better *than* rubies (are).
I see you oftener *than* (I see) him.
I am better acquainted with the country *than* you are.
I would rather suffer *than* that you should want.

412. **Lest** is used as a Subordinating Conjunction expressing a negative purpose, and is equivalent to 'in order that......not', 'for fear that' ; as,
Love not sleep, lest thou come to poverty.
Do not be idle, lest you come to want.
He fled lest he should be killed.
I was alarmed lest we should be wrecked.

Note 1—*Lest* is rare in modern English.

Note 2—The modern idiomatic construction after *lest* is *should.*

After certain expressions denoting fear or apprehension, *lest* was used as equivalent to *that* ; as,
I feared *lest* I might anger thee.

413. **While** is used to mean—

(1) *During the time that, as long as* ; as,

While he was sleeping, an enemy sowed tares.
While there is life there is hope.

(2) *At the same time that* ; as,

The girls sang *while* the boys played.
While he found fault, he also praised.

(3) *Whereas* ; as,

While I have no money to spend, you have nothing to spend on.
While this is true of some, it is not true of all.

414. **Only,** as a Conjunction, means *except that, but, were it not (that)*; as,

A very pretty woman, *only* she squints a little.
The day is pleasant, *only* rather cold.
He does well, *only* that he is nervous at the start.
I would go with you, *only* I have no money.

415. **Except** was once in good use as a Conjunction ; as,

Except (= unless) ye repent, ye shall all likewise perish.

Except a man be born again, he cannot see the kingdom of God.

In modern English its place has been taken by *unless*.

416. **Without.**—The use of *without* as a Conjunction meaning *unless* is now bad English ; as,

I shall not go *without* you do.

417. **Because, for, since.** —Of these three conjunctions, *because* denotes the closest causal conjunction, *for* the weakest, *since* comes between the two.

EXERCISE IN COMPOSITION 100

Fill the blanks with Conjunctions.

1. I am in the right, _____you are in the wrong.
2. The most exquisite work of literary art exhibits a certain crudeness and coarseness, _____we turn to it from nature.
3. _______he had not paid his bill, his electricity was cut off.
4. There never can be prosperity in any country _____ all the numerous cultivators of the soil are permanently depressed and injured.
5. Giving up wrong pleasure is not self-sacrifice, _____self-culture.
6. Conform thyself then to thy present fortune _____cut thy coat according to thy cloth.
7. Inconsistency consists in a change of conduct _____there is no change of circumstances which justify it.
8. The disgust felt towards any kind of knowledge is a sign ______that it is prematurely presented, _____that it is presented in an indigestible form.
9. _____do the learned know what sort of mortals inhabit beyond those mountains, _____whether they be inhabited at all.
10. His ambition was inordinate, _____he was jealous of every man of ability.
11. Just laws are no restraint upon the freedom of the good, _____the good man desires nothing which a just law will interfere with.
12. We judge ourselves by what we feel capable of doing, _____others judge us by what we have already done.
13. My worthy friend Sir Roger is one of those who are not only at peace with themselves, _____beloved and esteemed by all about them.
14. The fleets of the enemy were not merely defeated, _____destroyed.
15. As long as he (William of Orange) lived, he was the guiding-star of a brave nation ; _____he died the little children cried in the street.
16. No one likes puns, alliterations, antithesis. argument and analysis better than I do ; I sometimes had rather be without them.
17. It (the game of fives) is "the finest exercise for the body _____best relaxation for the mind."
18. He (Omar Khayyam) abhorred hypocrisy, _____he was not too stern with the hypocrite.
19. Our proudest title is not that we are the contemporaries of Darwin, _____that we are the descendants of Shakespeare.
20. He (Henry Bradshaw) knew more about printed books _____any man living.
21. Are you impatient with the lark _____he sings rather than talks ?
22. Trust the man who hesitates in his speech and is quick and steady in action, _____beware of long arguments and long beards.
23. Religion does not banish mirth _____only moderates and sets rules to it.
24. A man's real character will always be more visible in his household _____anywhere else.
25. _____grandfather was old and gray-haired, _____his heart leaped with joy whenever little Alice came fluttering, like a butterfly, into the room.
26. He that is slow to anger is better _____the mighty.
27. _____we approached the house, we heard the sound of music.
28. The ravine was full of sand now, _____it had once been full of water.
29. The harvest truly is plenteous, _____the labourers are few.

Lend every man thy ear but few thy voice.

30. A vessel that once gets a crack, _____it may be cunningly mended, will never stand such rough usage as a whole one.
31. Give every man thy ear, _____few thy voice.
32. Virtue _____wise action lies in the mean between the two extremes of too little and too much.
33. And God called the light Day, _____the darkness He called Night.

34. That is a good book which is opened with expectation, _____closed with profit.
35. _______ I was in Sri Lanka, I was particularly fascinated by the Coral Gardens of Hikkaduwa.
36. The restoration crushed for a time the Puritan party, _____placed supreme power in the hands of a libertine.
37. Of his voyage little is known, _____that he amused himself with books and with his pen.
38. _____she had given up novel writing, she was still fond of using her pen.
39. _____Addison was in Ireland, an event occurred to which he owes his high and permanent rank among British writers.
40. _____life _____property was safe, and the poor and the weak were oppressed by the strong.
41. _____Greek and Latin, _____all Aryan languages have their peaceful words in common.
42. He was an oppressor ; ______he had at least the merit of protecting his people against all oppression except his own.
43. People travelling in a spacecraft appear to be weightless ______can move about _______ there is no gravity in space.
44. The right of self-defence is founded in the law of nature, _____is not and cannot be superseded by the law of society.
45. Let the superstructure of life be enjoyment, _____let its foundation be in solid work.
46. _____I was not a stranger to books, I had no practical acquaintance with them.
47. Poetry takes me up so entirely _____I scarce see what passes under my nose.
48. A gentleman made it a rule in reading to skip over all sentences _____he spied a note of admiration at the end.
49. _____a fog rolled over the city in the small hours, the early part of the night was cloudless.
50. _____I were personally your enemy, I might pity and forgive you.

EXERCISE IN COMPOSITION 101

Fill the blanks with Conjunctions.

1. _____somewhat pompous, he was an entertaining companion.
2. "Mr. Johnson", said I, "I do indeed come from Scotland, _____I cannot help it."
3. The man that stands by me in trouble I won't bid him go _____the sun shines again.
4. _____you are upon Earth enjoy the good things that are here, _____be not melancholy.

5. The art of pleasing is a very necessary one to possess ; _____a very difficult one to acquire.
6. Never maintain an argument with heat and clamour, _____you think or know yourself to be in the right.
7. The crowd cheered loudly _________ The Prime Minister arrived.
8. I am persuaded _____the translators of the Bible were masters of an English style much fitter for that work _____any we see in our present writings.
9. He [Chaucer] must have been a man of most wonderful comprehensive nature, _____he has taken into the compass of his *Canterbury Tales* the various manners and humours of the whole English nation, in his age.
10. It is the common doom of man _____he must eat his bread by the sweat of his brow.
11. It is a sort of paradox, _____it is true : we are never more in danger _____when we think ourselves most secure.
12. I have imposed upon myself, _____I have been guilty of no other imposition.
13. One of the pleasantest things in the world is going on a journey ; _____I like to go by myself. I can enjoy society in a room ; _____, out of doors, nature is company enough for me.
14. It [the game of fives] is the finest exercise for the body, _____the best relaxation for the mind.

15. Religion does not banish mirth _____only moderates and sets rules to it.
16. Fit words are better _____fine ones.
17. I like political changes _____such changes are made as the result, not of passion, but of deliberation and reason.
18. Civilized man, _____let loose with the bonds of morality relaxed, is a far greater beast _____the savage, more refined in his cruelty, more fiend-like in every act.
19. The man who eats in a hurry loses both the pleasure of eating _____the profit of digestion.
20. Let a man sleep _____he is sleepy, _____rise _____the crow of the cock, _____the glare of the sun rouses him from his torpor.
21. It is a great loss to a man _____he cannot laugh.

22. Impure air can never make pure blood ; ____impure blood corrupts the whole system.
23. Never refuse to entertain a man in your heart ____all the world is talking against him.
24. ____you would be healthy, be good.
25. ____you have a sword ____a pen in your hand, wield ____the one ____the other in a spirit of insolent self-reliance.
26. A regular bath in the morning, ____with very feeble and delicate subjects, has always an invigorating effect.
27. There is no more sure sign of a shallow mind ____the habit of seeing always the ludicrous side of things.
28. An honest hater is often a better fellow ____a cool friend ; ____it is better not to hate at all.
29. There is no virtue that Dr. Arnold laboured more sedulously to instil into young men ____the virtue of truthfulness.
30. The teachers of morality discourse like angels, ____they live like men.
31. Massacres ____disorders never have the way to peace.
32. Natural thirst is more deliciously gratified with water, ____artificial thirst is with wine.
33. Woman was not meant to be ____an unthinking drudge, ____the merely pretty ornament of man's leisure.
34. The real dignity of a man lies in what he *has*, ____in what he *is*.
35. They say the Lion and the Lizard keep the Courts ____Jamshyd gloried and drank deep.
36. ____I am dead, my dearest, sing no sad songs for me.
37. ____he [Lord Beaconsfield] was ambitious, his ambition was a noble one.
38. Suffer the little children to come unto me, and forbid them not, ____of such is the Kingdom of God.
39. Heard melodies are sweet, ____those unheard are sweeter.
40. I awoke one morning ____found myself famous.
41. ____the blind lead the blind, both shall fall into the ditch.
42. One generation passeth away and other generation cometh, ____the earth abideth for ever.
43. A man has no more right to say an uncivil thing ____to act one.
44. Let us shun extremes, ____each extreme necessarily engenders its opposite.
45. ____this be madness, ____there is method in it.
46. The heavens declare the glory of God, ____the firmanent showeth His handi-work.
47. Every good tree bringeth forth good fruit, ____a corrupt tree bringeth forth evil fruit.
48. Small service is true service ____it lasts.
49. For my part, I was always bungler at all kinds of sport that required ____patience ____adroitness.
50. There are many truths of which the full meaning cannot be realized ____personal experience has brought it home.
51. He may be right ____wrong in his opinion, ____he is too clearheaded to be unjust.

Chapter 42 THE INTERJECTION

418. Examine the following sentences :—

Hello ! What are you doing there ?
Alas ! He is dead.
Hurrah ! We have won the game.
Ah ! Have they gone ?
Oh ! I got such a fright.
Hush ! Don't make a noise.

Such words as *Hello* ! *Alas* ! *Hurrah* ! *Ah* ! etc. are called **Interjections.**

They are used to express some sudden feeling or emotion. It will be noticed that they are not grammatically related to the other words in a sentence.

Def.—An Interjection is a word which expresses some sudden feeling or emotion.

Interjections may express—

(1) Joy ; as, *Hurrah* ! *huzza* !
(2) Grief ; as, *alas* !
(3) Surprise ; as, *ha* ! *what* !
(4) Approval ; as, *bravo* !

419. Certain groups of words are also used to express some sudden feeling or emotion ; as,
Ah me ! *For shame* ! *Well done* ! *Good gracious* !

Chapter 43 THE SAME WORD USED AS DIFFERENT PARTS OF SPEECH

420. The following are some of the most important words which may belong to different parts of speech according to the way in which they are *used*.

Always remember that it is the *function* or *use* that determines to which part of speech a word belongs in a given sentence.

About

Adverb.	They wandered *about* in sheepskins and goatskins.
Preposition.	There is something pleasing *about* him.

Above

Adverb.	The heavens are *above*.
Preposition	The moral law is *above* the civil.
Adjective.	Analyse the *above* sentence.
Noun.	Our blessings come from *above*.

After

Adverb.	They arrived soon *after*.
Preposition.	He takes *after* his father.
Adjective.	*After* ages shall sing his glory.
Conjunction.	We went away *after* they had left.

All

Adjective.	*All* men are mortal. It was *all* profit and no loss.
Adverb.	He was *all* alone when I saw him.
Pronoun.	*All* spoke in his favour.
Noun.	He lost his *all* in speculation.

Any

Adjective.	Are there *any* witnesses present ?
Pronoun.	Does *any* of you know anything about it ?
Adverb.	Is that *any* better ?

Give place to your better

As

Adverb.	We walked *as* fast as we could.
Conjunction.	*As* he was poor I helped him.
Relat. Pron.	She likes the same colour *as* I do.

Before

Adverb.	I have seen you *before*.
Preposition.	He came *before* the appointed time.
Conjunction.	He went away *before* I came.

Better

Adjective.	I think yours is a *better* plan.
Adverb.	I know *better*.
Noun.	Give place to your *betters*.
Verb.	The boxes with which he provided me *bettered* the sample.—*Froude*.

Both

Adjective.	You cannot have it *both* ways.
Pronoun.	*Both* of them are dead.
Conjunction.	*Both* the cashier and the accountant are Hindus.

But

Adverb. It is *but* (= only) right to admit our faults.
Preposition. None *but* (= except) the brave deserves the fair.
Conjunction. We tried hard, *but* did not succeed.
Relat. Pronoun. There is no one *but* likes him. (= *who* does *not* like him.)

Down

Adverb. *Down* went the "Royal George."
Preposition. The fire engine came rushing *down* the hill.
Adjective. The porter was killed by the *down* train.
Noun. He has seen the ups and *downs* of life.
Verb. *Down* with the tyrant !

Either

Adjective. *Either* bat is good enough.
Pronoun. Ask *either* of them.
Conjunction. He must *either* work or starve.

Else

Adjective. I have something *else* for you.
Adverb. Shall we look anywhere *else* ?
Conjunction. Make haste, *else* you will miss the train.

Enough

Adjective. There is time *enough* and to spare.
Adverb. You know well *enough* what I mean.
Noun. I have had *enough* of this.

Even

Adjective. The chances are *even*.
Verb. Let us *even* the ground.
Adverb. Does he *even* suspect the danger ?

Except

Verb. If we *except* Hari, all are to be blamed.
Preposition. All the brethren were in Egypt *except* Benjamin.
Conjunction. I will not let thee go *except* (= unless) thou bless me (§ 415)

For

Preposition. I can shift *for* myself.
Conjunction. Give thanks unto the Lord ; *for* He is good.

Less

Adjective. You are paying *less* attention to your studies than you used to do.
Adverb. The population of India is *less* than that of China.
Noun. He wants Rs. 500 for that watch. He won't be satisfied with *less*.

Like

Adjective. They are men of *like* build and stature.
Preposition. Do not talk *like* that.
Adverb. *Like* as a father pitieth his own children.
Noun. We shall not see his *like* again.
Verb. Children *like* sweets.

Little

Adjective. There is *little* danger in going there.
Noun. Man wants but *little* here below.
Adverb. He eats very *little.*

More

Adjective. We want *more* men like him.
Pronoun. *More* of us die in bed than out of it.
Adverb. You should talk less and work *more.*

Much

Adjective. There is *much* sense in what he says.
Pronoun. *Much* of it is true.
Adverb. He boasts too *much.*

Near

Adverb. Draw *near* and listen.
Preposition. His house is *near* the temple.
Adjective. He is a *near* relation.
Verb. The time *nears.*

Needs

Noun. My *needs* are few.
Verb. It *needs* to be done with care.
Adverb. He *needs* must come.

Neither

Conjunction. Give me *neither* poverty nor riches.
Adjective. *Neither* accusation is true.
Pronoun. It is difficult to negotiate where *neither* will trust.

Next

Adjective. I shall see you *next* Monday.
Adverb. What *next* ?
Preposition. He was sitting *next* to her.
Noun. I shall tell you more about it in my *next.*

No

Adjective. It is *no* joke.
Adverb. He is *no* more.
Noun. I will not take a *no.*

Once

Adverb. I was young *once.*
Conjunction. *Once* he hesitates we have him.
Noun. Please help me for *once.*

One

Adjective. *One* day I met him in the street.
Pronoun. The little *ones* cried for joy.
Noun. *One* would think he was mad.

Only

Adjective. It was his *only* chance.
Adverb. He was *only* foolish.
Conjunction. Take what I have, *only* (= but) let me go.

Over

Adverb.	Read it *over* carefully.
Noun.	In one *over* he took three wickets.
Preposition.	At thirty a change came *over* him.

Right

Verb.	That is a fault that will *right* itself.
Adjective.	He is the *right* man for the position.
Noun.	I ask it as a *right*.
Adverb.	Serves him *right* ! He stood *right* in my way.

Round

Adjective.	A square peg in a *round* hole.
Noun.	The evening was a *round* of pleasures.
Adverb.	He came *round* to their belief.
Preposition.	The earth revolves *round* the sun.
Verb.	We shall *round* the cape in safety.

Since

Preposition.	*Since* that day I have not seen him.
Conjunction.	*Since* there's no help, come, let us kiss and part.
Adverb.	I have not seen him *since*.

So

Adverb.	I am *so* sorry.
Conjunction.	He was poor, *so* they helped him.

Some

Adjective.	We must find *some* way out of it.
Pronoun.	*Some* say one thing and others another.
Adverb.	*Some* thirty chiefs were present.

Still

Verb.	With his name the mothers *still* their babes.
Adjective.	*Still* waters run deep.
Noun.	Her sobs could be heard in the *still* of night.
Adverb.	He is *still* in business.

Such

Adjective.	Don't be in *such* a hurry.
Pronoun.	*Such* was not my intention.

That

Demonst. Adjective.	What is *that* noise ?
Demonst. Pronoun.	*That* is what I want.
Adverb.	I have done *that* much only.
Relative Pronoun.	The evil *that* men do lives after them.
Conjunction.	He lives so *that* he may eat.

The

Def. Article.	*The* cat loves comfort.
Adverb.	*The* wiser he is, *the* better.

Till

Preposition.	Never put off *till* tomorrow what you can do today.
Conjunction.	Do not start *till* I give the word.

Up

Adverb.	Prices are *up*.
Preposition.	Let us go *up* the hill.
Adjective.	The next *up* train will leave here at 12.30.
Noun.	They had their *ups* and downs of fortune.

Well

Noun.	Let *well* alone.
Adjective.	I hope you are now *well*.
Adverb.	*Well* begun is half done.
Interjection.	*Well*, who would have thought it ? —

What

Inter. Adjective.	*What* evidence have you got ?
Interjection.	*What* ! you don't mean to say so ?
Inter. Pronoun.	*What* does he want ?
Relative Pronoun.	Give me *what* you can. *What* happened then, I do not know.
Adverb.	*What* by fire and *what* by sword, the whole country was laid waste.

While

Noun.	Sit down and rest a *while*.
Verb.	They *while* away their evenings with books and games.
Conjunction.	*While* a great poet, he is a greater novelist.

Why

Interro. Adverb.	*Why* did you do it ?
Relative Adverb.	I know the reason *why* he did it.
Interjection.	*Why*, it is surely Nanak !
Noun.	This is not the time to go into the *why* and the wherefore of it.

Yet

Adverb.	There is more evidence *yet* to be offered.
Conjunction.	He is willing, *yet* unable.

EXERCISE IN COMPOSITION 102

What part of speech is each of the words in italics ?

1. He kept the *fast* for a week.
2. Mohammedans *fast* in the month of Ramzan.
3. He is the *right* man in the *right* place.
4. God defend the *right* !
5. There is *much* truth in what he says.
6. *Much* cry and little wool.
7. Don't boast too *much*.
8. It is *hard* to understand.
9. Men who work *hard* enjoy life fully.
10. *Little* learning is a dangerous thing.
11. He is *little* known here.
12. It matters *little* what he says.
13. I have *long* thought so.

14. It is *long* since we met.
15. *Still* waters run deep.
16. He *still* lives in that house.
17. That boy gives *any* amount of trouble.
18. Is that *any* better ?
19. A *better* man than he never lived.
20. He knows *better* than to quarrel.
21. He spoke in a *loud* voice.
22. Do not speak so *loud*.
23. *Most* people think so.
24. What *most* annoys me is his obstinacy.
25. *Some* twenty boys were absent.
26. I will take *some*, but not all.

27.Please call me *early.*
28. The *early* bird catches the worm.
29. That can stand *over.*
30. Take this parcel *over* to the post office.
31. He has no command *over* himself.
32. He was only a yard *off* me.
33. Suddenly one of the wheels came *off.*
34. I must be *off.*
35. He told us all *about* the battle.
36. He lives *about* two miles from here.
37. Several men were standing *about.*
38. *After* the storm comes the calm.
39. The *after* effects of potash bromide are bad.
40. He went *after* I came.
41. The minstrels follow *after.*
42. May comes *after* April.

43. *All* fish are not caught with flies.
44. *All* is fair in love and war.
45. We shall lie *all* alike in our graves.
46. He that is warm thinks *all* so.
47. What is *all* this noise ?
48. *All* is not lost.
49. He is *all* for amusement.
50. *All* is good in a famine.

EXERCISE IN COMPOSITION 103

What part of speech is each of the words in italics?

1. He is not *any* the worse for it.
2. A thing you don't want is dear at *any* price.
3. I thought *as much.*
4. He is as deaf *as* a post.
5. He got the same result *as* before.
6. *As* he was ambitious, I slew him.
7. Men fear death *as* children to go in the dark.
8. There is no such flatterer *as* a man's self.
9. He did his *best.*
10. I like this *best.*
11. He is my *best* friend.
12. He is *but* a child.
13. Fear nought *but* sin.
14. *But* for his help, I could not have done it.
15. The paths of glory lead *but* to the grave.
16. *But* that I saw it I could not have believed it.
17. I change, *but* I cannot die.
18. There is no lane *but* has a turning.
19. The fool is busy in everyone's business *but* his own
20. *Enough* of this !
21. She sings well *enough.*
22. *Enough* is as good as a feast.
23. We have not men *enough.*
24. He is *like* his father.
25. I *like* the offer.

26. Did you ever hear the *like* of it ?
27. Do not talk *like* that.
28. I have heard *more* since.
29. This sum is *more* difficult.
30. *More* will be wanted.
31. He stood *next* me in class.
32. The *next* moment he was dead.
33. What happened *next* ?
34. We have *no* money.
35. He is *no* better, *no* worse.
36. His answer was a decided *no.*
37. *Right* the wrong.
38. He is in the *right.*
39. He is always *right.*
40. Set it *right.*
41. Use *right* words.
42. *Since* you say so, I believe it.
43. *He* has been ill *since* yesterday.
44. He has returned home long *since.*
45. What was *that* noise ?
46. He died so *that* he might save his country.
47. What is the so man *that* does not love his country ?
48. Give him *what* you can.
49. *What* nonsense is this !
50. *What* does it profit ?

Part I

Composition

Analysis, Transformation and Synthesis

This section leads you to a further study of the English grammatical system and seeks to help you build longer sentences.

A knowledge of different types of phrases, clauses and sentences (chapters 2 to 9) and practice in the use of conjunctions like **if, when, as, because, though, that, and, but,** etc. will extend your ability to construct sentences. If you learn clause analysis it will be easy for you to understand lengthy sentences which you sometimes meet in the language of eminent writers.

There are three very useful chapters (12, 13 and 14) containing exercises in synthesis or combination of sentences. Look at this passage :

There were three men. They were poor. One day they found a bag in the jungle. The bag contained money. It had evidently been lost by some traveller.

It sounds jerky. There are too many short sentences. They can be combined into a single sentence, as :

One day three poor men found a bag of money in the jungle, which had evidently been lost by some traveller.

This sounds much better, doesn't it ? This kind of exercises will strengthen your ability to build long, better sentences.

Chapters 10, 11 and 16 provide guidance and practice in forming a wide variety of sentences: exclamations (e.g. How beautiful the flower is!), rhetorical questions (e.g. Is this the way that a gentleman should behave ?), indirect speech (e.g. He asked where you had gone.), etc.

Now go on to read this section. Remember that you can learn more effectively by practising. Work through all the exercises.

PART I: ANALYSIS, TRANSFORMATION AND SYNTHESIS

Chapter 1 ANALYSIS OF SIMPLE SENTENCES

1. We have learnt that a **Sentence** is a set or group of words which makes *complete sense.*

We have also learnt that the first stage in the analysis of a sentence is to divide it into two main parts—the **Subject** and the **Predicate ;** as,

No.	SUBJECT	PREDICATE
1	Dogs	bark.
2	The sun	gives light.
3	The child	is dead.
4	The boys	made Rama captain.
5	My father	gave me a watch.
6	The flames	spread everywhere.
7	The flames	spread in every direction.
8	The hour to prepare lessons	has arrived.

The subject denotes the *person* or *thing* about which something is said.

The predicate is *what is said* about the person or thing denoted by the Subject.

We see that the Subject may consist of one word or several words. Thus, in sentence 1 the subject consists of one word, *viz.,* the Noun *dogs ;* in sentence 8 the Subject consists of five words of which the most important word is the Noun *hour.*

We also see that the Predicate may consist of one word or several words. Thus, in sentence 1 the Predicate consists of one word, *viz.,* the Verb *bark ;* in sentence 5 the Predicate consists of four words of which the essential word is the Verb *gave.*

EXERCISE 1

In the following sentences separate the Subject and the Predicate.

1. The cackling of geese saved Rome.
2. Stone walls do not make a prison.
3. All matter is indestructible.
4. No man can serve two masters.
5. A sick room should be well aired.
6. I shot an arrow in the air.
7. The shepherd hears barking sound.
8. Up went the balloon.
9. The naked everyday he clad.
10. Into the street the piper stepped.
11. Sweet are the uses of adversity.
12. Dear, gentle, patient, noble Nell was dead.

2. When the Subject of a sentence consists of several words, there is always one word in it which is more important than the other words. This chief word in the complete Subject is called the **Subject-word** or **Simple Subject.** Thus, in the sentence,

The little *child,* tired of play, / is sleeping,

the Noun *child* is the Subject-word.

The Subject-word is always a Noun, or a word or group of words *that does the work of a Noun* ; as,

He / tried his best.

The *rich* / are not always happy.

Talking overmuch / is a sign of vanity.

To err / is human.

To find fault / is easy.

3. In the complete Subject, the Subject-word is qualified by an Adjective or Adjective-equivalent* called its **Enlargement** or **Attribute**; as,

    1. New brooms / sweep clean.
    2. Barking dogs / seldom bite.
    3. Hari's father / is an engineer.
    4. My views / are quite different.
    5. Firdousi, the poet, / wrote the Shah Namah.
    6. A desire to excel / is commendable.
    7. A stitch in time / saves nine.

No.	SUBJECT		PREDICATE
	Subject-word	Attribute	
1	brooms	New	sweep clean.
2	dogs	Barking	seldom bite.
3	father	Hari's	is an engineer.
4	views	My	are quite different.
5	Firdousi	the poet	wrote the Shah Namah.
6	desire	(1) A (2) to excel	is commendable.
7	stitch	(1) A (2) in time	saves nine.

It will be noted that—

in 1, the Attribute is an Adjective ;

in 2, the Attribute is a Participle (or Participial Adjective) ;

in 3, the Attribute is a Noun in the Possessive or Genitive Case ;

in 4, the Attribute is a Possessive Adjective ;

in 5, the Attribute is a Noun in Apposition ;

in 6, the Attribute (*to excel*) is a Gerundial Infinitive ;

in 7, the Attribute (*in time*) is a group of words doing the work of an Adjective.

Note—*A* or *an* and the are really Attributes, but they are sometimes treated as parts of the Subject-word.

EXERCISE 2

In the following sentences, pick out the complete Subject; then separate Subject-word from its Attributes.

1. The boy, anxious to learn, worked hard.
2. A burnt child dreads the fire.
3. Birds of a feather flock together.
4. The attempt to scale the fort was an utter failure.
5. The days of our youth are the days of our glory.

I wish I were young again.

*A word or group of words which does the work of an Adjective is called an Adjective-equivalent.

6. Ill habits gather by unseen degrees.
7. The dog, seizing the man by the collar, dragged him out.
8. The streets of some of our cities are noted for their crookedness.
9. A house divided against itself cannot stand.
10. Deceived by his friends, he lost all hope.
11. The man carrying a hoe is a gardener.
12. One man's meat is another man's poison.
13. My days among the Dead are past.
14. With his white hair unbonneted, the stout old sheriff comes.

4. We have seen that the Predicate may consist of one word or several words.

When the Predicate consists of one word that word is always a Verb, because we cannot *say* anything without using a saying-word, *i.e.*, a Verb. (See sentence 1 in § 1)

When the Predicate consists of several words, the essential word in the Predicate is always a Verb. (As the Verb is the essential word in the Predicate it is sometimes called the Predicate-word.)

5. Just as the Subject-word may be qualified by an Adjective or Adjective-equivalent, the Verb in the Predicate may be qualified by an Adverb or Adverb-equivalent*, called, in analysis, its **Extension** or **Adverbial Qualification** ; as,

1. The flames spread everywhere.
2. He went home.
3. He rose to go.
4. The flames spread in every direction.
5. Spring advancing, the swallows appear.

No.	SUBJECT		PREDICATE	
	Subject-word	***Attribute***	***Verb***	***Adverbial Qualification***
1	flames	The	spread	everywhere
2	He		went	home
3	He		rose	to go
4	flames	The	spread	in every direction
5	swallows	The	appear	Spring advancing

It will be noted that—

in 1, the Adverbial Qualification is an Adverb ;
in 2, the Adverbial Qualification is an Adverbial Accusative ;
in 3, the Adverbial Qualification is a Gerundial Infinitive ;
in 4, the Adverbial Qualification is a group of words doing the work of an Adverb ;
in 5, the Adverbial Qualification is an Absolute Phrase.

EXERCISE 3

Point out the Adverbial Qualification in each of the following sentences and say whether it is an Adverb, an Adverbial Accusative, a Gerundial Infinitive, a group of words doing the work of an Adverb, or an Absolute Phrase.

1. She spoke distinctly.
2. He spoke in a distinct voice.
3. The boy ran a mile.
4. The postman called again.
5. He has come to stay.
6. Wait a minute.
7. The book is printed in clear type.
8. I recognized your voice at once.
9. Help a lame dog over a stile.

10. The tide having turned, the ship set sail.
11. He sold his horse below its value.
12. He leaves two children behind him.
13. He gets his living by trade.
14. He made his money by trade.
15. The enemy disputed the ground inch by inch.
16. He saw a new world spread about him.
17. The village life suited him in all respects.
18. Him will I follow to the ends of the earth.

6. When the Verb in the Predicate is an Intransitive Verb, it alone can form the Predicate ; as,

1. Dogs / bark. 2. Black clouds / are gathering 3. The boys / have been reading.

*A word or group of words which does the work of an Adjective is called an Adjective-equivalent.

Note— In sentence 1, the Verb consists of only one word. Often the Verb itself consists of a group of two or more words, as in 2 and 3.

7. Sometimes the Verb in the Predicate is an Intransitive Verb of Incomplete Predication, that is, an Intransitive Verb which requires a Noun, or an Adjective, or a Pronoun, etc., added to it to make the Predicate complete ; as,

The baby seems/happy.

If I simply say 'The baby seems' I do not make complete sense. The Intransitive Verb *seems* requires some word or words to make the Predicate complete.

What is thus required to complete the Predicate is called a **Complement.**

The Complement of an Intransitive Verb serves to describe the Subject, and is therefore called a **Subjective Complement.**

Now examine the Predicates in the following sentences.

1. The sky grew dark.
2. Venus is a planet.
3. It is me.
4. The man seems worried.
5. Your book is there.
6. The house is to let.
7. The building is in a dilapidated condition.

No.	SUBJECT		PREDICATE	
	Subject-word	***Attribute***	***Verb***	***Complement***
1	sky	The	grew	dark
2	Venus		is	a planet
3	It		is	me
4	man	The	seems	worried
5	book	Your	is	there
6	house	The	is	to let
7	building	The	is	in a dilapidated condition

It will be noticed that—

in 1, the Complement is an Adjective ;
in 2, the Complement is a Noun ;
in 3, the Complement is a Pronoun ;
in 4, the Complement is a Participle ;
in 5, the Complement is an Adverb ;
in 6, the Complement is an Infinitive ;
in 7, the Complement is a group of words doing the work of an Adjective.

Note— When the Predicate is completed by an Adjective, such an Adjective is said to be used Predicatively or to be a Predicative Adjective.

When the Predicate is completed by a Noun, the Noun is said to be a **Predicative Noun.**

EXERCISE 4

Pick out the Complement in each of the following sentences, and say whether it is a Noun, an Adjective, a Pronoun, etc.

1. John became a soldier.
2. Roses smell sweet.
3. The child appears pleased.
4. The workman seems tired.
5. The earth is round.

6. He looks happy.
7. Sugar tastes sweet.
8. The old woman is dead.
9. The weather was cold.
10. He became unconscious.

11. The old gentleman is of a gentle disposition.
12. The child is there.
13. The children look healthy.
14. Today she seems sad.
15. The cup is full to the brim.
16. His grammar is shocking.
17. He is a good type of the modern athlete.

18. Ugly rumours are about.
19. Gentle Evangeline was the pride of the village.
20. This morning he seemed in good spirits.
21. Giving to the poor is lending to the Lord.
22. The matter appears of considerable importance.
23. Every man is the architect of his own fortune.

8. Sometimes the Verb in the Predicate is a Transitive Verb, that is, a Verb which requires an Object to complete its sense.

For example, if I say 'Cats catch' I do not make complete sense. You want to know what the cats *catch.* The verb *catch* requires an Object, such as *mice,* to form a complete Predicate.

Now examine the Predicates in the following sentences.

1. Birds build nests.
2. I know him.
3. All good children pity the poor.
4. The Gurkhas love fighting.
5. The foolish crow tried to sing.
6. Our soldiers tried to scale the cliff.

No.	SUBJECT		PREDICATE	
	Subject-word	***Attribute***	***Verb***	***Object***
1	Birds	(1) All	build	nests
2	I	(2) good	know	him
3	children	The	pity	the poor
4	Gurkhas	(1) The	love	fighting
5	crow	(2) foolish	tried	to sing
6	soldiers	Our	tried	to scale the cliff

It will be noticed that—
in 1, the Object is a Noun ;
in 2, the Object is a Pronoun ;
in 3, the Object is an Adjective used as a Noun ;
in 4, the Object is a Gerund or Verbal Noun ;
in 5, the Object is an Infinitive ;
in 6, the Object is a group of words doing the work of a Noun.

9. The Object-word may have Attributes, just like the Subject-word ; as,
He shot a big panther.

SUBJECT	PREDICATE		
	Verb	***Object***	***Attribute***
He	shot	panther	(1) a (2) big

EXERCISE 5

In the following sentences point out the complete Object; then separate the Object-word from its attributes (if any).

1. The world knows nothing of its greatest men.
2. We should learn to govern ourselves.

3. Her arms across her breast she laid.
4. The architect drew a plan for the house.
5. Serpents cast their skin once a year.
6. God tempers the wind to the shorn lamb.
7. By their fruits ye shall know them.
8. Rock the baby to sleep.
9. He enjoys his master's confidence.

10. I recognized your voice at once.
11. Cut your coat according to your cloth.
12. The Eskimos make houses of snow and ice.
13. I had no answer to my letter.
14. The curfew tolls the knell of parting day.
15. Fear no more the heat of the sun.
16. Evil communications corrupt good manners.

10. Sometimes the Verb in the Predicate is a Transitive Verb that takes *two* Objects—a Direct Object and an Indirect Object.

If I say 'Rama gave a penknife', the noun *penknife* is the Object of the verb *gave.*

I may, however, by way of further information, say *to whom* Rama gave a penknife. Rama gave *me* a penknife.

The word *me* is called the **Indirect Object** of the Verb *gave* to distinguish it from the Object *penknife,* which is the **Direct Object.**

Now examine the Predicate in the following sentences.

I promised him a present.

He teaches us Geometry.

Father bought Mini a doll.

SUBJECT	PREDICATE		
	Verb	*Indirect Object*	*Direct Object*
I	promised	him	a present
He	teaches	us	Geometry
Father	bought	Mini	a doll

11. Some Transitive Verbs require a Complement in addition to the Object ; as,

The boys made Rama captain.

Here the noun *Rama* is the Object of the Transitive Verb *made* which here requires a word (*e.g., captain*) to make the sense complete.

If I say 'The boys made a snow-ball' the sense is complete. But it would be nonsense to say 'The boys made Rama.' The boys did not make Rama : they made Rama *captain.* The verb *made* is here a Transitive Verb of Incomplete Predication, because in the sense in which the verb *made* is here used, it cannot form a complete predicate unless it has a Complement besides an Object.

The Complement (*captain*) here refers to the Object *Rama.* It is therefore called an **Objective Complement.**

Now examine the Predicates in the following sentences.

1. The jury found him guilty.
2. His parents named him Hari.
3. He kept us waiting.
4. Nothing will make him repent.
5. His words filled them with terror.

No.	SUBJECT		PREDICATE		
	Subject-word	*Attribute*	*Verb*	*Object*	*Complement*
1	jury	The	found	him	guilty
2	parents	His	named	him	Hari
3	He		kept	us	waiting
4	Nothing		will make	him	repent
5	words	His	filled	them	with terror

EXERCISE 6

In the following sentences separate the Predicate from the Subject and then point out the different parts of the Predicate.

1. Abdul called his cousin a fool.
2. Exercise has made his muscles strong.
3. This will make you happy.
4. The Nawab appointed his own brother Vizier.
5. The Court appointed him guardian of the orphan child.
6. Time makes the worst enemies friends.
7. Sickness made the child irritable.
8. They elected him secretary of the club.
9. Do you take me for a fool ?
10. We saw the storm approaching.
11. I consider the man trustworthy.
12. They kept us in suspense.
13. The jury found him guilty of murder.
14. A thunderstorm often turns milk sour.

12. Let us now review the different forms of the Predicate.

(1) When the verb is Intransitive, the Predicate may consist of the verb alone (§ 6).

(2) When the verb is an Intransitive Verb of Incomplete Predication, the Predicate may consist of the Verb and its Complement (§ 7).

(3) When the verb is a Transitive Verb, the Predicate may consist of the Verb and its Object. (§ 8).

(4) When the verb is a Transitive Verb having two objects, the predicate may consist of the Verb and its two Objects —Indirect and Direct. (§ 10)

(5) When the verb is a Transitive Verb of Incomplete Predication, the Predicate may consist of the Verb, its Object and a Complement. (§ 11)

13. Carefully study the analysis of the following sentences :

The table is printed on page 156.

1. Abdul, quite pale with fright, rushed into the room.
2. Determination to do one's duty is laudable.
3. Around the fire, one wintry night,
   The farmer's rosy children sat.
4. Home they brought the warrior dead.
5. His friends elected him secretary of the club.
6. This circumstance certainly makes the matter very serious.
7. My uncle has been teaching me mathematics.
8. Jaffar, the Barmecide, the good Vizier,
   The poor man's hope, the friend without a peer,
   Jaffar was dead, slain by a doom unjust.
9. Who are you ?

EXERCISE 7

Analyse the following sentences.

1. A nod from a lord is breakfast for a fool.
2. A good paymaster never wants workmen.
3. Home they brought her warrior dead.
4. Sickness made the child irritable.
5. Gentle Evangeline was the pride of the village.
6. It is easy to find fault.
7. It is a miserable thing to live in suspense.
8. Wounds made by words are hard to heal.
9. Down went the Royal George.
10. Into the valley of death rode the six hundred.
11. Time makes the worst enemies friends.
12. Great is your reward in Heaven.

No.	SUBJECT		PREDICATE			
	Subject-word	*Attribute*	*Verb*	*Object*	*Complement*	*Adverbial Qualification*
1	Abdul	quite pale with fright	rushed			into the room
2	Determination	to do one's duty	is		laudable	
3	children	(1) the farmer's	sat			(1) Around the fire
		(2) rosy				(2) one wintry night
4	they		brought	the warrior dead		Home
5	friends	His	elected	him	secretary of the club	
6	circumstance	This	makes	the matter	very serious	certainly
			has	(1) mathematics		
7	uncle	My	been	(Direct)		
			teaching	(2) me		
				(Indirect)		
		(1) the Barmecide				
		(2) the good Vizier				
8	Jaffar	(3) the poor man's hope	was		dead	slain by a doom unjust
		(4) the friend without a peer				
9	you		are		Who	

Note:— It will be noticed that we have placed together in one column the Object-word and its Attributes.

13. In him India lost a true patriot.
14. The proof of the pudding is in the eating.
15. It is easy to be wise after the event.
16. A man he was to all the country dear.
17. Experience has taught us many lessons.
18. A man's first care should be to avoid the reproaches of his own heart.
19. All work and no play makes Jack a dull boy.
20. He showed a constant solicitude for his son's welfare.
21. Caesar, having conquered his enemies, returned to Rome.
22. To drive a car requires care and skill.
23. A great fortune in the hands of a fool is a great misfortune.
24. The postman looked very tired at the end of the day.

Note— In 6, "It" is a provisional subject ; the real subject is "to find fault". "It" should be entered in the subject-column in brackets.

"It" is a provisional subject in 7 and 15 also.

Chapter 2 PHRASES

I. Adjective Phrases

14. We have seen that sometimes a *group* of words does the work of an adjective (§ 3). Now examine the following pairs of sentences:

1. (*a*) The vizier was a *wealthy* man.
   (*b*) The vizier was a man *of great wealth.*
2. (*a*) The magistrate was a *kind* man.
   (*b*) The magistrate was a man *with a kindly nature.*
3. (*a*) The chief lived in a *stone* house.
   (*b*) The chief lived in a house *built of stone.*
4. (*a*) I like to see a *smiling* face.
   (*b*) I like to see a face *with a smile on it.*
5. (*a*) The coolies belonged to a *hill* tribe.
   (*b*) The coolies belonged to a tribe *dwelling in the hills.*

In each of the above pairs of sentences, we have first a *single word* describing the person or thing denoted by the noun, and then *a group of words* describing the person or thing denoted by the same noun.

For instance, the group of words *of great wealth* tells us what sort of *man* the vizier was. It qualifies the noun *man* just as an Adjective does. It therefore *does the work of an Adjective* and is called an **Adjective Phrase.**

Def— An Adjective Phrase is a group of words that *does the work of an Adjective.*

15. Study the following Adjectives and the Adjective Phrases that are equivalent to them.

Adjectives	**Adjective Phrases**
A *golden* crown.	A crown *made of gold.*
A *purple* cloak.	A cloak *of purple colour.*
A *white* elephant.	An elephant *with a white skin.*
A *jungle* track.	A track *through the jungle.*
A *blue-eyed* boy.	A boy *with blue eyes.*
A *deserted* village.	A village *without any inhabitants.*
A *blank* page.	A page *with no writing on it.*
The *longest* day.	The day *of greatest length.*
The *Spanish* flag.	The flag *of Spain.*
A *heavy* load.	A load *of great weight.*

EXERCISE 8

Pick out the Adjective Phrases in the following sentences.

1. A man in great difficulties came to me for help.
2. He is a person of very considerable renown.
3. Wild beasts in small cages are a sorry sight.
4. A man without an enemy is a man with few friends.
5. He tells a tale with the ring of truth in it.
6. A friend in need is a friend indeed.
7. A stitch in time saves nine.
8. A bird in the hand is worth two in the bush.

9. Gardens with cool shady trees surround the village.
10. Only a man with plenty of money buys a car of such beauty and power.
11. In a low voice he told the tale of his cruel wrongs.
12. Do you know the story of the noble Padmini ?
13. He was a lad of great promise.
14. He bore a banner with a strange device.
15. The police arrested a man of one of the criminal tribes.

EXERCISE 9

In each of the following sentences replace the Adjective in italics by an Adjective Phrase of the same meaning.

1. A *grey* cloud spread over the sky.
2. He dwelt in a *wooden* hut.
3. He had a *bald* head.
4. She wore a *diamond* necklace.
5. It was a *horrible* night.
6. They went by *Siberian* railway.
7. A *grassy* meadow stretched before us.
8. An *earthen* pitcher stood on a *three-legged* table.
9. The *French* flag flew at the top of the *highest* mast.
10. That was a *cowardly* act.
11. He is *well.*
12. A *valuable* ring was found yesterday.
13. *Heroic* deeds deserve our admiration.
14. Much has been said about the *Swiss* scenery.
15. *Numerical* superiority is a great advantage.
16. The Rajputs were *passionately* fond of martial glory.
17. I have passed two *sleepless* nights.
18. He is a *professional* cricketer.
19. This book contains many *biblical* quotations.
20. She wants *medical* advice.
21. A *tall* soldier stepped forth.

EXERCISE 10

Replace each of the following Adjective Phrases in italics by an Adjective of the same meaning.

1. He wore a turban *made of silk.*
2. He has done a deed *of shame.*
3. He led a life *devoid of blame.*
4. He is a man *without a friend.*
5. They came to a path *covered with mud.*
6. He carried a sword stained with *blood.*
7. I met a little girl *from a cottage.*
8. Balu was a man *with plenty of impudence.*
9. From this village *in the mountains* came a chieftain *of great fame.*

10. The Rajput leader was a soldier full of *hope* and *free from fear.*
11. Nelson was a boy *without fear.*
12. Nobody likes a person *with a bad temper.*
13. I admit that he is a man *of sense.*
14. The tops *of the mountains* were covered with snow.
15. He is an author *of great versatility.*
16. It is *of no use.*

Note—Not all Adjective Phrases can be replaced by Adjectives. For instance :

He never felt the witchery *of the soft blue sky.*

EXERCISE 11

Fill in the blanks with suitable Adjective Phrases.

1. An elephant ____ is considered sacred by some people.
2. Birds ____ flock together.
3. He leads a life ____.
4. Children like books ____.
5. He lost a diamond ____
6. The old sage spoke words ____.
7. She is a woman ____.
8. John Gilpin was a citizen ____.
9. Draw a picture ____.

10. The leaves ____ are glossy.
11. We heard the sound ____.
12. Listen to the sound ____.
13. The verdict ____ was in his favour.
14. The doors ____ closed upon him.
15. The water ____ is very deep.
16. The road ____ is very muddy.
17. The proprietor ____ died yesterday.
18. The paths ____ lead but to the grave.

EXERCISE 12

Write five sentences containing Adjective Phrases.

II. Adverb Phrases

16. Just as the work of an Adjective is often done by a group of words called an Adjective Phrase, so the work of an Adverb is often done by a group of words.

Study the following pairs of sentences carefully.

1. (*a*) Rama ran *quickly.* (*How* ?)
   (*b*) Rama ran *with great speed.* (*How* ?)
2. (*a*) He answered *rudely.* (*How* ?)
   (*b*) He answered *in a very rude manner.* (*How* ?)
3. (*a*) He does his work *carelessly.* (*How* ?)
   (*b*) He does his work *without any care.* (*How* ?)
4. (*a*) He is coming *now* (*When* ?)
   (*b*) He is coming *at this very moment.* (*When* ?)
5. (*a*) No such diseases were known *then.* (*When* ?)
   (*b*) No such diseases were known *in those days.* (*When* ?)
6. (*a*) The arrow fell *here.* (*Where* ?)
   (*b*) The arrow fell *on this spot.* (*Where* ?)
7. (*a*) You can buy it *everywhere.* (*Where* ?)
   (*b*) You can buy it *in all places.* (*Where* ?)
8. (*a*) He fell *down.* (*Where* ?)
   (*b*) He fell *to the ground.* (*Where* ?)

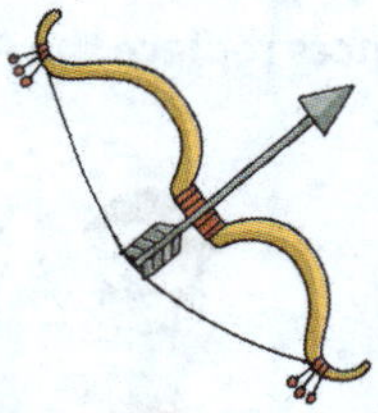

In each of the above pairs of sentences we have first a *single word* (an Adverb) modifying a verb, and then a *group of words* modifying a verb in the same way.

For instance, the group of words *with great speed* tells us how Rama *ran.* It modifies the verb *ran* just as the Adverb *quickly* does. It therefore *does the work of an Adverb* and is called an **Adverb Phrase.**

Def — An Adverb Phrase is a group of words that does the work of an Adverb.

Note—An Adverb Phrase, like an Adverb, may modify also an Adjective or Adverb : as,
Quinine is good for malaria.
I have done well on the whole.

17. Study the following Adverbs and the Adverb Phrases that are equivalent to them.

Adverbs	*Adverb Phrases*
Bravely	In a brave manner, *or* with bravery.
Unwisely	In an unwise manner, *or* without wisdom.
Swiftly	In a swift manner, *or* with swiftness.
Beautifully	In a beautiful style.
Formerly	In former times, *or* once upon a time.
Recently	Just now, *or* at a recent date.
Soon	Before very long, *or* at an early date.
There	At that place.
Away	To another place.
Abroad	To (in) a foreign country.

EXERCISE 13

Pick out the Adverb Phrases in the following sentences.

1. She lived in the middle of a great wood.
2. Nothing can live on the moon.
3. Come into the garden, Maud.
4. Three fishers went sailing over the sea.

5. O'er her hangs the great dark bell.
6. Down in a green and shady bed, a modest violet grew.
7. On your conscience this will lie.
8. They sat for a while on the bank.
9. Honesty is written on his face.
10. The gun went off with a loud report.
11. There dwelt a miller hale and bold, beside the river Dee.
12. I stood on the bridge at midnight.
13. To the northward stretched the desert.
14. Beside a green meadow a stream used to flow.
15. I have read Bacon to my great profit.
16. In her ear he whispers gaily.
17. Beside the ungathered rice he lay.
18. They fought to the last man.
19. He persevered in the face of all obstacles.
20. The shoe is pressing on my toe.
21. Keep him at arm's length.
22. Make yourself at home.
23. It must be done at any price.
24. Pauperism increases at a fearful rate.
25. He has painted him in his proper colours.
26. He has his finger on the pulse of the nation.
27. He lives by his pen.
28. The shepherd shouted to them at the top of his voice.
29. He strove with all his might to escape.
30. Without pausing to consider, he struck the blow.
31. Much water has run under the bridge since then.

EXERCISE 14

In each of the following sentences replace the Adverb in italics by an Adverb Phrase of the same meaning.

1. The pigeon flies *swiftly*.
2. Did Rama behave *well*?
3. Go *away*.
4. The dying man replied *feebly*.
5. *Gently* fell the rain.
6. We will pitch the tents just *here*.
7. He expects to get promotion *soon*.
8. He built his house *there*.
9. They have only *recently* arrived.

10. Although hungry, the soldiers worked *cheerfully*.
11. He spoke *eloquently*.
12. *Soon* the sun will set.
13. Do your work *thoroughly*.
14. They were *hurrying* homeward.
15. The door was *suspiciously* open.
16. *Formerly* he worked at the School of Economics.
17. He tried *hard*.

EXERCISE 15

Replace each of the following Adverb Phrases by an Adverb of the same meaning.

1. The bodies were mangled *in a terrible manner*.
2. Let us cease work *from this very moment*.
3. It was just *on this spot* that he died.
4. The child replied *with perfect truthfulness*.
5. He arrived *at that moment*.
6. I hope that he will come *at a very early date*.
7. He seems to have acted *with great promptitude*.
8. No one would dare to answer him *in an impudent way*.

9. I accept your statement *without reserve*.
10. I thank you with *all my heart*.
11. He succeeded *in the long run*.
12. He is ignorant *to a proverb*.
13. The post-boy drove *with fierce career*.
14. He has been painted *in his proper colours*.
15. The wind blew *with great violence*.
16. He has proved his case *to my satisfaction*.

Note—Not all Adverb Phrases can be replaced by Adverbs. For instance :—

I took him on the strength of your recommendation.

EXERCISE 16

Fill in the blanks with suitable Adverb Phrases.

1. The knight fought ____.
2. The Rajah treated his vizier ____.
3. The woodman struck the wolf ____.
4. Do not answer ____.
5. I agree ____.
6. He has behaved ____.
7. He does his homework ____.
8. He treated his relatives ____.
9. The police handled the bombs ____.
10. The sailor climbed ____.
11. That happened ____.
12. He reached school ____.
13. He does his homework ____.
14. He failed ____.
15. Old Mother Hubbard went ____.

EXERCISE 17

Write five sentences containing Adverb Phrases.

18. Compare

1. The crowd *in the bazaar* was very noisy.
2. The crowd halted *in the bazaar.*

In sentence 1, the phrase *in the bazaar* tells us *which* crowd was very noisy ; that is, it qualifies the noun *crowd.* It is therefore an Adjective Phrase.

In sentence 2, the phrase *in the bazaar* tells us *where* the crowd halted ; that is, it modifies the verb *halted.* It is therefore an Adverb Phrase.

Hence we see that the same phrase may be an Adjective Phrase in one sentence and an Adverb Phrase in another sentence.

We cannot say what kind of Phrase a given Phrase is until we examine *the work which it does in a sentence.*

EXERCISE 18

Say which of the following are Adverb Phrases and which are Adjective Phrases.

1. Have you heard of the man *in the moon* ?
2. How could a man be *in the moon* ?
3. They live *on an island.*
4. A house *on an island* was washed away.

5. Awful is the gloom *beneath her.*
6. Then why did she look *beneath her* ?
7. Is this the train *to Peshawar* ?
8. It usually goes *to Peshawar, Sir.*

EXERCISE 19

Use the following Phrases in sentences.

in a loud voice ; without further delay ; with one voice ; for certain ; just in time up in arms ; of no consequence ; out of fashion ; with great satisfaction ; in the twinkling of an eye ; on either side of the street ; in a shady nook ; to the last man ; with a smile ; at sixes and sevens ; at the eleventh hour ; on the top of the hill ; in future ; at nine o'clock.

III. Noun Phrases

19. Examine the following sentences.

1. The boy wants *something.*
2. The boy wants *to go home.*

The word *something* is a Noun and it is the Object of the verb *wants,* in sentence 1. Similarly the group of words, *to go home,* is the Object of the verb *wants,* in sentence 2. Hence this group of words *does the work of a Noun.* The group of words, *to go home,* is therefore a **Noun Phrase.**

Def.—A Noun Phrase is a group of words that does the work of a Noun.

Further examples of Noun Phrases:

Early to bed is a good maxim.
We enjoy *playing cricket.*
Did you enjoy *reading this book* ?
To win a prize is my ambition.

He hopes *to win the first prize.*
He loves *to issue harsh orders.*
I tried *to get the sum right.*
Standing about in a cold wet wind did me no good.

EXERCISE 20

Pick out the Noun Phrases in the following sentences.

1. His father wished to speak to the Headmaster.
2. The wicked vizier loves getting people into trouble.
3. The poor debtor intended to pay back every penny of the money.
4. He dislikes having to punish his servants.
5. Horses prefer living in dark stables.
6. I should hate to do such a thing.

7. Have you ever tried climbing a coconut palm ?
8. Thinking good thoughts precedes good actions.
9. He refuses to answer the question.
10. To write such rubbish is disgraceful.
11. Promise to come again.
12. Why do you like visiting such a man ?
13. Travelling in a hot dusty train gives me no pleasure.
14. He denies stealing the money.
15. Your doing such a thing surprises me.

EXERCISE 21

Supply a Noun Phrase.

1. I want ____.
2. ____delights me.
3. We all hope ____.
4. Pretend ____.
5. ____seems dishonest.
6. ____surprised my mother.
7. Do you wish ____?
8. My father hates ____.
9. ____gives me no pleasure.
10. I don't intend ____.
11. ____is not easy.
12. I do not expect ____.
13. I enjoy ____.
14. He wishes ____.
15. Cats like ____.
16. His father promised ____.

EXERCISE 22

Pick out the Phrases and say whether they are Adjective Phrases, Adverb Phrases, or Noun Phrases.

1. He speaks like a born orator.
2. It grieved me to hear of your illness.
3. Beyond a doubt this man is honest.
4. He failed in spite of his best efforts.
5. He won the prize by means of trickery.
6. Do not talk like that.
7. I have forgotten how to play this game.
8. He gained their affection in spite of many faults.
9. I do not expect such treatment at your hands.
10. He speaks too fast to be understood.
11. I do not know what to do.
12. I do not understand how to solve this problem.
13. He persevered amidst many difficulties.
14. He succeeded in the long run.
15. Birds of a feather flock together.
16. This is a matter of no importance.
17. The train is behind time.
18. He is a man of means.
19. It lies near his heart.

20. He keeps the necklace under lock and key.
21. He is a person of no importance.
22. I want to go to the cinema to-day.
23. I love to hear the watch-dog's honest bark.
24. I did it of my own free will.
25. Show me how to do it.
26. His car ran over a dog.
27. Things are in a bad way.
28. She is a woman of wonderful patience.
29. I have found the key to his secret.
30. The plan has the virtue of committing us to nothing.
31. I don't see the point of the story.
32. How to find the way to the ruins is the question.
33. Tubal Cain was a man of might.
34. He did it against his will.
35. I have no time to waste on trifles.
36. Don't do things by halves.
37. I enjoy walking in the fields.

Chapter 3 CLAUSES

I. Adverb Clauses

20. Look at the groups of words in italics in the following sentences.

1. They rested *at sunset.* [Rested *when* ?]
2. They rested *when evening came.* [Rested *when* ?]

It is evident that both the groups of words in italics, in 1 and 2, do the work of an Adverb as they modifiy the verb *rested,* showing when the action was performed.

We at once recognize the first group of words, *at sunset,* as an Adverb Phrase. Is the second group of words, *when evening came,* also an Adverb Phrase ?

No, it is not a Phrase for, unlike a Phrase, it has a Subject *(evening)* and a Predicate (*came when*) of its own, and is thus like a sentence. But though like a sentence it is part of a sentence.

Such a group of words that forms part of a sentence, and has a Subject and a Predicate of its own, is called a **Clause.**

Since the Clause, *when evening came,* does the work of an Adverb, it is called an **Adverb Clause.**

Def.—An Adverb Clause is a group of words which contains a Subject and a Predicate of its own, and does the work of an Adverb.

EXERCISE 23

Pick out the Adverb Clauses in the following sentences.

1. You may sit wherever you like.
2. He fled where his pursuers could not follow.
3. He behaves as one might expect him to do.
4. Because you have done this I shall punish you.
5. As he was not there, I spoke to his brother.
6. If you eat too much you will be ill.
7. He finished first though he began late.
8. Will you wait till I return ?
9. Just as he entered the room the clock struck.
10. They went where living was cheaper.
11. He does not always speak as he thinks.
12. Take a lamp because the night is dark.

13. I do it because I choose to.
14. If I make a promise I keep it.
15. You will pass if you work hard.
16. He advanced as far as he dared.
17. I forgive you since you repent.
18. I shall remain where I am.
19. We shall wait here until you come.
20. When I was younger, I thought so.
21. It was so dark that you could not see your hand.
22. Wherever one goes, one hears the same story.
23. If you do not hurry you will miss the train.
24. Since you have already decided, why do you ask my opinion ?

EXERCISE 24

Supply suitable Adverb Clauses.

1. Do not go ____.
2. He is not so clever ____.
3. I was so hurried ____.
4. He ran so fast ____.
5. He always does ____.
6. He spoke so low ____.
7. I shall do nothing ____.
8. Fools rush in ____.
9. Nobody likes him ____.
10. Open rebuke is better____.
11. He will succeed ____.
12. Make hay ____.
13. He is so busy ____.
14. Do not come ____.
15. The boy went out to play ____.
16. He does ____.
17. He always comes ____.
18. He did ____.
19. She sings exactly ____.
20. The earth is larger ____.
21. His father died ____.
22. He cannot see ____.
23. Do you work well ____.
24. I found my books____.
25. I will not go out ____.
26. You will succeed or fail ____.
27. Arithmetic is less difficult ____.
28. We shall miss the train ____..
29. Do_____.

21. Examine the following sentences.

1. The stolen property was found *in the dacoits' hiding place.*
2. The stolen property was found *where the dacoits were accustomed to hide.*

It will be noticed that both the groups of words in italics do the work of an Adverb.

But the group of words in italics in sentence 2 is a Clause, because it has a subject (*the dacoits*) and a Predicate (*were accustomed to hide where*) of its own; while the group of words in italics in sentence 1 is a Phrase.

We further notice that the Adverb Phrase, *in the dacoits' hiding place,* is equivalent to the Adverb Clause, *where the dacoits were accustomed to hiding,* and can therefore be replaced by it.

EXERCISE 25

In each of the following sentences replace each Adverb Phrase by an Adverb Clause.

1. On his return we asked him many questions.
2. Do it to the best of your ability.
3. The prince was met on his arrival by his secretary.
4. In spite of poverty he became distinguished.
5. Upon seeing the signal the troops set out.
6. Nobody must expect to become rich without hard work.
7. They were very grateful to him for his kindness.
8. In comparison with air water is heavy.
9. The weather is too bright to last.
10. My heart is too full for words.
11. The work is too much for any man to do single-handed.
12. With a view to early retirement he saved his money.
13. In the event of the president's death the vice-president succeeds him.
14. He always carried out his duties according to instructions.
15. The price is high for an old car.
16. He ran with all his might.
17. After such hard work, he requires a long rest.
18. He was base enough to accept the dishonourable terms.
19. Many ships were so shattered as to be wholly unmanageable.
20. A rose by any other name would smell as sweet.

EXERCISE 26

In each of the following sentences, replace each Adverb Clause by an Adverb or Adverb Phrase.

1. I have not been well since I returned from Chennai.
2. When the sun set he returned home.
3. They fought as heroes do.
4. When the righteous rule, the people rejoice.
5. Though I am poor, yet am I contented.
6. We have come so that we may help you.
7. When he entered the room he saw the vase broken.
8. The thief crept as a jackal does.
9. I am glad that he has recovered from his illness.
10. He works hard so that he may become rich.
11. He worked so hard that he succeeded.
12. As soon as I saw the cobra I ran away.
13. We ran so that we might arrive in time.
14. He jested even as he lay dying.
15. No man can become a great artist unless he applies himself continually to his art.
16. There was nothing he would not do if only he might make profit.
17. He was not so rich that he could buy a motor-car.
18. When he had uttered these words he sat down.
19. This exercise is so difficult that I cannot do it.
20. The news is so good that it cannot be true.
21. I did not pay him, as I had no money with me.
22. He lived carefully so that he might live long.
23. The steamer will leave as soon as the mails arrive.
24. He may go home after his work is finished.
25. As he was sick, he remained at home.
26. He was punished as he deserved.
27. This sum is right so far as the working is concerned.
28. It rained so hard that the streets were flooded.
29. I took him because you recommended him.
30. My parents were poor though they were of noble birth.
31. He refuses to work whatever I may say.
32. We will do the work as well as we can.
33. Robinson Crusoe was puzzled when he discovered the print of a foot on the sand.
34. Apollo was worshipped as long as the Roman Empire lasted.
35. He thought himself rich though his income was only Rs. 30,000 annually.
36. We are kind to you because you are kind to us.
37. The passage is so difficult that I cannot comprehend it.

II. Adjective Clauses

22. Look at the group of words in italics in the following sentences.

1. The umbrella *with a broken handle* is mine. [*Which* umbrella?]
2. The umbrella *which has a broken handle* is mine. [*Which* umbrella?]

The first group of words, *with a broken handle,* describes the umbrella ; that is, it qualifies the noun *umbrella,* and does the work of an Adjective. It is what we call an Adjective phrase.

The second group of words *which has a broken handle,* also describes the umbrella and so does the work of an Adjective. But because it contains a Subject and a Predicate of its own, it is called an **Adjective Clause.**

Def — An Adjective Clause is a group of words which contains a Subject and a Predicate of its own, and does the work of an Adjective.

EXERCISE 27

Pick out the Adjective Clauses in the following sentences, and tell what noun or pronoun each qualifies.

1. Mary had a little lamb whose fleece was white as snow.
2. The letter brought money which was badly needed.
3. The house that I live in belongs to my father.
4. I am monarch of all I survey.
5. I have a little shadow which goes in and out with me.
6. The dog that bites does not bark.
7. He tells a tale that sounds untrue.
8. It's an ill wind that blows nobody any good.
9. The boy stood on the burning deck whence all but he had fled.
10. They never fail who die in a great cause.
11. I remember the house where I was born.
12. He that climbs too high is sure to fall.
13. Here is the book you want.
14. Heaven helps those who help themselves.
15. He died in the village where he was born.
16. He never does anything that is silly.
17. People who live in glass houses should not throw stones.
18. It is a long lane that has no turning.
19. He laughs best who laughs last.
20. Thrice is he armed that hath his quarrel just.

EXERCISE 28

Supply suitable Adjective Clauses.

1. I know the place _____.
2. He is the man _____.
3. The house _____ is a hundred years old.
4. His offence is one _____.
5. Where is the book _____?
6. Boys _____ will not be promoted.
7. He has lost the book _____.
8. I found the book _____.
9. I know the man _____.
10. No man _____ shall suffer in any way.
11. The boy _____ gained the prize.
12. Students _____ get good marks.
13. Water _____ should be kept in a covered jar.
14. Any boy _____ will be punished.
15. He went away by the train _____.

23. Examine the following sentences.

    1. He met a girl *with blue eyes.*
    2. He met a girl *whose eyes were blue.*

The group of words, *with blue eyes,* qualifies the noun *girl.*

The group of words, *whose eyes were blue,* also qualifies the noun *girl.*

Hence both these groups of words do the work of an Adjective.

But the group of words, *with blue eyes,* is a Phrase, while the group of words, *whose eyes were blue,* is a Clause.

We further notice that the Adjective Phrase, *with blue eyes,* is equivalent to the Adjective Clause, *whose eyes were blue,* and can therefore be replaced by it.

EXERCISE 29

In each of the following sentences, replace each Adjective Phrase by an Adjective Clause.

1. A man of industrious habits is sure to succeed.
2. He told us the time of his arrival.
3. The time for departing has now arrived.
4. Do you know the road leading to the temple?
5. I have a box, filled with almonds.
6. We all admire a man of courage.
7. A city on a hill cannot be hid.
8. The people in the gallery could not hear.
9. You can have anything of your liking.
10. The houses of the Burmee are often built of bamboo.

EXERCISE 30

In the following sentences, replace Adjective Clauses by Adjectives or Adjective Phrases.

1. Do you know the woman who is wearing a blue sari ?
2. The boy who sits near me is my cousin.
3. That was the reason why he came late.
4. The reason why he failed is obvious.

5. The workers, who were weary with their exertions, lay down to rest.
6. The sun, which at mid-day was hot, made the traveller thirsty.
7. Which is the road that leads most quickly to the station?
8. People who eat too much die early.
9. Many men who have not been trained to write become journalists.

10. This is the place where our forefathers landed.
11. The explanation he gave was not satisfactory.
12. Such men as you cannot be easily disheartened.
13. This boy, who has been industrious, has earned a prize which he has well deserved.
14. A belief which is generally held is not necessarily one which is true.
15. An author who was famous during the freedom struggle lived in that cottage which overlooks the lake.

III. Noun Clauses

24. Examine the groups of words in italics in the following sentences.

1. I expect *to get a prize.* [Expect *what?*]
2. I expect *that I shall get a prize.* [Expect *what?*]

The first group of words, *to get a prize,* does not contain a Subject and a Predicate of its own. It is therefore a phrase. This phrase is object of the verb *expect* and hence does the work of a Noun. It is therefore a Noun Phrase.

The second group of words, *that I shall get a prize,* contains a Subject and a Predicate of its own. It is therefore a clause. This Clause is the object of the verb *expect* and so does the work of a Noun. We therefore call it a **Noun Clause.**

Now examine the sentence,
That you have come pleases me.

Here the Clause, *That you have come,* is the Subject of the verb *pleases.*
It therefore does the work of a Noun, and is what we call a Noun Clause.

Def.—A Noun Clause is a group of words which contains a Subject and a Predicate of its own, and does the work of a Noun.

EXERCISE 31

Point out the Noun Clauses in the following sentences.

1. I often wonder how you are getting on.
2. I fear that I shall fail.
3. He replied that he would come.
4. Do you deny that you stole the watch ?
5. I thought that it would be a fine day.
6. That you should cheat me hurts me.
7. No one knows who he is.
8. He saw that the clock had stopped.
9. That you should say this is very strange.
10. I don't see how you can get out of this mess.
11. I earn whatever I can.
12. I do not know what he wants.
13. There were no complaints except that the day was too hot.

14. I went to see what had happened.
15. I do not understand how it all happened.
16. Pay careful attention to what I am going to say.
17. It grieved me to hear that she was ill.
18. I want to know how far it is from here.
19. Where we were to lodge that night was the problem.
20. He begged that his life might be spared.
21. I think you have made a mistake.
22. Can you guess what I want ?
23. How the burglar got in is a mystery!
24. It is uncertain whether he will come.
25. I do not know what he will do.

EXERCISE 32

Complete the following by adding suitable Noun Clauses.

1. I cannot understand _____.
2. They all said _____.
3. I think _____.
4. This is just _____.

5. He told me _____.
6. _____ is a well known fact.
7. Do you know _____?
8. I wonder _____.

9. I do not know _____.
10. Please show me_____
11. _____is quite certain.
12. I feel certain _____.
13. Tell him _____.
14. Will you tell me _____?
15. His father was anxious _____.
16. You forget _____.
17. It is certain _____.
18. Have you heard _____?
19. _____do with your might.
20. He was pleased with _____.

EXERCISE 33

In each of the following sentences, replace the words in italics by suitable Noun Clauses.

1. *The time of his coming* no one can guess.
2. I heard *of his success.*
3. *The reason of his failure* will never be known.
4. I predict *a change in the weather.*
5. The jury believed *the man guilty.*
6. We expect *an improvement in business.*
7. Who can doubt *the truth of his statement*?
8. I know *him to be trustworthy.*
9. I do not believe the *account given* by him.
10. He confessed *his guilt.*
11. He described *the attack on the camp.*
12. *The place of their meeting* was known to the police.
13. The sailor told us *the direction of the wind.*
14. *His arrival* was quite unexpected.
15. His friends hoped *for his success.*
16. I know *your great regard for him.*

EXERCISE 34

In each of the following sentences, replace each Noun Clause by a Noun or Noun Phrase.

1. I hope that I shall be there in time.
2. He is sure that we will win the match.
3. I remarked that it was a fine day.
4. They do not know where he is concealed.
5. The police must know where he is living.
6. I believe what he says.
7. Tell me what you think about this.
8. The doctor is hopeful that she will soon recover.

9. It is to be regretted that he retired from the world so early in life.
10. I do not believe what he says.
11. He showed how the problem was done.
12. It seems that he is a swindler.
13. He does not know where I live.
14. Tell me why you did this.
15. It is not known who has written this book.
16. The law will punish whosoever is guilty.

25. We have now seen that there are three kinds of Clauses:

(1) Adverb Clauses which do the work of Adverbs.
(2) Adjective Clauses which do the work of Adjectives.
(3) Noun Clauses which do the work of Nouns.

26. Examine the following sentences, and notice the work done by the Clause in each.

1. I knew *where I could find him.*
2. I went to the place *where I could* find him.
3. I went *where I could find him.*

In sentence 1, the Clause does the work of a Noun, and is the Object of the verb *know.*

In sentence 2, the Clause does the work of an Adjective, and qualifies the noun *place.*

In sentence 3, the Clause does the work of an Adverb, and modifies the verb *went.*

We thus see that the same Clause may be a Noun Clause in one sentence, an Adjective Clause in another, and an Adverb Clause in yet another.

It is therefore clear that we cannot say what kind of Clause a Clause is unless we carefully examine *the work that it does in a sentence.*

EXERCISE 35

Pick out the clause in each of the following sentences, and say what kind of clause it is, and with what word it is connected.

1. Come when you like.
2. I know the man who is here.

3. He says that he met your brother.
4. The hand that rocks the cradle rules the world.
5. Before I die I intend to see Venice.

6. Let us rejoice as we go forward.
7. I was reading a book which I had read before.
8. Perhaps he thinks that I am a fool.
9. As I drew near I saw a very curious sight.
10. Where are the friends whom I knew ?
11. Can a man live whose soul is dead ?

12. I think that he will die.
13. I want to find the man who did this.
14. He made a vow that he would fast for a week.
15. Have you heard that Rama has won the prize ?
16. It was not the vizier whom the king suspected.
17. He admitted that he wrote the letter.
18. That he will do it, I have no doubt.
19. I know the place which you mention.
20. That such a thing could happen, I do not believe.
21. When he heard this he turned very pale.
22. Have you seen the horse that he has bought ?

23. My father hopes that you will visit us.
24. He behaved as a brave man should do.
25. I will wait until the next train comes.
26. The general feared that he would be surrounded.
27. He ate when he was hungry.
28. Since he has been in hospital he has improved greatly.
29. As I was going in my father came out.
30. There came a time when he was tired of waiting.
31. He spoke of a time when wars should cease.
32. They live where the climate is good.

33. I know a place where roses grow.
34. They have gone to a land whither few travellers go.
35. The wind bloweth whither it listeth.
36. They returned whence they had come.
37. The swallows will return to the country whence such birds migrate.
38. Let none follow me to the retreat whither I now depart.
39. I refer to the year when the monsoon failed.
40. This is not the sort of place where you'll get rich in a hurry.
41. Sadly they returned to the prison whence they had so hopefully set forth that morning.
42. You will always regret the day when you did this.
43. Another occupies the seat where once I sat.
44. He has gone to that bourne whence no traveller returns.

EXERCISE 36

In each of the following sentences write a Clause in place of the words in italics, and say whether the Clause is a Noun Clause, an Adjective Clause, or an Adverb Clause.

1. He cannot find a place *to sleep in*.
2. The girl *with long hair* is my cousin.

3. Have you heard *the news ?*
4. *In spite of his efforts* he failed.
5. He walked slowly *to avoid slipping*
6. This is *my home.*
7. He cried aloud *for joy.*
8. I am surprised at *your question.*
9. He works hard *for a living.*
10. *Being lame* he has to use crutches.
11. *The sun having set,* the army stopped to rest.
12. I heard *of his arrival.*
13. *The duration of the war* is uncertain.
14. *His remarks* were not received with approval.
15. He declared *his innocence.*

Can't find
a place to
sleep in.

16. I am hopeful *of his speedy recovery.*
17. Did he explain the *purpose of his coming?*
18. He ordered *the traitor to be executed.*
19. He remarked *on the boy's impudence.*
20. *His silence* proves his guilt.
21. I cannot tell you the *date of my return.*
22. *His share in the plot* was suspected.
23. He speaks *like a born orator.*
24. *Under existing conditions* railway travel is expensive.
25. He is not so foolish *as to accept your offer.*
26. *In my old home* we had many fruit trees.
27. I promise you a holiday *on condition of* your good behaviour.

Chapter 4 SENTENCES : SIMPLE, COMPOUND AND COMPLEX

27. Examine the following sentences.

1. His courage won him honour.
2. The moon was bright and we could see our way.
3. Night came on and rain fell heavily and we all got very wet.
4. They rested when evening came.
5. As the boxers advanced into the ring, the people said they would not allow them to fight.

We see that sentence 1 has only *one* Subject and *one* Predicate. Such a sentence is called a **Simple Sentence.**

Def —A Simple sentence is one which has only *one* Subject and *one* Predicate.

[Or] A Simple sentence is one which has only *one* Finite Verb.

Sentence 2 consists of two parts :

(*i*) The moon was bright.

(*ii*) We could see our way.

These two parts are joined by the Co-ordinating Conjunction *and.*

Each part contains a Subject and a Predicate of its own. Each part is therefore a sentence which is part of a large sentence. In other words, each part is what we call a Clause.

We further notice that each Clause makes good sense by itself, and hence can stand by itself as a complete sentence. Each Clause is therefore *independent* of the other or of the *same order* or *rank,* and is called a **Principal** or **Main Clause.**

A sentence, such as the second, which is made up of Principal or Main Clauses, is called a **Compound Sentence.**

Sentence 3 consists of three Clauses of the *same order* or *rank.* In other words, sentence 3 consists of three Principal or Main Clauses, *viz:*

(*i*) Night came on.

(*ii*) Rain fell heavily.

(*iii*) We all got very wet.

Such a sentence is also called a Compound sentence.

Def —A Compound sentence is one made up of two or more Principal or Main Clauses.

Note— The term *Double* is now used for a sentence which consists of *two* principal or main clauses, and the term *Multiple* for a sentence of *more than two* principal or main clauses.

Sentence 4 consists of two parts :

(*i*) They rested. (*ii*) When evening came.

Each part contains a Subject and a Predicate of its own, and forms part of a large sentence. Each part is therefore a Clause.

We further notice that the Clause, *They rested,* makes good sense by itself, and hence can stand by itself as a complete sentence. It is therefore called the **Principal** or **Main Clause.**

The Clause, *when evening came,* cannot stand by itself and make good sense. It is dependent on the Clause, *they rested.* It is therefore called a **Dependent** or **Subordinate Clause.**

Received with thanks.

A sentence, such as the fourth, is called a **Complex Sentence.**

Sentence 5 consists of the three Clauses:

(*i*) The people said. (Main Clause)
(*ii*) As the boxers advanced into the ring. (Subordinate Adverb Clause)
(*iii*) They would not allow them to fight. (Subordinate Noun Clause)

Such a sentence is also called a Complex sentence.

Def —A Complex sentence consists of one Main Clause and one or more Subordinate Clauses.

28. Look at the following Compound sentences, and notice the Co-ordinating Conjunctions joining clauses of equal rank.

I shall do it now *or* I shall not do it at all.
He gave them no money *nor* did he help them in any way.
He threw the stone *but* it missed the dog.
He neither obtains success *nor* deserves it.
He is *either* mad *or* he has become a criminal.
I *both* thanked him *and* rewarded him.

EXERCISE 37

State which of the following sentences are Compound, and which are Complex. In the case of a Compound sentence separate the co-ordinating clauses of which it is composed, and mention the conjunction, connecting these clauses. If a sentence is Complex divide it into its clauses, and state the Principal Clause and the Subordinate Clause or clauses.

1. The horse reared and the rider was thrown.
2. Walk quickly, else you will not overtake him.
3. The town in which I live is very large.
4. I called him, but he gave me no answer.
5. I agree to your proposals, for I think them reasonable.
6. I went because I was invited.
7. Either he is drowned or some passing ship has saved him.
8. I returned home because I was tired.
9. They always talk who never think.
10. He came oftener than we expected.
11. He blushes; therefore he is guilty.
12. A guest is unwelcome when he stays too long.
13. Whatever you do, do well.
14. He must have done his duty, for he is a conscientious man.
15. He rushed into the field, and foremost fighting fell.
16. Man proposes, but God disposes.
17. Where ignorance is bliss, 'tis folly to be wise.
18. Listen carefully and take notes.
19. The heavens declare the glory of God; and the firmament showeth His handiwork.

I was invited

20. He tried hard, but he did not succeed.
21. She must weep or she will die.
22. They serve God well who serve His creatures.
23. Man is guided by reason, and beast by instinct.
24. Quarrels would not last long if the fault were only on one side.
25. God made the country and man made the town.
26. He trudged on, though he was very tired.
27. There was one philosopher who chose to live in a tub.
28. The Commons passed the bill, but the Lords threw it out.
29. Tell me the news as you have heard.
30. He that has most time has none to lose.
31. Your arguments are weighty; still they do not convince me.
32. Everything comes, if a man will only work and wait.

33. The same day went Jesus out of the house, and sat by the seaside.
34. We must eat to live, but we should not live to eat.
35. Govern your passions or they will govern you.

36. They [rats] fought the dogs, and killed the cats.
And bit the babies in the cradles,
And ate the cheese out of the vats.
And licked the soup from the cook's own ladles.
37. My heart leaps up when I behold
A rainbow in the sky.

Chapter 5 MORE ABOUT NOUN CLAUSES

29. We have seen that there are three kinds of Subordinate Clauses:
The Noun Clause, the Adjective Clause, and the Adverb Clause.

We have also seen that a Noun Clause is a subordinate clause which does the work of a noun in a Complex sentence.

30. Since a Noun Clause does the work of a Noun in a Complex sentence, it can be :

1. The Subject of a verb.
2. The Object of a transitive verb.
3. The Object of a preposition.
4. In Apposition to a Noun or Pronoun.
5. The Complement of a verb of incomplete predication.

31. In each of the following Complex sentences, the Noun Clause is the Subject of a verb:

That you should say so surprises me.
That it would rain seemed likely.
What he said was true.
When I shall return is uncertain.
How he could assist his friend was his chief concern.
Why he left is a mystery.
Whether we can start to-morrow seems uncertain.

32. In each of the following Complex sentences, the Noun Clause is the Object of a transitive verb:—

He says *that he won't go.*
I hoped *that it was true.*
She denied *that she had written the letter.*
I cannot tell *what has become of him.*
I do not know *when I shall return.*
I asked the boy *how old he was.*
Tell me *why you did this.*
Tell me *where you live.*
No one knows *who he is.*
I earn *whatever I can.*
Ask *if he is at home.*

Where do you live?

33. In each of the following Complex sentences, the Noun Clause is the Object of a preposition:

Pay careful attention to *what I am going to say.*
There is no meaning in *what you say.*
There were no complaints except *that the day was too hot.*

34. In each of the following Complex sentences, the Noun Clause is in Apposition to a Noun or Pronoun:

Your statement *that you found the money in the street* will not be believed.
His belief *that some day he would succeed* cheered him through many disappointments.
You must never forget this, *that honesty is the best policy.*
It is feared *that he will not come.*
It was unfortunate *that you were absent.*

He failed to turn up.

35. In each of the following Complex sentences, the Noun Clause is used as the Complement of a verb of incomplete predication:

My belief is *that he will not come.*
Her constant prayer was *that the child might live.*
His great fear is *that he may fail.*
My wish is *that I may please you.*
Their request will be *that they may be allowed to resign.*
Life *is what we make it.*
This is *where I live.*

36. A Clause coming after a construction consisting of an intransitive verb (particularly the verb *to be*) and an adjective does the work of a noun and is, therefore, treated as a Noun Clause.

In each of the following Complex Sentences, the Noun Clause comes after an intransitive verb construction.

The child was afraid that he would fall down.
All of us are keen that you should succeed.
They felt sorry that they lost the match.
The patient was sure that he would recover.
She did not seem hopeful that he would arrive.

It will be seen that the preposition *of, about* or *for* necessary to connect the intransitive verb construction to the succeeding Noun Clause in each of the above sentences is omitted. If we put a noun or a gerund instead of the Clause, we would say *afraid of, keen about, sorry for, sure of, hopeful of,* and the noun or gerund would be the object of the preposition in each case. The Noun Clause in each of the Complex Sentences may also be regarded as the object of the missing preposition after the intransitive verb construction. However, such Noun Clauses are often said to be used *adverbially.*

Note— From the above examples it will be seen that a Noun Clause is generally introduced by the subordinating Conjunction *that.* Sometimes, however, the Conjunction that is omitted; as I know (that) he did it.

EXERCISE 38

Write down a dozen Complex sentences, each containing a Noun Clause. Make the Noun Clause the Subject in the first three, the Object in the next three, and in Apposition to a Noun or Pronoun in the next three. Use the Noun Clause predicatively in the last three.

EXERCISE 39

Point out the Noun Clause and say whether it is the Subject of some verb, or the Object of some verb, or the complement of some verb, or in Apposition to some noun or pronoun, or the Object of some preposition.

1. Tell me how you found that out.
2. That he will succeed is certain.
3. I think you have made a mistake.
4. She says her mother is ill.
5. How long I shall stay here is doubtful.
6. I did not know that he had come.
7. It is clear that he was guilty.
8. I do not understand how it all happened.
9. Can you tell who wrote *Shakuntala*?
10. All depends on how it is done.
11. Do you deny that you stole the purse?
12. The law will punish whosoever is guilty.
13. I think I know your face.
14. Ask if dinner is ready.
15. The report that he was killed is untrue.
16. He was very hopeful that he would succeed

17. Do whatever you think right.
18. I don't see how you can get out of this mess.
19. Do you know when the train will arrive?
20. Whoever came was made welcome.
21. I understand you want a situation.
22. My verdict is that the prisoners shall die.
23. I cannot express how sorry I am.
24. They guessed what he meant.
25. I am afraid that she will be angry.
26. Will you explain why you behaved so ?
27. No one can tell how this will end.
28. The truth is that we have been deceived.
29. It is not clear who has done this.
30. I do not know how I can deal with this rascal.
31. I did not know whether I should laugh or cry.
32. We are desirous that you should succeed.

37. Sometimes, instead of a Noun Clause introduced by *that,* the Accusative with the Infinitive is used.

1. (*a*) He thought *that he was safe there.*
   (*b*) He thought *himself to be safe there.*
2. (*a*) I believed *that he was a true friend.*
   (*b*) I believed *him to be a true friend.*
3. (*a*) This proved *that the man had stolen the horse.*
   (*b*) This proved *the man to have stolen the horse.*
4. (*a*) We know *that Rama is alive.*
   (*b*) We know *Rama to be alive.*

Chapter 6 MORE ABOUT ADJECTIVE CLAUSES

38. As we have seen, an Adjective Clause in a Complex sentence is a subordinate clause which does the work of an Adjective, and so qualifies some noun or pronoun in the main clause.

An Adjective Clause is introduced by a Relative Pronoun or by a Relative Adverb; as,

Uneasy lies the head *that wears a crown.*
He is the man *whom we all respect.*
The time *when the boat leaves* is not yet fixed.
The house *where the accident occurred* is nearby.
The reason *why I did it* is obvious.

39. Sometimes, however, a Relative Pronoun introduces a Co-ordinate clause; as,

I met Rama, *who* (= and he) gave me your message.

Here we are using the Relative Pronoun *who* to introduce a *co-ordinate* clause.

[It might appear, at first sight, that the clause, *who gave me your message,* is an Adjective clause and therefore Subordinate. It will be seen that this is not the case however, for it in no way identifies or describes *Rama.*

In the sentence,

He is the boy who broke the window.

the clause, *who broke the window,* clearly identifies and describes the *boy,* and is therefore an Adjective clause.]

40. Below are further examples of *who* (and *which)* used to introduce a co-ordinate clause.

1. I met Mr. Joshi, who (= and he) thereupon shook hands with me.
2. The prisoner was taken before the Captain, who (= and he) condemned him to instant death.
3. He gave me a message, which (= and it) is this.
4. He released the bird, which (= and it) at once flew away.

41. The Relative Pronoun or the Relative Adverb, introducing an Adjective clause, is sometimes understood, and not expressed; as,

1. Eat all ^ *you can.*
   [Here the Relative Pronoun *that* is understood.]
2. I saw a man ^ *I know.*
   [Here the Relative Pronoun *whom* is understood.]
3. Where's the book ^ *he left for me ?*
   [Here the Relative Pronoun *which* is understood.]
4. On the day ^ *you pass the examination* I shall give you a reward.
   [Here the Relative Adverb *when* is understood].
5. The reason ^ *I have come* is to ask for my money.
   [Here the relative Adverb *why* is understood.]

42. In older English *but* was used as a relative pronoun as in the sentences below. In such cases *but* is equivalent to a relative pronoun followed by *not.*

1. There was not a woman present *but* wept to hear such news.
   [That is, *who* did *not* weep to hear such news.]
2. And not a man of the three hundred at Thermopylae *but* died at his post.
   [That is, *who* did *not* die at his post.]

3. Nor is there a man here *but* loved our Caesar.
   [That is, *who* did *not* love our Caesar.]
4. There was not a widow *but* longed to die upon the pyre of her husband.
   [That is, *who* did *not* long to die, etc.]
5. There is no fireside *but* has one vacant chair.
   [*That* has *not* one vacant chair.]

43. Note that *than* is sometimes used as a Preposition before a Relative Pronoun in the Adjective Clause ; as,
They elected Rama *than* whom no better boy ever went to school.
We will follow Brutus *than* whom Rome knows no nobler son.
It was a blow *than* which no crueller was ever struck.
We came to a spot *than* which mine eyes have seldom seen a lovelier sight.

44. The infinitive with *to* is often used as the equivalent of an Adjective Clause.

1. (*a*) Give me some food *which I may eat.*
   (*b*) Give me some food *to eat.*
2. (*a*) He has no boots *which he can wear.*
   (*b*) He has no boots *to wear.*
3. (*a*) The doctor has given me medicine *which I must take.*
   (*b*) The doctor has given me medicine *to take.*
4. (*a*) I have work *which I must do.*
   (*b*) I have work *to do.*
5. (*a*) His mother gave him a rupee *which he might put in his money-box.*
   (*b*) His mother gave him a rupee to *put in his money-box.*

EXERCISE 40

Pick out each Adjective Clause in the following sentences and say which noun or pronoun in the main clause it qualifies.

1. This is the house that Jack built.
2. He that climbs too high is sure to fall.
3. She sleeps the sleep that knows no waking.
4. We obeyed the order the teacher gave us.
5. Servants that are honest are trusted.
6. They never fail who die in a great cause.
7. We love those who love us.
8. The moment which is lost is lost for ever.
9. I have a little shadow which goes in and out with me.
10. It is an ill wind that blows nobody good.
11. Youth is the time when the seeds of character are sown.
12. It was the schooner Hesperus that sailed the wintry sea.
13. They never pardon who have done the wrong.
14. He has a son who has made a name for himself.
15. A friend who helps you in time of need is a real friend.
16. All that glitters is not gold.
17. He could not answer the question I asked him.
18. He laughs best who laughs last.
19. All the blessings we enjoy come from God.
20. They that are whole have no need of the physician.

21. Little good work can be expected from men who are great boasters.
22. The plan you propose is a very good one.
23. The night is long that never finds the day.
24. It is a long lane that has no turning.
25. He gave me everything I asked for.
26. He failed in everything that he laid his hands upon.
27. He has tricks that remind me of his father.
28. I duly received the message you sent me.
29. The fox saw the grapes which hung over the garden wall.
30. The bark that held a prince went down.
31. He that is down need fear no fall.
32. We are such stuff as dreams are made on.
33. The man that hath no music in his soul is fit for treason.
34. True love's the gift which God has given to man alone beneath the heaven.
35. Not a soldier discharged his farewell shot
    O'er the grave where our hero we buried.
36. Who lives longest sees the most.
37. Often I think of the beautiful town
    That is seated by the sea.

EXERCISE 41

Make ten sentences, each containing an Adjective Clause, in which a Relative Pronoun is understood.

EXERCISE 42

Make ten sentences, each containing an Adjective Clause, in which a Relative Adverb is understood.

Chapter 7 MORE ABOUT ADVERB CLAUSES

45. We have seen that an Adverb clause is a subordinate clause which does the work of an Adverb. It may, therefore, modify some verb, adjective, or Adverb in the main clause; as,

Strike the iron *while it is hot.*
You are taller *than I thought.*
He ran so quickly that *he soon overtook me.*

46. Adverb clauses are of many kinds and may be classified as Adverb Clauses of–

1. Time 2. Place 3. Purpose
4. Cause 5. Condition 6. Result
7. Comparison 8. Supposition or Concession

1. Adverb Clauses of Time

47. Adverb Clauses of time are introduced by the Subordinating Conjunctions *whenever, while, after, before, since, as,* etc.

When you have finished your work you may go home.
I will do it *when I think fit.*
Don't talk *while she is singing.*
While I command this ship there will be good discipline.
He came *after night had fallen.*
After the law had been passed this form of crime ceased.
Do it *before you forget.*
Before you go bring me some water.
I have not been well *since I returned from Chennai.*
There was silence *as the leader spoke.*
As he came into the room all rose to their feet.
The doctor always comes *whenever he is sent for.*
They were commanded to wait *till the signal was given.*
The world always will be the same *so long as men are men.*
As soon as he heard the news he wrote to me.
Just as he entered the room the clock struck.
No sooner did he see us *than he disappeared.*

EXERCISE 43

Write five sentences containing Adverb Clauses of Time.

2. Adverb Clauses of Place

48. Adverb Clauses of Place are introduced by the Subordinating Conjunctions *where* and *wherever,*

I have put it *where I can find it again.*
They can stay *where they are.*
Where you live I will live.
He led the caravan *wherever he wanted to go.*
You can put it *wherever you like.*
Let him be arrested *wherever he may be found.*

In older English *whence* and *whither* were also used.

Go quickly *whence you came.*
The wind bloweth *whither it listeth.*

EXERCISE 44

Write three sentences containing Adverb Clauses of Place.

3. Adverb Clauses of Purpose

49. Adverb clauses of purpose are introduced by the subordinating conjunctions *so that, in order that* and *lest.* (*In order that* and *lest* are used in a formal style.)

I will give you a map *so that you can find the way.*
We eat *so that we may live.*
The UNO was formed *in order that countries might discuss world problems better.*
He was extra polite to his superiors *lest something adverse should be written into his records.*
'Sleep not *lest your Lord come in the night.*'

The conjunction *that* occurred in older English:

He drew the sword *that he might defend himself.*
'Come hither *that I may bless thee.*'

EXERCISE 45

Write three sentences containing Adverb Clauses of Purpose.

4. Adverb Clauses of Cause or Reason

50. Adverb Clauses of Cause or Reason are introduced by the Subordinating Conjunctions *because, as, since, that.*

Because I like you, I shall help you.
I did it *because I wanted to.*
I did not buy it *because I did not like the look of it.*
He thinks, *because he is rich,* he can buy justice.
Since you are so clever you will be able to explain this.
Since your father is not at home, I will ask you to take the message.
Since you swear to serve me faithfully, I will employ you.
I am glad *that you like it.*
He was very pleased *that you have passed.*
As he was not there, I spoke to his brother.

EXERCISE 46

Write five sentences containing Adverb clauses of cause or reason.

5. Adverb Clauses of Condition

51. Adverb Clauses of Condition are introduced by the Subordinating Conjunctions *if, whether, unless.*

If I like it, I shall buy it. Come *if you wish to.*
If it rains we shall stay at home.
If you have tears, prepare to shed them now.
You must go *whether you hear from him or not.*
Whether the Rajah gives him blows or money, he will speak the truth.
Unless you work harder you will fail.
I won't pay it *unless he sends me the bill again.*
I will forgive you *on condition that you do not repeat the offence.*

Note 1—Sometimes the Subordinating Conjunction is omitted in Adverb Clauses of Condition; as,

Had I not seen this with my own eyes I would not have believed it.
Had I the wings of a bird I would fly away.
He would be happier *were he more honest.*
Were an angel to tell me such a thing of you, I would not believe it.
What would you answer *did I ask you such a question* ?

Note 2—Clauses of Condition are sometimes introduced by a Relative Pronoun, or Adjective, or Adverb (without any antecedent) ; as,

Whatever happens keep calm.
Don't annoy him *whatever you do.*
Whatever may be the result, I shall refuse
Whichever road we take we shall be too late.
However cleverly you may cheat, you will be found at last.

EXERCISE 47

Write five sentences containing Adverb Clauses of Condition.

6. Adverb Clauses of Result or Consequence

52. Adverb Clauses of Result or Consequence are introduced by the Subordinating Conjunction *that.* Frequently *so* or *such* precedes it in the Principal Clause.

They fought so bravely *that the enemy were driven off.*/So bravely did they fight *that the enemy were driven off.* (Literary)
He is such a good man *that all respect him.*
So great a fire raged *that London was burnt down.*
The Romans built in such a way *that their walls are still standing.*
He spoke in such a low voice *that few could hear him.*
So terrible a disease broke out *that very few of the people survived.*
Very heavy rain fell *so that the rivers were soon in flood.*
Laws were quickly passed *so that this abuse was checked.*
He behaved in such a manner *that his reputation suffered.*
So cold was it *that many died.*

Note—The Subordinating Conjunction *that* is often dropped in informal English.

He was so weak *he could not speak.*
I am so deaf *I cannot hear thunder.*
It was so late *I waited no longer.*
He is so old *he can hardly walk.*
It was so small *I could not see it.*

EXERCISE 48

Write five sentences containing Adverb Clauses of Result or Consequence.

7. Adverb Clauses of Comparison

53. Adverb Clauses of Comparison are of two kinds:

(*i*) Adverb Clauses of Comparison of Degree.

(*ii*) Adverb Clauses of Comparison of Manner.

54. Adverb Clauses of Comparison of Degree are introduced by the Subordinating Conjunction *than,* or by the Relative Adverb *as;* as,

He is older *than he looks.*
No one can run faster *than Rama.*
It is later *than I thought.*

You must work harder *than I do.*
He is as stupid *as he is lazy.*
He is not so clever *as you think.*

Note—The verb of the Adverb Clause of Comparison of Degree is often understood and not expressed ; as,

Nobody knows it better than I [do].
Few are better leaders than he [is].
You like curry better than I [like it].
It will happen as sure as death [is sure].
Not many know the truth of this better than you [know it].

EXERCISE 49

Write five sentences containing Adverb Clauses of Comparison of Degree.

55. Adverb Clauses of Comparison of *Manner* are introduced by the Relative Adverb *as* ; as,

It all ended as I expected.

You may do as *you please.*
It all ended *as I expected.*
As you have made your bed so you must lie on it.
As he has lived so will he die.
As the twig is bent the branch will grow.

EXERCISE 50

Write five sentences containing Adverb Clauses of Comparison of Manner.

8. Adverb Clauses of Supposition or Concession

56. Adverb Clauses of Supposition or Concession are introduced by the Subordinating Conjunctions *though, although, even if.*

Though I am poor I am honest.
Though the heavens fall, justice must be done.
Though He slay me yet will I love Him.
He set sail *though the storm threatened.*
Although troops had marched all day they fought bravely all night.
Although I forbade this you have done it.
I shall be able to get in *although I have no ticket.*
Even if it rains I shall come.
Even if he is old he is able to do a great deal of work.
I would not do it *even if you paid me.*

EXERCISE 51

Write five sentences containing Adverb Clauses of Supposition or Concession.

EXERCISE 52

Pick out the Adverb clauses in the following sentences, tell the kind of each clause and point out the word in the main clause which it modifies.

1. Forgive us as we forgive our enemies.
2. We sow so that we may reap.
3. He did it as I told him.
4. I couldn't be angry with him, if I tried.
5. He arrived as we were setting out.
6. If this story were false, what should you do ?
7. It is ten hours since I had nothing to eat.
8. I make friends wherever I go.

9. In Rome we must do as the Romans.
10. If I were you I would do it at once.
11. The general was as good as his word.
12. My sight is as keen as yours.
13. Some seeds fell where there was no earth.
14. Since you say so, I must believe it.
15. Stand still if you value your life.
16. He labours so that he may become rich.
17. He lost more than he could afford.
18. It is so simple that a child can understand it.
19. He kept on writing as though he did not hear.
20. Boy as he was, he was chosen king.
21. He rides as a cowboy rides.
22. I will die before I submit.
23. He was caught in a shower as he was returning from school.
24. He speaks better than he writes.
25. He came in while I was out.
26. After the vote was taken the meeting broke up.
27. He wept as if he had been a child.
28. Apollo was worshipped as long as the Roman Empire lasted.
29. He consoled the unfortunate mother as best he might.
30. He ran so fast that I could not overtake him.
31. He knows that inasmuch as I have told him.
32. The younger man has more money than brains.
33. Since you desire it, I will look into the matter.
34. They set a strong guard, lest any one should escape.
35. He succeeded although his success was not expected.
36. The earth is larger than the moon.
37. It was dark when the cannonading stopped all of a sudden.
38. His pity gave ere charity began.
39. Wherever I went was my dear dog Tray.
40. He felt as if the ground were slipping beneath his feet.
41. Some people act as though they could do no wrong.
42. Fools rush in where angels fear to tread.
43. He dared not stir, lest he should be seen.
44. The movement was checked before it was fairly started.
45. A glutton lives so that he may eat.
46. Everything happened exactly as had been expected.
47. Robinson Crusoe was puzzled when he discovered the print of a foot on the sand.
48. Enough is as good as a feast.
49. He finished the work as the clock struck five.
50. As soon as you stand there, this young lady is your lawful wedded wife.
51. It's dull in our town since my playmates left.
52. Whilst I live, thou shalt never want a friend to stand by thee.
53. No sooner did this idea enter his head, than it carried conviction with it.
54. They have gone ahead with the plan, although there is widespread public opposition.
55. They were commanded to wait till the signal was given.
56. Rich as he is, one would scarcely envy him.
57. Open rebuke is better than secret love.
58. Have you turned a detective, that you keep your eye on me like this ?
59. He had not read half a dozen pages, when the expression of his face began to change.
60. My eldest son was bred at Oxford, as I intended him for the learned profession.
61. His behaviour was such that everybody liked him.
62. I had scarcely taken orders a year, before I began to think seriously of matrimony.
63. If you have tears, prepare to shed them now.
64. The world always will be the same, as long as men are men.

EXERCISE 53

Use each of the following clauses in a sentence, and say what work it does in your sentence.

1. that he was tired
2. where he was born
3. as he was told
4. what you say
5. whosoever is guilty
6. who laughs last
7. because he is generous
8. since you say so
9. as he deserved
10. before it was too late.
11. as soon as he heard the news.
12. that he soon overtook me
13. where he had left it
14. how old he was.
15. if you are diligent
16. because I was tired
17. what has become of him
18. when the train will arrive
19. who did it
20. whatever you think right
21. since I returned from Lahore
22. how this will end
23. what he wants
24. as he could
25. as he was not there
26. if I were you
27. that the streets were flooded
28. as I told him
29. before I submitted
30. that he is a millionaire
31. as she is beautiful
32. what you want
33. when his father died
34. as it was raining
35. as you please
36. than you are [strong]
37. although he is not rich
38. who works hard
39. that we shall win
40. when I shall return
41. if I had not helped you
42. although they fought most valiantly
43. when the cat is away
44. while it is hot
45. who help themselves
46. while the sun shines
47. till you are out of the wood
48. that wears a crown
49. who live in glass houses
50. where ignorance is bliss
51. that blows nobody good
52. no sooner did he see me

53. as dreams are made on
54. that has no turning
55. where angels fear to tread
56. so that we may live

EXERCISE 54

Use the following subordinate clauses in as many different ways as possible by attaching them to suitable principal clauses.

1. where he was buried
2. when the train will arrive
3. where he had left it
4. who did it
5. why he did it
6. that he might succeed in life
7. whom he had met
8. when the monsoon failed

EXERCISE 55

Complete the following sentences by supplying appropriate connecting words.

1. Small service is true service _______ it lasts.
2. It is a great loss to a man _______ he cannot laugh.
3. We there met a boy _______ had lost his way.
4. It is the common doom of man ___ he must eat his bread by the sweat of his brow.
5. Fit words are better _______ fine ones.
6. He makes no friend, _______ never made a foe.
7. The moment _______ is lost is lost for ever.
8. Forgive us our debts _______ we forgive our debtors.
9. The man _______ stands by me in trouble I won't bid him go until the sun shines again.
10. Money _______ is easily earned is soon spent.
11. _______ somewhat pompous, he was an entertaining companion.
12. Poetry takes me up so entirely _______ I scarce see what passes under my nose.
13. He _______ fights and runs away, lives to fight another day.

14. Never refuse to entertain a man in your heart _______ all the world is talking against him.
15. _______ you would be healthy, be good.
16. _______ I am dead, my dearest, sing no sad songs for me.
17. A man has no more right to say an uncivil thing _______ to act one.
18. _______ the blind lead the blind, both shall fall into the ditch.
19. _______ this be madness _______ there is method in it.
20. Consider the lilies _______ they grow.
21. _______ he has a car, he often goes to the office on foot.
22. _______ we approached the house, we heard the sound of music.
23. I have not been well _______ I returned from Delhi.
24. These are the books _______ I ordered last week.
25. They live _______ their fathers lived before them.

26. No one can tell _______ this will end.
27. _______ he had gone I remembered _______ he was.
28. A man _______ loses his temper continually is a nuisance.
29. Youth is the time _______ the seeds of character are sown.
30. The house _______ he was born lies in ruins.
31. _______ my mother died I was very young.
32. Do not halloo _______ you are out of the wood.
33. I shall see you tomorrow, _______ we will talk the matter over.
34. They always talk _______ never think.

35. I did not recognize him _______ he told me _______ he was.
36. They serve God well _______ serve His creatures.
37. I have a little shadow _______ goes in and out with me.
38. I met a boy _______ told me _______ I could find you.
39. We learn, _______ we may be able to make our way in the world.
40. _______ he was not there, I spoke to his brother.
41. A vessel that once gets a crack, _______ it may be cunningly mended, will never stand such rough usage _____ a whole one.
42. ______it journeys through space, the earth is not alone; spinning round with it is the moon.
43. Other planets have moons, ______ ours is very large compared to the earth.
44. I resolved _______ I would say nothing _______ I knew the worst.
45. _______ he was born, _______ brought him up, and _______ he lived, we are not told.
46. Nothing can describe the confusion of thought _____ I felt ____ I sank into the water.
47. ______ he was a strict disciplinarian he was loved by all _______ I served under him.
48. One great reason _______ we are insensible to the goodness of Creator is the fact _______ His bounty is so extensive.
49. Passengers are warned ______ it is dangerous to lean out of the window ______ the train is in motion.

Chapter 8 ANALYSIS OF COMPLEX SENTENCES (CLAUSE ANALYSIS)

57. Usually when a complex or compound sentence is given for analysing, detailed analysis is not required; the student is asked to give **clause analysis**, that is, he is asked to break up a given sentence into its several clauses and show their relation to one another.

58. In analysing a Complex sentence, the first step is to find out the Principal or Main Clause.

The next step is to find out the Subordinate Clause or Clauses, showing the relation which each Clause bears to the Principal Clause.

59. Now study carefully the following example of the analysis of a Complex sentence.

Whenever he heard the question, the old man who lived in that house, answered that the earth is flat.

Complex sentence containing three Subordinate clauses:

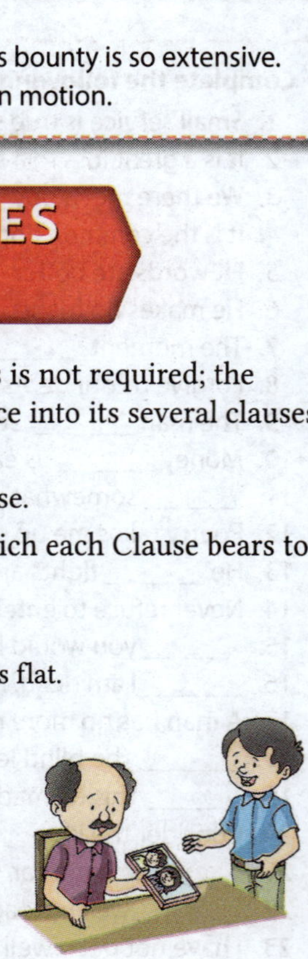

1. The old man.... answered (Principal clause)
2. Whenever he heard the question. (Adverb clause of time, modifying *answered* in 1.)
3. Who lived in that house. (Adjective clause, qualifying *man* in 1.)
4. That the earth is flat. (Noun clause, object of *answered* in 1.)

60. Sometimes a Subordinate clause has another Subordinate clause within it; that is, a Subordinate clause has another Subordinate clause dependent on it, *e.g.*,

(A) I think that he destroyed the letter which you sent there.

1. I think.... (Principal clause)
2. That he destroyed the letter ....(Noun Clause, object of *think* in 1.)
3. Which you sent there.....(Adjective clause, subordinate to 2, qualifying *letter.*)

(B) He replied that he worked whenever he liked.

1. He replied....(Principal clause)
2. That he worked... (Noun clause, object of *replied* in 1.)
3. Whenever he liked... (Adverb clause, subordinate to 2, modifying *worked.*)

(C) I know the man who said that this would happen.

1. I know the man....(Principal clause)

2. Who said....(Adjective clause, qualifying *man* in 1.)
3. That this would happen. (Noun clause, subordinate to 2, object *of said.*)

61. One afternoon, as in that sultry clime
It is the custom in the summer-time,
With bolted doors and window-shutters closed,
The inhabitants of Atri slept or dozed.
When, suddenly upon their senses fell
The loud alarm of the accusing bell !

Complex sentence, containing two subordinate clauses:

1. One afternoon, with bolted doors and window shutters closed, the inhabitants of Atri slept or dozed. (Principal clause)
2. As in that sultry clime it is the custom in the summer-time. (Adverb clause of manner, modifying *slept or dozed* in 1.)
3. When, suddenly, upon their senses fell the loud alarm of the accusing bell. (Adverb clause of time, modifying *slept* or *dozed* in 1)

62. Below are further examples:

(1) Breathes there the man with soul so dead
Who never to himself hath said,
'This is my own, my native land?'

Complex sentence, containing two subordinate clauses:

1. Breathes there the man with soul so dead...(Principal clause)
2. Who never to himself hath said..... (Adjective clause, qualifying *man* in 1.)
3. 'This is my own, my native land?' (Noun clause, subordinate to 2, object of *hath said.*)

(2) Everyone who knows you, acknowledges, when he considers the case calmly, that you have been wronged.

Complex sentence, containing three subordinate clauses:

1. Everyone acknowledges...(Principal clause)
2. Who knows you. (Adjective clause, qualifying *one* in 1.)
3. When he considers the case calmly. (Adverb clause, modifying *acknowledges* in 1.)
4. That you have been wronged. (Noun clause, object of *acknowledges* in 1.)

(3) Do the work that's nearest,
Tho' it's dull at whiles
Helping when you meet them.
Lame dogs over stiles.

Complex sentence, containing three subordinate clauses:

1. [You] do the work, helping lame dogs over stiles. (Principal clause)
2. That's nearest. (Adjective clause, qualifying *work* in 1.)
3. Tho' it's dull at whiles. (Adverb clause of concession, modifying *helping* in 1.)
4. When you meet them. (Adverb clause of time, modifying *helping* in 1.)

(4) I knew a man who believed that, if a man were permitted to make the ballads, he need not care who made the laws of a nation.

Complex sentence, containing four subordinate clauses:

1. I knew a man...(Principal clause)
2. Who believed....(Adjective clause, qualifying a *man* in 1.)
3. That he need not care. (Noun clause, subordinate to 2, object of *believed*)
4. Who made the laws of a nation. (Noun clause, subordinate to 2, object of *care.*)

5. If a man were permitted to make the ballads, Adverb clause of condition, subordinate to 3, modifying *need not care.*

(5) The man who can play most heartily when he has the chance of playing, is generally the man who can work most heartily when he must work.

Complex sentence, containing four subordinate clauses:

1. The man is generally the man...(Principal clause)
2. Who can play most heartily. [Adjective clause, qualifying *man* (subject) in 1.]
3. When he has the chance of playing. [Adverb clause, subordinate to 2, modifying *play.*)
4. Who can work most heartily. (Adjective clause, qualifying *man* (complement) in 1.]
5. When he must work. (Adverb clause, subordinate to 4, modifying *work.*)

I am a genius.

(6) Should you be so unfortunate as to suppose that you are a genius, and that things will come to you, it would be well to undeceive yourself as soon as it is possible.

Complex sentence, containing four Subordinate Clauses:

1. It would be well to undeceive yourself. (Principal clause)
2. As soon as it is possible. (Adverb clause of time, subordinate to 1.)
3. Should you be so unfortunate as to suppose...(Adverb clause of condition, sub ordinate to 1.)
4. That you are a genius. (Noun clause. Subordinate to 3, object of *to suppose.*)
5. And that things will come to you. (Noun clause, co-ordinate with 4, and subordinate to 3, object of *to suppose.*)

EXERCISE 56

Analyse the following sentences.

I read Milton when I was fourteen.

1. As my eldest son was bred a scholar, I determined to send him to town, where his abilities might contribute to our support and his own.
2. Clive had been only a few months in the army, when intelligence arrived that peace had been concluded between Great Britain and France.
3. I had a partial father, who gave me a better education than his broken fortune would have allowed.
4. He told us that he had read Milton, in a prose translation, when he was fourteen.
5. With whatever luxuries a bachelor may be surrounded, he will always find his happiness incomplete, unless he has a wife and children.
6. Among the many reasons which make me glad to have been born in England, one of the first is that I read Shakespeare in my mother tongue.
7. He [Pope] professed to have learned his poetry from Dryden, whom, whenever an opportunity was presented, he praised through his whole life with unvaried liberality.
8. We who are fortunate enough to live in this enlightened century hardly realize how our ancestors suffered from their belief in the existence of mysterious and malevolent beings.
9. We cannot justly interpret the religion of any people, unless we are prepared to admit that we ourselves are liable to error in matters of faith.
10. Milton said that he did not educate his daughters in the languages, because one tongue was enough for a woman.
11. The man who does not see that the good of every living creature is his good, is a fool.
12. Nothing can describe the confusion of thought which I felt when I sank into the water.
13. We had in this village, some twenty years ago, a boy whom I well remember, who from his childhood showed a strong liking for bees.
14. Considering that the world is so intricate, we are not to be surprised that science has progressed slowly.
15. You take my house when you do take the prop
    That doth sustain my house.
16. I heard a thousand blended notes,
    While in a grove I sat reclined
    In that sweet mood when pleasant thoughts
    Bring sad thoughts to the mind.

17. Much as we like Shakespeare's comedies, we cannot agree with Dr. Johnson that they are better than his tragedies.
18. Those who look into practical life will find that fortune is usually on the side of the industrious, as the winds and waves are on the side of the best navigators.
19. He who sits from day to day,
Where the prisoned lark is hung.
Heedless of its loudest lay,
Hardly knows that it has sung.

20. History says that Socrates, when he was given the cup of hemlock, continued to talk to the friends who were standing around him as he drank it.
21. I have no sympathy with the poor man I knew, who, when suicides abounded, told me he dared not look at his razor.

Chapter 9 ANALYSIS OF COMPOUND SENTENCES (CLAUSE ANALYSIS)

64. A compound sentence is made up of two or more *independent* sentences or *principal* or *main* clauses joined together by a Co-ordinating conjunction ; as,

1. The horse reared and the rider was thrown.
   [Here each Co-ordinate Clause is a Simple sentence.]
2. They were fond of music, played on various kinds of instruments and indulged in much singing.
   [Here each Co-ordinate Clause is a Simple sentence.]
3. They asked him how he received the wound, but he refused to answer.
   [Here the first clause is a Complex sentence, while the second clause is a Simple sentence.]
4. He says what he means, and he means what he says.
   [Here each Co-ordinate Clause is a Complex sentence.]

It will be thus seen that each main clause of a Compound sentence may be a Simple sentence or a Complex sentence.

It has been already pointed out (§ 27) that the term Double is now used for a sentence which is made up of *two* main clauses. and the term Multiple for a sentence of *more than* two main clauses.

65. In accordance with this new terminology, 1, 3, and 4 are Double sentences, and 2 is a Multiple sentence.

66. The connection between two main clauses of a Compound sentence may be one of the following four kinds:

(1) Copulative; as,

God made the country *and* man made the town.
Babar was *not only* a great soldier, he was *also* a wise ruler.
He cannot speak, *nor* can he write.
He plays the piano, he sings *also*.
The innocents were punished *as well as* the guilty.

Here in each sentence the main clauses are simply *coupled together.*

(2) Adversative ; as,

He is slow, *but* he is sure.
I did my best, *nevertheless* I failed.
He is rich, *yet* he is not happy.
He is vain, *still* his friends adore him.

Here in each sentence the two main clauses are *opposed* in meaning to each other.

(3) Alternative or Disjunctive; as,

She must weep, *or* she will die.
Either he is mad, *or* he feigns madness.
Neither a borrower *nor* a lender be.

Walk quickly, *else* you will not overtake him.

Here in each sentence the two main clauses are *disjoined* in meaning, and a *choice* between them is offered for acceptance.

(4) Illative ; as,

He is diligent, *therefore* he will succeed.
He is unwell, *so* he cannot attend office.
The angles are equal, *consequently* the sides are equal.

Here in each sentence the second clause *draws an inference from the first.*

67. Sometimes no connecting word is used to join two main clauses; as,

Temperance promotes health, intemperance destroys it.

Her court was pure; her life serene.

68. Sometimes a Subordinate Conjunction is used to join the clauses of a Compound sentence; as,

I shall see you tomorrow, *when* (= and then) we can finish the business.

I walked with him to the station, *where* (= and there) we parted.

69. Compared sentences are often contracted. For example, when the main clauses have:

(1) A common Subject; as,

He chid their wanderings, but relieved their pain.
= He chid their wanderings, but he relieved their pain.

(2) A common Verb; as,

Some praise the work, and some the architect.
= Some praise the work, and some praise the architect.

70. Study carefully the clause analysis of the following.

(1) One day Bassanio came to Antonio, and told him that he wished to repair his fortune by a wealthy marriage with a lady whom he dearly loved, whose father had left her sole heiress to a large estate.

Analysis–This is a Compound or Double sentence, consisting of–

A. One day Bassanio came to Antonio. (Principal clause)
B. Bassanio told him...(Principal clause, co-ordinate with A.)
b1. That he wished to repair his fortune by a wealthy marriage with a lady. (Noun clause, object of *told* in B.)
b2. Whom he dearly loved. (Adjective clause, subordinate to b1, qualifying *lady* .)
b3. Whose father had left her sole heiress to a large estate. (Adjective clause, subordinate to b1, qualifying *lady,* and co-ordinate with b2.)

(2) Before he died, the good Earl of Kent, who had still attended his old master's steps from the first of his daughters' ill-usage to this sad period of his decay, tried to make him understand that it was he who had followed him under the name of Caius; but Lear's care-crazed brain at that time could not comprehend how that could be, or how Kent and Caius could be the same person.

Analysis.– This is a Compound or Double sentence, consisting of–

A. The good Earl of Kent tried to make him understand...(Principal clause).
a1. Before he died. (Adverb clause, modifying *tried* in A).
a2. Who had still attended his old master's steps from the first of his daughters' ill-usage to this sad period of his decay. (Adjective clause, qualifying *Earl of Kent* in A.)
a3. That it was he. (Noun clause, object of *understand* in A.)
a4. Who had followed him under the name of Caius. (Adjective clause, subordinate to a3, qualifying *he.*)
B. But Lears's care-crazed brain at that time could not comprehend (Principal clause, coordinate with A.)
b1. How that could be. (Noun clause, object of *comprehend* in B.)
b2. Or how Kent and Caius could be the same person. (Noun clause, object of *comprehend* in B ; co-ordinate with b1.)

EXERCISE 57

Analyse the following.

1. I am satisfied with things as they are; and it will be my pride and pleasure to hand down this country to my children as I received it from those who preceded me.
2. Some politicians of our time lay it down as a self-evident proposition that no people ought to be free till they are fit to use their freedom.
3. He [a gentleman] never speaks of himself except when compelled, never defends himself by a mere retort; he has no ears for slander or gossip, is scrupulous in imputing motives to those who interfere with him, and interprets everything for the best.
4. Subhash Chandra Bose died before his aim was achieved, and yet he will always be remembered as a great hero, who fought and sacrificed his life for the freedom of the country.
5. The notice which you have been pleased to take of my labours, had it been early, had been kind; but it has been delayed till I am indifferent, and cannot enjoy it.
6. I hope it is no very cynical asperity not to confess obligations where no benefit has been received, or to be unwilling that the public should consider me as owing that to a patron, which Providence has enabled me to do for myself.
7. While I was doing this, I found the tide began to flow, though very calm, and I had the mortification to see my coat, shirt, and waistcoat, which I had left on shore upon the sand, swim away.
8. With reluctance he accepted the invitations of his kindly and faithful Persian friend, who scolded him for refusing meat; but he replied that too much eating led man to commit many sins.
9. Macaulay had wealth and fame, rank and power, and yet he tells us in his biography that he owed the happiest hours of his life to books.
10. A literary education is simply one of many different kinds of education and it is not wise that more than a small percentage of the people of any country should have an exclusively literary education.
11. The way into my parlour is up a winding stair, And I've many curious things to show when you are there.
12. They love to see the flaming forge,
And hear the bellows soar,
And catch the burning sparks that fly,
Like chaff from a threshing floor.
13. The friends who had left came back every one,
And darkest advisers looked bright as the sun.
14. She lived unknown and few could know,
When Lucy ceased to be.
15. Three wives sat up in the lighthouse tower,
And they trimmed the lamps as the sun went down.
16. His hair was yellow as hay,
But threads of a silvery grey
Gleamed in his tawny beard.

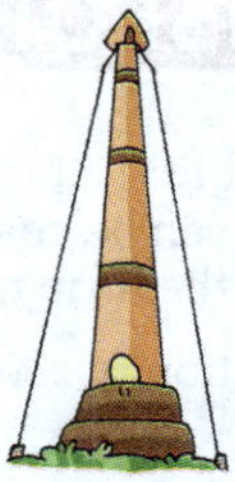

EXERCISE 58

(Miscellaneous) Analyse the following.

1. When Abraham sat at his tent door, according to his custom, waiting to entertain strangers, he espied an old man, stooping and leaning on his staff, weary with age and travel, coming towards him, who was a hundred years of age.
2. When the old man was gone, God called to Abraham and asked him where the stranger was.
3. He replied, I thrust him away because he did not worship Thee.
4. While you are upon Earth enjoy the good things that are here (to that end were they given) and be not melancholy, and wish yourself in heaven.
5. There is no saying shocks me so much as that which I hear very often that a man does not know how to pass his time.
6. You must observe, my friend, that it is the custom of this country, when a lady or gentleman happens to sing, for the company to sit as mute and as motionless as statues.

7. Mr. Burchell had scarce taken leave, and Sophia consented to dance with the chaplain, when my little ones came running out to tell us that the Squire was come with a crowd of company.
8. I hope it will give comfort to great numbers who are passing through the world in obscurity, when I inform them how easily distinction may be obtained.
9. All who have meant good work with their whole hearts, have done good work, although they may die before they have the time to sign it.
10. We are told that, while still a mere child, he stole away from his playfellows to a vault in St. James's Fields, for the purpose of investigating the cause of a singular echo which he had observed there.
11. The slave who was at his work not far from the place where this astonishing piece of cruelty was commited, hearing the shrieks of the dying person ran to see what was the occasion of them.
12. Every insignificant author fancies it of importance to the world to know that he wrote his book in the country, that he did it to pass away some of his idle hours, that it was published at the importunity of friends, or that his natural temper, studies, or conversation directed him to the choice of his subject.
13. I consider a human soul without education like marble in the quarry, which shows none of its inherent beauties, until the skill of the polisher fetches out the colours, makes the surface shine, discovers every ornamental cloud, spot, and view that run through the body of it.
14. When the Athenians in the war with the Lacedaemonians received many defeats both by sea and land, they sent a message to the oracle of Jupiter Ammon, to ask the reason why they who erected so many temples to the gods, and adorned them with such costly offerings, should be less successful than the Lacedaemonians, who fell so short of them in all these particulars.
15. He that holds fast the golden mean,
And lives contentedly between
The little and the great,
Feels not the wants that pinch the poor,
Nor plagues that haunt the rich man's door,
Embittering all his state.

Chapter 10 TRANSFORMATION OF SENTENCES

71. The student has already learnt that a phrase can be expanded into a clause and a clause contracted into a phrase; that is, the *form* of a sentence can be changed without changing the meaning. In this chapter we shall show some other ways of changing the form of a sentence.

The conversion or transformation of sentences is an excellent exercise as it teaches variety of expression in writing English.

1. Sentences containing the Adverb 'too'

72. We can change the form of a sentence containing the adverb 'too', as shown below.

1. The news is too good to be true.
   The news is so good that it cannot be true.
2. These mangoes are too cheap to be good.
   These mangoes are so cheap that they cannot be good.
3. He drove too fast for the police to catch.
   He drove so fast that the police could not catch him.

EXERCISE 59

Rewrite the following sentences so as to get rid of the Adverb 'too'.

1. It is never too late to mend.
2. He is too proud to beg.
3. My heart is too full for words.
4. He was too late to hear the first speech.

5. He is too ignorant for a postman.
6. The boy was too old for a whipping.
7. This tree is too high for me to climb.
8. He speaks too fast to be understood.
9. He is far too stupid for such a difficult post.

10. She was sobbing too deeply to make any answer.
11. This fact is too evident to require proof.
12. The work is too much for any man to do sing e-handed.
13. This shirt is too small for me.
14. The bag was too heavy for me too carry.

2. Interchange of the Degrees of Comparison

73. As the following examples show, it is possible to change the Degree of Comparison of an Adjective or Adverb in a sentence, without changing the meaning of the sentence.

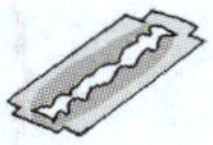

Positive.	I am as *strong* as him.
Comparative.	He is not *stronger* than me.
Positive.	This razor is not as *sharp* as that one.
Comparative.	That razor is *sharper* than this one.
Positive.	Few historians write as *interestingly* as Joshi.
Comparative.	Joshi writes more *interestingly* than most historians.
Positive.	No other metal is as *useful* as iron.
Comparative	Iron is *more useful* than any other metal.
Superlative.	Iron is the *most useful* of all metals.
Superlative.	India is the *largest* democracy in the world.
Comparative.	India is *larger* than any other democracy in the world.
Positive.	No other democracy in the world is as *large* as India.
Superlative.	Mumbai is one of the *richest* cities in India.
Comparative	Mumbai is *richer* than most other cities in India.
Positive.	Very few cities in India are as *rich* as Mumbai.
Superlative.	Usha Kiran is not the *tallest* of all the buildings in the city.
Comparative.	Usha Kiran is not *taller* than some other buildings in the city.
	OR
	Some other buildings in the city are perhaps *taller* than Usha Kiran.
Positive.	Some other buildings in the city are at least as *tall* as Usha Kiran.
	OR
	Usha Kiran is perhaps not as *tall* as some other buildings in the city.
Superlative.	Naomi is not one of the *cleverest* girls in the class.
Comparative.	Some girls of the class are *cleverer* than Naomi.
	OR
	Naomi is less *clever* than some other girls of the class.
Positive.	Naomi is not so *clever* as some other girls of the class.

EXERCISE 60

Change the Degree of Comparison without changing the meaning.

1. Abdul is as strong as his brother.
2. Akbar was one of the greatest kings.
3. Some boys are at least as industrious as Karim.
4. Mahabaleshwar is cooler than Mysore.
5. No other bowler in the eleven is so good as Rama.
6. Very few cities in India are as big as Chennai.
7. No other storybook is so popular as *The Arabian Nights*.
8. This pony is better trained than yours.

9. This church is the biggest in Mumbai.
10. This newspaper has a bigger circulation than any other morning paper.
11. Helen of Troy was more beautiful than any other woman.
12. The airplane flies faster than birds.
13. Hyderabad is one of the biggest of Indian cities.
14. Some beans are at least as nutritious as meat.
15. Samudra Gupta was one of the greatest of Indian kings.
16. Australia is the largest island in the world.

17. Very few Indo-Anglian novelists are as great as R.K. Narayan.
18. This is one of the hottest districts in India.
19. It is better to starve than beg.
20. He loves all his sons equally well.

3. Interchange of Active and Passive Voice

74. A sentence in the Active form can be changed into the Passive form, and *vice versa.*

Active.	Brutus stabbed Caesar.
Passive.	Caesar was stabbed by Brutus.
Active.	The people will make him President.
Passive.	He will be made President by the people.
Active.	Who taught you grammar ?
Passive.	By whom were you taught grammar?/Who were you taught grammar by? By whom was grammar taught to you ?
Active.	The Governor gave him a reward.
Passive.	He was given a reward by the Governor. A reward was given to him by the Governor.
Active.	The Romans expected to conquer Carthage.
Passive.	It was expected by the Romans that they would conquer Carthage.
Active.	One should keep one's promises.
Passive.	Promises should be kept.
Active.	I know her.
Passive.	She is known to me.
Active.	My captors were taking me to prison.
Passive.	I was being taken to prison by my captors.
Active.	His behaviour vexes me sometimes.
Passive.	I am sometimes vexed at his behaviour.
Active.	It is time to shut up the shop.
Passive.	It is time for the shop to be shut up.
Active.	The audience loudly cheered the Mayor's speech.
Passive.	The Mayor's speech was loudly cheered.

The enemy has defeated us.

Note— Whenever it is evident who the agent (i.e.,doer of the action) is, it is unnecessary to mention him in the passive form, and this omission gives a neater turn to the sentence. Thus in the last example the agent is not mentioned in the passive form because only those who heard the speech could have cheered it.

Passive.	My pocket has been picked.
Active.	Someone has picked my pocket.
Passive.	Our army has been defeated.
Active.	The enemy has defeated our army.
Passive.	I shall be obliged to go.
Active.	Circumstances will oblige me to go.

Note— The Active Voice is used when the agent, or actor, is to be made prominent ; the Passive, when the thing acted upon is to be made prominent. Hence the Passive Voice may be used when the agent is unknown, or when we do not care to name the agent ; as, 'The ship was wrecked.'

EXERCISE 61

Change the following sentences into the Passive form. (Omit the agent where possible.)

1. Premchand wrote this novel.
2. We admire the brave.
3. I bought the baby a doll.
4. They know me.
5. He invited me to his house yesterday.
6. They enjoy bathing.
7. I opened the door.
8. I read the book long ago.
9. Pakistan expected to win the match.
10. The master appointed him monitor.
11. Who taught you such tricks as these?
12. Brutus accused Caesar of ambition.
13. The boy is climbing the cliff.
14. He taught me to read Persian.
15. One expects better behaviour from a college student.
16. They showed a video of the 'Titanic'.
17. You must endure what you cannot cure.
18. The curator of the museum showed us some ancient coins.
19. The King reviewed the troops in the maidan.
20. They have pulled down the old house.
21. The rules forbid passengers to cross the railway line.
22. He made his wife do the work.
23. Nature teaches beasts to know their friends.
24. All desire wealth and some acquire it.
25. Lincoln emancipated four million African slaves.
26. We expect good news.
27. They propose to build a dam for irrigation purposes.
28. I offered him a chair.
29. The French surrendered Quebec to the English in 1759.
30. He showed me the greatest respect.
31. Alas ! we shall hear his voice no more.
32. Shall I ever forget those happy days ?
33. Do you not understand my meaning ?
34. We must listen to his words.

EXERCISE 62

Rewrite the following sentences in the Passive form. (Omit the agent where possible.)

1. Macbeth hoped to succeed Duncan.
2. Who taught you Urdu?
3. They found him guilty of murder.
4. The King immediately gave orders that he should be imprisoned.
5. Somebody has put out the light.
6. They laughed at his warnings and objected to all his proposals.
7. The Swiss regarded him as an impostor and called him a villain.
8. I have kept the money in the safe.
9. He pretended to be a baron.

Lock up this man or lock him up.

10. His subordinates accused him of various offences.
11. I saw him opening the box.
12. He ordered the police to pursue the thief.
13. One cannot gather grapes from thistles.
14. You never hear of a happy millionaire.
15. The public will learn with astonishment that war is imminent.
16. Did you never hear that name ?
17. The legend tells us how the castle received its name.
18. Do not insult the weak.
19. Why did he defraud you of your earnings ?

EXERCISE 63

Change the following sentences into the Active form.

1. The letter was written by the clerk.
2. Without effort nothing can be gained.
3. 'Shakuntala' was written by Kalidas.
4. I was struck by his singular appearance.
5. He was seen by my brother.
6. He was chosen leader.
7. Honey is made by bees.
8. The bird was killed by a cruel boy.
9. The steam-engine was invented by Watt.
10. The mouse was killed by the cat.
11. The boy was praised by the teacher.
12. The Exhibition was opened by the Prime Minister.
13. By whom was this jug broken ?

14. I was offered a chair.
15. We shall be blamed by everyone.
16. He will be gladdened by the sight.
17. The telephone was invented by Alexander Graham Bell.
18. My watch has been stolen.
19. A king may be looked at by a cat.
20. The telegraph wires have been cut.
21. Harsh sentences were pronounced on the offenders.
22. This question will be discussed at the meeting tomorrow.
23. Why should I be suspected by you?
24. Stones should not be thrown by those who live in glass houses.

25. He will be greatly surprised if he is chosen.
26. The ship was set on fire and abandoned by the crew.
27. He was arrested on a charge of theft, but for lack of evidence he was released.

4. Interchange of Affirmative and Negative Sentences

75. Study the following examples.

1. Brutus loved Caesar.
   Brutus was not without love for Caesar.
2. I was doubtful whether it was you.
   I was not sure that it was you.
3. Old fools surpass all other fools in folly.
   There's no fool like an old fool.
4. He is greater than me.
   I am not so great as him.
5. Alfred was the best king that ever reigned in England.
   No other king as good as Alfred ever reigned in England.

EXERCISE 64

Express the meaning of the following sentences in a negative form.

1. He was more rapacious than a griffin.
2. He was as rapacious as a griffin.
3. Akbar was the greatest of the Great Moghuls.
4. He was greater than Aurangzeb.
5. The rose by any other name would smell as sweet.
6. As soon as he came, he made objections.
7. These fishing nets are all the wealth I own.
8. I always love my country.
9. Everest is the highest mountain in the world.
10. He is sometimes foolish.
11. He failed to notice me when he came in.
12. Everybody will admit that he did his best.
13. Only a millionaire can afford such extravagance.
14. Every man makes mistakes sometimes.
15. I care very little what he says about me
16. As soon as he saw me he came up and spoke to me.
17. He must have seen the Taj Mahal when he went to Agra.

EXERCISE 65

Convert the following Negatives into Affirmatives.

1. Nobody was absent.
2. He did not live many years in India.
3. No one could deny that she was pretty.
4. God will not forget the cry of the humble.
5. I am not a little tired.
6. There was no one present who did not cheer.
7. I never in my life laid a plan and failed to carry it out.

8. Not many men would be cruel and unjust to a cripple.
9. No man could have done better.
10. The two brothers are not unlike each other.
11. He has promised never to touch wine again.
12. We did not find the road very bad.
13. There is no smoke without fire.
14. It is not likely that he will ever see his home again.

5. Interchange of Interrogative and Assertive Sentences

76. Study the following examples.

1. What though we happen to be late ?
   It does not matter much though we happen to be late.
2. Why waste time in reading trash ?
   It is extremely foolish to waste time in reading trash.
3. Were we sent into the world simply to make money ?
   We were not sent into the world simply to make money.
4. How can man die better than facing fearful odds ?
   Man cannot die better than facing fearful odds.
5. When can their glory fade ?

Their glory can never fade.

6. Was he not a villain to do such a deed ?
   He was a villain to do such a deed.

EXERCISE 66

Transform the following sentences into Assertive sentences.

1. Who can touch pitch without being defiled ?
2. Can any man by taking thought add a cubit to his stature ?
3. What though the field be lost ?
4. Is that the way a gentleman should behave ?
5. Who does not know the owl ?

6. Shall I ever forget those happy days ?
7. Who is so wicked as to amuse himself with the infirmities of extreme old age ?
8. Why waste time in this fruitless occupation ?.
9. Is this the kind of dress to wear in school ?
10. Can you gather grapes from thorns or figs from thistles ?

EXERCISE 67

Express the meaning of the following Assertions as Questions.

1. No one can be expected to submit for ever to injustice.
2. There is nothing better than a busy life.
3. Nowhere in the world will you find a fairer building than the Taj Mahal.
4. It is useless to offer bread to a man who is dying of thirst.
5. We could have done nothing without your help.
6. That was not an example to be followed.

6. Interchange of Exclamatory and Assertive Sentences

77. Study the following examples.

1. How sweet the moonlight sleeps upon this bank!
   The moonlight very sweetly sleeps upon this bank.
2. If only I were young again!
   I wish I were young again.
3. Alas that youth should pass away !
   It is sad to think that youth should pass away.
4. How beautiful is night !
   Night is very beautiful.
5. To think of our meeting here!
   [Or] That we should meet here !
   It is strange that we should meet here.

I wish I were young again.

EXERCISE 68

Transform the following Exclamatory sentences into Assertions.

1. What would I not give to see you happy !
2. Ah, what a sight was there !
3. What a piece of work is man !
4. What might be done, if men were wise !
5. What a wonderful creature an elephant is !
6. How awkwardly he manages his sword !
7. O that we two were infants playing !
8. If only I had the wings of a dove !
9. What a large nose !
10. If only I had a good horse !
11. If only I were safe at home !

How cold you are, by the way!

12. O what a fall was there, my countrymen !
13. What a delicious meal !
14. What sweet delight a quiet life affords !
15. How well fitted the camel is for the work he has to do !
16. How cold you are !
17. What a beautiful scene this is !
18. What a delicious flavour these mangoes have !
19. Shame on you to use a poor cripple so !
20. If only I knew more people !
21. How you have grown !
22. If only I had come one hour earlier !

EXERCISE 69

Transform the following into Exclamatory sentences.

1. It is a horrible night.
2. It was extremely base of him to desert you in your time of need.
3. It is hard to believe that he did such a deed.
4. I wish I had met you ten years ago.
5. It is very stupid of me to forget your name.
6. He leads a most unhappy life.

I wish I had met you ten years ago.

7. Interchange of One Part of Speech for Another

78. Study the following examples.

That kind of joke does not amuse me.

1. That kind of joke does not *amuse* me.
   That kind of joke does not give me any *amusement*.
2. It *costs* twelve rupees.
   The *cost* is twelve rupees.
3. He has *disgraced* his family.
   He is a *disgrace* to his family.
4. He *fought* bravely.
   He put up a brave *fight*.
5. The treaty of Salbai should be *remembered* as one of the landmarks in the history of India.
   The treaty of Salbai is worthy of *remembrance* as one of the landmarks in the history of India.
6. I cannot *consent* to your going.
   I cannot give my *consent* to your going.
7. He gave a curt *reply*.
   He *replied* curtly.
8. He showed *generosity* even to his enemies.
   He was *generous* even to his enemies.
9. There is a slight *difference* between the two shades.
   The two shades are slightly *different*.
10. The Act made the negro slaves *free*.
    The Act gave *freedom* to the negro slaves.
11. I see him every*day*.
    I see him *daily*.
12. He examined the document *carefully*.
    He examined the document with *care*.
13. We passed an *anxious* hour.
    We passed an hour *anxiously*.
14. Few historians have written in a more *interesting* manner than Gibbon.
    Few historians have written more *interestingly* than Gibbon.
15. He *presumptuously* ignored my advice.
    He *presumed* to ignore my advice.

Yeah... it's freedom...

EXERCISE 70

(a) In the following sentences replace the Nouns in italics by Verbs.

1. He rejected all our *proposals*.
2. Steel gains *strength* from the addition of nickel.
3. He made an *agreement* to supply me with firewood.
4. His *purpose* is not clear from his letter.
5. You cannot gain *admission* without a ticket.
6. He has no *intention* of leaving the city.
7. I have a *disinclination* for *work* today.
8. He made a *success* of all his *undertakings*.
9. These mangoes have a sweet *smell* but a sour *taste*.

Your wood Mr. Under Wood.

(b) Rewrite the following sentences so as to replace the Adverbs in italics by Verbs.

1. The defenders *successfully* repelled every attack on the city.
2. This scene is *surpassingly* beautiful.
3. He is *admittedly* the greatest general of the country.
4. They welcomed the good news most *joyfully*.

A quiz show ANT vs ELEPHANT

(c) Rewrite the following sentences so as to replace the Verbs and Adjectives in italics by corresponding Nouns.

1. Though the ant is small it is as *intelligent* as the elephant.
2. He said he *regretted* that he had *acted* so hastily.
3. He was so *active* in his old age that everybody *admired* him.
4. Before I pay you what is *due* you must *sign* this receipt.
5. The best way to be *healthy* is to be *temperate* in all things.

Rats give us a great deal of trouble.

(d) Rewrite the following sentences, replacing Nouns and Adverbs in italics by Adjectives of similar meaning.

1. In all *probability* the day will be fine.
2. The rats gave us a great deal of *trouble*.
3. He was dismissed for *negligence* rather than incompetence.
4. He was *admittedly* clever, but he *evidently* lacked industry.
5. The merchant had great *success* in all his dealings, and was naturally esteemed by his fellow citizens.

(e) Rewrite the following sentences replacing Nouns and Adjectives in italics by Adverbs of similar meaning.

1. Her dress was *poor* and mean.
2. He broke the rules without any intention of doing so, but it does not follow that his punishment was *wrong*.
3. His mistake was evident,but his sincerity was also *obvious*.
4. By a careful analysis of these substances you will see that they differ in *essence*.

Chapter 11 TRANSFORMATION OF SENTENCES (CONTD.)

1. Conversion of Simple Sentences to Compound (Double) Sentences

79. A Simple sentence can be converted into a Compound one by enlarging a word or a phrase into a co-ordinate clause.

Simple.	He must work very hard to make up for the lost time.
Compound.	He must work very hard and make up for the lost time.
Simple.	To his eternal disgrace, he betrayed his country.
Compound.	He betrayed his country, and this was to his eternal disgrace.
Simple.	Besides robbing the poor child, he also murdered her.
Compound.	He not only robbed the poor child but also murdered her.
Simple.	He must work very hard to win the first prize.
Compound.	He must work very hard, or he will not win the first prize.
Simple.	He must not attempt to escape, on pain of death.
Compound.	He must not attempt to escape, or he will be put to death.
Simple.	Notwithstanding his hard work, he did not succeed.
Compound.	He worked hard, yet did not succeed.
Simple.	Owing to ill-luck, he met with a bad accident on the eve of his examination.
Compound.	He was unlucky and therefore met with a bad accident on the eve of his examination.
Simple.	The teacher punished the boy for disobedience.
Compound.	The boy was disobedient, and so the teacher punished him.

EXERCISE 71

Rewrite the following Simple sentences as Compound (Double) ones.

1. In this tower sat the poet gazing on the sea.
2. To everyone's surprise, the project completely failed.
3. Seeing the rain coming on, we took shelter under a tree.
4. Besides educating his nephew, he also set him up in business.
5. The fog being very dense, the steamer sailed at less than half speed.
6. Raleigh, taking off his cloak politely, placed it in the muddy street.
7. Being occupied with important matters, he had no leisure to see us.
8. In spite of his popularity he cannot be called a great writer.
9. Rushing against Horatius, he smote with all his might.
10. With all his learning, he was far from being a pedant.
11. Little Jack Horner sat in a corner, eating his Christmas pie.
12. He must resign on pain of public dismissal.
13. Owing to drought the crop is short.
14. The men had not completed their work by sunset.
15. Notwithstanding several efforts, he failed.
16. By his pleasant manners he gained many friends.
17. In addition to pecuniary assistance he gave them much valuable advice.
18. The referee having whistled, the game was stopped.
19. On account of his negligence the company suffered heavy losses.
20. Running at top speed, he got out of breath.
21. Possessing all the advantages of education and wealth, he never made name.
22. Taking pity on the mouse, the magician turned it into a cat.
23. Being dissatisfied, he resigned his position.
24. Throwing off his coat, he plunged into sea.

EXERCISE 72

Convert the following Simple sentences to Compound sentences.

1. Hearing their father's footsteps, the boys ran away.
2. With a great effort he lifted the box.
3. The man, being very hungry, ate too much.
4. In spite of his great strength he was overcome.
5. Against the wishes of his family he left school.
6. He was universally respected on account of his virtue.
7. His friend having helped him, he is prospering.
8. Being a cripple, he cannot ride a horse.
9. The rain having washed away the embankment, the train was wrecked.
10. Finding himself in difficulty, he went to his teacher for help.
11. My friend being now in Mumbai, I shall go there to meet him.
12. In the event of such a thing happening, I should take long leave.
13. They are forbidden to enter the sacred place on pain of death.
14. To make certain of getting a place you must apply early.
15. He intends to try again notwithstanding his repeated failures.
16. In spite of all my advice he has done this foolish thing.
17. By reason of his great ability he has been able to win a high position.
18. Through no fault of his own he has become very poor.
19. Knowing no better, he used very inaccurate language.
20. His swords having broken, he was left defenceless.
21. He was rejected owing to ill-health.
22. I do not like him on account of his pride and boastfulness.
23. To avoid punishment he ran away.
24. In his ignorance he followed the wrong course.
25. Having made no provision for old age, he is very poor.
26. Out of a desire for revenge he agreed to this.
27. To add to their troubles, a tyre burst on the way.

2. Conversion of Compound (Double) Sentences to Simple Sentences

80. The following examples illustrate the chief ways of converting Compound sentences to Simple sentences.

Compound. He finished his exercise and put away his books.
Simple. Having finished his exercise, he put away his books.
Compound. Not only did his father give him money, but his mother did too.
Simple. Besides his father giving him money, his mother also did the same.
Compound. He was a mere boy but he offered to fight the giant.
Simple. In spite of his being a mere boy, he offered to fight the giant.
Compound. He must not be late, or he will be punished.
Simple. In the event of his being late, he will be punished.
Compound. You must either pay the bill at once or return the goods.
Simple. Failing prompt payment, the goods must be returned by you.
Compound. The men endured all the horrors of the campaign and not one of them complained at all.
Simple. The men endured all the horrors of the campaign without one of them making any complaint.
Compound. We must eat, or we cannot live.
Simple. We must eat to live.

EXERCISE 73

Rewrite the following Compound (Double) sentences as Simple ones.

1. They were poor, and often suffered great hardship.
2. He overslept himself, and so he missed the train.

3. The prince slew his brother and became king in his place.
4. This coat cannot be mine, for it is too big.
5. This general fought bravely, the king therefore made him commander-in-chief.
6. The camel pushed his head into the tent and asked to be allowed to warm his nose.
7. As a boy he had never been at school, and therefore he had no opportunity of learning to read or write.
8. This must not occur again, or you will be dismissed.
9. He granted the request, for he was unwilling to disappoint his friend.
10. They took every precaution ; still they ran aground.
11. He is rich, yet he is not contented.
12. Make haste, or else you will be late.
13. The steamer went down, yet the crew were saved.
14. The piper advanced, and the children followed.
15. The horse reared and the rider was thrown.
16. Walk quickly, else you will not overtake him.
17. I called him, but he gave me no answer.
18. Either he is drowned or some passing ship has saved him.
19. He must have done his duty, for he is a conscientious man.
20. He tried hard, but he did not succeed.
21. He tried again and again, but he did not succeed.
22. We decided not to go any further that day and put up at the nearest hotel.
23. Either you must help me or I must try to carry out my task alone.
24. His partner died, and this added to his difficulties.
25. He was horrified for he saw blood stains on the floor and no sign of his child.
26. Not only men, but women and children were put to death.
27. Everybody else went down to meet him in the train, but I did not.
28. He is a well-read man, but in matters of business he is a fool.
29. Work at least six hours a day, or you cannot make sure of success.
30. He is very poor, but he does not complain.
31. He neither returned the goods nor paid the bill.

EXERCISE 74

Convert the following Compound (Double) sentences to Simple sentences.

1. My friend arrived and we went for a walk.
2. The servant brought the lamp and I began my homework.
3. The ink had dried up and I could not write.
4. I have a lot of work and must do it now.
5. We must hurry and we shall escape the rain.
6. He has an unpleasant duty and must perform it.
7. He not only pitied him but relieved him.
8. He did this and so offended his master.
9. He had read the book carefully and could tell the story in his own words.
10. His object became known and everybody tried to help him.
11. He found a hundred rupee note and was delighted at his good luck.
12. Rama has hurt his ankle and will not be able to play today.
13. Be good and you will be happy.
14. He did not like the work and he began it unwillingly.
15. I ordered him to halt, but he took no notice.
16. He is a good steady worker, only he is rather slow.

17. I continually invited him to visit me, but he never came.
18. He served out his sentence in gaol and was released.
19. He worked exceedingly hard at school, for he was a good obedient boy.
20. The dacoits stopped to divide the booty and the police overtook them.
21. He practised daily and so became an expert player.
22. Your attempt can hardly be called successful, for it has had no good results.
23. The President came into the hall and everyone rose from his seat.
24. He escaped several times but was finally caught.
25. The horse fell heavily and his rider came down with him.
26. He found himself getting weaker and weaker; so he consulted a doctor.
27. The plague broke out in the city and the people moved out into the jungle.
28. I had no money with me, and I could not give the beggar anything.

3. Conversion of Simple Sentences to Complex

81. A Simple sentence can be converted to a Complex sentence by expanding a word or phrase into a Subordinate clause.

This clause may be a Noun, Adjective or Adverb clause.

Simple.	He confessed *his crime.*
Complex.	He confessed *that he was guilty.*
Simple.	His *silence* proves his guilt.
Complex.	The *fact that he is silent* proves his guilt.
Simple.	He bought *his uncle's* library.
Complex.	He bought the library *which belonged to his uncle.*
Simple.	*On the arrival of the mails* the ship will leave.
Complex.	The ship will leave *as soon as the mails arrive.*
Simple.	He owed *his success* to his father.
Complex.	It was owing to his father *that he succeeded.*
Simple.	He worked hard *to pass the examination.*
Complex.	He worked hard so *that he might pass the examination.*
Simple.	Cain, *being jealous of Abel,* struck him.
Complex.	Cain struck Abel *because he was jealous of him.*
Simple.	*Only Indians* are admitted.
Complex.	*If you are not an Indian* you cannot be admitted.
Simple.	He succeeded *unexpectedly.*
Complex.	He succeeded *although his success was not expected.*
Simple.	The management is *thoroughly bad.*
Complex.	The management is *as bad as it could be.*
Simple.	A man's modesty is in inverse proportion to his ignorance.
Complex.	The more ignorant a man is, the less modest he is.

EXERCISE 75

Convert the following Simple sentences to Complex sentences, each containing a Noun clause.

1. I expect to meet Rama tonight.
2. He hoped to win the prize.
3. His father is not likely to punish him.
4. He admitted stealing the watch.
5. Krishna wishes me to play for his team.
6. He believes their success to be certain in that case.
7. I overheard all his remarks.
8. I did not think fit to reply to his writings.
9. He confessed his fault.
10. His hiding place is still unknown.
11. I shall be glad of your advice in this matter.
12. He pleaded ignorance of the law.
13. Our friends will hear of our success.
14. You imply my guilt by your words and manner.
15. I request your help.
16. I cannot foretell the time of my departure.
17. I wish you to be quiet.
18. He is said to be a millionaire.
19. Tell the truth.
20. I have long suspected his poverty.

EXERCISE 76

Convert the following Simple sentences to Complex sentences, each containing an Adjective clause.

1. I saw a wounded bird.
2. Rama is happy in his present class.
3. The man near me is my brother.
4. Our guru is a man of blameless life.
5. Your father is the man to help you in this matter.
6. The value of exercise is great.
7. Was this the deed of a good man ?
8. I was the first to hear the news.
9. These are not the methods of business.
10. The classroom is not the place for boys to play in.
11. He is hardly the boy to do credit to the school.
12. He liked his former place.
13. Smoke, the certain indicator of fire, appeared in the mine.
14. I was the first to arrive.
15. That is not the way to answer.
16. It was the work of a wild animal.
17. He is the water-carrier.
18. I have nowhere to sit.
19. My friend, the magistrate of this place, is on leave.
20. He sat outside on a stone in the compound.

EXERCISE 77

Convert the following Simple sentences to Complex sentences, each containing an Adverb clause.

1. On being punished, he wept.
2. During Queen Victoria's reign there were many wars.
3. Being quite contented, he never grumbled.
4. Being ill-treated by his master, he ran away.
5. He was too dull to understand.
6. The tiger is feared for its fierceness.
7. With your permission I will go away.
8. The peon would be quite happy with a rise of Rs. 10 a month.
9. He replied to the best of his ability.
10. I can only tell you according to my memory.
11. Of Krishna and Rama the latter works the harder.
12. Owing to ill-health he has resigned.
13. He was annoyed at being rebuked.
14. He cannot be caught on account of his quickness.
15. He is too lazy to succeed.
16. He came in very quietly to avoid waking his father.
17. He waited there with a view to meeting me.
18. There is no admission without permission.
19. I will help you in any possible way.
20. Do not go out without leave.
21. In spite of the heat they marched quickly.
22. For all his youth he is very capable.
23. Till my arrival, wait here.

24. After the death of his father he left Mumbai.
25. Up to his thirtieth year he remained unmarried.
26. From the time of that illness he has been partly blind.
27. Previous to his death he made his will.
28. In anticipation of sanction I have issued the order.
29. He hindered the police in the execution of their duty.
30. This was done in my absence.
31. For fear of imprisonment they kept silence.
32. Notwithstanding my entreaties he shot the dog.
33. He wrote according to instructions.
34. He worked to the best of his ability.
35. Come back at six o'clock.
36. With every blow the body quivered.
37. Speaking honestly, I do not know.
38. I came today to take advantage of the special train.
39. He failed to my great surprise.
40. Till the day of the examination he did no more work.
41. The tiger having fallen, he climbed down from the tree.
42. In the time of Aurangzeb taxes were very heavy.
43. We eat to live.
44. Some people live to eat.
45. He has gone down to the river to bathe.
46. Have you come to see me ?
47. Does he wish me to go ?

EXERCISE 78

Rewrite the following Simple sentences as Complex sentences.

1. Can you tell me the time of his arrival ?
2. After seeing the King he departed.
3. Many ships were so shattered as to be wholly unmanageable.
4. England expects every man to do his duty.
5. The guests having departed, he went to bed.
6. Few know the date of Lucy's death.

7. The source of the Nile was difficult to discover.
8. I will meet you at any place convenient for you.
9. In spite of his earnest protestations, he was condemned.
10. He is proud of his high birth.
11. The prince was to be found in the hottest of the battle.
12. I rejoice at his good fortune.

13. But for his own confession, the crime could scarcely have been brought home to him.
14. He alone entered, the rest of us waiting outside.
15. Not feeling well, he decided to lie down.
16. The last of these voyages not proving very fortunate, I grew weary of the sea.

17. Considering the difficulties of his position, he has acted admirably.
18. Speak low, to prevent our being overheard.
19. He was too much excited to hear reason.
20. A letter from the butler brings to the club the news of Sir Roger's death.
21. My right there is none to dispute.
22. Accustomed to rule, he schooled himself to obey.
23. He saved the child at the risk of his life.
24. A good tree cannot bring forth evil fruit.
25. I convinced him of his mistake.
26. It all depends upon the manner of your doing it.
27. He can prove his innocence.
28. Everybody knows the author of *Gulliver's Travels.*
29. The date of his arrival is uncertain.
30. The duration of the war is uncertain.
31. There is no hope of his recovery.
32. The exact date of the birth of Buddha is unknown.
33. A daily bath is necessary to perfect health.
34. Success or failure depends largely on your own efforts.
35. In my hurry I forgot the most important letters.
36. Listeners never hear any good of themselves.
37. Finding the door unlocked, the thief entered the house.
38. It is impossible to trust the word of a habitual liar.
39. Gray, the author of the *Elegy,* lived in the eighteenth century.
40. The shepherd found the lost sheep.
41. The boy readily admitted his mistake.
42. Tell me your plans.
43. He could clearly remember the incidents of his youth.
44. On arriving at the foot of the hill, he blew his trumpet.
45. A spider saved Robert Bruce.
46. The prudent man looks to the future.
47. For want of money, he was unable to prosecute his studies.
48. All the money having been spent, we started looking for work.
49. The idle cannot hope to succeed.
50. Our orders were to show no mercy.
51. It was too late for retreat.
52. I must be cruel, only to be kind.

53. The men fought with desperation.
54. He is too truthful to be a successful courtier.
55. Your remuneration depends on the quality of your work.
56. He conducted himself madly to escape suspicion.
57. Good boys need not fear punishment.
58. The accused confessed his guilt.
59. I asked him the reason of his coming.
60. But for your folly you could have been a partner in the firm today.

61. Tell me your age.
62. I was glad to hear of your arrival.
63. Being a very diligent and clever lad, he soon distinguished himself.
64. He is too short for a soldier.
65. This is said to be the birthplace of Buddha.
66. His success went beyond his expectations.
67. In spite of his poor health, he worked hard.
68. Feeling out of sorts, he went to bed.
69. He complained of being unjustly treated.
70. He killed the hen to get the treasure.
71. An army of ants will attack large and ferocious animals.
72. A very miserly planter formerly lived in the island of Jamaica.
73. He often gave his poor slaves too little food.
74. Industry will keep you from want.
75. A drowning man will catch at a straw.

76. It is excellent to have a giant's strength.
77. Having finished our work, we went out for a walk.
78. With all thy faults I love thee still.
79. The news is too good to be true.
80. This tree is too high for me to climb.
81. He is too old to learn anything new.
82. The world's greatest men have not laboured with a view to becoming rich.

83. With a change of wind we shall have rain.
84. With all his wealth he is not happy.

4. Conversion of Complex Sentences to Simple Sentences

82. Study the following examples.

Noun Clause

Complex.	He said *that he was innocent.*
Simple.	He declared *his innocence.*
Complex.	*That you are drunk* aggravates your offence.
Simple.	*Your drunkenness* aggravates your offence.
Complex.	Tell me *where you live.*
Simple.	Tell me *your address.*

Complex. It is a pity *that we should have to undergo this disgrace.*
Simple. *Our having to undergo this disgrace* is a pity.
Complex. *It is proclaimed* that all men found with arms will be shot.
Simple. *According to the proclamation* all men found with arms will be shot.
Complex. He remarked *how impudent the boy was.*
Simple. He remarked *on the boy's impudence.*
Complex. *How long I shall stay* is doubtful.
Simple. *The duration of my stay* is doubtful.
Complex. *Except that he hurt his hand,* he was lucky.
Simple. *Except for the hurt to his hand,* he was lucky.

EXERCISE 79

Convert each of the following Complex sentences to a Simple sentence.

1. We believe that he is innocent.
2. It was much regretted that he was absent.
3. The consequence of his carelessness was that the game was lost.
4. He asked why I came.
5. He ordered that the traitor should be executed.
6. It is to be hoped that he escaped unhurt.
7. I do not know when I shall return.
8. We hope that better times will come.
9. The news that the enemy landed spread like wild fire.
10. That I was successful does not make me happy.
11. He ordered the police that they should imprison the rioters.
12. That you should be willing to believe this is incredible.
13. Whoever is prudent is respected.
14. It is reported that our troops have won a victory.
15. All believed that he was guilty of murder.
16. Tell me what you mean by this.

I don't know I shall return.

83. Study the following examples.

Adjective Clause

Complex. He died in the village *where he was born.*
Simple. He died in his *native village.*
Complex. The moment *which is lost* is lost for ever.
Simple. A *lost* moment is lost for ever.
Complex. Men *who have risen by their own exertions* are always respected.
Simple. *Self-made* men are always respected.
Complex. They *that are whole* have no need of the physician.
Simple. *Healthy* persons have no need of the physician.
Complex. We came upon a hut *where a peasant lived.*
Simple. *We came upon a peasant's hut.*
Complex. Youth is the time *when the seeds of character are sown.*
Simple. Youth is the time *for the formation of character.*
Complex. The exact time *when this occurred* has not been ascertained.
Simple. The exact time *of the occurrence* has not been ascertained.
Complex. The son *who was his chief pride in his old age* is dead.
Simple. His son, *the pride of his old age,* is dead.
Complex. *The place where Buddha was cremated* has recently been discovered.
Simple. *The place of Buddha's cremation* has recently been discovered.
Complex. I have no advice *that I can offer you.*
Simple. I have no advice *to offer you.*

I'm a self-made man.

EXERCISE 80

Convert each of the following Complex sentences to a Simple sentence.

1. He sold the horse which belonged to his brother.
2. As I was unable to help in any other way, I gave her some money.
3. I have no horse that I can lend you.
4. The marks that were left by the whip were still visible.
5. This is the place where we camp.
6. The heart that is full of grief is heavy.
7. The reply which you have made is foolish.
8. The evil that men do lives after them.
9. Do you not remember him who was formerly your friend ?

It's a foolish reply.

10. This is the needle with which she knits.
11. Have you nothing that you wish to say ?
12. He prospered by the help he got from his friends.
13. They were advised by a clever lawyer who was a High Court pleader.
14. He is weak from the illness which he had recently.
15. A man who is dead needs no riches.
16. I have seen the house which belongs to Rama.
17. He was the most learned of the judges who lived at that time.
18. He died in the village where he was born.
19. The horse which is an Arab of pure blood, is very swift.
20. The smell which comes from this drain, is very bad.
21. Can he get no work that he can do ?
22. Is there no place which is kept for bathing here ?
23. The birds have no water that they can drink.
24. He shot a tiger which was the scourge of the district.
25. That is the book that belongs to me.
26. I saw a man who was blind.
27. This is the bottle which is used for water.
28. The chief thing that Wycliffe and his friends achieved was the translation of the Bible into English.
29. I found the book which I had lost.
30. The boy who stood first got the prize
31. A city that is set on a hill cannot be hid.
32. People who live in glass houses must not throw stones.
33. The services he has rendered to the state cannot be over-estimated.
34. The place where they live is very unhealthy.
35. This idea on which he based his philosophy, is very difficult to comprehend.
36. I have no time that I can waste on idle talk.
37. A person who relies on his own efforts has the best chance to win success.
38. Here is a barrier that cannot be passed.
39. A person who has risen by his own exertions is always respected.
40. A boy who had been notoriously idle was awarded a prize.
41. Such men as you cannot be easily disheartened.
42. A man who is industrious is sure to succeed.
43. He told us the time when he expected to arrive.

84. Study the following examples.

Adverb Clause

Complex.	The Captain was annoyed *that he had not carried out his orders.*
Simple.	The Captain was annoyed *at his not having carried out his orders.*
Complex.	You can talk *as much as you like.*
Simple.	You can talk *to your heart's content.*
Complex.	Everything comes *if a man will only work and wait.*
Simple.	Everything comes *to a diligent and patient man.*
Complex.	I am pushing my business *wherever I can find an opening.*
Simple.	I am pushing my business *in every possible direction.*
Complex.	He will *not* pay *unless he is compelled.*
Simple.	He will pay *only under compulsion.*
Complex.	You have succeeded *better than you hoped.*
Simple.	You have succeeded *beyond your hopes.*
Complex.	*When the cat is away* the mice will play.
Simple.	*In the absence of the cat* the mice will play.
Complex.	He does not always speak *as he thinks.*
Simple.	He does not always speak *his thoughts.*
Complex.	A good boy will always do *as he is commanded by his superiors.*
Simple.	A good boy will always carry out (or execute) *the commands of his superiors.*
Complex.	I was surprised *when I heard him talk so.*
Simple.	I was surprised *to hear him talk so.*
Complex.	He was so tired *that he could not stand.*
Simple.	He was *too* tired *to stand.*
Complex.	If I make a promise *I keep it.*
Simple.	I make a promise *only to keep it.*
Complex.	*As the war was ended,* the soldiers returned.
Simple.	*The war being ended,* the soldiers returned.
Complex.	While there is life there is hope
Simple.	Life and hope are inseparable.
Complex.	As you sow, so you will reap.
Simple.	You will but reap the fruits of your sowing.

EXERCISE 81

Convert the following Complex sentences into Simple sentences.

1. As you are here you may as well see it.
2. He was angry when he heard the result.
3. Does he know the consequences if he refuses ?
4. He cannot go unless I consent.
5. You cannot always talk sense if you are always talking.
6. You never come here but you steal something.

7. The boy ran as fast as he could.
8. As it was beginning to rain we waited a while.
9. Although he has failed twice he will try again.
10. He made such good speed that he was in time.
11. Because he was ill he stayed at home.
12. As he felt cold he lit a fire.
13. Since I am unable to get much, I accept little.

14. He will pay you when he hears from me.
15. He was so tired that he could not sleep.
16. They rejoice that they are going.
17. I congratulated him because he had passed.
18. He can afford to be generous because he is rich.
19. As the hour had arrived they started.
20. Since I believed his word I did not ask for proof.
21. The dog jumped up when he saw the cat.
22. The horse is so old that it cannot work.
23. The tiger is renowned through all the countryside because he is so cunning and ferocious.
24. He was very angry when he had to pay again.
25. The longer we wait here, the darker it will become.
26. He is not so tall that he cannot enter the doorway.
27. When they heard the signal they sprang up.
28. As the truth is known, further lying is useless.
29. Wherever you go I shall follow you.
30. No sooner did he see us than he disappeared.

31. As soon as he heard the news he wrote to me.
32. Because you have done this I shall punish you.
33. As he was not there, I spoke to his brother.
34. They went where living was cheaper.
35. Wherever he preached the people gathered to listen.
36. She stood as though turned to stone.
37. We have come so that we may help you.
38. You will pass if you work hard.
39. He cannot see unless he wears glasses.
40. His father still trusted him though he had deceived him.
41. He is not so prudent as he ought to be .
42. It was so dark that you could not see your hand.
43. When the fraud was discovered, he was imprisoned after being tried.
44. He was so indolent that he could not be successful.
45. An honest boy speaks as he thinks.
46. Sit down where you please.
47. The larger the brain, the more vigorous the mind.

I'll buy it, cost what it may.

48. I shall give you my horse if you give me your silver.
49. We will do the work as well as we can.
50. Robinson Crusoe was puzzled when he discovered the print of a foot on the sand.
51. Though the sky falls, he will not be frightened.
52. Apollo was worshipped as long as the Roman Empire lasted.
53. I will buy it, cost what it may.
54. I am surprised that you should believe such nonsense.
55. Whatever you do, I will support.

EXERCISE 82

Turn each of the following Complex sentences into a Simple sentence.

1. It is terrible that people should die of starvation.
2. I was unable to hear what you were saying.
3. We did not go, as the weather was too stormy.
4. It is doubtful whether he will succeed.
5. He became so ill that he was unable to walk.
6. No one is promoted to a higher class unless he is examined.

Pardon me...

7. He ran as fast as he could.
8. He said that he would come tomorrow.
9. Tell me where you live.
10. He confessed that he was guilty.
11. It was so dark that we lost our way.
12. Tell me how old you are.
13. When he will arrive is not yet known.
14. Grant me what I ask.

15. We hope that better times will come.
16. I insist that you should not go.
17. I shall remain where I am.
18. If you turn to the right you will soon reach the temple.
19. He gave a graphic account of how he escaped.

20. We went half-an-hour earlier, so that we might get a good seat.
21. He complained that he had been unjustly treated.
22. It is certain that he will come.
23. The Commissioner gave rewards to such men as deserve them.
24. I asked him why he came.
25. A child who has lost his parents is to be pitied.
26. They left at six o'clock so that he might catch the early train.

27. Suspicion always haunts the mind of a person who is guilty.
28. He went to Ooty so that he might improve his health.
29. A book in which were pictures of animals, was presented to him by his uncle.

This is a complicated question.

30. When Caesar saw Brutus among the assassins, he covered his face with his gown.
31. John Bright once said that the safest place in England was a first-class carriage in an express train.
32. The question is so complicated that it cannot be settled immediately.

33. Had he been absent, the motion would have been carried.
34. The passage is so difficult that I cannot comprehend it.
35. We must do the work as well as we can.
36. Although they fought most valiantly, they were defeated.
37. If he wins the battle he will be crowned.
38. I wish to know the time when he died.
39. Those soldiers who survived have received medals.
40. This is a machine which is used for sewing.
41. He seemed very anxious that we should come.
42. The priests were satisfied when he offered the money.
43. You must be hungry if you have not dined.
44. It is time you went.
45. It is lucky that he came just then.
46. It is certain that he will help you.
47. You must write to me as soon as you reach Mumbai.
48. He gave away some books which belonged to his brother.
49. Can you tell me the name of the person who wrote the book ?
50. It is said that he died by his own hand.
51. While my parents are absent I cannot come.
52. This sum is so hard that I cannot do it.
53. As one man fell another took his place.

54. Work as hard as you can.
55. Drink while you may.
56. Such a man as he is should succeed.
57. The police know this from information which has been received by them.

5. Conversion of Compound Sentences to Complex

85. Study the following examples.

Compound.	Search his pockets and you will find the watch.
Complex.	If you search his pockets, you will find the watch.
Compound.	Do as I tell you, or you will regret it.
Complex.	Unless you do as I tell you, you will regret it.
Compound.	The lion was wounded but not killed.
Complex.	The lion was not killed although he was wounded. (=Although the lion was wounded, he was not killed.)
Compound.	Waste not, want not.
Complex.	If you do not waste, you will not want.
Compound.	He saw the danger, but pressed on.
Complex.	Although he saw the danger, he pressed on.
Compound.	He saw the danger and paused.
Complex	When he saw the danger he paused.
Compound	He aimed at winning the prize and worked hard.
Complex.	He worked hard so that he might win the prize.
Compound.	He had to sign, or be executed.
Complex.	If he had not signed, he would have been executed.
Compound.	He is buried near Rome and myrtles grow round his grave.
Complex.	He is buried near Rome in a place where myrtles grow.
Compound.	He wishes to become learned ; therefore he is studying hard.
Complex.	He is studying hard so that he may become learned.

EXERCISE 83

Transform from Compound into Complex sentences.

1. Spare the rod and spoil the child.
2. He put on his hat and went outside.
3. At length she woke and looked round.
4. Keep quiet, or you will be punished.
5. The ship was wrecked, but the crew were saved.

6. Either Shirin will come or she will send a letter.
7. Do your best, and you will never regret it.
8. He received your telegram and set off at once.
9. I must hurry back at once, or my business will greatly suffer.

10. Do this, or you will be punished.
11. Rama may not be clever but he is certainly industrious.
12. I put my hand into my pocket and gave him a rupee.
13. Only do the right, and you will have no reason to be ashamed.
14. The crow stole a piece of cheese and flew with it to a tree.
15. I called at your house yesterday but you were out.

16. This is the prisoner's first offence so h with a small fine.
17. We must do our work well, or our master will be angry with us.
18. You have earned his gratitude, so you shall not go unrewarded.
19. He failed in his first attempt and never tried again.
20. Time flies fast, yet it sometimes appears to move slowly.
21. Mosquitoes cause malaria, and this is well known.
22. She must weep, or she will die.
23. He ran to the station, but he missed the train.
24. The boy was tired, therefore he went to bed.
25. He is poor, but contented.
26. Life has few enjoyments ; still we cling to it.
27. Eat few suppers and you'll need few medicines.
28. He is working hard ; therefore he will succeed.
29. He wishes to succeed ; therefore he works hard.
30. He was going along this road, and met a dragon.
31. They were refused pay, but went on working.
32. I frowned upon him, yet he loves me still.
33. Do you find victories and we will find rewards ?
34. The archers were poorly armed, but they offered a stubborn resistance.
35. Cross this line and you will be captured.
36. You must be warmly clad, or you will catch cold.
37. Take care of the pence and the pounds will take care of themselves.
38. He adored his proud wife, but he was in mortal fear of her fierce temper.
39. We are few, but we are of the right sort.
40. Be diligent and you will succeed.
41. It seems too good to be true, nevertheless it is a fact.
42. Resist the devil, and he will flee from you.
43. I will recover it, or die in the attempt.
44. Take a farthing from a hundred pounds, and it will be a hundred pounds no longer.
45. He has lost all his teeth, consequently he cannot eat hard food.
46. Give him an inch and he'll take an ell.
47. Hear him out, and you will understand him the better.
48. Advance another step, and you are a dead man.
49. Send the deed after me and I will sign it.
50. He was very learned and seemed to know everything.
51. He was ambitious and therefore I killed him.
52. We landed at Karachi, and there we spent a very enjoyable week.
53. We called upon Mr. Pundit and he introduced us to his partner.
54. He was my friend, therefore I loved him.

EXERCISE 84

Convert the following Compound sentences to Complex sentences.

1. Give me the book and I will read it.
2. Take quinine and your fever will be cured.
3. I tell him to be quiet and he takes no notice.
4. He is deaf but he will always pretend to hear.
5. You have paid the bill but you will get no more credit.
6. I ran all the way to the station but I missed the train.
7. Rama is a better player than Krishna and therefore he must take his place in the team.
8. You called me and here I am.
9. The master is nearly blind and the boys are very sorry for him.
10. We will win or die.
11. Let me come in, or I will break down the door.
12. Be careful in your diet and you will keep health.
13. Listen and I will tell you all.
14. He is very agreeable but I don't like him.
15. It is cold, so I shall wear a coat.
16. Send me the gun and I will mend it.
17. Be good and you need not be clever.
18. Follow me, or you will lose your way.
19. You ordered the goods and so they have been sent.
20. You must pay, or else sign a chit.
21. I do not like his lectures and so I don't attend them.

22. He ran away, or they would have killed him.
23. He has injured me but I will forgive him.
24. Be quiet, or I shall punish you.
25. Be just and fear not.
26. He was never present, but he always sent a deputy.
27. Be kind and help me.
28. Pay heed to the small details and the general plan will surely succeed.
29. He is certain to be late, so why wait for him ?
30. You or I must go away.
31. Sri Lanka went in first on a very wet wicket, and so they lost the match.
32. They tried to bribe the peon but he was too clever for them.

6. Conversion of Complex Sentences to Compound

86. Study the following examples.

I hate loud sounds.

Complex. I am certain you have made a mistake.
Compound. You have made a mistake, and of this I am certain.
Complex. I am glad that he has recovered from illness.
Compound. He has recovered from illness, and I am glad of it.
Complex. We can prove that the earth is round.
Compound. The earth is round, and we can prove it.
Complex. I have found the book that I had lost.
Compound. I had lost a book, but I have found it.
Complex. As soon as he got the telegram, he left in a taxi.
Compound. He got the telegram, and immediately he left in a taxi.

You have made a mistake.

Complex. He worked hard so that he might win the prize.
Compound. He aimed at winning the prize and worked hard.
Complex. If he is at home, I shall see him.
Compound. He may be at home, and in that case I shall see him.
Complex. He lost more than he could afford.
Compound. He could afford to lose something, but he lost somewhat more.
Complex. He is more a philosopher than a poet.
Compound. He is something of a poet, but rather more of a philosopher.
Complex. If you do not hurry you will miss the train.
Compound. You must hurry, or you will miss the train.
Complex. Unless we do our work well our master will be angry with us.
Compound. We must do our work well, or our master will be angry with us.
Complex. We sow so that we may reap.
Compound. We desire to reap, therefore we sow.

EXERCISE 85

Convert from Complex to Compound sentences.

1. Once upon a time a man owned a hen which laid everyday a golden egg.
2. We selected this bicycle after we had tried several times.
3. It is surprising that he did not succeed.
4. If you do not take exercise, you will be ill.
5. If you run, you will be in time.
6. He ran away because he was afraid.
7. As he was not there, I spoke to his brother.
8. Although he saw the danger, he pressed on.
9. Though you try with all your might, you will not succeed.
10. I shall not go unless I am invited.
11. If you eat too much you will be ill.
12. A book's a book, although there's nothing in it.
13. Unless you keep quiet, you will be punished.
14. As Caesar loved me, I weep for him.
15. Because you have done this I shall punish you.
16. As soon as he heard the news he wrote to me.
17. When you have rested, go on with the work.
18. I forgave him because he was dying.
19. He stayed at home because he was ill.
20. His father still trusted him though he had deceived him.

21. Though the sky falls, he will not be frightened.
22. He was educated at a public school where he learnt Latin.
23. I struck him because he ventured to obstruct my path.
24. They went to war that they might extend their empire.
25. Although they fought most valiantly, they were defeated.
26. He writes so illegibly that I cannot read his letter.
27. I know what you told him.
28. The ship was steered so skillfully that it reached the harbour safely.
29. You must be respectable if you would be respected.
30. As he was ambitious, I killed him.
31. Though often capricious and impertinent, she was never out of temper.
32. Though the waves are raging high, I'll row you o'er the ferry.
33. He finished first though he began late.
34. Though he tries hard, he is seldom successful.
35. When the sun set he returned home.
36. Since duty calls us, we must obey.
37. He had a cow that gave enormous quantities of milk.
38. He failed because he was too rash.
39. We eat so that we may live.
40. He was so learned that he seemed to know everything.

EXERCISE 86

Convert the following Complex sentences to Compound sentences.

1. Rama went to school as soon as he had finished his meal.
2. If I ask a civil question I expect a civil reply.
3. They have never been poor since they opened that shop.
4. I could answer if I chose.
5. We might admire a bad man though we cannot admire a weak one.
6. I advise you to try although you may not succeed.
7. I spoke plainly so that you might understand.
8. He feigned sleep as he had an object in doing so.
9. He gave himself up because the flight was useless.
10. As we are here we will stay here.
11. I do not think he will come.
12. I know there is a rupee in your hand.
13. Come when you like.
14. I shall come when I am in better health.
15. I would have shot the snake if I had seen it.
16. His precept is as beautiful as his practice is disgraceful.
17. At Rome we must behave as the Romans do.
18. He fell as I fired.
19. If you come here you will repent it.
20. I have never heard from him since he left Mumbai.
21. He went to the house so that he might leave a message.
22. Unless we run we shall miss the train.
23. As soon as the sun touches the horizon darkness begins to settle upon the scene.
24. However clever you may be, you cannot succeed without industry.
25. Do this, lest a worse thing befall.
26. If you trust to the book you will find yourself in difficulties.
27. We may lose all without regret, if we may keep our honour sustained.
28. Bad as things are they might be worse.
29. You may go when you have finished your work.
30. His bark is worse than his bite.
31. If I am right you must be wrong.

EXERCISE 87

(Miscellaneous) Recast the following sentences as directed.

1. A soldier of the tenth legion leaped into the water as soon as the ship touched the shore. (Begin with *No sooner.*)
2. We have helped them with money as well as a body of workers, all well-trained and experienced. (Use the expression 'not only' and 'everyone'.)
3. Mrs. Smith is the wisest member of the family and of her four daughters Jane is the prettiest. (Use the comparatives of 'wise' and 'pretty'.)
4. The difficulty was solved by means of a special service devised for the occasion. (Make the word 'service' the subject.)
5. The lady was compelled by the doctor to drink such vile medicine that she was all but killed by him. (Use the active voice throughout.)
6. You are already as well acquainted with these affairs as I am. (Use 'known' for 'acquainted'.)
7. As soon as Sir Roger had seated himself, he called for wax candles. (Use 'no sooner' for 'as soon as'.)
8. When supper had been prepared, Robinson Crusoe sat down expecting to enjoy himself greatly. (Use noun forms instead of 'prepared' and 'expecting'.)
9. Nelson knew the value of obedience so well that he anticipated some censure for his act. (Rewrite this sentence, using 'too' for 'so'.)
10. The secretary sent me no reply for ten days. (Rewrite, using the verb 'reply' instead of the noun.)
11. Have a look at the newspaper and you will find a lot of space devoted to advertisements. (Begin with *if.*)
12. Her reason for not going with us was that she had no money. (Use *therefore.*)
13. Besides having a salary, he also has a private income. (Use *not only ..... but*)
14. His parents were compelled by poverty to send him abroad so that he might earn his own living. (Simple sentence, active voice)
15. His fondness for games increases with his proficiency. (Complex sentence, using 'the.......the' and adjectives to replace the abstract nouns.)
16. Of all the men I know none is less inclined than he is to believe ill of others. (Reduce to two clauses.)
17. When the monsoon broke, the temperature fell rapidly. (Simple sentence, 'break' as subject ; replace 'fell' by noun.)
18. He has squandered his fortune, estranged his friends and ruined his health by his recklessness and extravagance. (Use 'not only.....but'.)

19. He has discovered new facts and advanced new arguments, but my opinion is unchanged. (Complex sentence ; negative principal clause with verb in active voice; two adjectival clauses.)
20. He is notoriously mean in his treatment of his servants. (Rewrite in four ways–(1) Simple sentence with 'treatment' as subject; (2) Simple sentence with 'treat' as the verb ; (3) Complex sentence with a noun clause ; (4) Complex sentence with an adjective clause and 'meanness' as subject of the principal clause.)
21. You can imagine my annoyance on learning of the postponement of the football match. (Complex sentence ; three subordinate clauses.)
22. His sole income is what he earns by his pen. (Make the principal clause negative.)
23. A sailing ship was wrecked here last December. (Rewrite in three ways so as to emphasize (1) 'sailing', (2) 'here', (3) 'December'.)
24. It is probable that he will come back. (Simple sentence; replace 'probable' and 'come back' by nouns.)

Chapter 12 SYNTHESIS OF SENTENCES

Combination of Two or More Simple Sentences into a Single Simple Sentence

87. **Synthesis** is the opposite of Analysis and means the combination of a number of simple sentences into one new sentence–Simple, Compound or Complex.

88. The following are the chief ways of combining two or more Simple sentences into one Simple sentence.

(i) By using a Participle

1. He jumped up. He ran away.
   Jumping up, he ran away.
2. He was tired of play. He sat down to rest.
   Tired (*or,* being tired) of play, he sat down to rest.

(ii) By using a Noun or a Phrase in Apposition

1. This is my friend. His name is Rama.
   This is my friend Rama.
2. I spent two days in Cox's Bazar. It is one of the most attractive spots in Bangladesh.
   I spent two days in Cox's Bazar, one of the most attractive spots in Bangladesh.
3. This town was once a prosperous seaport. It is now a heap of ruins.
   This town, once a prosperous seaport, is now a heap of ruins.

(iii) By using a Preposition with a Noun or Gerund

1. The moon rose. Their journey was not ended.
   The moon rose before the end of their journey.
2. He has failed many times. He still hopes to succeed.
   In spite of many failures he hopes to succeed.
3. Her husband died. She heard the news. She fainted.
   On hearing the news of her husband's death, she fainted.

(iv) By using the Nominative Absolute Construction

1. The soldiers arrived. The mob dispersed.
   The soldiers having arrived, the mob dispersed.
2. The town was enclosed by a strong wall. The enemy was unable to capture it.
   The town having been enclosed by a strong wall, the enemy was unable to capture it.

(v) By using an Infinitive

1. I have some duties. I must perform them.
   I have some duties to perform.
2. We must finish this exercise. There are still three sentences.
   We have still three sentences of this exercise to finish.
3. He wanted to educate his son. He sent him to Europe.
   He sent his son to Europe to be educated.
4. He is very fat. He cannot run.
   He is too fat to run.

(vi) By using an Adverb or an Adverbial Phrase

1. He deserved to succeed. He failed.
   He failed undeservedly.
2. The sun set. The boys had not finished the game.
   The boys had not finished the game by sunset.

89. Several of these methods may be combined in the same sentence.
The sun rose. The fog dispersed. The general determined to delay no longer. He gave the order to advance.
At sunrise, the fog having dispersed, the general, determined to delay no longer gave the order to advance.

EXERCISE 88

Combine each set of sentences into one Simple sentence by using Participles. (You have to use the Nominative Absolute Construction in some of your sentences.)

1. He hurt his foot. He stopped.
2. The thief had been in prison before. He received severe sentences.
3. He was unwilling to go any further. He returned home.
4. They saw the uselessness of violence. They changed their policy.
5. He was weary of failure. He emigrated to Africa.
6. The King was warned of his danger. He made good his escape.
7. He lost a large sum of money. He gave up speculation.
8. I received no answer. I knocked a second time.
9. His wife encouraged him. He persevered.
10. He gave up his situation. He was not satisfied with his salary.
11. He felt tired. He laid his work aside.
12. He went straight on. He saw Hari on the path.
13. The stable door was open. The horse was stolen.
14. The hunter took up his gun. He went out to shoot the lion.
15. I went to Mumbai last year. I wished to see a dentist.
16. A crow stole a piece of cheese. She flew to her nest to enjoy the tasty meal.
17. The magician took pity on the mouse. He turned it into a cat.
18. A passenger alighted from the train. He fell over a bag on the platform.
19. My sister was charmed with the silk. She bought ten yards.
20. I did not hear his answer. It was spoken quietly.
21. The ship was delayed by a storm. She came into port a day late.
22. He had resolved on a certain course. He acted with vigour.
23. The letter was badly written. I had great difficulty in making out its contents.
24. A hungry fox saw some bunches of grapes
    They were hanging from a vine.
25. Cinderella hurried away with much haste.
    She dropped one of her little glass-slippers.
26. I was walking along the street one day.
    I saw a dead snake.
27. He was overpowered. He surrendered.
28. He ran at top speed. He got out of breath.
29. He possessed all the advantages of education and wealth. He never made a name.
30. He was occupied with important matters. He had no leisure to see visitors.
31. The Russians burnt Moscow. The French were forced to quit it.
32. The votes on each side were equal. The chairman gave his casting vote against the resolution.
33. Wolsey lost the favour of his master. He was dismissed from his high offices.
34. He is a big boy. He is very strong. He is in the foot-ball team.
35. He came to me. He wanted leave. He was ill.
36. I heard Abdul. He was shouting very loudly. He was calling me.
37. He raised his gun. He took aim. He shot the tiger.
38. He could not eat hard food. He was very old. He had lost his teeth.
39. I have told you the facts. I have nothing more to say. I will sit down.
40. I was returning home. I saw a man. He looked very ill. He was lying by the roadside.

EXERCISE 89

Combine each set of sentences into one Simple sentence by using Nouns or Phrases in Apposition.

1. There goes my brother. He is called Sohrab.
2. The cow provides milk. Milk is a valuable food.
3. Mr. Pundit was elected President. He is a well-known Sanskrit scholar.
4. Coal is a very important mineral. It is hard, bright, black and brittle.
5. We saw the picture. It is a very fine piece of work.

6. Geoffrey Chaucer was born in 1340. He is the first great English poet.
7. Tagore's most famous work is the *Gitanjali*. It is a collection of short poems.
8. His only son died before him. He was a lad of great promise.
9. His uncle was a millionaire. He sent him to England for his education.
10. The dog bit the man. He was a notorious burglar.
11. Bruno is my faithful dog. I love him.
12. Jawaharlal Nehru died in 1964. He was the first Prime Minister of India.
13. De Lesseps made the Suez Canal. This was a great work. He was a French engineer.
14. Mr. Pundit lives in Dustipore. He is the Collector. It is a large town.

EXERCISE 90

Combine each set of sentences into one Simple sentence by using Prepositions with Nouns or Gerunds.

1. He attended to his duties. He earned promotion.
2. He must confess his fault. He may thus escape punishment.
3. He was ill last term. He was unable to attend school.
4. I forgave him his fault. That has not prevented him from repeating it.
5. The bugle sounded. The weary soldiers leapt to their feet.
6. The word of command will be given. You will then fire.
7. He set traps every night. He cleared his house of rats.
8. The judge gave his decision. The court listened silently.
9. He expects to obtain leave. He has already bought his steamer ticket.
10. He has a good record. It is impossible to suspect such a man.
11. Even a bird will defend its young ones. It then shows great courage.
12. There was a want of provisions. The garrison could hold out no longer.
13. You helped me. Otherwise I should have been drowned.
14. I have examined the statement. I find many errors in it.
15. He is free from disease. At least he appears to be so.
16. His son died. This gave him a shock. He never fully recovered from it.
17. He took the law in his own hands. He was not justified in doing so.
18. It rained hard. The streets were flooded.
19. He made heroic efforts to succeed. He failed.
20. The weather is pleasant. It is a little cold however.
21. He was rude. I took no notice of it.
22. He has stolen the purse. There is no doubt about this.
23. She wants to marry a foreigner. Her father is opposed to this.
24. He entered the room with his hat on. His behaviour surprised me.
25. He got great honour. He saved the life of the Rajah.
26. There was an advertisement in the newspaper. His interest was aroused.
27. He amused us very much. He sang a funny song.
28. The prince was ill. The people heard of it. They crowded to the palace.
29. The prince recovered. The people received the news. They were very enthusiastic.
30. He makes a lot of money. He buys horses. He sells horses.
31. I saw a *soldier*. He had a lance in his hand. He had a sword by his side.
32. She stood there for hours. She did not move. She did not speak.
33. The discovery of his crime was a heavy blow. His reputation suffered. His business decreased.

EXERCISE 91

Combine each set of sentences into one simple sentence by using the Nominative Absolute construction.

1. His friend arrived. He was very pleased.
2. The rain fell. The crops revived.
3. The storm ceased. The sun came out.
4. The troops were ordered out. The police were unable to hold the mob in check.
5. The holidays are at an end. Boys are returning to school.
6. The wind failed. The crew set to work with a will.
7. It was a very hot day. I could not do my work satisfactorily.
8. His house has been burned down. He lives in an hotel.
9. The king died. His eldest son came to the throne.
10. His father was dead. He had to support his widowed mother.
11. Rain was plentiful this year. Rice is cheap.
12. The secretaryship was vacant. Nobody was willing to undertake duties of the post. I offered my services.
13. The prisoner was questioned. No witness came forward. The Judge dismissed the case.
14. The sun rose. The fog cleared away. The lighthouse was seen less than a mile away.
15. He fired his gun. The ball went high. The tiger sprang on him.
16. The master was out of the room. The door was shut. The boys made a lot of noise.

EXERCISE 92

Combine each set of sentences into one Simple sentence by using Infinitives.

1. He had no money. He could not give any away.
2. I have told you all. There is nothing more to be said.
3. He cannot afford a motor-car. He is too poor.
4. I heard of his good fortune. I was glad of that.
5. The information is of no use to us. It has come too late.
6. Your father will hear of your success. He will be delighted.
7. You did not invest all your savings in one concern. You were prudent.
8. He did not have even a rupee with him. He could not buy a loaf of bread.
9. The Pathan took out a knife. His intention was to frighten the old man.
10. I speak the truth. I am not afraid of it.
11. He wants to earn his livelihood. He works hard for that reason.
12. The strikers held a meeting. They wished to discuss the terms of the employers.
13. He has five children. He must provide for them.
14. Napoleon was one of the greatest of generals. This is universally acknowledged.
15. His Majesty desired to kill Gulliver secretly. Various means were employed for this purpose.
16. I will speak the truth. I am not afraid of the consequences.
17. He is very honourable. He will not break his word.
18. He has some bills. He must pay them.
19. He must apologise. He will not escape punishment otherwise.
20. He keeps some fierce dogs. They will guard his house. They will keep away robbers.

EXERCISE 93

Combine each set of sentences into one Simple sentence by using Adverbs or Adverbial Phrases.

1. I accept your statement. I do it without reserve.
2. He answered me. His answer was correct.
3. He forgot his umbrella. That was careless.
4. He is a bad boy. This is certain.
5. The train is very late. That is usual.

6. I shall come back. I shall not be long.
7. He kicked the goal-keeper. It was his intention to do so.
8. He was obstinate. He refused to listen to advice.
9. He spent all his money. This was foolish.
10. He was not at the meeting. His absence was unavoidable.
11. He applied for leave. It was not granted.
12. He admitted his error. He expressed his regret.
13. I met him only once. It was in a railway carriage.
14. He has succeeded. His success has been beyond my expectation.
15. It must be done. The cost does not count.
16. I have read Bacon. It has profited me greatly.
17. He persevered. He was not deterred by obstacles.
18. The door was open. It looked rather suspicious.
19. He is not qualified for the post. He is not qualified in any degree.
20. The blow dazed him. That condition lasted only for a time.
21. I did not eat any of the poisoned food. This was lucky.
22. He solved the problem. Its solution took him no time.
23. He visited Ooty. He did so for reasons of health.
24. He accomplished the task. He brought unflagging industry to his accomplishment.
25. Boys grow up to be men. The growth is very slow. It cannot be seen.
26. Rama struck Krishna. His blows were cruel. They were frequent. There was no reason for this.

EXERCISE 94

(Miscellaneous) Combine each set of sentences into one Simple sentence.

1. Homer was a great poet. He was born somewhere. Nobody knows where.
2. He was a leader. He did not follow other men. Such was his nature.
3. I bought this hat two years ago. It is still good. It is fit to wear.
4. He devoted himself to public affairs. He never took a holiday. This continued for thirty years.
5. Clive made proposals. Some opposed the proposals. The majority supported them. They were carried.
6. Clive was determined to reform the administration. Reforms were needed. He informed the council accordingly.
7. The man was innocent. He could have defended himself. He refused to speak. He was afraid of convicting his friend.
8. He was in prison. His friend was in the next cell. There was a brick wall between the cells. He made a hole in the wall. He was able to talk to his friend.
9. The boy was drowning. He shouted for help. A workman heard the boy's shouts. He plunged into the river. He risked his own life.
10. The traveller was toiling slowly over the desert. He suddenly turned round. He heard his companion's voice. His companion was crying for help.
11. We returned down the valley of the Jumna. We came first to Delhi. Delhi is the capital of India.
12. The art of printing was introduced into England during the reign of Edward IV. The art of printing was introduced by William Caxton. William Caxton was a native of Kent.
13. He struck his foot against a stone. He fell to the ground. He made his clothes very dirty.
14. The sun shone on the corn. The corn ripened. It did this in a short time. The farmer was filled with joy.
15. He opened his letters. He read them carefully. He sent for his clerk. He dictated answers to them.
16. He paid all his late father's debts. This was a very honest proceeding. It was very creditable to him.
17. He has two horses. He must feed them. He must water them. He must groom them. He must bring them to his master at 12 o'clock.
18. He goes to school. He wishes to learn. He wants to grow up honest, healthy and clever.
19. There was a man hiding in my garden. He was armed with a gun. He was a Pathan. My notice was drawn to it.

20. The soldiers were starving. Their ammunition was expended. Their clothes were in rags. Their leaders were dead. The enemy easily defeated them.
21. Napoleon was the first Emperor of the French. He was a great soldier. He inspired his armies with the most war-like spirit. This was the cause of their many victories.
22. Wellington was the greatest of English admirals. Napoleon was the greatest of French soldiers. They were contemporaries. They were the heroes of their respective countries.
23. The miser laughed. He found himself to be richer by a rupee. He saw his adversary outwitted.
24. He hardened his heart. He wished to punish the people mercilessly. He wanted to make an example of them once and for all.
25. He receives much gratitude. He performs kindly actions. He is not harsh in the execution of his duty. He does not oppress the poor.
26. His friends assembled. They offered him their congratulations upon his safe return. Everybody was comfortably seated. He described all his adventures.
27. The thieves poisoned the dog. He had brought it from England. He had trained it carefully to protect his property.
28. Vultures appeared one after another. They were wheeling round and round. They were descending towards the spot. They had cruel beaks and talons.
29. The room was covered with blood. It stained the walls and ceiling. It darkened the floor. It flowed in a stream under the door. It stood in puddles everywhere.
30. The house had been pulled down. Another had been built in its place. It was difficult to identify the exact spot.
31. He earned the hatred of all good men. He incited youths to crime. He furnished them with means. He himself kept safely out of the way in time of danger.
32. He copied from the next boy. This was a mean and dishonest action. It brought disgrace upon him. He was punished for it.
33. He had not sufficient courage. He could not face the opposition of his caste fellows. He could not go away from his native place to begin life afresh.
34. Rabindranath Tagore founded Shantiniketan. He was a Nobel laureate. He was the author of the national anthem.
35. He could not finish his work. He had no opportunity. He could not do much of it in fact. He was very often ill. He was frequently absent.
36. The criminal was a man of his own caste. He was an ungrateful and incorrigible wretch . He had often helped him.
37. He went for a walk one day. He saw a wounded bird. He picked it up. He brought it home. He carefully tended it for some time. It completely recovered. This gave him great joy.
38. I knew a boy at school. He is now famous as a soldier. He is known to the tribesmen as the 'Sleepless One'. He is greatly feared by them.
39. The water had boiled. The tea was made. The food was ready. The table was spread. They sat down to eat and drink.
40. He deserves my thanks. He found my purse. He returned it to me. He took nothing out of it.
41. I saw a dog. It had three legs. It had only one ear. It was a terrier. It was a well-bred little animal.
42. He must clean all the silver. He must put it away. He must lock it up. He must bring me the key of the box. These were my orders to him.
43. The horse had many of the points of a racer. It had slim legs. It had high withers. It had powerful quarters. It had a tremendous stride.
44. He was a great statesman. He had worked well for his country. He was very popular. He was awarded the title of 'Bharat Ratna'.
45. Wood was collected. Camp fires were lighted. Food was cooked. Food was eaten. The army lay down to sleep.
46. He alienated his friends. His conduct was disgraceful. He was put in gaol.
47. Rama had a wide knowledge of the business. Krishna had the necessary capital. They combined resources. They entered into partnership.
48. Their father had a large sum of money. He divided it equally between them by his will. The daughters were eagerly sought in marriage.
49. The ground is soft and marshy. There are many frogs. Snakes abound there. They are the enemies of mankind.
50. His hopes are high. His superiors are pleased with him. He is justified in hoping.
51. He rode along for hours. He did not strike his horse. He did not spur it.

52. I have some advice. I must give it to you. I must impress it strongly upon you.
53. I hear rumours about Laxman. He is an old pupil of mine. He is a good cricketer. He is a good football player. He is not a steady worker.
54. He was delighted with the intelligence and brightness of the scholars. He overlooked the fact of their knowing few things by heart.
55. He built a house. It had many large doors. It had many large windows. It had wide verandahs. It had a general air of coolness and comfort.
56. He told a story. It was about a man. The man had great strength. He was a famous warrior.
57. He came to Mumbai. He wished to see his father. He had some business to settle.
58. After the storm the boat had no mast. It could not keep before the wind. It could not return to port.
59. The cage contains a tiger. The cage was strongly built. It was so built for this purpose.
60. The ancient myths of India have been preserved in the minds of the people. They have been preserved with great care. This has been done by priests. It has also been done by the learned men. These are the guardians of the lamp of learning.

Chapter 13 SYNTHESIS OF SENTENCES (CONTD.)

Combination of Two or More Simple Sentences into a Single Compound Sentence

90. Simple sentences may be combined to form Compound sentences by the use of Co-ordinative Conjunctions. These are of four kinds–Cumulative, Adversative, Alternative, and Illative.

A. 1. Night came on. The room grew dark.
Night came on *and* the room grew dark.

2. He is a fool. He is a knave.
He is a fool *and* a knave.
[Or] He is *both* a fool *and* a knave.
[Or] He is *not only* a fool *but also* a knave.
[Or] He is a fool *as well as* a knave.

3. The wind blew. The rain fell. The lightning flashed.
The wind blew, the rain fell, *and* the lightning flashed.

It will be noticed that the conjunction *and* simply *adds* one statement to another.

The conjunctions *both....and, not only...but also, as well as* are emphatic forms of *and* and do the same work.

Conjunctions which merely *add* one statement to another are called **Cumulative.**

B. 1. He is slow. He is sure.
He is slow *but* he is sure.

2. I was annoyed. I kept quiet.
I was annoyed, *still* (or *yet)* I kept quiet.

3. He failed. He persevered.
He failed, *nevertheless* he persevered.

4. I shall not oppose your design. I cannot approve of it.
I shall not oppose your design; I cannot, *however,* approve of it.

5. He was all right. He was fatigued.
He was all right; *only* he was fatigued.

It will be noticed that the conjunctions *but, still, yet, nevertheless, however,* express a *contrast* between one sentence and the other. Some of these conjunctions (*still, yet, however, nevertheless*) are more emphatic than *but.*

Conjunctions which express opposition or *contrast* between two statements are called **Adversative**.

C. 1. Make haste. You will be late.
Make haste *or* you will be late.

2. Come in. Go out.
Come in *or* go out.
[Or more emphatically]. *Either* come in *or* go out.

3. Do not be a borrower. Do not be a lender.
Do not be a borrower *or* a lender.
Or : Be *neither* a borrower *nor* a lender.

It will be noticed that the conjunctions *or, either ....or, neither.....nor,* express a *choice* between two alternatives.

Conjunctions which express a *choice* between two alternatives are called **Alternative.**

D. 1. He was obstinate. He was punished.
He was obstinate; *therefore* he was punished.
2. I cannot see. It is very dark.
I cannot see, *for* it is very dark.
3. It is raining heavily. I will take an umbrella with me.
It is raining heavily, *so* I will take an umbrella with me.

It will be noticed that the conjunctions *therefore, for, so,* etc., join sentences in which one statement is *inferred* from the other.

Conjunctions which express an *inference* are called **Illative.**

1. Abdul is ill. He cannot study. He still attends school.
Abdul is ill and cannot study, yet he still attends school.
2. He saw the boy in the street. He stopped to speak to him. He gave him a rupee.
Seeing the boy in the street, he stopped to speak to him and gave him a rupee.

EXERCISE 95

Combine each set of Simple sentences into one Compound sentence.

1. He does well. He is nervous at the start.
2. The way was long. The wind was cold.
3. It is raining heavily. I will take an umbrella with me.
4. The harvest truly is plenteous. The labourers are few.
5. It was a stormy night. We ventured out.
6. Football is a vigorous and healthy game. Every boy should play it.
7. He is foolish. He is also obstinate.
8. I am in the right. You are in the wrong.
9. We can travel by land. We can travel by water.
10. The train was wrecked. No one was hurt.
11. The paper is good. The binding is very bad.
12. We must hasten. The robbers will overtake us.
13. The prince married the beautiful princess. They lived happily ever after.
14. The river is deep and swift. I am afraid to dive into it.
15. He was fined. He was sent to prison.
16. You may go to the theatre. Rama may go to the theatre.
17. Bruce was lying on his bed. He looked up to the roof. He saw a spider.
18. I cried out sadly. I beat my head and breast. I threw myself down on the ground.
19. You may play hockey. You may play football. You must do either of the two.
20. You may be wrong. Rashid may be wrong. You cannot both be right.
21. I got up. I looked about everywhere. I could not perceive my companions.
22. In Hyderabad I visited Charminar, Golkonda Fort and Birla Mandir. I could not visit Salar Jung Museum.
23. A is equal to B. B is equal to C. A is equal to C.
24. Most of the rebels were slain. A few escaped. They hid in the woods and marshes. The rebellion was quickly suppressed.
25. He was my school-fellow. He has become a great man. He has grown proud. He forgets his old friends.
26. I did not see you. I should have spoken to you. I had important news. Delay was dangerous.
27. Make haste. You will be late. There is no other train till midnight. That train is a slow one.
28. Their boats are made of a kind of bark. They are very light. They can easily be carried on the shoulders.

29. The emu, or Australian ostrich, does not sit on its eggs. It covers them up with leaves and grass. It leaves them to be hatched by the heat of the sun.
30. We must catch the 5 o'clock train. There is only half an hour left. We must start without further delay.
31. A timid dog is dangerous. He always suspects ill-treatment. He tries to protect himself by snapping.
32. A husbandman had sown some corn in his fields. He had only recently done so. Cranes came to eat the corn. The husbandman fixed a net in his fields to catch the cranes.
33. The monsoon failed. The tanks became almost empty. No grain could be sown. A famine was feared. The ryots looked anxiously for the next monsoon. It proved unusually abundant. The danger was averted.
34. The second class carriage is full. We may pay first class fare. We may not travel first class with second class tickets. That is forbidden.
35. He is a rich man. He did not earn his wealth. He does not appreciate the value of money. He squanders it.
36. He beat me in the race. He is a year older. He naturally runs faster. Next year I may do better.
37. The storm abated. The sun shone. The ship-wrecked mariners could see no sign of land. They were adrift in mid-ocean.
38. Generally your conduct is good. You have been guilty of an act of folly. You will not be punished. I advise you to be more prudent in future.

39. I lost my way. I asked a policeman to direct me. He was new to his work. He could not help me. He called a gentleman passing by to my assistance.
40. The engine-driver saw the danger. He applied the brakes. The line was greasy. The brakes failed to act quickly. The train crashed into the gates at the crossing. The engine left the rails.
41. The rain fell steadily for several days. The river overflowed its banks. The terrified villagers abandoned their homes. They fled to the higher ground. Soon the floods retired. The villagers were able to return.

Chapter 14 SYNTHESIS OF SENTENCES (CONTD.)

Combination of Two or More Simple Sentences into a Single Complex Sentence

I. Subordinate Clause a Noun Clause

91. In the following examples the Subordinate clause is a Noun clause.

1. You are drunk. That aggravates your offence.
   That you are drunk aggravates your offence.
2. He will be late. That is certain.
   It is certain that he will be late.
3. You are repentant. I will not forget it.
   I will not forget that you are repentant.
4. He may be innocent. I do not know.
   I do not know whether he is innocent.
5. He is short-sighted.Otherwise he is fit for the post.
   Except that he is short-sighted he is fit for the post.
6. The clouds would disperse. That was our hope. Our hope was cheering.
   Our hope that the clouds would disperse, was cheering.
7. The game was lost. It was the consequence of his carelessness.
   The consequence of his carelessness was that the game was lost.

II. Subordinate Clause an Adjective Clause

92. In the following examples the Subordinate clause is an Adjective clause:

1. A fox once met a lion. The fox had never seen a lion before.
   A fox who had never seen a lion before met him.
2. She keeps her ornaments in a safe. This is the safe.
   This is the safe where she keeps her ornaments.
3. A cottager and his wife had a hen. The hen laid an egg everyday. The egg was golden.
   A cottager and his wife had a hen which laid an egg everyday.

III. Subordinate Clause an Adverb Clause

93. In the following examples the Subordinate clause is an Adverb clause.

1. Indira Gandhi died in 1984. Rajiv Gandhi thereafter became Prime Minister.
   When Indira Gandhi died in 1984, Rajiv Gandhi became Prime Minister.
2. I waited for my friend. I waited till his arrival.
   I waited for my friend until he came.
3. He fled somewhere. His pursuers could not follow him.
   He fled where his pursuers could not follow him.
4. Let men sow anything. They will reap its fruit.
   As men sow, so shall they reap.
5. You are strong. I am equally strong.
   I am as strong as you are.
6. He was not there. I spoke to his brother for that reason.
   As he was not there, I spoke to his brother.
7. We wish to live. We eat for that purpose.
   We eat so that we may live.
8. He was quite tired. He could scarcely stand.
   He was so tired that he could scarcely stand.
9. Don't eat too much. You will be ill.
   If you eat too much you will be ill.
10. He began late. He finished first.
    He finished first though be began late.
11. I shall come. My being alone is a condition.
    I shall come if I am alone.
12. I must know all the facts. I cannot help you otherwise.
    Before I can help you, I must know all the facts.
13. He is superstitious. He is equally wicked.
    He is as superstitious as he is wicked.

EXERCISE 96

Combine each set of Simple sentences into one Complex sentence containing a Noun clause.

1. He is wrong. I am sure of it.
2. You deceived him. That was his complaint.
3. The train will arrive at a certain time. Do you know the time?
4. All the planets except for Pluto travel round the sun the same way and in the same plane. I have often told you this truth.
5. He will waste his time. That is certain.
6. Where have you put my hat ? Tell me.
7. He is short-tempered. I like him all the same.
8. Is it time for the train to start ? Ask the guard.
9. It is going to rain. I am sure of it.
10. Something may be worth doing. It is only worth doing well.
11. He is a sincere worker. No one can doubt this fact.
12. He said something. I did not hear it.
13. How did you find that out ? Tell me.
14. You have made a mistake. I think so.
15. Who wrote *Shakuntala* ? Can you tell me that ?
16. You stole the purse. Do you deny it ?
17. I am very sorry. I cannot adequately express my sorrow.
18. We have been deceived. That is the truth.
19. How did Netaji Subhash Chandra Bose die? It is a mystery.
20. He will succeed. We expect it.
21. What have you done ? Tell me.

22. We wished to know. We were going somewhere.
23. We were nearing some waterfall. It was evident from the distant roar of water.
24. A certain number of the enemy escaped. We do not know this number.
25. The two friends quarrelled. I want to know the reason.
26. He is a great orator. This fact cannot be denied.
27. Columbus made an egg stand on its end. I will show you his method.
28. I have seen this man somewhere before. I cannot remember the place.
29. He will arrive some time. I do not know the time of his arrival.
30. He distrusts his own sons. It is difficult to understand the reason.

EXERCISE 97

Combine each set of Simple sentences into one Complex sentence containing an Adjective clause.

1. The theft was committed last night. The man has been caught.
2. The French and Italian languages are different from the Latin language. Latin was once spoken in almost every part of Europe.
3. The time was six o'clock. The accident happened then.
4. You are not keeping good health lately. Can you tell me the reason ?
5. He has many plans for earning money quickly. All of them have failed.
6. A lion was proud of his strength. He despised the weakness of the mouse.
7. The grapes hung over the garden wall. The fox saw the grapes.
8. That is the school. I was taught there.
9. You put it somewhere. Show me the place.
10. My travelling companion was an old gentleman. His name is Mr. Haq. I met him in Basra.

EXERCISE 98

Combine each set of Simple sentences into one Complex sentence containing an Adverb clause.

1. The nurse must be very tired. She had no sleep last night.
2. A gentleman may call. Please ask him to wait.
3. He ran so quickly. He soon overtook me.
4. I will get ready. Do not go till then.
5. He mended in a very low voice. Nobody could hear him.
6. I wound my watch this morning. It has stopped.
7. It was very stuffy last night. I could not sleep.
8. The monsoon may break this month. Otherwise the wells will run dry.
9. I may help you. I may not help you. You are sure to lose the game.
10. The fireman came out of the house. The roof collapsed that very moment.
11. Success attends hard work. Failure attends bad work.
12. You must hurry. You will miss the train otherwise.
13. The delegates arrived. The discussion was resumed.
14. He is very old. He enjoys good health.
15. No more funds are available. The work has been stopped.
16. He saw me coming. He immediately took to his heels.
17. I may be blunt. I am at least honest.
18. He was contradicted. He was annoyed.
19. He bled profusely. He died.
20. This may be true of some. It is not true of all.
21. He ran quickly. He soon overtook me.
22. I had left home. Your letter arrived afterwards.

23. He saw us. He disappeared immediately.
24. He will not go out in the rain. He is afraid of getting wet.
25. The bandits fought desperately. They could not bear the idea of being taken alive.
26. The sailors cast anchor. They did so to prevent the ship from drifting on the rocks.
27. You make a good deal of noise. I cannot work.
28. We may sail tomorrow. It depends on the weather.
29. It is very simple. Even a child can understand it.
30. He was returning from school. He was caught in a shower.
31. Robinson Crusoe discovered the print of a foot on the sand. He was puzzled.
32. He finished the work. Just then the clock struck five.
33. He is being lionized. He still keeps a level head.
34. Why do you keep your eye on me like this ? Have you turned detective ?
35. We travelled together as far as Kolkata. We parted company there.
36. He is a rich man. No other man in our community is equally rich.
37. You may wish to do the work. You may not wish to do the work. You must still do it.
38. He was sick. He remained at home.
39. You have tears. Prepare to shed them now.
40. He may slay me. I will trust him.
41. He saw me. He ran away then.
42. He came to my house. I was out.
43. His father died. He has been very poor from that time.
44. He grew weaker and weaker. He died.
45. We take off our clothes. We go to bed.
46. He was hanged. He had committed murder.
47. All will respect you. Your being honest is a condition.
48. He is old. He cannot walk.
49. He won the race. He was the swiftest.
50. Life lasts a certain time. Let us be honest during that time.
51. The wolf is larger. The jackal is smaller.
52. Arjun is clever. His cleverness equals Rama's.

94. Carefully study the following sentences.

1. He had read Milton. He had read it in a prose translation. He had read it when he was fourteen. He told us this.
   He told us that he had read Milton, in a prose translation, when he was fourteen.
2. A bachelor may be surrounded with all sorts of luxuries. In spite of that he will always find his happiness incomplete. He must have a wife and children.
   With whatever luxuries a bachelor may be surrounded, he will always find his happiness incomplete, unless he has a wife and children.
3. Pope professed to have learned his poetry from Dryden. Through his whole life he praised him with unvaried liberality. He did so whenever an opportunity was presented.
   Pope professed to have learned his poetry from Dryden, whom, whenever an opportunity was presented, he praised through his whole life with unvaried liberalilty.
4. Milton did not educate his daughters in the languages. He said that one tongue was enough for a woman.
   Milton said that he did not educate his daughters in the languages, beecause one tongue was enough for a woman.
5. I sank into the water. I felt confused. Nothing can describe that confusion.
   Nothing can describe the confusion of thought which I felt when I sank into the water.
6. We had in this village an idiot boy. I well remember that boy. From a child he showed a strong propensity for bees. This was some twenty years ago.
   We had in this village, some twenty years ago, an idiot boy, whom I well remember, who from a child showed a strong propensity for bees.

EXERCISE 99

Combine each of the following sets of Simple sentences into one Complex sentence.

1. That is the man. He gave me a dog. It went mad.
2. Rama will not play in the match. The notion is foolish. He is the best player in the school.
3. I wrote the letter. It contained the truth. He praised me for it.
4. Honesty is the best policy. Have you never heard it ?
5. He came to see me. He wanted to tell me something. His father was dead. He had been ill for a long time.
6. The horse has killed a man. I wished to sell it to you. The man was trying to steal it.
7. He took the medicine. He then felt better. It cured his headache.
8. He gave an order. He is obeyed. They fear to offend him.
9. The absence of the girl from her home was unusual. Inquiries were made. They led to no result.
10. Your conduct is very peculiar. I am unable to understand it. It has been described to me.
11. He played exceedingly well in the match. His team won in consequence. The match was played yesterday.
12. He wrote a letter. He wrote it for a certain reason. He wrote it to his superior. He told me about this.

13. I visited his garden. In it there were some beautiful rose trees. The trees were full of bloom. These were red and white in colour.
14. He forsook his dishonest ways. No one would give him work. His dishonest ways had brought him to the depths of poverty.
15. He is sure to receive his pay. It is due to him. Why then does he worry ?
16. He has very bad health. He lives very carefully. It is inexplicable to the doctor. The doctor has attended him for years. He told me this.
17. His servants disliked him. They flattered him. He was very harsh to them.
18. I carefully sighted the rifle. I did not wish to miss. A miss might have cost me my life.
19. The speed of the boat was remarkable. It was going against the current. It was going against the wind. These facts should be kept in mind.
20. He stole a book. It had the owner's name written in it. I was told this. The name was well known to him.
21. They had marched the whole journey at top speed. They wished to surprise the enemy. The journey was very long.
22. My friend is going to Europe. He has got long leave. His brother is already there. He wishes to become a doctor.
23. Rama will not play against the Hindu school. It has a very strong team. He has declared this to be his intention. He does not wish to tire himself before the cup-match. It takes place the next day.
24. The man talks most. That man does least. This very often happens.
25. A man did this. He must have been very strong. There is no doubt of it. Our father says so.
26. He paid a sum of money for the information. He paid it to a certain person. He paid it for some reason. I should like to know the sum, the person and the reason. I could then prosecute him.
27. They had the treasure in some place. The treasure was very valuable. The place was never discovered. They feared pursuit and capture. They hid it in a jungle.
28. He endeavoured to hide the traces of the crime. He had committed it. The reason is not difficult to see.
29. He had not learned to read and write. He was very ignorant. He could not even talk fluently. Such a man should not pretend to be a doctor.

30. The boy had many accomplishments. The father fully described a large number of these to the teacher. He wished to get him admitted to the school.
31. The jackal was pursued by the dogs. It was very hungry. They were well fed. It was caught.
32. He waited longer. He got more angry. He had ordered them to be punctual.
33. You may like it. You may not like it. In either case I shall send you there. It is my duty to do so.
34. Your father succeeded well. Would you like to succeed equally well ? He worked hard. You must work equally hard.
35. You have failed. I am sorry to hear it. You deserved to pass. I think it.
36. You will be allowed to enter for the examination. Your working hard is a condition. The orders are to that effect. They were issued by the Principal.
37. Rama is more clever. Krishna is less clever. I think it. I judge by the results of the examination.

38. There is a will. There is a way too. This is generally true.
39. I heard the news. I went to the hospital. I wished to discover the extent of his injuries. The hospital is not far from my house.
40. You may please him. You may displease him. He will promote you sooner or later accordingly. This is only right.
41. You sow in a certain way. You will reap in the same way. The proverb says this.
42. You may look everywhere. There you will see signs of industry. These signs speak well for the prosperity of the people.
43. I have done much sword-play. The sight of a sword gives pleasure to a man like me. This is undeniable.
44. They played the game very skilfully. No one could have played it more skilfully. They had been thoroughly well trained.
45. He is an idle and careless boy. The report was to this effect. His father received the report. He was very grieved to receive it.

EXERCISE 100

Combine each of the following groups of sentences into one Compound or one Complex sentence in any way you like.

1. I offered him help. He needed help. He persisted in refusing help. I left him to his fate.
2. A famished traveller was toiling over the desert. He found a bag. He was highly delighted. He opened the bag. He found nothing but pearls.
3. Hundreds of men and women have travelled in space. Some have travelled in space for a few days. Others have done it for several months.
4. I was in Sri Lanka in May last. I visited Mihintale. It is regarded as the cradle of Buddhism.
5. Once an oarsman was rowing by himself. He did not look behind him. He met another boat. He crashed into it. He was upset.
6. A dog was running away with a piece of meat. He passed some deep still water. He saw there the reflected image of the meat. He dropped the meat into the deep water. He snatched in vain at the shadow.
7. A fox saw a crow sitting on a tree with a piece of cheese in his mouth. The fox praised the crow's singing. The crow was pleased by the flattery. The crow began to sing. The crow dropped the cheese.
8. A lion was proud of his strength. He despised the weakness of the mouse. He was caught in a net. He could not escape from the net. He was set free by the exertions of the mouse.

9. John signed. John was King of England. He signed a document called the Magna Carta. He was afraid of his barons. He did not care about liberty. He signed the document at Runnymede. Runnymede is on the Thames. It is not far from Windsor.
10. The train ran down the incline. The train attained great speed. The train turned a sharp curve at the bottom. The train oscillated under the influence of the brakes. The train threw all the passengers into a panic.
11. A half-starved mouse managed to creep into a basket of corn. The mouse rejoiced in his good fortune. The mouse fed greedily on the corn. The mouse tried to get out of the basket. His body was now too big to pass through the hole.
12. It would not be possible for any life to survive on Venus and Mercury. They are nearer to the sun than the earth. They are very hot planets.
13. A band of ruffians entered a village. The ruffians were well armed. They entered the village at night. Some of the ruffians were escaped convicts. The ruffians stole the cattle of the villagers. The villagers were asleep.
14. My fellow-traveller had a gun. He was boasting of his bravery. Suddenly a bear came behind a rock close in front of us. It stood in our way. It was growling angrily.
15. Mungo Park explored the interior regions of Africa. He was employed by the African Association. The undertaking was hazardous. He suffered many distresses. Those distresses were often alleviated by the compassion of the negroes.
16. A lion was drinking in a clear pool. His stately mane was reflected by the pool. The lion saw the reflection. He greatly admired his mane. He was afterwards pursued by hunters with their guns. He was pursued through a thick wood. He then found his mane useless and of no avail.
17. The King ordered me to go to a distant village. It was not possible to disobey. I set off for the village. There I was mortified to find no one willing to admit me into his house. I was regarded with astonishment and fear. I was obliged to sit the whole day without victuals. A tree protected me against the heat and the sun.
18. The night was very threatening. The wind rose. There were heavy rain clouds. The wild beasts were numerous thereabout. To escape them it would have been necessary to climb a tree and sit among the branches.

19. The sun set. I was preparing to pass the night in a tree. A negro woman stopped to observe me. She was returning from the labour of the field. She perceived my weariness and dejection. She inquired into my situation. I briefly explained it to her. With a look of compassion she told me to follow her.
20. She conducted me to her hut. She told me to remain there for the night. Then she found me hungry. She procured from outside a fine fish. She caused it to be half boiled upon some embers. She then gave it to me for supper.
21. He had made war on Saxony. He had set the Roman crown upon his own head. He had become famous throughout the whole world. But his fame had not prevented his hair from becoming grey.
22. Augustus probably died a natural death. He was in his seventy-eighth year. He had been reduced to despondency by the disaster in Germany. He was travelling at an unhealthy time of the year. He had exposed himself imprudently to the night air. And all the other particulars are quite opposed to the poison theory.
23. This is not the least part of our happiness. We enjoy the remotest products of the north and south. At the same time we are free from extremities of the weather. Our eyes are refreshed with the green fields of Britain. At the same time our palates are refreshed with tropical fruit.
24. He was a man of haughty and vehement temper. He was treated very ungraciously by the court. He was supported very enthusiastically by the people. He would eagerly take the first opportunity of showing his power and gratifying his resentment. This might be expected.
25. Bonaparte was born a Corsican. He distinguished himself at school. He joined the republican army. He started as corporal. His bravery was remarkable. His mental powers were great. He became the head of the army of Italy. He conquered Egypt. He set aside the republic. He was proclaimed Emperor.
26. He is now gone to his final reward. He was full of years and honours. These honours were especially dear to his heart for the following reasons. They were gratefully bestowed by his pupils. They bound him to the interests of that school. He had been educated in that school. His whole life had been dedicated to its service.

Chapter 15 THE SEQUENCE OF TENSES

95. The **Sequence of Tenses** is the principle in accordance with which the Tense of the verb in a subordinate clause *follows* the Tense of the verb in the principal clause. (*Sequence* is connected with the Latin verb *sequor*, follow.)

The Sequence of Tenses applies chiefly to Adverb Clauses of Purpose and Noun Clauses.

96. A Past Tense in the principal clause is followed by a Past Tense in the subordinate clause ; as,

He *hinted* that he *wanted* money.
She *replied* that she *felt* better.
I *found* out that he *was* guilty.
He *saw* that the clock *had* stopped.
He *replied* that he *would* come.
I never *thought* that I *should* see him again.
I *took* care that he *should* not hear me.
They *climbed* higher so that they *might* get a better view.
I *worked* hard so that I *might* succeed.

There are, however, two exceptions to this rule:

(*i*) A Past Tense in the principal clause *may* be followed by a Present Tense in the subordinate clause when the subordinate clause expresses a universal truth ; as,

Newton *discovered* that the force of gravitation makes apples fall.
Galileo *maintained* that the earth *moves* round the sun.
Euclid *proved* that the three angles of a triangle are equal to two right angles.
He *said* that honesty is always the best policy.

(*ii*) When the subordinate clause is introduced by *than,* even if there is a Past Tense in the principal clause, it may be followed by any Tense required by the sense in the subordinate clause ; as,

He *liked* you better than he *likes* me.
He *helped* him more than he *helps* his own children.
I then *saw* him oftener than I *see* him now.
He *valued* his friendship more than he *values* mine.

97. A Present or Future Tense in the principal clause may be followed by any Tense required by the sense ; as,

He *thinks* that she *is* there.
He *thinks* that she *was* there.
He *thinks* that she *will be* there.
He *will think* that she *is* there.
He *will think* that she *was* there.
He *will think* that she *will be* there.

But in sentences where the subordinate clause denotes *purpose,* if the verb in the principal clause is Present or Future the verb in the subordinate clause must be Present ; as,

I *eat* so that I *may* live.
I *shall* nurse him so that he *may* live.

EXERCISE 101

Insert the correct tense of verb in the following.

1. I waited for my friend until he______ . (To come)
2. So long as the rain______, I stayed at home. (To continue)
3. I did not know it until you______. (To speak)
4. He speaks as one who ______. (To know)
5. He ran as quickly as he______. (Can or could)
6. He went where he______find work. (Can or could)
7. Wherever there is coal you______find iron. (Will or would)
8. He behaves as one______expect him to do. (May or might)
9. He ran away because he______afraid. (To be)
10. He fled where his pursuers______not follow. (Can or could)
11. As he______not there, I spoke to his brother. (To be)
12. The notice was published in order that all______know the facts. (May or might)
13. He was so tired that he______scarcely stand. (Can or could)
14. You make such a noise that I______not work. (Can or could)
15. He finished first though he______late. (To begin)
16. His health has improved since he______India. (To leave)
17. As soon as he______the news he wrote to me. (To hear)
18. After the shower______over, the sun shone out again. (To be)
19. Whenever we______we talk of old times. (To meet)
20. Answer the first question before you______further. (To proceed)
21. Just as he______the room the clock struck. (To enter)
22. Now that we______safe we stopped to take breath. (To feel)
23. Wherever he______the people gathered to listen. (To preach)
24. He speaks as though he______very angry. (To be)
25. He ran because he______in a hurry. (To be)
26. I do it because I______to. (To choose)
27. He advanced as far as he______. (To dare)
28. He lost more than he ______afford. (Can or could)
29. He eats as much as he______. (Can or could)
30. He rode as swiftly as he______. (Can or could)
31. He locked the papers up so that they______be safe. (May or might)
32. He walked as though he______slightly lame. (To be)
33. He stayed at home because he______feeling ill. (To be)
34. I forgive you since you______. (To repent)
35. He labours hard so that he______become rich. (May or might)
36. We shall wait here until you______. (To come)
37. He rested his horse, for it______. (To limp)
38. You may sit wherever you______. (To like)
39. He went to Kolkata so that he______find work. (May or might)
40. I would die before I______. (To lie)
41. They come to see us as often as they______. (Can or could)
42. I studied hard in order that I______succeed. (May or might)
43. He ______so hard that he is certain to succeed. (To work)
44. She told me that she______come. (Will or would)
45. He would succeed if he______. (To try)
46. I asked him what I______do. (Can or could)
47. He came oftener than we______. (To expect)
48. I would not attempt it if you______me. (To ask)
49. He walked so fast than I______not overtake him. (Can or could)

EXERCISE 102

Fill in the blanks with an appropriate auxiliary. (Remember to observe the sequence of tenses.)

1. He died so that he______save the flag.

2. They erected signposts in order that the road______be known.
3. We eat so that we______live.
4. Even if he paid me to do so, I______not live in his house.
5. You______go only if you have permission.
6. On the understanding that you return soon, you______go out.
7. A bridge was built in order that the dangerous ferry______be avoided.
8. He begs from door to door so that he______keep body and soul together.
9. He was so tired that he______scarcely stand.
10. He went to England in order that he______become a barrister.
11. You make such a noise that I______not work.
12. He asked again whether supper______be ready soon.
13. In order that he______learn the language quickly, he engaged a teacher.
14. He said that he______do it.
15. The thieves stole whatever they______find in the house.
16. He begged that we______pardon him.
17. I wished that I______come earlier.
18. He said that he______try again.
19. He worked hard so that he______win the prize.
20. We ran so that we______arrive in time.
21. He said that he______give an early reply.

EXERCISE 103

Supply Verbs in correct concord in the following complex sentences.

1. They sold the house because it______old.
2. He solemnly assured them that they______quite mistaken.
3. I come home when it______to rain.
4. The soldiers advanced when the bugle______.
5. I asked him what his name______.
6. He had a cow that______enormous quantities of milk.
7. When the sun set he______home.
8. He told them that they______wrong.
9. I heard that there______a disturbance in the city.
10. Could you doubt that there______a God ?

Chapter 16 DIRECT AND INDIRECT SPEECH

98. We may report the words of a speaker in two ways:

(*i*) We may quote his *actual words.* This is called **Direct Speech.**

(*ii*) We may report what he said without quoting his exact words. This is called **Indirect** (or **Reported) Speech.**

Direct. Rama said, 'I am very busy now.'

Indirect. Rama said that he was very busy then.

It will be noticed that in Direct Speech, we use inverted commas to mark off the exact words of the speaker. In Indirect Speech we do not.

It will be further noticed that in changing the above Direct Speech into Indirect certain changes have been made. Thus :

(*i*) We have used the conjunction *that* before the Indirect statement.*

(*ii*) The pronoun *I* is changed to *he.* (The Pronoun is changed in Person.)

(*iii*) The verb *am* is changed to *was.* (Present Tense is changed to Past.)

(*iv*) The adverb *now* is changed to *then.*

Rules for Changing Direct Speech into Indirect

99. When the reporting or principal verb is in the Past Tense, all Present tenses of the Direct are changed into the corresponding Past Tenses. Thus :

(*a*) A *simple present* becomes a *simple past.*

Direct. He said, 'I *am* unwell.'

Indirect. He said (that) he *was* unwell.

(*b*) A *present continuous* becomes a *past continuous.*

Direct. He said,'My master *is writing* letters.'

Indirect. He said (that) his master *was writing* letters.

(*c*) A *present perfect* becomes a *past perfect.*

Direct. He said,'I *have passed* the examination.'

Indirect. He said (that) he *had passed* the examination.

Note—The shall of the Future Tense is changed into should.

The *will* of the Future Tense is changed into *would* or *should.*

As a rule, the *simple past* in the Direct becomes the *past perfect* in the Indirect.

Direct. He said,'The horse *died* in the night.'

Indirect. He said that the horse *had died* in the night.

99A. The tenses may not change if the statement is still relevant or if it is a universal truth. We can often choose whether to keep the original tenses or change them.

Direct. 'I know her address,' said Gopi.
Indirect. Gopi said he *knows/knew* her address.
Direct. The teacher said, 'The earth *goes* round the sun.'
Indirect. The teacher said the earth *goes/went* round the sun.
Direct. 'German is easy to learn', she said.
Indirect. She said German *is/was* easy to learn.

The past tense is often used when it is uncertain if the statement is true or when we are reporting objectively.

100. If the reporting verb is in the Present Tense, the tenses of the Direct Speech do not change. For example, we may rewrite the above examples, putting the reporting verb in the Present Tense, thus:

He says he is unwell.
He has just said his master is writing letters.
He says he has passed the examination.
He says the horse died in the night.

101. The pronouns of the Direct Speech are changed, where necessary, so that their relations with the reporter and his hearer, rather than with the original speaker, are indicated. Observe the following examples.

Direct. He said to me, 'I don't believe you.'
Indirect. He said *he* didn't believe *me.*
Direct. She said to him, 'I don't believe you.'
Indirect. *She said she* didn't believe *him.*
Direct. I said to him,'I don't believe you'
Indirect. I said *I* didn't believe *him.*

*The *that* in often omitted specially in spoken English.

Direct.	I said to you, 'I don't believe you.'				
Indirect.	I said *I* didn't believe *you*.				

102. Words expressing *nearness* in time or place are generally changed into words expressing *distance*. Thus:

now	becomes	*then*	*today*	becomes	*that day*
here	"	*there*	*tomorrow*	"	*the next day*
ago	"	*before*	*yesterday*	"	*the day before*
thus	"	*so*	*last night*	"	*the night before*

Direct. He says, 'I am glad to be here this evening.'
Indirect. He says that he is glad to be *there this* evening.

The changes do not occur if the speech is reported during the same period or at the same place ; *e.g.*,

Direct. He said, 'I am glad to be here this evening.'
Indirect. He said he was glad to be *here that* evening.

103. Similarly, *this* and *these* are changed to *that* and *those* unless the thing pointed out is near at hand at the time of reporting the speech.

Questions

104. In reporting questions the Indirect Speech is introduced by some such verbs as *asked, inquired,* etc.

When the question is not introduced by an interrogative word, the reporting verb is followed by *whether* or *if.*

Direct. He said to me,'What are you doing ?'
Indirect. He asked me what I was doing.
Direct. 'Where do you live ?' asked the stranger.
Indirect. The stranger enquired where I lived.
Direct. The policeman said to us,'Where are you going ?'
Indirect. The policeman enquired where we were going.
Direct. He said,'Will you listen to such a man ?'
Indirect. He asked them whether they would listen to such a man.
[Or] Would they, he asked, listen to such a man ?
Direct. 'Do you suppose you know better than your own father ?' jeered his angry mother.
Indirect. His angry mother jeered and asked whether he supposed that he knew better than his own father.

Commands and Requests

105. In reporting commands and requests, the Indirect Speech is introduced by some verb expressing *command* or *request,* and the imperative mood is changed into the Infinitive.

Direct. Rama said to Arjun,'Go away.'
Indirect. Rama ordered Arjun to go away.
Direct. He said to him,'Please wait here till I return.'
Indirect. He requested him to wait there till he returned.
Direct. 'Call the first witness,' said the judge.
Indirect. The judge commanded them to call the first witness.
Direct. He shouted,'Let me go.'
Indirect. He shouted to them to let him go.
Direct. He said,'Be quiet and listen to my words.'
Indirect. He urged them to be quiet and listen to his words.

Exclamations and Wishes

106. In reporting exclamations and wishes, the Indirect Speech is introduced by some verb expressing *exclamation* or *wish.*

Direct. He said,'Alas ! I am undone.'
Indirect He exclaimed sadly that he was undone.
Direct Alice said, 'How clever I am !'
Indirect Alice exclaimed that she was very clever.
Direct He said, 'Bravo ! You have done well.'
Indirect. He applauded him, saying that he had done well.

Direct. 'So help me, Heaven!' he cried, 'I will never steal again.'
Indirect. He called upon Heaven to witness his resolve never to stealagain.

EXERCISE 104

Turn the following into Indirect Speech.

1. He said to me, 'I have often told you not to play with fire.'
2. 'You have all done very badly !' remarked the teacher.
3. They wrote, 'It is time we thought about settling this matter.'
4. The teacher promised, 'If you will come before school tomorrow, I will explain it.'
5. She wrote,'I am waiting and watching and longing for my son's return.'
6. The examiner's orders were, 'No one is to bring books into the room nor ask me questions about what I have told you to do.'
7. The dwarf said to her, 'Promise me that when you are Queen you will give me your first-born child.'
8. 'That is my horse,' said he, 'and if I do not prove it in a few minutes I will give up my claim.'
9. 'I will avenge your wrongs,' he cried, 'I will not enter Athens until I have punished the king who had so cruelly treated you.'
10. He wrote and said, 'I am unable to come just now because I am ill, but I will certainly start as soon as I am well enough to do so.'
11. One day he sent for Cassim and said to him, 'You are now old enough to earn your living, so you must set off, and make your own way in the world.'

EXERCISE 105

Turn the following into Indirect Speech.

1. 'What do you want?' he said to her.
2. He said, 'How's your father ?'
3. 'Are you coming home with me ?' he asked.
4. He enquired, 'When do you intend to pay me ?'
5. He said to us, 'Why are you all sitting about there doing nothing ?'
6. 'Do you really come from China ?' said the prince.
7. The poor man exclaimed, 'Will none of you help me ?'
8. 'Which way did she go ?' asked the young Rakshas.
9. Aladdin said to the magician, 'What have I done to deserve so severe a blow?'
10. 'Don't you know the way home ?' asked I.
11. 'Do you write in a good hand ?' he said.
12. 'Have you anything to say on behalf of the prisoner ?' said the judge finally.
13. 'Which is the proper way to answer this question, father ?' the boy enquired.
14. 'Have you anything to tell me, little bird ?' asked Ulysses.
15. The young sparrow said, 'Mother, what is that queer object ?'
16. Then aloud he said, 'Tell me, boy, is the miller within ?'
17. 'Who are you, sir, and what do you want ?' they cried.
18. 'Dear bird,' she said, stroking its feathers, 'have you come to comfort me in my sorrow ?'
19. The Rajah was deeply grieved, and said to his wife, 'What can I do for you?'
20. When the sun got low, the king's son said, 'Jack, since we have no money, where can we lodge this night ?'
21. She said to him, 'What is it that makes you so much stronger and braver than any other man ?'
22. When the Brahmin approached, the first thief said, 'Why do you carry a dog on your back ? Are you not ashamed ?'

EXERCISE 106

Put the following in Indirect Speech.

1. 'Bring me a drink of milk,' said the swami to the villagers.

2. 'Sit down, boys,' said the teacher.
3. 'Halt !' shouted the officer to his men.
4. 'Take off your hat,' the king said to the Hatter.
5. The teacher said to him, 'Do not read so fast.'
6. He said to me, 'Wait until I come.'
7. 'Hurry up,' he said to his servant, 'do not waste time.'
8. 'Run away, children,' said their mother.
9. He said, 'Daughter, take my golden jug, and fetch me some water from the well.'
10. 'Go down to the bazaar. Bring me some oil and a lump of ice.' ordered his master.

EXERCISE 107

Put the following in Indirect Speech.

1. 'What a rare article milk is, to be sure, in London !' said Mr. Squeers with a sigh.
2. 'What a stupid fellow you are !' he angrily remarked.
3. He said, 'My God ! I am ruined.'
4. He said, 'Alas ! our foes are too strong.'
5. He said, 'What a lazy boy you are ! How badly you have done your work !'
6. 'How smart you are!' she said.
7. He said, 'Oh ! that's a nuisance.'
8. He said, 'How cruel of him !'
9. He said, 'What a pity you did not come !'
10. 'Ah me !' exclaimed the Queen, 'What a rash and bloody deed you have done !'

Conversion of Indirect into Direct

107. The conversion of Indirect into Direct generally presents no special difficulties, as the following examples will show.

Indirect. He inquired whether his name was not Ahmed.

Direct. He said to him, 'Is your name not Ahmed ?'

Indirect. As the stranger entered the town, he was met by a policeman, who asked him if he was a traveller. He replied carelessly that it would appear so.

Direct As the stranger entered the town, he was met by a policeman, who asked, 'Are you a traveller?' 'So it would appear,' he answered carelessly.

Indirect. She asked how she, a girl, who could not ride or use sword or lance, could be of any help. Rather would she stay at home and spin beside her dear mother.

Direct. She said, 'How can I, a girl, who cannot ride or use sword or lance, be of any help ? Rather would I stay at home and spin beside my dear mother?'

EXERCISE 108

Put the following in Direct Speech.

1. He asked Rama to go with him.
2. Rama replied that he could not do so.
3. He asked his father when the next letter would come.
4. His father replied that there might not be another that year.
5. Rama asked me what had become of Hari.
6. I told him that I had not seen him for months.
7. The master requested that they would attend carefully to what he was saying.
8. I wrote that I would visit him next day.
9. He observed that he had never liked doing that.

10. I told them to be quiet.11.He asked me if I had anything to say.
12. Rama asked Hari if he would change places with him.
13. He said that he was tired, and that he wished to go to bed.
14. An old mouse asked who would bell the cat.
15. John said that he wanted to be a soldier.
16. He asked me where I was going.17.He asked me what I wanted.
18. Abdul said that he had seen that picture.
19. The boy said that he would go with us.
20. He said that the earth moves round the sun.
21. The stranger asked Alice where she lived.
22. I asked Mary if she would lend me a pencil.
23. He told us that he had waited an hour.
24. The lady inquired if he was now quite well again.
25. He said that he had come to see them.
26. He said that though he had come, it was against his will.
27. The speaker said that it gave him great pleasure to be there that evening.
28. He asked them whether they would listen to such a man.
29. He asked me if I would accompany him.
30. He ordered him to leave the room and forbade him to return.
31. The mother asked her boy where he had been all the afternoon.
32. Hari asked Rama if he had read the letter.
33. The King asked the philosopher whom he considered the happiest man living.
34. The magistrate asked the prisoner what he was doing with his hand in the gentleman's pocket.
35. The fox cried out to the goat that a thought had just come into his head.
36. He advised his sons not to quarrel amongst themselves, when he was dead but to remain united.
37. The lion told the fox that he was very weak, that his teeth had fallen out, and that he had no appetite.
38. He replied that he had promised to reward his soldiers and that he had kept his word.

108. Study the following examples, and in each case carefully note the changes made while turning from Direct into Indirect Speech.

Direct. The Prince said, 'It gives me great pleasure to be here this evening.'
Indirect. The Prince said that it gave him great pleasure to be there that evening.

Direct. He said, 'I shall go as soon as it is possible.'
Indirect. He said that he would go as soon as it was possible.

Direct. He said, 'I do not wish to see any of you; go away.'
Indirect. He said that he did not wish to see any of them and ordered them to go away.

Direct. My teacher often says to me, 'If you don't work hard, you will fail.'
Indirect. My teacher often says to me that if I don't work hard I shall fail.

Direct. He said, 'We are all sinners.'
Indirect. He said that we are all sinners.

Direct. The lecturer said, 'Akbar won the respect of all races and classes by his justice.'
Indirect. The lecturer said that Akbar won the respect of all races and classes by his justice.

Direct. He said, 'Let us wait for the award.'
Indirect. He proposed that they should wait for the award.

Direct. 'Saint George strike for us !' exclaimed the Knight, 'do the false yeomen give way ?'
Indirect. The Knight prayed that Saint George might strike for them and asked whether the false yeomen gave way.

Direct. 'Curse it !' exclaimed the driver. 'Who could have foreseen such ill-luck ? But for accident we should have caught the train easily.'
Indirect. The driver exclaimed with an oath that nobody could have foreseen such ill-luck. But for the accident they would have caught the train easily.

Direct. The general, addressing his mutinous troops, said, 'You have brought disgrace upon a famous regiment. If you had grievances, why did you not lay them before your own officers ? Now you must first suffer punishment for your offence, before your complaints can be heard.'

Indirect. The general told his mutinous troops that they had brought disgrace upon a famous regiment. If they had grievances, why had they not laid them before their own officers? Now they must suffer punishment for their offence before their complaints could be heard.

Direct. The traveller said, 'Can you tell me the way to the nearest inn ?' 'Yes,' said the peasant, 'do you want one in which you can spend the night?' 'No,' replied the traveller, 'I only want a meal.'

Indirect. The traveller asked the peasant if he could tell him the way to the nearest inn. The peasant replied that he could, and asked whether the traveller wanted one in which he could spend the night. The traveller answered that he did not wish to stay there, but only wanted a meal.

Remark– It will be noticed that we have avoided the ugly phrases 'replied in the affirmative' and 'replied in the negative.'

EXERCISE 109

Turn the following into Indirect Speech.

1. 'Cheer up, mother, I'll go and get work somewhere,' said Jack.
2. But the sea-god cried, 'Do not be afraid, noble prince. I have taken pity on you and will help you.'
3. 'No,' said the child; 'I won't kneel, for if I do, I shall spoil my new breeches.'
4. 'What a horse they are losing for want of skill and spirit to manage him !' exclaimed Alexander.
5. Telemachus replied, 'How can I drive away the mother, who bore me and nourished me ?'
6. 'Call no man happy,' was the reply of the philosopher, 'until he has ended his life in a fitting manner.'
7. Then said the wolf to the fox, 'Now either yield thyself as vanquished, or else certainly I will kill thee.'
8. 'I believe,' said he, 'that we are in this country among a people whom we like and who like us.'
9. He said, 'Take that bird away. Its gilded cage reminds me of my father whom I imprisoned.'
10. 'I have just one word to say to you,' said the dealer. 'Either make your purchase, or walk out of my shop.'
11. 'My hour is come,' thought he. 'Let me meet death like a man.'
12. 'Be not cast down,' said Mentor, 'remember whose son thou art, and all shall be well with thee.'
13. Bhishma said: 'Boys ! boys ! remember you play a game. If it be Arjuna's turn let him have it.'
14. 'Friends,' said the old man, 'sit down and rest yourselves here on this bench. My good wife Baucis has gone to see what you can have for supper.'
15. 'Ah ! you don't know what these beans are,' said the man; if you plant them over-night, by morning they grow right up to the sky.'
16. 'How clever I am !' he said. 'All my life I have been talking prose without knowing it.'
17. 'I am old and lonely,' said she. 'Hast thou no pity on my lonelines ? Stay with me, my best son, for thou art yet more boy than man.'
18. 'I do not practise', Goldsmith once said; 'I make it a rule to prescrible only for my friends.' 'Pray, dear doctor,' said Beauclerk, 'alter your rule, and prescribe only for your enemies.'
19. He said : 'Who are you to speak to me like this ? I am the master. Why should I help you ? It is your work, not mine, to draw the cart.'
20. 'I cannot hope to see these trees which I am planting come in perfection,' said the duke, 'but it is right for me to plant for the benefit of my successors.'
21. 'Are you angry, my friends,' said the king, 'because you have lost your leader ? I am your king; I will be your leader.'
22. Said an old Crab to young one, 'Why do you walk so crooked, child ? Walk straight !' 'Mother,' said the young Crab, 'show me the way, will you ?'
23. 'Who are you ?' said the Deer. The Jackal replied : 'I am Kshudrabuddhi the Jackal. I live in this forest all by myself; I have neither friend nor relation.'
24. One summer some elephants were very much distressed by the heat, and said to their leader : 'We are absolutely perishing, for want of water. The smaller animals have bathing-places but we have none. What are we to do ? Where are we to go ?'
25. When the king saw him coming he said, 'Pray' who are you, and what do you want ?' The Rabbit said, 'I am an ambassador from His Majesty Chandra–the Moon.' The Elephant King replied, 'Declare your errand.'
26. A young Rajah once said to his Vizier, 'How is it that I am so often ill ? I take great care of myself; I never go out in the rain; I wear warm clothes; I eat good food. Yet I am always catching cold or getting fever.'

27. 'My sons,' said he, 'a great treasure lies hidden in the estate I am about to leave you.' 'Where is it hid ?' said the sons. 'I am about to leave you.' said the old man, 'but you must dig for it.'

28. 'How very well you speak French !' Lady Grizzel said. 'I ought to know it,' Becky modestly said. 'I taught it in a school, and my mother was a Frenchwoman.'

29. 'What are you going to do with the tinder-box?' asked the soldier. 'That's no business of yours,' said the witch; 'You've got your money ; give me my tinder-box.'

30. 'My name is Noman,' said Ulysses, 'my kindred and friends in my own country call me Noman.' 'Then,' said the Cyclops, 'this is the kindness I will show thee, Noman ; I will eat thee last of all thy friends.'

31. 'I am a dead man, Hardy,' said Nelson; 'I am going fast ; it will be all over with me soon. Come nearer to me. Let my dear Lady Hamilton have my hair, and all other things belonging to me.'

32. He said to the shoemaker : 'You are a big blockhead; you have done the reverse of what I desired you. I told you to make one of the shoes larger than the other, and, instead of that, you have made one of them smaller than the other.'

33. 'I can extend no other mercy to you,' said the Raja, 'except permitting you to choose what kind of death you wish to die. Decide immediately, for the sentence must be carried out.' 'I admire your kindness, noble Prince,' said the jester, 'I choose to die of old age.'

34. Her mother said, 'You must go straight to your grandmother's cottage and not loiter on the way. There is a wolf in the wood through which you are going ; but if you keep to the road he won't do you any harm. Now, will you be a good girl and do as I tell you ?'

35. Next morning at breakfast his wife said to him, 'George, I think I can tell what is amiss with our clock.' 'Well, what is it?' he sharply asked. 'It wants winding up,' said his partner.

36. A fawn one day said to her mother, 'Mother, you are bigger than a dog, and swifter and better winded, and you have horns to defend yourself; how is it that you are so afraid of the hounds ?' She smiled and said, 'All this, my child, I know fully well ; but no sooner do I hear a dog bark, than, somehow or other, my heels take me off as fast as they can carry me.'

37. Said a young mole to her mother, 'Mother, I can see.' So her mother put a lump of frank incense before her, and asked her what it was. 'A stone,' said the young one. 'O my child !' said the mother, 'not only do you not see, but you cannot even smell.'

38. 'What are you doing, good old woman ?' said the princess. 'I'm spinning, my pretty child.' 'Ah, how charming ! Let me try if I can spin also.'

39. 'You say,' said the judge, 'that the bag you lost contained one hundred and ten pounds.' 'Yes, your honour,' replied the miser. 'Then as this one contains one hundred pounds it cannot be yours.'

40. He answered slowly, 'Alas ! my dear son, why do you ask the one thing I cannot grant you ? Your hands are too weak to rein those fiery beasts ; you do not know the path. Come, ask something else, anything but that.'

41. The speaker said, 'I entirely object to the proposal. I object to it as founded on a wrong principle, and I object to it as highly inconvenient at this time. Have you considered all that this proposal involves ? Gentlemen, I entreat you to be cautious.'

42. Kausalya said to Rama, 'Do not desire, O my child, to possess the moon, because it is thousands of miles off, and it is not a plaything for children and no child ever got it. If you wish I will bring some jewels that are brighter than the moon, and you can play with them.'

43. The hen bird was just about to lay, and she said to her mate : 'Cannot you find me some place convenient for laying my eggs ?' 'And is not this,' he replied, 'a very good place for the purpose?' 'No,' she answered. 'for it is continually overflowed by the tide.' 'Am I, then, become so feeble,' he exclaimed, 'that the eggs laid in my house are to be carried away by the sea?' The hen bird laughed and said, 'There is some considerable difference between you and the sea.'

44. A cat hearing that a hen was laid up sick in her nest, paid her a visit of condolence, and creeping up to her, said : 'How are you, my dear friend ? What can I do for you ? What are you in want of ? Only tell me. Is there anything in the world that I can bring you ? Keep up your spirits, and do not be alarmed.' 'Thank you,' said the hen. 'Do you be good enough to leave me, and I have no fear but I shall soon be well.'

45. 'Sweet child,' he answered, 'do not fret, for I can make you happier here than ever you could have been on the earth ; I will give you beautiful things to play with, which a queen would envy. Rubies and diamonds shall be your toys, and your plates shall be of solid gold. All the beautiful things you see, belong to me, for I am king of this rich underworld.' But she only replied, 'I was happy playing with the pebbles on the seashore, and I care only for the sparkle of the little waves on the shining sand. Here there are no flowers, no sun,' and she wept anew.

Part II

Composition

Correct Usage

This section largely focuses on the areas of usage which are often trouble some to non-native speakers of English, especially Indian students.

Nouns like **advice, news, information, furniture, luggage, scenery,** etc. are often wrongly used with a/an and in the **plural**. (This point is explained in chapter 18.) We should say :

He gave me **some advice**. (not **an advice**)

This is **good news**. (not **a good news**)

He sold all the **furniture**. (not **furnitures**)

And so on.

Many students say **to discuss about something, to order for something, to stress on a point,** etc. These expressions are wrong. (Chapter 114) The verbs **discuss, describe, order, request, stress** and **emphasize** are transitive and cannot therefore be used with prepositions. For example, we should say :

We **discussed** the matter yesterday.

I **have ordered** five cups of tea.

She requested my help. (not **requested for my help**)

Where necessary, the differences between formal and informal English are pointed out. For example, '**Whom** did you meet ?' is grammatically correct, but today **whom** is not used except in literary or formal English. **Who** is used instead of **whom** in speech and informal writing. (Chapter 18) We say :

Who did you meet ?

Who are you going with ?

Who was the book written by ? (Formal: By **whom** was the book written ?)

There is a chapter on spelling rules. Can you spell these words correctly ? Do you put **ei** or **ie**?

bel--ve	rec--ve	ach--ve
dec--ve	rel--ve	conc--ve

Remember this rule : **i** comes before **e** except after **c.** (Chapter 27)

This section also includes very valuable material dealing with punctuation, idioms, word formation and figures of speech. Work through all the material.

PART II: CORRECT USAGE

Chapter 17 AGREEMENT OF THE VERB WITH THE SUBJECT

109. A Verb must agree with its Subject in Number and Person.

Often, by what is called the "Error of Proximity", the verb is made to agree in number with a noun near it instead of with its proper subject. This should be avoided as shown in the following examples.

The quality of the mangoes *was* not good.
The introduction of tea and coffee and such other beverages *has* not been without some effect.
His knowledge of Indian vernaculars *is* far beyond the common.
The state of his affairs *was* such as to cause anxiety to his creditors.
If it were possible to get near when one of the volcanic eruptions *takes* place, we should see a grand sight.
The results of the recognition of this fact *are* seen in the gradual improvement of the diet of the poor.

110. Two or more singular nouns or pronouns joined by *and* require a plural verb ; as,

Gold and silver *are* precious metals.
Fire and water *do* not agree.
Knowledge and wisdom *have* of times no connection.
Are your father and mother at home ?
In him *were* centred their love and their ambition.
He and I *were* playing.

But if the nouns suggest *one idea* to the mind, or refer to the *same* person or thing, the verb is singular ; as,

Time and tide *waits* for no man.
The horse and carriage *is* at the door.
Bread and butter *is* his only food.
Honour and glory *is* his reward.
The rise and fall of the tide *is* due to lunar influence.
My friend and benefactor *has* come.
The novelist and poet *is* dead.

111. Words joined to a singular subject by *with, as well as,* etc., are parenthetical. The verb should therefore be put in the singular ; as,

The house, with its contents, *was* insured.
The Mayor, with his councillors, *is* to be present.
The ship, with its crew, *was* lost.
Silver, as well as cotton, *has* fallen in price.
Sanskrit, as well as Arabic, *was* taught there.
Justice, as well as mercy, *allows* it.
The guidance, as well as the love of a mother, *was* wanting.

112. Two or more singular subjects connected by *or* or *nor* require a singular verb; as.

No nook or corner *was* left unexplored.
Our happiness or our sorrow *is* largely due to our own actions.
Either the cat or the dog *has* been here.
Neither food nor water *was* to be found there.

Neither praise nor blame *seems* to affect him.

But when one of the subjects joined by *or* or *nor* is plural, the verb must be plural, and the plural subject should be placed nearest the verb ; as,

Neither the Chairman nor the directors *are* present.

113. When the subjects joined by *or* or *nor* are of different persons, the verb agrees with the nearer ; as,

Either he or I *am* mistaken. Either you or he *is* mistaken.

Neither you nor he *is* to blame. Neither my friend nor I *am* to blame.

But it is better to avoid these constructions, and to write.

He is mistaken, or else I am. You are mistaken, or else he is.

He is not to blame, nor are you. My friend is not to blame, nor am I.

114. *Either, neither, each, everyone, many a,* must be followed by a singular verb ; as,

He asked me whether *either* of the applicants *was* suitable.

Neither of the two men *was* very strong.

Each of these substances *is* found in India.

Everyone of the prisons *is* full.

Everyone of the boys *loves* to ride.

Many a man *has* done so.

Many a man *does* not know his own good deeds.

Many a man *has* succumbed to this temptation.

Yes, the news is true.

115. Two nouns qualified by *each* or *every,* even though connected by *and,* require a singular verb ; as,

Every boy and every girl *was* given a packet of sweets.

116. Some nouns which are plural in form, but singular in meaning, take a singular verb ; as,

The *news is* true.

Politics was with him the business of his life.

The *wages* of sin *is* death.

Mathematics is a branch of study in every school.

117. *Pains* and *means* take either the singular or the plural verb, but the construction must be consistent ; as,

Great pains *have* been taken. Much pains *has* been taken.

All possible means *have* been tried. The means employed by you *is* sufficient.

In the sense of *income,* the word *means* always takes a plural verb ; as,

My means *were* much reduced owing to that heavy loss.

His means *are* ample.

Great pains have been taken.

118. Some nouns which are singular in form, but plural in meaning take a plural verb ; as,

According to the present market rate twelve *dozen cost* one hundred rupees.

119. *None,* though properly singular, commonly takes a plural verb (see § 132) ; as,

None *are* so deaf as those who will not hear.

Cows are amongst the gentlest of breathing creatures ; none *show* more passionate tenderness to their young.

120. A Collective noun takes a singular verb when the collection is thought of as one whole ; plural verb when the individuals of which it is composed are thought of ; as,

The Committee *has* issued *its* report.

The Committee *are* divided on one minor point.

But we must be consistent. Thus, we should say :

The Committee *has* appended a note to *its* (not *their*) report.

121. When the plural noun is a proper name for some single object or some collective unit, it must be followed by a singular verb ; as,

The Arabian Nights is still a great favourite.

The *United States has* a big navy.

Plutarch's Lives is an interesting book.

Gullliver's Travels was written by Jonathan Swift.

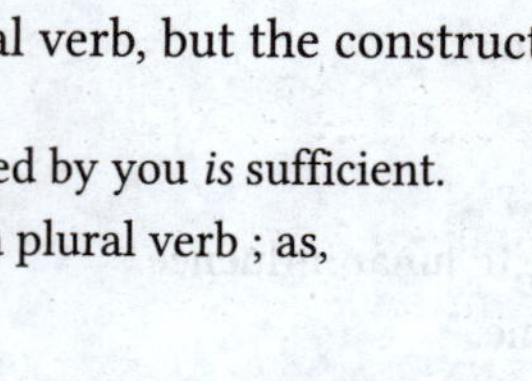
Fifty thousand is a large sum.

Gulliver's Travels

122. When a plural noun denotes some specific quantity or amount considered as a whole, the verb is generally singular ; as,

Fifteen minutes is *allowed* to each speaker.

Ten kilometers *is* a long walk.

Fifty thousand rupees *is* a large sum.

Three parts of the business *is* left for me to do.

EXERCISE 110

In each of the following sentences supply a Verb in agreement with its Subject.

1. To take pay and then not to do work____dishonest.
2. The cost of all these articles____risen.
3. The jury____divided in their opinions.
4. That night every one of the boat's crew____down with fever.
5. One or the other of those fellows____stolen the watch.
6. The strain of all the difficulties and vexations and anxieties____more than he could bear.
7. No news____good news.
8. The accountant and the cashier_____absconded.
9. A good man and useful citizen_____passed away.
10. The famous juggler and conjurer____too unwell to perform.
11. *The Three Musketeers*____written by Dumas.
12. Each of the suspected men____arrested.
13. The ebb and flow of the tides____explained by Newton.
14. Ninety rupees _____ too much for this bag.
15. The cow as well as the horse _____ grass.
16. Neither his father nor his mother _____ alive.
17. There _____ many objections to the plan.
18. Two-thirds of the city _____ in ruins.
19. The formation of paragraphs _____ very important.
20. Man's happiness or misery _____ in a great measure in his own hands.

Chapter 18 NOUNS AND PRONOUNS

123. Words like *book, table, flower* and *apple* are "countable nouns" : they are things that can be counted. Such nouns can have plural forms and are used with *a/an*.

Words like *ink, milk, gold* and *wisdom* are "uncountable nouns" : they are things that cannot be counted. Normally uncountable nouns do not have plural forms and cannot be used with *a/an*.

Note that the following nouns are usually uncountable in English: *advice, news, information, furniture, luggage, work, business, weather, traffic, scenery, paper* (= writing material), *soap, bread*. Most of these are countable in Indian languages and therefore Indian students often wrongly use them with *a/an* and in the plural.

Wrong: He gave me *an advice*.
Right: He gave me *some advice* (or: *a piece of advice*).
Wrong: The *sceneries* here are very good.
Right: The *scenery* here is very good.

If you are thinking of one separate item or unit of an uncountable thing, you may say *a piece of/a bottle of*, etc. a piece of advice, a piece of work, a piece/bar of soap, a bottle of milk

124. The use of the Possessive (or Genitive) Case should be confined to the following :—

(1) Names of living beings and personified objects ; as,
The Governor's bodyguards ; the lion's mane ; Nature's laws ; Fortune's favourite.

(2) A few stereotyped phrases ; as,
For conscience' sake, for goodness' sake, at his fingers' ends, out of arm's way, the boat's crew.

(3) Nouns of space or time denoting an amount of something ; as,
A day's work, a hand's breadth, in a year's time.

125. When two nouns in the possessive case are in apposition the apostrophe with *s* is added to the last only ; as,

This is my uncle, the engineer's office.
My brother Harry's watch.
For thy servant David's sake.

125A. When one noun is qualified by two possessive nouns both must have the possessive sign, unless joint possession is indicated.

The King and Queen's journey to India.
Huntley and Palmer's biscuits.

126. Grammarians formerly recommended that the complement of the verb *to be*, when it is expressed by a pronoun, should be in the nominative case. Today the use of the nominative form is considered extremely formal and over-correct. We usually use the objective form.

It is *me*. (Rare: It is *I*.)
It was *him*.

127. The Object of a verb or of a preposition, when it is a Pronoun, should be in the Objective form; as,

Between you and *me* (not *I*) affairs look dark.
There is really no difference between you and *me*.
Let you and *me* (not I) do it.
Please let Jack and *me* go to the theatre.
Her (not *she*), who had been the apple of his eye, he now began to regard with something like distrust. *Him* (not *he*), who had always inspired in her a respect which almost overcame her affection, she now saw the object of open pleasantry.
He has given great trouble to my father and *me* (not *I*).

128. A pronoun directly after *than* or *as* is usually in the objective case unless there is a verb after it. If a verb follows it, the nominative form is used.

He is taller than *me*.
[Or] He is taller than *I* am. (More formal)
I swim better than *him*.
[Or] I swim better that *he* does. (More formal)
I am as tall as *her*.
[Or] I am as tall as *she* is. (More formal)
The nominative form without a verb after it (*e.g.* 'He is taller than *I*') is old-fashioned.

129. A Pronoun must agree with its Antecedent in person, number and gender.

All *passengers* must show *their* tickets.
Every *man* must bear *his* own burden.
Each of the girls gave *her* own version of the affair.
I am not one of *those* who believe everything *they* (not *I*) hear.

130. In referring to *anybody, everybody, everyone, anyone, each*, etc., the pronoun of the masculine or the feminine gender is used according to the context ; as,

I shall be glad to help *everyone* of my boys in *his* studies.

What pronoun should be used to refer back to *anybody, everyone, each*, etc. when the sex is not determined? Some grammarians recommend that the pronoun of the masculine gender should be used as there is no singular pronoun of the third person to represent both male and female, *e.g.*,

Anybody can do it if *he* tries.
Everyone ran as fast as *he* could.

In present-day English, *anybody, everyone*, etc. are often followed by a plural pronoun (*they/them/their*) except in very formal speech or writing.

Anybody can do it if *they* try.

Everyone ran as fast as *they* could.
Each of them had *their* share.

131. The indefinite pronoun *one* should be used throughout, if used at all.

One cannot be too careful about what *one* (not *he*) says.
One cannot be too careful of *one's* (not *his*) good name.
One does not like to have *one's* word doubted.
One must not boast of *one's* own success.
One must use *one's* best efforts if *one* wishes to succeed.
Cannot *one* do what *one* likes with *one's* own ?

It is better to change the form of the sentence than to keep on repeating *one*.

132. *None* is construed in the singular *or* plural as the sense may require ; as,

Did you buy any mangoes ? There *were none* in the market.
Have you brought me a letter ? There *was none* for you.

When the singular equally well expresses the sense, the plural is commonly used ; as,

None of these words *are* now currently used.
None of his poems *are* well known. *None* but fools *have* believed it.

133. *Anyone* should be used when *more than two* persons or things are spoken of ; as,

She was taller than *anyone* (not *either*) of her five sisters.

134. *Each, either,* and *neither* are distributive pronouns calling attention to the individuals forming a collection, and must accordingly be followed by verbs in the singular.

Each of the scholars *has* (not *have*) done well.
Each of the men *was* (not *were*) paid twenty rupees.
Neither of them *was* invited to the party. *Neither* of the accusations is true.
Either of the roads *leads* to the railway station.
He asked whether *either* of the brothers *was* at home.

135. Be careful to use *who* (Nominative) and *whom* (Objective) correctly.

There's Mr. Dutt, *who* (not *whom*) they say is the best portrait painter in the town.
Who (not *whom*) they were I really cannot specify.
I was the man *who* (not *whom*) they thought was dead.
He was the man *who* (not *whom*) they determined should be the next mayor.
There are some *who* (not *whom*) I think are clever.
There are many *who* (not *whom*) we know quite well are honest.

One evening of each week was set apart by him for the reception of *whosoever* (not *whomsoever*) chose to visit him.
Who (not *whom*) did you say was there ?
Who (not *whom*) do you think she is ?
They were a people *whom* it was not advisable to excite.
The student, *whom* (not *who*) you thought so highly of, has failed to win the first prize.
Whom do you wish to see ?
Who (not *whom*) do you believe him to be ?

Note that today *whom* is not usual except in formal English. *Who* replaces *whom* in spoken English.
Who did you meet?
Who are you going with?
This is the man *who* I talked about this morning.

As a relative pronoun *who* replaces *whom* only in defining clauses.

136. When the subject of a verb is a relative pronoun care should be taken to see that the verb agrees in number and person with the antecedent of the relative ; as,

This is one of the most interesting novels that *have* (not *has*) appeared this year.
[The antecedent of *that* is *novels,* not *one.*]
He is one of the cleverest boys that *have* passed through the school.
One of the greatest judges that *have* ever lived laid this down as law.
It was one of the best speeches that *have* ever been made in the Parliament.
This is the only one of his poems that *is* (not are) worth reading.
[Here the antecedent of *that* is *one.* "Of his poems this is the only one that is worth reading."]

137. A definite word as the antecedent of the relative pronoun *which* make the sentences easier to understand than is possible otherwise. Thus the sentence, "His foot slipped, which caused him to fall heavily," would be easier reading, and hence better, as ;

His foot slipped, *and this* caused him to fall heavily.

Similarly we should say :

I went home for my umbrella, *and this* (rather than *which)* prevented me from being in time.
I gave him a sovereign, *and this* left me penniless.
He fell heavily, *and this* caused him great pain.

138. *And which, but which*—The relative itself fulfils the purpose of a conjunction ; hence no conjunction should be placed before it except to join together two relative clauses referring to the same antecedent ; as,

He possessed a sandalwood table *which* was of excellent workmanship, *and which* had been in his family for generations.

But the following sentences are *incorrect.*

He has a wardrobe of wonderful carving, *and* which has been in his family for generations.
They wished me to drink with them, *but* which I declined.

EXERCISE 111

Fill in each blank with "who" or "whom".

1. I met a man today ____ I had just heard was on the continent.
2. Any of you may take it ; I don't care ____.
3. ____ did you give that letter to ?
4. The man ____ I thought was my friend deceived me.
5. There was no doubt as to ____ the speaker meant.
6. The vacancy was filled by Mr. Rao ____ the manager said ought to be promoted.
7. The vacancy was filled by Mr. Rao ____ the manager thought worthy of promotion.
8. It is Sohrab ____ I think is the better of the two at swimming.
9. Ali was the man ____ they intended should be our captain next year.
10. ____ do you think is the better of the two at tennis ?
11. Enoch Arden, ____, his wife thought, had died many years before, suddenly reappeared.
12. The boy ____ I trusted proved worthy of my confidence.
13. ____ do you take me for ?
14. ____ are you speaking to ?
15. ____ do men declare me to be ?
16. A boy ____ I believed to be him just passed this way.
17. I ____ am most concerned, was not consulted.
18. The man ____ you wished to see is here.
19. Where is the boy about ____ you were speaking ?

EXERCISE 112

Correct the following sentences.

1. Please give me a soap.
2. What beautiful sceneries!
3. Can you give me an advice?
4. He has eaten two breads.
5. I have an important work to do.
6. What an awful weather!

EXERCISE 113

Tell which of the italicized forms is right, and give the reason.

1. She is one of the best mothers that (*has* or *have)* ever lived.
2. You are not the first man that (*has* or *have*) been deceived by appearances.
3. One of his many good traits that (*comes* or *come*) to my mind was his modesty.
4. This is one of the things that (*kills* or *kill*) ambition.
5. *Treasure Island* is one of the best pirate stories that (*was* or *were*) ever written.
6. Ambition is one of those passions that (*is* or *are*) never satisfied.
7. This is one of the songs that (*was* or *were*) most popular.
8. We lament the excessive delicacy of his ideas, which (*prevents* or *prevent*) one from grasping them.
9. Tyranny is one of those evils which (*tends* or *tend*) to perpetuate (*itself* or *themselves*).

EXERCISE 114

Fill in the blanks.

1. All failed except ____. (he, him)
2. That is a matter between you and ____. (I, me)
3. Leave Nell and ____ to toil alone. (I, me)
4. It is not ____ who are to blame. (we, us)
5. You and ____ are invited to tea this morning. (I, me)
6. Between you and ____, he drinks heavily. (I, me)

139. Sometimes a Pronoun is inserted where it is not required; as,
The applicant, being a householder, he is entitled to a vote. *(Incorrect)*
Here the pronoun *he* is not required.

140. A noun or pronoun in the Possessive case should not be used as the antecedant to a relative pronoun ; as,
Do not forget *his* enthusiasm who brought this movement so far. *(Incorrect)*
Change the construction to –
Do not forget the enthusiasm of him who brought this movement so far. *(Correct)*.

141. The relative pronoun is sometimes wrongly omitted when it is the Subject of the clause ; as,
He has an impudence would carry him through anything. *(Incorrect)*
Say:
He has an impudence *that* would carry him through anything. *(Correct)*

142. When the antecedent is *same,* the consequent should be *as* or *that.*
That is the *same* man *that* (or *as*) we saw yesterday.
I played with the *same* bat *that* you did.

143. Pronouns of the third person plural should not be used as antecedents to *who* and *that* ; as,
They that are whole have no need of a physician.
Here *those* is to be preferred to *they.*

144. Avoid the use of *same* as a substitute for the personal pronoun.
When you have examined these patterns please return *them* (not *same*) to us.

Chapter 19 ADJECTIVES

145. The Adjective is correctly used with a verb when some quality of the subject, rather than of the action of the verb, is to be expressed; as,
The flowers smell *sweet* (not *sweetly*).
She looks *dainty.*
That statement sounds *queer.*
It tastes *sour.*
He feels *sad.*

As a general rule, if any phrase denoting manner could be substituted, the adverb should be used ; but if some part of the verb *to be* could be employed as a connective, the Adjective is required.
The ship appeared *suddenly.*
The decision appears *unjust.*
His friends now began to look *coldly* upon him.
He looks *cold.*
We feel *warmly* on the subject.
We feel *warm.*
He spoke *angrily.*
He looked *angry.*

146. The plural forms *these* and *those* are often used with the singular nouns *kind* and *sort* ; as,
These kind of things.
Such a form of expression is, however, constanly heard and occurs in good writers.

Some grammarians insist that we should say:
"This kind of things" or, better, "Things of this kind."

147. The words, *superior, inferior, senior, junior, prior, anterior,* and *posterior,* take *to* instead of *than;* as,
As a novelist Jane Austen is *superior* to Mrs. Henry Wood.
Hari is *inferior* to Rama in intelligence.
The death of King Edward VII was *prior* to World War I.
He is *senior* to me.

148. In comparing two things or classes of things the Comparative should be used ; as,

Of the two suggestions, the former is the *better.*
Of the two novels, this is the *more interesting.*
Which is the *cheaper* of the two ?
He is the *taller* of the two.

This rule is, however, not strictly observed. In informal English the superlative is often used when we talk about one of only two items. We can use *best,most interesting, cheapest* and *tallest* in the sentences above.

149. When a comparison is instituted by means of a Comparative followed by *than,* the thing compared must be always *excluded* from the class of things with which it is compared, by using *other* or some such words ; as,
He is stronger than any *other* man living.
[The sentence "He is stronger than any man living" suggests that the person referred to is stronger than himself, which is of course, absurd.]
Mussolini may be said to have done more for the unity of Italy than any *other* man.
The Nile is said to be longer than all *other* rivers in the eastern hemisphere.
The Taj is more beautiful than all *other* mausoleums.
Solomon was wiser than all *other* men.

150. In a comparison by means of a Superlative, the latter term should *include* the former ; as,
Solomon was the wisest of all men (not *all other men.*)
The crocodile is the largest of all reptiles.
The Amazon is the largest of all rivers.
Of all men he is the strongest.

151. *Of any* is often used incorrectly in conjunction with a Superlative ; as,
He has the lightest touch of any musician.
This should be rewritten as follows:—
He has a lighter touch than any other musician.
[Or] No other musician has so light a touch.

152. A very common form of error is exemplified in the following sentence.
The population of London is greater than any city in India.
Say :
The population of London is greater than *that of* any city in India.
The comparison is between :
(*i*) the *population* of London and
(*ii*) the *population* of any city in India.

153. *Double* Comparatives and Superlatives are to be avoided, though their use was once common in English. Thus, we have in Shakespeare—
It was the *most unkindest* cut of all.
The following sentence is *incorrect.*
Seldom had the little town seen a *more costlier* funeral. [Omit *more*]
But *lesser* (a double comparative) is used even by the best authors.
The *lesser* of the two evils.

154. *Preferable* has the force of a Comparative, and is followed by *to.* We must not say *more preferable.*
He has a scheme of his own which he thinks *preferable to* that of any other person.

155. *Less* (the comparative of *little*) is used before uncountable nouns, while *fewer* (the comparative of *few*) is used before plural nouns. However, *less* is also often used before plural nouns in informal English.

No *fewer* (or *less*) than fifty miners were killed in the explosion.

156. Certain adjectives do not really admit of comparison because their meaning is already superlative ; as,

Unique, ideal, perfect, complete, universal, entire, extreme, chief, square, round.

Do *not* therefore say :

Most unique, quite unique, chiefest, extremist.

But we still say, for instance:

This is the *most* perfect specimen I have seen.

157. *Older* and *oldest* may be said either of persons or of things, while *elder* and *eldest* apply to persons only, and are besides, strictly speaking, confined to members of the same family.

Gladstone was *older* than Morley.
He will succeed to the title in the event of the death of his *elder* brother.
Patricia is the *eldest* of the Vicar's family.
Old Farmer Giles is the *oldest* inhabitant in our village.

158. The *two first* is a meaningless expression, for it implies that two things may be first. We should say "the first two."

The *first two* chapters of the novel are rather dull.
The *first two* boys were awarded gold medals.

159. *Few* and a *few* have different meanings.

Few is negative, and equivalent to *not many, hardly any.*

A few is positive, and equivalent to *some.*

Few persons can keep a secret.
A few words spoken in earnest will convince him.

Similarly *little* = not much ; *a little* = some, though not much.

There is *little* hope of his recovery.
A little tact would have saved the situation.

160. *Latter* is often wrongly used for *last.* Use *latter* when there are two only, *last* when there are more.

Of the three, tea, coffee and cocoa, the *last* (not *latter*) is his favourite.

161. *Verbal* is often wrongly used for *oral.*

Verbal means 'of or pertaining to *words*'; *oral* means, 'delivered by word of mouth', *not written.* Hence the opposite of *written* is *oral,* not *verbal.*

His written statement differs in several important respects from his *oral* (not *verbal*) statement.
The lad was sent with an *oral* message to the doctor.
There are a few *verbal* differences in the two manuscripts (*i.e.,* differences in *words,* not in sense).
The photograph will give the reader a far better notion of the structure than any *verbal* description.
Were your instructions *oral* or *written* ?

162. Do not say 'our *mutual* friend.' The proper expression is 'our *common* friend'.

They were introduced to each other by a *common* (not *mutual*) friend.
We happened to meet at the house of a *common* friend.

Chapter 20 VERBS

163. The subject of the sentence should not be left without a verb. The following sentence is *incorrect.*

He who has suffered most in the cause, let him speak.

Recast as shown below.

Let him who has suffered most in the cause speak.
[Or] He who has suffered most in the cause should speak.

164. A verb should agree with its subject, and not with the complement ; as,

What is wanted *is* (not *are*) not large houses with modern conveniences, but small cottages.

The details *are* a matter for future consideration.

Our followers *are* but a handful.

165. In a compound sentence a single verb can be made to do duty for two subjects, only when the form of the verb is such as to permit of it ; as,

Not a drum was heard, not a funeral note [was heard].

But the following sentence is *incorrect*, because the subjects are not in the same number:

His diet was abstemious, his prayers long and fervent.

We should rewrite it as follows:

His diet was abstemious, his prayers *were* long and fervent.

[In a sentence like this, Mr. Fowler regards the ellipsis as permissible.]

166. Two auxiliaries can be used with one principal verb, only when the form of the principal verb is appropriate to *both* the auxiliaries; as,

I never have hurt anybody, and never will.

No state can or will adopt this drastic measure.

But the following sentence is *incorrect :*

He never has, and never will, take such strong measures.

Rewrite it as follows:

He never has taken, and never will take, such strong measures.

167. When there is only one auxiliary to two principal verbs, it should be such that it may be correctly associated with both; as,

Ten rioters have been sentenced, and five acquitted.

But the following sentence is *incorrect.*

Ten new members have been enrolled, and seven resigned.

Rewrite it as follows :

Ten new members have been enrolled and seven *have* resigned.

168. Carefully distinguish between the verbs *lay* and *lie.* The verb *lay* is transitive and is always followed by an object; the verb *lie* is intransitive and cannot have an object.

Lay, laid, laid.

Lay the child down to sleep.

I *laid* the book on the table.

The hen has *laid* an egg.

Lie, lay, lain

Let me *lie* here.

He *lay* under that pipal tree.

169. An Infinitive should be in the present tense unless it represents action prior to that of the governing verb ; as,

I should have liked *to go* (not *to have gone*).

But we correctly say—

He seems *to have enjoyed* his stay at Mahabaleshwar.

170. A common blunder is to leave the Participle without proper agreement or with no agreement at all ; as,

Sitting on the gate, a scorpion stung him.

Here the word "scorpion" to which the participle "sitting" refers grammatically is not that with which it is meant to be connected in sense ; in other words, the Participle is left without proper agreement.

We should therefore recast it as shown below.

Sitting on the gate, *he* was stung by a scorpion.

[Or] While *he* was sitting on the gate, a scorpion stung him.

Now read the following sentence where the Participle is left with no agreement at all.

Being a very hot day, I remained in my tent.

Here the sentence contains no word to which the Participle can possibly refer. We should therefore write :

As it was a very hot day, I remained in my tent.

171. Usage, however, permits in certain cases constructions like the following :—

Considering his abilities, he should have done better.
Roughly *speaking,* the distance from here to the nearest railway station is two miles.
Taking everything into consideration, his lot is a happy one.

It will be noticed that in each sentence the unexpressed subject is indefinite. Thus,

Taking everything into consideration=If *one* should take everything into consideration.

172. A present participle should not be used to express an action which is not contemporaneous with the action of the principal verb.

The following sentence is therefore *incorrect.*

He sailed for New York on Monday, *arriving* there on Saturday.

Rewrite it as follows.

He sailed for New York on Monday, *and arrived* there on Saturday.

173. The Subjunctive Mood is sometimes wrongly used for the Indicative. When the statement introduced by *if* or *though* is an *actual fact,* or what is *assumed as a fact,* the proper Mood to be used is the Indicative and not the Subjunctive.

Though the war is over, there is much discontent.
If he was there, he must have heard the talk.

But the Subjunctive is correctly used in the following sentences.

Mere supposition {
If I *were* you [but I am not], I should agree.
If he *were* here, he would support me.
Though he were the Prime Minister, I would say the same.

174. The verb *make* is followed by noun/pronoun + plain infinitive (= infinitive without *to*). Many students wrongly use it with the *to*-infinitive.

She made the boy *do* the whole work. (not: *to do* the whole work)

175. When used in the passive, *make* is followed by the *to*-infinitive.

The boy *was made* to do the whole work.

176. The following verbs are often wrongly used with the *to*-infinitive: *enjoy, avoid, miss, postpone, suggest.* They should be used with the gerund.

Hi I'm
Jojo

He enjoys *swimming.* (not: *to swim*)
She avoids *meeting* people. (not: *to avoid*)
We missed *seeing* the Prime Minister. (not: *to see*)

Note the following.

1. *Wrong:* Suresh *told to* me about it.
Right: Suresh *told* me about it.

The verb *tell* is followed by an indirect object (*me, him, her,* etc.) without *to.*

2. *Wrong:* She *told* she wouldn't come.
Right: She *told* me she wouldn't come./She *said* she wouldn't come.

When used with a *that*-clause, *tell* takes an indirect object, while *say* does not.

I want to
meet him.

3. *Wrong:* I *want* that you should meet him.
Right: I *want* you to meet him.

The verb *want* should not be used with a *that*-clause. It is used with the *to*-infinitive.

4. *Wrong:* I *suggest* you to apply for the post.
Right: I *suggest* that you (should) apply for the post.

The verb *suggest* should be used with a *that*-clause. It cannot be used with the *to*-infinitive.

177. The verbs *discuss, describe, order* and *request* are transitive verbs. Students often wrongly use these verbs with a preposition.

Wrong:	We *discussed about* the matter yesterday.
Right:	We *discussed* the matter yesterday.
Wrong:	He *described about* the scenery.
Right:	He *described* the scenery.
Wrong:	I have *ordered for* three cups of coffee.
Right:	I have *ordered* three cups of coffee.
Wrong:	She *requested for* my help.
Right:	She *requested* my help.

EXERCISE 115

Recast the following sentences.

1. Being condemned to death, the scaffold was erected for his execution.
2. Born in Surat, a part of his education was received in Mumbai.
3. Observing the house on fire, the engines were sent for.
4. Being a wet day, I wore my mackintosh.
5. Having gone to bed very late, the sun woke me at about nine o'clock.
6. Referring to your esteemed inquiry, the prices of the articles are as follows.
7. Standing on the top of the hill, the eye roams over the beautiful landscape.
8. Having failed in the first attempt, no further attempts were made.
9. Bearing this in mind, no particular difficulty will be found.
10. Travelling from Karjat to Khandala, the line is most beautifully laid.
11. Being his sole companion, he naturally addressed himself to me.
12. Crossing the channel, a heavy storm arose.
13. Hoping to hear from you soon, yours sincerely.
14. Calling upon him yesterday, he subscribed a handsome sum to the Famine Relief Fund.
15. Going up the hill, an old temple was seen.
16. Resting in cool shelter, the hours were beguiled with desultory talk.
17. Having obtained information, he was arrested for complicity in the plot.
18. Weary with travelling, the destination seemed a hundred miles away.
19. Meeting my friend in the park, he told me all the news.
20. Entering the room, the light was quite dazzling.

For a detailed treatment of the uses of the Tenses and Auxiliaries, see chapters **25, 26 and 32,** Book I.

Chapter 21 ADVERBS

178. Adverbs should be so placed in a sentence as to make it quite clear which word or words they are intended to modify. Hence Adverbs should come, if possible, next to the word or words they modify.

He had got *almost* to the top when the rope broke.

179. As a general rule, *only* should be placed immediately *before* the word it is intended to modify ; as,

I worked *only* two sums.

Only Balu succeeded in scoring a century.

I praise him *only* when he deserves it.

In spoken English, however, it is usually put before the verb. The required meaning is obtained by stressing the word which the *only* modifies ; *e.g.,*

He only worked two sums. (The word *two* is stressed.)

180. The adverbs *ever, never, scarcely, ever* are often misplaced, as in the following sentence :

Quite the most remarkable article we ever remember to have read.
[Say : we remember ever......]

181. Two negatives destroy each other. Hence two negatives should not be used in the same sentence unless we wish to make an affirmation. We should say :

I haven't got *any* (not *none*).
I could not find it *any*where (not *no*where).
I have not got *any* (not *no*) paper for my exercise.
I can't see *any* (not *no*) wit in her.
Scarcely any one believes in such ghost stories nowadays.
(*Not,* No one scarcely believes ....)

182. Adjectives should not be used for Adverbs. We should say, for instance :

He ate the sweets greedily (not *greedy*).
He will pay *dearly* (not *dear*) for his mistake.

183. *Ever* is sometimes misused for *never.*

We seldom or *never* (not *ever*) see those forsaken who trust in God.
Such goods are made for export, and are seldom or *never* (not *ever)* used in the country.

Note—Seldom or never and seldom if ever are both correct but seldom or ever is incorrect.

184. *Else* should be followed by *but.*

It is nothing *else but* (not *than*) pride.

185. The use of *never* for *not* is incorrect.

We met the other day, but he *never* referred to the matter. [Say : he *did not* ever refer....]
Kipling was *never* born in London. [Say : Kipling was *not* born......]
I *never* remember having met him. [Say: I *do not* remember *ever* having met him.]

186. Except colloquially, *so* as an adverb of degree must not be used absolutely. (*i.e.,* without a correlative)
We should say :

He is *very* (not *so*) weak.
Cricket is *very* (not *so*) uncertain. I was *very* (not *so*) lonely.

187. *That* should not be used instead of *so* as an adverb. We should say :

He went only *so* (not *that*) far.
He was *so* (not *that*) tired that he could scarcely stand.
He was *so* (not *that*) angry that he slammed the book on the table.

188. The adverb *too* means "more than enough" and should not be used instead of *very* or *much.*
In the following sentences *too* is used correctly.

The news is *too* good to be true.
My heart is *too* full for words.
The work is *too* much for any man to do single-handed.
He is *too* much exhausted to speak.

189. *Of course* is often loosely used for *certainly, undoubtedly.* Strictly speaking, *of course* should be used to denote a *natural* or an *inevitable* consequence.

Does she sing well ? *Certainly* (not *of course*) she does.

EXERCISE 116

Correct the following sentences and state your reasons for so doing.

1. It was bitter cold.
2. I couldn't help not laughing at the joke.
3. I never remember to have seen a more excited football match.
4. This novel is too interesting.

5. I haven't got no money.
6. My friend said he never remembered having read a more enjoyable book.
7. This hardly won liberty was not to be lightly abandoned.
8. I am much glad to see you.
9. No one can write as neatly as he does.
10. I cannot by no means allow you to do so.
11. The flowers smell sweetly.
12. I don't know nothing whatever of the matter.

Chapter 22 CONJUNCTIONS

190. *Except* is not now used as a conjunction equivalent to *unless*.

I shall not come *unless* (not *except*) you need me.
Do not trouble yourself about writing to me, *unless* (not *except*) you are quite in the humour for it.

191. The use of *without* as conjunction equivalent to *unless* is now bad English.

Unless (not *without*) you apologize I shall punish you.
I shall not go *unless* (not *without*) you do.

192. The adverb *like* is often wrongly used as a conjunction instead of *as*.

He speaks *as* (not *like*) his father does.

But it is quite correct to say :

He speaks *like* his father. [*Like* is here a preposition.]

193. *Directly* should not be used as a conjunction where *as soon as* would in every way be better.

As soon as [not *directly*] the session of 1999 commenced, the Government was pressed to do something for the unemployed.

According to Fowler, "the conjunctional use of *directly* is quite defensible, but is chiefly colloquial."

194. The conjunction *that* is sometimes redundantly repeated; as,

He must remember that, although the first people in Europe would like his society, and place him on an equality with themselves, [*that*] none of them would either give or lend him a farthing.

195. Instead of repeating the conjunction used in the preceding clause, some writers have a trick of introducing a subsequent clause by *that;* as,

If I do not speak of them it is *because* they do not come within my subject, and not *that* they are lightly esteemed by me.[Use *because* instead of *that*.]

196. *Scarcely* should be followed by *when*, and not by *than.*

Scarcely had he gone, *when* (not *than*) a policeman knocked at the door.

197. *No sooner* is followed by *than*, and not by *but.*

No sooner had he returned *than* (not *but*) he was off again.

198. The phrase "seldom or ever" is meaningless. We should say "seldom or never".

Such goods are made for export, and are *seldom or never* used in this country.

199. Say:

I gave no more than I could *not* help (not *than I could* help).

200. Examine the following sentence.

This is as good if not better than that.

You will notice that *as* is omitted after "as good".

It is better to say :

This is as good as, if not better than, that.

But the best way to correct the sentence is to recast it, thus:

This is as good as that, if not better.

201. Care should be taken, when using correlative conjunctions, such as *either.....or, neither.....nor, not only....but also*, that they are followed by the same part of speech ; as,

He lost *not only* his ticket, *but also* his luggage.

But the following is *incorrect :*

He not only lost his ticket, but also his luggage.

202. *Neither* is followed by *nor*, not by *or*.

He washed *neither* his hands *nor* (not *or*) his face.

Chapter 23 ORDER OF WORDS

203. In English, owing to the fewness of the inflexions, the order (or arrangement) of the words in a sentence is of the first importance.

The following is the usual order of words in an English sentence.

(1) The subject usually comes before the verb; as,

The *dog* bit the horse.

The *people* rang the bell for joy.

(2) The object usually comes after the verb; as,

The horse bit the *dog*.

The King wears a *crown*.

(3) When there is an indirect object and also a direct object, the indirect precedes the direct; as,

Lend *me* your *ears*.

(4) When the adjective is used attributively it comes before the noun which it qualifies ; as,

Few cats like *cold* water.

I like the *little* pedlar who has a *crooked* nose.

King Francis was a *hearty* king, and loved a *royal* sport.

(5) When the adjective is used predicatively it comes after the noun; as,

The child is *asleep*.

The horse became *restive*.

(6) The adjective phrase comes immediately after the noun; as,

Old Tubal Cain was a man *of might*.

The tops *of the mountains* were covered with snow.

(7) The adverb is generally placed close to the word which it modifies; as,

Nothing *ever* happens by chance.

John is a *rather* lazy boy.

He worked *only* two sums.

He *never* tells a lie.

Note—When an adverb is intended to modify the sentence as a whole, it is placed at the beginning of a sentence; as,

Certainly he made a fool of himself.

(8) All qualifying clauses are placed as close as possible to the words which they qualify; as,

He died in the village *where he was born*.

The dog *that bites* does not bark.

People *who live in glass houses* should not throw stones.

204. The normal order of words in a sentence is sometimes altered for *emphasis;* as,

Uneasy lies the head that wears a crown.
Monkeys I detest.
Money you shall have.
Blessed are the merciful.
Great is Diana of the Ephesians.
Great is the struggle, and great is also the prize.
Just and true are all Thy ways.
Fallen, fallen is Babylon !
Silver and gold have I none, but such as I have give I unto thee.

205. Owing to faulty arrangement of words a sentence may be turned into perfect nonsense; as,

Few people learn anything that is worth learning easily.
He blew out his brains, after bidding his wife goodbye with a gun.
A gentleman has a dog to sell who wishes to go abroad.

It is, therefore, essential that *all qualifying words, phrases and clauses should be placed as near as possible to the words to which they refer.*

EXERCISE 117

Rewrite the following sentences, improving the arrangement.

1. For sale, piano, the property of a musician, with carved legs.
2. He tore up the tender letter which his mother had written him in a fit of peevish vexation.
3. The captain took the things which the gods provided with thankful good humour.
4. Sometimes you will see an alligator lying in the sunshine on the bank eight feet long.
5. All the courtiers told the Queen how beautiful she was all the day long.
6. Mrs. Jeremy Daud was sitting with her husband on the steps of the hotel when Amy and Dulce came up, with her lap full of newspapers.
7. The man ought to be brought before a magistrate who utters such threats.
8. He visited the battlefield where Napoleon was defeated in his holidays.
9. He killed the sparrow which was eating some crumbs with a gun.
10. No magnanimous victor would treat those whom the fortune of war had put in his power so cruelly.
11. The constable said that the prisoner seizing a bolster full of rage and fury had knocked the prosecutor down.
12. A nurse maid is wanted for a baby about twenty years old.
13. I spent the three last days of my holiday in a chair with a swollen leg.
14. This monument has been erected to the memory of John Brown who was accidentally shot by his brother as a mark of affection.
15. In thirty-seven wrecks only five lives were fortunately lost.
16. The following verses were written by a young man who has long since been dead for his own amusement.
17. Many works must close if the strike lasts over the weekend owing to lack of fuel.
18. There will be a meeting of all boys who play cricket and football in the long room at 4 o'clcok.

EXERCISE 118

Rewrite the following sentences improving the arrangement.

1. These acts were pushed through Parliament in spite of opposition with but little modification.
2. The beaux of that day painted their faces as well as the women.
3. He saw countless numbers of the dead riding across the field of battle.
4. They only work when they have no money.
5. He refused to relieve the beggar with a frown on his face.
6. His body was found floating lifeless on the water at a short distance from where the boat was upset by a fisherman.
7. He was very fond of her; he thought of marrying her more than once.
8. It is proposed to construct a bath for males 99 feet long.

9. One day the bird did not perform certain tricks which had thought it to his satisfaction.
10. I have lately received permission to print the following tale from the author's son.
11. They left the hotel where they had been staying in a motor-car.
12. The Board of Education has resolved to erect a building large enough to accommodate 500 students three storeys high.
13. He spoke of the notion that the national debt might be repudiated with absolute contempt.
14. One of the combatants was unhurt, and the other sustained a wound in the arm of no importance.
15. Girl wanted for telephone of nice manners and appearance.
16. He repeated the whole poem after he had read it only once with perfect accuracy.
17. He was shot by a secretary under notice to quit with whom he was finding fault very fortunately without effect.
18. A clever judge would see whether a witness was deliberately lying a great deal better than a stupid jury.
19. I was rather impressed by the manner of the orator than by his matter.
20. He was driving away from the church where he had been married in a coach and six.
21. Stories have been related of these animals which are of an entirely fictitious character.

Chapter 24 IDIOMS

206. Idioms may be defined as expressions peculiar to a language. They play an important part in all languages.

207. Many verbs, when followed by various prepositions, or adverbs, acquire an idiomatic sense; as,

He backed up (supported) his friend's claim.

The present disturbances will soon blow over (pass off).

The police produced evidence to bear out (substantiate) the charge of murder.

You must not build your hopes upon (rely upon) his promises.

The matter has been cleared up (explained).

I readily closed with (accepted) his offer.

He is ready to dispose of (sell) his car for Rs.1,50,000.

Rust has eaten away (corroded) the plate.

They fixed upon (chose) him to do the work.

My good behaviour so far gained on (won the favour of) the emperor that I began to conceive hopes of liberty.

The habit of chewing tobacco has been growing upon (is having stronger and stronger hold over) him.

Please hear me out (*i.e.,* hear me to the end).

I have hit upon (found) a good plan to get rid of him.

About an hour ago I saw a fellow hanging about (loitering about) our bungalow.

These events led up to (culminated in) the establishment of a republic.

During excavations one of the workmen lighted upon (chanced to find, discovered) a gold idol.

During her long illness she often longed for (desired) death.

I could not prevail on (persuade, induce) him to attend the meeting.

For years I could not shake off (get rid of) my malaria.

I threatened to show him up (expose him).

All eyes turned to him because he was the only person who could stave off (prevent, avert) the impending war.

He is sticking out for (persists in demanding) better terms.

I must think the matter over (*i.e.,* consider it).

Train up (educate) a child in the way he should go; and when he is old he will not depart from it.

That fellow trumped up (concocted, fabricated) a story.

He seems to be well off (in comfortable circumstances).

Bear

Satish bore away (won) many prizes at the school sports.
The new leader has been able to bear down (overthrow, crush) all opposition.
His evidence bears out (confirms, corroborates) the evidence of the first witness.
In his misfortune God gave him strength to bear up (to keep up spirits, not to despair).
A religious hope bears up (supports) a man in his trials.
His evidence did not bear upon (was not relevant to) the inquiry.
I trust you will bear with (have patience with, show forbearance to) me a few minutes more.

Break

He broke down (failed) in the middle of his speech.
He broke off (stopped suddenly) in the middle of his story.
I gave him no cause to break with (quarrel with) me.
The burglars broke into (entered by force) the house.

Bring

His folly has brought about (caused) his ruin.
Idleness and luxury bring forth (produce, cause) poverty and want.
He brought forward (adduced) several cogent arguments in support of his scheme.
That building brings in (yields as rent) Rs. 7000 a month.
Our teacher often tells us a story to bring out (show) the meaning of a lesson.
The publishers have recently brought out (published) a cheap edition of their new dictionary.
He found great difficulty in bringing her round (converting her) to his views.
She brought up (reared) the orphan as her own child.

Call

His master called for (demanded) an explanation of his conduct.
New responsibilities often call out (draw forth) virtues and abilities unsuspected before.
Call in (summon, send for) a doctor immediately.
He called on me (paid me a brief visit) yesterday.
The old man could not call up (recollect) past events.

Carry

He agreed to carry out (execute) my orders.
His passion carried him away (*i.e.,* deprived him of self-control).
His son carried on (managed) his business in his absence.
Many persons were carried off (killed) by plague.

Cast

The ship was cast away (wrecked) on the coast of Africa.
He was much cast down (depressed) by his loss.

Come

How did these things come about (happen) ?
How did you come by (get) his purse ?
When does the Convocation come off (take place) ?
At last the truth has come out (transpired).
The taxes come to (amount to) a large sum.
The question came up (was mooted or raised for discussion).
before the Municipal Corporation last week.

I expect he will come round (recover) within a week.
I hope he will come round (agree) to our views.

Cry

Men of dissolute lives cry down (depreciate) religion, because they would not be under the restraints of it.
He cried out against (protested against) such injustice.
That young author is cried up (extolled) by his friends.

Cut

He was cut off (died) in the prime of life.
You must cut down (reduce) your expenditure.
He is cut out for (specially fitted to be) a sailor.
His wife's death cut him up (afflicted him, distressed him) terribly.

Do

I am done for (ruined).
Having walked twenty miles, he is quite done up (fatigued, exhausted).

Fall

At last the rioters fell back (retreated, yielded).
At my friend's tea-party I fell in with (met accidentally) a strange fellow.
The measure falls in with (happens to meet) the popular demand.
The scheme has fallen through (failed) for want of support.
I am told the two brothers have fallen out (quarrelled).
It is said that the standard of efficiency in public service has recently fallen off (deteriorated).
In the second school-term the attendance fell off (diminished).

Get

His friends expected that he would get off (escape) with a fine.
It is hard to get on with (agree or live sociably with) a suspicious man.
The thief got away (escaped) with my cash-box.
I can't get out (remove) this stain.
The revolt of the tribal chiefs has been got under (subdued).
The dog tried to get at (attack) me.
He has got through (passed) his examination.
They soon got the fire under (under control) by pouring buckets of water over it.
You were lucky to get out of (escape from) his clutches.

Give

We are credibly informed that the murderer has given himself up (surrendered himself) to the police.
The doctors have given him up (*i.e.,* have no hope of his recovery).
Soon after it was given forth (published, noised abroad), and believed by many, that the King was dead.
The fire gave off (emitted) a dense smoke.
The strikers seem determined, and are not likely to give in (submit, yield).
It was given out (published, proclaimed) that he was a bankrupt.
The horses gave out (were exhausted) at the next milestone.
The rope gave way (broke, snapped) while the workmen were hauling up the iron pillar.
He would not listen to me at first, but at last he gave way (yielded).
The Governor gave away (distributed, presented) the prizes.

Give over (abandon) this foolish attempt.

In his cross-examination, he ultimately gave himself away (betrayed himself).

Go

You cannot always go by (judge from) appearances.

It is a good rule to go by (to be guided by).

He promised to go into (examine, investigate) the matter.

Have you anything to go upon (*i.e.,* any foundation for your statement) ?

We have no data to go upon (on which to base our conclusions).

The story won't go down (be believed).

The concert went off well (was a success).

The auditor went over (examined) the balance sheet.

The poor woman has gone through (suffered) much.

I must first go through (examine) the accounts.

Hold

The rebels held out (offered resistance) for about a month.

He holds out (gives) no promise of future prospects.

They were held up (stopped on the highway and robbed) by bandits.

The subject is held over (deferred, postponed) till next meeting.

Keep

A few boys were kept in (confined after school-hours).

I was kept in (confined to the house) by a bad cold.

They kept up (carried on) a long conversation.

Little disputes and quarrels are chiefly kept up (maintained) by those who have nothing else to do.

He is trying his best to keep up (maintain) the reputation of his family.

The rubber syndicate keeps up (maintains) the price.

She kept on (continued) talking.

I shall keep back (conceal) nothing from you.

Knock

He has knocked about (wandered about) the world a great deal.

The dressing-table was knocked down (sold at an auction) for Rs. 900.

We were greatly knocked up (exhausted) after our steep climb.

Lay

The rebels laid down (surrendered) their arms.

He had laid out (invested) a large sum in railway shares.

Foolish people, who do not lay out (spend) their money carefully, soon come to grief.

He is laid up (confined to his bed) with fever.

He resolved to lay by (save for future needs) a part of his income.

Let

I was let into (made acquainted with) her secret.

This being his first offence he was let off (punished leniently) with a fine.

Look

His uncle looks after (takes care of) him.
He looks down upon (despises) his poor cousins.
Look up (search for) the word in the dictionary.
The old man is looking forward to (expecting with pleasure) the visit of his grandchildren.
I will look into (investigate) the matter.
I look on (regard) him as my son.
Some look to (rely on) legislation to hasten the progress of social reforms.
Look to (be careful about) your manners.
Prices of piece-goods are looking up (rising).
Things are looking up (improving).
His friends look up to (respect) him.
He will not look at (*i.e.*, will reject) your offer.

Make

Contentment makes for (conduces to) happiness.
He made over (presented, gave in charity) his bungalow to the Islam Orphanage.
I cannot make out (discover) the meaning of this verse.
I cannot make out (read, decipher) his handwriting.
You have failed to make out (prove) your case.
Some time ago the two brothers quarrelled, but they have now made it up (become reconciled).

Pass

He generally passed by (overlooked) the faults of his subordinates.
The crew of the boat passed through (underwent) terrible sufferings.
He passed himself off as (pretended to be) a nobleman.
He poses all for (is regarded as) a great Sanskritist.

Pick

The Committee picked out (selected) the best players for the team.
He lost twenty pounds in sickness, but is now picking up (regaining or recovering health).

Pull

Unless we pull together (co-operate, work together in harmony) we cannot succeed.
My cousin pulled through (passed with difficulty) the examination.
The doctor says the patient will pull through (recover from his illness).
It is far easier to pull down (demolish) than to build up.
He was pulled up (scolded, rebuked) by the President.

Put

He puts on (assumes) an air of dignity.
Please put out (extinguish) the light.
He was put out (vexed, annoyed) when I refused his request for a loan.
The plaintiff was put out (disconcerted) when the suit was dismissed.
He tried to put me off (evade me, satisfy me) with promises.
He has put in (made, sent in) a claim for compensation.
While travelling I had to put up with (endure) a good deal of discomfort.
I cannot put up with (tolerate) his insolence.

They put him up to (incited him to) mischief.

I am sorry to put you to (give you) so much trouble.

He put off (postponed) his departure for a week.

The measure was put through (passed) without opposition.

Run

On account of overwork he is run down (enfeebled).

He always runs down (disparages) his rivals.

The lease of our premises has run out (expired, come to an end).

He has run through (squandered away) his fortune.

The tailor's bill has run up to (amounted to) a large amount.

He has run into (incurred) debt.

While turning the corner I ran against (chanced to meet) an old friend.

Recently my expenses have run up (increased) considerably.

The cistern is running over (overflowing).

See

I saw through (detected) the trick.

It is hard to see into (discern) his motive.

His friends were present at the station to see him off (witness his departure).

Set

The High Court set aside (annulled) the decree of the lower court.

He immediately set about (took steps towards) organizing the department.

He set off (started) for Peshawar early this morning.

The frame sets off the picture (*i.e.,* enhances its beauty by contrast).

He has set up (started business) as a banker.

I have enough capital to set me up (establish myself) in trade.

He hired a palatial bungalow and set up for (pretended to be) a millionaire.

I was obliged to set him down (snub him).

You may set down (charge) his loss to me.

Who set you on (instigated you) to do it ?

These seats are set apart (reserved) for ladies.

In his speech on prohibition, he set forth (explained, made known) his views at length.

The robbers set upon (attacked) the defenceless travellers.

Winter in England sets in (begins) about December.

Speak

In this city there is no free library to speak of (worth mentioning).

I was determined to speak out (express my opinion freely).

Stand

They are determined to stand up for (vindicate, maintain) their rights.

Let this matter stand over (be deferred or postponed) for the present.

It is hard but I think I can stand it out (endure it to the end without yielding).

He is always standing up for (championing the cause of) the weak and oppressed.

We shall be formidable if we stand by (support) one another.

Strike

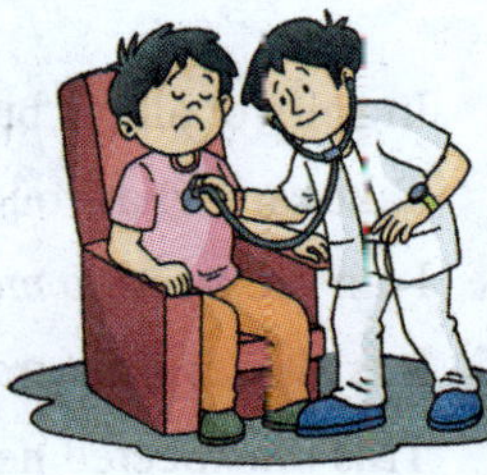

He is struck down with (attacked by) paralysis.

The Medical Council struck off (removed) his name from the register of medical practitioners.

While we were planning a family picnic, my sister struck in (interrupted) with the suggestion that we invite our neighbour's children as well.

Take

The piano takes up (occupies) too much room.

It would take up (occupy) too much time to tell you the whole story.

He takes after (resembles) his father.

At present I am reading the Essays of Bacon, but it is sometimes difficult to take in (comprehend, understand) his meaning.

Recently he has taken to (become addicted to) opium eating.

Talk

We talked over (discussed) the matter for an hour.

I hope to talk him over (convince him by talking) to our view.

Tell

I am afraid your antecedents will tell against you (*i.e.*, prove unfavourable to you).

The strain is telling upon (affecting) his health.

Throw

My advice was thrown away (wasted) upon him, because he ignored it.

The bill was thrown out (rejected) by the Assembly.

In disgust he threw up (resigned) his appointment.

When he became rich he threw over (abandoned or deserted) all his old friends.

Turn

The factory turns out (produces, manufactures) 20,000 lbs of cloth a day.

If he is lazy, why don't you turn him off (dismiss him)?

He turned out (proved) to be a sharper.

His very friends turned against (became hostile to) him.

Who can say what will turn up (happen) next ?

He promised to come, but he never turned up (appeared).

Work

We tempted him with many promises, but nothing would work on (influence) him.

He worked out (solved) the problem in a few minutes.

He is sure to work up (excite) the mob.

He worked upon (influenced) the ignorant villagers.

Chapter 25 IDIOMS (CONTD.)

208. The student who studies the following selection of English idioms will notice that metaphor enters largely into idiomatic phraseology.

1

In spite of all his brag he had *to eat humble pie* (to apologize humbly, to yield under humiliating circumstances).

Take care what you say! You will have *to eat your words* (to retract your statements, to take back what you have said).

I am prepared *to meet you half-way* (come to a compromise with you).

It is silly *to meet trouble half-way (i.e.,*to anticipate it ; to worry about it before it comes).

This unexpected new difficulty *put me on my mettle* (roused me to do my best.)

This is *of a piece with* (in keeping with) the rest of his conduct.

He is *not worth his salt* (quite worthless) if he fails at this juncture.

The cost of living has increased so much that he finds it difficult *to make both ends meet* (to live within his income).

As a social reformer, *he set his face against* (sternly opposed) nautch parties.

At the battle of Marengo, Napoleon was *within an ace of* (on the point of) defeat (*i.e.,* he was very nearly defeated).

2

The belief in witchcraft is *losing ground* (becoming less powerful or acceptable).

Lord Roberts first *won his laurels* (acquired distinction or glory) in India.

It was in parliamentary debate that he *won his spurs* (made his reputation as a politician).

When the prodigal returned to his father's house, he was received *with open arms* (with a warm welcome).

How can you trust a man who *plays fast and loose* (says one thing and does another) ?

I *took him to task* (rebuked him) for reading "penny dreadfuls".

He *turned a deaf ear to* (disregarded) my advice.

That argument will not *hold water* (stand scrutiny *i.e.,* it is unsound).

He is determined to achieve his object *by hook or by crook* (by fair means or foul; by any means he can).

To all intents and purposes (practically, virtually) the Prime Minister of Nepal was the ruler of the country.

3

The singer, having a slight cough, was *not in voice* (unable to sing well) at the concert.

These two statements *do not hang together (i.e.,* are not consistent with each other).

This is more than *flesh and blood* (human nature) can endure.

He accepted my statement *without reserve* (fully, implicitly).

I must *take exception to* (object to) your remark.

He is indulgent *to a fault (i.e.,* he is *over*-indulgent; so indulgent that his indulgence is a fault).

The belief in efficacy of vaccination is *gaining ground* (becoming more general).

From his attitude it is clear that he wants *to pay off old scores* (to have his revenge).

He has been working *on and off* (at intervals) several years to compile a dictionary.

He visits me *off and on* (now and then, occasionally).

4

At least on the question of child-marriage we are *at one* (of the same opinion).

He took my advice *in good part* (without offence ; *i.e.,* he did not resent it).

It was he who *put a spoke in my wheel* (thwarted me in the execution of my design).

At an early age he *made his mark* (distinguished himself) as a chemist.

I *have it at my fingers' ends* (know it thoroughly).

The new play has *fallen flat* (met with a cold reception).

Where discipline is concerned I *put my foot down* (take a resolute stand).

It is a matter of gratification to me that he has *turned over a new leaf* (changed for the better; begun a different mode of life).

I have *made up my mind* (resolved, decided) to retire from business.

This *puts me in mind* (reminds me) of an amusing incident.

5

There's *no love lost between them* (*i.e.*, they are not on good terms, they dislike each other).

Many people in that country live *from hand to mouth* (*i.e.*, without any provision for the future).

Steady work is sure to be rewarded *in the long run* (eventually, ultimately).

Whatever else one may say of him, no one dare *call in question* (challenge, express a doubt about) his honesty of purpose.

The police came to the scene *in the nick of time* (just at the right moment, opportunely).

She stood by him *through thick and thin* (under all conditions, undaunted by anything).

His partner *threw cold water on* his scheme (discouraged him by showing indifference to it).

He can *turn his hand to* (adapt or apply himself to) anything.

The Sultan rules his subjects *with a high hand* (oppressively).

He is *hand and glove* (on very intimate terms) with my cousin.

6

He *turns* even his errors *to account* (*i.e.*, profits by them).

He is accused of *sitting on the fence* (halting between two opinions, hesitating which side to join).

It is *all one* (just the same) to me whether he lives in Mumbai or Kolkata.

What is the point *at issue* (in dispute) ?

The inquiry has *brought to light* (disclosed) some startling facts.

He is *not fit to hold a candle to* (not to be named in comparison with) his predecessor.

He *burnt his fingers* (got himself into trouble) by interfering in his neighbour's affairs.

I suspect the fellow *lives by his wits* (*i.e.*, he has no settled means of subsistence but picks up a living by deceit or fraud).

He *bids fair* (seems likely) to rival his father as a lawyer.

He *strained every nerve* (used his utmost efforts) to get his friend elected.

7

When I saw him last he was *beside himself* (out of his mind) with grief.

He spent over it much time and energy, and lost a large sum *into the bargain* (in addition, besides).

When I entered the house everything was *at sixes and sevens* (in disorder or confusion).

Recently he has been *giving himself airs* (behaving arrogantly).

The attack might be launched at any time, so you must be *on the alert* (on your guard, ready to act).

Retrenchement is *the order of the day* (the prevailing state of things) in every public and private office.

In the manufacture of dyes the Germans *bear the palm* (are pre-eminent).

Agriculture in America has *kept pace* with (progressed at equal rate with) industrial activities.

This text-book of chemistry is quite *out of date* (obsolete).

This is the most *up-to-date* (modern, recent) book on the subject.

8

What you say has no bearing on the subject *in hand* (under discussion or consideration).

It *speaks volumes for* (serves as a strong testimony to) Dr. Johnson's industry that he should have compiled the dictionary without anyone's help.

Poor fellow ! he is *hoping against hope* (hoping even when the case seems hopeless).

I am told he has got *into hot water* (into trouble).

Ultimately I *got the better of him* (overcame him).

He was found guilty, but, he *got off easy* (got a light sentence).

I *wash my hands of* the whole matter (*i.e.*, I refuse to have anything more to do with it).

The situation seems to have got quite *out of hand* (beyond control).

It is said that he *has a finger in the pie* (has something to do with the affair, is mixed up in the affair).

That fellow *sets* everybody *by the ears* (*i.e.*, he is a mischief-maker).

9

You have *hit the nail on the head* (said or done exactly the right thing).

Today he is *in high spirits* (cheerful, joyful).

How is that ? You seem *out of spirits* (gloomy, sad).

Hello ! my lad; you look as if you've *been in the wars* (hurt yourself).

I suspect he has *an axe to grind* (private ends to serve, a personal interest in the matter).

The news of the Amir's death *spread like wild fire* (spread rapidly).

He *took to heart* (was deeply affected by) the death of his wife.

He was disappointed, but he *took heart* (cheered himself up) and tried again.

He *has his heart in the right place* (means well, is of a kindly and sympathetic disposition).

He is *coming to the front* (attaining prominence, becoming conspicuous) in public life.

10

He is not a great lawyer but he has *the gift of the gab* (a talent for speaking).

Prohibition is *gall and wormwood* (hateful) to distillers.

The strikers have thrown out of gear (disturbed the working of) many of our important industries.

Though he addressed his boys for a few minutes only, the earnestness with which he spoke *went home to them* (deeply appealed to them).

Just now he is simply *coining money* (making money very rapidly, earning large sums easily).

The screen is *in character* (in keeping) with the rest of the furniture.

He is not *in the good books of* (in favour with) his master.

I am afraid I am *in his bad books* (out of favour with him).

I am quite *at sea* (perplexed, at a loss what to do or how to act).

He does not understand that he *stands in his own light* (acts against his own interests, hinders his own advancement).

11

Although he denies it, I think he is *behind the scenes* (in the secret, in possession of facts not generally known).

You are sure *to put your foot in it* (to blunder, to get into a scrape) if you meddle in his affairs.

I begged him to reconsider his decision, but he *put his foot down* (remained firm ; refused to yield).

He asked me to dine with him, but I had to *foot the bill* (pay for it).

We shall fight *tooth and nail* (with all our power) for our rights.

The property belonged to a Nawab, but recently it *changed hands* (became someone else's property).

He is *by long odds* (most decidedly) the greatest of living mathematicians.

The thief *took* to his heels (ran off) on seeing a policeman.

Our school is *within a stone's throw of* (at a short distance from) the railway station.

A few days before his death, he *made a clean breast of* (confessed without reserve) everything connected with that affair.

12

He *stood his ground* (maintained his position) against his adversary.

He *keeps in touch with* (has intimate knowledge of) the latest developments in wireless.

That is *where the shoe pinches* (where the difficulty or trouble lies).

I told him that I was prepared *to show my hand* (to reveal my plan of action, to let out my designs) provided he agreed to do the same.

The medical graduates *to a man* (*i.e.*, everyone without exception) voted in favour of him.

He insisted on his orders being carried out *to the letter* (exactly, with adherence to every detail).

For a long time he kept his father *in the dark* (in ignorance) about the true state of affairs.

Success has *turned his head* (made him quite vain).

His *star is in the ascendant* (*i.e.*, fortune favours him).

13

The scheme appears worthless *at the first blush* (at first sight).

It was his constant prayer that he might *die in harness* (continue to the last in his business or profession).

He *has too many irons in the fire (i.e.,* he is engaged in too many enterprises at the same time).

The Sikh soldiers were *true to their salt* (faithful to their employers).

The latest police report says that the situation is now well *in hand* (under control).

He was *at his wit's end* (quite puzzled, at a complete loss how to act).

What's the matter with him ? He is *falling foul of* (quarrelling with) everybody.

I am sure he won't *go back on* (fail to keep) his word.

The directors of the company *put their heads together* (consulted one another) to formulate a new scheme.

Do not *give ear to* (listen to) a tale-bearer.

14

So far as I could see there was nothing *out of the way* (strange, eccentric) in the behaviour of that stranger.

A spirit of unrest is *in the air* (prevalent, found everywhere).

The controversy is likely to create *bad blood* (ill-feeling, bitterness) between the two communities.

The rebels surrendered *at discretion* (unconditionally).

The letter is meant *to be read between the lines (i.e.,* it has a hidden or unexpressed meaning, not apparent on the surface).

He was murdered *in cold blood (i.e.,* not in the heat of passion or excitement, but deliberately).

Let us have your terms *in black and white* (in writing).

On the approach of a policeman the bully *showed a clean pair of heels* (ran away).

He has politics *on the brain* (constantly in his thoughts, as a sort of monomania).

This will suit you *to a T* (exactly).

15

His eldest son, a spendthrift, is *a thorn in his side* (a constant source of annoyance to him).

I *smell a rat* (have reason to suspect something).

I *nipped* his scheme *in the bud (i.e.,* made it fail before it could mature).

What you propose is *out of the question* (not to be thought of, impossible).

The performance was not *up to the mark* (quite satisfactory).

The long and the short of it (the simple fact, the whole matter in a few words) is that I do not want to deal with that new firm.

I am told he is *in the running (i.e.,* he has good prospects in the competition).

Now that he has nothing to fear from me, he is *showing his teeth* (adopting a threatening attitude).

He *changed colour* (turned pale) when I questioned him about his antecedents.

He had made a great mistake in championing their cause, but, having done it, he *stuck to his guns* (remained faithful to the cause).

16

This is the time *to take stock of* (to survey) the whole situation.

What's the good of entering into negotiations with *a man of straw* (a man of no substance or consequence)?

The election campaign is just now *in full swing* (very active).

He is not wise enough *to keep his own counsel* (to preserve a discreet silence, to be reticent about his opinions or affairs).

That young fellow was *born with a silver spoon in his mouth* (born in wealth and luxury).

It *stands to reason* (is quite clear, is an undoubted fact) that the rich never have justice done them in plays and stories; for the people who write are poor.

This suitcase *has stood me in good stead* (proved useful to me) in my travels.

You have *taken the wind out of my sails* (made my words or actions ineffective by anticipating them).

I *took him to task* (reproved him) for his carelessness.

I have *a bone to pick with you* (some cause of quarrel with you).

17

It will do *at a pinch* (in case of emergency, if hard pressed).

When the opportunity came I *paid him back in his own coin* (treated him in the same way as he had treated me).

Just now *my hands are full* (I am very busy).

It is generally believed that he *had a hand* (was concerned) in the plot.

Explorers in the arctic regions *take their lives in their hands* (undergo great risks).

Naturally he *fights shy of* (avoids from a feeling of mistrust, dislikes) his young nephew, who is a gambler.

All his schemes *ended in smoke* (came to nothing).

The police *left no stone unturned* (used all available means, adopted every possible method of search) to trace the culprits.

Later on he became unpopular because he tried *to lord it over* (to domineer over) his followers.

As he was growing old, his friends persuaded him *to rest on his laurels* (to retire from active life).

18

The champion will have to *look to your laurels* (take care not to lose your pre-eminence).

I am tired of hearing him *harp on the same string* (dwell tediously on the same subject).

His blood ran cold (i.e., he was horrified) when he heard that his friend was murdered.

I *gave him a piece of my mind* (scolded him).

The dog is *as good as* (practically) dead.

He was *as good as his word (i.e.,* kept his promise).

The child was *as good as gold (i.e.,* very good).

You will have *to make good the loss* (to compensate me for the loss).

He *kicked up a row* (made great noise or fuss).

He seems *ill at ease* (uneasy, anxious, uncomfortable).

19

The old man is *hard of hearing* (somewhat deaf).

It *will go hard with him* (*i.e.,* he will suffer severely) if he keeps company with that fellow.

People say that Mr. X, the banker, is *on his last legs* (on the verge of ruin).

I can make *neither head nor tail* (nothing) of it.

You'll never *get the better of* (gain an advantage over) that rascal : with him it's always, *'Heads I win, tails you lose'* (*i.e.,* in any case he will be the winner).

By his advocacy of widow-remarriage, he *stirred up a hornet's nest* (excited the hostility or adverse criticism of a large number of people).

He made great claims for his discovery; but it turned out to be a *mare's nest* (a delusion, a worthless thing).

On the very first night she *brought down the house* (called forth general and loud applause) by her superb acting.

He is *every inch* (entirely, completely) a gentleman.

You have *done the handsome thing by him* (behaved towards him in a magnanimous manner) in accepting his apology and foregoing the claim for damages.

20

He proved his worth by *rising to the occasion* (showing himself equal to dealing with the emergency). For some days the new professor lectured *over the heads of* (above the comprehension of) his pupils.

He knows *the ins and outs* (the full details) of that affair.

He is *over head and ears* (deeply) in love (or, in debt).

Beyond all question (undoubtedly) she is a great singer.

You want to see him ? *Out of the question !* (*i.e.,* impossible).

The two friends *agreed to differ* (gave up trying to convince each other) after discussing the question for about an hour.

Since that day he has been *in bad odour* (out of favour, in bad repute) with his neighbours.

Intimate friends need not *stand on ceremony* (act with reserve, insist on strict rules of etiquette being observed).

He *went out of his way* (took special trouble) to oblige me.

21

I am afraid you two *are at cross-purposes* (misunderstand each other).

I trusted him and he *played me false* (deceived me, betrayed me).

He is a shrewd man, and it will not be easy *to draw him out* (to elicit information from him).

He *made light of* (treated lightly) his friend's warning.

The proposal was rejected *with one voice* (unanimously).

The figures which he quoted were shown to be incorrect, and this *took the edge off his argument* (made his argument ineffective).

We had on the way tea *of a kind* (of a poor kind, *i.e.,* tea that scarcely deserved the name).

I repaid his insolence *in kind* (in the same way, *i.e.,* with insolence).

Beware of that fellow ! he *will stick at nothing* (is unscrupulous and will do anything to accomplish his purpose).

He is not the man *to pocket an affront* (to receive or submit to it without retaliating or showing resentment).

22

I am *out of pocket* (a loser) by the transaction.

The fate of the accused *hangs in the balance* (is undecided).

He is a man of *well-balanced* (reasonable, moderate) opinions.

He *was carried off his feet* (was wild with excitement) when he was declared to have won the first prize.

He *made the most of his* opportunity (*i.e.,* used it to the best advantage).

That house is *put on the market* (offered for sale).

He sometimes works nine hours *at a stretch* (continuously).

By his skill in arguing he *carried his point* (defeated his adversaries in debate).

He is *serving his time* (going through an apprenticeship) in a bank.

Serves you right (i.e., you've got what you deserved) !

23

I shall manage *to serve him out* (to retaliate upon him, to have my revenge on him).

He is working *against time* (with utmost speed).

This year the mango-crop has *fallen short of my expectations* (*i.e.,* has disappointed me).

While the members of the committee were discussing questions of finance, I felt *like a fish out of water* (like one out of his element ; *i.e.,* in a strange situation).

A good student works steadily, not *by fits and starts* (irregularly, capriciously, without steady application).

He has made his fortune and now *takes things easy* (does not work hard).

Mr. X first introduced the system of payments by instalments, and shortly afterwards others *took a leaf out of his book* (imitated him, profited by his example).

The Secretary of the Company was charged with *cooking the accounts* (preparing false accounts).

You should *take into account* (consider) his past services.

You must *lie in the bed you have made* (take the consequences of your own acts; suffer for your own misdeeds).

24

He *thinks better of* it now (*i.e.,* he has thought more carefully about it and come to a wiser decision).

I am sure he *means business* (is in earnest).

I cannot give you a definite reply *on the spur of the moment* (at once, without deliberation).

It is *the thing* (the proper thing) to do.

I see you *know a thing or two* (are wise or cunning).

He *took* his failure *to heart (i.e.,* felt it deeply; grieved over it).

It *goes to his heart* (touches him deeply) to see so much misery.

The offer *holds good* (remains binding, is valid) for two days.

He is leaving India *for good* (permanently).

It will *go hard with him* (prove a serious matter for him) if his partner retires from business.

25

Do you expect me to be *at your beck and call* (under your absolute control) ?

I am afraid he is *burning the candles at both ends* (overtaxing his energies).

Let us now *bury the hatchet* (cease fighting, make peace), and work for the advancement of the country.

Mr. X, who is one of the trustees of a certain big charity, is suspected of *feathering his won nest* (making money unfairly).

It is reported that some ruffians *laid hands on* (assaulted) him while he was returning home.

It is suspected that he *had a hand in* (was concerned in) the plot.

As usual he is *blowing his own trumpet* (praising himself).

The excuses *will not pass muster* (will not be accepted as satisfactory).

As a diplomat he was *head and shoulders* (very much) above his contemporaries.

Old sets of the Encyclopaedia Britannica are *a drug in the market* (unsaleable from lack of demand).

26

The foolish young man *made ducks and drakes of* (squandered) his patrimony.

She knows French *after a fashion* (to a certain degree, not satisfactorily).

It is all *Greek* (or *Hebrew*) to me (*i.e.,* something which I do not understand).

The thief was caught *red-handed* (in the very act of committing the theft).

Late in life he *tried his hand* (made an attempt) at farming.

What you say is *neither here nor there* (foreign to the subject under discussion, irrelevant).

Even his old friend Smith, who had been indebted to him for many favours in the past, *gave him the cold shoulder* (treated him in a cold and distant manner).

If we are to give credence to rumours, another great war is *on the cards* (not improbable).

While he spoke, the audience *hung on his lips* (listened eagerly to his words).

The Speaker urged the Committee to take drastic action, but they *hung fire* (were reluctant ; hesitated).

27

He *stands well with* (is well thought of by) his master.

He claims that he has given *chapter and verse* (full and precise reference to authority) for every statement made in his book.

The editor of that paper is accused of *giving a false colouring to* (misrepresenting) the incident.

Throughout his speech the boys were *all ears* (deeply attentive).

I was *all eyes* (eagerly watching) to see what he would do.

I know my friend *keeps a good table* (provides luxurious food, entertains his guests sumptuously).

With a small income and a large family to maintain, he finds it rather difficult *to keep his head above water* (to keep out of debt).

He will never *set the Thames on fire* (do some remarkable or surprising thing).

The scheme *came to grief* (failed) owing to want of foresight.

You will *come to grief* (be ruined) if you follow his advice.

28

I keep the fellow *at arm's length* (at a distance ; *i.e.,* I hold aloof from him).

He is *keeping up appearances* (keeping up an outward show of prosperity) although he has lost his whole fortune.

Last year when the prince *came of age* (reached the age of twenty-one) he was installed on his father's throne.

Don't trust those men ; they are villains *to the backbone* (in every way).

You shall go, *bag and baggage* (with all your belongings. *i.e.,* altogether, completely).

The account of the murder *made her blood creep* (filled her with horror).

That territory is *a bone of contention* (a subject of dispute) between the two countries.

He *took away my breath* (very much surprised me) when he coolly proposed that I should buy votes.

Since his easy succcess in the elections, he has become *swollen-headed* (conceited).

29

Wherever he addressed public meetings he *carried all before him* (was completely successful).

The cashier, having admitted defalcation, was *given in charge* (handed over to the police).

"If thine enemy be hungry, give him bread to eat, and if he be thirsty, give him water to drink ; for thou shalt *heap coals of fire upon his head* (return good for evil, and make him ashamed of his enmity) and the Lord shall reward thee."

It is mean *to crow over* (to triumph over) a fallen foe.

He *took up the cudgels for* (defended vigorously) his friend.

He is *currying favour* (using mean acts to ingratiate himself) with his rich neighbour.

If you endorse that promissory note, you will *cut your own throat* (ruin yourself).

His father *cut him off with a shilling* (disinherited him by bequeathing a trifling sum).

While he was speaking his father *cut him short* (interrupted him).

30

The witness *cut a poor figure* (produced a poor impression) in his cross-examination.

When he met me in the street, he *cut me dead* (deliberately insulted me by ignoring me).

That Act is *a dead letter* (no longer in force).

A great many faults may be *laid at his door* (imputed to him), but he is certainly not dishonest.

We must *draw the line* (fix the limit) somewhere. The cost of the new building should not exceed two lakhs.

Printing *is not in my line* (is out of my province).

He *is in the cotton line* (*i.e.,* he follows that trade).

I don't expect him *to see eye to eye* (to be in complete agreement) with me on the question of Prohibition.

He failed to get elected, but *put a good face on* (bore up courageously) his defeat.

His speech on economic reform *fell flat* (caused no interest, produced no effect).

31

The joke *fell flat* (caused no amusement).

It is *a far cry* (a long way off) from Delhi to New York.

It is *a far cry* (no easy transition) from autocracy to democracy.

He is *far and away* (very much) the better of the two players.

The story of the shipwreck, as narrated by one of the survivors, *made my flesh creep* (horrified me).

A Pathan is *an ugly customer* (a formidable person to deal with) when *his blood is up* (he is excited).

She is a delicate woman but has *to rough it* (to endure hardship) to support her family.

He *pins his faith to* (places full reliance upon) technical education.

He sometimes tells lies, so people *take* his statements *with a grain of salt* (doubt).

He is not the sort of man *to let the grass grow under his feet* (to remain idle, to procrastinate).

32

It's no use *splitting hairs* (disputing over petty points, quibbling about trifles).

He is *a great hand at* (expert at) organizing public meetings.

By your strange conduct you will *give a handle to* (furnish an occasion for) suspicion and scandal.

He *knows what he is about* (is far-sighted and prudent).

You can rely on him ; he *knows what's what* (is shrewd and experienced, knows the ways of the world).

Mussolini seems *to bear a charmed life* (to be invulnerable, as he escapes death in an almost miraculous manner).

When the Arabs conquered Persia, some Persians, it is safe to say, embraced Islam for *loaves and fishes* (material benefits).

It never occurred to me that you would *leave me in the lurch* (desert me in my difficulties, leave me in a helpless condition).

In everything that he does *he has an eye to the main chance* (his object is to make money, he regards his own interests).

The bank won't accept the guarantee of *a man of straw* (a man of no substance).

33

His observations were *beside the mark* (not to the point, irrelevant).

Not to mince matters (to speak unreservedly), some of these pundits are mere charlatans.

His adversaries *moved heaven and earth* (made every possible effort) to get him dismissed.

Do your worst ! I *nail my colours to the mast* (refuse to climb down or surrender).

Stick to your colours (refuse to yield, be faithful to the cause), my boys !

The murdered man was found *in a state of nature* (naked).

This coat fits you *to a nicety* (exactly).

He refused *to be led by the nose* (to follow submissively).

His wife, who was the daughter of a millionaire, *turned up her nose at* (regarded with contempt) her husband's proposal to buy a Ford car.

Don't *thrust your nose into* (meddle officiously in) my affairs.

34

He is such an absent-minded fellow that he does not know what passes *under his nose* (in his very presence).

Successive ministers have found the question of employment *a hard nut to crack* (a difficult problem to solve).

This gentleman, having worked successfully in the business line for several years, is now *resting on his oars* (stopping work for a time and having rest).

A dispute in that colliery *came to a head* (reached a crisis) this week.

The recent outbursts of murderous rioting should warn the labour agitators that they are *playing with fire* (trifling ignorantly with matters liable to cause trouble or suffering).

During the War, he *made a pile* (made a fortune).

The famous libel case *brought into play* (gave an opportunity for the exercise of) his forensic abilities.

I admit that he pleaded the cause of the poor very eloquently; but will he *put his hand in his pocket* (give money in charity) ?

To small purpose (without much practical benefit) was the Commission appointed, if its main recommendations are not adopted.

Nowadays flying is *all the rage* (extremely popular).

35

He is rather blunt, but *his heart is in the right place* (he is faithful and true-hearted).

He is regarded as his chief's *right-hand man* (most efficient assistant).

His letters to his ward *speak volumes for* (serve as strong testimony to) his forbearance and good sense.

The new cotton mill is mortgaged *up to the eyes* (completely, to its full extent).

You don't look quite *up to the mark* (in excellent health) this evening.

Now, don't you call me any names, or you will find that *two can play at that game* (*i.e.*, I can retaliate in the same way).

He was a man who could *put two and two together* (draw a correct inference, reason logically).

You see he *has two strings to his bow* (has two sources of income to rely upon) ; he deals in curios, and also does miniatures.

Her uncle has taken her *under his wing* (under his protection).

I suspect that fellow has sent us on *a wild-goose chase* (a foolish and fruitless search).

36

The policeman, having disarmed the thief, *had the whip-hand of* (was in a position to control) him.

I did not notice in him anything *out of the way* (strange, eccentric).

I am told your cousin is *in hot water* (in trouble) over that speech.

There is nothing so bad as *washing one's dirty linen in public* (discussing unpleasant private matters before strangers).

If their demands are not granted, the strikers threaten *war to the knife* (a bitter and deadly struggle).

They are *at daggers drawn* (*i.e.*, their relations are strained) ever since the dissolution of the partnership between them.

When plague first broke out in Mumbai, Dr. X did *yeoman service* (excellent work).

He is still in the vigorous health, although he is *on the wrong side of sixty* (more than sixty years of age).

You can safely trust him ; he is *a man of his words* (a man to be depended on, a trustworthy man).

He finds no little difficulty in *keeping the wolf from the door* (keeping off starvation).

37

Beware of that *wolf in sheep's clothing* (hypocrite) !

The doctor says the patient has *turned the corner* (passed the crisis).

He very cleverly *turned the tables* on his opponent *(i.e.,* brought him to the position of disadvantage lately held by himself).

I am afraid you have *caught a Tartar* in him *(i.e.,* found him more formidable than you expected).

I should like to have that matter settled immediately, because it keeps a man *on tenterhooks* (in a state of suspense and anxiety).

He is *under the thumb of* (completely under the influence of) his wife.

He carried out his project *in the teeth of* (in defiance or regardless of) opposition from his community.

Only ten years ago he was a junior barrister, but he is now *at the top of the tree* (at the head of his profession).

We must avoid saying or writing anything that would *tread on their toes* (give offence to them).

His master *put the screw on* (brought pressure to bear on) him to vote for his friend.

38

In the contest he *came off second-best* (was defeated, got the worst of it).

I *sent him about his business* (dismissed him peremptorily) as I could stand his insolence no longer.

People who *talk shop* (talk exclusively about their business or professional affairs) are generally unbearable.

He appears *to have an old head on young shoulders* (to be wise beyond his years).

As a rule, they eat but one *square meal* (full meal) a day.

In his travels he claims to have *rubbed shoulders* (come into close contact) with people of all sorts and conditions.

Although much remains to be done in this direction, the gradual increase in the number of schools clearly shows that *the school master is abroad* (education is spreading in every direction and ignorance is diminishing).

His boorish manners occasionally *set* his refined cousin's *teeth on edge (i.e.,* irritated him).

When the Inspector entered the class some of the pupils *shook in their shoes* (trembled with fear).

39

There are *black sheep* (bad characters, scoundrels) in every community.

One of our best workers was ill, so we had to *make shift* (get along as best as we could) without him.

I threatened *to show him up* (to disclose his villainy) if he did not mend his ways.

That solicitor is guilty of *sharp practice* (underhand or questionable dealings).

The usurper cannot maintain his position without *the sinews of war* (money).

As a writer he has often *snapped his fingers at* (defined) convention.

The speaker was unmercifully heckled, but he manfully *stood to his guns* (*i.e.,* maintained his own opinion).

Chapter 26 PUNCTUATION

209. **Punctuation** (derived from the Latin *punctum*, a point) means the right use of putting in Points or Stops in writing. The following are the principal stops.

(1) Full Stop or Period (.)
(2) Comma (,)
(3) Semicolon (;)
(4) Colon (:)
(5) Question Mark (?)
(6) Exclamation Mark (!)

Other marks in common use are the Dash –; Parentheses ( ); Inverted Commas or Quotation Marks" ".

210. The **Full Stop** represents the greatest pause and separation. It is used to mark the end of a declarative or an imperative sentence ; as,

Dear, patient, gentle, noble Nell was dead.

We like non-stop things.

211. The Full Stop can be used in abbreviations, but they are often omitted in modern style.

M.A. or MA
M.P. or MP
U.N.O. or UNO

Note that in current English *Mr* and *Mrs* occur without a full stop, as these have come to be regarded as the full spellings.

Lost every thing.

212. The **Comma** represents the shortest pause, and is used :–

(1) To separate a series of words in the same construction ; as,

England, France and Italy formed an alliance.
He lost lands, money, reputation and friends.
It was a long, dull and wearisome journey.

Note–A comma is generally not placed before the word preceded by *and*.

(2) To separate each pair of words connected by *and* ; as,

We should be devout and humble, cheerful and serene.
High and low, rich and poor, wise and foolish, must all die.

(3) After a Nominative Absolute ; as,

This done, she returned to the old man with a lovely smile on her face.
The wind being favourable, the squadron sailed.
The genius making me no answer, I turned about to address myself to him a second time.

(4) To mark off a Noun or Phrase in Apposition ; as,

Paul, the apostle, was beheaded in the reign of Nero.
Milton, the great English poet, was blind.
Pandit Nehru, the first Prime Minister of India, died in 1964.

(5) To mark off words used in addressing people

Come into the garden, Maud.
How are you, Mohan?
Lord of the universe, shield us and guide us.

But when the words are emphatic, we ought to use the Note of Exclamation; as,

Monster ! by thee my child's devoured !

(6) To mark off two or more Adverbs or Adverbial phrases coming together ; as,

Then, at length, tardy justice was done to the memory of Oliver.

(7) Before and after a Participial phrase, provided that the phrase might be expanded into a sentence, and is not used in a merely qualifying sense; as,

Caesar, having conquered his enemies, returned to Rome.

(8) Before and after words, phrases, or clauses, let into the body of a sentence; as,

He did not, however, gain his object.
It is mind, after all, which does the work of the world.
His behaviour, to say the least, was very rude.
His story was, in several ways, improbable.
Let there be no strife, I pray thee, between thee and me.
The essay-writers, whose works consisted in a great measure of short moral dissertations, set the literary taste of the age.
The people of Orleans, when they first saw her in their city, thought she was an angel.

(9) To indicate the omission of a word, especially a verb ; as,

Rama received a Parker pen ; Hari, a watch.
He was a Brahmin ; she, a Rajput.
He will succeed ; you, never.

(10) To separate short co-ordinate clauses of a Compound sentence ; as,

The rains descended, and the floods came.
Men may come and men may go, but I go on for ever.
I came, I saw, I conquered.
The way was long, the wind was cold.
The minstrel was infirm and old.

When there is a conjunction the comma is sometimes omitted ; as,

He came and saw me.

(11) To mark off a direct quotation from the rest of the sentence; as,

"Exactly so," said Alice.
He said to his disciples, "Watch and pray."
"Go then," said the ant, "and dance winter away."

(12) Before certain co-ordinative conjunctions ; as,

To act thus is not wisdom, but folly.

(13) To separate from the verb a long Subject opening a sentence; as,

The injustice of the sentence pronounced upon that great scientist and discoverer, is now evident to us all.
All that we admired and adored before as great and magnificent, is obliterated or vanished.

(14) To separate a Noun clause–whether subject or object–preceding the verb ; as,

Whatever is, is right.
How we are ever to get there, is the question.
That he would succeed in his undertaking, no one ever doubted.

(15) To separate a clause that is not restrictive in meaning, but is co-ordinate with the Principal clause ; as,

Sailors, who are generally superstitious, say it is unlucky to embark on a Friday.
During my stay in Sri Lanka I visited Mihintale, which is regarded as the cradle of Buddhism.

When the Adjective clause is restrictive in meaning the comma should not be applied; as,

This is the house that Jack built.
The Lord is nigh up to them that are of a broken heart.
The echoes of the storm which was then raised I still hear grumbling round me.

The design was disapproved by everyone whose judgement was entitled to respect.

(16) To separate an Adverbial clause from its Principal clause ; as,

When I was a bachelor, I lived by myself.

If thou would'st be happy, seek to please.

When the Adverbial clause follows the Principal clause the comma is frequently omitted; as,

Seek to please if thou would'st be happy.

213. The **Semicolon** represents a pause of greater importance than that shown by the comma. It is used:

(1) To separate the clauses of Compound sentence, when they contain a comma; as,

He was a brave, large-hearted man; and we all honoured him.

(2) To separate a series of loosely related clauses; as,

Her court was pure ; her life serene;

God gave her peace; her land reposed.

Today we love what tomorrow we hate; today we seek what tomorrow we shun; today we desire what tomorrow we fear.

214. The **Colon** marks a still more complete pause than that expressed by the Semicolon. It is used (sometimes with a dash after it):

(1) To introduce a quotation ; as,

Bacon says : "Reading makes a full man, writing an exact man, speaking a ready man."

(2) Before enumeration, examples, etc; as,

The principal parts of a verb in English are : the present tense, the past tense, and the past participle.

The limitation of armaments, the acceptance of arbitration as the natural solvent of international disputes, the relegation of wars of ambition and aggression to the categories of obsolete follies : these will be milestones which mark the stages of the road.

(3) Between sentences grammatically independent but closely connected in sense; as,

Study to acquire a habit of thinking : no study is more important.

215. The **Question Mark** is used, instead of the Full Stop, after a direct question ; as,

Have you written your exercise ?

If you prick us, do we not bleed ? If you tickle us, do we not laugh ? If you poison us, do we not die? And if you wrong us, shall we not have revenge ?

But the Question Mark is not used after an indirect question; as,

He asked me whether I had written my exercise.

216. The **Exclamation Mark** is used after Interjections and after Phrases and Sentences expressing sudden emotion or wish ; as,

Alas ! Oh dear !

What a terrible fire this is !

O,what a fall was there, my countrymen ! Long live the King !

Note– When the interjection O is placed before the Nominative of Address, the Exclamation Mark, if employed at all, comes after the noun; or it may be placed at the end of the sentence; as,

O father ! I hear the sound of guns.

O Hamlet, speak no more !

217. **Inverted Commas** are used to enclose the exact words of a speaker, or a quotation; as,

"I would rather die," he exclaimed, "than join the oppressors of my country."

Babar is said by Elphinstone to have been "the most admirable prince that ever reigned in Asia."

If a quotation occurs within a quotation, it is marked by single inverted commas; as,

"You might as well say," added the March Hare, "that 'I like what I get' is the same thing as 'I get what I like.'"

218. The **Dash** is used:

(1) To indicate an abrupt stop or change of thought ; as,

If my husband were alive–but why lament the past ?

(2) To resume a scattered subject; as,.

Friends, companions, relatives–all deserted him.

219. The **Hyphen** –a shorter line than the Dash –is used to connect the parts of a compound word; as,

Passer-by, man-of-war, jack-of-all-trades.

It is also used to connect parts of a word divided at the end of a line.

220. **Parentheses** or Double Dashes are used to separate from the main part of the sentence a phrase or clause which does not grammatically belong to it; as,

He gained from Heaven (it was all he wished) a friend.

A remarkable instance of this kind of courage–call it, if you please, resolute will–is given in the history of Babar.

221. The **Apostrophe** is used:

(1) To show the omission of a letter or letters; as,

Don't, e'er, I've.

(2) In the Genitive Case of Nouns.

(3) To form the plural of letters and figures.

Dot your *i's* and cross your *t's*.

Add two 5*'s* and four 2*'s*.

Capital Letters

222. **Capitals** are used:

(1) To begin a sentence.

(2) To begin each fresh line of poetry.

(3) To begin all Proper Nouns and Adjectives derived from them : as,

Delhi, Rama, Africa, African, Shakespeare, Shakespearian.

(4) For all nouns and pronouns which indicate the Deity; as,

The Lord, He is the God.

(5) To write the pronoun *I* and the interjection *O*.

EXERCISE 119

Insert commas, where necessary, in the following sentences.

1. The necessity of amusement made me a carpenter a bird-cager a gardener.
2. Speak clearly if you would be understood.
3. Even a fool when he holdeth his peace is counted wise.
4. When we had dined to prevent the ladies leaving us I generally ordered the table to be removed.
5. My orchard was often robbed by schoolboys and my wife's custards plundered by the cats.
6. Whenever I approached a peasant's house towards night-fall I played one of the most merry tunes.

7. By conscience and courage by deeds of devotion and daring he soon commended himself to his fellows and his officers.
8. Wealth may seek us but wisdom must be sought.
9. Beware lest thou be led into temptation.
10. Brazil which is nearly as large as the whole of Europe is covered with a vegetation of incredible profusion.
11. We judge ourselves by what we feel capable of doing while others judge us by what we have already done.
12. Some are born great some achieve greatness and some have greatness thrust upon them.
13. I therefore walked back by the horseway which was five miles round.
14. Read not to contradict nor to believe but to weigh and consider.

15. The leaves as we shall see immediately are the feeders of the plant.
16. A public speaker should be cool collected and precise.
17. Sir I would rather be right than be President.
18. In fact there was nothing else to do.
19. At midnight however I was aroused by the tramp of horse's hoofs in the yard.
20. Spenser the great English poet lived in the time of Queen Elizabeth.
21. One of the favourite themes of boasting with the Squire is the noble trees on his estate which in truth has some of the finest that I have seen in England.
22. When he was a boy Franklin who afterward became a distinguished statesman and philosopher learned his trade in the printing office of his brother who published a paper in Boston.
23. We had in this village some twenty years ago an idiot boy whom I well remember who from a child showed a strong propensity for bees.
24. Margaret the eldest of the four was sixteen and very pretty being plump and fair with large eyes plenty of soft brown hair a sweet mouth and white hands of which she was rather vain.
25. A letter from a young lady written in the most passionate terms wherein she laments the misfortune of a gentleman her lover who was lately wounded in a duel has turned my thoughts to that subject and inclined me to examine into the causes which precipitate men into so fatal a folly.

EXERCISE 120

Insert commas, where necessary, in the following sentences.

1. In the old Persian stories Turan the land of darkness is opposed to Iran the land of light.
2. History it has been said is the essence of innumerable biographies.
3. Attention application accuracy method punctuality and dispatch are the principal qualities required for the efficient conduct of business of any sort.
4. When I was in Delhi I visited the Red Fort Qutab Minar Raj Ghat India Gate and Chandni Chowk.
5. He was now in the vigour of his days forty-three years of age stately in person noble in his demeanour calm and dignified in his deportment.
6. Your wife would give you little thanks if she were present to hear you make this offer.
7. A high-bred man never forgets himself controls his temper does nothing in excess is courteous dignified and that even to persons whom he is wishing far away.
8. All that I am all that I hope to be I owe to my angel mother.
9. We all or nearly all fail to last our "lease" owing to accidents violence and avoidable as well as unavoidable disease.
10. Nuclear bomb testing fills the air with radioactive dust and leaves many areas uninhabitable for centuries.
11. In a strict and legal sense that is properly the domicile of a person where he has his true fixed permanent home and principal establishment and to which whenever he is absent he has the intention of returning.

EXERCISE 121

Punctuate the following.

1. As Caesar loved me I wept for him as he was fortunate I rejoice at it as he was valiant I honour him but as he was ambitious I slew him.
2. The shepherd finding his flock destroyed exclaimed I have been rightly served why did I trust my sheep to a wolf.
3. However strange however grotesque may be the appearance which Dante undertakes to describe he never shrinks from describing it he gives us the shape the colour the sound the smell the taste.
4. Perhaps cried he there may be such monsters as you describe.
5. Sancho ran as fast as his ass could go to help his master whom he found lying and not able to stir such a blow he and Rozinante had received mercy on me cried Sancho did I not give your worship fair warning did I not tell you they were windmills and that nobody could think otherwise unless he had also windmills in his head
6. Modern ideas of government date back to the 1960s when for the first time people began to question a kings right to rule once thought to be god given.

7. When I look upon the tombs of the great every emotion of envy dies in me when I read the epitaphs of the beautiful every inordinate desire goes out when I meet with the grief of parents upon a tombstone my heart melts with compassion when I see the tomb of the parents themselves I consider the vanity of grieving for those whom we must quickly follow.
8. They had played together in infancy they had worked together in manhood they were now tottering about and gossiping away in the evening of life and in a short time they will probably be buried together in the neighbouring churchyard.
9. Take away that bauble said Cromwell pointing to the mace which lay upon the table and when the House was empty he went out with the key in his pocket

10. One day walking together up a hill I said to Friday do you not wish yourself in your own country again yes he said what would you do there said I would you turn wild and eat mens flesh again he looked full of concern and shaking his head said no
11. When a great office is vacant either by death or disgrace which often happens five or six of these candidates petition the emperor to entertain his majesty and the court with a dance on the rope and whoever jumps the highest without falling succeeds to the office
12. That familiarity produces neglect has been long observed the effect of all external objects however great or splendid ceases with their novelty the courtier stands without emotion in the royal presence the rustic tramples under his foot the beauties of the spring with little attention to their colours or their fragrance and the inhabitant of the coast darts his eye upon the immense diffusion of waters without awe wonder or terror.
13. If you look about you and consider the lives of others as well as your own if you think how few are born with honour and how many die without name or children how little beauty we see and how few friends we hear of how many diseases and how much poverty there is in the world you will fall down upon knees and instead of repining at one affliction will admire so many blessings which you have received from the hand of God
14. We thank Thee for the place in which we dwell for the love that unites us for the peace accorded us this day for the hope with which we expect the morrow for the health the work the food and the bright skies that make our life delightful for our friends in all parts of the earth
15. Androcles who had no arms of any kind now gave himself up for lost what shall I do said he I have no spear or sword no not so much as a stick to defend myself with
16. My quaint Ariel said Prospero to the little sprite when he made him free I shall miss you yet you shall have your freedom thank you my dear master said Ariel but give me leave to attend your ship with prosperous gales before you bid farewell to the assistance of your faithful spirit.
17. O master exclaimed Ananda weeping bitterly and is all the work undone and all by my fault and folly that which is built on fraud and imposture can by no means endure returned Buddha
18. Wretch said the king what harm did I do thee that thou shouldst seek to take my life with your own hand you killed my father and my two brothers was the reply

EXERCISE 122

Punctuate the following.

1. Nothing is so easy and inviting as the retort of abuse and sarcasm but it is a paltry and an unprofitable contest
2. Think how mysterious and often unaccountable it is that lottery of life which gives to this man the purple and fine linen and sends to the other rags for garments and dogs for comforters

3. The human mind is never stationary it advances or it retrogrades
4. The laws of most countries today are spilt into two kinds criminal law and civil law
5. Islam is one of the worlds largest religions with an estimated 1100-1300 million believers it was founded in the 7th century by the Prophet Mohammad
6. There is a slavery that no legislation can abolish the slavery of caste
7. Truly a popular error has as many lives as a cat it comes walking long after you have imagined it effectually strangled
8. So far from science being irreligious as many think it is the neglect of science that is irreligious it is the refusal to study the surrounding creation that is irreligious
9. None of Telleyrand's mots is more famous than this speech was given to man to conceal his thoughts
10. There is only one cure for the evils which newly acquired freedom produces and that cure is freedom
11. If you read ten pages of a good book letter by letter that is to say with real accuracy you are for evermore in some measure an educated person

Chapter 27 SPELLING RULES

Final Consonant

223. One-syllable words ending in single vowel + single consonant double the consonant before a suffix beginning with a vowel.

beg + ed = begged | rob + er = robber
run + ing = running | sad + est = saddest

but:
wish + ed = wished (two consonants)
fear + ing = fearing (two vowels)

224. Words of two or three syllables ending in sigle vowel + single consonant double the final consonant if the last syllable is stressed.

begin + ing = beginning | occur + ed = occurred
permit + ed = permitted | control + er = controller

The consonant is not doubled if the last syllable is not stressed.
benefit + ed = benefited | suffer + ing = suffering

These words are exceptions: *worship, kidnap, handicap.*
worship + ed = worshipped | handicap + ed = handicapped
kidnap + er = kidnapped

225. In British English the consonant *l* is doubled, even if the stress does not fall on the last syllable.
quarrel + ed = quarrelled | signal + ing = signalling
travel + er = traveller | distil + er = distiller

Note the exception:
parallel + ed = paralleled

226. If the word to which the suffix *ful* is added ends in *ll*, the second *l* is dropped.
skill + ful = skilful | will + ful = wilful

Final e

227. Words ending in silent *e* drop the *e* before a suffix beginning with a vowel.
live + ing = living | move + ed = moved
hope + ing = hoping | drive + er = driver

The *e* remains before a suffix beginning with a consonant.
hope + ful = hopeful | engage + ment = engagement

Note the exceptions:
true + ly = truly | whole + ly = wholly
due + ly = duly | nine + th = ninth
argue + ment = argument | awe + ful = awful

228. Notice the special case of words ending in *ce* and *ge* which keep the *e* when adding *able* and *ous*.
notice + able = noticeable | peace + able = peaceable
change + able = changeable | courage + ous = courageous

In such words, the *c* and *g* are pronounced soft before *e*. Sometimes the *e* is retained to avoid confusion with a similar word.
singe + ing = singeing (avoids confusion with *singing*)
swinge + ing = swingeing (avoids confusion with *swinging*)

229. Words ending in *ee* do not drop an *e* before a suffix.
see + ing = seeing | agree + ment = agreement

230. Words ending in *ie* change the *ie* to *y* when *ing* is added.

die, dying   tie, tying,   lie, lying

Final y

231. A final *y* following a consonant changes to *i* before a suffix except *ing*.

happy + ly = happily   carry + ed = carried

beauty + ful = beautiful   marry + age = marriage

But:

carry + ing = carrying   marry + ing = marrying

But *y* following a vowel does not change.

pray + ed = prayed play + er = player

Notice a few exceptions:

pay + ed = paid   day + ly = daily

say + ed = said   gay + ly = gaily

lay + ed = laid

ie or ei

232. When *ie* or *ei* is pronounced like *ee* in 'jeep', *i* comes before *e* except after *c*.

believe	receive
relieve	receipt
achieve	deceive
grieve	deceit
yield	conceive
field	conceit

Some exceptions :

seize	protein	counterfeit
weird	surfeit	plabeian

Chapter 28 THE FORMATION OF WORDS

233. Words which are not derived or compounded or developed from other words are called **Primary Words.** They belong to the original stock of words in the language.

(*i*) **Compound Words,** formed by joining two or more simple words; as,

Moonlight, nevertheless, undertake, man-of-war.

(*ii*) **Primary Derivatives,** formed by making some change in the body of the simple word; as,

Bond from *bind, breach* from *break, wrong* from *wring.*

Note– The most important class of words formed by internal change consists of the Past Tenses of Primary Verbs, which are not usually classed as Derivatives.

(*iii*) **Secondary Derivatives**, formed by *an addition* to the beginning or the end ; as,

*Un*happy ; good*ness.*

An addition to the beginning of a word is a **Prefix**, an addition to the end is a **Suffix.**

(I) Compound Words

234. Compound words are, for the most part, Nouns, Adjectives and Verbs.

235. **Compound Nouns** may be formed from:

(1) Noun + Noun ; as,

Moonlight, chess-board, armchair, postman, railway, airman, manservant, fire-escape, jailbird, horse-power, shoemaker, ringleader, screwdriver, tax-payer, teaspoon, haystack, windmill.

(2) Adjective + Noun ; as,

Sweetheart, nobleman, shorthand, blackboard, quicksilver, stronghold, halfpenny.

(3) Verb + Noun ; as,

Spendthrift, makeshift, breakfast, telltale, pickpocket, cut-throat, cutpurse, daredevil, scarecrow, hangman.

(4) Gerund + Noun ; as,

Drawing-room, writing-desk, looking-glass, walking-stick, blotting paper, stepping-stone, spelling-book.

(5) Adverb (or Preposition) + Noun ; as,

Outlaw, afterthought, forethought, foresight, overcoat, downfall, afternoon, bypass, inmate, off-shoot, inside

(6) Verb + Adverb ; as,

Drawback, lock-up, go-between, die-hard, send-off.

(7) Adverb + Verb ; as,

Outset, upkeep, outcry, income, outcome.

236. **Compound Adjectives** may be formed from:

(1) Noun+Adjective (or Participle) ; as,

Blood-red, sky-blue, snow-white, pitch-dark, breast-high, skin-deep, purse-proud, lifelong, world-wide, headstrong, homesick, stone-blind, seasick, note-worthy, heart-rending, ear-piercing, time-serving, moth-eaten, heart-broken, bed-ridden, hand-made, sea-girl, love-lorn.

(2) Adjective + Adjective ; as,

Red-hot, blue-black, white-hot, dull-grey, lukewarm

(3) Adverb + Participle ; as,

Long-suffering, everlasting, never-ending, thorough-bred, well-deserved, outspoken, down-hearted, far-seen, inborn.

237. **Compound Verbs** may be formed from:

(1) Noun+Verb ; as,

Waylay, backbite, typewrite, browbeat, earmark.

(2) Adjective+Verb ; as,

Safe-guard, whitewash, fulfil.

(3) Adverb+Verb ; as,

Overthrow, overtake, foretell, undertake, undergo, overhear, overdo, outbid, outdo, upset, ill-use.

Note— In most compound words, it is the first word which modifies the meaning of the second. The accent is placed upon the modifying word when the amalgamation is complete. When the two elements of the compound are only partially blended, a hyphen is put between them, and the accent falls equally on both parts of the compound.

EXERCISE 123

Explain the formation of the following Compound words.

newspaper, football, moonstruck, turncoat, brand-new, jet-black, onlooker, soothsayer, stronghold, ice-cold, worldly-wise, tempest-tossed, race-horse, ear-ring, cooking-stove, over-dose, fire-proof, top-heavy, heaven-born, skin-deep, widespread, snake-charmer, lifelong, upland

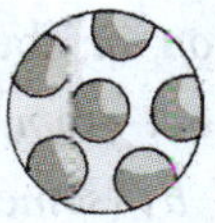

238. **(II) PRIMARY DERIVATIVES**

(1) Formation of Nouns from Verbs and Adjectives.

Verbs	*Nouns*	*Verbs*	*Nouns*
Advise	advice	Gape	gap
Bear	bier	Gird	girth
Bind	bond	Grieve	grief

Bless	bliss	Live	life
Break	breach	Lose	loss
Burn	brand	Prove	proof
Choose	choice	Sing	song
Chop	chip	Sit	seat
Deal	dole	Speak	speech
Deem	doom	Strike	stroke
Dig	ditch dike	Strive	strife
		Wake	watch
Float	fleet	Weave	web woof

Adjectives	*Nouns*
Dull	dolt
Hot	heat
Proud	pride

(2) Formation of Adjectives from Verbs and Nouns.

Verbs	*Adjectives*	*Nouns*	*Adjectives*
Float	fleet	Milk	Milch
Lie	low	Wit	wise

(3) Formation of Verbs from Nouns and Adjectives.

Nouns	*Verbs*	*Nouns*	*Verbs*
Bath	bathe	Gold	gild
Belief	Believe	Grass	graze
Blood	bleed	Half	halve
Breath	breathe	Knot	knit
Brood	breed	Price	prize
Cloth	clothe	Sale	sell
Drop	drip	Sooth	soothe
Food	feed	Tale	tell
Glass	glaze	Thief	thieve
Adjectives	***Verbs***	Wreath	wreathe
Cool	chill		
Hale	heal		

239. **(III) SECONDARY DERIVATIVES**

English Prefixes

A-, *on, in*; abed, aboard, ashore, ajar, asleep

A-, *out, from,* arise, awake, alight

Be-, *by* (*sometimes intensive*); beside, betimes, besmear, bedaub

For-, *thoroughly* ; forbear, forgive

Fore-, *before* ; forecast, foretell

Gain-, *against* ; gainsay

In-, *in* ; income, inland, inlay

Mis-, *wrong, wrongly* ; misdeed, mislead, misjudge

Over-, *above, beyond* ; overflow, overcharge

To-, *this*; today, tonight, tomorrow

Un-, *not*; untrue, unkind, unholy

Un-, *to reverse an action* ; untie, undo, unfold

Under-, *beneath, below* ; undersell, undercharge, undergo, underground

With-, *against, back* ; withdraw, withhold, withstand

> **Note**— There are only two prefixes of English origin that are still applied freely to new words, *mis* and *un*, the former with the force of the adjective *bad* and the latter with the force of a negative.

Latin Prefixes

Ab, (a, abs), *from, away* ; abuse, avert, abstract.

Ad (ac, af, ag, al, an, ap, ar, as, at, a), *to*; adjoin, accord, affect, aggrieve, allege, announce, appoint, arrest, assign, attach, avail

Ambi (amb, am), *on both sides, around;* ambiguous, ambition, amputate

Ante (anti, an), *before ;* antedate, anticipate, ancestor

Bene, *well ;* benediction, benefit

Bis, (bi, bin), *twice, two ;* biscuit, bisect, binoculars

Circum (circu), *around ;* circumnavigate, circumference, circuit

Con (col, com, cor), *with, together ;* contend, collect, combine, correct

Contra (counter), *against ;* contradict, counteract, counterfeit

De, *down ;* descend, dethrone, depose

Dis, (dif, di), *apart ;* disjoin, differ, divide

Demi, *half* ; demigod

Ex (ef, e), *out of ;* extract, effect

Extra, *beyond, outside, of;* extraordinary, extravagant

In (il, im, ir, en, em), *in, into*; invade, illustrate, immerse, irrigate, enact, embrace

In (il, im, ir), *not ;* insecure, illegal, imprudent, irregular

Inter (intro, enter), *among, within ;* intervene, introduce, entertain

Male (mal), *ill, badly ;* malevolent, malcontent

Non, *(not); nonsense*

Ob (oc, of), *in the way of, against;* object, occupy, offend

Pen, *almost ;* penultimate, peninsula

Per (pel), *through* ; pervade, pellucid

Post, *after ;* postscript, postdate, postpone

Pre, *before ;* prefix, prevent, predict

Preter, *beyond* ; preternatural

Pro (por, pur), *for;* pronoun, portray, pursue

Re, *back, again ;* reclaim, refund, renew, return

Retro, *backwards ;* retrospect, retrograde

Se (sed) ; *apart ;* secede, separate, seduce, sedition

Semi, *half ;* semicircle, semicolon

Sine, *without ;* sinecure

Sub (suc, suf, sug, sum, sup, sur, sus), *under ;* subdue, succeed, suffer, suggest, summon, support, surmount, sustain

Subter, *beneath ;* subterfuge

Super, *above ;* superfine, superfluous

Trans (tra, tres), *across* ; transmit, traverse, trespass
Vice, *in the place of* ; viceroy, vice-president

Greek Prefixes

A (an), *without, not* ; atheist, apathy, anarchy
Amphi, *around, on both sides* ; amphitheatre, amphibious
Ana, *up, back* ; anachronism, analysis
Anti (ant), *against* ; antipathy, antagonist
Apo (ap) *from* ; apostate, apology
Arch (archi) *chief* ; archbishop, archangel, architect
Auto, *self* ; autocrat, autobiography, autograph

Cata, *down* ; cataract, catastrophe, catalogue
Di, *twice* ; dilemma
Dia, *through* ; diagonal, diameter
Dys, *badly* ; dyspepsia, dysentery
En (em), *in,* ; encyclopaedia, emblem
Epi, *upon* ; epilogue, epitaph
Eu, *well* ; eulogy, euphony, eugenics
Ex (ec), *out of* ; exodus, eccentric

Hemi, *half* ; hemisphere
Homo (hom), *like* ; homogeneous, homonym
Hyper, *over, beyond* ; hyperbole, hypercritical
Hypo, *under* ; hypothesis, hypocrite
Meta (met), *implying change* ; metaphor, metonymy
Mono, *alone, single* ; monoplane, monopoly
Pan, *all* ; panacea, panorama, pantheism
Para, *beside, by the side of* ; parallel, paradox, parasite
Peri, *round* ; period, perimeter, periscope
Philo (Phil), *love* ; philosophy, philanthropy
Pro, *before* ; prophescy, programme
Syn, (sym, syl, sy), *with, together* ; synonym, sympathy, syllable, system

English Suffixes

Of Nouns

(1) Denoting agent or doer
–er (-ar, -or, -yer) ; painter, baker, beggar, sailor, lawyer
–ster ; spinster, punster, songster
–ter (-ther) ; daughter, father

(2) Denoting *state, action, condition, being,* etc
–dom ; freedom, martyrdom, wisdom
–hood (-head) ; manhood, childhood, godhead
–lock (-ledge) ; wedlock, knowledge
–ness ; darkness, boldness, goodness, sweetness
–red ; kindred, hatred
–ship ; hardship, friendship, lordship

–**th** ; health, stealth, growth

(3) Forming *Diminutives*

–**el (-le)** ; satchel, kernel, girdle, handle

–**en** ; maiden, kitten, chicken

–**ie** ; dearie, birdie, lassie

–**kin** ; lambkin, napkin

–**let** ; leaflet

–**ling** ; duckling, darling, stripling, weakling

–**ock** ; hillock, bullock

Of Adjectives

–**ed,** *having* ; gifted, talented, wretched, learned

–**en,** *made of* ; wooden, golden, woollen, earthen

–**ful,** *full of* ; hopeful, fruitful, joyful

–**ish,** *somewhat like* ; boorish, reddish, girlish

–**less,** *free from, without* ; fearless, shameless, hopeless, senseless, boundless

–**ly,** *like* ; manly, godly, sprightly

–**some,** *with the quality of* ; wholesome, meddlesome, gladsome, quarrelsome

–**ward,** *inclining* to ; forward, wayward

–**y,** *with the quality of* ; wealthy, healthy, windy, slimy, greedy, needy, thirsty, dirty

Of Verbs

–**en,** *causative, forming transitive verbs* ; weaken, sweeten, gladden, deaden, strengthen

–**se,** *to make* ; cleanse, rinse

–**er,** *intensive or frequentative* : chatter, glitter, glimmer, fritter, flutter

Of Adverbs

–**ly,** *like* ; boldly, wisely

–**long,** headlong, sidelong

–**ward, (-wards),** turning to ; homeward, backwards, upwards

–**way, (-ways)** ; straight a way, anyway, always

–**wise,** *manner, mode* ; likewise, otherwise

Note—We still feel the force of a few English suffixes. These are:

–**er,** *denoting the actor or agent* ; as, driver

–**hood,** *indicating rank or condition* ; as, boyhood

–**kin, ling,** *diminutives,* as, lambkin, yearling

–**ness, ship, th,** *indicating abstract nouns* ; as, loveliness, friendship, truth

–**en, ful, ish, less, ly, some, ward, y,** *adjective and adverb endings* ; as, golden, hopeful, oldish, helpless, manly, lonesome, homeward, mighty

Latin Suffixes

Of Nouns

(1) Denoting chiefly the *agent* or *doer of a thing*

–**ain (-an, -en, -on)** ; chieftain, artisan, citizen, surgeon

–**ar, (-er, -eer, -ier, -ary**); scholar, preacher, engineer, financier, missionary
–**ate (-ee, -ey, -y)** ; advocate, trustee, attorney, deputy
–**or, (-our, -eur, -er)** ; emperor, saviour, amateur, interpreter

(2) Denoting *state, action, result of an action*

–**age** ; bondage, marriage, breakage, leakage
–**ance (-ence)** ; abundance, brilliance, assistance, excellence, innocence
–**cy** ; fancy, accuracy, lunacy, bankruptcy
–**ion** ; action, opinion, union
–**ice (-ise)** ; service, cowardice, exercise
–**ment** ; punishment, judgement, improvement
–**mony** ; parsimony, matrimony, testimony
–**tude** ; servitude, fortitude, magnitude
–**ty ;** cruelty, frailty, credulity
–**ure ;** pleasure, forfeiture, verdure
–**y ;** misery, victory

(3) Forming *diminutives*

–**cule (-ule, -cel, -sel, -el, -le) ;** animalcule, globule, parcel, damsel, chapel, circle
–**et ;** owlet, lancet, trumpet
–**ette ;** cigarette, coquette

(4) Denoting *place*

–**ary (-ery, -ry) ;** dispensary, library, nunnery, treasury
–**ter (tre) ;** cloister, theatre

Of Adjectives

–**al** ; national, legal, regal, mortal, fatal
–**an (-ane) ;** human, humane, mundane
–**ar** ; familiar, regular
–**ary ;** customary, contrary, necessary, ordinary, honorary
–**ate ;** fortunate, temperate, obstinate
–**ble (-ible, able) ;** feeble, sensible, laughable
–**esque ;** picturesque, grotesque
–**id ;** humid, vivid, lucid
–**ile ;** servile, fragile, juvenile
–**ine ;** feminine, canine, feline, divine
–**ive ;** active, attentive, shortive
–**lent** ; corpulent, indolent, turbulent, virulent
–**ose (ous) ;** verbose, dangerous, onerous, copious

Of Verbs

–**ate;** assassinate, captivate, exterminate
–**esce;** acquiesce, effervesce
–**fy** ; simplify, purify, fortify, sanctify, terrify
–**ish ;** publish, nourish, punish, banish

Greek Suffixes

–**ic (-ique) ;** angelic, cynic, phonetic, unique
–**ist** ; artist, chemist

–**isk ;** asterisk, obelisk
–**ism (-asm) ;** patriotism, despotism, enthusiasm
–**ize ;** civilize, sympathize, criticize
–**sis (-sy) ;** crisis, analysis, heresy, poesy
–**e (-y) ;** catastrophe, monarchy, philosophy

Note—We still feel the force of a number of suffixes of foreign origin. These are:

ee (French), added to nouns to denote, usually, the person who takes a passive share in an action; as, employee, payee, legatee, mortgagee, trustee, referee.

or, ar, er, eer, ier, denoting a person who perfoms a certain act or function ; as, emperor, scholar, officer, engineer, gondolier.
ist, denoting a person who follows a certain trade or pursuit; as, chemist, theosophist, artist, nihilist.
ism, forming abstract nouns ; as, patriotism.
ble, forming adjectives that have usually a passive sense; as, tolerable, bearable.
ize or *ise,* forming verbs from nouns and adjectives; as, crystallize, moralize, baptize.

EXERCISE 124

(a) *Give examples showing the use and meaning of the following prefixes.*
super-, trans-, con-, sub-, auto-, mis-, ante-, post-, vice-, extra-, pre-, arch-

(b) *Give examples of adjectives formed from nouns by the addition of the suffixes* -en, -ish, -less,*and explain the meaning of the suffixes.*

(c) *Show by the use of suffixes that we can use a single word to express the meaning of each of the following groups of words.*
a little river, the state of being a child, to make fat, that which cannot be read, unfit to be chosen

(d) *Give the meanings of the prefixes and suffixes in the following words.*
incredible, antidote, anarchy, misconduct, monarch, sympathy, manhood, hillock, archbishop, amiss, bicycle, dismantle, freshen

(e) *Form Adjectives from the following nouns.*
circumstance, habit, stone, miser, irony, labour, circuit

(f) *Form Verbs from :–*
friend, bath, fertile, grass, clean, sweet, critic

(g) *Form Nouns from.*
sustain, attain, confess, attach, fortify, oblige, give, cruel, hate, govern, sweet

(h) *Form Adjectives from.*
muscle, hazard, worth, quarrel, admire, thirst, god

(i) *Add to each of the following words a prefix which reverses the meaning.*
fortune, legible, visible, agreeable, ever, fortunate, practicable, honour, patience, sense, truth, resolute, legal, capable, organize, credible, creditable

(j) *What is the force or meaning of the (1) Prefixes :* in-, bene-, post-, dys-, dis-, *(2) Suffixes :*-en, -fy, -ness, -isk, -ing ? *Name the language from which each is derived.*

(k) *Mention two prefixes which denote (1) reversal of an action ; (2) something good ; (3) something bad ; (4) a negative.*

(l) *Name the primary derivatives of the following words.*
hale, glass, high, sit, dig, strong, deep

(m) *By means of a suffix turn each of the following words into an abstract noun.*
grand, discreet, supreme, rival, certain, warm, desolate, dense

240. **A Root** is the simple element common to words of the same origin.

A Few Latin Roots

Đquus, *equal* : equal, equator, equivalent, adequate
Ager, *a field* : agriculture, agrarian
Ago, actus, *I do* : agent, agile. active, actor
Alius,*another* : alien, aliquot, alias, alibi
Amo, *I love* : amiable, amateur, amorous, inimical
Angulus, *a corner* : angle, triangle
Anima, *life* ; **animus,** *mind* : animal, animate, unanimous, magnanimous
Annus, *a year* : annual, biennial, perennial
Aperio, apertus, I open : aperture, April
Aqua, water : aquatic, aquarium, aqueduct
Appello, *I call* : appeal, repeal
Ars, artis, art : artist, artisan, artifice
Audio, I hear : audible, audience, auditor
Bellum, *war* : belligerent, rebel, rebellious
Bene, *well* : benefit, benevolent, benefactor
Brevis, *short* : brevity, abbreviate, abridge
Caedo, caesus, *I cut, kill* : suicide, homicide, concise
Candeo, *I shine*: candle, candid, candour, incandescent
Capio, captus, *I take* : captive, capacious, accept
Caput, capitis, *the head* : capital, decapitate, captain
Caro, carnis, *flesh* : carnivorous, carnage
Cedo, cessum, *I go, yield* : concede, proceed, accede
Centrum, *centre* : eccentric, centralize, concentrate
Centum, *a hundred* : cent, century, centipede
Cerno, cretus, *I distinguish* : discern, discreet
Civis, *citizen* : civil, civilize
Clamo, *I shout* : clamour, claim, exclaim
Claudo clausus, *I shut* : exclude, conclude, closet
Colo, cultus, *I till* : colony, culture, cultivate, agriculture
Cor, cordis, *the heart* : core, cordial, concord, discord, accord, courage
Corpus, *the body* : corpse, corps, corporation, corpulent
Credo,*I believe* : creed, credible, credence, miscreant
Cresco, *I grow* : increase, decrease, crescent
Crux, a cross : crucify, crusade
Culpa, *a fault* : culprit, culpable
Cura, *care* : curator, sinecure, accurate, secure, incurable
Deus, *God* : deity, deify, divine
Dico, dictus *I say* : dictation, contradict, predict, verdict
Dies, *a day* : diary, daily, meridian
Do, datus, *I give* : add, date, tradition, addition, condition
Doceo, doctus, *I teach* : docile, doctrine
Dominus, *a lord* : dominion, dominant
Duco, ductus, *I lead* : adduce, conduit, product, education
Duo, *two* : dual, duel, double, duplicate, duodecimal
Durus, *hard lasting* : durable, obdurate, duration
Eo, itum, *I go* : exit, circuit, transition, ambition
Esse, *to be* : essence, essential, present, absent
Facio, *I make* : fabric, counterfeit, manufacture
Fero, latus, *I carry* : infer, confer, refer, relate

Fido, *I trust* : confide, infidel, defy
Finis, *an end* : finite, infinite, confine
Flecto flexus, *I bend* : inflict, inflexible, reflection
Forma, *a form* : formal, deformed, reform
Fortis, *strong* : fort, fortress, fortify, fortitude, reinforce
Frango, fractus, *I break* : fragment, fragile, fraction, infringe
Frater, *a brother* : fraternal, fratricide
Frons, frontis, *forehead* : front, affront, frontier, confront
Fugio, *I flee* : fugitive, refugee, refuge, subterfuge
Fundo, fusus, *I pour* : profuse, diffuse, confuse, refund
Fundus, *the bottom* : found, foundation, profound, fundamental, founder
Gens, gentis, *a race* : congenial, indigenous
Gradior, grassus, *I go:* grade, degrade, transgress, progress
Gratia, *favour* : gratitude, gratis, ingratiate, grateful
Gravis, *heavy* : gravity, gravitation, grief, grievous
Habeo, *I have* : habit, habitable, habituate, exhibit, inhabit, prohibit
Homo, *a man* : homage, homicide, human, humane
Impero, *I command:* imperative, imperial, emperor, empire
Jacio, jactus, *I throw* : ejaculate, reject
Judex, judicis, *a judge* : judicial, judgment, judicious, prejudice
Jungo, junctus, *I join* : junction, conjunction, juncture
Labor, lapsus, *I glide,* lapse, collapse, relapse, elapse
Laus, laudis, *praise* : laudable, laudatory
Lego, lectus, I *gather, read* : collect, neglect, select
Lego, legatus, *I send* : delegate, legation
Levis, *light* : levity, alleviate, elevate, leaven
Lex, legis, *a law* : legal, legislate, legitimate, loyal
Liber, *free* : liberal, libertine, deliver
Ligo, *I bind* : ligature, ligament, religion, league, obligation
Litera, *a letter* : literal, literary, literate, literature
Locus, *a place* : local, locality, locomotive
Loquor, locutus, I speak : loquacious, elocution, eloquence
Ludo, lusum, *I play* : elude, delude, ludicrous
Lumen, *a light* : luminous, luminary
Luo, lutus, *I wash* : lotion, ablution, deluge, dilute, pollute
Lux, lucis, *light* : lucid, elucidate
Magnus, *great* : major, mayor, magnate, magnify, magnitude
Malus, *bad* : malady, malice, maltreat, malaria
Manus, *hand* : manuscript, amanuensis, manual
Mare, *the sea* : marine, mariner, submarine, maritime
Mater, *a mother* : maternal, matriculate, matron, matrimony
Medius, *the middle* : medium, mediate
Memor, *mindful* : memory, memorable, memoir
Miles, militis, *a soldier* : military, militia, militant
Mitto, missus, *I send* : admit, missionary, promise
Moneo monitus, *I advise* : monitor, admonish
Mons, montis, *a mountain* : mount, dismount, surmount
Moveo, motus, *I move* : motor, motion, commotion, promote
Multus, *many* : multitude, multiple
Munus, muneris, *a gift* : munificent, remunerate
Navis, *a ship* : navy, nautical
Noceo, *I hurt* : innocent, noxious, nuisance
Novus, *new* : novel, novice, innovation
Nox, noctis, *night* : nocturnal, equinox

Omnis, *all :* omnipotent, omnipresent, omnibus
Pando, passus, *I spread out :* expand, compass, trespass
Pars, partis, *a part :* part, partial, particle
Pater, *a father :* paternal, patron, patrimony
Patior, passus, *I suffer :* passive, patient
Pello, pulsus, *I drive :* compel, expel, repel
Pendeo, pensum, *I hang :* depend, suspend
Pes, pedis, *a foot :* biped, quadruped, pedestrian, pedestal
Peto, petitus, *I seek :* petition, competition, impetuous
Pleo, *I fill :* complete, replete, replenish, supplement
Pono, positus, *I place :* position, preposition, composition
Porto, *I carry :* portable, portmanteau, import, export
Primus, *first :* primary, primitive, prince, premier, principal
Probo, *I try :* probation, probable, approval
Puto, putatus, *I cut, think :* amputate, dispute, compute
Rapio, raptus. *I seize :* rapacious, ravenous
Rego, rectus, *I rule :* regal, regent, correct, regulate
Rumpo, ruptus, *I break :* rupture, rout, bankrupt, eruption
Sanctus, *holy :* sanctuary, sanctify, saint
Scio, *I know :* science, conscience, omniscience
Scribo, scriptus, *I write :* describe, scribble, postscript, inscription, manuscript
Seco, *I cut :* bisect, dissect, sickle
Sentio, *I feel :* sentiment, sensation, nonsense, sensual
Sequor, secutus, *I follow :* sequel, sequence, consequence, prosecute, execute
Servio, *I serve :* servant, serf, service, servitude
Signum, *a sign :* signal, significant, design
Similis, *tike :* similar, dissimilar, resemblance
Solvo, solutus, *I loose :* solution, resolution, absolve, dissolve, resolve
Specio, spectus, *I see :* specimen, spectator, suspicion
Spiro, *I breathe :* aspire, conspire, inspire, expire
Stringo, strictus, *I bind :* stringent, strict, restrict
Struo, structus, *I build :* structure, construction
Sumo, sumptus, *I take :* assume, presume, resume
Tango, tactus, *I touch :* tangent, contact, contagion
Tempus, temporis, *time :* tense, temporal, contemporary
Tendo, tensus, *I stretch :* tend, contend, attend, extend
Teneo, tentus, *I hold :* tenant, tenure, content, retentive
Terminus, *an end :* term, terminate, determination
Terra, *the earth :* inter, subterranean, terrestrial
Texo, textus, I weave : textile, texture, context
Torqueo, tortus, *I twist :* distort, torture, torment
Traho, tractus, *I draw :* contract, abstract, portrait
Tribuo, *I give :* tribute, contribute
Unus, *one :* union, unique, unanimous
Valeo, *I am well :* valid, invalid, equivalent, valiant
Venio, *I come :* venture, adventure, convene, prevent
Verbum, *a word :* verb, adverb, proverb, verbose, verbal
Verto, versus, *I turn :* convert, converse, reverse, diversion
Verus, true : verify, verdict, aver, veracious
Video, visus, *I see :* vision, survey, evident, television
Vinco, victus, *I conquer :* victor, invincible, convince
Vivo, victum, *I live :* vivid, vivacious, revive, survive
Voco, vocatus, *I call :* vocal, vocation, vociferous, invoke, revoke
Volo, *I wish :* voluntary, benevolent, malevolence

Volvo, *I roll* : revolve, involve, revolution
Voro, *I eat* : voracious, omnivorous, carnivorous, devour
Voveo, votus, *I vow* : vote, devote, devotee, votary
Vulgus, *the common people* : vulgar, divulge

A Few Greek Roots

Ago, *I lead* : demagogue, pedagogue, stratagem
Agon, *a contest* : agony, antagonist
Anthropos, *a man* : anthropology, misanthrope, philanthropist
Aster, astron, *a star* : asterisk, astronomy, astrology
Autos, *self* : autocrat, autograph, autonomy, autobiography
Biblos, *a book* ; Bible, bibliography, bibliomaniac
Bios, *life* : biology, biography
Chole, *bile* : choleric, melancholy
Chronos, *time* : chronicle, chronology, chronometer, chronic
Deka, *ten* : decagon, decade
Demos, *the people* : democracy, demagogue, epidemic
Doxa, *opinion* : orthodox, dogmatic
Gamos, *marriage* : monogamy, bigamy, polygamy
Geo, *the earth* : geology, geography, geometry
Gonia, *an angle* : diagonal, polygon, hexagon
Grapho, I write : biography, telegraph, telegram, phonograph
Helios, *the sun* : heliograph, heliotrope
Hippos, *a horse* : hippopotamus, hippodrome
Hodos, *a way* : period, method, episode
Homos, *the same* : homogeneous, homonym
Hudor, *water* : hydrogen, hydrophobia, hydrant
Idios, *one's own* : idiot, idiom, idiosyncrasy
Isos, *equal* : isosceles
Kosmos, *the world* : cosmopolite
Kratos, *strength* : democrat, autocrat, aristocrat, plutocrat
Kuklos, *a circle* : cycle, cyclone, encyclopaedia
Lithos, *a stone* : lithography, aerolite
Logos, *a word, speech* : dialogue, catalogue, astrology
Luo, *I loosen* : analysis, paralysis
Meter, *a mother* : metropolis
Metron, *a measure* : thermometer, barometer
Mikros, *little* : microscope
Monos, *alone* : monarch, monopoly
Nomos, *a, law* : astronomy, economy, autonomy
Ode, *a song* : prosody, parody
Onoma, *a name* : anonymous, synonymous
Orthos, *right* : orthodoxy, orthography
Pan, *all* : pantheist, pantomime, panacea
Pathos, *feeling* : pathetic, sympathy, antipathy,
Petra, *a rock* : petrify, petroleum
Phileo, *I love* : philosophy, philanthropy
Phone, *a sound* : phonograph, telephone
Phos, photos, *light* ; phosphorus, photograph
Phrasis, *a speech* : paraphrase, phraseology
Poleo, *I make* : poem, onomatopoeia
Polis, *a city* : police, policy, politic, metropolis
Polus, *many* : polygamy, polygon
Pous, podos, *a foot* : antipodes, tripod
Rheo, *I flow* : rheumatic, diarrhoea, catarrh

Skopeo, *I see* : telescope, microscope
Sophia, *wisdom* : philosopher, sophist
Techne, *an art* : technical, architect, pyrotechnics
Tele, *far*: telegraph, telegram, telephone, telescope.
Temno, *I cut* : anatomy, epitome
Theos, *a god* : theism, theology, theosophy
Thermos, *warm* : thermometer
Thesis, *a placing* : hypothesis, synthesis, parenthesis
Treis, *three* : triangle, tripod, trinity
Tupos, *impression* : type, stereotype, electrotype
Zoon, *an animal* : zoology, zodiac

Chapter 29 FIGURES OF SPEECH

241. A Figure of Speech is a departure from the ordinary form of expression, or the ordinary course of ideas in order to produce a greater effect.

242. Figures of Speech may be classified as under:

(1) Those based on Resemblance, such as Simile, Metaphor, Personification and Apostrophe.
(2) Those based on Contrast, such as Antithesis and Epigram.
(3) Those based on Association, such as Metonymy and Synecdoche.
(4) Those depending on Construction, such as Climax and Anticlimax.

263. **Simile**–In a Simile a comparison is made between two objects of *different* kinds which have however at least one point in common.

The Simile is usually introduced by such words as *like, as* or *so.*

Examples:

1. The Assyrian came down like a wolf on the fold.
2. The righteous shall flourish as the palm tree.
3. As the hart panteth after the water-brooks, so panteth my soul after Thee, O God.
4. Words are like leaves : and where they most abound,
   Much fruit of sense beneath is rarely found.
5. How far that little candle throws his beams !
   So shines a good deed in a naughty world.
6. Life is as tedious as a twice-told tale
   Vexing the dull ear of a drowsy man.
7. Thy soul was like a star, and dwelt apart:
   Thou hadst a voice whose sound was like the sea.
8. O my Love's like a red, red rose
   That's newly sprung in June;
   O my Love's like the melodie
   That's sweetly played in tune.

The following are some common similes of everyday speech.

mad as a March Hare; as proud as a peacock; as bold as brass; as tough as leather; as clear as crystal; as good as gold; as old as the hills; as cool as a cucumber.

Note–A comparison of two things of the *same* kind is not a Simile.

244. **Metaphor**– A Metaphor is an *implied* Simile. It does not, like the Simile, state that one thing is *like* another or acts *as* another, but takes that for granted and proceeds as if the two things were one.

Thus, when we say, 'He fought *like* a lion' we use a Simile, but when we say, 'He *was* a lion in the fight', we use a Metaphor.

Examples:

1. The camel is the ship of the desert.
2. Life is a dream.
3. The news was a dagger to his heart.
4. Revenge is a kind of wild justice.

Note 1— Every Simile can be compressed into a Metaphor and every Metaphor can be expanded into a Simile.

Thus, instead of saying,

Richard fought *like* a lion (Simile),

we can say,

Richard was a lion in the fight (Metaphor).

Similarly, instead of saying,

The camel is the ship of the desert (Metaphor).

we may expand it and say,

As a ship is used for crossing the ocean, so the camel is used for crossing the desert (Simile).

Other examples:

Variety is the spice of life (Metaphor).

As spice flavours food, so variety makes life more pleasant (Simile).

The waves broke on the shore with a noise like thunder (Simile).

The waves thundered on the shore. (Metaphor)

Note 2— Metaphor should never be *mixed.* That is, an object should not be identified with two or more different things in the same sentence.

The following is a typical example of what is called a *Mixed Metaphor.*

I smell a rat ; I see it floating in the air ; but I will nip it in the bud.

245. **Personification**– In Personification inanimate objects and abstract notions are spoken of as having life and intelligence.

Examples:

1. In Saxon strength that abbey frowned.
2. Laughter holding both her sides.
3. Death lays his icy hand on kings.
4. Pride goeth forth on horseback, grand and gay,
   But cometh back on foot, and begs its way.

246. **Apostrophe**–An Apostrophe is a direct address to the dead, to the absent, or to a personified object or idea. This figure is a special form of Personification.

Examples:

1. Milton ! thou should'st be living at this hour.
2. O Friend ! I know not which way I must look.

For comfort.

3. Roll on, thou deep and dark blue Ocean–roll !
4. O death ! where is thy sting ? O grave ! where is thy victory ?
5. O liberty, what crimes have been committed in thy name ?
6. Wave, Munich, all thy banners wave,
   And charge with all thy chivalry !
7. O judgement ! thou art fled to brutish beasts.
8. O Solitude ! where are the charms
   That sages have seen in thy face ?

247. **Hyperbole**–In Hyperbole, a statement is made emphatic by overstatement.

Examples :

1. Here's the smell of blood still ; all the perfumes of Arabia will not sweeten this little hand.
2. Why, man, if the river were dry, I am able to fill it with tears.
3. O Hamlet ! thou hast cleft my heart in twain.
4. Surely never lighted on this orb, which she hardly seemed to touch, a more delightful vision than Marie Antoinette.
5. I Loved Ophelia ; forty thousand brothers
   Could not with all their quantity of love
   Make up the sum.

248. **Euphemism–** Euphemism consists in the description of a disagreeable thing by an agreeable name.

Examples:

1. He has fallen asleep (*i.e.,* he is dead).
2. You are telling me a fairy tale (*i.e.,* a lie).

249. **Antithesis–** In antithesis a striking opposition or contrast of words or sentiments is made in the same sentence. It is employed to secure emphasis.

Examples:

Man proposes, God disposes.

1. Man proposes, God disposes.
2. Not that I loved Caesar less, but that I loved Rome more.
3. Better fifty years of Europe than a cycle of Cathay.
4. Give every man thy ear, but few thy voice.
5. Speech is silvern, but silence is golden.
6. To err is human, to forgive divine.
7. Many are called, but few are chosen.
8. He had his jest, and they had his estate.
9. The Puritans hated bear-baiting, not because it gave pain to the bear, but because it gave pleasure to the spectators.
10. A man's nature runs either to herbs or weeds ; therefore, let him seasonably water the one and destroy the other.

250. **Oxymoron–** Oxymoron is a special form of Antithesis, whereby two contradictory qualities are predicted at once of the same thing.

Examples:

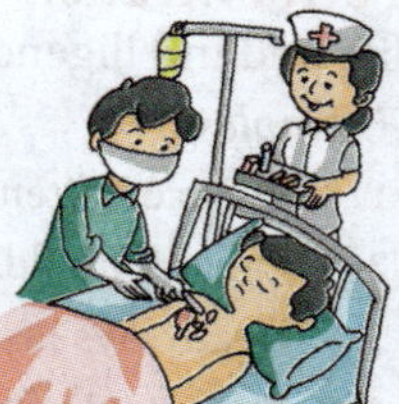

1. His honour rooted in dishonour stood.
   And faith unfaithful kept him falsely true.
2. So innocent arch, so cunningly simple.
3. She accepted it as the kind cruelty of the surgeon's knife.

251. **Epigram–** An Epigram is a brief pointed saying frequently introducing antithetical ideas which excite surprise and arrest attention.

Examples:

1. The child is the father of the man.
2. A man can't be too careful in the choice of his enemies.
3. Fools rush in where angels fear to tread.
4. In the midst of life we are in death.
5. Art lies in concealing art.
6. He makes no friend, who never made a foe.
7. Know then thyself, presume not God to scan;
   The proper study of mankind is man.
8. The fool doth think he is wise, but the wise man knows himself to be a fool.
9. Lie heavy on him, earth, for he*
   Laid many a heavy load on thee.
10. Here lies our Sovereign Lord the King
    Whose word no man relies on,
    Who never said a foolish thing
    And never did a wise one.

---

* Vanburgh, the architect

252. **Irony**–Irony is a mode of speech in which the real meaning is exactly the opposite of that which is literally conveyed.

Examples:

1. No doubt but ye are the people, and wisdom shall die with you.
2. The atrocious crime of being a young man, which the honourable gentleman has, with such spirit and decency, charged upon me. I shall neither attempt to palliate nor deny.
3. Here under leave of Brutus and the rest
(For Brutus is an honourable man:
So are they all, all honourable men)
Come I to speak in Caesar's funeral.
He was my friend, faithful and just to me;
But Brutus says he was ambitious,
And Brutus is an honourable man.

253. **Pun**–A Pun consists in the use of a word in such a way that it is capable of more than one application, the object being to produce a ludicrous effect.

Examples:

1. Is life worth living ?–It depends upon the *liver.*
2. An ambassador is an honest man who *lies* abroad for the good of his country.

254. **Metonymy**– In Metonymy (literally, *a change of name)* an object is designated by the name of something which is generally associated with it.

Some familiar examples:

The Bench, for the judges.
The House, for the members of Lok Sabha.
The laurel, for success.
Red-coats, for British soldiers.
Bluejackets, for sailors.
The Crown, for the king.

Since there are many kinds of association between objects, there are several varieties of Metonymy. Thus a Metonymy may result from the use of–

(*i*) The sign for the person or thing symbolized ; as,

You must address the *chair* (*i.e.,* the chairman).
From the *cradle* to the *grave* (*i.e.,* from infancy to death).

(*ii*) The container for the thing contained ; as,

The whole *city* went out to see the victorious general.
The *kettle* boils.
Forthwith he drank the fatal *cup.*
He keeps a good *cellar.*
He was playing to the *gallery.*
He has undoubtedly the best *stable* in the country.

(*iii*) The instrument for the agent ; as,

The pen is mightier than the sword.

(*iv*) The author for his works ; as,

We are reading *Milton.*
Do you learn *Euclid* at your school ?

(*v*) The name of a feeling or passion for its object ; as,

He turn'd his charger as he spake
Upon the river shore,
He gave the bridle-reins a shake,
Said 'Adieu for evermore,
My *love* !
And adieu for evermore.'

255. **Synecdoche**–In Synecdoche a part is used to designate the whole or the whole to designate a part.

(*i*) A part used to designate the whole ; as,

Give us this day our daily *bread* (*i.e.*, food),

All *hands* (*i.e.*, crew) to the pumps.

Uneasy lies the *head* that wears a crown.

A fleet of fifty *sail* (*i.e.*, ships) left the harbour.

All the best *brains* in Europe could not solve the problem.

He has many *mouths* to feed.

(*ii*) The whole used to designate a part ; as,

England (*i.e.*, the English cricket eleven) won the first test match against Australia.

256. **Transferred Epithet**–In this figure an epithet is transferred from its proper word to another that is closely associated with it in the sentence.

Examples:

1. He passed a *sleepless* night.
2. The ploughman homeward plods his *weary* way.
3. A lackey presented an *obsequious* cup of coffee.

257. **Litotes**–In Litotes an affirmative is conveyed by negation of the opposite, the effect being to suggest a strong expression by means of a weaker. It is the opposite of Hyperbole.

Examples:

1. I am a citizen of *no mean* (= a very celebrated) city.
2. The man is *no fool* (= very clever).
3. I am *not a little* (= greatly) surprised.

258. **Interrogation**–Interrogation is the asking of a question not for the sake of getting an answer, but to put a point more effectively.

This figure of speech is also known as **Rhetorical Question** because a question is asked merely for the sake of rhetorical effect.

Examples:

1. Am I my brother's keeper ?
2. Do men gather grapes of thorns, or figs of thistles ?
3. Shall I wasting in despair.
   Die because a woman's fair ?
4. Who is here so vile that will not love his country ?
5. Breathes there the man with soul so dead
   Who never to himself hath said,
   This is my own, my native land ?
6. Can storied urn or animated bust
   Back to its mansion call the fleeting breath ?

259. **Exclamation**–In this figure the exclamatory form is used to draw greater attention to a point than a mere bald statement of it could do.

Examples:

1. What a piece of work is man !
2. How sweet the moonlight sleeps upon this bank !
3. O what a fall was there, my countrymen !

260. **Climax**–Climax (Gk. *Klimax* = a ladder) is the arrangement of a series of ideas in the order of increasing importance.

Examples:

1. Simple, erect, severe, austere, sublime
2. What a piece of work is man ! How noble in reason, how infinite in faculties ! In action, how like an angel ! In apprehension, how like a god!

261. **Anticlimax**–Anticlimax is the opposite of Climax–a sudden descent from higher to lower. It is chiefly used for the purpose of satire or ridicule.

Examples:

1. Here thou, great Anna ! whom three realms obey,
   Dost sometimes counsel take–and sometimes tea.
2. And thou, Dalhousie, the great god of war,
   Lieutenant-Colonel to the Earl of Mar.

EXERCISE 125

Name the various Figures of Speech in the following.

1. The more haste, the less speed.
2. I must be taught my duty, and by you !
3. Plead, Sleep, my cause, and make her soft like thee.
4. Charity suffereth long, and is kind.
5. He makes no friend, who never made a foe.
6. He that planted the ear, shall He not hear ? He that formed the eye, shall He not see ?
7. Let not ambition mock their useful toil.
8. To gossip is a fault ; to libel, a crime ; to slander, a sin.
9. Oh ! what a noble mind is here overthrown!
10. Excess of ceremony shows want of breeding.
11. Why all this toil for triumphs of an hour ?
12. Fools who came to scoff, remained to pray.
13. The Puritan had been rescued by no common deliverer from the grasp of no common foe.
14. The cup that cheers but not inebriates.
15. You are a pretty fellow.
16. Hasten slowly.
17. Hail ! smiling morn.
18. Can two walk together, except they be agreed?
19. Curses are like chickens ; they come home to roost.
20. A thousand years are as yesterday when it is past.
21. The prisoner was brought to the dock in irons.
22. We had nothing to do, and we did it very well.
23. Boys will be boys.
24. The cloister opened her pitying gate.
25. Lowliness is young Ambition's ladder.
26. Language is the art of concealing thought.
27. Must I stand and crouch under your testy humour ?
28. Exult, O shores, and ring, O bells !
29. He followed the letter, but not the spirit of the law.
30. One truth is clear : whatever is, is right.
31. I came, I saw, I conquered.
32. Labour, wide as the earth, has its summit in heaven.
33. Just for a handful of silver he left us.
34. They were swifter than eagles ; they were stronger than lions.
35. Swiftly flies the feathered death.
36. It is a wise father that knows his own child.
37. Brave Macbeth, with his brandished steel, carved out his passage.
38. Sweet Thames ! run softly, till I end my song.
39. There is only one cure for the evils which newly acquired freedom produces–and that cure is freedom.
40. Sweet Auburn, loveliest village of the plain,
    Where health and plenty cheered the labouring swain.
41. So spake the seraph Abdiel faithful found.
    Among the faithless, faithful only he.
42. Youth is full of pleasure,
    Age is full of care.

Youth is full of pleasure.

43. Like the dew on the mountain,
    Like the foam on the river,
    Like the bubble on the fountain,
    Thou art gone and for ever.
44. Can Honour's voice provoke the silent dust,
    Or Flattery soothe the dull cold ear of Death?
45. Golden lads and girls all must,
    As chimney-sweepers, come to dust.
46. Sweet are the uses of adversity,
    Which, like the toad, ugly and venomous,
    Wears still a precious jewel in its head.
47. The naked every day he clad
    When he put on his clothes.
48. O mischief, thou art swift
    To enter in the thoughts of desperate men.
49. Knowledge is proud that it knows so much,
    Wisdom is humble that it knows no more.
50. At once they rush'd
    Together, as two eagles on one prey
    Come rushing down together from the clouds,
    One from east, one from west.
51. Errors, like straws, upon the surface flow,
    He who would search for pearls must dive below.
52. The best way to learn a language is to speak it.
53. Sceptre and crown
    Must tumble down,
    And in the dust be equal made
    With the poor crooked scythe and spade.
54. O Solitude ! where are the charms
    That sages have seen in thy face ?
55. I thought ten thousand swords must have leapt from their scabbards to avenge a look that threatened her with insult.
56. The soldier fights for glory, and
    a shilling a day.

Sceptre and crown.

57. His honour rooted in dishonour stood,
    And faith unfaithful kept him falsely true.
58. They speak like saints, and act like devils.
59. He was a learned man among lords,
    and a lord among learned men.
60. Speech was given to man to conceal his thoughts.

Part III

Composition

Structures

Different verbs are used in different patterns. The verb **suggest** is used with a **that**-clause, e.g. I suggest that you should see him. The verb **want** can't be used in the same way. The sentence 'I want that you should see him' is wrong. The correct pattern is 'I want you to see him' (**want** + noun/pronoun + to-infinitive). The verb **suggest** can't be used in this pattern. We should not say, 'I suggest you to see him.' The verbs **say** and **tell** nearly mean the same, but they can't be used in the same pattern. We can say, 'He **said** that he was very tired', but we can't say, 'He **told** that he was very tired.' When used with a **that**-clause, **tell** takes a personal object (like **me, him, her, us**). We should say, 'He **told us** that he was very busy.' Chapter 30 presents the main patterns in which verbs are used. Make a careful study of the material, noting which verbs are used in which pattern.

Chapter 31 deals with the kind of structures most commonly used in everyday conversation. Question tags are not always easy to form. There are some peculiarities **like the** following, which need special attention:

I am right, **aren't I** ? (not **amn't I**)

Let's go out, **shall we** ?

Somebody has called, haven't they ? (not **hasn't he**)

Wait a minute, **can you** ?

Chapter 32 presents further structures - the sorts of structures which have not been talked about in the preceding chapters. They include the three types of conditionals:

1. If you **work** hard you **will pass** the exam. (The condition may or may not be fulfilled.)
2. If you **worked** hard you **would pass** the exam. (Improbable condition. I don't expect you will work hard. Here the past tense refers to the future.)
3. If you **had worked** hard you **would have** passed the exam. (= You didn't work hard, so you didn't pass.)

A careful study of the structures and practice in using them will help to strengthen your communicative skill in the language.

PART III: STRUCTURES

Chapter 30 VERB PATTERNS

Pattern 1

Subject+Verb.

This is the simplest of verb patterns. The subject is followed by an intransitive verb, which expresses complete sense without the help of any other words.

	Subject	Verb
1.	Birds	fly.
2.	Fire	burns.
3.	The moon	is shining.
4.	The baby	is crying.
5.	Kamala	was singing.
6.	The bell	has rung.
7.	The sun	rose.

Pattern 2

Subject+verb+subject complement

The complement usually consists of a noun (examples 1 & 2), a pronoun (3 & 4), or an adjective (5,6, 7 & 8).

	Subject	Verb	Subject Complement
1.	This	is	a pen.
2.	His brother	became	a soldier.
3.	It	is	me.
4.	That book	is	mine.
5.	Gopal	looks	sad.
6.	My father	grew	angry.
7.	The children	kept	quiet.
8.	The milk	has turned	sour.

Pattern 3

Subject + verb + direct object

	Subject	Verb	Direct Object
1.	I	know	his address.
2.	The boy	has lost	his pen.
3.	Mohan	opened	the door.
4.	Who	broke	the jug ?
5.	Mr. Pitt	has bought	a car.
6.	You	must wash	yourself.
7.	We	should help	the poor.

Pattern 4

Subject + verb + indirect object + direct object

	Subject	Verb	Indirect Object	Direct Object
1.	I	lent	her	my pen.
2.	The teacher	gave	us	homework.
3.	We	have paid	him	the money.
4.	The old man	told	us	the whole story.
5.	You	must tell	the police	the truth.
6.	I	have bought	my sister	a watch.
7.	He	didn't leave	us	any.
8.	–	Show	me	your hands.

Pattern 5

Subject + verb + direct object+ preposition + prepositional object

	Subject	Verb	Direct Object	Preposition	Prepositional object
1.	I	lent	my pen	to	a friend of mine.
2.	The teacher	gave	homework	to	all of us.
3.	We	have paid	the money	to	the proprietor.
4.	He	told	the news	to	everybody in the village.
5.	He	promised	the money	to	me (not to you).
6.	I	have bought	a watch	for	my sister.
7.	Mr. Raman	sold	his car	to	a man from Mumbai.
8.	She	made	coffee	for	all of us.

Many verbs can be used both in Pattern 4 and in Pattern 5. Pattern 5 is preferred when the direct object is less important or when the indirect object is longer than the direct object.

Pattern 6

Subject + verb + noun/pronoun + adjective

	Subject	Verb	Noun/ Pronoun	Adjective
1.	The boy	pushed	the door	open.
2.	The smith	beat	it	flat.
3.	She	washed	the plates	clean.
4.	The thief	broke	the safe	open.
5.	He	turned	the lamp	low.
6.	You	have made	your shirt	dirty.
7.	I	like	my coffee	strong.
8.	We	found	the trunk	empty.

In examples 1—6, the adjective denotes a state that results from the action expressed by the verb. In the last two examples the noun and the adjective combine to be the object of the verb.

Verbs used in this pattern include *get, keep, beat, drive, make, paint, leave, turn, find, like, wish.*

Pattern 7

Subject + verb + preposition + prepositional object

	Subject	Verb	Preposition	Prepositional Object
1.	We	are waiting	for	Suresh.
2.	He	agreed	to	our proposal.
3.	You	can't count	on	his help.
4.	These books	belong	to	me.
5.	His uncle	met	with	an accident.
6.	She	complained	of	his rudeness.
7.	He	failed	in	his attempt.

Pattern 8

Subject + verb + to-infinitive (as object of the verb)

	Subject	Verb	to-infinitive, etc. (object of the verb)
1.	She	wants	to go.
2.	I	forgot	to post the letter.
3.	He	fears	to speak in public.
4.	They	intend	to postpone the trip.
5.	Ramesh	proposes	to go into business.
6.	We	would like	to visit the museum.
7.	I	hoped	to get a first class.
8.	He	decided	not to go there.

The commonest verbs used in this pattern are : *like, love, prefer, begin, start, agree, try, attempt, choose, continue, intend, propose, desire, wish, want, hate, dislike, hope, expect, promise, refuse, fear, remember, forget, offer, learn.*

Pattern 9

Subject + verb + noun/pronoun + to-infinitive

	Subject	Verb	Noun/ Pronoun	to-infinitive, etc.
1.	I	would like	you	to stay.
2.	We	asked	him	to go.
3.	He	helped	me	to carry the box.
4.	She	advised	him	to study medicine.
5.	The doctor	ordered	Gopi	to stay in bed.
6.	They	warned	us	not to be late.
7.	I	can't allow	you	to smoke.
8.	Who	taught	you	to swim ?

The chief verbs used in this pattern include *ask, tell, order, command, persuade, encourage, urge, want, wish, request, intend, expect, force, tempt, teach, invite, help, warn, like, love, hate, allow, permit, remind, cause, mean, dare.*

Pattern 10

Subject + verb + gerund

	Subject	Verb	Gerund, etc.
1.	She	began	singing.
2.	He	has finished	talking.
3.	I	hate	borrowing money.
4.	You	mustn't miss	seeing him.
5.	Mr Bannerjee	loves	teaching.
6.	My brother	enjoys	playing cricket.
7.	I	suggest	burning that letter.
8.	—	Don't keep	saying that.

In this pattern, the gerund is the object of the verb. The chief verbs used in this pattern include *begin, start, love, like, hate, stop, finish, enjoy, prefer, fear, remember, forget, mind, miss, suggest, practise, try, understand, keep, help, advise, admit, avoid, consider, intend, delay, deny.*

Pattern 11

Subject + verb + noun/pronoun + present participle

	Subject	Verb	Noun/Pronoun	Present Participle
1.	I	saw	him	crossing the bridge.
2.	We	smell	something	burning.
3.	We	noticed	the boy	walking down the street.
4.	She	caught	him	opening your letters.
5.	They	found	him	playing cards.
6.	She	kept	the fire	burning.
7.	—	(Please) start	the clock	going.

The verbs used in this pattern include *see, hear, smell, feel, watch, notice, find, observe, listen, get, catch, keep, leave, set, start.*

Pattern 12

Subject + verb + noun/pronoun + plain infinitive

	Subject	Verb	Noun/ Pronoun	Plain infinitive
1.	I	saw	him	go out.
2.	She	watched	him	steal the watch.
3.	We	heard	her	sing.
4.	The thief	felt	someone	touch his arm.
5.	—	Let	me	go.
6.	We	made	Tom	behave well.
7.	He	bade	them	leave the house.

The chief verbs used in this pattern are : *see, watch, notice, observe, hear, listen, feel, make, let, help, bid.*

Pattern 13

Subject + verb + noun/pronoun + past participle

	Subject	Verb	Noun/ Pronoun	Past Participle
1.	I	heard	my name	called.
2.	I	want	this letter	typed.
3.	She	felt	herself	lifted up.
4.	You	should get	that tooth	pulled out.
5.	He	had	his suit	cleaned.
6.	We	found	the house	deserted.

The verbs used in this pattern are : *see, hear, find, feel, want, wish, like, make, prefer, get, have.*

Pattern 14

Subject + verb + noun/pronoun + (to be +) complement

The complement may be an adjective, adjective phrase or noun.

	Subject	Verb	Noun/ Pronoun	(to be +) Complement
1.	I	consider	the plan	(to be) unwise.
2.	We	thought	him	(to be) foolish.
3.	People	supposed	him	(to be) a patriot.
4.	They	reported	Robert	(to be) a reliable person.
5.	The court	appointed	her	guardian of the orphan child.
6.	The club	chose	Mr Sunder	treasurer.
7.	She	called	him	a fool.

The chief verbs used in this pattern are : *appoint, choose, elect, make, call, name, nominate, crown, christen.*

Pattern 15

Subject + verb + that-clause (object of the verb)

	Subject	Verb	that-clause (object of the verb)
1.	I	suppose	(that) he is not at home.
2.	I	expect	(that) it will rain.
3.	We	hoped	(that) you would succeed.
4.	He	says	(that) he has met your uncle.
5.	The teacher	said	he was very busy.
6.	Padma	suggested	that we should go to the park.
7.	He	admitted	that he had written the letter.
8.	They	complained	that they had not been fairly treated.

That is often omitted, especially after *say, think, suppose, hope, expect.*

Among the important verbs used in this pattern are *say, think, suppose, imagine, know, believe, admit, confess, declare, suggest, complain, hope, expect, fear, feel, hear, intend, notice, propose, show, understand, wonder.*

Pattern 16

Subject + verb + noun/pronoun + that-clause

	Subject	Verb	Noun/ Pronoun	that-cluase
1.	He	told	me	(that) he was coming on Sunday.
2.	I	warned	him	that there were pickpockets in the crowd.
3.	She	has assured	me	that she is ready to help.
4.	Venu	promised	us	that he would be here at five.
5.	We	have informed	him	that we are leaving this afternoon.
6.	He	satisfied	me	that he could do the work well.

The chief verbs used in this pattern are *tell, inform, promise, warn, remind, teach, assure, satisfy.*

Pattern 17

Subject + verb + interrogative + clause

	Subject	Verb	Interrogative + clause
1.	I	asked	where he was going.
2.	Nobody	knows	when he will arrive.
3.	I	wonder	what he wants.
4.	She	showed	how annoyed she was.
5.	Tom	could not decide	what he should do next.
6.	I	can't imagine	why she has behaved like that.
7.	–	Find out	when the train is due.

The important verbs used in this pattern are *say, ask, wonder, know, believe, imagine, decide, discuss, understand, show, reveal, find out, suggest, tell* (especially in the interrogative and negative).

Pattern 18

Subject + verb + noun/pronoun + interrogative + clause

	Subject	Verb	Noun/ Pronoun	Interrogative + clause
1.	She	asked	me	when you had gone.
2.	–	Tell	us	what it is.
3.	I	showed	them	how they should do it.
4.	–	(Please) advise	me	what I should do.
5.	–	(Please) inform	me	where I should turn off the road.
6.	Can	you tell	me	where he lives?

The chief verbs used in this pattern are *tell, ask, show, teach, advise, inform.*

Pattern 19

Subject + verb + interrogative + to-infinitive

	Subjet	Verb	Interrogative + to-infinitive, etc.
1.	I	don't know	how to do it.
2.	I	wonder	where to spend the weekend.
3.	She	knows	how to drive a car.
4.	He	forgot	when to turn.
5.	Tom	couldn't decide	what to do next.
6.	We	must find out	where to put it.
7.	–	Remember	how to do it.

The commonest verbs used in this pattern are *know, understand, wonder, remember, forget, decide, settle, find out, enquire, see, explain, guess, learn, consider.*

Pattern 20

Subject + verb + noun/pronoun + interrogative + to-infinitive

	Subject	Verb	Noun/ Pronoun	Interrogaive + to-infinitive
1.	I	shall show	you	how to operate it.
2.	He	has taught	me	how to play chess.
3.	They	informed	us	where to turn off the road.
4.	–	(Please) advise	me	what to do.
5.	–	(Please) tell	us	how to get there.
6.	We	asked	him	where to get tickets.

The chief verbs used in this pattern are those illustrated in the table.

EXERCISE 126

Make up five sentences on each of the patterns. (Do not copy the examples given in the tables.)

Chapter 31 QUESTION TAGS, SHORT ANSWERS, ETC.

(1) **Question Tags.** It is a common practice in conversation to make a statement and ask for confirmation ; as, 'It's very hot, isn't it?' The later part ('isn't it ?') is called a question tag. The pattern is (*i*) auxiliary+*n't* +subject, if the statement is positive, (*ii*) auxiliary + subject, if the statement is negative.

(*i*) It's raining, isn't it ?
You are free, aren't you ?
She can swim well, can't she ?
Gopi broke the glass, didn't he ?
Your sister cooks well, doesn't she ?

(*ii*) You aren't busy, are you ?
She can't swim, can she ?
Mohan doesn't work hard, does he ?
They haven't come yet, have they ?

Note that the subject of the question tag is always a pronoun, never a noun.

Note these peculiarities:

I am right, aren't I?
Let's go to the beach, shall we?
Wait a minute, can you?
Have some more rice, will you?
There is a mosque in that street, isn't there?
There are some girls in your class, aren't there?
Somebody has called, haven't they?

(2) **Short Answers.** The following is the most usual form of short answers to verbal questions (*i.e.,* questions beginning with an auxiliary).

Yes + pronoun + auxiliary
Or : *No* + pronoun + auxiliary + *n't* (*not*)

Are you going to school ?	Yes, I am. / No, I am not.
Can you drive a car ?	Yes, I can. / No, I can't.
Is your son married ?	Yes, he is. / No, he isn't.
Does Venu work hard ?	Yes, he does. / No, he doesn't.
Did he say anything ?	Yes, he did. / No, he didn't.

(3) **Agreements and Disagreements with Statements.** Agreements with affirmative statements are made with *Yes/So/Of course* + pronoun + auxiliary.

It is a good film. —Yes, it is.
Mohan has already come. —So he has.

He can speak Hindi very well. —Of course he can.

He looks dishonest. —Yes, he does.

Agreements with negative statements are made with *No* + *pronoun* + auxiliary + *n't/not.*

The apples aren't good. — No, they aren't.
She doesn't like fish. No, she doesn't.
He can't help coughing. No, he can't.
They haven't played well. No, they haven't.

Disagreements with affirmative statements are made with *No/Oh no* + pronoun + auxiliary + *n't/not. But* is used in disagreement with a question or an assumption.

He is drunk. —No, he isn't.
You are joking. —Oh no, I'm not.
Why did you beat him ? —But I didn't.
I suppose she knows Bengali. —But she doesn't.

Disagreements with negative statements are made with (*Oh*) *yes*/(*Oh*) *but* + pronoun + auxiliary.

You can't undestand it. —Yes, I can.
He won't come again. —But he will.
You don't know him. —Oh yes, I do.
I didn't break it. —Oh but you did.

(4) **Additions to Remarks.** Affirmative additions to affirmative remarks are made with *So* + auxiliary + subject.

Anand likes oranges. So do I.
She must go home. So must I.
He was late for the meeting. So were you.
I've finished my homework. So has my sister.

Negative additions to negative remarks are made with *Nor/ Neither* + auxiliary + subject.

Ramesh doesn't like sweets. Nor do I.
He didn't believe it. Neither did I.
I can't do the sum. Nor can my father.
Tom wasn't there. Neither was Peter.

Negative additions to affirmative remarks are made with *But* + subject + auxiliary + *n't/not.*

He knows German. But I don't.
I understood the joke. But Mary didn't.
He knows how to cook. But his wife doesn't.
I can play chess. But my brother can't.

Affirmative additions to negative remarks are made with *But* + subject + auxiliary.

He doesn't know her. But I do.
I didn't see the film. But Gopi did.
He can't play cricket. But I can.
She wasn't late. But you were.

EXERCISE 127

Add question tags to the following.

1. It's very hot today, _____?
2. You like him, _____?
3. Kishore will come, _____?
4. We must hurry, _____?
5. He will never give up, _____?
6. Your father is a doctor, _____?
7. You have tea for breakfast, _____?
8. I didn't hurt you, _____?

9. You aren't going out, _____?
10. They have sold the house, _____?
11. I needn't get up early tomorrow, _____?
12. It isn't ready yet, _____?
13. Gopal hasn't passed the exam. _____?
14. They will go home soon, _____?
15. He didn't paint it himself, _____?

EXERCISE 128

Answer the following questions (*a*) in the affirmative, (*b*) in the negative.

1. Can you swim ?
2. Do you like sweets ?
3. Are you angry with me ?
4. Is it going to rain ?
5. Am I in your way ?
6. Does your father smoke ?
7. Did you go to college yesterday ?
8. Will they be at the cinema ?
9. Is Suresh staying with his uncle ?
10. Has he met you ?

EXERCISE 129

I. Agree with the following statements, using *Yes/So/Of course* + pronoun + auxiliary.

1. Children like playing.
2. He has left already.
3. My aunt came yesterday.
4. They are playing beautiful music.
5. Mr. Mukherji knows ten languages.
6. Abdul has come to see you.

II. Agree with the following statements, using *No* + pronoun + auxiliary + *n't/not*.

1. He doesn't like tea.
2. You haven't played well.
3. Your brother doesn't look his age.
4. She didn't complain.
5. He can't speak English fluently.
6. Ramesh didn't attend the party.

III. Disagree with the following statements. (Use the pattern *No/Oh no/But* + pronoun auxiliary + *n't/not*).

1. He lied.
2. She has promised to obey you.
3. Why have you spoiled my pen ?
4. The boy will hurt himself.
5. I suppose he is honest.
6. You are in the wrong.

IV. Disagree with the following statements, using the pattern (*Oh*) *yes*/(*Oh*) *But* + pronoun + auxiliary).

1. You can't do the sum.
2. Radha doesn't like you.
3. He isn't reading.
4. She won't come.
5. I am not in your way.
6. I don't know where you went.

EXERCISE 130

I. Add to the following remarks either freely or using the suggestions in brackets. (Pattern : *So* + auxiliary + subject)

1. Venu came late. (Gopi)
2. My friend lives in Mumbai. (his sister)
3. Oranges were very dear. (bananas)
4. I've read the book. (my brother)
5. Madhu can speak Tamil. (his wife)
6. I must leave today. (you)

II. Add to the following remarks, either freely or using the suggestions in brackets. (Pattern : *Nor/Neither* + auxiliary + subject)

1. I don't like meat. (my wife)
2. She could't help laughing. (I)
3. This book doesn't belong to me. (that)
4. Monday's debate wasn't very interesting. (Wednesday's)
5. She doesn't know me quite well. (her husband)
6. You didn't notice him. (I)

III. Add contradictory statements to the following, either freely or using the suggestions in brackets. (Pattern : *But* + subject + auxiliary + *n't/not*)

1. He can type well. (I)
2. I won the election. (my friend)
3. My sister can speak Marathi. (I)
4. I like playing chess. (she)
5. He knows me well. (his brother)
6. Hindi is easy to learn. (English)

IV. Add contradictory statements to the following either freely or using the suggestions in brackets. (Pattern : *But*+subject+auxiliary)

1. I don't know Telugu. (my wife)
2. My sister doesn't like films. (I)
3. He won't leave tomorrow. (We)
4. I didn't do the homework. (others)
5. He didn't thank me. (she)
6. I didn't know the way. (my friend)

Chapter 32 MORE STRUCTURES

(1) Preparatory *There* + *be* + subject

	There + be	*Subject, etc.*
1.	There is	a book on the desk.
2.	There is	a hotel near the station.
3.	There is	a lamp beside the bed.
4.	There was	someone at the door.
5.	There are	twelve months in a year.
6.	There are	plenty of pins in a drawer.

The structure '*There* + *be* ......' is generally used when the subject is indefinite, *i.e.*, when the subject is preceded by *a, an, some, much, many, a few,* etc.

(2) *to*-infinitive after adjectives expressing emotion or desire.

	Subject + verb	*Adjective*	*to-infinitive, etc.*
1.	We were	glad	to see him.
2.	She is	afraid	to go alone.
3.	My brother is	eager	to join the army.
4.	I shall be	happy	to accept your invitation.
5.	He was	anxious	to meet you.
6.	They are	impatient	to start.

(3) *It* + *be* + adjective + *of* + noun/pronoun + *to*-infinitive.

	It + be	*Adjective*	*Of + noun/ pronoun*	*to-infinitive, etc.*
1.	It is	kind	of you	to help us.
2.	It was	clever	of Mohan	to find his way here.
3.	It was	careless	of her	to make a mistake.
4.	It was	unwise	of me	to lend him money.
5.	It was	foolish	of Mr Ramesh	to accept the offer.
6.	It is	wicked	of him	to say such things.

The following adjectives can be used in this pattern : *kind, good, generous, considerate, foolish, stupid, unwise, clever, wise, nice, wrong, polite, brave, cowardly, silly, wicked, cruel, careless,* etc.

(4) *to*-infinitive after *easy, difficult, hard, impossible,* etc.

	Subject + verb	*Adjective*	*to-infinitive, etc.*
1.	This book is	easy	to read.
2.	This rug is	difficult	to wash.
3.	His actions are	impossible	to justify.
4.	The subject is	hard	to understand.
5.	His speech was	difficult	to follow.
6.	The food is	difficult	to digest.
7.	This medicine is	pleasant	to take.

(5) *It* + *be* + adjective + *to*-infinitive

	It + be	*Adjective*	*to-infinitive, etc.*
1.	It is	easy	to learn Hindi.
2.	It will be	difficult	to give up smoking.
3.	It may be	difficult	to get the job.
4.	It is	bad	to borrow money.
5.	It is	cruel	to treat animals in that way.
6.	It was	impossible	to lift the box.

(6) *It* + *be* + *no good, etc.* + gerundial phrase

	It + be	*Gerundial Phrase*
1.	It is no good	asking him for help.
2.	It was no good	talking to her.
3.	It's no use	worrying about it.
4.	It is worth	seeing the film.
5.	It was worthwhile	seeing the exhibition.
6.	It is amusing	watching monkeys.
7.	It has been a pleasure	meeting you.

(7) *It* + *be* + *adjective/noun* + *noun clause*

	It + be	*Adjective/ Noun*	*Noun Clause*
1.	It is	strange	that he should have behaved like that.
2.	It is	likely	that there will be rain this afternoon.
3.	It is	possible	that he doesn't understand Hindi.
4.	It is	doubtful	whether he will be able to come.
5.	It is	a pity	that you didn't try harder.
6.	It was	fortunate	that you escaped the accident.
7.	It is	a mystery	who can have taken my book.

(8) *It* + *to take* + *me, him, etc.* + *time phrase* + *to-infinitive*

	It + to take	*Time phrase*	*to-infinitive, etc.*
1.	It took me	fifteen minutes	to reach the stadium.
2.	It will take you	only five minutes	to walk to the park.
3.	It took him	two months	to recover from his illness.
4.	It will take us	ten minutes	to get there.
5.	It took me	one year	to learn Kannada.
6.	It has taken me	one hour	to write my composition.

(9) *too* + *adjective/adverb* + *to-infinitive*

	Subject + verb	*too + Adjective/ Adverb*	*to-infinitive, etc.*
1.	She is	too weak	to carry the box.
2.	I am	too busy	to attend the party.
3.	He talks	too fast	to be understood.
4.	My sister is	too young	to go to school.
5.	She is	too proud	to listen to me.
6.	The boy is	too lazy	to work.
7.	He worked	too slowly	to be of much use to me.

(10) *Adjective/Adverb + enough + to-infinitive*

	Subject + verb	*Adjective/ Adverb + enough*	*to-infinitive, etc.*
1.	She is	strong enough	to carry the box.
2.	He is	clever enough	to understand it.
3.	The police ran	fast enough	to catch the burglar.
4.	You are	old enough	to know better.
5.	She was hit	hard enough	to be knocked down.
6.	He is	tall enough	to reach the picture.
7.	She is	stupid enough	to believe us.

(11) *So + adjective/Adverb + that-clause*

	Subject + Verb	*so + adjective/ adverb*	*that-clause*
1.	It is	so dark	that I can see nothing.
2.	He talks	so fast	that you can hardly follow him.
3.	The box fell	so heavily	that it was broken.
4.	It was	so hot	that we had to postpone our trip.
5.	He was	so furious	that he couldn't speak.
6.	He walked	so quickly	that we couldn't catch him up.
7.	I was	so tired	that I couldn't walk any further.

(12) *Patterns of exclamatory sentences*

(i) *What + (adjective +) noun (+ subject + verb)*

	What(+Adjective+) Noun	*(Subject+Verb)*
1.	What a charming girl	(she is) !
2.	What a lovely garden	(it is) !
3.	What a good idea !	
4.	What a terrible noise !	
5.	What a fool	you are !.
6.	What a (large) nose	he has !
7.	What beautiful music	they are playing !
8.	What a pity !	

(ii) *How + Adjective/Adverb + Subject + Verb*

	How+Adjective/Adverb	*Subject+Verb*
1.	How charming	she is !
2.	How lovely	the garden is !
3.	How clever	you are !
4.	How sweet	the song is !
5.	How tall	you have grown !
6.	How well	she dances !
7.	How quickly	the holiday has passed !

(13) *Conditionals* : *Type* 1 (*open condition*)

	If-clause *Simple Present*	*Main clause* *Will/shall/can may+plain infinitive*
1.	If you study hard	you will get a first class.
2.	If it rains	we shall postpone our picnic.
3.	If I find the pen	I shall give it to you.
4.	If he runs all the time	he can get there in time.
5.	If her uncle arrives	she may not come with you.
6.	If you hit the dog	it will bite you.

Conditionals of this type tell us that something will happen if a certain condition is fulfilled. The condition may or may not be fulfilled.

(14) *Conditionals* : *Type 2* (improbable or imaginary condition)

	If-clause *Simple Past (subjunctive)*	*Main clause* *would/should/could/might + plain infinitive*
1.	If you studied hard	you would get a first class.
2.	If I were you	I should not do that.
3.	If we started now	we could be in time.
4.	If you were a millionaire	how would you spend your time ?
5.	If he stopped smoking	he might get fat.
6.	If I had a degree	I could get a job easily.

Conditionals of this type are used when we talk about something which we don't expect to happen or which is purely imaginary.

(15) *Conditionals* : *Type 3* (Unfulfilled condition)

	If-clause *Past perfect*	*Main clause* *would/should/could/might +* *perfect infinitive*
1.	If you had studied hard	you would have got a first class.
2.	If I had tried again	I should have succeeded.
3.	If I had seen him	I could have saved him from drowning.
4.	If you had left that wasp alone	it might not have stung you.
5.	If you had come to me	I would not have got into trouble.

Conditionals of this type say that something did not happen because a certain condition was not fulfilled.

EXERCISE 131

Make up five sentences on each of the patterns.

Part IV

Composition

Written Composition

The knowledge of grammar and sentence construction acquired in the preceding sections can be put to real use in this section. The following chapters aim to help you build up your communication skills.

Good communication skills will increase your chances of success in many aspects of life. You can't communicate effectively if you are merely able to produce correct sentences. You should be able to form a number of related or connected sentences in real-life situations. You should learn to write a paragraph, a letter, an essay, a story, etc. This section provides plenty of guidance and practice in such forms of composition. Unity, order and clarity: these are the main characteristics of good writing in general. You must practise a lot. You can learn to write **by writing.**

The chapters on comprehension and precis writing contain ample practice material. Precis writing is a good exercise in both reading and writing. Practice in precis writing is of great value for practical life. In any position of life the ability to grasp what is read or heard, and to reproduce it clearly and briefly, is of the utmost value.

The chapter on dialogue writing is specially geared towards students who need to improve their spoken English. For further guidance in conversational English, read H. Martin's **English Dialogues** (S. Chand & Co. Ltd.).

Exercises in paraphrase, expansion of passages and reproduction of story poems integrate comprehension and writing skills.

It is hoped that when you finish this book you will find yourself capable using English effectively and confidently in all situations.

PART IV: WRITTEN COMPOSITION

Chapter 33 PARAGRAPH–WRITING

If you look at any printed prose book, you will see that each chapter is divided up into sections, the first line of each being indented slightly to the right. These sections are called Paragraphs. Chapters, essays and other prose compositions are broken up into paragraphs, to make the reading of them easier, for the beginning of a new paragraph marks a change of topic, or a step in the development of an argument or of a story. In writing essays or other compositions, it is important to know how to divide them properly into paragraphs; for an essay not so broken up, looks uninteresting and is not easy to read.

Definition— A paragraph is a number of sentences grouped together and relating to one topic; or, a group of related sentences that develop a single point.

These definitions show that the paragraphs of a composition are not mere arbitrary divisions. The division of a chapter into paragraphs must be made according to the changes of ideas introduced.

There is, therefore, no rule as to the length of paragraphs. They may be short or long according to the necessity of the case. A paragraph may consist of a single sentence, or of many sentences.

Note— In this respect, the paragraphs of a piece of prose differ from the stanzas or verses of a poem. The stanzas of a poem are usually of the same length and pattern; but paragraphs are long or short according to the amount of matter to be expressed under each head.

Principles of Paragraph Structure

1. *UNITY*—The first and most important principle to be observed in constructing a paragraph is that of *Unity.* Just as each sentence deals with one thought, each paragraph must deal with *one topic or idea*— and *with no more than one.* In writing an essay, for example, every head, and every sub-head, should have its own paragraph to itself. And every sentence in the paragraph must be closely connected with the main topic of the paragraph. The paragraph and every part of it must be the expression of one theme or topic.

   Note— A good practice is to read a chapter in a book, and give a short heading or title to each paragraph, which will express in a word or brief phrase the subject of the paragraph.

   The topic, theme or subject of a paragraph is very often expressed in one sentence of the paragraph—generally the first. This sentence is called the *topical sentence* (because it states the topic), or the *key-sentence* (because it unlocks or opens the subject to be dealt with in the paragraph).

2. *ORDER*—The second principle of paragraph construction is *Order* —that is, *logical sequence of thought* or development of the subject. Events must be related in the order of their occurrence, and all ideas should be connected with the leading idea and arranged according to their importance or order.

Note— The two most important sentences in the paragraph are the first and the last. The first, which should as a rule be the topical sentence, should arouse the interest of the reader; and the last should satisfy it. The first, or topical, sentence states the topic—a fact, a statement, or a proposition; the last should bring the whole paragraph on this topic to a conclusion, or summing up.

3. *ARIETY*—A third principle of paragraph construction is ***Variety***; by which is meant that, to avoid monotony, the paragraph of a composition should be of different lengths, and not always of the same sentence construction.

To sum up: the essentials of good paragraph construction are— (1) Unity. (2) A good topical sentence. (3) Logical sequence of thought. (4) Variety. (5) A full and rounded final sentence in conclusion.

EXAMPLES

Now let us examine a few paragraphs by standard authors, in illustration of these principles of paragraph construction.

1. "Hence it is that it is almost a definition of a gentleman to say he is one who never inflicts pain. This description is both refined and, as far as it goes, accurate. He is mainly occupied in merely removing the obstacles which hinder the free and unembarrassed action of those about him; and he concurs with their movements rather than takes the initiative himself. His benefits may be considered as a parallel to what are called comforts or conveniences in arrangements of a personal nature, like an easy chair or a good fire, which do their part in dispelling cold and fatigue, though nature provides both means of rest and animal heat without them." *—J.E. Newman.*

This is a paragraph from Cardinal Newman's famous description of a "Gentleman" in his *The Idea of a University.* Notice that the paragraph is confined to *one point* in the character of a gentleman, which is clearly stated in the first, or *topical sentence viz.,* that "he is one who never inflicts pain." The rest of the paragraph is simply a development and illustration of the topical sentence. And the concluding sentence drives home the statement of the subject with its similies of the easy chair and the good fire.

2. "The Road is one of the great fundamental institutions of mankind. Not only is the Road one of the great human institutions because it is fundamental to social existence, but also because its varied effects appear in every department of the State. It is the Road which determines the sites of many cities and the growth and nourishment of all. It is the Road which controls the development of strategies and fixes the sites of battles. It is the Road that gives its framework to all economic development. It is the Road which is the channel of all trade, and, what is more important, of all ideas. In its most humble function it is a necessary guide without which progress from place to place would be a ceaseless experiment; it is a sustenance without which organised society would be impossible, thus the Road moves and controls all history." *—Hilaire Belloc.*

In this paragraph, the first sentence states the subject. It is the topical sentence. The body of the paragraph consists of examples which prove the statement in the first sentence. The final sentence sums up the whole.

3. "Poetry is the language of the imagination and the passions. It relates to whatever gives immediate pleasure or pain to the human mind. It comes home to the bosoms and businesses of men; for nothing but what comes home to them in the most general and intelligible shape can be a subject for poetry. Poetry is the universal language which the heart holds with nature and itself. He who has a contempt for poetry cannot have much respect for himself, or for anything else. Wherever there is a sense of beauty, or power, or harmony, as in the motion of a wave of the sea, in the growth of a flower, there is poetry in its birth." *—William Hazlitt.*

Here again, the first sentence is the topical sentence. The sentences that follow enforce or restate the statement that "poetry is the language of the imagination and the passions"; and the concluding sentence reinforces it by showing that poetry exists wherever men feel a sense of beauty, power or harmony.

In all these paragraphs, the principles of Unity and Order are observed, and also the general rules about the place of the topical sentences and the rounding off the whole with a good conclusion.

The Writing of Single Paragraphs

So far we have been treating of paragraphs which are sections of a more or less lengthy composition, like an essay or the chapter of a book. But students are often asked in examinations to write short separate paragraphs, instead of essays, on subjects of ordinary interest. Such single paragraphs are really miniature essays ; but the same principles as we have discussed above (except the principle of variety), must be followed in their construction. Each paragraph must be a unity, treating of one definite subject, and must follow a logical order of thought. In most cases, too, the rules about the topical sentences and the conclusion should be borne in mind.

A few examples should make this clear. Suppose, for example, you are asked to write a paragraph on "The Cat." It is obvious that you cannot treat this subject fully, as you might in a long essay. And yet you must, according to the principle of unity, confine your paragraph to one definite topic. You must, therefore, choose one thing to say about a cat, and stick to it throughout. You might, for example, write of one characteristic of the cat, say, its love of comfort and attachment to its home. In that case, you might write a paragraph something like this:–

The Cat

There is some truth in the common saying that while dogs become attached to persons, cats are generally attached to places. A dog will follow his master anywhere, but a cat keeps to the house it is used to ; and even when the house changes hand, the cat will remain there, so long as it is kindly treated by the new owners. A cat does not seem to be capable of the personal devotion often shown by a dog. It thinks most of its own comfort, and its love is only cupboard love.

Notice the construction of this paragraph. It begins with the topical sentence, which clearly states the subject. The following sentence explains the statement by expanding it; and the last sentence, by giving a reason for the attachment of a cat to a particular house forms a fitting conclusion. The paragraph is therefore a Unity, treating of one characteristic of cat character: and it follows an orderly plan.

The paragraph on the cat is descriptive. Now take an example of a narrative paragraph, in which you are required to tell a story. Suppose the subject is to be a motor-car accident ; you might treat it in this way.

A Car Accident

It is the mad craze for speed that is responsible for many motor accidents. Only last year I witnessed what might have been a fatal accident on the Kashmir Road. I was motoring down from Srinagar; and as I was nearing Kohala, I came upon the wreckage of two cars on the road. The smash had been caused by a car coming down, which swept round a sharp corner at forty miles an hour and crashed into a car coming up. Happily no one was killed ; but several were badly injured, and the two cars were wrecked. To drive at such a speed down a twisting mountain road is simply to court disaster.

In this paragraph, the topical sentence is again first ; the narrative that follows is simply an illustration of the statement in the topical sentence that many accidents are caused by a mad craze for speed; and the concluding sentence sums the paragraph up by a restatement of the topical sentence in other words.

The following is an example of a reflective paragraph ; that is, one that expresses some reflection or thought on an abstract subject.

Mercy

To forgive an injury is often considered to be a sign of weakness ; it is really a sign of strength. It is easy to allow oneself to be carried away by resentment and hate into an act of vengeance; but it takes a strong character to restrain those natural passions. The man who forgives an injury proves himself to be the superior of the man who wronged him, and puts the wrong-doer to shame. Forgiveness may even turn a foe into a friend. So mercy is the noblest form of revenge.

The topical sentence of a paragraph is usually the first, or at latest the second; and this is the best place for it. But for the sake of variety it may be placed in a different position. In this paragraph, it comes last—"So mercy is the noblest form of revenge". But the opening sentence is also a good introduction to the subject, and is calculated to arouse interest by stating an apparent paradox.

To sum up: In writing single paragraphs, the principles of Unity and Order must be kept in mind, and also the rules of the topical and concluding sentences. The language should be simple, the style direct, and the sentences short; and, as a paragraph is limited, all diffuseness must be avoided.

EXERCISE 132

Write short paragraphs on the following subjects.

1. A Rainy Day. 2. A Walk. 3. The Cow. 4. Trees. 5. Politeness. 6. Anger. 7. A Picnic. 8. A Fire. 9. A Flood. 10. Some Pet Animal. 11. Rivers. 12. Cricket. 13. Contentment. 14. Gymnastics. 15. Gratitude. 16. A Holiday. 17. The Elephant. 18. The Cobra. 19. The Tailor. 20. The Astronaut. 21. Revenge. 22. Thrift. 23. Stars. 24. The Crow. 25. Robots. 26. To-day's Weather. 27. Your Hobby. 28. Humility. 29. The Mango. 30. Examinations.

Chapter 34 STORY WRITING

To tell even a simple story well requires some practice. An uneducated person generally tells a tale badly. He does not mentally look ahead as he tells it and plans it out. So he repeats himself, omits important items, which he drags in afterwards out of place, and dwells too long on minor details and fails to emphasise the leading points. To write a good story, you must have the whole plot clear in your mind, and the main points arranged in their proper order.

In this exercise you are not asked to make up a story. The plot of each story is given to you, more or less fully, in the outlines provided. But an outline is only a skeleton; it is your work to clothe the skeleton with flesh and breathe life into it. You must try to produce a connected narrative, and to make it as interesting as you can.

HINTS

1. As has been already said, see that you have a clear idea of the plot of the story in your mind before you begin to write.
2. Follow the outline given; *i.e.,*do not omit any point, and keep to the order in which the points are given in the outline.
3. Be careful to connect the points given in the outline naturally, so that the whole will read well as a connected piece of good composition. Otherwise the whole will be disconnected and jerky. You must use your imagination in filling in the details of action, gesture and conversation that should connect one point with the next.
4. Where possible, introduce dialogue or conversation; but be careful to make it natural and interesting.
5. The conclusion of a story is important. The whole story should be made to lead up to it naturally, and then it should come as a bit of surprise.
6. If you are asked to supply a heading or title to the story, you may choose the main character, object or incident of the story (*e.g.,*"The Barber of Baghdad," or "The Pot of Olives,"or "An Accident"); or, a proverb or well-known quotation that suits the story (*e.g.,*"No pains, no gains," "Sorrow's Crown of Sorrow", etc.)
7. See that your composition is grammatical and idiomatic and in good simple English. Revise your work, and if necessary rewrite it, until it is as good as you can make it.

Specimen Outline

Boy set to guard sheep—told to cry "Wolf!" if he sees a wolf near the flock—watches the sheep for several days—gets tired of the monotonous work—so one day shouts "Wolf !" as a joke—all the villagers hasten to his help-they find no wolf—boy laughs at them—villagers angry—plays the same joke a few days later—some villagers take no notice-some come runing—finding nothing, they beat the boy—at last wolf really comes—boy is terrified and shouts "Wolf ! Wolf'—villagers take no notice—wolf kills several sheep

Complete Story

The Boy Who Cried "Wolf !"

One of the boys in a village was sent out into fields to look after the sheep.

"Mind you take care of them and don't let them stray," said the villagers to him.. "And keep a good look out for wolves. Don't go far away : and if you see a wolf coming near the sheep, shout out 'Wolf!' as loudly as you can, and we will come at once to help you."

"All right !" said the boy, "I will be careful."

So every morning he drove his sheep out to the hillside and watched them all day. And when evening came, he drove them home again.

But after a few days he got rather tired of this lonely life. Nothing happened and no wolves came. So one afternoon he said to himself: "These villagers have given me a very stupid job. I think I will play a trick on them just for fun."

So he got up and began shouting as loudly as he could, "Wolf ! Wolf !"

The people in the village heard him, and at once they came running with sticks.

"Wolf ! Wolf !" shouted the boy; and they ran faster. At last they came up to him, out of breath.

"Where is the wolf ?" they panted. But the boy only laughed and said: "There is no wolf. I only shouted in fun. And it was fun to see you all running as hard as you could !"

The men were very angry.

"You young rascal !" they said. "If you play a trick like that again, we will beat you instead of the wolf."

And they went back to their work in the village.

For some days the boy kept quiet. But he got restless again, and said to himself: "I wonder if they will come running again if I cry 'Wolf !' once more. It was such fun the last time."

So once more he began shouting , "Wolf ! Wolf !"

The villagers heard him. Some said, "That boy is up to his tricks again." But others said, "It may be true this time ; and if there really is a wolf, we shall lose some of our sheep."

So they seized their sticks, and ran out of the village to the hillside.

"Where is the wolf ?" they cried, as they came up.

"Nowhere !" said the boy laughing. "It was fun to see you running up the hill as fast you could."

"We will teach you to play jokes," shouted the angry men; and they seized the boy and gave him a good beating, and left him crying instead of laughing.

A few days later a wolf really did come. When the boy saw it, he was very frightened and began shouting "Wolf ! Wolf ! Help ! Help !" as loudly as he could.

The villagers heard him, but they took no notice.

"He is playing his tricks again," they said. "We won't be made fools for a third time. You can't believe a boy after you have caught him lying twice."

So no one went to his help, and the wolf killed several sheep and frightened the boy nearly out of his wits.

EXERCISE 133

Construct readable stories from the following outlines.

1. An old lady becomes blind—calls in a doctor —agrees to pay large fee if cured, but nothing if not—doctor calls daily—covets lady's furniture—delays the cure—every day takes away some of her furniture—at last cures her—demands his fees—lady refuses to pay, saying cure is not complete—doctor brings a court case—judge asks lady why she will not pay—she says sight not properly restored—she cannot see all her furniture—judge gives verdict in her favour—moral
2. A jackal wants crabs on the other side of a river—wonders how to get across—tells camel there is sugarcane the other side—camel agrees to carry him across in return for the information—they cross—jackal finishes his meal—plays trick on camel—runs round the fields howling—villagers rush out—see camel in sugarcane—beat him with sticks—camel runs to river—jackal jumps on his back—while crossing, camel asks jackal why he played him such a trick—jackal says he always howls after a good mea —camel replies he always takes a bath after a good meal—rolls in the river—jackal nearly drowned—tit-for-tat

3. A son is born to a Rajah—the mother dies in childbirth—a young mother with a baby is chosen as nurse—she nurses both babies together—enemies of the Rajah plot to kill his son—they bribe the guards and get into the palace—the nurse is warned just in time—quickly changes the children's dresses—leaves her own child dressed as prince and flies with real prince—murderers enter room and kill the child left behind—so prince is saved—Rajah offers nurse rewards—she refuses them and kills herself—Rajah grieved—erects splendid tomb for the faithful nurse

4. A miser loses a purse of a hundred pieces of gold—in great distress—goes to town crier—crier says he must offer a reward—offers reward of ten pieces of gold—the crier announces this —a few days later a farmer comes to the miser—he has picked up the purse—returns it to miser—miser counts the money—a hundred pieces of gold—thanks the farmer—the farmer asks for the reward—miser says there were a hundred and ten pieces in the purse, so the farmer has already taken his reward of ten pieces—they quarrel—farmer appeals to the judge—the judge hears the case, and asks for the purse—sees that it only just holds a hundred pieces—decides it cannot be the miser's purse—so gives the purse to farmer—the miser had overreached himself
5. A king distressed—his people lazy—to teach them a lesson he had a big stone put in the middle of the road one night—next day merchants pass and go round it—an officer driving in his carriage did the same—a young soldier came riding, did the same—all cursed the stone and blamed the government for not removing it—then the king had the stone removed—under it was an iron box, marked, "*For the man who moves away the stone*"—inside a purse full of money—the people were ashamed

6. Tiger kills an Indian lady travelling through the jungle—as he eats her body, he notices her gold bangle—keeps it as he thinks it may be useful—later he hides himself by a pool—traveller comes to pool, dusty and tired—strips and bathes in cool water—sees the tiger in bushes watching him—terrified—tiger greets him with a mild voice—says he is pious and spends time in prayer—as a sign of goodwill, offers the traveller the gold bangle—traveller's greed overcomes his fear—crossed pool to take bangle—tiger springs on him and kills him

7. A young man setting out on a journey—accompanied part way by an old man—they part under a pipal tree—young man asks old man to keep Rs. 100 for him till he returns—old man agrees and takes money—old man says he never gave him any to keep—young man takes him before judge—judge sends young man to summon tree to court—a long time away—judge asks old man, "Why?"—old man says tree is long way off—judge sees that the old man knows which tree it is—when young man returns, judge gives verdict in his favour
8. A poor Brahmin travelling through forests—comes across a tiger caught in a trap—tiger begs him to let him out—Brahmin in pity does so—tiger knocks him down—Brahmin pleads for his life and says the tiger is ungrateful—tiger agrees that he may appeal to three things against tiger—Brahmin first asks a pipal tree—tree says all men are ungrateful—tree gives them shade and they cut its branches—Brahmin next asks the road—the road says that in return for its services men trample on it with heavy boots—Brahmin then asks a buffalo—buffalo says her master beats her and makes her turn a Persian wheel—Brahmin in despair—consults a jackal—jackal asks how tiger got into cage—tiger jumps in to show him—jackal shuts cage and walks away with Brahmin
9. Baghdad merchant, about to go with a caravan to Damascus, suddenly falls ill—entrusts his bales of silk to a camel-driver—says he will go to Damascus as soon as he is well—will pay camel-driver when he arrives—camel-driver waits in Damascus—merchant does not come—camel-driver sells the silk for a large sum—shaves his beard, dyes his hair and dresses in fine clothes—Baghdad merchant at last arrives—searches all Damascus for camel-driver—one day recognises him—camel-driver pretends to be a merchant of Samarkand—Baghdad merchant brings him before the judge—judge decides he can do nothing, as there are no witnesses—as camel-driver leaves court, judge suddenly calls out "Camel-driver !"—he stops and turns round—judge puts him in prison, and makes him pay money to Baghdad merchant

10. A slave in ancient Carthage—cruel master—slave runs away into desert—sleeps that night in a cave—waked up by terrible roar—sees lion coming into cave—terrified—but lion quite gentle—holds up wounded paw—slave takes out a big thorn—lion grateful and wags his tail—slave and lion live together as friends—at last slave homesick—goes back to Carthage—is caught by his master—condemned by judge to be thrown to lions—thousands go to amphitheatre to see man fight lion— slave brought out—lion rushes to attack him—but when he sees slave lies down and licks his feet—same lion—great astonishment—governor sends for slave—hears his story—frees slave and gives him the lion

11. King Solomon noted for his wisdom—Queen of Sheba heard of his fame—came to visit him—impressed by his wealth and grandeur—wanted to test his power of solving puzzles—showed him two garlands of flowers, one in right hand and one in left—one real, the other artificial—asks, "Which is which?"—courtiers puzzled—both garlands look the same—Solomon silent—Queen feels triumphant—Solomon ordered windows to be opened—bees flew in from garden—buzzed about the Queen—all settled on garland in her right hand—Solomon said the flowers in right hand real, in left hand artificial—Queen impressed with his wisdom

12. Ship of pirate becalmed near rocky coast—pirate sees bell fastened to dangerous submerged rock—asks what it is—is told it was placed there to warn sailors in storms—thinks it would be a joke to take the bell—rows across in boat to rock—they cut the chain and sink the bell—wind rises and they sail away—years after pirate returns to same coast—sea covered with fog and storm rising—pirate does not know where he is—a terrible crash—ship strikes on the same rock—as they go down the pirate realizes his ship wrecked on the same rock—wishes he had left the bell alone

13. Rich nobleman gives a grand feast—many guests—his steward tells him a fisherman has brought a fine fish—nobleman tells him to pay him his price—steward says his price is a hundred lashes—nobleman thinks this a merry jest—sends for fisherman—fisherman confirms steward's report—nobleman agrees—fisherman quietly receives fifty lashes—then stops—says, he has a partner to whom he promised half the price—"Who is he ?"— nobleman's porter—"Why ?"—porter refused to let him in if he did not agree—porter brought in and given the other fifty lashes—guests enjoy joke—nobleman rewards fisherman

14. Ali, a barber in Baghdad—Hassan, a wood-seller—Hassan brings Ali load of wood on a donkey—they bargain about the price—at last Ali offers so much for "all the wood on the donkey's back"—Hassan agrees—unloads the wood—Ali claims donkey's wooden saddles—Hassan protests—quarrel—Ali seizes saddle and drives Hassan away with blows—Hassan appeals to Khalif—Khalif gives him advice—some days later Hassan goes to Ali's shop—asks Ali to shave him and a friend for so much—Ali agrees—shaves Hassan first—"Where is your friend?"—"Outside"—Hassan fetches in his donkey—Ali refuses to shave donkey—drives Hassan away—Hassan reports to Khalif—Khalif sends for Ali—forces him to fulful his bargain—Ali has to shave Hassan's friend, the donkey, before all the courtiers—great laughter, and shame for Ali

Chapter 35 REPRODUCTION OF A STORY-POEM

What you have to do in these exercises, is to tell in your own words the story which is told in a poem. The first thing, then, is to read the poem as a story, so that you know what the story is; and the next is, to tell the same story over again in your own words and your own way.

HINTS

1. Read the whole poem through, slowly and carefully. If after the first reading, the story is not quite clear, read the poem again, and yet again, until you feel you understand it thoroughly.

2. Write down briefly the chief facts of the story, in order to guide you in your narration. Do not leave out any important point.
3. Now try to write out the story in simple, straightforward English, telling the incidents of the story in their natural order.
4. Do not copy the language of the poem. You must use your own words in telling the story. But do not try to use the fine language; be simple and choose plain words.
5. When you have finished the exercise, read it through to see whether you have left out any important fact, or have stated any wrongly.
6. Finally, examine your composition for mistakes in spelling, grammar and punctuation. And see that your sentences are properly constructed, and that the whole composition reads well.

Specimens

1. Tell concisely in the form and style appropriate to a prose-narrative the story of the following poem.

The Glove And The Lions

King Francis was a hearty king, and loved a royal sport ;
And one day, as his lions strove, sat looking on the court ;
The nobles filled the benches round, the ladies by their side,
And 'mongst them Count de Lorge, with one he hoped to make his bride.
And truly 'twas a gallant thing, to see the crowning show.
Valour and love, and a king above, and the royal beasts below.
Ramped and roared the lions, with horrid laughing jaws ;
They bit, they glared, gave blows like beams, and went with their paws ;
With wallowing might and stifled roar they rolled one on another,
Till all the pit, with sand and mane was in a thund'rous smother ;
The bloody foam above the bars came whizzing through the air ;
Said Francis then, "Good gentlemen, we're better here than there !"
De Lorge's love o'erheard the king, a beauteous lively dame,
With smiling lips, and sharp bright eyes, which always seemed the same ;
She thought, "The Count, my lover, is as brave as brave can be ;
"He surely would do desperate things to show his love of me !
"King, ladies, lovers all look on ; the chance is wondrous fine ;
"I'll drop my glove to prove his love ; great glory will be mine !"
She dropped her glove to prove his love ; then looked on him and smiled;
He bowed, and in a moment leaped among the lions wild ;
The leap was quick ; return was quick ; he soon regained his place–
Then threw the glove, but not with love, right in the lady's face !
"Well done!" cried Francis, "bravely done !" and he rose from where he sat :
"No love," quoth he, "but vanity, sets love a task like that !"

Reproduction

The Glove and the Lions

King Francis was a great lover of all kinds of sport ; and one day he and his courtiers, noblemen and ladies, sat watching wild savage lions fighting each other in the enclosure below. Amongst the courtiers sat Count de Lorge beside a beautiful and lively lady of noble birth whom he loved and hoped to marry. The lions roared, and bit and tore each other with savage fury, until the king said to his courtiers, "Gentlemen, we are better up here than down there !"

The lady, hearing him, thought she would show the king and his court how devoted her lover was to her : so she dropped her glove down among the fighting lions, and then looked at Count de Lorge and smiled at him. He bowed to her, and leaped down among the savage lions without hesitation, recovered the glove, and climbed back to his place in a few moments. Then he threw the glove right in the lady's face.

King Francis cried out, "Well and bravely done ! But it was not love that made you lady set you such a dangerous thing to do, but her vanity !"

2. Tell the story of Leigh Hunt's "Plate of Gold" in five short paragraphs.

THE PLATE OF GOLD

One day there fell in great Benares' temple-court
A wondrous plate of gold, whereon these words were writ :
"To him who loveth best, a gift from Heaven."
Thereat
The priests made proclamation : "At the midday hour,
Each day, let those assemble who for virtue deem
Their right to heaven's gift the best ; and we will hear
The deeds of mercy done, and so adjudge."
The news
Ran swift as light, and soon from every quarter came
Nobles and munshis, hermits, scholars, holy men,
And all renowned for gracious or for splendid deeds,
Meanwhile the priests in solemn council sat and heard
What each had done to merit best the gift of Heaven.
So for a year the claimants came and went.
At last,
After a patient weighing of the worth of all,
The priests bestowed the plate of gold on one who seemed
The largest lover of the race—whose whole estate,
Within the year, had been parted among the poor.
This man, all trembling with his joy, advanced to take
The golden plate—when lo! at his first finger touch
It changed to basest lead ! All stood aghast ; but when
The hapless claimant dropped it clanging on the floor,
Heaven's guerdon was again transformed to shining gold.
So for another twelve months sat the priests and judged,
Thrice they awarded—thrice did Heaven refuse the gift
Meanwhile a host of poor, maimed beggars in the street
Lay all about the temple gate, in hope to move
That love whereby each claimant hoped to win the gift.
And well for them it was (if gold be charity),
For every pilgrim to the temple gate praised God.
That love might thus approve itself before the test.
And so the coins rained freely in the outstretched hands ;
But none of those who gave, so much as turned to look
Into the poor sad eyes of them that begged.
And now
The second year had almost passed, but still the plate
Of gold, by whomsoever touched, was turned to lead.
At length there came a simple peasant—not aware
Of that strange contest for the gift of God—to pay
A vow within the temple. As he passed along
The line of shrivelled beggars, all his soul was moved
Within him to sweet pity, and the tears welled up
And trembled in his eyes.

Now by the temple gate
There lay a poor, sore creature, blind, and shunned by all ;
But when the peasant came, and saw the sightless face
And trembling, maimed hands, he could not pass, but knelt,
And took both palms in his, and softly said ; "O thou,
My brother ! bear the trouble bravely. God is good.''
Then he arose and walked straightway across the court,
And entered where they wrangled of their deeds of love
Before the priests.
A while he listened sadly ; then
Had turned away ; but something moved the priest who held
The plate of gold to beckon to the peasant. So
He came, not understanding, and obeyed, and stretched
His hand and took the sacred vessel. Lo ! it shone
With thrice its former lustre, and amazed them all !
"Son", cried the priest, "rejoice. The gift of God is thine.
Thou lovest best !'' And all made answer, "It is well."
And, one by one, departed. But the peasant knelt
And prayed, bowing his head above the golden plate ;
While o'er his soul like morning streamed the love of God.

Reproduction

The Plate of Gold

One day a wonderful plate made of gold fell from Heaven into the court of a temple at Benares ; and on the plate these words were inscribed: "A gift from Heaven to him who loves best." The priests at once made a proclamation that every day at twelve o'clock, all who would like to claim the plate should assemble at the temple, to have their kind deeds judged.

Everyday for a whole year all kinds of holy men, hermits, scholars and nobles came, and related to the priests their deeds of charity, and the priests in solemn council heard their claims. At last they decided that the one who seemed to be the greatest lover of mankind was a rich man who had that very year given all his wealth to the poor. So they gave him the plate of gold. but when he took it in his hand, it turned to worthless, lead; though, when he dropped it in his amazement on to the floor, it became gold again. For another year claimants came; and the priests awarded the prize three times. But the same thing happened, showing that Heaven did not consider these men worthy of the gift.

Meanwhile a large number of beggars came and lay about the temple gate, hoping that the claimants who came would give them alms to prove they were worthy of the golden plate. It was a good time for the beggars, because the pilgrims gave them plenty of money ; but they gave them no sympathy, nor even a look of pity.

At last a simple peasant, who had heard nothing about the plate of gold, came ; and he was so touched by the sight of the miserable beggars, that he wept ; and when, he saw a poor blind and maimed wretch at the temple gate, he knelt at his side and took his maimed hands in his and comforted him with kind words. When this peasant came to the temple, he was shocked to find it full of men boasting of their kind deeds and quarrelling with the priest. One priest, who held the golden plate in his hand, seeing the peasant standing there, beckoned to him ; and the peasant came, and knowing nothing about the plate, took it in his hands. At once it shone out with three times its former splendour, and the priests said : "Son, the gift is yours : for you love best."

EXERCISE 134

1. Tell in your own words the story of Leigh Hunt's "Abou Ben Adhem," What is the moral of the legend? [Wren's "Lotus Book of English Verse", No. 128. Wren's "Story Poems", No. 20.].
2. Imagine yourself to be King Bruce, and tell the story of "King Bruce and the Spider" ["Lotus", No. 5. "Story Poems", No. 10]
3. Tell the story of "Bishop Hatto" in a letter to a friend ["Lotus", No. 59. "Story Poems", No. 37]
4. Tell at length the story told in Campbell's "Adelgitha," supplying details left out by the poet. ["Story Poems" No. 62]

5. Tell in your own words the story of "The Blind Men and the Elephant" as told by J.G. Saxe. ["Lotus", No. 16. "Story Poems", No. 1.]
6. Tell the story of Southey's "Inchcape Rock" in your own words. ["Lotus", No. 60. "Story Poems", No. 9]
7. Tell the story of "Androcles and the Lion", as related by Androcles. ["Story Poems", No. 14.]
8. Tell the story of Browning's "Incident of the French Camp" in your own words. ["Lotus", No. 108. "Story Poems", No. 21.]
9. Relate in a few plain sentences the bare facts narrated in W. R. Spencer's "Beth Gelert". ["Lotus", No. 51. "Story Poems", No. 36.]
10. Rewrite the story of "The Fisherman and the Porter", as told by the fisherman. ["Story Poems", No. 39.]
11. Tell the story of Leigh Hunt's "Mahmoud", using the dialogue form for the conversational parts. ["Lotus", No. 61. "Story Poems", No. 41]
12. Put yourself in the place of Ibrahim, and tell the story told in Lowell's "Yussouf" from his point of view. ["Lotus", No. 62. "Story Poems", No. 42.]
13. Tell the story narrated in Trench's "Harmosan," as told by a member of the Caliph's retinue. ["Lotus", No. 63. "Story Poems", No. 43.]
14. Read the poem "John Maynard", and then describe in your own words the heroism of John Maynard. ["Story Poems", No. 55]
15. Imagine yourself to be the country mouse ; then tell the story of "The Town and the Country Mouse". ["Story Poems," No. 57]
16. The two poems, Campbell's "Earl March" and Scott's "Maid of Neidpath", are two versions of the same incident. Read both these poems and then tell in simple language the one story which both relate. ["Story Poems', Nos. 94 and 95.]
17. Tell in your own words the story of Thackeray's "Canute and the Tide". ["Lotus", No. 18. "Story Poems", No. 64.]
18. Tell in your own words the beautiful legend related in W. Bruce's poem "The Stranger". ["Story Poems", No. 81.]
19. Relate in your own words, the Talmudic legend about Solomon and the Bees as narrated in verse by J.G. Saxe. ["Lotus", No. 64. "Story Poems", No. 89.]
20. Relate in simple language and in the form of a dialogue the incident told in J. Merrick's "Chameleon". ["Lotus", No. 17. "Story Poems". No. 77.]

21. Tell the story of Hay's "Enchanted Shirt" in your own words. ["Lotus", No. 8. "Story Poems", No. 65.]
22. Tell in your own words the story of the jester who, condemned to death, saved his life by his wits. ["Story Poems". No. 72.]
23. Read Lowell's "Dara" : then relate in four paragraphs (*a*) the early life and rise of Dara ; (*b*) the jealousy which his rise excited ; (*c*) the incident of the chest and (*d*) the clearing of the suspicion about his integrity. ["Lotus", No. 66. "Story Poems". No. 66.

Chapter 36 LETTER–WRITING

Every educated person should know how to write a clear and readable letter. Everyone has sometimes to write business letters of some sort, and may have to face the problem of writing an important letter that will vitally affect his interests in life. The art of letter-writing is, therefore, no mere ornamental accomplishment, but something that every educated person must acquire for practical reasons.

I. The Form Of Letters

Letters are messages, and certain *letter-forms* have been established by experience and custom as the most useful forms learned and used by every letter-writer, for neglect of them is a sign of ignorance and carelessness. There are several different kinds of letters (such as friendly letters, business letters, etc.) each of which has its own particular form ; but there are certain matters of form which apply to all, and these may be explained first.

In all kinds of letters there are six points of form to be attended to, namely :–

1. The Heading consisting of *(a)* the writer's address and *(b)* the date.
2. The courteous Greeting or Salutation.
3. The Communication or Message—The body of the letter.
4. The Subscription, or courteous Leave-taking, or Conclusion.
5. The Signature.
6. The Superscription on the envelope.

1. ***The HEADING***— This informs the reader *where* you wrote the letter, and *when.* The *where* (which should be the writer's full postal address) gives the address to which the reader may reply ; and the *when* is for reference, as it gives him the *date* on which you wrote.

The position of the heading is the top right-hand corner of the first page—the address above and the date just below it. The heading and the date may alternatively go on the left.

24 Poorvi Marg
New Delhi 110 057
10 October 2001

The date may be written in any of the following ways:

4 June 2001	4-6-2001	To a British person this means the fourth of
4th June 2001	4.6.2001	June; to an American it means the sixth of April.
June 4, 2001	4/6/2001	(Americans put the month before the day.)

2. ***SALUTATION or Greeting***— The form of Greeting will depend upon the relation in which you stand to the person to whom you are writing.

To members of your family, for example, it will be–
Dear Father, My dear Mother, Dear Uncle, Dear Hari, etc.
To friends, it will be–
Dear Shri Desai, or *Dear Desai,* or *Dear Ramchandra, etc.*
To business people, it will be–
Dear Sir, Dear Sirs, etc.
[Full examples will be given for each kind of letter later.]

Note— The use of the term *Dear* is purely formal, and is a mere polite expression, not necessarily implying any special affection.

The position of the Salutation is at the left-hand of the first page, at a lower level than the Heading.

3. ***The COMMUNICATION or Body of the letter***— This is, of course, the letter itself, and the style in which it is written will depend upon the kind of letter you wish to write. The style of a letter to an intimate friend will be very different from that of a purely business letter or an official communication. But a few hints that apply to all letters are given below.

(a) *Divide your letter* (unless it is very short) *into paragraphs,* to mark changes of Subject-matter, etc.

(b) *Use simple and direct language* and short sentences. Do not try to be eloquent, and drag in long words, just because they are long words. Be clear about what you want to say, and say it as directly as possible.

(c) *Try to be complete.* It is a sign of slovenly thinking when you have to add postscripts at the end of a letter. Think out what you want to say *before* you begin to write ; and put down your points in some logical order.

(d) *Write neatly.* Remember that your correspondent has to read what you write, and do not give him unnecessary trouble with bad penmanship and slovenly writing.

(e) *Mind your punctuation,* and put in commas and semicolons and fullstops in their proper places. Incorrect punctuation may alter the whole meaning of a sentence.

4. ***The SUBSCRIPTION or courteous Leave-taking***—A letter must not end abruptly, simply with the writer's name. This would look rude. So certain forms of polite leave-taking are prescribed. Such as—

Yours sincerely, Your sincere friend, Yours faithfully, etc.

[Different leave-taking forms are used in different kinds of letters, and these will be given under their proper heads.]

The subscription, or Leave-taking phrase, must be written below the last words of the letter, and to the right side of the page. This is the traditional method. Note that today there is a growing tendency to place the subscription on the left side.

> **Note**—The first word of the Subscription must begin with a capital letter ; e.g.,

Sincerely yours

5. ***The SIGNATURE or name of the writer.***— This must come below the Subscription. Thus :

Yours sincerely,

K.R. Deshpande

In letters to strangers, the signature should be clearly written, so that the reader may know whom to address in reply. A woman should prefix to the name *Miss* or *Mrs* (or: *Kumari* or *Smt*) in brackets. *Ms* can be used by a woman who does not wish to be called Miss or Mrs.

Yours faithfully,

(Mrs.) J.L. Desai

6. ***The address on the envelope (or postcard):*** The address on the envelope or postcard should be written clearly, like this:

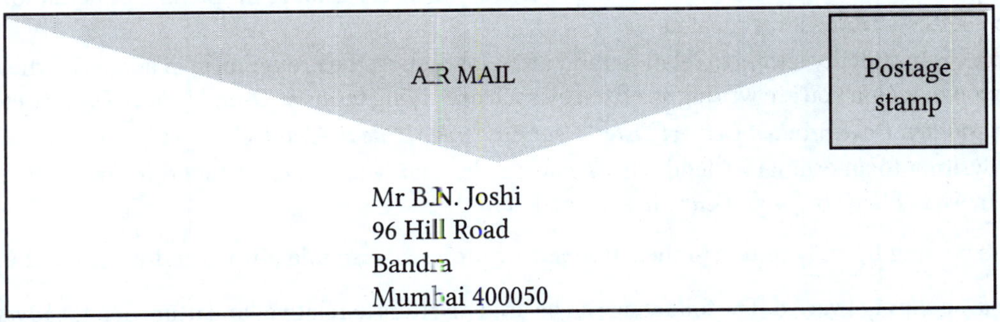

To sum up:

In writing a letter, first write your address and under it the date in the top right-hand corner of the first page. You may alternating write them on the left.

Then write the Salutation (*e.g., Dear Shri Desai,*) lower down at the left side of the page, beginning with a capital and putting a comma after it.

Next begin your letter (with a capital letter) on the next lower line, to the right of the salutation.

At the end of the letter write the Subscription, or words of leave-taking (*e.g., Yours sincerely*), at right/left side of the page, with your signature below it.

For example:

16 North Usman Road
Chennai 600 017
4 October 2001

Dear Sir,

I shall be much obliged if you send me as soon as possible the books which I ordered a week ago.

Yours faithfully,

Abdul Ghani

II. Classification Of Letters

Letters may be classified according to their different purposes. Thus :

(1) Social Letters, including Friendly Letters and Notes of Invitations.

(2) Business Letters; including Letters of Application, Letters to Government Officers and Letters to Newspapers.

These have different characteristics which must be considered.

I. Social Letters

1. FRIENDLY LETTERS

Letters to relations and intimate friends should be written in an easy, conversational style. They are really of the nature of friendly chat; and, being as a rule unpremeditated and spontaneous compositions, they are informal and free-and-easy as compared with essays. Just as in friendly talk, so in friendly letters, we can touch on many subjects and in any order we like ; and we can use colloquial expressions which would in formal essays be quite out of place. But this does not mean that we can be careless and slovenly in dashing off our letters, for it is insulting to ask a friend to decipher a badly-written, ill-composed and confused scrawl; so we must take some care and preserve some order in expressing our thoughts. Above all, it must be remembered that, however free-and- easy may be our style, we are just as much bound by the rules of spelling, punctuation, grammar and idiom in writing a letter as we are in writing the most formal essay. Such ungrammatical expressions as "an advice" "those sort of things" and "he met my brother and I," are no more permissible in a friendly letter than in a literary article. Mistakes in spelling, punctuation and grammar at once stamp a letter-writer as uneducated.

Forms of address—In friendly letters to relations and intimate friends, the proper form of address is the name (without title) of the person to whom you are writing, prefixed by such qualifying terms as *Dear, My dear, Dearest,* etc. For example: *Dear Father* or *Mother, Dear Brother, Dearest Sister, Dear Edward, My dear Abdul,* etc.

But if you are writing to an ordinary friend who is much older than you are, or of superior rank, it is respectul to use a prefix like Mr, Mrs, Shri etc., *e.g. Dear Mr Krishna Rao.*

N.B.—Students writing friendly letters to their teachers or professors, should always address them thus.

The forms of subscription are varied. The following can be used in letters to relatives and near friends : *Yours affectionately, Your affectionate* (or *loving*) *son,* or *brother* or *friend, Yours very sincerely* (to friends) ; or you can use some such form as this :

With love and best wishes,
From your affectionate friend,
Ahmad Hassan

In concluding letters to friends or acquaintances whom you address as "Shri or Mr ......" (*e.g., My Dear Shri Durga Prasad*) you should use the word *sincerely* or *very sincerely,* in the subscription ; and this may be preceded by *With kind* (or *very kind* or *kindest*) *regards.* Thus:

With kind regards,
Yours sincerely,
Chaman Lal

N.B.— *Sincerely* should not be used in letters beginning with the formal *Dear Sir,* after which the proper word of subcription is *faithfully* or *truly.*

[To your uncle on his 70th birthday]

18 Patel Road,
Mumbai 400014.
24 Sept. 2001

My dear Uncle,

I have just remembered that it is your birthday on Saturday and so I must send you a birthday letter at once. And I begin with the old greeting, Many happy returns of the day ! I hope the day itself will be peaceful and happy for you and that you will be spared in happiness and health to us all for years yet. You have always been a kind and generous uncle to me, and I take this opportunity of thanking you from the bottom of my heart for all you have done for me. And I know all your nieces and other nephews feel the same.

I was so glad to hear from father that you are still hale and hearty, and can take your four-mile walk every day, and still play a good set of tennis.

I am sending you a book which I think you will like. You were always a great reader, and I am glad that your eyesight remains as good as ever—so father says.

I am getting on well in my business and hope to enlarge it considerably before the end of the year.

With love and best wishes,

Your loving nephew,

Sohrab

[From a boy in a boarding-school to his mother, telling her that he dislikes the life of a boarder.]

St. Dominics,
Pune 411 002.
24th October, 2001

Dearest Mother,

I was so glad to get your letter yesterday. Thank you so much! I read it just after morning school ; but it made me feel very homesick. It seems years since I left home though it is really only about a month. It seems ages to the Christmas holidays, when I shall be able to come home. It was much nicer when I was at the day-school, and came home every afternoon.

I do hate being a boarder. I am in a big dormitory, with about twenty other boys. Some of them are all right ; but the bigger boys are always playing nasty jokes on us smaller ones ; and we daren't say anything, or we should get a most awful kicking. The master comes round to see all lights out, but all the larking goes on after he has gone; so he knows nothing about it. And I don't like the masters. They simply make you work all day, and cane you for every fault. Most of the boys are horrid ; but I like two or three.

Please ask Dad to put me into a day-school again. I would be much happier there.

With Love,

Your loving son,

Tommy

[The mother's reply]

Hill-top House,
Matheran,
26th October, 2001

My dear Tommy,

Thank you for your letter. But I am sorry you are so unhappy at St. Dominic's. I don't wonder you feel rather home-sick, for it is the first time you have been away from home ; and I, too, often want you home again, my child. But you know, we can't always have what we want in life. If I were selfish, I would keep you always at home. for I don't like any of my children to be away ; but then how would you ever get your education and grow up to be a man able to manage your own life ? Your father thinks that a few years at a boarding-school is necessary for all boys, to make men of them ; and he knows best.

So my dear boy, you must be brave and stick to your school. I am sure you will soon get to like it, as other boys do. Don't mind the jokes boys play on you, and if you do, don't let them know you do. When they see you don't mind, they will soon get tired of teasing you. So cheer up ! and be a brave laddie.

With much love,

Yours lovingly

Mummy

EXERCISE 135

Write a short letter.

1. To your cousin, requesting the loan of a camera during your holidays.
2. From a boy in a boarding-school to his mother who is keeping poor health.
3. To your father, who has been away from home for a fortnight, about anything of interest that has taken place in his absence.
4. To your cousin about what particularly pleased you at the circus.
5. From a boy at a boarding-school to his parents on the approaching vacation.
6. From a son to his father, stating how he hopes to fare in the approaching School-Leaving Examinat
7. To your younger brother, scolding him for having neglected his studies.
8. Reply to the above.
9. From a mother to her daughter, on receiving a bad report from her boarding-school.
10. Reply to the above.
11. You have recovered from a long illness. Write about your experience in bed etc., to your cousin.
12. You have been delayed one night by a railway accident near a small country out-station. Write a letter home relating your experience.

[To a friend in a hospital]

Race Cottage
Lucknow-226 003
28th December, 2001

Dear Mela Ram,

I have only just heard from your brother that you have been ill in the hospital for the last two weeks. I am very sorry. If I had known, I should have written before. But I am glad to know that the worst is now over, and you are much better. He says he saw you the other day, and you were quite comfortable and cheery. I hope you will soon be all right, and coming out again. As soon as you can, write and let me know how you are.

Yours very sincerely,

Sant Ram

[To a friend, about your favourite game]

18 East Road,
Junglepore.
6th March, 2001

Dear Sharif,

Thanks for your letter, with your praises of cricket as the finest game in the world. I don't want to dispute that; but it is not my favourite. I have two favourite games, one for out-of-doors, and one for indoors.

For exercise and interest, I like tennis best of all outdoor games. Football and hockey are too violent to suit me ; cricket is too slow ; badminton is childish. But tennis gives you plenty of exercise ; it develops quickness of eye and limb ; and it calls your brain, your thinking power, into action. A few sets of tennis in the evening keep me physically and mentally fit.

For indoors, chess is the queen of games. I take no interest in card games ; and draughts after chess is like water after wine. People say chess is a selfish game, because only two can play at a time. Well, I don't see that bridge is only less selfish, simply because four play instead of two. They also say it is slow. No chess-player ever says this. For an outsider it may look slow to see two men sitting silent and making a move only every few minutes. But to the two players, it is all the time intensely exciting. There is no game that so absorbs you like chess.

You will probably scoff; but I don't mind.
Yours very sincerely,
Lal Khan

[To a friend, describing a football match in which you were referee]

54 Khazanchi Road,
Patna 800 004.
5 Jan. 2001

Dear Devi Prasad,

My advice to those who are about to act as football referees is—Don't! Why? Hear my sad story.

We have here two local teams called the Brilliants and the Valiants. They are easily the best teams in the district and in every tournament the fight in the end is between these two. And when their blood is up, they both fight to win, by fair means or foul— mostly foul. Moreover, the town is divided into two bitterly opposed factions—Brilliants and Valiants, who roll up, to the matches to cheer and jeer, and to see "fair" play.

The game had not long begun, before I had to turn off one of the Brilliants for foul play. The team protested, the crowd roared and things looked ugly ; but I stuck to my point, and they settled down. But they were sulky. Then the Valiants scored ; and the Brilliants looked sulkier still.

But the fun began when I awarded the Valiants a penalty kick close to goal, by which they promptly scored again. Then all the Brilliants rushed on to the field, yelling and shouting, and went for me. I was jostled, struck and kicked and knocked down; and the match came to an end in free fight between the two parties.

I am sitting up, nursing my wounds, and vowing, "No more refereeing for me!"

Yours in sorrow,

Kartikey

[To a friend, greeting him on the occasion of the Independence Day.]

Satpura Hostel,
Vindhyachal Block,
Varanasi - 221001.
10th July, 2002

Dear Satish

I hope this letter finds you in the best of spirits. It's time we exchanged greetings, for our nations will soon be celebrating the fifty-fifth Independence Day. My friends and I of Himalayan Academy, Rajganj would like to express our spirit of brotherhood and oneness on the occasion of the Independence Day.

May the internal and communal disturbances give way to religious tolerance, harmony and space. Since you are in a residential school, I suppose we will be celebrating it with a sense of patriotic discipline.

Let's nourish the spirit of Solidarity for now and all times to come.

Your loving friend,

Caramel Moghbelpoor

[Reply to the above]

Godavari House,
Sainik School,
Bhubaneshwar.
18th July, 2002

Dear Caramel

It was wonderful to see your letter in my mail box. As you rightly said, the future month August will soon see us marching for the Independence Day parade in our school as well as on the streets leading to the Governor's House.

The rehearsal session has started and we have little time to spare for other activities. Truly we have to motivate our little ones with patriotic favour and enthusiasm. Our country has withstood external aggressions and internal conflicts. We need to stand united in all such circumstances. I'm grateful to you for kindling the spirit of an ideal child as we would all be tomorrow's citizens.

Hope Martha is fine. I conclude this letter like a typical citizen of an honourable country.

JAI HIND

Satish Triphul

EXERCISE 136

Write a short letter.

1. To a friend, telling him how you play your favourite game, assuming that he knows nothing about it.
2. To a friend, describing your favourite hobby.
3. To a friend, describing a recent exciting cricket match in which your side won.
4. To a friend, describing a football match.
5. To a friend, describing a tennis tournament.
6. To your friend whom you are sending a photograph recently taken of your school football team, referring to some common friends in the group.
7. Reply to the above.
8. To a friend, describing your mishaps in an obstacle race in the shcool.
9. To a friend, describing a magic performance.
10. To a friend, describing a film which appealed to you very much.
11. To an English boy, describing the Indian Juggler.
12. To your friend, about some memory feats you have witnessed or heard about.
13. To a friend who has failed to take his defeat well.
14. Friend's reply to the above.
15. To your friend who did not "play fair".
16. Friend's reply to the above.
17. To a friend, expressing your preference for outdoor games.
18. Friend's reply, expressing preference for indoor games.
19. To your sister, about a real or imaginary flight in an aeroplane.

[To a friend, arranging for an excursion together]

5 Railway Road,
Allahabad.
15th May, 2001

Dear Smith,

We both have a holiday next Monday. What do you say to a trip to Murree and a ramble in the gullies? We could start early, say 6 a.m., in my car, and take some grub with us, and make a day of it up in the cool. It would be a change from this heat down here. If you agree, I will arrange the picnic, and be round at your house at quarter to six on Monday morning. Bring your camera with you.

Yours sincerely,

R.P. Brown

[Reply, accepting]

Circular Avenue,
Allahabad.
16th May, 2001

Dear Brown,

Many thanks for your invitation. I shall be delighted to go, and shall be ready for you at 5-45 a.m., next Monday. A day in Murree will be a grand change. Yes, I'll bring my camera, and hope to get some good snapshots.

Yours forever,

A.B. Smith

[Reply, regretting inability to join]

Circular Avenue,
Allahabad.
16th May, 2001

Dear Brown,

It is awfully good of you to propose a day's picnic at Murree. I only wish I could join you as I am sick of this heat. But I am sorry to say I shall not be able to get away, as I have already promised to see a friend in Jhelum next Monday. Thanks all the same.

Yours very sincerely,

A.B. Smith

[Write a letter of introduction for a friend to take to another friend who lives in a different part of the country. Say why you think each will enjoy knowing the other.]

5 Armernian Lane,
Kolkata 700 005.
7th February, 2001

My dear Haider Ali,

You have often heard me speak of my friend, Abdul Latif, who is a barrister here. He is an old friend of mine, and one for whom I have a great admiration. Well, he is going to Mumbai in a few days and will probably make a fairly long stay there. And as I want you two to meet and get to know each other, I am giving him this letter for you as an introduction. I am sure you will do your best to make his stay in Mumbai happy. At first you will do it for my sake ; but in the end you will do it for his also. For I know you will like him and both of you will find you have many interests in common.

Abdul Latif is, like you, very interested in social reform of all kinds. He also makes Islamic history a hobby, as you do. And, perhaps above all, he plays chess ; and you are a chess enthusiast. He is also a good tennis-player. So you should get on well together.

I hope you have got rid of your cold, and are keeping quite well.

Yours very sincerely,

Ghulam Samdani

[To your sister/friend about a real or imaginary flight in a space shuttle]

Cleveson Buildings,
North Campus,
FIIT, New Delhi.
28th Feb. 2000

Dear Anjali,

Hi.

I am delighted to know that you are going to do a project on Space Voyages. The other day, my teacher Shalini asked us to go on a Phantasy flight in a space shuttle to Venus.

Well, as advised by the NASA scientists, we did not eat anything in the first place. Before we went off into space we went through a rigorous 14-day training programme developed by the engineers of Russian Space Agency and tour operator Space Adventures. We also underwent an extensive medical examination and training on the Soyuz Simulator.

The first space traveller was Dennis Tito from the United States. Well, dear, fancying a holiday in space costs quite a fortune: twenty million United States dollars and a 14-day rigorous training programme.

Since one needs to wear a spacesuit. I had to bear the the heaviness of it with an oxygen cylinder and a mask. Added to the mask were helmets. The garment is designed to allow an astronaut to survive in space. However, there I enriched my vocabulary, by prefixing everything to 'space'. Space telescope, space time, space travel and space vehicle were perhaps some of the words which I learnt and I will be explaining the terms at length at a later date.

In short, I travelled in a space shuttle which is a rocket launched space craft able to land like an unpowered aircraft, used to make repeated journeys between the earth and the space station.

More in my next letter.

Yours lovingly,

Mahima

EXERCISE 137

Write a short letter.

1. To a friend, giving a brief description of a holiday tour you intend to make.
2. To a friend, telling him how you spent your summer vacation.
3. To your friend, about the longest journey made by you.
4. To an English friend giving him an idea of the life in your town or village.
5. To a friend, describing your visit to some notable public building.
6. A friend writes to say that he is spending a week in your town. Write a letter saying how sorry you are that you will be away, but telling him what he ought to see.

[From a boy to his friend who has met with an accident]

Old Gate,
Rampur,
1st April, 2001

My dear Ahmad,

Razak told me this morning that you had been knocked off your bicycle by a tonga yesterday and badly hurt. I am awfully sorry ; but I hope it is not really as bad as Razak made out. If you can write, please let me know how you are. Those tongawallas are awfully careless beggars. I had a nasty spill myself a few weeks ago in the same way. Happily no bones were broken. Mind you let me know how you are getting on.

Yours forever,

Karim

EXERCISE 138

Write a short letter.

1. To a friend, giving details of a railway accident (real or imaginary).
2. From a boarding-school girl to her friend, describing a terrible accident that happened to some of her friends while swinging.
3. To a friend, giving an account of a striking incident which happened to you or another.
4. To a friend, describing a thunderstorm in which you were recently caught.
5. To a friend, giving an account of a brave deed, real or imaginary, noticed by you in your street.
6. To a friend, about a striking example (real or imaginary) of presence of mind.

[To a schoolfellow who has been absent from school for a week]

High School,
Junglepore.
16th February, 2001

Dear Yaqub,

What is the matter with you ? You have not been at school for a week, and the Headmaster is asking where you are and what you are up to. I hope you are not ill. Please write, and say when you are coming back.

You missed the football match against the Mission School last Monday, and I can tell you the Captain was jolly cross when he found you were not there. Salim took your place. However, in spite of your absence, we won by two goals to one.

I hope you will soon be back again.

Yours sincerely,

Ahmed Din

EXERCISE 139

1. Write to a friend who needlessly runs down the school he used to attend some time ago.
2. It is a fortnight to your examination, and you are unprepared. Write to your friend about your difficulty.
3. Reply to the above.
4. Write a letter to your friend who works on Sundays as well as on other holidays.
5. "It is better to wear out than to rust out." Discuss this saying in a letter to a friend who holds this view.
6. "A short life and a merry one." Write a reply to a friend who holds this view.
7. Write to a friend who is exclusively occupied with his studies, advising him to take part in athletic games.
8. Write a letter of advice to a friend who complains that he does not know how to spend his spare time.
9. In a letter to your very intimate friend, write plainly about his faults ; also dwell upon the good points of his character.

[To the Subdivisional Officer Seeking for a Telephone Connection]

Aman Pandit,
G-114 B, Lajpat Nagar,
New Delhi.

To

The Sub Divisional Officer,
The Mahanagar Telecommunication Network Limited
Vikaspuri
New Delhi

Dear Sir,

I am a resident of Vikas Apartments at Lajpat Nagar, New Delhi. I am a new inhabitant of this region. I would be extremely grateful if you could kindly consider my application for installation of a new telephone connection as early as possible. Since I am a doctor by profession serving at the Indra Prastha Apollo Hospitals, I need the telephone connection urgently. My profession falls under the ESMA category (Essential Services Maintenance Act) which is of prime importance.

Thank you

Yours faithfully,

Aman Pandit

(Dr. Aman Pandit)

New Delhi

8th March, 2001

[Letter for issue of a Driving License]

From

Prema Vindhyachal,
66-B, Hill Part Drive,
I.I.T., Powai,
Mumbai.

To

The Transport Commissioner,
(Ministry of Road Transport),
Chatrapati Shivaji Building,
Mumbai.

Dear Sir,

I'm a resident of Powai and since I will be shortly driving to my place of work I need a driving license.

The registration number of my car is MLZ 9999. I'd be extremely grateful if you could kindly grant me a driving license. I can be contacted at the address given above. I would appreciate an early reply so that I can take a day off for my driving test.

Yours faithfully,

P. Vindhyachal

(Prema Vindhyachal)

Mumbai.

16th June 2001

[Letter accompanying a birthday present]

42 Ashok Marg
Lucknow 226 001
16 December 2001

My dear Charley,

It is your birthday on Saturday, so—Many happy returns of the day ! I am sending you a camera to celebrate the event, as I know you are keen on photography, and hope you will find it useful.

With all best wishes for the best of luck from your friend.

Tom

[Reply to the above]

26 M.G. Street
Ahmedabad 380 005
18 December 2001

My dear Tom,

Ever so many thanks for your good wishes and your jolly present. The camera is a beauty—just the kind I have been wanting for a long time. I shall be able to take some really fine pictures with it. Thank you very much !

Yours affectionately,

Charley

[To a friend who has recently lost his mother]

72 Patel Street
Mumbai 400 014
6 Jan. 2001

Dear Fred,

It was with real sorrow that I heard this morning of your great loss. I knew your mother was ill, for your brother told me several weeks ago ; but, as he at that time did not seem to think the illness was very serious, the news of your mother's death came to me as a shock. You have my sincere and heartfelt sympathy, my dear fellow, in your sorrow. I know you will feel it deeply, for you always thought so much of your mother and loved her so truly. I feel it also as a personal loss to myself ; for your mother was always very kind to me, and I admired her as a good and noble woman. Her death must be a terrible grief to your father, too ; please assure him also of my sincere sympathy.

Words, I know, are poor comforters. "The heart knoweth its own sorrow," and in such sorrows we are always alone. But it is not mere words when I say that I feel with you in your sorrow.

Your sincere friend,
Jack

[Reply to the above]

16 Church Street
Pune 411 003
9 Jan. 2001

My dear Jack,

Thank you very much for your most kind and sympathetic letter. You say that words are poor comforters; but the sympathy of true friends like yourself is a great comfort in times of sorrow ; and I am grateful to you for its expression.

Mother's death was a great shock to me, though I do not fully realize it even yet. We were always so much to each other ; and it is hard to face the fact that I must live the rest of my life without her.

Happily her end came very peacefully. She had no pain, and passed away quietly in her sleep.

She was fond of you, and spoke of you several times towards the end.

You will excuse me from writing more at present. I don't feel equal to it.

With many thanks, again from,

Your sincere friend,

Fred

[To a friend, from a girl who is going abroad with her father and mother]

Jaiprakash Nagar
Goregaon
Mumbai 400 062
10th March, 2001

My dear Nora,

I am awfully excited ! My daddy and mummy are going abroad on a long tour; and I am going with them. We shall be away for about two months. We are leaving on 20th.

We are going first to Hong Kong, where my father has some business. Then we are travelling to Japan. Think of it ! I shall see the Japanese and all their interesting ways. We shall stay there some time, and then fly to San Francisco. After that we are to travel to New York, and stay there for some time. Then we shall travel to England.

By the time we get home, I shall have seen half the world and will be a much travelled person.

I shall write you long letters from all the places we stay in and tell you of all the new and strange things we see.

With best wishes,

Very sincerely yours,

Naomi

EXERCISE 140

Write a short letter.

1. From a young man who has recently become possessed of a fortune left him by his uncle, to his intimate friend.
2. To a friend, advising him to insure his life.
3. To the same giving information about life-insurance.
4. To a friend, proposing the formation of a debating union.
5. Reply to the above.
6. To a friend, describing a pleasant dream.
7. To a friend, describing a horrid dream.
8. To a friend, giving an account of your favourite story-book or author.
9. To a friend, asking him to return a book which you lent him a long time ago. Couch your letter in such terms that your friend will not take offence.

10. To a friend, apologizing for not having kept an appointment.
11. To a sick friend, congratulating him on the good progress he is making.
12. To a sick friend in a hospital.
13. To a friend who has long been silent.
14. Reply to the above.
15. From a sister to her brother, decribing her visit to an orphanage.
16. To your uncle in Japan, asking for information about the habits and customs of the Japanese.
17. Reply to the above.
18. From a son to his father, asking permission to become a lawyer.
19. The father's reply to the above.

EXERCISE 141

1. Write a letter to a village-boy, your cousin, telling him what your town is like.
2. An uncle has sent you a present of Rs. 300. Write a letter thanking him and telling him how you propose to spend it.
3. Write a letter to your American friend to accompany a small model of the Taj Mahal at Agra which you are sending him.
4. Reply, referring to the sky-scrapers of New York.
5. Your friend is a member of a large family ; you are not. Write to him.
6. Reply to the above.
7. Write a letter to a friend, telling him that you have shifted to a new house, and describe your new neighbourhood.
8. In a letter to your sick friend, advise him to go to a hospital as, owing to various circumstances, he cannot be looked after properly at home.
9. Imagine that you have returned from a visit to your uncle. Write a letter, thanking him for his kindness and describing your journey.
10. Write a letter to a friend, describing a book you have just read and strongly recommending it to him.

2. Notes Of Invitations

A formal invitation is generally written in the third person, and should contain no heading, no salutation, and no complimentary close. The writer's name should appear in the body of the letter. The address of the writer and the date should be written to the left, below the communication.

The reply to such a note should also be in the third person, and should repeat the date and time mentioned in the invitation.

[Formal note of invitation]

Mr and Mrs V.A. Paul request the pleasure of Mr K. Gopalan's company at dinner on Friday, 14 July, at eight o'clock.

18 Peters Road

Chennai 600 014

[Formal note of acceptance]

Mr K. Gopalan has pleasure in accepting the kind invitation of Mr and Mrs V.A. Paul to dinner on Friday, 14 July, at eight o'clock.

12 Kamaraj Salai

Chennai 600 005

[Formal note of refusal]

Mr K. Gopalan regrets that a previous engagement prevents his accepting the kind invitation of Mr and Mrs V.A. Paul to dinner on Friday, July.

12 Kamaraj Salai

Chennai 600 005

Informal notes of invitation, acceptance and refusal are like ordinary friendly letters, though using more formal language. They are addressed to the recipient by name (My dear Shri Joshi), and the formal close is usually any of the following :—

Sincerely yours, Yours sincerely, Yours very sincerely, Yours affectionately (to relations, or intimate friends)

[Informal note of invitation]

12 Alwarpet
22 November

Dear Pramila,

Will you give me the pleasure of your company at dinner on Sunday, the 27th at 8 o'clock?

Yours sincerely,

V. Saroja

[Informal note of acceptance]

Poes Garden

23 November

My dear Saroja,

I shall be pleased to be with you at dinner on Sunday, the 27th. Thanks a lot for your invitation.

Yours sincerely,

S. Pramila

[Informal note of refusal]

Poes Garden
23 November

My dear Saroja,

I am very sorry that a previous engagement will prevent me from joining you at dinner on Sunday. Thank you very much for your kind invitation.

sincerely,

S. Pramila

II. Business Letters

Business letters should be terse, clear, and to the point. Businessmen are busy men, and have no time to read long, rambling and confused letters.

Business letters are naturally much more formal in style than friendly letters. Certain forms of polite expression are used, such as—

"I shall be much obliged if you will send me."

"Please despatch at your earliest convenience." etc.

At the same time certain phrases of business "jargon" should be avoided. They are commonly used, but are not good English ; and the meaning can be conveyed as clearly in simple, everyday language. Examples of such expressions are—

"Yours of even date to hand."

"Despatch same at once."

Avoid so far as possible abbreviations (like *advt.* for advertisement, *exam.* for examination, etc.) and the omission of *I* or *we* (*e.g.*, "Have received" instead of "We have received").

In business letters ordering goods, care should be taken to give clear and exact descriptions of the articles wanted. An itemized list of the goods wanted should be supplied, with the quality and quantity required.

Directions for forwarding should be given (by rail, post, etc.) and the manner in which payment will be made indicated (by Money Order, V.P.P., cheque, or by debiting to the writer's account). Everything should be clear and precise.

FORM—The form of business letters is the same as already described, with one addition, *viz.,* the Address (*i.e.,* the name of the firm or businessman to whom the letter is addressed), which should be written on the first page, lower down than the Heading and to the left of the page. (It may be placed at the end of the letter lower than the signature and at the left side of the page, but the usual position is at the beginning.)

MODES OF ADDRESS—The modes of address vary.

(1) To a tradesman:

Shri B.V. Rao
Bookseller
12 Ring Road
Bangalore

Begin *Dear Sir,* and conclude *Yours faithfully.*

(2) To a firm:

Messrs K.R. Das & Co.
Tea Merchants
24 Ring Road
Kolkata

Begin *Dear Sirs,* and conclude with *Yours faithfully.*

Note— If the firm has an impersonal title, Messrs should not be prefixed. For example : Eurasia Publishing House, Vijay Trading Co.

(3) To professional men or private gentlemen:

Mr. K. Bhaskar
Chartered Accountant
Pratibha House
Thiruvananthapuram 695 002
Mr. K.R. Misra
32 Bhandarkar Road
Pune 411 004

Begin *Dear Sir* or *My dear Sir,* and conclude *Yours faithfully, Yours truly,* etc. (not *Yours sincerely*).

When a clerk signs a business letter on behalf of his employer, he puts the letter p.p. (Latin *per pro* = on behalf of) or *for* before the name of the firm, and writes his signature beneath. For example:

Yours faithfully
For R. Gomes & Sons
K.S. Kumar

If a gentleman is entitled to be called *Honourable,* he is addressed, for example, as *The Hon. Shri K.R. Patil.*

N.B.—The title *The Hon.* cannot be used by itself ; you must not write *The Hon. K.R. Patil.*

REPLIES—In replying to a business letter, always quote the number of reference (if there is one) and the date of the letter you are answering. For example :

"In reply to your letter No. 502/P, dated July 26, 20......, I would like to say," etc.

[Example to show the form of a business letter]

16 Church Street
Anaparthi 533 341
14 Dec. 2001
The Manager

Southern Agency
Rajahmundry 533 101

Dear Sir,

I shall be grateful if you will kindly supply the following items of Godrej furniture:

1 almirah – model 2
3 chairs – model 4
2 chairs – model 6

1 table – model 101

Please send them carriage forward to the above address, and your bill will be paid on receipt.

Yours faithfully,

V.J. Manohar

(Letter to a bank manager asking him to stop payment of a cheque)

37 Nrupatunga Road

Bangalore 560 001

3 December 2001

The Manager

Indian Bank

Bengaluru 560 001

Dear Sir,

Would you please stop the payment of cheque 104662 dated 2 December ? I signed it in favour of Mr K. Ramakrishna, the sum was Rs. 500.

Yours faithfully,

K.V. Gokak

(Account no. 986)

Note—A cheque has to be stopped only where there is some good reason for it, such as fraud.

[Ordering a journal]

23 Patel Nagar
Gurgaon 122 001
Haryana
1 December 2001
The Business Manager
'Employment News'
East Block IV
Level-7, R.K. Puram
New Delhi 110 066

Dear Sir,

I enclose a draft for Rs. 120 for one year's subscription to your journal *Employment News*. Kindly arrange to put this order into effect immediately so that I may receive the next issue.

Yours faithfully,

Abdul Rahim

[From a shopkeeper to a customer, asking for the settlement of an overdue account]

Fashion and Style Ltd.
R.G. Street
Mumbai 400 012
5 Jan. 2001
Mr. V.N. Patil
43 Park Lane
Pune 411 004

Dear Sir,

We wish to call your attention to our bill for Rs. 16,500, payment of which is long overdue. We have sent you several reminders, but have received from you no reply. We must ask you to settle this account without further delay, or we shall be obliged to take legal steps to recover the amount due to us.

Yours faithfully,

S. Nazeeruddin

Manager

(Order for books)

16 Ring Road
Ravulapalem 533 238
30 November 2001
The Manager
Sudhitha Book Centre
Kakinada 533 001

Dear Sir,

I shall be grateful if you will send me by VPP one copy each of the following books (Collin's Retold classics, published by Messrs S. Chand & Company Ltd.) as early as possible.

1. David Copperfield
2. Huckleberry Finn
3. Treasure Island
4. Monte Cristo
5. Pickwick Papers

My address is as above.

Yours faithfully,

N. Chaitanya

EXERCISE 142

1. Write a letter to Messrs Babcock and Singer, complaining that the watch lately bought from them does not keep good time.
2. Write a letter to a landlord, asking that certain repairs be done to the house in which you are living.
3. During the last two weeks your baker has been supplying bread of a quality inferior to what you were getting previously. Write a letter calling his attention to this.
4. Draft out the baker's apology.
5. Write a letter to your baker, telling him not to deliver any bread while you are away on a holiday.
6. Shri Ramesh Bannerjee sends a letter to a firm, asking for their catalogues. The firm reply that the catalogues are being reprinted, and that they will send one as soon as possible. Write these two letters.
7. Write on behalf of your father to a house-agent about a suitable flat, stating clearly your requirements.

8. Write the house-agent's reply.
9. Write to the local Gas or Electric Company, saying that you need the light, etc., on your premises, and asking them to forward the lowest estimate. Do not forget to supply full particulars of your requirements.
10. You have sprained your ankle while playing football. Copy out the letter your father writes to your family doctor.
11. M.O. of Rs. 100 to your aunt—no reply from aunt—no receipt from Post Office. Write to the Post Master.
12. Write a letter to a railway company, complaining that your furniture has been damaged in transit, and claiming damages.
13. Write a letter to the manager of a factory, asking permission for a party to visit the factory.
14. Write a letter to the secretary of a joint-stock company of which you are a shareholder, notifying your change of address.

Letters Of Application

A letter applying for employment should contain:

(*a*) A short introduction stating whether the writer is answering an advertisement or is applying on his own responsibility.

(*b*) A statement of his age, education and experience.

(*c*) A conclusion giving references, testimonials, or an expression of the applicant's earnestness of purpose.

Letters of application should be in the form of business letters.

[Reply to an advertisement for a junior clerk]

24 Old Gate
Saranpur
3rd October, 2001
Messrs Abdul Rahim & Sons
Merchants
Saranpur

Gentlemen,

I wish to apply for the position of junior clerk, advertised in today's The Hindu.

I am eighteen years old, and have just passed the Matriculation Examination from the Saranpur High School. I have also taken a course in type-writing and book-keeping.

I enclose some testimonials, and would refer you to the Principal of the Saranpur School for my character.

If I am given the post, I can assure you I will do my best to give you satisfaction.

Yours faithfully,
Nathu Ram Baxi

EXERCISE 143

1. Answer the following advertisement.
   Wanted a clerk with a good knowledge of English and Arithmetic. Apply, Manager, New Press, Allahabad.
2. Apply for position as book-keeper, advertised in a daily paper, stating age, education, experience, qualification, reasons for leaving last position, references, previous salary, salary required, etc.
3. Speaking to a friend, a prominent businessman said, "I require a successful applicant for employment under me to demonstrate that he is sober, energetic and adaptable, and that he possesses practical knowledge of the work he proposes to undertake." Make an application to the gentleman, saying you possess the required qualifications.
4. Sir, having tried very earnestly to fit myself for advancement in your employ, I would like to approach you in the matter of an advance in salary. In support of my request, I would like to point out the following facts :—
   Finish this letter, referring to the length of your service, last promotion, why you deserve promotion, etc.

Further Official Letters

(Request to the Postmaster)

46 Kingsway
Nagpur 440 001
18 Jan. 2001
The Postmaster
Head Post Office
Nagpur 440 001

Dear Sir,

I have recently shifted from 25 Park Street, Nagpur 440 002 to 46 Kingsway, Nagpur 440 001. I shall be grateful if you will kindly redirect my letters to the new address.

Yours faithfully,

K. Joseph

(Letter of inquiry to an educational institution)

Desaipeta
Vetapalem 523187
21 May 2001
The Director
APTECH
4/7 Brodipet
Guntur 522 002

Dear Sir,

I have passed the B.Sc. degree examination with Electronics as the main subject. I intend to have a course in Computer Science and would like to know the details of the courses taught at your institution. Could you please send me a copy of your prospectus?

Yours faithfully,

N. Mahesh

EXERCISE 144

Write:

1. To the Director of Education, applying for appointment as a teacher in the Educational Service.
2. To the Commissioner of Police, about the grant for an appointment as Sub-Inspector.
3. To the Commissioner of Police, about the grant of licence to carry arms, stating reasons.
4. To the Municipal Commissioner on the necessity of public parks in a crowded city like Mumbai.
5. To the Postmaster of your town, asking for particulars about Post Office Cash Certificates.
6. To the Superintendent, Government Central Press, asking for a list of Government publications relating to dairying in India, and inquiring if any periodical is published on the subject.
7. To the Jailor, Yerawada Prison, as from a prisoner's mother, asking permission to see her son.

Letters To Newspapers

These should always be addressed to "The Editor," and they usually end with *Yours faithfully.*

The form of Salutation is *Sir/Dear Sir.*

If the writer gives his address for publication, it is often placed below the letter and to the left of the signature.

If the writer does not wish his name to be published, he can sign his letter with a *non-de-plume* (such as "Interested", "Anxious", "One who knows", etc.) ; but in any case he must give his name and address (in a covering letter) to the Editor, for no respectable newspaper will publish anonymous letters.

[To a newspaper, about a bad piece of road that is in need of repair.]

To
The Editor
The Hindu

Sir,

Our Municipality wants waking up ; and, as private appeals to their office have had no effect, perhaps a little publicity will do no harm. For the last month Chetty Road has been almost impassable. The surface is badly broken up by the heavy rains, and on a dark night it is positively dangerous for motors or carriages to pass that way. Moreover, there are heaps of roadmetal on both sides of the road, which leave very little room in the middle. It is scandalous that we should be inconvenienced in this way for weeks, and I hope the public will bring pressure to bear on those responsible so that the road may be put in thorough repair without further delay.

Yours faithfully,

Anirudh Kumar

EXERCISE 145

Write:

1. To the Editor of a newspaper, on reckless driving.
2. To a newspaper, drawing attention to the insanitary condition of the city bazaars.
3. To a newspaper, protesting against street noises.
4. To a newspaper, advocating the establishment of a Free Library in your town.
5. To a newpaper, appealing for the funds for an orphanage.
6. To a newspaper, complaining of the bad quality and inadequate supply of Municipal water in your town.
7. To a newspaper, suggesting to the public the desirability of a Social Service League in your town.
8. To a newspaper, on the evils of street-begging.
9. To a newspaper, appealing for funds to relieve the sufferers from a flood.

More Letters

[To a very near neighbour about quiet for the benefit of a person who is seriously ill]

21 Osborne Street

7th May, 2001

Dear Shri Naik,

I am sorry to have to worry you with my troubles, but when I have explained I am sure you will understand. I regret to say that Mrs. Pradhan is seriously ill. The doctor, who has just been, says she is in a critical condition, and that absolute quiet is essential for her recovery. She has had several bad nights, and cannot get sufficient sleep. I am sure you will not be offended if, in the circumstances, I ask you to tell your servant and your children to make as little noise as they can during the next few days. Our houses are so close together that we cannot help hearing shouting, and even talking ; and the slightest noise disturbs my wife, who is in a very low, nervous state. If she can only have a few days and nights of quiet, I think it will work wonders.

Apologizing for putting you to this inconvenience.

Yours sincerely

Satish Pradhan

[A father reports to the police that his son has not returned home from school, giving particulars of the boy, his dress, etc.]

35 Patel Street
Ahmednagar
4 Jan. 2001
The Inspector of Police
Police Station II
Ahmednagar

Dear Sir,

My son, Abdur Rashid, a lad twelve years old, is missing, and I am very anxious about him. As all my efforts to trace him have failed, I must appeal to you for help. He went to school this morning as usual, but although it is eight o'clock, he has not returned. He generally comes home before 4-30 p.m., everyday. I have made inquiries at the school (the Government High School), but the headmaster cannot throw any light on the matter. He says Abdur Rashid left school as usual at about 4-15 p.m., and he was quite well. The only clue I can find is from one of his school friends (a boy called Mhd. Hussain) who says he saw my son going along the canal bank at about 4-30 p.m., with a man whom he did not know. He cannot describe this man, but says he was wearing a white pagri and a brown jacket.

Abdur Rashid was wearing a red fez, a white coat and trousers. He is rather tall for his age, and walks with a slight limp.

I cannot think he has got into mischief, as he has always been a good boy and most regular in his habits. In view of the kidnapping case a few weeks ago, I am naturally very anxious lest he may have suffered from some foul play. Please do your best to trace him, and let me know as soon as you have anything to report.

Yours faithfully,

Abdur Rahim

[Certificate to a pupil]

Ideal College
Varanasi
12 May 2001

Ahmad Hasan has studied in this college for two years, and has just appeared in the Intermediate Examination. As he has worked well and is intelligent, he stands a good chance of passing. His conduct has been most satisfactory and he bears a good character. Physically he is robust and active, and was a member of the college football team. I am sure he will do any work entrusted to him conscientiously and efficiently.

N. Solomon

Principal

EXERCISE 146

1. Write a courteous letter to a neighbour whose dog annoys you by barking at night.
2. Reply to the above.
3. Write as from the father of a boy to a gentleman who rescued his son from drowning.
4. Your father thinks you are a precious boy; so he writes, "There have been many men whose early life was full of brilliant promise, but whose careers have ended in failure, owing to lack of industry." Write to him, assuring him that you will not belie the promise of your boyhood.
5. Write, as from a father to his son, about a drunkard and his unhappy family.
6. Write an imaginary letter as from a great-grandfather to his great-grandson about the means of communication in his days.
7. You have left school and are seeking a situation. Write to your Headmaster, asking for a testimonial.
8. Write to your Headmaster, asking for a letter of recommendation and explaining what you want.
9. Write a letter to your Headmaster, thanking him for the testimonial.
10. Write to the Society for the Prevention of Cruelty to Animals about a case of cruelty to a bullock, giving details including the date and place and name and address of the guilty person.
11. "It is often the steady plodder who gets prizes." Write as from a father to his son.
12. Write to a friend, setting forth your views on prize-giving in schools.

13. It is wonderful how a rumour grows. In an imaginary letter to your friend, give a story which, though foolish enough, was accepted by a large number of credulous people.
14. Write to a friend who, you think, is "a rolling stone".
15. Write as from a grandfather to his grandson who lives beyond his income.
16. Write a letter to your younger brother, advising temperance.
17. "It is often at school that life-friendships are made." A father makes this observation when writing to his son at a boarding school. Imagine the letter and copy it out.
18. Write as from a father to his son, asking him to make a habit of reading the daily newspaper, and pointing out what portions he should particularly read, etc.

19. Write to a prince, as from his teacher who believes, "There is no royal road to learning."
20. Write a letter from a shopkeeper to another shopkeeper about "cut-throat competition."
21. Write to your sportmaster, criticising the decision of the referee in a hockey match.
22. Write a letter to the manager of a local paper, enclosing an advertisement of your school concert.
23. You have advertised your bicycle for sale. Reply to an inquirer, and give him full details.
24. You see in a local paper an advertisement offering a second-hand bicycle. Write to the advertiser, asking for an appointment, as you wish to inspect the bicycle with a view to purchase.
25. Draft these advertisements.
    (*i*) Seeking a cheap second-hand computer.
    (*ii*) Offering for the sale of your car.
    (*iii*) Announcing the loss of your dog and offering a substantial reward.

Chapter 37 COMPREHENSION

A comprehension exercise consists of a passage, upon which questions are set to test the student's ability to understand the content of the given text and to infer information and meanings from it.

Here are a few hints:

1. Read the passage fairly quickly to get the general idea.
2. Read again, a little slowly, so as to know the details.
3. Study the questions thoroughly. Turn to the relevant portions of the passage, read them again, and then rewrite them in your own words, neatly and precisely.
4. Use complete sentences.
5. If you are asked to give the meaning of any words or phrases, you should express the idea as clearly as possible in your own words. Certain words require the kind of definition that is given in a dictionary. Take care to frame the definition in conformity with the part of speech.

SPECIMEN

Read the passage below and then answer the questions which follow it.

It has been part of Nelson's prayer that the British fleet might be distinguished by humanity in the victory which he expected. Setting an example himself, he twice gave orders to cease firing upon the *Redoubtable,* supposing that she had struck because her great guns were silent ; for as she carried no flag, there was no means of instantly ascertaining the fact. From this ship, which he had thus twice spared, he received his death. A ball fired from her mizzen-top which, in the then situation of the two vessels was not more than fifteen yards from that part of the deck where he was standing, struck the epaulette on his left shoulder about a quarter after one, just in the heat of action. He fell upon his face on the spot which was covered with his poor secretary's blood. Hardy, who was a few steps from him turning round, saw three men raising him up. "They have done for me at last, Hardy !" said he. "I hope not !" cried Hardy. "Yes," he replied ; "my back-bone is shot through !" Yet even now not for a moment losing his presence of mind, he observed as they were carrying him down the ladder, that the tiller-ropes which had been shot away, were not yet replaced and ordered that new ones should be roped immediately. Then that he might not be seen by the crew, he took out his handkerchief and covered his face and his stars. Had he but concealed these badges of honour from the enemy, England perhaps would not have had cause to receive with sorrow the news of the battle of Trafalgar. The cockpit was crowded with wounded and dying men ; over whose bodies he was with some difficulty conveyed, and laid upon a pallet in the midshipmen's berth. It was soon perceived, upon examination, that the wound was mortal. This, however, was concealed from all, except Captain Hardy, the chaplain, and the medical attendants. He himself being certain, from the sensation in his back, and the gush of blood he felt momently within his breast, that no human care could avail him, insisted that the surgeon should leave him and attend to those to whom he might be useful.

QUESTIONS

1. What is meant by 'supposing that she had struck' ?
2. How can Nelson be said to have been partly responsible for his own death?
3. What do you understand by the 'mizzen-top' ?
4. Why did Nelson insist that the surgeon should leave him and attend to others ?
5. What qualities in Nelson's character are revealed by this passage ?

Answers

1. 'Supposing that she had struck' means 'thinking that the men in the ship had surrendered'.
2. Nelson ordered his men two times to cease firing on the *Redoubtable.* From the same ship a ball was fired at him and brought about his death. He was thus partly responsible for his death.
3. The 'mizzen-top' is the platform round the lower part of the mast nearest the stern.
4. Nelson was certain that it would be impossible to save his life. He, therefore, insisted that the surgeon should leave him and attend to others.
5. His patriotism, his humanity and his powers of endurance are revealed by this passage.

EXERCISE 147

Read each of the passages carefully and answer the questions given below it.

1

People talk of memorials to him in statues of bronze or marble or pillars and thus they mock him and belie his message. What tribute shall we pay to him that he would have appreciated ? He has shown us the way to live and the way to die and if we have not understood that lesson, it would be better that we raised no memorial to him, for the only fit memorial is to follow reverently in the path he showed us and to do our duty in life and in death.

He was a Hindu and an Indian, the greatest in many generations, and he was proud of being a Hindu and an Indian. To him India was dear, because she had represented throughout the ages certain immutable truths. But though he was intensely religious and came to be called the Father of the Nation which he had liberated, yet no narrow religious or national bonds confined his spirit. And so he became the great internationalist, believing in the essential unity of man, the underlying unity of all religions, and the needs of humanity, and more specially devoting himself to the service of the poor, the distressed and the oppressed millions everywhere.

His death brought more tributes than have been paid at the passing of any other human being in history. Perhaps what would have pleased him best was the spontaneous tributes that came from the people of Pakistan. On the morrow of the tragedy, all of us forgot for a while the bitterness that had crept in, the estrangement and conflict of these past months and Gandhiji stood out as the beloved champion and leader of the people of India, of india as it was before partition cut up this living nation. What was his great power over the mind and heart of man due to ? Even we realize, that his dominating passion was truth. That truth led him to proclaim without ceasing that good ends can never be attained by evil methods, that the end itself is distorted if the method pursued is bad. That truth led him to confess publicly whenever he thought he had made a mistake—Himalayan errors he called some of his own mistakes. That truth led him to fight evil and untruth wherever he found them, regardless of the consequences. That truth made the service of the poor and the dispossessed the passion of his life, for where there is inequality and discrimination and suppression there is injustice and evil and untruth. And thus he became the beloved of all those who have suffered from social and political evils, and the great representative of humanity as it should be. Because of that truth in him wherever he sat became a temple and where he trod was hallowed ground.

—Jawaharlal Nehru

QUESTIONS

1. About whom is the passage written ?
2. Why does Nehru make the difference about being a "Hindu" and an "Indian"? Is there any difference really ?
3. What great lesson did this great man show us for life ?
4. Mention some of the virtues of "the great internationalist."
5. Nehru seems to suggest that his hero was "the beloved champion and leader of the people of India" only before the partition of Pakistan and India. Do you agree with that ? Explain.
6. What did "truth" mean to this great man ?
7. Give the meaning of the following : memorials, immutable, essential, estrangement, spontaneous, discrimination, dominating, Himalayan.

2

The Voice had to be listened to, not only on account of its form but for the matter which it delivered. It gave a message to the country that it needed greatly. It brought to the common people a realization of their duty to concern themselves with their affairs. The common people were made to take an interest in the manner in which they were governed, in the taxes they paid, in the return they got from those taxes. This interest in public affairs—politics as you may call it—was to be the concern no longer of the highly educated few but of the many—the poor, the propertyless, the workingmen in town and country. Politics was not to be the concern of a small aristocracy of intellect or property of the masses. And with the change in the subjects of politics that Voice brought about also a change in the objects of politics. Till then politics had busied itself mainly with the machinery of Government towards making its personnel more and more native, with proposals for a better distribution of political power, with protests against the sins of omission and of commission of the administration. This Voice switched politics on to concern for the needs of the common people. The improvement of the lot of the poor was to be the main concern of politics and the politician. The improvement, especially of the lives of the people of the neglected villages, was to be placed before Governments and political organizations as the goal of all political endeavour. The raising of the standard of living of the people of the villages, the finding of subsidiary occupations which would give the agricultural poor work for their enforced leisure during the off season and an addition to their exiguous income, the improvement of the housing of the poor, the sanitation of the villages—these were to be the objectives to be kept in view. In the towns, the slums and *cheries* were to receive especial attention. There was especially a class of the poor for which that compassionate Voice pleaded and protested. This was for the so-called depressed class, the outcastes of Hindu society. The denial of elementary human rights to this class of people is considered the greatest blot on Hindu society and history. It raised itself in passionate protest against the age-old wrongs of this class and forced those that listened to it to endeavour to remove the most outrageous of them like untouchability. It caused a revolution in Hindu religious practice by having Hindu temples thrown open to these people. It made the care of them a religious duty of the Hindus by re-naming them Harijans.

—Mr Ruthnasami

QUESTIONS

1. Why had people to listen to "The Voice" of Mahatma Gandhi ?
2. Why had people to take an interest in politics ?
3. What was the change brought about in the objects of politics ?
4. What improvements were made for the common man ?
5. Explain:
   (*a*) Sins of omission and of commission of the administration.
   (*b*) No longer the monopoly of the classes, but the property of the masses.

3

The next ingredient is a very remarkable one : *Good Temper.* "Love is not easily provoked". Nothing could be more striking than to find this here. We are inclined to look upon bad temper as a very harmless weakness. We speak of it as a mere infirmity of nature, a family failing, a matter of temperament, not a thing to take into very serious account in estimating a man's character. And yet here, right in the heart of this analysis of love, it finds a place ; and the Bible again and again returns to condemn it as one of the most destructive elements in human nature. The peculiarity of ill temper is that it is the vice of the virtuous. It is often the one blot on an otherwise noble character. You know men who are all but perfect, and women who would be entirely perfect, but for an easily ruffled quick-tempered or "touchy" disposition. This compatibility of ill temper with high moral character is one of the strangest and saddest problems of ethics. The truth is there are two great classes of sins—sins of the *Body,* and sins of *Disposition.* The Prodigal son may be taken as a type of the first, the Elder Brother of the second. Now society has no doubt whatever as to which of these is the worse. Its brand falls, without a challenge, upon the Prodigal. But are we right ? We have no balance to weigh one another's sins, and coarser and finer are but human words ; but faults in the higher nature may be less venial than those in the lower, and to the eye of Him who is Love, a sin against Love may seem a hundred times more base. No form of vice, not worldliness, not greed of gold, not drunkenness itself does more to un-christianise society than evil temper. For embittering life, for breaking up communities, for destroying the most sacred relationships, for devastating homes, for withering up men and women, for taking the bloom off childhood ; in short for sheer gratuitous misery-producing power, this influence stands alone. Jealousy, anger, pride, uncharity, cruelty, self-righteousness, touchiness, doggedness, sullenness—in varying proportions these are the ingredients of all ill temper. Judge if such sins of the disposition are not worse to live in, and for others to live with than sins of the body. There is really no place in Heaven for a disposition like this. A man with such a mood could only make Heaven miserable for all the people in it.

—Henry Drummond

QUESTIONS

1. What is the popular notion about "bad temper"?
2. How is bad temper "the vice of the virtuous"?
3. Which class of sins is worse, and why—sins of the body, sins of the disposition?
4. Mention some evils of bad temper.
5. Why, according to the author, will there be no place in Heaven for bad-tempered folk?
6. Find words from the passage which mean: breaking up ; running ; scandalising ; souring; easily or quickly offended.

4

Yes, there were giants before the Jam Sahib (the great Indian cricketer, Kumar Shree Ranjitsinhji, better known to the world of cricket as Ranji). And yet I think it is undeniable that as a batsman the Indian will live as the supreme exponent of the Englishman's game. The claim does not rest simply on his achievements although, judged by them, the claim could be sustained. His season's average of 87 with a total of over 3,000 runs, is easily the high-water mark of English cricket. Thrice he has totalled over 3,000 runs and no one else has equalled that record. And is not his the astonishing achievement of scoring two double centuries in a single match on a single day—not against a feeble attack, but against Yorkshire, always the most resolute and resourceful of bowling teams?

But we do not judge a cricketer so much by the runs he gets as by the way he gets them. "In literature as in finance," says Washington Irving, "much paper and much poverty may co-exist." And in cricket too many runs and much dullness may be associated. If cricket is menaced with creeping paralysis, it is because it is losing the spirit of joyous adventure and becoming a mere instrument for compiling tables of averages. There are dull, mechanic fellows who turn out runs with as little emotion as a machine turns out pins. There is no colour, no enthusiasm, no character in their play. Cricket is not an adventure to them ; it is a business. It was so with Shrewsbury. His technical perfection was astonishing ; but the soul of the game was wanting in him. There was no sunshine in his play, no swift surprise or splendid unselfishness. And without these things without gaiety, daring, and the spirit of sacrifice cricket is a dead thing. Now, the Jam Sahib has the root of the matter in him. His play is as sunny as his face. He is not a miser hoarding up runs, but a millionaire spending them, with a splendid yet judicious prodigality. It is as though his pockets are bursting with runs that he wants to shower with his blessings upon the expectant multitude. It is not difficult to believe that in his litttle kingdom Nawangar where he has power of life and death in his hands he is extremely popular for it is obvious that his pleasure is in giving pleasure.

—A.G. Gardiner

QUESTIONS

1. Correct the following statistics, if necessary.
   (*a*) His season's average of 87 with a total of over 3,000 runs is easily the high-water mark of English cricket.
   (*b*) Thrice he has totalled over 3,000 runs, and no one else has equalled that record.
   (*c*) He scored two double centuries in a single match on a single day.
2. "Many runs and much dullness may be associated." Prove this.
3. Mention some reasons why cricket is losing its lustre.
4. What gives cricket its "character"?
5. How should real cricket be played ?
6. Describe in your own words the secret of the Jam Sahib's wizardry with the bat.
7. Make a list of "do's" and "don'ts" for a promising cricketer.

5

Supposing you have to make a payment of Rs. 100, you can do so in rupee-coins ; but it would be cumbersome to pay in nickel or copper coins, because they are heavy to carry and also because it takes much time to count them. The Government therefore permits you to make the payment in rupee-notes. What are these rupee-notes really? They are a kind of money, right enough, although they are made of paper instead of metal. You can use them in just the same way that you use ordinary money. The reason why they are made of paper and used is that they save the trouble of carrying metal coins about—of course, paper is lighter than metal—and they also save using silver and other metals when they are scarce.

What makes these mere pieces of paper bear the value of the number of rupees that is printed upon them? Why should a piece of paper, with "100" printed on it be worth twenty times as much as a piece of paper with "five" printed on it—and also worth a hundred times as much as a silver rupee-coin ? The reason is that Government *guarantees* that the piece of paper is worth the amount printed on it and promises to pay that amount to anybody who wishes to exchange this paper for the rupee-coins. Also, if you think about it you can easily realize that crores and crores more of rupee-coins would have to be minted, if all paper-money were abolished.

Perhaps you may ask, "Then why not have paper money only ? Why use silver and nickel and copper at all?" The answer is—because money must, as we have already said, be something so useful that everyone wants. Also because the metals are the best form of money ; and thirdly because it would be impossible to print just the right amount of paper money that would keep prices at their proper natural level. If any Government prints too much paper money, then prices go up at once. The *supply* of money is increased and therefore its value (in food, clothes, books, houses, land, tools and everything else) goes down.

You may think at first that it is queer to talk of having too much paper money and that money is so nice and useful that you cannot have too much of it. But if you think that, I am afraid you are forgetting that money is only useful for what it will buy ; so it is no good at all having more money if there are no more things to buy with it. The more money there is, the higher will be the prices of everything. The same thing happens with rupee-coins as with paper money. But it is not likely to happen, for this reason : it is very easy to print a great deal of paper money, but not at all easy to increase the amount of rupee-coins. Silver has to be dug out of mines, and very difficult to get ; so the amount there is if it keeps very steady and changes very little. In fact that is one of the chief reasons why it was chosen to make coins of.

—Ernest F. Row

QUESTIONS

1. Why does the Government allow payment to be made in paper notes ?
2. What is more valuable, to have 100 rupee-coins in silver or a Rs. 100 note in paper ?
3. If metal is so cumbersome, why should we not have only paper money ? Why should we not print as much of it as possible ?
4. What is the real use of money ?
5. Why should the prices of commodities go up when there is plenty of paper money ?
6. Why does the Government print only a certain number of paper notes, and not as many as it likes arbitrarily ?

6

You seemed at first to take no notice of your school-fellows, or rather to set yourself against them because they were strangers to you. They knew as little of you as you did of them; so that this would have been the reason for their keeping aloof from you as well, which you would have felt as a hardship. Learn never to conceive a prejudice against others because you know nothing of them. It is bad reasoning, and makes enemies of half the world. Do not think ill of them till they behave ill to you ; and then strive to avoid the faults which you see in them. This will disarm their hostility sooner than pique or resentment or complaint. I thought you were disposed to criticize the dress of some of the boys as not so good as your own. Never despise any one for anything that he cannot help—least of all, for his poverty. I would wish you to keep up appearances yourself as a defence against the idle sneers of the world, but I would not have you value yourself upon them. I hope you will neither be the dupe nor victim of vulgar prejudices. Instead of saying above "Never despise anyone for anything that he cannot help," I might have said, "Never despise anyone at all" ; for contempt implies a triumph over and pleasure in the ill of another. It means that you are glad and congratulate yourself on their failings or misfortunes.

You have hitherto been a spoilt child, and have been used to have your own way a good deal, both in the house and among your playfellows, with whom you were too fond of being a leader ; but you have good nature and good sense, and will get the better of this in time. You have now got among other boys who are your equals, or bigger and stronger than yourself and who have something else to attend to besides humouring your whims and fancies, and you feel this as a repulse or piece of injustice. But the first lesson to learn is that there are other people in the world besides yourself. The more airs of childish self-importance you give yourself, you will only expose yourself to be the more thwarted and laughed at. True equality is the only true morality or wisdom. Remember always that you are but one among others and you can hardly mistake your place in society. In your father's house you might do as you pleased ; in the world you will find competitors at every turn. You are not born a king's son, to destroy or dictate to millions; you can only expect to share their fate, or settle your differences amicably with them. You already find it so at school, and I wish you to be reconciled to your situation as soon and with as little pain as you can.

—William Hazlitt

QUESTIONS

1. Can you tell who is writing to whom in this passage ? What would you call this kind of writing—a speech, a diary, a letter, a sermon ?
2. What reasons does the author give for not harbouring a prejudice against others ?
3. What are some of the blessings of living with others in the same class or the same school?
4. Paraphrase:

(*a*) True equality is the only true morality or true wisdom.

(*b*) To be the dupe or victim of vulgar prejudices.

(*c*) Settle your differences amicably with them.

5. "Contempt implies a triumph over and pleasure in the ill of another." Who are those who feel like this and why ?
6. The author says that "in the world you will find competitors at every turn." But competition is a very good thing. Why does he seem to warn his son about it?

7

Unquestionably a literary life is for the most part an unhappy life ; because, if you have genius, you must suffer the penalty of genius ; and, if you have only talent, there are so many cares and worries incidental to the circumstances of men of letters, as to make life exceedingly miserable. Besides the pangs of composition, and the continuous disappointment which a true artist feels at his inability to reveal himself, there is the ever-recurring difficulty of gaining the public ear. Young writers are buoyed up by the hope and the belief that they have only to throw that poem at the world's feet to get back in return the laurel-crown ; that they have only to push that novel into print to be acknowledged at once as a new light in literature. You can never convince a young author that the editors of magazines and the publishers of books are a practical body of men, who are by no means frantically anxious about placing the best literature before the public. Nay, that for the most part they are mere brokers, who conduct their business on the hardest lines of a Profit and Loss account. But supposing your book fairly launches, its perils are only beginning. You have to run the gauntlet of the critics. To a young author, again, this seems to be as terrible an ordeal as passing down the files of Sioux or Comanche Indians, each one of whom is thirsting for your scalp. When you are a little older, you will find that criticism is not much more serious than the bye-play of clowns in a circus, when they beat around the ring the victim with bladders slung at the end of long poles. A time comes in the life of every author when he regards critics as comical rather than formidable, and goes his way unheeding. But there are sensitive souls that yield under the chastisement and, perhaps after suffering much silent torture, abandon the profession of the pen for ever. Keats, perhaps, is the saddest example of a fine spirit hounded to death by savage criticism ; because, whatever his biographers may aver, that furious attack of Gifford and Terry undoubtedly expedited his death. But no doubt there are hundreds who suffer keenly hostile and unscrupulous criticism, and who have to bear that suffering in silence, because it is a cardinal principle in literature that the most unwise thing in the world for an author is to take public notice of criticism in the way of defending himself. Silence is the only safeguard, as it is the only dignified protest against insult and offence.

—P.A. Sheehan

QUESTIONS

1. Why is the Literary Life mostly an unhappy one ?
2. What are the ambitions of a young author ?
3. Are editors and publishers sympathetic to young authors ?
4. What are some of the ordeals awaiting the young authors from the critics?
5. What attitude should an author adopt in the face of bitter critics ?
6. Explain : Sioux Indians ; abandon the profession of the pen ; laurel-crown ; to run the gauntlet ; hounded to death.
7. Write in simple English : the pangs of composition ; buoyed up by the hope ; mere brokers; thirsting for your scalp.

8

Then one day there passed by that way a Pashupata ascetic. And he said to the Brahman : "My son, what are you doing here ?" So he replied : "Reverend Sir, I am performing penance, for the expiation of sin, on the banks of the Ganges." Then the ascetic said: "What has this miserable puddle to do with the Ganges." And the Brahman said :"Is this then, not the Ganges ?" And the ascetic laughed in his face, and said :"Truly, old as I am, I did not think that there had been folly like this in the world. Wretched man, who has deluded you ? The Ganges is hundreds of miles away, and resembles this contemptible brook no more than Mount Meru resembles an ant-hill." Then the Brahman said :"Reverend Sir, I am much obliged to you." And taking his pot and staff, he went forward, till at length he came to a broad river. And he rejoiced greatly, saying : "This must be the sacred Ganges." So he settled on its banks and remained there for five years, bathing every day in its waters. Then one day there came by a Kapalika, who said to him, "Why do you remain here, wasting precious time over a river of no account or sanctity, instead of going to the Ganges ?" But the Brahman was amazed, and said ; "And is this, then not the Ganges ?" Then the Kapalika replied :"This is the Ganges ! Is a jackal, lion or a Chandala a Brahman ? Sir, you are dreaming." Then the Brahman sighed deeply. And he said, "Sir, I am enlightened by you." And he took his pot and staff, and went forward.

But he was now very old and feeble. And long penance had weakened his frame and exhausted his energies. And as he toiled on in the heat of the day over the burning earth, the sun beat on his head like the thunderbolt of Indra, and struck him with fever. Still he gathered himself together and struggled on, growing weaker and weaker day by day, till at last he got no further, but fell down and lay dying on the ground. But collecting all his remaining strength, with a last desperate effort he dragged himself up a low hill in front of him. And lo! there before him rolled the mighty stream of Ganges, with countless numbers of pilgrims doing penance on its banks and bathing in its stream. And in his agony he cried aloud : "O Mother Ganges ! alas ! alas ! I have pursued you all my life and now I die here helpless in sight of you." So his heart broke, and he never reached its shore.

—F.W. Bain

QUESTIONS

1. Explain the allusion to Mount Meru and the comparison between it and an ant-hill. What was "the thunderbolt of Indra" ?
2. What is a "Pashupata" ascetic, a Kapalika or a Chandala ?
3. What do you surmise is the intiention of the author in telling this very sad story ? Quote phrases from the text to show the pathos.
4. Comment on the significance and the author's use of the following expressions.
   (*a*) "This is the Ganges ! Is a jackal a lion ____?"
   (*b*) "O Mother Ganges ! alas ! alas !"
5. What is the purpose of the words : "Reverend Sir, I am performing penance, for the expiation of sin ____?

9

One common mistake that many people have made is this : they have thought that it would be a very good thing if everybody had exactly the same amount of money, no matter whether they worked hard or lived quite idly. They forget that very few people would work at all if it were not for the money their work brings them, and that without work there would be no money. And they have imagined that if all the money in the country were equally divided everybody would be rich. Now that is a very great mistake, because there simply is not enough money to make everybody rich. If it were shared equally all round every one then would, on the basis of the calculations made in 1935, receive only about Rs. 65 a year. Today with a rise in the price level it might be Rs. 150 a year. That may be more than you receive now or it may be less, but would certainly not make you really rich. It is quite true that there are in this country a small number of very rich people ; but they are so few in comparison with the whole population that even if they were to share out all their wealth among the rest, it would make very little difference. It is said that if you flattened out that great French mountain Mont Blanc, the highest mountain in Europe, and spread it over the whole of France you would only raise the level of the land by about six inches. See if you can think out what that has to do with the question I have been talking about.

Many people, unfortunately, seem to think also that Government can always pay out money quite easily and in any quantity, and they forget, or else they do not know, that the Government can only pay out money that it has received in taxes—money that the tax-payer has had to work for.

And now here is one final mistake that I should like to warn you against. Don't ever imagine that there is any thing to be ashamed of, or anything undignified, to grumble about in having to work hard for your living. If when you start work you can go into a job that suits you, so that you can really enjoy the work itself, so much the better : I hope that is what will happen. But if the work is not exactly the kind that you would choose, you must try to remember that you are helping to produce the things that other people need ; you are "doing your bit" and playing your part in the work of the world. You are like a wheel, even if it is only a very tiny wheel, in the great world-machinery of trade and industry that is always busily at work providing for the wants of hundreds of millions of people, and you must "put your back into it" and see to it that your particular task is always done as well as you can possibly do it.

—Ernest F. Row

QUESTIONS

1. Why is it really necessary to work ?
2. If all the money in the world were equally divided, everybody would be very happy. Do you agree ?
3. The author tells us about flattening Mont Blanc and the little difference it would make in raising the level of France. What is his point in giving us this example ?
4. Which is the best job in the world ? Why must you embrace it lovingly?
5. What is the meaning of :"put your back into it ?" :"doing your bit"?
6. Paraphrase "You are like a wheel......millions of people."

10

All Great Thinkers live and move on a high plane of thought. It is only there they can breathe freely. It is only in contact with spirits like themselves they can live harmoniously and attain that serenity which comes from ideal companionship. The studies of all great thinkers must range along the highest altitudes of human thought. I cannot remember the name of any illuminative genius who did not drink his inspiration from fountains of ancient Greek and Hebrew writers ; or such among the moderns as were pupils in ancient thought, and, in turn, became masters in their own. I have always thought that the strongest argument in favour of the Baconian theory was, that no man, however indubitable his genius, could have written the plays and sonnets that have come down to us under Shakespeare's name who had not the liberal education of Bacon. How this habit of intercourse with the gods makes one impatient of mere men. The magnificent ideals that have ever haunted the human mind, and given us our highest proofs of a future immortality by reason of the impossibility of their fulfilment here, are splintered into atoms by contact with life's realities. Hence comes our sublime discontent. You will notice that your first sensation after reading a great book is one of melancholy and dissatisfaction. The ideas, sentiments, expressions, are so far beyond those of ordinary working life that you cannot turn aside from one to the other without an acute sensation and consciousness of the contrast. And the principles are so lofty, so super-human that it is a positive pain, if once you become imbued with them, to come down and mix in the squalid surroundings of ordinary humanity. It may be spiritual or intellectual pride that is engendered on the high plane of intellectual life . But whatever it is, it becomes inevitable. A habitual meditation on the vast problems that underline human life, and are knit into human destinies—thoughts of immortality, of the littleness of mere man, of the greatness of man's soul, of the splendours of the universe that are invisible to the ordinary traffickers in the street, as the vastness of St. Peter's is to the spider that weaves her web in a corner of the dome—these things do not fit men to understand the average human being, or tolerate with patience the sordid wretchedness of the unregenerate masses. It is easy to understand, therefore, why such thinkers fly to the solitude of their own thoughts, or the silent companionship of the immortals ; and if they care to present their views in prose or verse to the world, that these views take a sombre and melancholy setting from "the pale cast of thought" in which they were engendered.

—P.A. Sheehan

QUESTIONS

1. On what plane must great thinkers live and move ?
2. Is a liberal education necessary to produce great literature ?
3. Why does the reading of a great book, according to the author, make one melancholy and disappointed ?
4. What are the things that make it hard to understand the average human being?

11

Although religion does not inhibit the acquistion of wealth, although it does not hold up large fortunes as evil,the tenor of its teaching, by and large, is to induce an attitude of indifference to worldly things, things which gratify one's lower self and keep one engrossed in money-making. The student should be made to realize that the real goods of life are spiritual, love of things of the spirit and service of one's fellowmen, joy of an ordered disciplined life. These are blessings money cannot buy. What is wealth before such things of the spirit ? Of all religious teachers Jesus Christ has dealt more comprehensively than any other with the problem of wealth in all its aspects. He may be called the greatest exponent of the science of the wealth. With only four words "Blessed are ye poor!" he changed altogether the values which man attached to human existence and human happiness and acquisition and possession of wealth. Real bliss consisted, he taught, not in riches nor in anything else which the world regarded as prosperity or felicity, but in the joy and happiness derived from being at peace with one's fellowmen through perfect love and fellowship and selfless service and sacrifice.

The word "poor" on the lips of the Master had a spiritual significance—the poor so far as they were poor in spirit, humble before God, simple, God-fearing, teachable, faithful. It could surely not have been his intention to hold up destitution and privation as a blessing in itself. That would have turned life into a terrible ordeal and it would have been heartless to exhort the poor to believe that money was not necessary for one's sustenance or the joys and blessings of life. Even things of the spirit cannot be had without money. Extreme poverty is as liable to lead to the stagnation and impoverishment of the soul as excessive wealth. Not outward poverty but inward spirit was what Jesus Christ desired and demanded. Every religion asks a man to regard his wealth as a trust. Giving in charity for the relief of the poor and public welfare is not merely an act of compassion, not merely a religious duty, but also an act of social justice. All the gospels of wealth are based on the fundamental concept that none can claim an absolute or inherent right to property. Everyone holds it in trust from God to promote the good of mankind. All rights to private property are subject to this primary obligation to God and man.

—R.P. Masani

QUESTIONS

1. What, according to the author, is the meaning of "indifference" ? Is it applicable to all religions ?
2. Which are some of the real goods of spiritual living ? Is it easy to make the student realise this ?
3. In what sense can it be said that Jesus Christ has dealt more comprehensively with the problem of wealth ? Did Mahatma Gandhi teach a similar doctrine ?
4. What do you understand by the phrase : "poor in spirit" ? In that case, would it be more perfect to give away all your belongings and property and live like a pauper ?
5. Describe some of the drawbacks of poverty and show how money is absolutely necessary in life.
6. Write a short paragraph in which you develop the idea contained in the following : "Every religion asks a man to regard his wealth as a trust."
7. Bernard Shaw has said that poverty is a crime. Do you agree ?

12

The third great defect of our civilization is that it does not know what to do with its knowledge. Science has given us powers fit for the gods, yet we use them like small children. For example, we do not know how to manage our machines. Machines were made to be man's servants ; yet he has grown so dependent on them that they are in a fair way to become his masters. Already most men spend most of their lives looking after and waiting upon machines. And the machines are very stern masters. They must be fed with coal, and given petrol to drink, and oil to wash with, and they must be kept at the right temperature. And if they do not get their meals when they expect them, they grow sulky and refuse to work, or burst with rage, and blow up, and spread ruin and destruction all round them. So we have to wait upon them very attentively and do all that we can to keep them in a good temper. Already we find it difficult either to work or play without the machines, and a time may come when they will rule us altogether, just as we rule the animals.

And this brings me to the point at which I asked, "What do we do with all the time which the machines have saved for us, and the new energy they have given us ?" On the whole, it must be admitted, we do very little. For the most part we use our time and energy to make more and better machines ; but more and better machines will only give us still more time and still more energy, and what are we to do with them ? The answer, I think, is that we should try to become mere civilized. For the machines themselves, and the power which the machines have given us, are not civilization but aids to civilization. But you will remember that we agreed at the beginning that being civilized meant making and linking beautiful things, thinking freely, and living rightly and maintaining justice equally between man and man. Man has a better chance today to do these things than he ever had before ; he has more time, more energy, less to fear and less to fight against. If he will give his time and energy which his machines have won for him to making more beautiful things, to finding out more and more about the universe, to removing the causes of quarrels between nations, to discovering how to prevent poverty, then I think our civilization would undoubtedly be the greater, as it would be the most lasting that there has ever been.

—C.E.M. Joad

QUESTIONS

1. Instead of making machines our servants the author says they have become our masters. In what sense has this come about ?
2. The use of machines has brought us more leisure and more energy. But the author says that this has been a curse rather than a blessing. Why ?
3. What exactly is the meaning of "civilization" ? Do you agree with the author's views ?
4. "Making more beautiful things" – What does this expression mean? Make a list of the beautiful things that you would like to make and how you would make them.
5. Mention some plans you may have to prevent poverty in the world. Who would receive your most particular attention, and why ?
6. The author uses phrases like "fed with coal" ; "given petrol to drink"; "oil to wash" ; "kept at the right temperature". What machines would require these things?

13

The other day we heard someone smilingly refer to poets as dreamers. Now, it is accurate to refer to poets as dreamers, but it is not discerning to infer, as this person did, that the dreams of poets have no practical value beyond the realm of literary diversion. The truth is that poets are just as practical as people who build bridges or look into microscopes ; and just as close to reality and truth. Where they differ from the logician and the scientist is in the temporal sense alone ; they are ahead of their time, whereas logicians and scientists are abreast of their time. We must not be so superficial that we fail to discern the practicableness of dreams. Dreams are the sunrise streamers heralding a new day of scientific progress, another forward surge. Every forward step man takes in any field of life, is first taken along the dreamy paths of imagination. Robert Fulton did not discover his steamboat with full steam up, straining at a hawser at some Hudson River dock; first he dreamed the steamboat, he and other dreamers, and then scientific wisdom converted a picture in the mind into a reality of steel and wood. The automobile was not dug out of the ground like a nugget of gold ; first men dreamed the automobile and afterward, long afterward, the practical-minded engineers caught up with what had been created by winging fantasy. He who looks deeply and with a seeing eye into the poetry of yesterday finds there all the cold scientific magic of today and much which we shall not enjoy until some tomorrow. If the poet does not dream so clearly that blueprints of this vision can immediately be drawn and the practical conversions immediately effected, he must not for that reason be smiled upon as merely the mental host for a sort of harmless madness. For the poet, like the engineer, is a specialist. His being, tuned to the life of tomorrow, cannot be turned simultaneously to the life of today. To the scientist he says, "Here, I give you a flash of the future." The wise scientist thanks him, and takes that flash of the future and makes it over into a fibre of today.

—Glen Falls

QUESTIONS

1. Are poets dreamers ? In what sense ?
2. Is a poet a practical man ? In what way ?
3. Are dreams, according to the author, useful to the world ? Why ?
4. What was Fulton's achievement ?
5. If the poet did not dream, what would happen ?
6. In what way is the poet a specialist ?

14

This romantic life in Kashmir was drawing to its end after three glorious months. Miss Joan was leaving a week earlier than Mrs. Rhodes, and about two days before she left I took her alone to the hotel for dinner. We walked to the hotel in perfect silence, a silence so heavy that I could hardly breathe. The hotel seemed to be far away and yet not far enough. That night, as I served her at table the temptation to touch her was overpowering, and I had almost forgotten myself when I dropped her coffee cup, which made me pull myself together and realize my position and my caste. On the way home there was a bridge over the canal to be crossed. She stopped on the bridge without a word, so I stopped beside her looking on to the calm water of the canal shining between the gigantic chenar trees. In the distance a gramophone was playing and the music floated over the water. We stood for a long time without saying a word to each other. I think the parting was disturbing her. There was something which she could not have explained and which she was trying to express. It might have been just a fancy of her own, or it may have been the subconscious knowledge of the secret, consuming passion of her attendant that was affecting her on this calm and beautiful night as we tarried on the bridge. It seemed to me that we stood there for ages, as if neither of us dare break the magic spell of night and music. Our houseboat was only a few yards from the bridge, and the Goodnight was the only word that passed between us as we parted—everything then went into the darkness. The Mail lorry came up to the bridge to take her away from the romantic city of Srinagar—and away from me. After she had taken her seat I put a woollen rug over her knees to keep her warm on the journey, and she handed me a ten-rupee note as a parting gift and sweetly said Good-bye. I watched her wave her hand till the lorry was out of sight. Then I realized what I had lost, and lost for ever.

—Hazari

QUESTIONS

1. What was the matter with the attendant as he walked with Miss Joan to the hotel ? Why did they not talk to each other ?
2. After reading the passage can you give reasons to show what caste the attendant belonged to ?
3. The author mentions the chenar trees of Kashmir. Give a brief but graphic description of these trees.
4. "I think the parting was disturbing her." Was it the romantic atmosphere of the surroundings, the thought of having to leave Kashmir, the kindness of her attendant, or thoughts of home that were the cause of the disturbance ?
5. Why does the author call Srinagar a romantic city ? Give the meaning of "romantic." Show how it may apply to Srinagar.
6. Why did Miss Joan give the attendant a ten-rupee note ? Do friends do such things?

15

Long years ago we made a tryst with destiny, and now the time comes when we shall redeem our pledge, not wholly or in full measure, but very substantially. At the stroke of the midnight hour, when the world sleeps, India will awake to life and freedom. A moment comes, which comes but rarely in history, when we step out from the old to the new, when an age ends, and when the soul of a nation, long suppressed, finds utterance. It is fitting that at this solemn moment we take the pledge of dedication to the service of India and her people and to the still larger cause of humanity.

At the dawn of history India started on her unending quest, and trackless centuries are filled with her striving and the grandeur of her success and her failures. Through good and ill fortune alike she has never lost sight of that quest or forgotten the ideals which gave her strength. We end today a period of ill fortune and India discovers herself again. The achievement we celebrate today is but a step, an opening of opportunity, to the greater triumphs and achievements that await us. Are we brave enough and wise enough to grasp this opportunity and accept the challenge of the future ?

Freedom and power bring responsibility. That responsibility rests upon this Assembly, a sovereign body representing the sovereign people of India. Before the birth of freedom we have endured all the pains of labour and our hearts are heavy with the memory of this sorrow. Some of those pains continue even now. Neverthless, the past is over and it is the future that beckons to us now. That future is not one of ease or resting but of incessant striving so that we may fulfil the pledges we have so often taken and the one we shall take today. The service of India means the service of the millions who suffer. It means the ending of poverty and ignorance and disease and inequality of opportunity. The ambition of the greatest man of our generation has been to wipe every tear from every eye. That may be beyond us, but as long as there are tears and suffering , so long our work will not be over.

—Jawaharlal Nehru

QUESTIONS

1. Express in your own words : (*a*) we made a tryst with destiny ; (*b*) at the stroke of the midnight hour ; (*c*) when the world sleeps ; (*d*) when we step out from the old to the new ; (*e*) we take the pledge of dedication ; (*f*) at the dawn of history ; (*g*) India discovers herself again ; (*h*) with the memory of sorrow.
2. In what does the "service of India" consist, according to the author ?
3. What are the ideals which India has never forgotten ?
4. Mention some of the responsibilities of freedom and power.
5. This speech is concerned with the living as well as the dead. In what way does Nehru appeal to his listeners ? What motive urges Nehru to rouse the India of today to action ?
6. Quote the line that has a direct reference to Mahatma Gandhi.

16

The Artist co-operates with God in making increasingly larger numbers of people see the beauty of the world which these people could never see for themselves. The world is, of course, God's artistic masterpiece ; but it is the artist who lends people eyes to see it with. Browning's Fra Lippo has the last word on the subject :—

For, don't you mark, we're made so that we love
First when we see them painted, things we have passed
Perhaps a hundred times nor cared to see ?

In this sense, Oscar Wilde's paradox is perfectly true : that Nature imitates Art; for the majority of men see in Nature what Art has taught them to see in Nature. The fogs of London, said Wilde, were the invention of Whistler. To love beauty therefore becomes to the artist, as an artist, his first duty. To love beauty, that is, to see it for himself first, and then to communicate it to others ; for love implies at once vision and reproduction. It must be the first article in an artist's creed, as an artist, that beauty is the best interpreter of God to man ; that, when he has got hold of beauty, he has got hold of the surest key to the knowledge of God. Keats has said that Beauty is Truth. Now, this is not true. But to us here, Beauty is, as Plato said, the splendour of Truth. The artist, as an artist, must be content with the splendour and, through this splendour strive to convey the truth. He has no business with truth as such as the philosopher, for instance, has. He has no concern with conduct as such, as the moralist, for instance, has. It is not his function to exhort men to good works, or to prove things ; but merely to exhibit them. Plato thought a picture, for instance, was just a copy of an object—a copy of the idea. It was Aristotle, Plato's pupil, who pointed out that, though a picture was in one sense certainly a copy and therefore something *less* than the object, in another sense it was something *more* than the object. It was, briefly, the *idea* of the object made visible to the eye. Art, therefore, does not consist merely in line and colour, sound and image ; but primarily in *ideas.* Beauty may not be useful. Beauty may not improve our minds. But beauty must *please.* Indeed, such is the inherent delightfulness of beauty that, by its magic touch, not only the ugly becomes pleasureable, but even sorrow becomes a joy. That is the explanation of the pleasure we feel in tragedy. What would shock us in actual life gives us pleasure in a tragedy. For tragedy makes experience significant ; and by making it significant, it makes it beautiful ; and by making it beautiful, it makes it pleasant. And yet, it does not *aim* at pleasing ; it only aims at exhibiting. Pleasure is not its aim ; it is its effect.

—Armando Menezes

QUESTIONS

1. What does the artist do for most of us ?
2. Why does the artist "lend" his eyes to people ?
3. Explain : "Nature imitates Art."
4. What is the artist's first duty ? Why ?
5. What is the surest key to the knowledge of God ? Why ?
6. What is the artist's real function ?
7. In what does Art primarily consist ?
8. When does sorrow become a joy ?

Chapter 38 PRECIS-WRITING

A precis* is a summary, and precis-writing means summarising. Precis-writing is an exercise in compression. A precis is the gist or main theme of a passage expressed in as few words as possible. It should be lucid, succinct, and full (*i.e.*

including all essential points), so that anyone on reading it may be able to grasp the main points and general effect of the passage summarised.

Precis-writing must not be confused with paraphrasing. A paraphrase should reproduce not only the substance of a passage, but also all its details. It will therefore be at least as long as, and probably longer than, the original. But a precis must always be much shorter than the original ; for it is meant to express only the main theme, shorn of all unimportant details, and that as tersely as possible. As the styles of writers differ, some being concise and some diffuse, no rigid rule can be laid down for the length of a precis ; but so much may be said, that a precis should not contain more than a third of the number of words in the original passage.

I. Uses of Precis-Writing

1. Precis-writing is a very fine exercise in *reading*. Most people read carelessly, and retain only a vague idea of what they have read. You can easily test the value of your reading. Read in your usual way a chapter, or even a page, of a book ; and then, having closed the book try to put down briefly the substance of what you have just read. You will probably find that your memory of it is hazy and muddled. Is this because your memory is weak ? No; it is because your attention was not fully centred on the passage while you were reading it. The memory cannot retain what was never given it to hold ; you did not remember the passage properly because you did not properly grasp it as you read it. Now precis-writing forces you to pay attention to what you read ; for no one can write a summary of any passage unless he has clearly grasped its meaning. So summarizing is an excellent training in concentration of attention. It teaches one to read with the mind, as well as with the eye, on the page.
2. Precis-writing is also a very good exercise in *writing* a composition. It teaches one how to express one's thoughts clearly, concisely and effectively. It is a splendid corrective of the common tendency to vague and disorderly thinking and loose and diffuse writing. Have you noticed how an uneducated person tells a story ? He repeats himself, brings in a lot of irrelevant matter, omits from its proper place what is essential and drags it in later as an after-thought, and takes twenty minutes to say what a trained thinker would express in five. The whole effect is muddled and tedious. In a precis you have to work within strict limits. You must express a certain meaning in a fixed number of words. So you learn to choose your words carefully, to construct your sentences with an eye to fullness combined with brevity, and to put your matter in a strictly logical order.
3. So practice in precis-writing is of great value for *practical life*. In any position of life the ability to grasp quickly and accurately what is read, or heard, and to reproduce it clearly and concisely, is of the utmost value. For lawyers, businessmen, and government officials it is essential.

II. Method of Procedure

You must make up your mind from the beginning that precis-writing means intensive brain-work. There is no easy short cut to summarising a passage. To tear the heart out of a passage means concentrated thought, and you must be prepared for close attention and hard thinking.

1. **Reading** **(*a*)** First read the passage through carefully, but not too slowly, to get a general idea of its meaning. If one reading is not sufficient to give you this clearly, read it over again, and yet again. The more you read it, the more familiar will it become to you, and the clearer will be **(*i*)** its subject, and **(*ii*)** what is said about that subject. Ask yourself, "What is it I am reading ? What does the author mean ? What is his subject ? What is he saying about it ? Can I put in a few words the pith of what he says ?"

   (*b*) Usually you are required to supply a *title* for your precis. This is a good stage at which to do this. Think of some word, phrase or short sentence that will sum up briefly the main subject of the passage. Sometimes this is supplied by what we may call a *key-sentence.* This key-sentence may be found at the beginning or at the end of the passage. For example, look at Exercise 148, No. 20, in which the first sentence gives the subject, all the rest of the passage being an expansion and illustration of it : "Hospitality is a virtue for which the natives of the East in general are highly and deservedly admired". This at once suggests the short title of "Eastern Hospitality". But you will not always find such convenient key-sentences in the passage you have to summarise. In their absence, you must get a clear idea of the subject from the passage as a whole, and then sum it up in a suitable heading.

The effort to find a suitable title at this stage will help you to define in your mind what exactly the subject, or main theme, of the passage is.

(c) Further reading is now necessary to ensure that you understand the *details* of the passage as well as its main purport. Take it now sentence by sentence, and word by word. If the meanings of any words are not clear, look them up in a dictionary. Detailed study of this kind is necessary, because a phrase, a sentence, or even a single word, may be of prime importance, and the misunderstanding of it may cause you to miss the whole point of the passage.

(d) You should now be in a position to decide what parts of the passage are essential and what parts are comparatively unimportant and so can be omitted without any loss. This process of *selection* is not so easy as some people think. Beginners select ; but they often select in a haphazard or mechanical way. It requires some practice to be able to say, "*This* is essential to the meaning of the passage, and *that* is only incidental and unimportant." The best guide, of course, is the subject or main theme of the passage. If you have a clear and correct idea of that you will soon see what is important and what is unimportant.

At this stage it is useful to jot down your conclusions in brief notes—writing down the subject, the title, and the details which you consider essential or important. (This is a better plan than underlining sentences and phrases in the original.)

2. **Writing** ***(a) Rough Drafts***—You should now be ready to attempt the writing of the precis ; but be sure of the limits within which it must be compressed. If the number of words is given you, this is easy; but if you are told to reduce the passage to say, a third of its length, count the number of words in the passage and divide by three. You may use fewer words than the number prescribed, but in no case may you exceed the limit.

It is not likely that your first attempt will be a complete success. The draft will probably be too long. In fact you may have to write out several drafts before you find how to express the gist of the passage fully within the limits set. A good deal of patience and revision will be required before you get it right. It is a good plan to write the first draft without having the actual words of the originial passages before one's eyes.

(b) Important Points—The following points must be kept in mind:

(i) The precis should be *all in your own words.* It must not be a patchwork made up of phrases and sentences quoted from the original.

(ii) The precis must be *a connected whole.* It may be divided into sections or paragraphs, according to changes in the subject-matter, but these must not appear as separate notes, but must be joined together in such a way as to read continuously.

(iii) The precis must be *complete* and *self-contained* ; that is, it must convey its message fully and clearly without requiring any reference to the original to complete its meaning.

(iv) It is only the gist, main purport, or general meaning of the passage which you have to express. There is no room in a precis for colloquial expressions, circumlocutions, periphrasis or rhetorical flourishes. All redundancies of expression must be rigorously pruned. If faithful reproduction of the main theme is the first essential of a summary, *conciseness* is the second.

(v) The precis must be in simple, direct grammatical and idiomatic English.

(c) The Art of Compression—You are not bound to follow the orginal order of thought to the passage to be summarised, if you can express its meaning more clearly and concisely by transposing any of its parts.

In *condensing,* aim rather at remodelling, than at mere omission. We may omit mere repetitions, illustrations and examples ; but we change figures of speech into literal expressions, compress wordy sentences, and alter phrases to words.

Take a few examples:

"His courage in battle might without exaggeration be called lion-like". He was very brave in battle.

"The account the witness gave of the incident moved everyone that heard it to laughter."
The witness's story was absurd.

"There came to his recollection."
He remembered.

"The clerk who is now in his employ."
His present clerk.

"They acted in a manner that rendered them liable to prosecution."
They acted illegally.

"He got up and made a speech on the spur of the moment."
He spoke off-hand.

"John fell into the river and, before help could reach him, he sank."
John was drowned in the river.

"He was hard up for money and was being pressed by his creditor."
He was in financial difficulties.

"The England of our own days is so strong and the Spain of our own days is so feeble, that it is not possible, without some reflection and care, to comprehend the full extent of the peril which England had from the power and ambition of Spain in the 16th century." (51 words.)

We cannot nowadays fully realise what a menace Spain was to England in the 16th century. (16 words.)

(d) *Indirect Speech*—As a rule, a precis should be written in indirect speech, after a "verb of saying" in the past tense. For example:

"Whether we look at the intrinsic value of our literature, or at the particular situation of this country, we shall see the strongest reason to think that of all foreign tongues the English tongue is that which would be the most useful to our native subjects."

—*Macualay*

Condensed in indirect speech:

Lord Macaulay said that England's noble literature and the universality of her language made English the foreign language most useful for India.

The change from direct to indirect speech calls for attention to the following points:

(*i*) Correct sequence of tenses after the "verb of saying" in the past tense.

(*ii*) Clear differentiation of the various persons mentioned in the passage. Care must be taken with pronouns *he, she* and *they*. To avoid confusion proper names should be used occasionally.

(*iii*) Correct use of adverbs and other words indicating time.

(*iv*) Proper choice of "verbs of saying", to indicate questions, commands, warnings, threats or exhortations.

Great care must be taken to avoid lapsing into direct speech—a very common fault.

Some passages, however, are best summarised in direct speech.

3. **Revision**—When you have made your final draft, carefully *revise* it before you write out the fair copy. Be sure that its length is within the limits prescribed. Compare it with the original to see that you have not omitted any important point. See whether it reads well as a connected whole, and correct any mistakes in spelling and punctuation, grammar and idiom.

Then write out the fair copy neatly, prefixing the title you have chosen.

III. To Sum Up

1. First carefully read the passage, if necessary, several times, apprehend clearly its main theme or general meaning.
2. Examine the passage in detail, to make sure of the meaning of each sentence, phrase and word.
3. Supply a short title which will express the subject.
4. Select and note down the important points essential to the expression of the main theme.

5. Note the length of number of words prescribed for the precis, and write out a first draft.

6. In doing this remember that you are to express the gist of the passage in your own words, and not in quotations from the passage ; that you should condense by remodelling than by mere omission ; and that your precis must be self-contained and a connected whole. Add nothing ; make no comment ; correct no facts.

7. Revise your draft. Compare it carefully with the original to see that you have included all the important points. If it is too long, still further compress it by omitting unnecessary words and phrases or by remodelling sentences. Correct all mistakes in spelling, grammar and idiom, and see that it is properly punctuated. Let the language be simple and direct.

8. Write out neatly the fair copy under the heading you have selected.

SPECIMEN — 1

One great defect of our civilization is that it does not know what to do with its knowledge. Science, as we have seen, has given us powers fit for the gods, yet we use them like small children.

For example, we do not know how to manage our machines. Machines were made to be man's servants; yet he has grown so dependent on them that they are in a fair way to become his masters. Already most men spend most of their lives looking after and waiting upon machines. And the machines are very stern masters. They must be fed with coal, and given petrol to drink, and oil to wash with, and must be kept at the right temperature. And if they do not get their meals when they expect them, they grow sulky and refuse to work, or burst with rage, and blow up, and spread ruin and destruction all round them. So we have to wait upon them very attentively and do all that we can to keep them in a good temper. Already we find it difficult either to work or play without the machines, and a time may come when they will rule us altogether, just as we rule the animals.

(C.E.M. Joad)

Summary

Men and Machines

We do not know what to do with our knowledge. Science has given us superhuman powers, which we do not use properly. For example, we are unable to manage our machines. Machines should be fed promptly and waited upon attentively; otherwise they refuse to work or cause destruction. We already find it difficult to do without machines. In the course of time they may rule over us altogether.

SPECIMEN — 2

A stamp is, to many people, just a slip of paper that takes a letter from one town or country to another. They are unable to understand why we stamp collectors find so much pleasure in collecting them and how we find the time in which to indulge in our hobby. To them it seems a waste of time, a waste of effort and a waste of money. But they do not realise that there are many who do buy stamps, many who find the effort worth-while and many who, if they did not spend their time collecting stamps, would spend it less profitably. We all seek something to do in our leisure hours and what better occupation is there to keep us out of mischief than that of collecting stamps? An album, a packet of hinges, a new supply of stamps, and the time passes swiftly and pleasantly.

Stamp-collecting has no limits and a collection never has an end; countries are always printing and issuing new stamps to celebrate coronations, great events, anniversaries and deaths. And the fascination of collecting is trying to obtain these stamps before one's rivals. Every sphere of stamp-collecting has its fascination – receiving letters from distant countries and discovering old stamps in the leaves of dusty old books. A stamp itself has a fascination all its own. Gazing at its little picture we are transported to the wilds of Congo, the homes of the Arabs, and the endless tracks of the Sahara desert. There is a history in every stamp. The ancient Roman Empire and the Constitution of America, India's Independence and the Allied victory, are all conveyed to our mind's eye by means of stamps. We see famous men, pictures, writers, scientists, soldiers, politicians and famous incidents. Stamps, so small and minute, contain knowledge that is vast and important.

Summary

Stamp-collecting

To many people a stamp is merely something necessary for sending a letter. They regard stamp-collecting as a waste of time, effort and money. But there are many people who love buying stamps and find this hobby worthwhile and more profitable than other leisure pursuits. Collecting stamps helps to pass the time quickly and pleasantly.

Stamp-collecting is limitless and endless. Countries are always issuing stamps to celebrate important events. It is fascinating to receive letters from distant countries and to discover stamps in old books. A stamp itself has a charm. Stamps show us geographical and historical pictures, famous people and incidents. These small things contain vast knowledge.

EXERCISE 148

Write summaries of the following passages of about one-third of the original length.

1. In every country people imagine that they are the best and the cleverest and the others are not so good as are not so good as they are. The Englishman thinks that he and his country are the best; the Frenchman is very proud of France and everything French. The Germans and Italians think no less of their countries and many Indians imagine that India is in many ways the greatest country in the world. This is wrong. Everybody wants to think well of himself and his country. But really there is no person who has not got some good and some bad qualities. In the same way, there is no country which is not partly good and partly bad. We must take the good wherever we find it and try to remove the bad wherever it may be. We are, of course, most concerned with our own country, India. Unfortunately, it is in a bad way today. Many of our people are poor and unhappy. They have no joy in their lives. We have to find out how we can make them happier. We have to see what is good in our ways and customs and try to keep it, and whatever is bad we have to throw away. If we find anything good in other countries, we should certainly take it.

2. There are hundreds of superstitions which survive in various parts of the country, and the stury of them is rather amusing. We are told, for example, that it is unlucky to point to the new moon or to look at it through glass, but if we bow nine times to it we shall have a lucky month.

   Now suppose you tell a scientist that you believe a certain superstition – let us say, that the howling of a dog is a sign of death. The scientist will immediately require evidence before he can accept your belief. He will want figures to prove it. It will be useless to quote two or three cases; he will want hundreds. He will want also to know (*a*) if it ever happens that the howling of dogs is not followed by a death, (*b*) if ever a person's death is predicted by the howling of dogs. The answer to the former question is in the affirmative, and to the latter in the negative. Your superstition will not bear investigation. It may impress an ignorant person; but it cannot face the light of facts. Your case would not carry conviction in a court of law.

   Apart from this process of testing by results, any intelligent man will want to know the "reason why". What connection can there be between a howling dog and an approaching death? Can it be cause and effect? Can it be that the dog has a gift of foreseeing such events? Or is the dog the instrument employed by some uncanny power that moves invisibly in our midst?

3. Over-eating is one of the most wonderful practices among those who think that they can afford it. In fact, authorities say that nearly all who can get as much as they desire, over-eat to their disadvantage. This class of people could save a great more food than they can save by missing one meal per week and at the same time they could improve their health.

   A heavy meal at night, the so-called "dinner", is the fashion with many and often it is taken shortly before retiring. It is unnecessary and could be forgone, not only once a week but daily without loss of strength. From three to five hours are needed to digest food. While sleeping, this food not being required to give energy for work, is in many cases converted into excess fat, giving rise to over-weight. The evening meal should be light, taken three or four hours before retiring. This prevents over-eating, conserves energy and reduces the cost of food.

4. Trees give shade for the benefit of others and while they themselves stand in the sun and endure scorching heat, they produce the fruit by which others profit. The character of good men is like that of trees. What is the use of this perishable body, if no use of it is made for the benefit of mankind? Sandalwood – the more it is rubbed the more scent does it yield. Sugarcane – the more it is peeled and

cut into pieces, the more juice does it produce. Gold — the more it is burnt, the more brightly does it shine. The men who are noble at heart do not lose these qualities even in losing their lives. What does it matter whether men praise them or not? What difference does it make whether riches abide with them or not? What does it signify whether they die at this moment or whether their lives are prolonged? Happen what may, those who tread in the right path will not set foot in any other. Life itself is unprofitable to a man who does not live for others. To live for the mere sake of living one's life is to live the life of dogs and cows. Those who lay down their lives for the sake of a friend, or even for the sake of a stranger, will assuredly dwell forever in a world of bliss.

5. We must insist that free oratory is only the beginning of free speech; it is not the end, but a means to an end. The end is to find the truth. The practical justification of civil liberty is not that the examination of opinion is one of the necessities of man. For experience tells us that it is only when freedom of opinion becomes the compulsion to debate that the seed which our forefathers planted has produced its fruit. When that is understood, freedom will be cherished not because it is a vent for our opinions but because it is the surest method of correcting them.

'The unexamined life', said Socrates, 'is unfit to be lived by man'. This is the virtue of liberty, and the ground on which we may best justify our belief in it, that it tolerates error in order to serve the truth. When more men are brought face to face with their opponents, forced to listen and learn and mend their ideas, they cease to be children and savages and begin to live like civilized men. Then only is freedom a reality, when men may voice their opinions because they must examine their opinions.

The only reason for dwelling on all this is that if we are to preserve democracy we must understand its principles. And the principle which distinguishes it from all other forms of government is that in a democracy the opposition not only is tolerated as constitutional but must be maintained because it is in fact indispensable.

The democratic system cannot be operated without effective opposition. For, in making the great experiment of governing people by consent rather than by coercion, it is not sufficient that the party in power should have a majority. It is just as necessary that the party in power should never outrage the minority. That means that it must listen to the minority and be moved by the criticisms of the minority.

6. I designed, after my first voyage, to spend the rest of my days at Baghdad, but it was not long ere I grew weary of an indolent life, and I put to sea a second time, with merchants of known probity. We embarked on board of a good ship, and after recommending ourselves to God, set sail. One day we landed on an Island covered with several sorts of fruit-trees, but we could see neither man nor animal. We walked in the meadows, along the streams that watered them. Whilst some diverted themselves with gathering flowers, and others fruits, I took my wine and provisions, and sat down near a stream betwixt two high trees, which afforded a delightful shade. I made a good meal, and afterwards fell asleep. I cannot tell how long I slept, but when I awoke the ship was no longer in view.

In this sad condition, I was ready to die with grief. I cried out in agony, beat my head and breast, and threw myself upon the ground, where I lay some time, overwhelmed by a rushing current of thoughts, each more distressing than the last. When I gazed towards the sea I could discern nothing but sky and water ; but looking over the land I beheld something white ; and coming down, I took what provision I had left, and went towards the object, which was so distant that at first could not distinguish what it was.

As I approached, I thought it to be a white dome, of a prodigious height and extent. I drew near to it, and walked round it ; but found no door to it ; and I found that I had not strength nor activity to climb it, on account of its exceeding smoothness. I made a mark at the place where I stood, and went round the dome, measuring its circumference ; and lo ! it was fifty full paces ; and I meditated upon some means of gaining an entrance into it ; but no means of accomplishing this occurred to me.

By this time the sun was about to set, and all of a sudden the sky became as dark as if it had been covered with a thick cloud. I was much astonished at this sudden darkness but much more when I found it occasioned by a bird of a most extraordinary size, that came flying towards me. I remembered that I had often heard mariners speak of a miraculous bird called the roc, and conceived that the great dome which I so much admired must be her egg. Shortly afterwards, the bird alighted, and sat over the egg.

7. It is very easy to acquire bad habits, such as eating too many sweets or too much food, or drinking too much fluid of any kind, or smoking. The more we do a thing, the more we tend to like doing it ; and, if we do not continue to do it, we feel unhappy. This is called the *force of habit,* and the force of habit should be fought against.

Things which may be very good when only done from time to time, tend to become very harmful when done too often and too much. This applies even to such good things as work or rest. Some people form a bad habit of working too much, and others of idling too much. The wise man always remembers that this is true about himself, and checks any bad habit. He says to himself, "I am now becoming idle," or "I like too many sweets," or "I smoke too much" and then adds, "I will get myself out of this bad habit at once."

One of the most widely spread of bad habits is the use of tobacco. Tobacco is now smoked or chewed by men, often by women, and even by children, almost all over the world. It was brought into Europe from America by Sir Walter Raleigh, four centuries ago, and has thence spread everywhere. I very much doubt whether there is any good in the habit, even when tobacco is not used to excess ; and it is extremely difficult to get rid of the habit when once it has been formed.

Alcohol is taken in almost all cool and cold climates, and to a very much less extent in hot ones. Thus, it is taken by people who live in the Himalaya Mountains, but not nearly so much by those who live in the plains of India. Alcohol is not necessary in any way to anybody. Millions of people are beginning to do without it entirely ; and once the United States of America have passed laws which forbid its manufacture or sale throughout the length and breadth of their vast country. In India it is not required by the people at all, and should be avoided by them altogether. The regular use of alcohol, even in small quantities, tends to cause mischief in many ways to various organs of the body. It affects the liver, it weakens the mental powers, and lessens the general energy of the body.

8. The great advantage of early rising is the good start it gives us in our day's work. The early riser has done a large amount of hard work before other men have got out of bed. In the early morning the mind is fresh, and there are few sounds or other distractions, so that work done at that time is generally well done. In many cases the early riser also finds time to take some exercise in the fresh morning air, and this exercise supplies him with a fund of energy that will last until the evening. By beginning so early, he knows that he has plenty of time to do thoroughly all the work he can be expected to do, and is not tempted to hurry over any part of it. All his work being finished in good time, he has a long interval of rest in the evening before the timely hour when he goes to bed. He gets to sleep several hours before midnight, at the time when sleep is most refreshing and after a sound night's rest, rises early next morning in good health and spirits for the labours of a new day.

It is very plain that such a life as this is far more conducive to health than that of the man who shortens his waking hours by rising late, and so can afford in the course of the day little leisure for necessary rest. Any one who lies in bed late, must, if he wishes to do a full day's work, go on working to a correspondingly late hour, and deny himself the hour or two of evening exercise that he ought to take for the benefit of his health. But, in spite of all his efforts, he will probably produce as good results as the early riser, because he misses the best working hours of the day.

It may be objected to this that some find the perfect quiet of midnight by far the best time for working. This is no doubt true in certain cases. Several great thinkers have found by experience that their intellect is clearest, and they can write best, when they burn the midnight oil. But even in such cases the practice of working late at night cannot be commended. Few men, if any, can exert the full power of their intellect at the time when nature prescribes sleep, without ruining their health thereby ; and of course the injury done to the health must in the long run have a bad effect on the quality of the work done.

9. The human race is spread all over the world, from the polar regions to the tropics. The people of which it is made up, eat different kinds of food, partly according to the climate in which they live, and partly according to the kind of food which their country produces. Thus, in India, the people live chiefly on different kinds of grain, eggs, milk, or sometimes fish and meat. In Europe the people eat more flesh and less grain. In the Arctic regions, where no grain and fruits are produced, the Eskimo and other races live almost entirely on flesh, especially fat.

The men of one race are able to eat the food of another race, if they are brought into the country inhabited by the latter ; but as a rule they still prefer their own food, at least for a time—owing to custom. In hot climates, flesh and fat are not much needed ; but in the Arctic regions they seem to be very necessary for keeping up the heat of the body.

The kind of food eaten also depends very often on custom or habit, and sometimes upon religion. Brahmins will not touch meat ; Mohammedans and Jews will not touch the flesh of pigs. Most races would refuse to eat the flesh of many unclean animals, although, quite possibly, such flesh may really be quite wholesome.

All races of mankind have their own different ideas on this matter. Thus the English used to laugh at the French because the latter ate frogs' legs and some kind of snails; the Australians dislike rabbits although the English eat them ; and the Burmese eat the flesh of crocodiles and elephants.

Neverthless there are many reasons for these likes and dislikes. Thus, swine in eastern countries are very dirty feeders, whereas in Europe they are kept on clean food. The result is that their flesh is eaten in Europe but not in India. Men dislike eating the flesh of all draught animals. Hence the Englishman will not eat horse-flesh, and the Hindu will not touch the flesh of cattle.

Lastly, certain savage peoples used to be cannibals—that is to say, they ate human flesh—though this custom has now fortunately almost ceased throughout the whole world.

There is another reason for disliking certain kinds of flesh, and a very good reason too. It is because these kinds are apt to contain dangerous parasites, which may get into the blood of those who eat the flesh. Certain kinds of swine, for example, are dangerous as food, as their flesh contains a parasite in the form of a little worm.

10. Dear boy, now that you are going a little more into the world I will take this occasion to explain my intentions as to your future expenses, that you may know what you have to expect from me, and make your plan accordingly. I shall neither deny nor grudge you any money that may be necessary for either your improvement or pleasures ; I mean the pleasures of a rational being. Under the head of improvement I mean the best books, and the best masters cost what they will ; I also mean all the expense of lodgings, coach, dress, servants, etc., which, according to the several places where you may be, shall be respectively necessary to enable you to keep the best company. Under the head of rational pleasures I comprehend, first, proper charities to real and compassionate objects of it ; secondly, proper presents to those to whom you are obliged, or whom you desire to oblige ; thirdly, a conformity of expense to that of the company which you keep ; as in public spectacles, your share of little entertainments, a few pistoles at games of mere commerce and other incidental calls of good company. The only two articles which I will never supply are, the profusion of low riot, and the idle lavishness of negligence and laziness. A fool squanders away without credit or advantage to himself, more than a man of sense spends with both. The latter employs his money as he does his time, and never spends a shilling of the one, nor a minute of the other, but in something that is either useful or rationally pleasing to himself or others. The former buys whatever he does not want, and does not pay for what he does want. He cannot withstand the charms of a toy-shop ; snuff-boxes, watches, heads or canes, etc., are his destruction. His servants and tradesmen conspire with his own indolence to cheat him, and in a very little time he is astonished, in the midst of all the ridiculous superfluities, to find himself in want of all the real comforts and necessaries of life. Without care and method the largest fortune will not, and with them almost the smallest will, supply all necessary expenses. Keep an account in a book, of all that you receive, and of all that you pay ; for no man, who knows what he receives and what he pays, ever runs out.

11. A great part of Arabia is desert. Here there is nothing but sand and rock. The sand is so hot that you cannot walk over it with your bare feet in the daytime. Here and there in the desert are springs of water that come from deep down under the ground—so deep that the sun cannot dry them up. These springs are few and far apart, but wherever there is one, trees grow tall and graceful, making a cool, green, shady place around the spring. Such a place is called an oasis.

The Arabs who are not in the cities live in the desert all the year round. They live in tents that can be put up and taken down very easily and quickly so that they can move from one oasis to another, seeking grass and water for their sheep, goats, camels and horses. These desert Arabs eat ripe, sweet figs, and also the dates that grow upon the palm trees ; they dry them, too, and use them as food all the year round.

These Arabs have the finest horses in the world. An Arab is very proud of his riding horse, and loves him almost as much as he loves his wife and children. He never puts heavy loads upon his horse, and often lets him stay in the tent with his family.

The camel is much more useful to the Arab than his beautiful horse, however, for he is much larger and stronger. One camel can carry as much as or more than two horses. The Arab loads the camel with goods and rides him, too, for miles and miles across the desert—just as if he were really the "Ship of the Desert," which he is often called.

12. Ferdinand and Isabella, informed of the return and discoveries of their admiral, awaited him at Barcelona with honour and munificence worthy of the greatness of his services. The nobility came from all the provinces to meet him. He made a triumphal entry as a prince of future kingdoms. The Indians brought over as a living proof of the existence of new races in these newly-discovered lands, marched at the head of the procession, their bodies painted with divers colours, and adorned with gold necklaces and pearls. The animals and birds, the unkonwn plants, and the precious stones collected on these shores, were exhibited in golden basins, carried on the heads of Moorish or Negro slaves. The eager crowd pressed close upon them, and wondrous tales were circulated about the officers and companions of Columbus. The admiral himself, mounted on a richly charger presented by the king, next appeared, accompanied by a numerous caparisoned cavalcade of courtiers and gentlemen. All eyes were directed toward the man inspired of Heaven, who first had dared lift the veil of Ocean. People sought in his face for a sign of his mission and thought they could discern one. The beauty of his features, the majesty of his countenance, the vigour of eternal youth joined to the dignity of age the combination of thought with action, of strength with experience, a thorough appreciation of his worth combined with piety, made Columbus then appear (as those relate who saw him enter Barcelona) like a prophet, or a hero of Holy Writ or Grecian story.

"None could compare with him," they say ; "all felt him to be the greatest or most fortunate of men."

Ferdinand and Isabella received him on their throne, shaded from the sun by a golden canopy. They rose up before him, as though he had been an inspired messenger. They then made him sit on a level with themselves, and listened to the circumstantial account of his voyage. At the end of his recital, which habitual eloquence had coloured with his exuberant imagination, the king and queen, moved to tears, fell on their knees and repeated the *Te Deum,* a thanksgiving for the greatest conquest the Almightly had yet vouchsafed to sovereigns.

13. Up the River Hudson in North America are the Catskill Mountains. In a certain village at the foot of these mountains, there lived long ago a man named Rip Van Winkle. He was a simple and good-natured person, a very kind neighbour and a great favourite among all the good wives of the village. Whenever there was a squabble in the family of Rip, the women in the village always took his part and laid all the blame on Dame Van Winkle.

The children of the village too would shout with joy, whenever they saw him. He helped at their sports, made playthings for them, taught them to fly kites and shoot marbles and told them long stories of ghosts, witches and Indians.

Rip had no love for labour, if it would bring him profit. He would sit for a whole day on a wet rock and fish without a murmur, even though he did not catch a single fish. He would carry a light gun on his shoulder for hours together and shoot only a few squirrels or wild pigeons.

He would never refuse to assist a neighbour even in roughest toil. The women of the village often employed him to run their errands and to do little jobs for them. In a word, Rip was ready to attend to anybody's business but his own. He was, however, one of those men who take the world easy. He would eat coarse bread or fine, whichever could be got with least thought or trouble. And he would rather starve on a penny than work for a pound.

If left to himself, Rip would have whistled away life in perfect contentment. But his wife always kept drumming in his ears about his idleness, his carelessness and the ruins he was bringing on his family. Rip had but one way of replying to all her lectures—he shook his head, cast up his eyes and said nothing. He had one good friend at home and that was his dog Wolf which was as idle as the master.

14. The man who is perpetually hesitating which of the two things he will do first, will do neither. The man who resolves, but suffers his resolution to be changed by the first counter-suggestion of a friend, – who fluctuates from opinion to opinion, from plan to plan, and veers like a weather-cock to every point of the compass, with every breath of caprice that blows—can never accomplish any thing great or useful. Instead of being progressive in any thing, he will be at best stationary, and more probably retrograde in all. It is only the man who first consults wisely, then resolves firmly, and then executes his purpose with flexible perseverance, undismayed by those petty difficulties which daunt a weaker spirit, that can advance to eminence in any line. Take your course wisely, but firmly ; and having taken it, hold upon it with heroic resolution, and the Alps and Pyrenees will sink before you.

15. Nature seems to have taken a particular care to disseminate her blessings among the different regions of the world with an eye to this mutual intercourse and traffic among mankind, that the natives of the several parts of the globe might have a kind of dependence upon one another, and be united together by their common interest. Almost every degree produces something peculiar to it. The food often grows in one country, and the sauce in another. The fruits of Portugal are corrected by the products of Barbadoes, and the infusion of a China plant is sweetened by the pith of an Indian cane. The Philippine islands give a flavour to our European bowls. The single dress of a woman of quality is often the product of a hundred climates. The muff and the fan come together from the different ends of the earth. The scarf is sent from the torrid zone, and the tippet from beneath the pole. The brocade petticoat rises out of the mines of Peru, and the diamond necklace out of the bowels of Indostan.

16. It is the height of selfishness for men, who fully appreciate in their own case the great advantage of a good education, to deny these advantages to women. There is no valid argument by which the exclusion of the female sex from the privilege of education can be defended. It is argued that women have their domestic duties to perform, and that, if they were educated, they would bury themselves in their books and have little time for attending to the management of their households. Of course it is possible for women, as it is for men, to neglect necessary work in order to spare more time for reading sensational novels. But women are no more liable to this temptation than men, and most women would be able to do their household work all the better for being able to refresh their minds in the intervals of leisure with a little reading. Nay, education would even help them in the performance of the narrowest sphere of womanly duty. For education involves knowledge of the means by which health may be preserved and improved, and enables a mother to consult such modern books as will tell her how to rear up her children into healthy men and women and skilfully nurse them and her husband when disease attacks her household. Without education she will be not unlikely to listen with fatal results to the advice of superstitious quacks, who pretend to work wonders by charms and magic.

But according to a higher conception of woman's sphere, woman ought to be something more than a household drudge. She ought to be able not merely to nurse her husband in sickness, but also to be his companion in health. For this part of her wifely duty education is necessary, for there cannot well be congenial companionship between an educated man and an uneducated wife, who can converse with her husband on no higher subjects than cookery and servants' wages. Also one of a mother's highest duties is the education of her children at the time when their mind is most amenable to instruction. A child's whole future life, to a large extent, depends on the teaching it receives in early childhood, and it is needless to say, that this first foundation of education cannot be well laid by an ignorant mother. On all these grounds female education is a vital necessity.

17. The effect produced on the mind by travelling depends entirely on the mind of the traveller and on the way in which he conducts himself. The chief idea of one very common type of traveller is to see as many objects of interest as he possibly can. If he can only after his return home say that he has seen such and such a temple, castle, picture gallery, or museum, he is perfectly satisfied. Therefore, when he arrives at a famous city, he rushes through it, so that he may get over as quickly as possible the task of seeing its principal sights, enter them by name in his note-book as visited or, in his own phraseology 'done', and then hurry on to another city which he treats in the same unceremonious way.

Another kind of traveller in all he sees finds entertainment for his foolish spirit of ridicule. The more hallowed any object is from historical and religious associations or artistic beauty, the more he delights to degrade it by applying to it familiar terms of vulgar slang that he mistakes for

wit. Such a one brings disgrace upon his nation by the rude insolence with which he laughs at foreigners and their ways, and everything else that attracts the notice of his feeble understanding. At the end of his wanderings he returns to his home a living example, showing

How much the fool that hath been taught to roam

Excels the fools that hath been kept at home.

Far different is the effect of travels upon who leave their native country with minds prepared by culture to feel intelligent admiration for all the beauties of nature and art to be found in foreign lands. Their object is not to see much, but to see well. When they visit Paris or Athens or Rome, instead of hurrying from temple to museum, and from museum to picture gallery, they allow the spirit of the place to sink into their minds, and only visit such monuments as the time they have at their disposal allows them to contemplate without irreverent haste. They find it more profitable and delightful to settle down for a week or so at centres of great historical and artistic interest or of remarkable natural beauty, than to pay short visits to all the principal cities that they pass by. In this way they gain by their travels refreshment and rest for their minds, satisfaction to their intellectual curiosity or artistic tastes, and increased knowledge of the world and its inhabitants. Such people, who have travelled with their eyes open, return to their native land with a greater knowledge of its glories and defects than the stay-at-home can ever have.

18. It is in the temperate countries of northern Europe that the beneficial effects of cold are most manifest. A cold climate seems to stimulate energy by acting as an obstacle. In the face of an insuperable obstacle our energies are numbed by despair ; the total absence of obstacles, on the other hand leaves no room for the exercise and training of energy ; but a struggle against difficulties that we have a fair hope of overcoming, calls into active operation all our powers. In like manner, while intense cold numbs human energies, and a hot climate affords little motive for exertion, moderate cold seems to have a bracing effect on the human race. In a moderately cold climate man is engaged in an arduous, but no hopeless struggle with the inclemency of the weather. He has to build strong houses and procure thick clothes to keep himself warm. To supply fuel for his fires, he must hew down trees and dig coal out of the bowels of the earth. In the open air, unless he moves quickly, he will suffer pain from the biting wind. Finally, in order to replenish the expenditure of bodily tissue caused by his necessary exertions, he has to procure for himself plenty of nourishing food.

Quite different is the lot of man in the tropics. In the neighbourhood of the equator there is little need of clothes or fire, and it is possible with perfect comfort and no danger to health, to pass the livelong day stretched out on the bare ground beneath the shade of a tree. A very little fruit or vegetable food is required to sustain life under such circumstances, and that little can be obtained without much exertion from the bounteous earth.

We may recognize much the same difference between ourselves at different seasons of the year, as there is between human nature in the tropics and in temperate climes. In hot weather we are generally languid and inclined to take life easily ; but when the cold season comes, we find that we are more inclined to vigorous exertion of our minds and bodies.

19. One of the peculiarities which distinguish the present age is the multiplication of books. Everyday brings new advertisements of literary undertakings, and we are flattered with repeated promises of growing wise on easier terms than our progenitors

I would face the world manly.

How much either happiness or knowledge is advanced by this multitude of authors, is not very easy to decide.

He that teaches us anything which we know not before, is undoubtedly to be loved as a benefactor; and he that supplies life with innocent amusement, will be certainly caressed as a pleasing companion.

But few of those who fill the world with books, have any pretensions to the hope either of pleasing or instructing. They have often no other task than to lay two books before them out of which they compile a third, without any new materials of their own, and with little application of judgement to those which former authors have supplied.

That all compilations are useless, I do not assert. Particles of science are often very widely scattered upon topics very remote from the principal subject, which are often more valuable than formal treatises, and which yet are not known because they are not promised in the title. He that collects those under proper heads is very laudably employed ; for though he exerts no great abilities in the work, he facilitates the progress of others, and, by making that easy of attainment which is already written, may give some mind more vigorous or more adventurous than his own, leisure for new thoughts and original designs.

But the collections poured lately from the press have seldom been made at any great expense of time or inquiry, and therefore only serve to distract choice without supplying any real want.

20. Hospitality is a virtue for which the natives of the East in general are highly and deservedly admired ; and the people of Egypt are well entitled to commendation on this account. A word which signifies literally "a person on a journey" ("musafir") is the term most commonly employed in this country in the sense of a visitor or guest. There are very few persons here who would think of sitting down to a meal, if there were a stranger in the house without inviting him to partake of it unless the latter were a menial ; in which case, he would be invited to eat with the servants. It would be considered a shameful violation of good manners if a Muslim abstained from ordering the table to be prepared at the usual time because a visitor happened to be present. Persons of the middle classes in this country, if living in a retired situation, sometimes take their supper before the door of their house, and invite every passenger of respectable appearance to eat with them. This is very commonly done among the lower order. In cities and large towns, claims on hospitality are unfrequent ; as there are many wekalehs, or khans, where strangers may obtain lodging ; and food is very easily procured ; but in the villages, travellers are often lodged and entertained by the Sheykh or some other inhabitant ; and if the guest be a person of the middle or higher classes, or even not very poor he gives a present to his host's servants, or to the host himself. In the desert, however, a present is seldom received from a guest. By a Sunneh law, a traveller may claim entertainment from a person able to afford it to him, for three days.

21. Day by day her influence and dignity increased. First of all she received the title of *Noor Mahal,* 'Light of the Harem' but was afterwards distinguished by that of *Noor Jahan Begam,* 'Light of the World.' All her relations and connexions were raised to honour and wealth......No grant of lands was conferred upon any one except under her seal. In addition to giving her the titles that other kings bestowed, the Emperor granted Noor Jahan the rights of sovereignty and government. Sometimes she would sit in the balcony of her palace, while the nobles would present themselves, and listen to her dictates. Coin was struck in her name, with this superscription : 'By order of the King Jehangir, gold has a hundred splendours added to it by receiving the impression of the name of Noor Jahan, the Queen Begam.' On all *farmans* also receiving the Imperial signature, the name of 'Noor Jahan, the Queen Begam,' was jointly attached. At last her authority reached such a pass that the King was such only in name. Repeatedly he gave out that he had bestowed the sovereignty on Noor Jahan Begam, and would say, 'I require nothing beyond a *sir* of wine and half a *sir* of meat.' It is impossible to describe the beauty and wisdom of the Queen. In any matter that was presented to her, if a difficulty arose, she immediately solved it. Whoever threw himself upon her protection was preserved from tyranny and oppression ; and if ever she learnt that any orphan girl was destitute and friendless, she would bring about her marriage, and give her a wedding portion. It is probable that during her reign not less than 500 orphan girls were thus married and portioned.

22. Dante was of moderate height and after reaching maturity, was accustomed to walking somewhat bowed, with a slow and gentle pace, clad always in such sober dress as befitted his ripe years. His face was large, and the lower lip protruded beyond the upper. His complexion was dark, his hair and beard thick, black, and curled, and his expression ever melancholy and thoughtful.

In both his domestic and his public demeanour he was admirably composed and orderly, and in all things courteous and civil beyond any other. In food and drink he was most temperate, both in partaking of them at the appointed hours and in not passing the limits of necessity. Nor did he show more epicurism in respect of one thing than another, He praised delicate viands, but ate chiefly of plain dishes, and censured beyond measure those who bestow a great part of their attention upon possessing choice things, and upon the extremely careful preparation of the same, affirming that such persons do not eat to live, but rather live to eat.

None was more vigilant than he in study and in whatever else he undertook, insomuch that his wife and family were annoyed thereby, until they grew accustomed to his ways, and after that they paid no heed thereto. He rarely spoke unless questioned, and then thoughtfully, and in a voice suited to the matter whereof he treated. When, however, there was cause he was eloquent and fluent in speech, and possessed of an excellent and ready delivery. In his youth he took the greatest delight in music and song, and enjoyed the friendship and intimacy of all the best singers and musicians of his time. Led on by this delight he composed many poems, which he made them clothe in pleasing and masterly melody.

23. People moan about poverty as a great evil ; and it seems to be an accepted belief that if people only had plenty of money, they would be happy and useful and get more out of life. As a rule, there is more genuine satisfaction in life and more obtained from life in the humble cottage of the poor man than in the palaces of the rich. I always pity the sons and daughters of rich men, who are attended by servants, and have governesses at a later age ; at the same time I am glad to think that they do not know what they have missed.

It is because I know how sweet and happy and pure the home of honest poverty is, how free from perplexing care and from social envies and jealousies—how loving and united its members are in the common interest of supporting the family that I sympathize with the rich man's boy and congratulate the poor man's son. It is for these reasons that from the ranks of the poor so many strong, eminent, self-reliant men have always sprung and always must spring. If you will read the list of the "Immortals who were not born to die," you will find that most of them have been born poor.

It seems nowadays a matter of universal desire that poverty should be abolished. We should be quite willing to abolish luxury ; but to abolish honest, industrious, self-denying poverty would be to destroy the soil upon which mankind produces the virtues that will enable our race to reach a still higher civilization than it now possesses.

24. The situation of Columbus was daily becoming more and more critical. In proportion as he approached the regions where he expected to find land, the impatience of his crews augmented. The favourable signs which increased his confidence were decided by them as delusive ; and there was danger of their rebelling and obliging him to turn back, when on the point of realizing the object of all his labours. They beheld themselves with dismay still wafted onward over the boundless wastes of what appeared to them a mere watery desert surrounding the habitable world. What was to become of them should their provisions fall ? Their ships were too weak and defective even for the great voyage they had already made, but if they were still to press forward, adding at every moment to the immense expanse behind them, how should they ever be able to return, having no intervening port where they might victual and refit? Were they to sail in until they perished, or until all return became impossible ? In such case they would be the authors of their own destruction.

On the other hand, should they consult their safety and turn back before too late, who would blame them ? Any complaints made by Columbus would be of no weight ; he was a foreigner, without friends or influence ; his schemes had been condemned by the learned and discountenanced by people of all ranks. He had no party to uphold him, and a host of opponents whose pride of opinion would be gratified by his failure. Or, as an effectual means of preventing his complaints, they might throw him into the seas and give out that he had fallen overboard while busy with his instruments contemplaing the stars, a report which no one would have either the inclination or the means to controvert.

Columbus was not ignorant of the mutinous disposition of his crew, but he still maintained a serene and steady countenance—soothing some with gentle words, endeavouring to stimulate the pride or avarice of others, and openly menacing the refractory with signal punishment, should they do anything whatever to impede the voyage.

25. The great Roman orator, Cicero, in his celebrated treatise on Friendship, remarks with truth that it increases happiness and diminishes misery by the doubling of our joy and the dividing of our grief. When we do well, it is delightful to have friends who are so proud of our success that they receive as much pleasure from it as we do ourselves. For the friendless man the attainment of wealth, power, and honour is of little value. Such possessions contribute to our happiness most by enabling us to do good to others but if all those whom we are able to benefit are strangers, we take far less pleasure in our beneficence than if it were exerted on behalf of friends whose happiness is as dear to us as our own. Further, when we do our duty in spite of temptation, the mental satisfaction obtained from the approval of our consciences is heightened by the praise of our friends ; for their judgement is as it were a second conscience, encouraging us in good and deterring us from evil. Our amusements have little zest and soon pall upon us if we engage in them in solitude, or with uncongenial companions, for whom we can feel no affection. Thus in every case our joys are rendered more intense and more permanent by being shared with friends.

It is equally true that, as Cicero points out, friendship diminishes our misery by enabling us to share the burden of it with others. When fortune has inflicted a heavy unavoidable blow upon us, our grief is alleviated by friendly condolence and by the thought that as long as friends are left to us, life is still worth living.

But many misfortunes which threaten us are not inevitable and in escaping such misfortunes, the advice and active assistance of our friends may be invaluable. The friendless man stands alone, exposed, without protection to his enemies and to the blows of fortune ; but whoever has loyal friends is thereby provided with a strong defence against the worst that fortune can do to him.

26. The best friend a man has in this world may turn against him and become his enemy. His son or his daughter, that he has reared with loving care, may prove ungrateful. Those who are nearest and dearest to us, those whom we trust with our happiness and our good name, may become traitors to their faith.

The money that a man has he may lose. It flies away from him perhaps when he needs it most.

A man's reputation may be sacrificed in a moment of ill-considered action. The people who are prone to fall on their knees to do us honour when success is with us, may be the first to throw stones of malice when failure settles its cloud upon our heads.

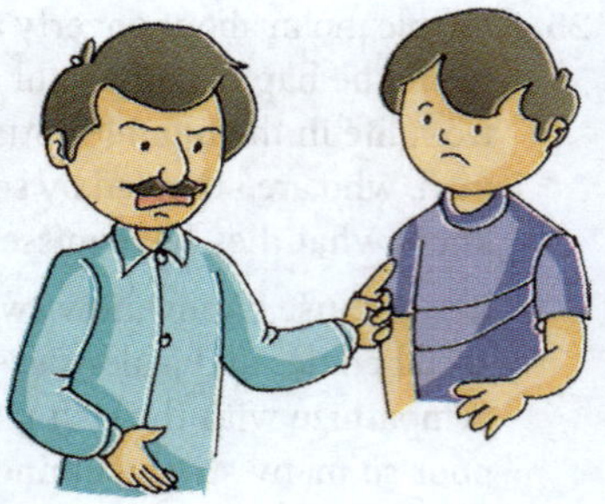

The one absolutely unselfish friend that man can have in this selfish world, the one that never deserts him, the one that never proves ungrateful or treacherous is his dog.

A man's dog stands by him in prosperity and in poverty, in health and in sickness. He will sleep on the cold ground, where the wintry winds blow and the snow drives fiercely, if only he may be by his master's side. He will kiss the hand that has no food to offer, he will lick the wounds and sores that come in encounter with the roughness of the world.

He guards the sleep of his pauper master as if he was a prince. When all other friends desert he remains.

When riches take wings and reputation falls to pieces, he is as constant in his love as the sun in its journey through the heavens. If fortune drives the master forth an outcast in the world, friendless, homeless, the faithful dog asks no higher privilege than that of accompanying him to guard against danger, to fight against his enemies. And when the last scene of all comes, and death takes the master in his embrace, and his body is laid away in the cold ground, no matter if all other friends pursue their way, there by the graveside will the noble dog be found, his head between his paws, his eyes sad but open in alert watchfulness, faithful and true even to death.

Chapter 39 EXPANSION OF PASSAGES

This exercise is the exact opposite of Precis-writing. In Precis-writing we have to compress; and in these exercises we have to expand. A sentence, or a short passage, has to be enlarged into a paragraph by the fuller and more elaborate expression of its meaning, or by adding illustrations, details or proofs to a simple statement. Such exercise practically amounts to the writing of miniature essays on the subject of the original sentence or passage. No strict rule can be laid down for the length of the expansion ; it must not be too short, or it will scarcely be an expansion, or so long as to become an essay. On the average, eighty to one hundred words should be aimed at.

METHOD OF PROCEDURE

1. Carefully read the original sentence or passage, until you feel that you clearly understand its meaning. (It is a good practice to try to express the main idea in a word or a phrase ; *e.g.*, the real subject of the second specimen is, "Pride in One's Work.")
2. Having grasped the subject and meaning of the passage, proceed to expand it by adding details, illustrations, proofs, examples etc., until it is a tiny essay only long enough to make a paragraph.
3. The expansion must contain all that was in the original passage; and more can be added, so long as it is *strictly relevant to the subject.* [For instance, in Specimen No. 3 (Let thy secret, unseen acts, etc.) the story of the Greek sculptor is not in the original, but it well illustrates the meaning of the passage.]
4. The sentence for expansion is a conclusion or finished product: and it is your work to trace the steps by which this thought has been arrived at.
5. If it is a metaphor, explain its full meaning in plain language, and give reasons to support it.
6. Your expansion should read as a complete piece of composition, expressed in good English ; such that it can be clearly understood apart from the original passage. So, when you have written it, go over it carefully to see that nothing essential has been omitted or left obscure.
7. Correct all mistakes in spelling, grammar and punctuation.

SPECIMENS

1

A great deal of talent is lost in the world for the want of a little courage.

EXPANSION

SELF-CONFIDENCE

Timidity and self-distrust are almost as great faults as conceit and over-confidence. There are many people who have real talent in different lines and yet who never accomplish anything, because they are afraid to make the first venture ; and in this way good and useful things are lost to the world. A reasonable amount of confidence in one's own powers is necessary for success.

2

If I were a cobbler, it would be my pride
The best of all cobblers to be ;
If I were a tinker, no tinker beside
Should mend an old kettle like me.

EXPANSION

PRIDE IN ONE'S WORK

It is a great thing to take a pride in our work. Anything that is worth doing at all, is worth doing well. Even in the humblest task we should be ambitious to do it as well as we can, if possible better than anyone else. For example, a cobbler should not think that because his job is a humble one, it can be scamped and done anyhow ; he should be determined to make better shoes than any other cobbler ; and a tinker should take pride in mending even an old kettle better than any other tinker can.

3

Let thy secret, unseen acts,
Be such as if the men thou prizest most
Were witnesses around thee.

EXPANSION

TOWARD GOODNESS

A Greek sculptor, when he was asked why he carved the backs of his statues, which no man would ever see, as carefully as he carved the front, said : "The gods will see them !" So it is not enough for us to live outwardly good lives while in secret we allow evil in our hearts, for God knows even if men do not ! We should never do in secret what we should be ashamed of doing in the presence of our most valued friends.

4

However mean your life is, meet it and live it ; do not shun it and call it hard names.

EXPANSION

MAKING THE BEST OF LIFE

Men who are always grumbling about their poverty, complaining of their difficulties, whining over their troubles, and thinking that their lot in this world is mean and poor, will never get any happiness out of life or achieve any success. However mean our life may be, if we face it bravely and honestly and try to make the best of it, we shall find that after all it is not so bad as we thought : and we may have our times of happiness and the joys of success. There is nothing common or unclean, until we make it so by the wrong attitude we adopt towards it.

5

Peace hath her victories
No less renowned than war.

EXPANSION
THE VICTORIES OF PEACE

The word victory is generally associated in our minds with war, and calls up visions of battles, bloodshed, and conquest by force : and we think of war as a glorious thing because of its famous victories and splendid triumphs. But when we think of the achievements of great men–statesmen, scholars, social reformers, scientists, philanthropists, explorers, discoverers and honest workers–for the betterment of the human race and the progress and civilization of the world, we realize that the victories of peace are even more glorious than the victories of war.

EXERCISE 149

Expand the idea contained in each of the following.

1. It is a great loss to a man when he cannot laugh.
2. Charity is a universal duty, which it is in every man's power sometimes to practise.
3. Slow and steady wins the race.
4. He who follows two hares catches neither.
5. A great city is, to be sure, the school for studying life.
6. Mid pleasures and palaces though we may roam,
   Be it ever so humble, there's no place like home.
7. The noblest men that live on earth,
   Are men whose hands are brown with toil.
8. Where there's a will there's a way.
9. Perseverance is the very hinge of all virtues.
10. Honour and shame from no condition rise :
    Act well your part ; there all the honour lies.
11. They are slaves who dare not be
    In the right with two or three.
12. Great talkers are never great doers.
13. The crown and glory of life is Character.
14. Life indeed would be dull, if there were no difficulties.
15. Only the actions of the just
    Smell sweet, and blossom in their dust.
16. Tell me not, in mournful numbers,
    Life is but an empty dream.
17. To anyone who wishes to amend his life there is no time like the present.
18. The real dignity of a man lies, not in what he *has,* but in what he *is.*
19. He that is humble, ever shall
    Have God to be his guide.
20. What is this life, if full of care,
    We have no time to stand and stare?

21. Home-keeping youths have ever homely wits.
22. Houses are built to live in and not to look on.
23. Nothing was ever achieved without enthusiasm.
24. Train up a child in the way he should go.
25. Whatever is worth doing at all, is worth doing well.
26. Custom reconciles us to everything.
27. Do the work that's nearest,
    Though it's dull at whiles,
    Helping when we meet them,
    Lame dogs over stiles.
28. Each man's belief is right in his own eyes.
29. The good are always the merry, save by an evil chance.
30. The heights by great men reached and kept,
    Were not attained by sudden flight ;
    But they, while their companions slept,
    Were toiling upwards in the night.
31. One crowded hour of glorious life.
    Is worth an age without a name.
32. Breathes there the man with soul so dead
    Who never to himself hath said,
    This is my own, my native land ?
33. Full many a gem of purest ray serene
    The dark unfathomed caves of ocean bear ;
    Full many a flower is born to blush unseen,
    And waste its sweetness on the desert air.

Chapter 40 ESSAY-WRITING

The word Essay is defined in "The Concise Oxford Dictionary" as "a literary composition (usually prose and short) on any subject." Properly speaking, it is a written composition giving expression to one's own personal ideas or opinions on some topic ; but the term usually covers also any writtten composition, whether it expresses personal opinions, or gives information on any given subject, or details of a narrative or description.

In fact the word "Essay" is somewhat loosely applied to a variety of compositions, from Bacon's compressed "Essays" on the one hand, to those so called "Essays" of Macaulay, some of which are lengthy articles, almost as big as small books, on the other.

[Addison's Essays are good models for Indian students, because of their brevity and simple directness of style.]

So far as we are concerned here, an essay is an exercise in composition ; and it is well to remember that the word *essay* means, literally, an *attempt.* (Compare the verb "to essay", with the accent on the second syllable, meaning to attempt or try.) The essays you write at school are trial exercises or "attempts" to express your thoughts in good English. (School essays of this kind are sometimes called "themes," from the fact that such an essay is a composition written upon a given theme, or subject).

CHARACTERISTICS OF A GOOD SCHOOL ESSAY

1. ***Unity.*** An essay must be a *unity,* developing one theme with a definite purpose. The subject must be clearly defined in the mind and kept in view throughout. Nothing that is not relevant to it should be admitted to the essay. At the same time, the subject may be treated in a variety of ways and from different points of view.
2. ***Order.*** The essay should follow a certain ordered line of thought and come to a definite conclusion. It should not consist of haphazard reflections put down anyhow. There should be not only unity of subject but also unity of treatment. Hence the necessity for thinking out a line of thought before beginning to write.
3. ***Brevity.*** School essays should not be long. The limit should be about three hundred words ; though, of course, there can be no strict rule as to length, which will depend a good deal on the nature of the subject. But an essay should be a brief exercise, concisely expressed.
4. ***Style.*** In friendly letters, the style should be conversational—easy, natural and familiar ; and in writing such letters we may use colloquial terms which would be out of place in a book. But the style of an essay must be more dignified and literary. Slang, colloquial terms and free and easy constructions are not proper in an essay. At the same time it is a mistake to attempt any flights of fine writing. The language and sentence construction should be simple, direct and natural. The secret of clear writing is clear thinking. "If you clearly understand all about your matter, you will never want thoughts, and thoughts instantly become words." This was said by Cobbett, a writer whose style is a model of clearness, simplicity and directness.
5. ***The Personal Touch.*** An essay should reveal the personal feelings and opinions of the writer. It should have his individuality in it. Strictly speaking, as has been already said, an essay is a written composition giving expression to one's personal ideas or opinions on a subject ; and this personal touch should not be lost, or the essay will be colourless and devoid of individuality. So do not be afraid to express in your essays your own views, and do not be content with repeating the opinions of others. Let there be a note of sincerity in all that you write.

To sum up: An essay must be a *unity,* treating in *an orderly manner* of one subject ; it should be *concisely written* and *not too long,* and the style should by *simple, direct and clear ;* and it should have an individuality, or show the *personal touch* of the writer.

Three features are necessary in a good essay—suitable subject-matter, proper arrangement, and adequate power of expression. Where all these three are present, the essay will be a success.

CLASSIFICATION OF ESSAYS

Essays may be classified as Narrative Essays, Descriptive Essays, Expository Essays, Reflective Essays and Imaginative Essays. The classification is useful, so long as it is remembered that these classes are not mutually exclusive, and that some essays may partake of the peculiarities of more than one class. For example, a narrative essay may contain a good deal of description ; and essays of all classes should be more or less reflective, for the original idea of this form of composition is an expression of the writer's own feelings and opinions about a given subject. For this reason, let us begin with–

1. *Reflective Essays*–A reflection is a thought on some subject–on an idea arising in the mind. So a reflective essay consists of reflections or thoughts on some topic, which is generally of an abstract nature ; for example ; *(a) habits, qualities,* etc., such as truthfulness, thrift, temperance, cowardice, heroism, patriotism, industry, etc., *(b) social, political and domestic topics,* such as riches and poverty, caste, democracy, liberty, government, family life, education, marriage, business, etc., *(c) philosophical subjects,* such as right and wrong, reality, consciousness, the meaning of the universe, etc. ; or *(d) religious and theological topics.*

   In treating such themes, you should try *(i)* to explain, for example, the importance or advantages of possessing good habits and qualities, and the risks and disadvantages of lacking them ; and quote stories, fables, or historical or literary references in support of your statements; *(ii)* discuss the importance of social institutions etc. ; *(iii)* expound and discuss philosophical and theological theories. You should *reason* and support your statements with arguments and facts.

2. *Narrative Essays*–A narrative essay consists mainly in the narration of some event, or series of events. I say "mainly" because a narrative essay must not be confused with a short story or bits of history. The narrative it relates should be treated as a subject for thought and comment, and so the essay should be more or less reflective. Narrative essays may treat of–*(a) historical stories* or *legends* (*e.g.,* the reign of Akbar, the story of Rama and Sita) ; *(b) biographies* (*e.g.,* life of Shivajee, or of Babar) ; *(c) incidents* (*e.g.,* a street quarrel, a festival, a marriage) ; *(d) an accident* or *natural disaster* (*e.g.,* a flood, a fire, a ship-wreck, an earthquake ; *(e) a journey* or *voayge* ; *(f) a story* (real or imaginary).

3. *Descriptive Essays*– A descriptive essay consists of a description of some place or thing ; *e.g., (a) animals, plants, minerals* (such as the elephant, the pipal tree, coal); *(b) towns, countries, buildings,* etc., (*e.g.,* Mumbai, Italy, the Taj Mahal); *(c) aspects and phenomena of nature* (such as volcanoes, the monsoon, sunlight, organic life); and *(d) manufactured articles* (such as motor-cars, steam-engines, silk, paper, etc.).

4. *Expository Essays*–An expository (or explanatory) essay consists of an exposition or explanation of some subject; *e.g.* : *(a) institutions, industries, occupations* (*e.g.,* parliament, the press, silk-weaving, farming, etc.): *(b) scientific topics* (such as gravitation, evolution, astronomy, etc.) ; *(c) literary topics* (such as the nature of poetry, prose styles, the genius of Shakespeare, the novels of Scott, history of fiction, etc.).

5. *Imaginative Essays*–Essays on subjects such as the feelings and experiences of the sailor wrecked on a desert island may be called imaginative Essays. In such the writer is called to place himself in imagination in a position of which he has had no actual experience. Such subjects as "If I were a king," or "The autobiography of a horse," would call for imaginative essays.

HINTS ON ESSAY-WRITING

1. *General Preparation*–One of the chief difficulties young people feel in essay-writing is lack of matter. They do not easily find anything to say about a subject. This is natural, because their experience and general reading are limited. But it may be remedied by reading, and by training the power of observation.

   (a) *Reading*–Bacon said, "Reading maketh a full man"; that is, a person who reads much and widely stores his mind with a large variety of facts, thoughts, illustrations and general information. If you want to write good essays you must acquire a love of reading–not simply reading stories for amusement, but reading good books of history, travel, biography and science. Fill your mind with fine thoughts and accurate information. By so doing you will become "a full man", and "a full man" can always find plenty to say on most subjects.

(*b*) ***Observation***–But all knowledge does not come from books. We may learn much from the life around us—what we see and hear and observe for ourselves. Keep eyes and ears open, and learn from your own experience. Practise writing short descriptions of what you see in everyday life—the people you meet, bits of scenery that strike you, buildings, street scenes, trees and flowers, hills and valleys, the habits of animals and birds. Don't be content with reading other people's description of such things, but see them for yourself. It is surprising what a lot may be learnt from personal observation.

(*c*) ***Conversation***–Books are written by men and women ; and if we can learn from the books they write, we can learn also from the words they say. Listen to people's conversation ; get them to talk to you about the things they know, and discuss subjects that interest you, with your friends. In this way, also, you may learn much.

A writer reads, observes, and gets people to talk ; and in these ways he is always enriching his mind with ideas and knowledge.

2. ***Special Preparation***–Now we come to the special preparation needed for writing an essay on some particular subject ; and the first thing we must do is to define the subject.

(*a*) ***Defining the Subject***–It is very important that you should have a clear and accurate conception of the subject of the essay before you attempt to write on it—what exactly it is and (equally important) what it is not. Some subjects are so simple that you can scarcely make a mistake about them ; but some want looking into to define them exactly. For example, "The Uses of Computers". The subject is not how computers work. Nor is it the history of computers. Yet some students, carelessly reading the subject, might easily take up a large part of their essay with such topics. In a short school-essay there is no room for irrelevant matter. You have to come to the point at once, and start away with the subject. The subject in this case is the uses of computers in offices, in industries, in aircraft, in spacecraft, etc. It is, therefore, very necessary that you should define the subject clearly in your own mind, or you may waste much time and paper in writing on more or less irrelevant matters.

(*b*) ***Collecting materials***–**(*i*) Reading up the Subject**–When you have got a clear idea of your subject, the next step will be to think of what you can say about it. Some subjects are so simple that a little reflection should supply you with sufficient material for a short essay ; but for others, special information will be needed for which you may have to do some special reading. For instance, if you have to write about some historical subjects, or give a description of some country you have seen, you will have to get hold of some book and read the subject up. But in any case, you have to *collect materials* for your essay before you can write it. In schools, class-discussions on the subject, under the guidance of the teacher, are very helpful in this stage of special preparation. In any case, do not attempt to write the essay before you have given some time to thinking over what you can say on the subject. The common habit of beginning to write down the first thing that comes into one's head, without knowing what is to come next, is fatal to good essay-writing.

(*ii*) ***Collection***–As you think over the subject, ideas, facts, and illustrations will pass through your mind. But if you don't catch them as they come, you may forget them just when you want them. So, as you catch birds and put them in a cage, catch and cage these fleeting thoughts by jotting them down on a piece of paper just as they come into your head, without troubling yourself at this stage about their order or suitability. You can examine the birds thus caught at your leisure later. (To save time afterwards, and for convenience of reference, number these notes as you jot them down.)

(*iii*) ***Selection***–When you think you have collected enough material for your essay, or you can't think of any more points, read over the notes you have jotted down to *select* the points most suitable for your purpose. Examine at your leisure the birds in the cage, to see what they are worth. You may find that some points are not very relevant or won't fit in; cross them out. You may find that some are mere repetitions of others ; and others may be simply illustrations to be brought under main heads. This process of selection will probably suggest to you in a general way the line of thought you may follow in the essay.

(c) ***Logical Arrangement***–Now you should be ready to decide on the line of thought of the essay, *i.e.,* the logical order in which you can arrange the points you have selected. The necessity of thus arranging your thoughts according to some ordinary plan cannot be too strongly insisted upon. Without it, the essay will probably be badly arranged, rambling, disproportioned, and full of repetitions and irrelevancies.

(*i*) **Making the outline**–Bearing your subject definitely in your mind and with your purpose clearly before you, sketch out a bare outline of the main heads, under which you will arrange your various materials in a natural, logical and convincing order–from a brief Introduction to an effective Conclusion.

(*ii*) **Filling in the Outline**–Having thus mapped out the main points with which you are going to deal, arrange the ideas you have collected each under its proper main head, rejecting all those not really relevant to your subject or which simply repeat other thoughts, and taking care that each really belongs to the division in which you place it.

You will now have a full outline, which is to be a guide to you in writing the essay. But this is not the essay, but only its well-articulated skeleton. You must now clothe the skeleton with flesh, and (most difficult of all) breathe into it the breath of life, before you can call your production an essay.

EXAMPLE

To illustrate this method of collecting materials and drawing up an outline, let us work out together a simple example for an essay on, say, "The Elephant."

The subject is so simple that we need not spend any time defining it. What is wanted is evidently a Descriptive Essay, and all we have to do is to think of all we can say about the Elephant.

So we can set to work at once catching and caging our birds, or, in other words, jotting down, as they come into our mind, all we can remember about elephants. The thoughts may come to us something like this, and we will put them down and number them as they occur to us.

THE ELEPHANT

1. Largest of all animals.
2. Used in tiger-hunting.
3. Revengeful–story of tailor and elephant.
4. Its trunk and large ears.
5. Found in India and Africa–two kinds.
6. Its skill in piling logs.
7. Its great strength.
8. In India, used in state processions.
9. How caught and tamed.
10. Mad elephants.
11. Elephant grass.
12. Its tusks–hunted for ivory.
13. Howdah and mahout.
14. Story of blind men and elephant.
15. In old times used in war.
16. Its intelligence.
17. Feeds on leaves and grass.

18. Decoy elephants, and *Keddahs.*

19. Can draw heavy loads.

Here is plenty of material ; but it is in no order, and it will want a lot of sifting before it can be used. We must examine all these details to see which are suitable and arrange them.

A little scrutiny will show that they may be *arranged in groups* under different headings.

Nos. 1, 4, 7, 12, and 16 are parts of a *description* of an elephant.

Nos. 2, 6, 8 (with 13), 12, 15 and 19 refer to different ways in which elephants are of *use* to man.

Nos. 7 and 16 give reasons why the elephant is useful to man.

Nos. 9, 12 and 18 refer to the *hunting* of the elephant.

Nos. 5 and 17 mention the *habitat* and food of the elephant.

We have now classified all the points except Nos. 3, 10, 11 and 14. As to No. 11, it is of no use to us, as the grass referred to gets its name simply from its great size. No. 14 would be too long ; and besides the story is not so much about the elephant as an illustration of the fact that truth is many-sided. No. 10 might be brought in incidentally, and perhaps taken along with No. 3 ; but we may have more than enough material without them.

Already something like an outline is emerging from the disorderly mass of material. We see how we may group the different items under such heads as Description, Habitat, Uses, Hunting, etc. Very soon some such provisional bare outline as this may suggest itself.

BARE OUTLINE

1. Description
2. Habitat and food
3. How and why hunted
4. Strength and intelligence, making elephant useful to man
5. Its different uses

Now we must fill in this bare outline by grouping the various points under the main heads. In doing this, we may find occasion to modify or alter the bare outline, and additional details may suggest themselves.

FULL OUTLINE
THE ELEPHANT

1. *Description*–(Nos. 1, 4, 7, 12)

   Great size and strength ; trunk (its uses) ; big ears ; small tail ; tusks ; speed

2. *Habitat*–(Nos. 5 and 17)

   Found in Africa and India ; two kinds ; lives in herds ; feeds on leaves and grass in jungles

3. *Of great use to man* (because of its strength and intelligence)–(Nos. 7 and 16)

   Different uses :

   (*a*) Draws heavy loads (No. 19)

   (*b*) Piles logs (No. 6)

   (*c*) Used in tiger-hunting (No. 2) ; howdah and mahout (No. 13)

   (*d*) Used in battles in old days (No. 15)

   (*e*) Used in state processions in India (No. 8)

4. *Elephant hunting*–Why and how

   (*a*) Hunted for ivory with elephant guns (No. 12)

(*b*) Caught alive to be tamed (No. 9)–Decoy elephants entice herd into *Keddahs* (No. 18)

The outline will be quite long enough for an ordinary school essay; so we had better omit some of the points we first jotted down and marked as doubtful, *viz.*, Nos. 3, 10, 11 and 14. This illustrates the necessity for selection.

When we come to write the essay, we must keep this outline before us as a guide ; but, unless we are required to do so, the outline should not appear in the fair copy of the essay. (In examinations, the outline can be written on the left-hand page of the answer-book, on which scribbling is allowed.)

WRITING THE ESSAY

1. ***Paragraphs***–Every essay should be divided into paragraphs, and each heading should have at least one paragraph to itself. An essay not thus paragraphed looks unattractive, and is not easy to read.

   [A paragraph is a group of related sentences that develop a single point. In constructing a paragraph these principles should be kept in view :–(*i*) *Unity.* The paragraph must treat of one subject only. (*ii*) *Variety.* Paragraphs should not all be of the same length or of the same monotonous structure . (*iii*) *Logical sequence of thought.* (*iv*) *Topical sentence.* The most important sentences of a paragraph are the first and the last. In many paragraphs the first sentence states the subject, and is called the *topical sentence* (or key-sentence). The concluding sentence may sum up effectively what has been said in the paragraph.]

2. ***Structure of an Essay***–We may divide an essay into three parts—the Introduction, the Body of the Essay, and the Conclusion.

   (*a*) ***The Introduction***–This, in a short essay, must be very brief. It would be absurd to have the porch bigger than the building itself. It may be simply a sentence, or a very short paragraph. But it should always be arresting and pertinent to the subject. The introduction may consist of a definition or a quotation, proverb, very brief story, or general remark, leading up to the subject.

   (*b*) ***The Body of the Essay***–This is really the essay itself—the house to which the introduction is the front door, and the conclusion the back door, or exit.

   In arranging the body of the essay *observe proportion* ; that is, let each part have due weight given to it. If the subject is "The good and bad influence of Newspapers," do not devote three-quarters of the essay to good influences and so leave only a quarter for the bad. Closely follow your full outline throughout.

   The *paragraphs* should be well constructed and should be related to one another according to the direction of your outline ; and, as far as possible, the connection between one and another should be shown. Avoid "padding" and keep to the point.

   Take pains in selecting *words* and *phrases* which exactly express the ideas which you have in mind ; and frame your *sentences* so that they are quite clear and forceful.

   Avoid the use of unneccessary words. In revising your essay, look out for useless repetitions and redundant expressions, and strike them out.

   Match the words to the sense, and adapt the style to the subject-matter. Do not write frivolously on a serious subject, or ponderously on a light and humorous subject.

   (c) ***The Conclusion***–As the introduction should arouse interest, the conclusion should satisfy it. An effective and satisfying end to an essay is as important as an arresting beginning. An abrupt or feeble ending may spoil the whole effect of the essay. A good conclusion may consist of :– (*a*) a summing up of the arguments of the essay ; (*b*) final conclusion drawn from the subject-matter ; (*c*) a suitable quotation ; (*d*) a sentence that strikingly expresses the main point you want to drive home.

3. **Finally, a few words about your *Style in Writing***–To acquire a simple, direct and forceful style in writing calls for constant practice. It does not come "by nature." As the poet Pope says:

   "True ease in writing comes from art, not chance ;

   As those move easiest who have learned to dance."

   The secret of clear writing is clear thinking. So, be perfectly clear about what you want to say, and then *say it*–as directly, as simply, as concisely as possible. *Be direct* : use short sentences in preference to long and involved periods. *Be simple* : don't attempt any oratory or flowery language but use simple words and constructions and avoid elaborate and superfluous words ; say what you want to say as tersely as is consistent with making your meaning clear. Never use two words where one (the *right* one) will do. *Be natural*: don't try to imitate any author's style, however eloquent, but *be yourself*.

SUMMARY OF METHOD OF PROCEDURE

To sum up:

1. Clearly define your subject in your own mind.
2. Think over it, until ideas about it come into your mind, and jot the points down on paper as they occur to you–numbering them.
3. Classify these points in groups under suitable headings, rejecting any that are unsuitable.
4. Arrange these headings in a bare outline.
5. Fill in the ouline, making a full outline.
6. Now begin to write the essay, dividing it into paragraphs.
7. The essay should consist of introduction, body and conclusion.
   (*a*) Make the introduction arresting.
   (*b*) Keep the parts of the body of the essay in proper proportion; and take pains in choosing words, constructing sentences and building up paragraphs.
   (*c*) Make the conclusion effective and satisfying.
8. Write in a simple, concise, clear, direct and natural style.

1. HOLIDAYS

There is not much need of proving to most schoolboys that holidays are necessary. They are quite convinced that they are–and most desirable, too. They welcome a holiday from school with hilarious joy, and plague the headmaster on the least excuse to let them off their lessons. It would be more in place to try to convince them of the necessity of work and study. Yet it may be desirable to show that regular intervals of rest, recreation, or a change of occupation are really necessary. As the old rhyme says,

> "All work and no play,
> Makes Jack a dull boy."

> Holidays at proper intervals are especially necessary for young people, and for those engaged in hard mental work; for continuous work, without a break, will injure the health, and may cause a nervous breakdown. A short holiday, rightly used, will send us back to our work with renewed zest and vigour.

"Rightly used." It all depends upon that. For holidays may be abused. If the holiday is spent in stupid idleness, or in an exhausting round of exciting amusements, or shut up in close stuffy rooms drinking and playing, or in any other unhealthy way, the boy or man will come back to his work tired, listless, and uninterested. The holiday, instead of doing good, has done harm, much more harm than steady work could ever do.

How can a holiday, then, be best used, so that at the end of it we shall come back to or work with energies renewed and interest keener than ever ? If we are students, or have been shut up in stuffy offices, we should get away into the pure air of the country and live a healthy, open air life, enjoying games or sports. We should avoid unhealthy amusement, keep early hours and get plenty of refreshing sleep. And we should not be completely idle. Change of occupation is a rest. And if we have a little regular work to do, work that we take an interest in, it will make our holiday not only healthier, but more enjoyable.

2. BOOKS AND READING

Happy is the man who acquires the habit of reading when he is young. He has secured a life-long source of pleasure, instruction and inspiration. So long as he has his beloved books, he need never feel lonely. He always has a pleasant occupation of leisure moments, so that he need never feel bored. He is the possessor of wealth more precious than gold. Ruskin calls books. "Kings' Treasures"–treasuries filled, not with gold and silver and precious stones, but with riches much more valuable than these–knowledge, noble thoughts and high ideals. Poor indeed is the man who does not read, and empty is his life.

The blessings which the reading habit confers on its possessor are many provided we choose the right kind of books. Reading gives the highest kind of pleasure. Some books we read simply for pleasure and amusement–for example, good novels. And novels and books of imagination must have their place in everybody's reading. When we are tired, or the brain is weary with serious study, it is a healthy recreation to lose ourselves in some absorbing story written by a master hand.

But to read nothing but books of fiction is like eating nothing but cakes and sweetmeats. As we need plain, wholesome food for the body, so we must have serious reading for the mind. And here we can choose according to our taste. There are many noble books on history, biography, philosophy, religion, travel, and science which we ought to read, and which will give us not only pleasure but an education. And we can develop a taste for serious reading, so that in the end it will give us more solid pleasure than even novels and books of fiction. Nor should poetry be neglected, for the best poetry gives us noble thoughts and beautiful imaginings clothed in lovely and musical language.

Books are the most faithful of friends. Our friends may change, or die ; but our books are always patiently waiting to talk to us. They are never cross, peevish, or unwilling to converse, as our friends sometimes are. No wonder a reader becomes a "book-lover."

3. A VISIT TO A BOOK FAIR

The year 2002 was declared "The year of Books" by the National Book Trust of India. With this note the nation's capital played the host to the World Book Fair at the Trade Fair Pragati Maidan.

On hearing this my friends and I expressed our eagerness to go and watch this mega festival. Our principal readily agreed and students went by batches to be a part of this grand event. The inaugural day was marked with a walk from the Parliament House to the Trade Fair Grounds.

The book fair was indeed a spectacle to watch. There were hoardings everywhere "All for books and books for all". Each hall was segmented into many stalls managed by the respective publishing houses. Over the years I was told by our principal about the increasing number of publishing houses. We had local publishers, national publishers and international publishers. The book fair attracted a large number of men and women and a much larger number of children.

While the stalls, had the art of finesse, each stall was a delight to watch. They displayed children's books, subject oriented books, books on language and literature, books on performing arts, science and technology books, software and hardware books, books on Finance and Management, books on anatomy and medicine, books on law and income tax, academic books and sponsored books. To top them all was a huge collection of dictionaries.

While every stall was impressive, what attracted us most was the special seating arrangement made for enthusiastic readers by S. Chand and Company Ltd,. To add to this we were all served with a cup of coffee, everyone of us. The coffee relieved our fatigue and we were two steps and thirty miles away from the rest of the world. There were cafeterias and ice cream parlours, I bought some books which appealed to me. As the clock struck eight. I walked home with the feeling of Francis Bacon's memorable words: "Reading maketh a full man, conference a ready man and writing an exact man".

I wish we hosted to such book fairs three times a year so that we can be stimulated to read more and more books and broaden our visions.

4. A HOUSE ON FIRE

I had never seen a house on fire before. So, one evening when I heard fire engines with loud alarm bells rushing past my house, I quickly ran out and, a few streets away, joined a large crowd of people ; but we could see the fire only from a distance because the police would not allow any one near the building on fire.

What a terrible scene I saw that day ! Huge flames of fire were coming out of each floor, and black and thick smoke spread all around. Every now and then tongues of fire would shoot up almost sky-high, sending huge sparks of fire round-about.

Three fire engines were busily engaged and the firemen in their dark uniform were playing the hose on various parts of the building. The rushing water from several hoses soaked the building but it did not seem to have any effect on the flames. Then the tall red ladders of the fire engine were stretched upwards and I could see some firemen climbing up with hoses in their hands. On reaching almost the top of the ladder, they began to pour floods of water on the topmost part of the building. This continuous flooding brought the fire under control but the building was completely destroyed.

While fire is a blessing in many ways, it can also be a great danger to human life and property.

5. THE ELEPHANT

Now that the mammoth is extinct, the elephant is the largest of all animals living. and the strongest. It is a strange-looking animal, with its thick legs, huge sides and back, large hanging ears, small tail, little eyes, long white tusks, and, above all, its long nose, called the trunk. The trunk is the elephant's peculiar feature, and it puts it to various uses. It draws up water by its trunk, and can squirt it all over its body like a shower bath; and with it, it picks leaves from the trees and puts them into its mouth. In fact its trunk serves the elephant as a long arm and hand. Elephants look very clumsy and heavy, and yet they can move very quickly when they like.

Elephants are found in India and in Africa. The African elephant differs in some points from the Indian, being larger, with longer tusks and bigger ears. In fact, the two are considered to be different species. In both countries, they live in herds in the jungles, and are naturally shy animals that keep away from men. Elephants, with their great size and strength, are fine advertisement for vegetarianism, for they live entirely on leaves of trees, grass, roots and bulbs.

The elephant is a very intelligent animal, and its intelligence combined with its great strength, makes it, when tamed, a very useful servant to man ; and it has been trained to serve in various ways.

Elephants can carry heavy loads about a thousand seers each ; and they are used to draw heavy wagons and big guns that would require many horses. They are very skilful, too, in piling timber. The trained elephant will kneel down, lift a heavy log of wood with its tusks, carry it to the place where it is wanted, and lay it exactly in position.

Elephants are also trained for tiger-hunting. The huntsmen sit in the *howdah* on the back of the elephant, which is driven and guided by the driver, called the *mahout,* who squats on its neck. In this way the hunters are carried through the thickest, and at such a height that they can see and fire at the tiger when it is driven out.

In old days elephants were used in battles, and all Indian Rajas had their regiments of trained fighting elephants. And they still have their place in state processions, when they are painted with bright colours and covered with silk and velvet clothes.

In Africa elephants are hunted mainly for their tusks, which are made of ivory and are very valuable. Their skins are so thick that an ordinary bullet will not pierce them ; and so large guns, called elephant-guns, are used to kill the animals.

Many elephants are caught alive to be tamed and trained. But catching elephants alive is difficult and dangerous work ; for, though the elephant is a shy, wild animal when left alone, it can be a dangerous enemy when attacked. Elephants are generally caught alive in great traps or enclosures, called *keddahs.* They are either driven into these *keddahs,* or led into them by tame elephants, called decoys, which are trained to lead their wild brothers into captivity.

6. POPULATION GROWTH

One major problem that faces the world today is the rapid growth of population, often referred to as population explosion. Until about 800 AD the world's population stayed below 200 million. Since then it has risen dramatically. The rise has been greatest in the 20th century. The population has recently risen to about six billion: it is three times as large as it was in 1960. It is not so much the actual population as its rate of increase that is alarming. Experts predict that by 2020 there will be about ten billion people, causing serious problems of hunger, overcrowding and environmental pollution.

This enormous increase of population is due to better food, better hygiene and, above all, the advances made in medicine. Rapid developments in modern medicine have conquered many diseases and consequently the death rate has decreased. Until the beginning of the 19th century most people died before the age of 50. Today in developed countries the average lifespan has risen to more than 70 years. The population goes on increasing at an alarming rate in spite of the practice of birth control in many parts of the world. Thomas Malthus, a British mathematician and economist, went to the extent of declaring that, if unchecked, human population would grow in geometric progression (*i.e.* 1, 2, 4, 8 and so on) while food production could only grow in arithmetic progression (*i.e.* 1, 2, 3, 4 and so on). He was, of course, very pessimistic.

With a population of over one billion, India is the second most populous country in the world. (China is the first.) India's population has risen drastically since 1950: the population today is 2½ times as large as it was in 1950. It is rising by 2.9 per cent per year, and in consequence, every year an extra 26 million people have to be provided for. The government is taking measures to check the population growth and a large percentage of people practise birth control. Recent advances in farming have made the country productive enough to feed the present population. Failure to arrest further increase of population may have disastrous effects, though there seems to be some truth in the statement made by Julian Simon of the University of Maryland: according to him, although population growth means there will be more mouths to feed, there will be "more hands to work and more brains to think."

7. "SPREADING GREENERY FOR A HEALTHY LIVING"

'A thing of beauty is a joy for ever'

John Keats

The grandeur of a drawing room and a living room is best felt when there is an element of nature's pride possession - a tree, or an indoor plant, or even for that matter a sapling. Children as of now get to see less of greenery and more of technologically driven software parks. Fortunately we have come to a point where we can bring the world of flora to our homes.

In the emerging world scenario, interior decoration has become a passion and a dictum for healthy living. The art of planting in small pots with its branches neatly trimmed gives rise to small neat structures of plants. These plants are easy to grow indoors as long as they have soil, air, light and water. Plants can be grown in the house all year round. Of late Bonsai have attracted the attention of one and all. Botanists say that bonsai are ornamental trees or shrubs grown in a pot and artifically prevented from reaching their normal size. The Japanese specialise in bonsai and Ikebana. The latter flowers are displayed according to strict rules.

EXERCISE 150

Write a short essay on:

1. Old Custom. 2. The Kangaroo. 3. School Games. 4. Fairy Tales. 5. Space Travel. 6. The Pleasures of Reading. 7. Popular Superstitutions. 8. The Use and Abuse of Leisure. 9. Life in a Big City : Its Advantages and Disadvantages. 10. Advertising : Its Uses and Abuses. 11. The Book You Like Best. 12. Travel as a Part of Education. 13. My Role Model. 14. The Best Way of Spending Holidays. 15. The Telephone. 16. The Internet. 17. Pollution. 18. The Narmada. 19. Traffic Jams. 20. Your Favourite Hobbies. 21. Counselling in Schools. 22. The Importance of the Study of Geography. 23. No Man is a Judge of His Own Merits. 24. Safety First. 25. The Use and Abuse of Strikes. 26. Scouting for Boys. 27. The Uses of Paper. 28. India in the New Millennium. 29. Hijacking of an Aeroplane. 30. My Greatest Wish. 31. The Influence of Cable Television Network in India. 32. The Cyber Revolution. 33. Nuclear Disarmament. 34. A Metro Station. 35. A Wet Day. 36. The Uses of Rubber. 37. A Visit to a Place of Historic Interest. 38. India in 2020.

EXERCISE 151

Write a short essay on:

1. Should boys learn to cook ? 2. Is life for us better than it was for our forefathers ? 3. The Olympic Games. 4. Is life in the city preferable to life in the country ? 5. Street hawkers. 6. Should games be compulsory for schoolboys ? 7. An important day in my life. 8. How you hope to continue your education when you leave school? 9. What do you think is the most enjoyable month of the year ? Say why you think so. 10. Playing the game. 11. Examination day. 12. Good manners. 13. How to keep fit? 14. The conquest of the air. 15. Ghosts and ghost stories. 16. An Excursion. 17. The dream I should like to have. 18. Milk. 19. Adventure in a Space Craft. 20. Fresh air. 21. Pocket-money. 22. My country. 23. Aeroplanes. 24. The care of the teeth. 25. Our duty to the backward communities in our country. 26. Some desirable improvements in your home town. 27. An English dictionary. 28. Walking tours. 29. The influence of the cinema. 30. Electricity in the service of man.

31. The Influence of Television on our Lives. 32. The value and purpose of a school debating society. 33. The housing of the working classes. 34. "The man who will succeed in life is he who can adapt himself easily." 35. Some wonders of modern science. 36. The educational possibilities of "broadcasting." 37. "Gluttony kills more than a sword."
38. The fascination of a great city.

Chapter 41 AUTOBIOGRAPHIES

A Biography is the history of the life of a person written by someone else (*e.g.*, Southey's "Life of Nelson," Boswell's "Life of Johnson," etc.). An Autobiography is the history of the life of a person written by himself (*e.g.*, John Stewart Mill's "Autobiography").

In the following exercises, the pupil is asked to use his imagination by pretending to be another person, an animal, or an inanimate object, and to invent an autobiography of him or it. He must consider himself to be the animal or object, and, in the first person, write as that particular animal or object might be supposed to tell its own story.

The story must be made as interesting as possible and told in simple language, such as in everyday talk.

SPECIMENS

1. THE AUTOBIOGRAPHY OF A EURO

As soon as I entered this fascinating world I was looked upon with great expectations. The world was full of racism yet [and even if I occupy a place] I was held in high esteem. People from the United States of America to Antartica looked at me as I soon rolled out from the parentage of Europeans. Since economists, raging bulls and bears did not know much about me, I caught the apprehension of my parents, the share market holders, the financial experts, scholars, students and so on. On my birth I was placed on the lap of my mother the Federal Bank.

Frankly, my brother Lira, my sister sterling and my extended family members like the Deutsche Mark the Yen were quite jealous of me. I know my worth I reveal this secret of mine. I am a form of money held or traded outsided the country, in whose currency its value is stated. In future I would be globally acceptable by the members of all the the nations.

I now take pride of place in the Euromarket, a financial market which deals with European currencies. I do not want to roll over but I'd love to be accepted by the developing as well as underdeveloped nations.

2. THE AUTOBIOGRAPHY OF A HORSE

Now that I am getting old and stiff in the joints, I like to meditate, while grazing in the pasture, on my foal days. I think that was the happiest part of my life. I had no work to do, and could run about after my mother, who was a fine white Arab mare, without any restraint. Most of my time was spent in the fields, where I nibbled the tender grass and capered about, while my mother was steadily grazing.

But that could not last for ever. When I was old enough, the trainer came and, to my great indignation, fastened a long rope to my head, and then began driving me round and round in circles with his long whip. I was frightened and angry, but he went on till I was so tired that I could scarcely stand. However, my mother told me that it was no use my resisting, and to make a long story short, I was at last thoroughly trained as a riding-horse.

I was bought by a young officer as a polo pony, and I soon got to love the game. He was a kind master, and a good rider ; and in the end I would do anything for him, and was quite proud when his side won the game. But he got into debt, and had to sell me ; and I was bought by a gentleman and a lady who kept a buggy, and was trained to run in shafts. I hated this work ; and I am afraid I gave a lot of trouble, by going as slowly as I could.

When my driver gave me the whip, I started shying at any object on the road. And then I found that jibbing was a very good trick, and whenever I was whipped, I simply backed. My owner got disgusted at last, and sold me to a gentleman who was fond of hunting.

I was delighted to get back to saddle-work ; and thoroughly enjoyed my gallops with the hounds after the jackal in open country. But an accident put a stop to that jolly life; for one day my master pressed me to a big jump which I knew I could not do. I did my best but fell short, and fell. My master was thrown and broke his arm, and I badly sprained one of my legs.

I was in hospital for weeks, and then was sold to a gentleman who wanted a quiet riding-horse. He was a kind master, and used me well ; and I was in his service for a good number of years. Now I am old, he gives me very little work, and I spend most of my time grazing in the pasture, and leading a quiet, contented life.

EXERCISE 152

Write autobiographies of the following.

1. **A Bee**–(Read up something about the habits of hive-bees ; then bring in the various duties of the worker-bee ; feeding and tending larvae (young), strong honey, sweeping hive, guarding, fetching nectar from flowers to make honey, etc.)
2. **An Ant**–(On the same lines.)
3. **A St. Bernard Dog**–(Training as a puppy by monks of St. Bernard to rescue travellers lost in snow ; describe the dog ; sent out with flask of brandy fastened round its neck ; some of the dog's adventures)
4. **A Sheep Dog**–(Training by the shepherd to look after flock ; as young dog, imitates his mother in her work; learns to understand the shepherd's sign and verbal orders ; knows each sheep, and can pick out and bring whichever the shepherd wants ; can separate certain numbers from others ; drives sheep to pastures, and into fold at night ; guards flock against enemies)
5. **An Elephant**–(Wildlife in jungle when young ; how caught in *keddah* by decoy; training ; its work : carrying loads, piling logs, drawing carts, carrying hunters in tiger-shooting, marching in state processions, etc.)
6. **A Rose Tree**–[Early cultivation ; the first pruning resented ; learns later it is necessary for producing fine flowers ; gets rich manure ; learns that cultivation makes it different from wild rose ; suffers from disease, like greenfly, blight, etc. ; how gardener cures it ; produces splendid red roses ; much admired ; next year, some blooms gain prize at Flower Show ; cuttings taken (its children), etc.]
7. **A Watch**–(Describe–silver watch ; in jeweller's shop ; other watches its companions ; *e.g.,* proud gold watch, humble gun-metal watch, repeating watches, wrist watches, etc. Bought as present for young man ; stolen out of his pocket ; sold by thief; put in pawnshop ; bought by man ; falls sick and goes to hospital. *i.e.,* jeweller's–new main spring)
8. **A River**–(Rises as spring in mountains, or from a glacier ; mountain torrent, rocky bed, water-falls, tributaries, swollen when snow melts ; reaches plains ; slow steady river ; cultivated fields on banks ; irrigation canals taken off ; passes villages and small towns ; flows through a big town ; pollution of waters ; boats and ships; fall into sea at big port, etc.)
9. **A Kite or Hawk**–(Young in a nest in a tall tree, fed by mother and fatherkite ; how it learns to fly ; hunting its prey–mice, chickens, small birds ; teased by crows and minas ; chooses mate ; builds nest ; etc.)
10. **A Fish** (Salmon)–(Its youth as a smelt in river ; journey to the sea ; returns up river leaping weirs ; chooses a mate ; grows big ; fished for ; how it is deceived by bait; nearly hooked ; escapes and vows to take no more baits; its enemies ; proud of being king of river fishes, etc.)

EXERCISE 153

Write autobiographies of:

1. A Camel. 2. A Spider. 3. A Donkey. 4. A Tiger. 5. A Seagull 6. A Kingfisher. 7. A Caterpillar and Butterfly. 8. A Sword. 9. A Steam-engine. 10. A House. 11. A Motor-car. 12. An Aeroplane. 13. A Crocodile. 14. A Crow. 15. A Steamship. 16. A Cobra. 17. A Buffalo. 18. A Plough. 19. A Child's Toy. 20. A Rifle.

EXERCISE 154

Tell the life-story of each one of the following as told by itself.

1. A Piece of Coal. 2. An Owl. 3. A Pariah Dog. 4. A Parrot. 5. A Cocoanut Tree. 6. A Banyan Tree. 7. A Television 8- Supermarket 9. An Airport. 10. A Stadium.

Chapter 42 DIALOGUE-WRITING

A Dialogue literally means "talk between two people". Dialogue-writing is a useful form of composition, especially for the Indian student who is trying to gain a command of spoken English. Under proper guidance, it should introduce him to the colloquial way of talking English, and train him to express his thoughts in easy and natural constructions. The spoken English of the Indian school-boy is too often rather stilted and bookish, owing to the fact that he has not much chance of talking with English people ; and anything that will help him to acquire naturalness and ease in speaking in English is of value.

To write a dialogue successfully, calls for a little dramatic power; for the writer has not only to see both sides of a question, but has also to put himself, so to speak, inside two imaginary persons so as to make them express their opposite opinions naturally and in keeping with their characters. He has in turn to be each one, and see the point of view of each on the question.

A written dialogue should be so composed that it appears to be spontaneous or impromptu. The reader of it should not feel that it is premeditated, stilted and dull.

At the same time, careful preparation is necessary for writing a dialogue, though this must not appear. The writer must have the art to conceal his art. It is always advisable to make a plan or outline of the dialogue before beginning to write ; otherwise the dialogue may be rambling and pointless.

METHOD OF PROCEDURE

1. Carefully think over the subject given, and jot down briefly the arguments or opinions about it which might reasonably be expressed by the imaginary persons who are supposed to be talking.
2. Arrange these ideas in some logical order, so that one will arise naturally from another in the course of the conversation. (It is well to write down these points in the form of an outline, or numbered heads, as a guide to follow in writing the dialogue.)
3. Try to imagine what would be the way in which each character in the dialogue would express his views. To do this, you must have in your mind a clear idea of the imaginary persons taking part in the conversation, so as to make them speak in character. (For instance, in Specimen No. 2, Swarup, the bookish student talks in a different way from Dulip Singh, the athletic student.)
4. Keep in mind that your dialogue, when completed, should read like a real, spontaneous conversation. So try to make your imaginary characters talk in an easy, familiar and natural manner. Avoid stilted and bookish phrases. Try to remember how real people talk in friendly conversation, and reproduce that conversational style as well as you can.

SPECIAL HINTS

1. (*a*) Don't let any of your characters monopolize the conversation, as if he were giving a public lecture. Give all a chance, and keep the ball rolling. Let the conversation be brisk and rapid.

   (*b*) In real conversation, one person sometimes interrupts the other, or breaks in on what he is saying. A sparing use of such interruptions in written dialogue is quite permissible, and adds to its naturalness.

For example:

A.–"I am perfectly certain he would never do such thing. Why, only the other day he told me–"

B.–"I don't care what he told you ! I know for a fact that he did it."

(*c*) In real conversation, a speaker often answers a question by asking another ; or sometimes, seeing what is coming, he answers a question before it is asked. You may enliven your dialogue by making your characters do the same now and then.

For example:

(*i*) A.–"What will you do if he does not answer your letter ?"

B.–"Well, what would *you* do ?"

(*ii*) D.–"I heard something about you the other day, John."

J.–"I know ! You are going to ask me why I was absent from office last Monday. Well, I will tell you–etc."

(*d*) In real conversation, people often use exclamations, surprise (*e.g.*, "My word !" "Good heavens !" "You don't say so !" "Well" etc.); irritation (*e.g.*, "Bother !" "O dear !" "Confound it !"); pleasure ("How nice !" "Splendid !")–and so on. Such interjections may be introduced from time to time, *sparingly* ; but the use of them should not be overdone. (*Note*–Slang and profane words should be avoided.)

2. The dialogue should begin in an interesting way, so that the reader's attention may be arrested from the very first. And the conversation should lead up to some definite conclusion. It should not end abruptly and in the air, so to speak. Special attention should be paid to the opening sentences and the conclusion.

3. The fact that language should be as far as possible colloquial does not, of course, mean that it may be ungrammatical. However free-and-easy the style in which the persons in the dialogue are made to talk, they must talk good English. They must not, for example, be made to use such expressions as, "He asked my brother and *I* to tea," or "Can I give you *an advice*?"

4. Keeping these points in view, write your dialogue in as natural, interesting and realistic a manner as possible. The whole conversation should be brief, and the questions and replies as concise and pointed as possible.

SPECIMENS

1. *A conversation between two boys, one of whom is habitually despondent and thinks that luck is against him, whereas the other is of a more practical turn of mind.*

Nasarullah Jan–Come, Hussain, you are taking your failure too much to heart. I know it is a great disappointment, and I sympathize with you ; but you must not allow it to make you so unhappy.

Mohd. Hussain–It is all very well for a lucky chap like you, Nasarullah. You have passed the first time, and this is my second failure. You would not feel so cheery if you were in my place.

N.J.–I know ; but you must pull yourself together, and make up your mind you will pass next time. Remember the old saying "If at first you don't succeed, try, try, again!"

M.H.–I think the other version of the saying has more sense in it,"If at first you don't succeed, quit, quit, quit, at once !"

N.J.–Oh nonsense ! You'll never do anything if you don't persevere. Now why do you think you failed ?

M.H.–All this year fate has been against me. First, I was ill with enteric, which lost me a whole term. Then just before my examination, my father died, and that so upset me that I could not prepare properly.

N.J.–Well, you certainly did have bad luck, I am sorry. But I am sure you will succeed next time ; so you must make up your mind to win through.

M.H.–It's no use. I think I was born unlucky. I seem to fail in everything I touch. I tried several times to get a scholarship, but some other boy always got it instead. I shall give it up.

N.J.–Indeed, you must not. Remember it's the darkest hour before the dawn. Often when things are at the worst, they begin to improve. I don't believe in all the talk about bad and good luck. A brave man makes his own luck. You have a year before you ; you have brains, and if you will only pull yourself together and put your heart into your work, you will win through.

M.H.–I wish I had your disposition. Still, I will take your advice and have another try.

N.J.–That's the style ! And I am sure you will succeed and break your so-called "bad luck" once for all.

2. *An imaginary conversation between a bookish student and an athletic student on the comparative merits of mental and physical culture.*

Dulip Singh–Hello, Swarup ! Swotting away as usual. Come out, man ; shut up your old books, and come and have a game of tennis.

Swarup–I am sorry I cannot do that, Dulip. The examination is drawing near, and I want every hour I can get for study.

Dulip Singh–Oh! hang all examinations ! I do not worry about mine. What is the use of them, anyway ?

Swarup–Well, you can't get a degree if you don't pass the examination; and I have set my heart on being a B.A.

Dulip Singh–And pray what good will B.A. do you ? You may get a clerkship in a government office ; but that's all. And there are hundreds of fellows who have got their degrees, and are no nearer getting jobs of any sort.

Swarup–That may be so; but I am not studying so much to pass my examination and obtain my degree, as to store my mind with knowledge and develop my intellectual faculties.

Dulip Singh–My word ! How fine you "highbrows" can talk !Develop my intellectual faculties,! I tell you, all a man wants to get on in the world is some brains, plain common sense, and plenty of push. And you can't learn these things from books. And while you are "developing your intellectual faculties," you are spoiling your health. You will soon be a thin, white, narrow-chested, half-blind weakling if you stick to your beloved books like this. Look at my broad chest and feel my biceps ! Anyway, I am developing my physical powers with my games and athletics.

Swarup–Well, if I have to choose, I would rather have a learned and cultivated mind than a strong and well-developed body ; for the mind is far more important than the body.

Dulip Singh–Oh ! I see ! You mean to say that a man who plays football and hockey and is as strong as a horse, cannot have any brains ?

Swarup–I did not say that ; but you may remember what Kipling said about "Muddied oafs and flannelled fools."

Dulip Singh–Well, I must say you are very complimentary ! Kipling must have been an ass if he said that. Anyway I would rather be "a muddied oaf" than a whitefaced, spectacled bookworm, as blind as an owl.

Their teacher (coming in).–Hello! What are you two fellows quarreling about?

[*They explained.*]

Teacher–I see. Well, you are both right and both wrong. Swarup, a little more physical exercise will do you good and will not interfere with your mental culture ; and Dulip Singh, a little more study will not in any way spoil your physical strength. So, go and have a game of tennis, Swarup ; and afterwards you, Dulip, settle down to a few hours' study.

3. *A dialogue between a countryman and a townsman, bringing out the comparative advantages of town and country life.*

Smith–Good morning, Mr. Jones. It is a long time since I saw you in town. Are you staying long ?

Jones–Good morning. No, Mr. Smith, I only came up on business for a few hours, and hope to get home again this evening.

Smith–Running away so soon ? Why not stay a few days and enjoy yourself ?

Jones–Not me. I don't find much enjoyment in the smoky air of a town, and all its noise and racket. Give me the clean air, the sunshine, and the quiet of the country.

Smith–Well, I grant you have the advantage of purer air in the ountry; but as for noise, you soon get used to it. In fact, I could not stand your quiet–it would drive me crazy. I like to feel plenty of life and movement about me.

Jones–Really ? Why, I could not get a wink of sleep in a noisy town. And towns are so ugly–nothing to see but ugly smoke-grimed houses, dreary streets, hideous advertisements on every hoarding, factory chimneys belching smoke, and a dull, smoky sky. I have the beauty of the green fields and shady woods and flowery meadows of the country.

Smith–Ah ! my friend, but do not forget what Dr. Johnson said : "When you have seen one green field you have seen all green fields ; come with me down Fleet Street and study man."

Jones–Well, all I can say is that Dr. Johnson never saw a green field in his life, or he would have known that there is an infinite variety in nature if you have the eyes to see it.

Smith–But what in the world do you do with yourself in your village ? It must be a very dull and slow life, with no theatres, no concerts, no cinemas, no public lectures, no exciting political meetings. You must lead a stupid vegetable life, like a cabbage.

Jones–Not so stupid and dull as you imagine. I have my garden, which is a great source of pleasure ; and there is fishing, and a little hunting. And then I love tramping over the hills, and seeing the beautiful scenery. And in the evenings I have my books.

Smith–Well, every man to his taste ; but to me yours would be a dull life.

Jones–Dull or not, it is much healthier. In the pure country, we do not get the epidemics and dirt-produced diseases you have in the towns. And our quiet habits give us longer lives.

Smith–Yes, you may live longer in the country. But you don't get so much out of life as we do in town. A short life and a merry one, I say.

4. *A dialogue between two boys discussing their hobbies.*

George–I am in luck, Will. My uncle has just sent me a letter from Japan, where he is on business, with some Japanese stamps. He knows I collect them and often sends me foreign stamps from the places he visits.

Will–They look rather nice. Are you going to paste them in your album ?

George–Yes, here it is. I have got quite a nice collection now.

Will–What a lot ! French, Italian, Dutch, German, American, Turkish. You seem to have some from almost every country.

George–Oh ! there are a lot I have not got yet. And some rare ones are very expensive, and cost pounds of money.

Will–But what is the use of collecting stamps ?

George–Oh ! Well, it's a hobby. And it teaches you some geography ; and sometimes it brings money.

Will–How is that ?

George–Why, a really good collection sometimes sells for hundreds of pounds. Why don't you go in for stamp-collecting ?

Will–I like something more active. My hobby is collecting ferns and wild flowers. And to get these you have to go long country walks, and explore the woods, and climb the hills. It is quite an adventure when you find a rare plant or fern in some wild place.

George–But what do you do with them when you get them ?

Will–I press them, and then mount them neatly on sheets of paper, and name them. I have got quite a nice collection.

George–How do you press them ?

Will–I lay the fern or plant between sheets of blotting-paper, and put them in a press, or under a board with heavy weights. You have to change the blotting-paper every day, and in about a week the plant is dried and pressed, and will last like that for years.

George–And what is the good of your hobby ?

Will–Well, it teaches me a lot of botany ; and takes me into beautiful country; and does me good physically, because it means exercise in the open air.

5. *A dialogue between a master and a pupil on public speaking.*

Master–Well Ram Narain, I hear you are taking part in the speaking competition.

Pupil–Yes, Sir ; and I came to ask you to give me some hints on the art of the public speaking.

Master–With pleasure, Ram Narain. Have you prepared your speech ?

Pupil–Yes, Sir ; and now I am learning it by heart.

Master–Oh ! but that is a great mistake. Always carefully prepare what you want to say, but never try to learn it off by heart.

Pupil–But why, Sir ?

Master–Because when you are speaking, you should watch your audience to see whether they are following what you say. You can see by their faces whether they understand and are interested ; and if they are not, you can then win their attention by adding, or emphasizing, or changing something. But if your speech is learnt by heart, you can't alter it.

Pupil–But it seems so much easier to learn it.

Master–It is not so in the end. Memorising is a great strain. Also, if you forget one sentence, you may break down altogether.

Pupil–Well, I might manage if I could have my notes with me when I speak.

Master–At first you may take a short note of outline, or main points, of your speech, lest you should forget; but when you get used to speaking in public, it is best to do without notes altogether.

Pupil–But if I don't use notes, and must not learn my speeches off by heart how can I remember what to say?

Master–You must prepare carefully, and think out what you want to say ; and learn the main points, or outline of your speech. Then, when you get up to speak, you will find that the words will come.

Pupil–But I feel so nervous when I have to speak.

Master–That is natural, especially at first. But as you get used to speaking in public, you will overcome that. Even practised speakers often feel very nervous before they begin to speak ; but when they get on to their feet, they forget all about it.

Pupil–When I am nervous, I think I speak too fast.

Master–Well, you must practise speaking slowly and distinctly. And don't shout–it strains your voice and prevents people hearing you ; and don't speak too low. Speak naturally, so that all can hear.

Pupil–Thank you, Sir, for your hints. I will try to follow them.

6. *A dialogue on the choice of a profession–law or medicine.*

Jai Dyal–Thank goodness ! our examinations are over at last.

Sain Das–What a relief ! I hope I shall pass ; for I have just got a letter from my father promising to send me to the Medical College if I get through Class 12.

Jai Dyal–Oh ! are you going to be a doctor ?

Sain Das–Yes ; and I am very glad. My father is a doctor, you know, and I have always wanted to be one too. It seems a very interesting profession. What are you going to do ?

Jai Dyal–My ambition is to be a lawyer ; and when I have got my B.A., I am to go to the Law College to study for my LL.B.

Sain Das–Law ! That never had any attractions for me. Why do you want to be a lawyer ?

Jai Dyal–Well, it is a very respectable profession. One can be a gentleman and hold a good position, anyway.

Sain Das–So can a doctor. The medical profession is just as respectable as the legal.

Jai Dyal–Oh ! yes, of course. But I think a lawyer can make more money than a doctor.

Sain Das–I am not so sure of that. A few lawyers who get to be leaders of the bar, of course, do make fortunes. But what about the crowd of pleaders and even barristers who can scarcely make a living ? The law is terribly overcrowded.

Jai Dyal–Oh ! well, there is always plenty of room at the top, you know.

Sain Das–What I like about the medical profession, apart from its scientific interest, is that the work is so humanitarian. A doctor is always doing good to his fellows–relieving suffering, curing diseases, restoring health, and so making folk happy. This makes a doctor's life a sort of social service.

Jai Dyal–Well, a lawyer is doing good work too. He is helping to detect and prevent crime, defending the innocent from false charges, and helping people in distress.

Sain Das–Yes; but a lawyer's life is full of temptations. He is tempted to defend criminals for big fees, and to get them off from just punishment. I don't see how a lawyer can help being a liar, too !

Jai Dyal–Now you are joking. It is as possible for a lawyer to be an honest man as it is for a doctor to be a rogue.

EXERCISE 155

Compose imaginary conversations on the following subjects:

1. Between a father and his son on thrift.

   (*Hints*–The son has been wasting his allowance extravagantly and got into debt ; his father rebukes him, and warns him of the danger of extravagance, telling him how to spend economically, and save for his old age.)

2. Between a temperance advocate and a young man on the evils of intemperance.

   (*Hints*–The young man sees no harm in drinking ; argues it is a jolly social custom, makes him lively and happy, drowns care, revives him when tired, is a manly habit, etc. The temperance man warns him against danger of becoming a drunkard ; the terrible power of the drink craving ; argues alcoholic drink is a slow poison, and damages health; appeals to him to set an example to others by signing the pledge,etc.)

3. Between a soldier and a shopkeeper on the merits of their respective occupations.

   (*Hints*–The soldier argues that his is a noble profession ; superior to civilian in rank ; calls for courage and manly qualities ; he is the defender of his country ; whereas a tradesman's job is mean and despised ; no job for a man, etc. The shopkeeper argues that the soldier produces nothing ; he simply destroys ; it is a butcher's job ; food for powder, etc. ; whereas the tradesman is a useful member of society, who is doing a public service ; can become rich, while a soldier must always be poor, etc. The dignity of labour.)

4. Between a huntsman and a gardener on their respective pursuits.

   (*Hints*–The huntsman defends his sport as manly, exciting, and needing courage ; tries to show the benefits others by killing pests like tigers and bears ; says gardening is a tame and effeminate hobby. The gardener argues hunting is a cruel sport ; it means killing and torturing many of God's innocent creatures ; purely destructive. Whereas he is productive ; making two blades of grass grow where only one grew before ; making the world more beautiful. (*Hints.*–The refining effect of gardening.)

EXERCISE 156

Write a short imaginary conversation:

1. Between a horse and an ass.
2. Between a cage-bird and a crow.
3. Between a pen and a pencil.
4. Between a pet-dog and a pariah-dog.
5. Between a film actor and yourself.
6. Between an aeroplane and a train.
7. Between a gas stove and a microwave oven.

8. Between an the president of the BCCI and you.
9. Between a spider and a fly.
10. Between Cinderella and her two sisters just before t e ball.

EXERCISE 157

Write in the form of a dialogue:

1. The table of "The Hare and the Tortoise".
2. The fable of "The Lion and the Mouse."
3. The fable of "The Country Mouse and the Town Mouse."
4. The fable of "The Blind Man and the Lame Man."
5. The fable of "The Dog in the Manger."
6. The fable of "The Ant and the Grasshopper."
7. The fable of "The Wolf and the Lamb."
8. The story of "The Sun and the Wind".

EXERCISE 158

Write a short dialogue:

1. Between two friends about dreams.
2. Between a miser and a spendthrift.
3. Between a railway-guard and an engine-driver.
4. Between two class-fellows about the visit of the Inspector..
5. Between two boys discussing their hobbies.
6. Between a credulous man and an impostor.
7. Between two friends on a topic of common interest.
8. Between two friends–the one a believer, and other a disbeliever, in ghost stories.
9. Between two boys about the approaching examination.
10. Between two class-fellows on a poem they have read in the class.
11. Between a hypochondriac and his friend.
12. Between two boys who have just come out of the Examination Hall.
13. Between two friends who have lost their way in a jungle.
14. Between two friends discussing holiday plans.
15. Between two friends about their neighbours.
16. Between two boys caught in a shower on their way from school. One looks on the bright side of matters, and the other on the dark side.
17. Between two friends on life in flats.
18. Between two friends discussing the "theatre-manners" of latecomers, who mar the pleasure of the audience.
19. Fan and an airconditioner.
20. An earthquake and a cyclone.

EXERCISE 159

Write short dialogues on the following.

1. The use and abuse of athletics.
2. The advantages and disadvantages of solitude.
3. The uses and abuses of advertisement.
4. The advantages and disadvantages of cheap literature.
5. The pleasures and perils of speed.
6. The pleasures and disadvantages of life in a school hostel.
7. The advantages and disadvantages of life in a great city.

8. The influence of the Cinema.
9. The necessity to save Religious Institutions.
10. The advantages and disadvantages of life in a great city.
11. The influence of Television Channels
12. Terrorism and Fanaticism.

EXERCISE 160

Discuss in the form of a dialogue the pros and cons of the following subjects.

1. Prohibition.
2. Alms-giving.
3. Corporal punishment.
4. The caste system.
5. Luck.
6. The United Nations.
7. Lotteries.
8. Hand-industries.
9. Asceticism.
10. Geography as a class-subject.
11. Entrance Examinations.
12. Making Global Friendship through the Internet.
13. Awards and Recognitions.

EXERCISE 161

Discuss each of the following subjects in the form of a dialogue.

1. Is luxury an evil ?
2. Is poverty a handicap ?
3. Which should be the medium of education in our school–English or the vernaculars ?
4. Ought everyboy to become a Scout ?
5. Which is worse–flood or fire ?
6. Which should we use in a big town–well water or tap-water ?
7. Which is better–hockey or cricket ?
8. War–is it necessary ?
9. Which is better–to wear out or to rust out ?
10. Should Hygiene be made a compulsory school-subject ?

EXERCISE 162

Finish the following conversations.

Krishna–Hurrah ! only ten days to the holidays !
Rama–I know. I have been counting the days. I am just sick of school.
Krishna–So am I. What are you going to do with yourself in the holidays ?
Patient–Good morning, doctor ! Can you spare me a few minutes ?
Doctor–Certainly ! Come in and sit down. Now, what is the matter with you?
Abdul–What is that roaring noise ? It sounds like a train.
Kabali–More likely an aeroplane. Yes ! Up there ! Six of them.
Bepin–Oh, yes ! They seem to be a great height up.
Feroz Din–Well, Abdul Latif, only three weeks more to the Matriculation examination!

Abdul Latif–Yes, it is coming very near now. I wish it were all over.

F.D.–So do I ! And then, no more school.

A.L.–Hurrah ! What are you going to do when you leave school, Feroz Din ?

Father–I am sorry to hear you have failed the examination, Hari.

Hari–So am I, father ; it was just my bad luck. Look at Govind–lucky fellow! He passed in the second division.

Father–So you think it is all a matter of good luck and bad luck ?

Rashid–Here is a puzzle for you, Ghulam ; which would you rather be–a sick millionaire or a healthy beggar?

Ghulam–Well, that wants some thinking over. I suppose you mean, which is more important for our happiness–health or wealth ?

Bepin–So you object to corporal punishment in schools ?

Ramesh–Yes, I do. I think it ought to be abolished.

Bepin–But why ?

Chapter 43 THE APPRECIATION OF POETRY

What is poetry ? : Though many have tried to define poetry, no one has succeeded in giving a satisfactory definition of it. Poetry seems to elude all attempts to describe it. Yet we should know something about poetry, and learn to cultivate our feeling for it, so that we may gradually come to recognize it, and know when it is present. The best we can do is to point out some essential characteristics of true poetry.

Before we discuss these essential characteristics, let us try and understand the connection between poetry and verse. Verse is the *form* of poetry. Poets generally (but not always) write their poetry in verse-form. But there is a lot of verse written which is no poetry at all. Verse is the body, and the poetry is the soul ; and body without a soul is a dead body. We shall undestand this better as we go on.

Verse is usually printed in a particular way, so that you can tell it from prose at a glance. But it is the ear, not the eye, which is the true test of verse ; for when verse is read aloud it *sounds* quite different from prose. Just listen to the different sounds of these two passages, one in prose and the other in verse:–

(*i*)"The untrodden snow lay all bloodless on Linden, when the sun was low; and the flow of Iser, rolling rapidly, was dark as winter."

(*ii*) "On Linden, when the sun was low,
All bloodless lay the untrodden snow ;
And dark as winter was the flow
Of Iser, rolling rapidly."

The two passages are exactly the same in meaning. In fact, the very words are the same. No. (*ii*) contains the first four lines of Campbell's poem called "Hohenlinden". No. (*i*) contains the same lines with the same words differently arranged. Yet how differently they sound when read aloud ! If we can *hear* this difference, we shall soon be able to tell the difference between prose and verse.

The first two points about the *verse-form* of the passage that we notice are its–

(1) Regular Rhythm–As you read it, can you not *hear* the regular beat of sound, like the regular tramp of soldiers marching ; or the regular beat of the feet of people dancing ? There is nothing like this regular swing in prose passage. It is caused by the fact that the poet arranges his words in such a way that the accented syllables, on which we naturally lay stress in speaking, come at equal intervals. If all the accented syllables in the first line are italicized you will see that every *second* syllable must be pronounced more loudly or emphatically than the others.

"On *Linden when* the *sun* was *low*."

The regular rising and falling in the flow of sounds in poetry, these recurring intervals of strong and light sounds, like the beat of a drum regulating dance movements, is called *rhythm* ; and rhythm is the chief, and an essential characteristic of verse, as distinguished from prose. This will be made clear later on.

(2) Rhyme–The next point we notice is that the words at the end of the first three lines all have the same sound–*low, snow, flow.* When words have the same vowel sound and end with the same consonant sound, they are said to *rhyme, e.g., keep, peep; jump, lump; hate, late; crew, few ; glide, slide.* Rhyme is not necessary to verse (*i.e.,* you can have verse without rhyme) ; but generally verse is rhymed. Rhyme serves two purposes; it makes verse more musical, by giving it pleasing sounds, like the chimes of bell ; and it serves to preserve the verse-form in which the poem is arranged by marking the ends of the lines.

Stanzas–If you look at the whole of the poem, "The Daffodils", given on page 399, you will notice another characteristic of verse. You will see that the poem is divided up into units and that all the units are exactly alike in form. Each unit is of six lines, the first line rhyming with the third, the second with the fourth and the fifth with the sixth. Such units or divisions in a poem are called stanzas. Most poems, though not all, are written in stanzas all of which are of the same pattern.

Verse, then, is characterized by regular rhythm, rhyme and stanzas. Of these characteristics, *rhythm* is essential. You cannot have verse or poetry without rhythm. But while most poems have rhyme and stanza-forms, these are not essential characteristics of poetry, for we have poems written in blank verse, *i.e.,* verse in which each line has ten syllables but there are no rhymes at the end.

Having discussed the connection between verse and poetry, we shall now consider some essential characteristics of true poetry.

(1) Music–The first Characteristic of poetry is *verbal music.* The poet chooses instinctively words of beautiful sound, and so arranges them that the words near each other will harmonise in sound, so as to produce what may be called "word music." And he varies this music to suit the subject, so that the sound of the lines helps to make their meaning clearer.

But verbal music depends not only on the musical sound of the words, but also on rhythm. It is the combination of lovely rhythms with sweet-sounding words that gives us the music of poetry. Here are two verses from Dryden's "Song for St. Cecilia's Day". The rapid rhythm of the first verse well expresses the excitement caused by the war alarm given by trumpet and drum ; the slow and quiet rhythm of the second verse suits the soft and tender music of the flute and the lute.

"The trumpet's loud clangour
Excites us to arms,
With shrill notes of anger,
And mortal alarms.
The double double double beat
Of the thundering drum
Cries, Hark ! the foes come ;
Charge, charge, 'tis too late to retreat
The soft complaining flute,
In dying notes, discovers
The woes of hopeless lovers,
Whose dirge is whisper'd by the warbling lute."

Now let us examine in detail how poets obtain some of the musical effects.

(a) *Rhyme*–Words rhyming together give a musical chime of sound, and this is one reason why rhyme is so much used in poetry. Listen to the chime of the rhymes in this verse :–

"Strew on her roses, roses,

And never a spray of yew,

In quiet she reposes :

Ah ! would that I did too !'' (*M. Arnold*)

Internal rhymes (*i.e.*, rhymes written within a line and not merely at the ends of lines) also add music (and a slight apparent acceleration of the rhythm) to a verse ; *e.g.*,

"The ice was here, the ice was there,

The ice was all around ;

It cracked and growled, and roared and howled.

Like noises in a swound !'' (*Coleridge*)

(b) ***Vowel and Consonant Sounds***–Words with long open vowels and soft consonants (like l, m, n, v, w, z. etc.) produce sweet, soft, soothing music in these lines :–

"Season of mists and mellow fruitfulness." (*Keats*)

"Then in a wailful choir the small gnats mourn." (*Keats*)

"To dream and dream, like yonder amber light." (*Tennyson*)

"The murmurous haunt of flies on summer eves." (*Keats*)

(c) ***Onomatopoeia***–This is the name given to the figure of speech by which the sound of the words is made to suggest or echo the sense. There are many onomatopoeic words in English ; *e.g.*, roar, bang, crash, clap, bump, bubble, screen, pop, moan, hum, murmur, etc. When they are talking of sounds, poets will use words to represent those sounds if they can. For instance :–

"The moan of doves in immemorial elms

And murmuring of innumerable bees.'' (*Tennyson*)

Can you not hear the cooing of the doves and the humming of the bees ? How is it done ? Some of the words are onomatopoeic, *e.g.*, moan, murmuring ; in others the soft vowels, and above all the *m* and *n* sounds, give a humming murmur, *e.g.*, immemorial, innumerable.

(d) ***Alliteration***–This is another figure of speech used in poetry. It brings together words which begin with the same consonant (or vowel) sound. For example :–

"The fair breeze below, the white foam flew

The furrow followed free.'' (*Coleridge*)

Here the *f* sounds give the impression of wind blowing.

"I hear *l*ake water *l*apping with *l*ow sounds by the shore." (*Yeats*)

Here the *l* sounds represent the liquid sounds of little waves, and the *s* and *sh* sounds help.

A *r*eeling *r*oad, a *r*olling *r*oad, that *r*ambles *r*ound the shire.'' (*Chesterton*)

The *r* sounds help the description of a wandering road.

(e) ***Repetition***–Repetition of words and phrases not only serves to emphasise the meaning, but often also to increase the musical effect of a poem.

"*The woods decay, the woods decay* and fall." (*Tennyson*)

"What hope of answer, or redress ?

Behind the veil, behind the veil..'' (*Tennyson*)

"A *weary* time ! A *weary* time !

How glazed each weary eye !'' (*Coleridge*)

"*In ever climbing* up a *climbing* wave." (*Tennyson*)

"*The western tide crept up along the sand.*

And o'er and o'er *the sand.*'' (*Kingsley*)

And round and round *the sand.*''

(*f*) ***Refrains.***– A refrain is a form of repetition. In some poems the same line, or part of it, is repeated at the end of each verse. Such a repeated line or phrase is called a *burden* or *refrain.*

(2) Vision. The second characteristic of poetry is vision. A great poet is a "seer", *i.e.,* a "see-er" ; one who has spiritual insight and can see truths that others do not. The ordinary unimaginative man is aware only of what he perceives by his senses, and sees only the outward aspect of what he sees. But the poets see much more. They have, in moments of vision, the power of understanding, by a kind of instinct, things, their qualities and the relations between them, which ordinary people cannot see. All true poetry is the product of vision or imagination for it is the expression of it. Wordsworth wrote a poem about a matter-of-fact, unimaginative man, called Peter Bell. Peter Bell saw nothing but what he saw with his physical eyes. He had no "vision."

"A primrose by a river's brim
A yellow primrose was to him,
And it was nothing more.''

Now see what a primrose, or any common wild flower, is to a real poet. Wordsworth himself says :–

"To me the meanest flower that blows can give
Thoughts that do often lie too deep for tears.

The poet idealises the real. He helps us to see natural objects "Apparelled in celestial light, the glory and the freshness of a dream."

There is suggestiveness in great poetry. It suggests or implies much more than it says. It has a depth of meaning that cannot be fathomed by one or two readings.

(3) Imagery. The suggestion of vivid mental pictures, or images, by the skillful use of words, is called "imagery." A poet can create or suggest beautiful *sight-effects,* as well as beautiful sound-effects, by means of words. This capacity is, of course, part of a poet's gift of imagination. Poetry, much more than prose, produces much of its effect by images. It often talks in pictures. The poet's pictures may be drawn from the real world, or the ideal world of imagination in which he dwells.

Poets have three ways of making us see mental pictures.

(a) By Description– He may, as a prose-writer does, describe a scene, real or ideal, in words. Here is Gray's description of the evening of a summer day :–

"The curfew tolls the knell of parting day,
The lowing herd wind slowly o'er the lea,
The ploughman homeward plods his weary way,
And leaves the world to darkness and to me.
Now fades the glimmering landscape on the sight,
And all the air a solemn stillness holds.
Save where the beetle wheels his droning flight,
And drowsy tinklings lull the distant folds.''

[For examples of verbal descriptions see, "The Sands of Dee" (2nd verse); "Hohenlinden", "Rain in Summer."]

(*b*) By certain Figures of Speech such as *simile, metaphor,* and *personification* about which you have learnt in Chapter 29. Read carefully the examples of *simile, metaphor* and *personification* given in that chapter. A poet compares one thing with another, and so suggests some important point about it by an image.

(c) *By Picturesque Epithets* –A poet can also call up a picture with a single illuminating word or phrase. Just examine the epithets of adjectives in these lines–

"All in a hot and *copper* sky,
The *bloody* sun, at noon."
(*Coleridge*)

–What a picture of colour these two epithets call up

(4) Emotion–The third essential of poetry is emotion. Ordinary prose writing (other than fiction) appeals more to the head than to heart; but the function of poetry is to touch the heart ; that is, to arouse emotion. Who can read such lines as these without emotion ?

"And the stately ships go on
To their haven under the hill;
But O for the touch of a vanish'd hand,
And the sound of a voice that is still !"
(*Tennyson*)

But it is only emotion that can rouse emotion. If the poet feels nothing when he writes a poem, his readers will feel nothing when they hear it. Heart must speak to heart.

To sum up, therefore, the essentials of poetry are music, vision (including imagery), and emotion. So we may say that *poetry springs from imagination roused by emotion, and is expressed in music and imagery.* This is not a definition for, as we have seen, we cannot define poetry, but a description of its essential characteristics.

Let us now take the well-known poem "Daffodils" by William Wordsworth to try and find out what essentials of good poetry are contained in it.

I wandered lonely as a cloud
That floats on high o'er vales and hills,
When all at once I saw a crowd,
A host of golden daffodils,
Beside the lake, beneath the trees,
Fluttering and dancing in the breeze.

Continuous as the stars that shine
And twinkle on the milky way,
They stretched in never-ending line
Along the margin of a bay :
Ten thousand saw I at a glance
Tossing their heads in sprightly dance.

The waves beside them danced, but they
Outdid the sparkling waves in glee :
A poet could not but be gay
In such a jocund company !
I gazed–and gazed–but little thought
What wealth the show to me had brought.

For oft when on my couch I lie
In vacant or in pensive mood,
They flash upon that inward eye
Which is the bliss of solitude ;
And then my heart with pleasure fills,
And dances with the daffodils.

APPRECIATION OF THE POEM

(1) *Substance* The first thing we must do is to read the poem through, carefully. Then we must ask ourselves : What is it all about ? What is the subject ? And what does the poet say about the subject ?

The poet tells us that as he was taking a solitary walk beside a lake one bright and breezy Spring morning, he suddenly came upon a sight that filled him with delighted wonder at its beauty, and with gaiety of heart. There stretched before his wondering gaze thousands and thousands of yellow daffodils under the trees beside the sparkling waters of the lake, "Fluttering and dancing in the breeze." The sight filled him with pleasure ; but he did not know at the time all that the experience had added to his life. For many times afterwards, memory brought back that beautiful scene as a mental picture, which gave him over and over again the same sense of gladness.

(2) *Language* The poem is in very simple language and there are really no difficult words. (*Daffodil* is a bulbous plant of the lily family bearing a yellow trumpet-shaped flower that grows wild in English woods and flowers in Spring).

(3) *Imagery*–(*a*) The first three verses are a description of a host of daffodils under the trees by the side of a lake, lit up by the sun and dancing in the wind.

(*b*) There are two *similes* : The comparison between the solitary poet and a lonely cloud in the first stanza, and the comparison between the endless line of daffodils and innumerable stars in the milky way given in the second stanza.

(*c*) There is also an example of *personification* in the second stanza and again in the third stanza. The daffodils are described as dancing in glee and tossing their heads like human beings and are said to be "such a jocund company."

The statement, "Ten thousand saw I at a glance", is a figure of speech known as *hyperbole*; it is a poetic exaggeration not intended to be taken literally.

(4) *Sound effects* (*a*) The quickened movement of line 6 of the first stanza, in comparison with the stately movement of the preceding lines, well echoes and reinforces the sense.

(*b*) There is an example of *alliteration* in line 6 of the fourth stanza. "And dances with the daffodils". Note also the *repetition* in line 5 of the third stanza, "I *gazed*–and *gazed*"; it emphasises the length of time the poet stood looking in delighted wonder at the beautiful scene.

(5) *Striking lines* The most striking lines are lines 3 and 4 of the last stanza. The "inward eye" is the faculty of visualising, or calling up mental pictures from memory or the imagination. Such mind-pictures give us joy when we are alone and at leisure.

We have given here a somewhat detailed appreciation of the poem, "The Daffodils". The points amplified above in connection with Wordsworth's beautiful poem will make you understand what you should look for in good poetry in order that you may enjoy in a better way. But at the high school stage, a continuous description of all the essential qualities of a good poem is not required. A student's appreciation of a particular piece of poetry may be judged by asking specific questions like the following : What is the central idea of the poem? What is the poet's attitude to life, or to nature, or to whatever is the subject of the poem ? What is the significance of certain given lines or expressions in the poem ? What picture is sketched in the lines specified ? How are certain sound effects produced by the poet ? What figures of speech are to be found in the poem and how can they be explained ? What title (or alternative title) can be given to the poem ?

SPECIMENS

Here are two short poems with certain questions on appreciation given below each of them and the answers worked out.

(*a*) She dwelt among the untrodden ways
Beside the springs of Dove ;
A maid whom there were none to praise
And very few to love.
A violet by a mossy stone
Half-hidden from the eye !
–Fair as a star, when only one

Is shining in the sky.
She lived unknown, and few could know
When Lucy ceased to be ;
But she in her grave, and, oh,
The difference to me

–W. Wordsworth

QUESTIONS

1. Give a suitable title to the poem.
2. Name and explain the figure of speech used in the second stanza.
3. Which lines in the poem show intense feeling ? What feeling has the poet expressed in these lines ?
4. What do you think of the language used in the poem ?

ANSWERS

1. "The Lost Love" or "She Dwelt Among the Untrodden Ways."
2. The figure of speech is *simile.* The girl is compared to the half hidden violet and the lonely star to emphsise (*a*) her solitude and obscurity, and (*b*) her beauty of soul as well as body.
3. The last two lines. They express the feeling of love and bereavement.
4. The most striking feature of the language is its simplicity. The poet has used simple, everyday words, mostly of one syllable; yet they produce a poem that has a magic charm.

(*b*) Laugh and be merry, better the world with a song.
Better the world with a blow in the teeth of a wrong.
Laugh, for the time is brief, a thread the length of a span.
Laugh and be proud to belong to the old proud pageant of man.
Laugh and be merry : remember, in olden time,
God made Heaven and Earth for joy. He took in a rhyme,
Made them, and filled them with the strong red wine of His mirth.
The splendid joy of the stars ; the joy of the earth.
So we must laugh and drink from the deep blue cup of the sky.
Join the jubilant song of the great stars sweeping by,
Laugh, and battle, and work, and drink of the wine outpoured
In the dear green earth, the sign of the joy of the Lord.
Laugh and be merry together, like brothers akin,
Guesting awhile in the rooms of a beautiful inn,
Glad till the dancing stops, and the lilt of the music ends.
Laugh till the game is played : and be you merry, my friends.

–John Masefield

QUESTIONS

1. What is the central idea of the poem ?
2. What is the "blow" with which the poet wants us to better the world ?
3. Quote three striking examples of *metaphors* used in the poem.
4. Explain:
   (*a*) "the old proud pageant of man."
   (*b*) "Guesting awhile in the rooms of a beautiful inn"

ANSWERS

1. Life is short and we must therefore laugh and be cheerful, and enjoy all the beauty and happiness that can be found on this earth.
2. It is our laughter and merriment that will serve as a blow and hit out boldly against wrong and injustice in the world.
3. (*i*) "Laugh, for the time is brief, a *thread* the length of a span."

   (*ii*) "Made them and filled them with the *strong red wine* of *His mirth*."

   (*iii*) "Laugh till the *game is played*."
4. (*a*) We are part of the spectacular progress of mankind which is marked with many glorious achievements.

   (*b*) We should be happy and cheerful together during the short time we are in this beautiful world in the same way as brothers who are staying for a short while in a beautiful inn where there is dancing and music.

EXERCISE 163

Read each of the following poems and answer the questions set below it.

1. What is this life if, full of care,
We have no time to stand and stare ?
No time to stand beneath the boughs
And stare as long as sheep or cows ?
No time to see, when woods we pass,
Where squirrels hide their nuts in grass ?
No time to see, in broad daylight,
Streams full of stars, like skies at night ?
No time to turn at Beauty's glance,
And watch her feet, how they can dance ?
No time to wait till her mouth can
Enrich that smile her eyes began ?
A poor life this if, full of care,
We have no time to stand and stare.

–*William Henry Davies*

(*a*) What kind of life does the poet condemn ?
(*b*) What are the "stars" of which the streams are full ?
(*c*) Name and explain the figures of speech in lines 9-10.
(*d*) Explain :
"No time to wait till her mouth can
Enrich that smile her eyes began".

2. My days among the Dead are past ;
Around me I behold,
Wherever these casual eyes are cast,
The mighty minds of old ;
My never-failing friends are they,
With whom I converse day by day;
With them I take delight in weal
And seek relief in woe ;
And while I understand and feel
How much to them I owe,
My cheeks have often been bedew'd
With tears of thoughtful gratitude.

–*Robert Southey*

(*a*) What is the central idea of the poem ?
(*b*) Who are the "mighty minds" ?

(c) Who are the poet's friends and how are they never-failing ?
(d) Explain :
My cheeks have often been bedew'd
With tears of thoughtful gratitude."

3. We scatter seeds with careless hand
And dream we ne'er shall see them more :
But for a thousand years
Their fruit appears
In weeds that mar the land,
Or healthful store.
The deeds we do–the words we say
Into still air they seem to float ;
We count them ever past–
But they shall last,
In the dread judgement, they
And we shall meet !

(a) What is the central idea of the poem ?
(b) Explain the imagery of the first stanza.
(c) Show how wrong we are about the consequences of our words and our deeds.
(d) Explain :
"In the dread judgement, they
And we shall meet."

4. Oh, sweet content, that turns the labourer's sweat
To tears of joy, and shines the roughest face;
How often have I sought you high and low
And found you still in some quiet place ;
Here in my room, when full of happy dreams
With no life heard beyond that merry sound
Of moths that on my lighted ceiling kiss
Their shadows as they dance and dance around;
Or in a garden, on a summer's night
When I have seen the dark and solemn air
Blink with the blind bat's wings, and heaven's bright face
Twitch with the stars that shine in thousands there.

(a) Where does the poet seek sweet content ? Where does he find it ?
(b) What striking word-pictures are contained in the poem ?
(c) Name and explain the figures of speech in the last two lines.
(d) Give a suitable title to the poem.

5. Much have I travell'd in the realms of gold
And many goodly states and kingdoms seen;
Round many western islands have I been
Which bards in fealty to Apollo hold.
Oft of one wide expanse had I been told.
That deep-brow'd Homer ruled as his demesne;
Yet did I never breathe its pure serene
Till I heard Chapman speak out loud and bold;
Then felt I like some watcher of the skies
When a new planet swims into his ken ;
Or like stout Cortez, when with eagle eyes
He stared at the Pacific–and all his men

Look'd at each other with a wild surmise–
Silent, upon a peak in Darien.

–*John Keats*

(*a*) What idea is expressed in the first four lines of the sonnet ?
(*b*) Explain the significance of the phrase "deep-browed Homer".
(*c*) What striking pictures are presented in the last six lines of the poem ?
(*d*) Quote the line which you think produces the greatest musical effect.
(*e*) Explain : "pure serene"; "eagle eyes"; "wild surmise".

6. Strew on her roses, roses,
And never a spray of yew !
In quiet she reposes;
Ah, would that I did too ;
Her mirth the world required;
She bathed it in smiles of glee
But her heart was tired, tired,
And now they let her be.
Her life was turning, turning,
In mazes of heat and sound.
But for peace her soul was yearning,
And now peace laps her round,
Her cabin'd, ample spirit,
It flutter'd and fail'd for breath.
To-night it doth inherit
The vasty hall of death.

–*Matthew Arnold*

(*a*) Does the poet show any grief at the person's death ?
What exactly are his feelings on the occasion ?
(*b*) Quote examples of *repetition* from the poem.
(*c*) What do you gather about the life of the dead person from the poem ?
(*d*) Explain :
(*i*) "Her cabin'd, simple spirit,
It flutter'd and fail'd for breath."
(*ii*) "To-night it doth inherit
The vasty hall of death."

7. Books ! 'tis a dull and endless strife :
Come, hear the woodland linnet,
How sweet his music ! on my life
There's more of wisdom in it.
And hark ! how blithe the throstle sings,
He too is no mean preacher :
Come forth into the light of things,
Let Nature be your teacher...
Enough of Science and of Art;
Come forth, and bring with you a heart
That watches and receives.

(*a*) Name and explain the figure of speech in the sixth line.
(*b*) What feelings does the poet seek to awaken in you by the following exclamations?
"Books!" "hark!"
(*c*) What kind of teaching does Nature give ?
(*d*) Explain : "the light of things"; "a heart that watches and receives".

–*S.S.C. Examination*

8. They tell us of an Indian tree
Which, howsoe'er the sun and the sky
May tempt its boughs to wander free
And shoot and blossom wide and high
Far better loves to bend its arms
Downwards again to that dear earth,
From which the life that fills and warms
Its grateful being first had birth.
'Tis thus, though wooed by flattering friends
And fed with fame (if fame it be),
This heart, my own dear mother, bends
With love's true instinct back to thee.

(a) Name the figures of speech in the second and third lines.
(b) Why is the tree considered "grateful"?
(c) In what respect is the poet like the tree?
(d) Explain : "Wooed by flattering friends"; "Shoot and blossom wide and high."

–S.S.C. Examination

Chapter 44 PARAPHRASING

The word "parapharse" (from the Greek, meaning literally "equivalent sentence") is defined as "restatement of the sense of a passage in other words." It is "the reproduction in one's own natural idiom or style of the full sense of a passage written in another idiom or style."

I. USES OF PARAPHRASING

Someone has said, with a sneer, that paraphrase "usually takes the form of converting good English into bad." But this need not be so; and if in any case it is so, then the paraphrase in question is a bad paraphrase. It should be the aim of the pupil to improve his English by the practice of paraphrasing, and of the teacher to see that the English in which his pupil's paraphrases are written is good English.

Paraphrasing has two important uses :–

(*a*) *As an Exercise in Composition.* (*i*) It is, first, a good test of a pupil's ability to understand what he reads; and is, therefore, an excellent method of training the mind to concentrate on what one reads and so to *read intelligently.* For it is impossible to paraphrase any passage without a firm grasp of its meaning.

(*ii*) It is, secondly, a fine training in the art of *expressing,* what one wants to say, simply, clearly and directly. Incidentally, it gives valuable practice in grammatical and idiomatic composition.

A man who has once acquired the art of *intelligent reading* and of *lucid expression,* has received no mean measure of education.

(*b*) A second use of paraphrase is that it forms a valuable method of *explanation.* Indeed, it is often the best way of explaining an involved or ornate passage of prose or of an obscure piece of poetry. So annotators of poems often make use of it. For example, take the note in Palgrave's "Golden Treasury" (Oxford University Press) on this verse from Browning's "Rabbi Ben Ezra" :–

Enough now, if the Right
And Good and Infinite
Be named here, as thou callest thy hand thine own.
With knowledge absolute,
Subject to no dispute.
From fools that crowded youth, nor let these feel alone.

Note–"It is enough if in age we can get as absolute a knowledge of Right and Wrong, Good and Evil, the Changing and the Eternal, as we have of our own hands."

II. CHARACTERISTICS OF A GOOD PARAPHRASE

1. Translation–Paraphrasing is really a species of *translation* ; for though a paraphrase is not a translation from one tongue into another (as from Urdu or Tamil into English), it is a translation of one man's words into the words of another in the same language. And as a translation must be accurate and explanatory to be of any value, so a paraphrase must faithfully reproduce and interpret the thought of the original passage.

A passage written in a very terse or compressed style has to be expanded in translation. For instance, this saying from Bacon's "Essays." :–

Prosperity doth best discover vice, but Adversity doth best discover virtue.

Paraphrase.–When a man is prosperous, there is more chance of his bad qualities coming to light ; but when he is unfortunate or in trouble, his good qualities are more likely to show themselves.

A verbose passage needs compression in translation. Here is a humorous illustration given by Ruskin in a lecture at Oxford. He said that, whereas in his youth he might have informed a man that his house was on fire in the following way–"Sir, the abode in which you probably passed the delightful days of your youth is in danger of inflammation," then, being older and wiser, he would say simply, "Sir, your house is on fire."

In the following passage by Sydney Smith, the long words and humorously ornate sytle need translating into simple language :–

Whoever had the good fortune to see Dr. Parr's wig, must have observed that, while it trespasses a little on the orthodox magnitude of perukes in the anterior parts, it scorns even episcopal limits behind, and swells out into a boundless convexity of frizz.

Paraphrase.–All who have seen Dr. Parr's wig must have been struck with its enormous size. Even in front it is larger than the usual style of wig; but behind it is fuller even than the wigs worn by bishops, and swells out into a gigantic round of curls.

2. Fullness–Paraphrasing differs from summarising or precis-writing, inasmuch as a paraphrase must reproduce, not only the substance or general meaning, but also the details, of a passage. Nothing in the original may be left unrepresented in the paraphrase. It is, therefore, a *full reproduction.* The difference between a summary and a paraphrase may be illustrated by giving both of the following verse:–

The glories of our blood and state
Are shadows, not substantial things :
There is no armour against fate ;
Death lays his icy hand on kings ;
Sceptre and Crown
Must tumble down.
And in the dust be equal made
With the poor crooked scythe and spade.

Summary.–High birth and rank are nothing ; for in death, which claims all, peasants are equal with kings.

Paraphrase.–Nobility of birth and exalted rank, of which men so proudly boast, are mere illusions and quickly pass away. They cannot protect their proud possessors from the common fate of all mankind–death. Even kings, like the meanest of their subjects, must die ; and in the grave the poor peasant is equal with the haughty monarch.

While nothing in the original is to be unrepresented in the paraphrase, nothing is to be added to it. To insert ideas or illustrations of your own is not allowed. The paraphrase must be "the truth, the whole truth, and nothing but the truth."

There is no rule for the length of a paraphrase as compared with the length of the original passage ; but, as in paraphrasing we have frequently to expand concise sentences to make their meaning clear, a paraphrase is usually as long as, and is often longer than, the original. In the above example, for instance, the verse has 45 words, the summary 17 but the paraphrase has 56.

3. Wholeness–In paraphrasing, the passage to be paraphrased must be treated *as a whole.* The practice of taking the original line by line, or sentence by sentence, and simply turning these into different words is not paraphrasing at all. Until the passage is grasped as a whole, no attempt should be made to paraphrase it. What we have to try to do is to get behind the words to the idea in the author's mind which begot them. This is not an easy task, and calls for imagination and concentration of thought ; but unless we can do it, we shall never produce a good paraphrase.

Suppose, for example, you are asked to paraphrase this sonnet :

Much have I travelled in the realms of gold,
And many goodly states and kingdoms seen ;
Round many western islands have I been
Which bards in fealty to Apollo hold.
Oft of one wide expanse had I been told
That deep-browed Homer ruled as his demesne ;
Yet did I never breathe its pure serene
Till I heard Chapman speak out loud and bold ;
–Then felt I like some watcher of the skies
When a new planet swims into his ken ;
Or like stout Cortez, when with eagle eyes
He stared at the Pacific–and all his men
Looked at each other with a wild surmise–
Silent, upon a peak in Darien.

–*J. Keats*

The mechanical line by line method of paraphrasing is of no use here. Before any satisfactory paraphrase can be produced *the central meaning of the whole* must be grasped. What is it ? Well, it may be expressed thus :

Keats had read widely in English literature, especially poetry, but he knew nothing of the poetic literature of ancient Greece until he read Chapman's translation of Homer's *Illiad.* This was a revelation to him ; and as he read, he felt all the wonder and joy felt by an astronomer when he discovers a new star, or an explorer when he discovers an unknown ocean.

4. A Complete Piece of Prose–Lastly, a good paraphrase is so well constructed and written that it will read as an independent and complete composition in idiomatic English. It should in itself be perfectly clear and intelligible, without any reference to the original passage. A paraphrase should be a piece of good prose that anyone would understand and read with pleasure, even if he had never seen the original upon which it is based.

Note— Explanatory notes, either attached to, or inserted in the body of, the paraphrase, must *never* be resorted to. All the explanation required must be in the paraphrase itself. The insertion of explanatory notes is a confession of failure in paraphrasing.

To be successful in paraphrasing, it is necesary to keep these four points always in mind; for, if they are forgotten, the mere changing of the words and constructions of a passage will never make a real paraphrase. If your paraphrase is not a faithful translation of the original passage into your own words ; if it does not reproduce all the details, omitting nothing if it does not reproduce the passage as a whole; and if it is not a self-contained composition, intelligible without reference to the original–then, your paraphrase is a failure.

III. THE PARAPHRASE OF POETRY

These are some special points in the paraphrasing of poetry that may be explained separately.

One thing must be made clear to start with and that is that, as poetry in one language can never be translated into another without losing much, if not all, of its charm, so poetry can never be *translated* into prose. It is impossible to give in prose the same *impression* as is conveyed by a poem. The reason for this is that the matter and the form, the spirit and the letter, the soul and the body, of a poem are so inextricably intermingled that you cannot change the form without losing the spirit–that is, the poetry itself. The rhythm and the verbal music in which lies much of the magic of poetry, must be lost. Even the finest prose paraphrase of a poem is not, and can never be, a poem. All that a paraphrase can convey is the *meaning* of a poem. Nevertheless, the paraphrasing of poetry is a useful exercise in composition, and may often be a valuable help in interpreting the meaning of poems.

The peculiar difficulty of paraphrasing poetry lies in the difference between the language of verse and prose.

(a) *Difference in words*–Poets often use archaic or unusual words that are no longer in use in colloquial speech, and which are not generally found in prose writing. Examples :–*brand,* for sword ; *carol,* for song ; *a cot,* for a cottage ; *argosy,* for merchantship ; *ere,* for before; *o'er,* for over ; of *yore,* for in the past ; I *ween,* for I think ; *oft-times,* for often; I *trow,* for I am of opinion ; *aught,* for anything ; *anent,* for about ; *chide,* for scold ; *save,* for except; *forefathers,* for ancestors ; *perchance, belike* and *haply,* for perhaps ; *albeit,* for although *; damsel,* for girl ; *dame,* for lady ; *sire,* for father; *quoth,* for said ; *withal,* in addition; *to boot,* as well ; *well-nigh,* almost–and many more. Modern poets generally avoid such words, but they are frequent in older poetry. In paraphrasing, modern equivalents should always be substituted for such words.

(b) *Difference in the order of words*–Inversion, *i.e.,* any change in the normal grammatical order of words in a sentence–subject, verb, object–is much more common in poetry than in prose.

For example :

"Mine be a cot beside a hill;"
instead of,–May a cot beside a hill be mine.
"A barking sound the shepherd hears;"
instead of,–The shepherd hears a barking sound.
"Not, Celia, that I juster am
Or better than the rest;''
instead of,–Not that I am juster, etc.

Note–This getting rid of inversion is the chief thing we have to do in giving the *prose order* of a verse. In "prose order" exercises we retain all the words of the original, simply rearranging them in the usual grammatical sequence. Words may be added here and there to complete the grammatical construction where necessary. These should be put in brackets. Of course this is not paraphrasing. For example, take this verse:

"On Linden, when the sun was low,
All bloodless lay the untrodden snow
And dark as winter was the flow
Of Iser, rolling rapidly.''

There is an inversion in each sentence. Change these, and the prose order will be :

The untrodden snow lay all bloodless on Linden when the sun was low, and the flow of (the) rapidly rolling Iser was (as) dark as winter.

(c) *Flowery and ornamental language.* Such language, frequent in verse, should be simplified in prose. For example :

"Now the golden morn aloft
Waves her dew-bespangled wing,
With vermile cheek and whisper soft
She woos the tardy Spring."

(d) *Rhythm and Rhyme,* so characteristic of verse, have no place in prose, and must be avoided in paraphrasing.

IV. SPECIAL HINTS

(a) *Direct and Indirect Speech*–A paraphrase may be written in either; but (unless indirect speech is definitely required), it is better to use direct speech, for indirect speech (especially for Indian students writing in English) is full of traps for the unwary.

(b) *Metaphors*– The best way to deal with metaphors, is to resolve them into similes. For example–

"Silently, one by one, in the infinite *meadows* of Heaven,

Blossomed the lovely stars, the *forget-me-nots* of the angels."

This might be paraphrased thus–

The stars came out one by one silently in the vast sky, like forget-me-nots flowering in the fields.

In some cases the metaphor may be dropped altogether, and the literal meaning given instead. For instance, the first line of Keats' sonnet (see above, p. 407-408), "Much have I travelled in the realms of gold" may be rendered,–I have read widely in classical literature.

(c) *Abstract used for concrete*–When the abstract is used for the concrete, the concrete should be restored. For example, "Let not ambition mock their useful toil," should become,– Ambitious men should not despise the useful labour of poor peasants.

(d) *Rhetorical questions*–These should be changed into direct affirmations or negations. For example, "Are we not better armed than our foes ?" should become,–We are better armed than our enemies; and, "Is thy servant a dog that he should do this thing ?" may be paraphrased,–I am not so contemptible a creature as to commit such a crime.

(e) *Exclamations*–These should be turned into simple statements. For example, "O for a lodge in some vast wilderness !" can be paraphrased,–I wish I had a secluded refuge remote from human society.

(f) *Apostrophe*–In paraphrasing poems addressed in the second person, it is better to use the plural *you* than the singular *thou,* partly because *thou* is not used in ordinary prose, and partly because the construction of verbs in the second person plural is simpler. But whichever is adopted, must be kept to consistently throughout. It is a very bad form to begin with *thou* and later drop into *you.* Such passages may be rendered in the third person also; for instance, the first line of Matthew Arnold's sonnet *Shakespeare,* "Others abide our question–Thou art free !" may be rendered,–We can freely criticise other authors, but Shakespeare is beyond our criticism.

V. METHOD OF PROCEDURE

1. Because *no one can paraphrase a passage which he does not undestand,* first *read the passage* slowly and carefully until you feel you have firmly grasped its *general meaning.* If one reading does not make this clear, read it again and yet again, and study it until you thoroughly understand it. This first step is all important. (It is a good thing to write down at this stage a brief summary, concisely expressing the gist or main theme of the passage.)
2. Next, read the passage again *with a view to its details.* Note all uncommon or difficult words, and all idioms and unusual grammatical constructions, metaphors and figures of speech, remembering that you are to express, not only the substance, but also the details, of the passage in your own way.
3. Now, keeping clearly in mind the main purport of the passage, prepare to reproduce the passage in your own words, in simple and direct English, not leaving anything in the original unrepresented in your paraphrase.
4. Treat the passage *as a whole.* Do not work word by word, or line by line ; but from the beginning keep the end in view.
5. You may rearrange the order of sentences, and even of the whole passage, if this can make the meaning clear.
6. Break up a long sentence into several short ones, or combine several short sentences into one long, if by so doing you can make the whole more easily understood.
7. Do not change words simply for the sake of change. No word can ever *precisely* take the place of another ; and when a word in the original is perfectly simple in meaning and the best word in that place, it is a mistake to alter it. But all words and phrases that are at all archaic, obscure, technical, or uncommon should be changed into suitable synonyms. **N.B.**–Never substitute a difficult or unusual word for a simple and familiar word ; *e.g.,* do not put "ratiocination" for "argument."
8. Explanatory notes are altogether out of place in a paraphrase, and their presence is a confession of failure in paraphrasing. All explanations of difficulties must be intrinsic parts of the paraphrase itself. If any sentence in the paraphrase requires a note to explain it, you must rewrite the sentence until it explains itself.
9. A common fault in using indirect speech is the constant repetition of the "saying verb"–*e.g.,* "The poet says that'–''The poet further says'–'' The poet again remarks that', and so on. The "verb of saying', if used at all, should come once, at the beginning and not again.
10. Write out a rough draft of your paraphrase first. (You may have to write several drafts before you get the paraphrase to your satisfaction.) Revise this carefully, comparing it with the original to see that you have omitted nothing, over- (or under-) emphasised

nothing, nor imitated the original too closely. Correct any mistakes in spelling, punctuation, grammar or idiom. Read it *aloud* (for the ear sometimes can detect a blemish which the eye overlooks) to hear if it reads well as a piece of good English.

11. If, after taking pains, you feel the paraphrase is as good as you can make it, finally write out the fair copy neatly and legibly.

SPECIMENS

1

Breathes there the man, with soul so dead,
Who never to himself hath said,
This is my own, my native land ?
Whose heart hath ne'er within him burn'd.
As home his footsteps he hath turn'd.
From wandering on a foreign strand ?
If such there breathe, go, mark him well ;
For him no Minstrel raptures swell;
High though his titles, proud his name,
Boundless his wealth as wish can claim;
Despite those titles, power, and pelf,
The wretch, concentred all in self,
Living, shall forfeit fair renown,
And, doubly dying, shall go down
To the vile dust, from whence he sprung.
Unwept, unhonour'd, and unsung.

–Scott

PARAPHRASE

It is difficult to believe that any man can be so spiritually dead as to have no love for his native country after travelling in foreign lands. But if such an unpatriotic person does exist, take careful note of his career ; and you will find that he will never inspire poets to celebrate him in deathless song. He may be a man of high rank, of noble family and of riches beyond the dreams of avarice; but these great advantages will not save him from oblivion. In spite of them all, he will win no fame during his lifetime; and when he dies he will die in a double sense. His body will return to the dust whence it came, and his name will be forgotten. None will weep for him, none will honour him, and no poet will keep his name alive in immortal poetry.

2

Heaven from all creatures hides the book of fate,
All but the page prescribed, their present state :
From brutes what men, from men what spirits know;
Or who could suffer being here below ?
The lamb thy riot dooms to bleed to-day,
Had he thy reason, would he skip and play ?
Pleas'd to the last, he crops the flow'ry food,
And licks the hand just rais'd to shed his blood.
Oh, blindness to the future ! kindly giv'n,
That each may fill the circle mark'd by Heav'n,
Who sees with equal eyes, as God of all,
A hero perish, or a sparrow fall.

–Pope

PARAPHRASE

It would be impossible for us to continue living in this world if each of us knew exactly what fate had in store for him. So God in His mercy conceals the future from all His creatures, and reveals only the present. He hides from the animals what men know, and He hides from men what the angels know. For example, if a lamb had reason like a man, it could not gambol happily, knowing it was destined to be killed for human food. But, being quite ignorant of its fate, it is happy to the last minute of its short life contentedly grazing in the flowery meadow, and even in its innocence licks the hand of the butcher who is about to slaughter it. What a blessing it is that we are ignorant of the future ! God, to Whom the death of a sparrow is of equal importance with the death of a hero, has in His mercy thus limited our knowledge, so that we might fulfil our duty in the sphere to which He has appointed us.

3

Perseverance is the very hinge of all virtues. On looking over the world, the cause of nine-tenths of the lamentable failures which occur in men's undertakings, and darken and degrade so much of their history, lies not in the want of talents, or the will to use them, but in the vacillating and desultory mode of using them, in flying from object to object, in staring away at each little disgust, and thus applying the force which might conquer any one difficulty to a series of difficulties, so large that no human force can conquer them. The smallest brook on earth, by continuing to run, has hollowed out for itself a considerable valley to flow in. Commend me therefore to the virtue of perseverance. Without it all the rest are little better than fairy gold, which glitters in your purse, but when taken to market proves to be slate or cinders.

–Carlyle

PARAPHRASE

All the virtues depend on the one virtue of perseverance. It is lack of perseverance, not lack of ability, that is the cause of most of the sad failures that stain the history of mankind. It is because men do not persevere in overcoming one difficulty at a time, that they fail. Instead of sticking to one aim in life until it is realized, they hesitate, get discouraged at every small rebuff, change from one aim to another, and so create for themselves such a series of difficulties as can never be overcome by human power. Hence they fail to accomplish anything. Even a small stream will carve out for itself a deep and wide channel simply by constantly flowing. Without perseverance, all the other virtues are like the deceitful fairy gold of the fairy-tales, which turns to worthless stones when you try to use it as money in the shops.

EXERCISE 164

Paraphrase the following.

1. Some murmur, when their sky is clear
And wholly bright to view,
If one small speck of dark appear
In their great heaven of blue :
And some with thankful love are filled,
If but one streak of light,
One ray of God's good mercy, gild
The darkness of their night.

–Trench

2. Lives of great men all remind us
We can make our lives sublime,
And, departing, leave behind us,
Footprints on the sands of time;
Footprints, that perhaps, another,
Sailing o'er life's solemn main;
A forlorn and shipwreck'd brother
Seeing, shall take heart again.

–Longfellow

3. More things are wrought by prayer
Than this world dreams of. Wherefore, let thy voice
Rise like a fountain for me night and day.
For what are men better than sheep or goats
That nourish a blind life within the brain,
If, knowing God, they lift not hands of prayer.
Both for themselves and those who call them friends !

–Tennyson

4. In such a world ; so thorny, and where none
Finds happiness unblighted; or, if found,
Without some thistly sorrow at its side;
It seems the part of wisdom, and no sin
Against the law of love, to measure lots
With less distinguish'd than ourselves, that thus
We may with patience bear our moderate ills,
And sympathize with others suffering more.

–Cowper

5. Children we are all
Of one great father, in whatever clime
Nature or chance hath cast the seeds of life–
All tongues, all colours; neither after death
Shall we be sorted into languages
And tints, white, black, and tawny, Greek and Goth,
Northmen, and offspring of hot Africa ;
The All-father, He in Whom we live and move;
He, the indifferent Judge of all, regards
Nations, and hues, and dialects alike :
According to their works shall they be judged
When even-handed Justice in the scale
Their good and evil weighs.

–Southey

6. Beside yon straggling fence that skirts the way,
With blossom'd furze unprofitably gay,
There, in his noisy mansion, skill'd to rule,
The village master taught his little school ;
A man severe he was, and stern to view,–
I knew him well, and every truant knew,
Well had the boding tremblers learn'd to trace
The day's disasters in his morning face;
Full well they laugh'd with counterfeited glee,
At all his jokes,–for many a joke had he;
Full well the busy whisper, circling round,
Convey'd the dismal tidings when he frown'd;
Yet he was kind; or if severe in aught,
The love he bore to learning was in fault.

7. Hark ! 'tis the twanging horn. O'er yonder bridge,
That with its wearisome but needful length
Bestrides the wintry flood, in which the moon
Sees her unwrinkled face reflected bright,
He comes, the herald of a noisy world,
With spattered boots, trappped waist and frozen locks.
News from all nations lumbering at his back,
True to his charge, the close-packed load behind,
Yet careless what he brings, his one concern
Is to conduct it to the destined inn,
And, having dropped the expected bag, pass on
He whistles as he goes, light-hearted wretch,
Cold and yet cheerful : messenger of grief
Perhaps to thousands and of joy to some,
To him indifferent whether grief or joy.

–Cowper

8. Be it a weakness, it deserves some praise,
We love the play-place of our early days,
The scene is touching and the heart is stone
That feels not at the sight, and feels at none;
The wall on which we tried our graving skill,
The very name we carved subsisting still,
The bench on which we sat while deep-employed.
Though mangled, hacked, and hewed, not yet destroyed;
The little ones, unbuttoned, glowing hot,
Playing our games and on the very spot;
The pleasing spectacle at once excites
Such recollection of our own delights,
That viewing it, we seem almost to obtain
Our innocent sweet simple years again.

–Cowper

9. Since trifles make the sum of human things,
And half our misery from our foibles springs ;
Since life's best joys consist in peace and ease,
And few can save or serve, but all may please;
Oh ! let th' ungentle spirit learn from hence,
A small unkindness is a great offence.
Large bounties to restore, we wish in vain,
But all may shun the guilt of giving pain.
To bless mankind with tides of flowing wealth,
With power to grace them, or to crown with health,
Our little lot denies, but heaven decrees
To all the gift of minist'ring ease ;
The mild forbearance at another's fault ;
The taunting word, suppress'd as soon as thought ;
On these Heaven bade the bliss of life depend,
And crush'd ill fortune when it made a friend.

–Hanmah More

10. Now came still Evening on, and Twilight grey
Had in her sober livery all things clad.
Silence accompanied–for beast and bird,
They to their grassy couch, those to their nests,
Were slunk–all but the wakeful nightingale ;
She all night long her amorous descant sung.
Silence was pleased. Now glow'd the firmament
With living sapphires. Hesperus, that led
The starry host, rode brightest, till the moon,
Rising in clouded majesty at length.
Apparent queen, unveil'd her peerless light,
And o'er the dark her silver mantle threw.

11. These few precepts in thy memory
See thou character. Give thy thoughts no tongue,
Nor any unproportioned thought his act :
Be thou familiar, but by no means vulgar.
Those friends thou hast, and their adoption tried,
Grapple them to thy soul with hoops of steel;
But do not dull thy palm with entertainment
Of each new-hatched, unfledged comrade. Beware
Of entrance to a quarrel, but being in,
Bear't that the opposed may beware of thee.
Give every man thy ear, but few thy voice,

Take each man's censure, but reserve thy judgement.
Costly thy habit as thy purse can buy,
But not expressed in fancy; rich, not gaudy;
For the apparel often proclaims the man.
Neither a borrower nor a lender be;
For loan oft loses both itself and friend,
And borrowing dulls the edge of husbandry.

12. If misery be the effect of virtue, it ought to be reverenced; if of ill-fortune, to be pitied; and if of vice, not to be insulted; because it is, perhaps, itself a punishment adequate to the crime by which it was produced; and the humanity of that man can deserve no panegyric who is capable of reproaching a criminal in the hands of the executioner.

–Johnson

13. We are all short-sighted, and very often see but one side of a matter ; our views are not extended to all that has a connection with it. From this defect I think no man is free. We see but in part, and we know but in part, and therefore it is no wonder we conclude not right from our partial views. This might instruct the proudest esteemer of his own parts how useful it is to talk and consult with others, even such as come short of him in capacity, quickness, and penetration; for since no one sees all, and we generally have different prospects of the same thing, according to our different, as I may say, positions to it, it is not incongruous to think, nor beneath any man to try, whether another man may not have notions of things which have escaped him, and which his reason would make use of if they came into his mind.

–Locke

14. All the performances of human art, at which we look with praise or wonder, are instances of the resistless force of perseverance; it is by this that the quarry becomes a pyramid, and that distant countries are united by canals. If a man was to compare the effect of a single stroke of a pickaxe, or of one impression of the spade, with the general design and last result, he would be overwhelmed by the sense of their disproportion; yet those petty operations, incessantly continued, in time surmount the greatest difficulties, and mountains are levelled, and oceans bounded, the slender force of human beings.

–Johnson

15. The proverbial oracles of our parsimonious ancestors have informed us that the fatal waste of fortune is by small expenses, by the profusion of sums too little singly to alarm our caution, and which we never suffer ourselves to consider together. Of the same kind is prodigality of life; he that hopes to look back hereafter with satisfaction upon past years must learn to know the present value of single minutes, and endeavour to let no particle of time fall useless to the ground. An Italian philosopher expressed in his motto that time was his estate; an estate indeed, that will produce nothing without cultivation, but will always abundantly repay the labours of industry, and satisfy the most extensive desires, if no part of it be suffered to lie waste by negligence, to be overrun by noxious plants, or laid out for show rather than for use.

–Johnson

16. Mr. Hampden was a gentleman of a good extraction and a fair fortune, who from a life of great pleasure and license had on a sudden retired to extraordinary sobriety and strictness, and yet retained his usual cheerfulness and affability; which, together with the opinion of his wisdom and justice and the courage he had shewed in opposing the ship-money, raised his reputation to a very great height, not only in Buckinghamshire where he lived, but generally throughout the kingdom. He was not a man of many words, and rarely began than discourse, or made the first entrance upon any business that was assumed; but a very weighty speaker, and after he had heard a full debate, and observed how the House was like to be inclined, took up the argument, and shortly and clearly and craftily so stated it that he commonly conducted it to the conclusion he desired; and if he found he could not do that, he was never without the dexterity to divert the debate to another time and to prevent the determining of anything in the negative which might prove inconvenient in the future.

–Clarendon

COMMON ABBREVIATIONS

A, ampere; argon.
Å, angstrom unit.
A.A.A., Amateur Athletic Association.
A.B., Bachelor of Arts (L *artium baccalaureus*).
A.E.A., Atomic Energy Authority.
A.F.C., A.F.M., Air Force Cross (Medal)
Ag, silver.
Al, aluminium.
As, arsenic.
Aslib, Association of Special Libraries and Infor-mation Bureaux.
Au, gold.
B, boron.
B.A., Bachelor of Arts.
Ba, barium.
Be, beryllium.
Bi, bismuth.
b.p., boiling point.
Br., bromine.
C, carbon.
c., L *circa, about* (with dates, numbers etc.).
Ca, calcium.
CaCO3, calcium, carbonate, chalk.
CaO, calcium oxide, lime.
cal., calorie.
Cantab., of Cambridge University (L *Canta-brigiensis*).
Cb, columbium.
c.c., cm3, cubic centimetre.
C.C.P.R., Central Council of Physical Recreation.
Cd, cadmium.
Cdr, Commander.
Ce, cerium.
cg, centigram(s).
c.g.s., centimetre-gram-second system of units.
Cl, chlorine.
C.I.S., Common wealth of Independent States.
Cm, curium.
cm, centimetre(s).
Co, cobalt.
C.P., Communist Party.
Cr, chromium.
Cs, caesium.
Cu, copper.
d.c., direct current.
D.g., by the grace of God (L *Dei gratia*).
D.Lit., Doctor of Literature.
D.Litt., Doctor of Letters (L *doctor literarum*).
D.M., Doctor of Medicine.
DNA, deoxyribonucleic acid.
D.P.H., Diploma in Public Health.
D.Ph., D.Phil., Doctor of Philosophy.
D.Sc., Doctor of Science.
ECG, electrocardiogram.
EEC, electro-encephalogram.
E.P.N.S., electroplated nickel silver.
E.P.T., excess profits tax.
Esro, European Space Research Organization.
e.s.u., electrostatic unit(s).
eV, electron volt(s).
F, fluorine.
F.A., Football Association.
F.A.O., Food and Agriculture Organization.
F.C.A., Fellow of the Institute of Chartered Accountants.
Fe, iron.
Fr, Father.
F.R.S., Fellow of the Royal Society.
F.W.A., Family Welfare Association.
F.Z.S., Fellow of the Zoological Society.
g, acceleration due to gravity; gram(s).
GATT, Gatt, General Agreement on Tariffs and Trade.
Ge, germantum.
gm, gram(s).
G.P., general practitioner.
gr, grain(s).
H, hydrogen.
H.A., hardy annual.
Hants, Hampshire.
HCL, hydrochloric acid.
He, helium.
Hf, hafnium.
Hg, mercury.
h.t., high tension.
H.W.M., high-water mark.
I, iodine.
I.L.O., International Labour Organization.
I.M.F., International Monetary Fund.
Ind., Indiana.
I.Q., intelligence quotient.
K, potassium.
kc/s, kilocycles per second.
kg, kilo(s), Kilogram(s).
kilo-, a thousand.
km, kilometre(s).
K.O., knock-out.
Kr, krypton.
kV, kilovolt(s).
kW, kilowatt(s).
kWh, kilowatt-hour(s).
La, lanthanum; Louisiana.
Li, lithium.
Linn., Linnaean system of classification.
Lit, Hum., Literae Humanpres, see dictionary.
L.T.A., Lawn Tennis Association.
L.W.M., low-water mark.
M, (in metric units) mega–, a million; (in Roman numerals) 1,000.
m, micro-, × 10–6. one-millionth; micron.
mm, micromicro-, × 10–12, one billionth.
M.B., Bachelor of Medicine (L *medicinae baccalaureus*).
mb, millibar(s).
M.C.C., Marylebone Cricket Club.
M.Ch., Master of Surgery (L *magister chirurgiae*).
M.D., Doctor of Medicine (L *medicinae doctor*):
MeV, million electron-volts.
Mg, magnesium.
mg, milligram(s).
M.I., Military Intelligence.
Mich., Michigan.
Minn., Minnesota.
ml, millilitre(s).
M.M., Military Medal.
mm, millimetre(s).
Mn, manganese.
Mo, molybdenum; Missouri.
M.O.H., Medical Officer of Health.
m.p., melting point.
M.R.C.P., M.R.C.S., M.R.C.V.S., Member of the Royal College of Physicians (Surgeons. Veterinary Surgeons).
M.Sc., Master of Science.
Mus. B., Mus.D., Mus.M., Bachelor (Doctor, Master) of Music (L musicae baccalaureus, etc.).

Mx, Middlesex.
N, Nitrogen.
n.a., not available; not applicable.
Na, sodium.
NaCl, sodium chloride, common salt.
Ne, neon.
Neb., Nebr., Nebraska.
N.F.S., National Fire Service.
N.H.I., National Health Insurance.
N.H.S., National Health Service.
Ni, nickel.
n.p., net personality.
N.P.L., National Physical Laboratory.
N.T., New Testament; National Trust.
N.U.R., National Union of Railwaymen.
N.U.T., National Union of Teachers.
O, Oxygen.
O., Ohio.
Okla., Oklahoma.
O.M., Order of Merit.
Ont., Ontario.
O.R., other ranks.
Ore., Oreg., Oregon.
Os, osmium.
O.T., Old Testament.
P, phosphorus.
Pa, Penn., Pennsylvania.
Pb, Lead.
P.C., Privy Councillor.
p.d., (elect.) potential difference.
Pd. palladium.
P.D.S.A., People's Dispensary for Sick Animals.
P.E.P., Political and Economic Planning.
Ph.D., Doctor of Philosophy (L *philosophiae doctor*)
P.L.A., Port of London Authority.
P.N.E.U., Parents National Educations Union.
P.O.W., prisoner of war.
P.R., proportional representation; public relations.
P.R.O., public relations officer.
Pt., platinum.
Pu, plutonium.
Q.B., Queen's Bench.
Q.C., Queen's Counsel.
Que., Quebec.
Ra, radium.
R.A.D.A., Royal Academy of Dramatic Art.
Rb, rubidium.
R.B.A., Royal (Society of) British Artists.
R.D., refer (cheque) to drawer.
R.D.C., Rural District Council.
R.I., Rhode Island.
R.I.P., may he/she/they rest in peace (L *requiesca(n) t in pace*).
R.M., Royal Marines; Royal Mail; Resident Magistrate.
R.M.A., Royal Military Academy, Sandhurst (formerly Woolwich).
R.M.C., Royal Military College, Sandhurst (now R.M.A.).
Rn, randon.
RNA, ribonucleic acid.
R.N.(V).R., Royal Naval (Volunteer) Reserve.
R.N.Z., Royal New Zealand (A.f., etc.).
R.O.C., Royal Observer Corps.
R/T., radio-telegraphy, -telephony.
Ru, ruthenjum.
S, Sulphur.
Sb, antimony.
Sc, scandium.
Sc.D., Doctor of Science (L *scientiae doctor*).
S.C.R., Senior Common (Combination) Room.
Se, selenium.
Seato, South East Asia Treaty Organization.
SF, science fiction.
Si, silicon.
Sn, tin.
S.P.G., Society for the Propagation of the Gospel.
Sr, strontium.
STD, subscriber trunk dialling.
s.t.p., standard temperature and pressure.
s.v., (see) under the word (specified), L *sub verbo or sub voce*.
T.A., Territorial Army.
Tenn., Tennessee
Tex., Texas.
Th, thorium.
Ti, titanium.
U, uranium; upper-class usage.
U.A.E., United Arab Emirates.
UHF, ultra-high frequency.
Uno, United Nations Organization.
V, vanadium; volt.
Va, Vuginia.
V.A.D., Voluntary Aid Detachment.
VE, Victory in Europe (VE day, May 8, 1945).
VHF, very high frequency, see dictionary under VERY.
V.I.P., very important person, see dictionary under VERY.
v.l., variant reading. alternative version (L *varia Lectio*).
vt, Vermont.
Vulg., Vulgate.
W, tungsten (wolfram).
W.A.A.F., Women's
Auxiliary Air Force.
W.D., War department.
WHO, World Health Organization.
Xe, xenon.
Yb, ytterbium.
Y.H.A., Youth Hostels Association.
Yt, yttrium.
Zn, zinc.
Zr, zirconium.